D1114979

# INTERNATIONAL ENTERTAINMENT LAW

# INTERNATIONAL ENTERTAINMENT LAW

**LIONEL S. SOBEL**
*Editor, Entertainment Law Reporter*
*Distinguished Scholar, Berkeley Center for Law & Technology, University of California, Berkeley, Boalt Hall School of Law*

**DONALD E. BIEDERMAN**
*Professor of Law and Director, National Entertainment & Media Law Institute*
*Southwestern University School of Law, Los Angeles*

**Westport, Connecticut**
**London**

**Library of Congress Cataloging-in-Publication Data**

Sobel, Lionel S.
International entertainment law/Lionel S. Sobel and Donald E. Biederman.
p. cm.
Includes bibliographic references and index.
ISBN 0-275-97616-5 (alk. paper)
1. Performing arts—Law and legislation. 2. Entertainers—Legal status, laws, etc.
I. Biederman, Donald E. II. Title
K3780.S66 2003
343'.0787902—dc21 2002072844

British Library Cataloguing in Publication Data is available.



Library of Congress Catalog Card Number: 2002072844
ISBN: 0-275-97616-5

First published in 2003

Praeger Publishers, 88 Post Road West, Westport, CT 06881
An imprint of Greenwood Publishing Group, Inc.
www.praeger.com

Printed in the United States of America

The paper used in this book complies with the
Permanent Paper Standard issued by the National
Information Standards Organization (Z39.48 – 1984)

10 9 8 7 6 5 4 3 2 1

# CONTENTS

**For Marna**
*DEB*

**For Carol**
*LSS*

# ACKNOWLEDGMENTS

These Acknowledgments were to have been written in two separate parts, one by my co-author Don Biederman, and the other by me. As most people in the worlds of entertainment law and legal education know by now, Don passed away last August, just weeks after we finished the manuscript for this book. He had been battling skin cancer, as well as the after-effects of treatments for it, for years. But his passing came as an unexpected shock.

Don was regarded, by all who knew him, as one of the very nicest, most pleasant-to-deal-with lawyers in the entertainment industry. When it came to his cancer, however, he was the toughest fighter I have ever known or heard about. He underwent more than fifty surgeries, some of which disfigured him quite badly. But he complained less about his physical condition than most people do (certainly than I do) about getting a computer virus. To the very end, Don went about his life and work as though he were the healthiest and strongest man on the planet. And insofar as his publicly displayed state of mind was concerned, he was. He simply refused to acknowledge there was any reason for him to slow down, let alone stay in. And for that reason, I – along with his countless friends – were certain that Death would be afraid to approach let alone take him.

I do and will continue to miss Don enormously, not only because we were friends, and not only because we worked together on this book, but also because he was proof that the type of law we loved and taught to students could in fact be practiced with humility and respect, as well as skill. And that is important proof to have.

Don was the co-author of this book as well as the reason it came to exist in this handsome volume you now hold in your hands. In the beginning, the spark that became this book was struck by Professor Herbert Lazerow of the University of San Diego School of Law, and I thank him for striking it. As the Director of USD's Institute on International and Comparative Law, Professor Lazerow invited me to teach international entertainment law in the Institute's London program during the summer of 1999 – an invitation I happily accepted. This book began as materials compiled for that course. In addition to giving me a reason to create this book, the USD summer-abroad program also provided me with terrific students, too numerous to acknowledge individually by name. Some were from the University of San Diego itself and other American law schools from Boalt to NYU, as well as Puerto Rico. Other students were from Canada, Germany, Israel, Italy and Mexico. For an American law professor, few pleasures in legal education can measure up to teaching an international law course, in a city like London, to a group of students whose homes literally ring the world. I thank all of my former students for their enthusiastic response to these materials and to this subject.

Don taught the International Entertainment Law course for the University of San Diego during the summer of 2000, in Paris, using the materials I had first compiled for USD's 1999 program. Don and his wife Marna always loved Paris, he told me. Better still, from my point of view, his experience in Paris with those materials led him to conclude, enthusiastically, that they could be expanded into a publishable book. Don was the lead author of *Law and Business of the Entertainment Industries*, a casebook then going into its Fourth Edition, so his enthusiasm was infectious. Don acted as our mutual literary agent in selling Praeger on the idea of publishing this book, and then as my collaborator in preparing the text you now hold. It would not have been published without him, and I wish I could thank him for all that he did to bring that about.

I also want to thank Bernie Gold of Proskauer Rose in Los Angeles who provided me with documents and his insights (more than once), and Professor Edith Friedler of Loyola Law School in Los Angeles whose valuable advice was enormously helpful in an area that was (until her advice was given, on short notice) entirely foreign to me.

When we finished the manuscript, Don told me he wanted to gratefully acknowledge assistance he had received from Ken Dearsley and Josh Crome of Denton Wilde Sapte, London; Shane Simpson of Simpsons Solicitors, Sydney; Dr. Ulrich Michael of Noerr Stiefenhofer Lutz, Berlin; and David A. Basskin, President of the Canadian Mechanical Rights Reproduction Agency, Ltd., Toronto. "Each of these gentlemen provided clues that helped me find stuff," Don emailed me, and "while not all of it made it into the book," he wrote that he "certainly made use of it."

Finally, both Don and I want to thank Vito Torchia, Jr., for tracking down copies of important materials that, despite their importance, were not online or on library shelves. And we would like to thank Tamara Moore and Martha Fink of Southwestern University School of Law for their valued assistance in preparing these materials for publication.

*Lionel S. Sobel*
October 2002

# INTRODUCTION

## OVERVIEW

### The international nature of today's entertainment business

Until its last decade, the 20th Century was the American Century in the entertainment industries. In the early years, Hollywood, jazz and Broadway musicals ruled the entertainment world. Authors like Hemingway, Fitzgerald, Faulkner and Steinbeck attracted worldwide audiences. Rock 'n roll burst on the scene in the mid-50s, and although the "English invasion" of the 60s was long and strong, beginning with the Beatles in 1964, and continuing through such artists as the Rolling Stones, The Who, Rod Stewart, Elton John, and ELO, American music and American record companies dominated the worldwide market. Exports of American television programming were ubiquitous.

While the United Sates remains the single most important producer of entertainment products, the rest of the world has made great strides. Countries which had but one or two, government-owned and operated, television channels a few years ago, now bristle with commercial broadcast channels, cable systems, and satellite delivery. China, long a haven for film and record piracy, has adhered to the Berne Convention, adopted copyright legislation, and has joined the World Trade Organization.

Although many foreign film stars and directors did most of their important work in Hollywood (e.g., actors Rex Harrison, Deborah Kerr, David Niven, directors Alfred Hitchcock and John Ford, in the early years, to today's actors Mel Gibson, Russell Crowe and Nicole Kidman (all Australian), Sean Connery (Scotland), and Pierce Brosnan (Ireland) as well as directors Tony and Ridley Scott (UK), Peter Weir, Bruce Beresford and Fred Schepisi (Australia)), there are many notable film personnel who have done all or most of their work in their home countries and/or in other locations outside the U.S. A few recent examples are actors such as Gerard Depardieu (France), Michael Caine, Bob Hoskins, Judi Dench, Joan Plowright and Ben Kingsley (all UK), Roberto Benigni (Italy) and Chow Yun Fat (Hong Kong), directors Gillian Armstrong (Australia), Peter Jackson (New Zealand), Ang Lee (Taiwan) and Franco Zeffirelli (Italy). Foreign recording artists such as ABBA (Sweden), Andrea Bocelli (Italy), Celine Dion (Canada), Enya (Ireland), Julio Iglesias (Spain), Antonio Carlos Jobim (Brazil), U2 (Ireland), and Vangelis (Greece/UK) are but a few of the marquee musical artists to achieve sustained worldwide fame and major sales in the U.S.

Until the last ten or fifteen years, however, the U.S. companies were the enduring worldwide powerhouses. While foreign film production companies, record distributors, and book and music publishers frequently prospered, and while they might achieve success in other countries, that was rarely replicated in the U.S., which accounted for a substantial majority of worldwide revenues in almost every entertainment industry. For example, the UK's EMI, Germany's Ariola, and the German/Dutch PolyGram all enjoyed major foreign success, but they were usually far behind CBS Records, RCA Records, Capitol Records and the WEA (Warner/Atlantic/Elektra) Group in U.S. market share and revenues. The major U.S. studios (Universal, Paramount, Columbia, MGM, Walt Disney, 20th Century Fox and Warner Bros.) commanded virtually the entire U.S. theatrical film market. Companies like Random House, Doubleday, and Simon & Schuster dominated the U.S. literary publishing scene.

How things have changed!

For one thing, U.S. sales are no longer the lion's share. In films, more than half the theatrical film revenues of American movies come from non-U.S. sources. In a number of cases (e.g., "Titanic," "Jurassic Park" and "Schindler's List") foreign revenues have exceeded blockbuster U.S. revenues. According to the annual survey of the industry conducted by the National Music Publisher's Association, some 70% of American music publishers' revenues come from non-U.S. sources. Aggressive programs of tax credits, development, production and marketing subsidies, screen-time quotas and other quotas requiring high percentages of local content, have led to the creation and/or expansion of local production facilities featuring up-to-date technology and well-trained personnel, often available at bargain rates due to the strength of the dollar (e.g., at this writing the Australian and Canadian dollars are worth, respectively, approximately 52 and 62 cents) and, consequently, to "runaway productions." The majority of movies-of-the-week shown on U.S. television (as well as such popular series as "The X-Files") are shot in Canada. The Canadian industry takes in some $2.8 billion annually from U.S.-based productions. Another source of support for the foreign film and television industries is the network of international co-production treaties, under which producers from two or more countries can avail themselves of tax breaks and/or subsidies from each of their respective countries. The U.S. is not party to any co-production treaty.

U.S. box office dominance is under challenge. In 2001, for example, French films accounted for some 43% of the French theatrical box office, a remarkable change from a succession of years in which the French share was less than 10%.

And it doesn't end there: Whereas, in prior years, all of the major studios were American-owned, this is no longer the case. Columbia Pictures is now Sony Pictures Entertainment. Universal Studios is part of France's Vivendi, and 20th Century Fox is now owned by Australia's News Corp. (although CEO Rupert Murdoch became a U.S. citizen in order to qualify for ownership of the Fox Network; indeed, only federal legislation prohibiting foreign ownership has prevented foreign multinationals from bidding on U.S. networks). Germany's Bertelsmann is now the largest U.S. book publisher. And four of the remaining five major record companies are foreign-owned: Sony (formerly CBS Records), Capitol (owned for many years by UK's EMI), RCA (part of BMG, also owned by Bertelsmann) and Universal Music Group (which includes the former PolyGram, and is also owned by Vivendi).

### Legal problems resulting from international nature of the entertainment business

The American entertainment industries thus face severe economic and creative challenges. But there are legal problems as well. In addition to the tax/subsidy/quota programs referred to above, foreign countries have their own legal systems, cultures and customs. Some elements of entertainment materials which would be acceptable in the U.S. may cause trouble in other lands. In the UK, for example, there is no "actual malice" rule as there is in U.S. media libel cases. Moreover, if a defendant unsuccessfully raises truth as a defense, it may be subject to punitive damages. (Indeed, to use Prof. Rodney Smolla's phrase, the UK has become something of a "libel haven.") Germany and France prohibit the sale or distribution of Nazi material, activity which would be protected here by the First Amendment. Canada's definition of obscenity may cover film scenes which would not meet the test articulated by our Supreme Court.

Of course, not all the problems are of foreign origin. For example, the U.S. has very complicated rules governing foreign entertainers and sports figures who want to come to the U.S. to perform, whether on a temporary basis or permanently. Unions (such as Actors' Equity, and the three principal film unions, the Screen Actors Guild, the Writers Guild of America and the Directors Guild of America), impose staffing levels through their contracts with producers. The Production Loan Guarantee program of the Export-Import Bank offers help to independent producers of small to medium-budget films produced principally for export. Southern California-based guilds and companies are pressuring Congress and the California government to enact tariffs (at the federal level) and/or tax breaks to counteract runaway production. And it may be possible, depending upon the flexibility of the U.S. producer and the strength and quality of the producer's foreign relationships, for a U.S. producer to enjoy some of the tax/subsidy programs available to foreign producers.

Substantial economic success in the entertainment industries thus requires an understanding of how business is done elsewhere, and of the ways in which assumptions as to the similarity of other legal systems to our own may be erroneous. "Entertainment law" is an amalgam of copyright, trademark, rights of privacy and publicity, contract law (for example, few countries besides the U.S. recognize the "work for hire" doctrine, while almost all foreign countries recognize "moral rights," which can permit U.S. talent to prevent producers from taking actions which would be perfectly legal in the U.S. under the terms of the applicable contracts), with a little tax, administrative law and antitrust thrown in. In the pages that follow, we attempt to survey important cases and materials which illustrate the need to anticipate the potential fate of American entertainment product in other countries.

## THIS BOOK

### The organization of this book

Because "entertainment law" is an amalgam of many types of law, there are at least three ways an entertainment law course – and casebook – could be organized.

It could be organized by type of law, with separate chapters devoted to mini-explorations of copyright law, trademark law and so forth. However, in the actual practice of entertainment law, legal issues do not present themselves as "copyright" or "labor" law questions. Indeed, some very important questions – like who is the "author" of an American-produced motion picture – is answered, in the United States, by a blend of copyright and labor law, while in Europe, it is a question of copyright law alone. Moreover, if organized by type of law, each chapter would present an unrealistically brief picture of its subject, and might actually mislead readers about what the law is in that area.

An entertainment law casebook also could be organized industry by industry, with a chapter devoted to motion pictures and television, another to music, a third to the stage, and so forth. That organization, however, might require the time- and page-consuming repetition of certain topics, because certain legal issues arise in the same or similar fashion in all entertainment businesses.

The fact that certain legal issues do arise in the same or similar fashion in all entertainment businesses suggests a third method of organizing an entertainment law casebook, and that is the method used in this book. Every entertainment project – from motion pictures to music to ballet and even sports – passes through six stages of development, as it moves from conception by its creator to enjoyment by its audience. These six stages are: acquisition of rights; employment of talent; finance; production; distribution; and performance, exhibition or sale.

The importance of these stages varies from business to business. Acquisition of rights is a very important stage in the movie business, and not very important in professional sports. But every entertainment project passes, at least briefly, through all six of these stages. And specific legal issues arise at each stage – issues that are the same or similar in all entertainment businesses. That is why this book has been organized into six chapters, one for each of these six stages.

This method of organization does result in some legal subjects – like copyright law – showing up in more than one chapter. But the specific copyright issues that arise during the acquisition of rights stage are not the same as those copyright issues that arise during the finance stage, or during the distribution stage, or during the performance, exhibition and sale stage. As a result, there is little or no repetition from chapter to chapter, even of copyright law issues. Instead – as in the actual practice of law – there is merely the need to revisit certain types of law, because they play a continuing role throughout the lives of some types of entertainment projects.

### The scope and depth of the material in this book

Each of the topics covered in this book is worthy of a multi-volume treatise by itself. The leading treatise (for Americans) on international copyright law (*International Copyright Law and Practice*, by Paul Edward Geller and Melville B. Nimmer) is two volumes. And a leading treatise on international sports law (*International Sports Law and Business*, by Aaron N. Wise and Bruce S. Meyer) is three volumes.

Quite obviously, a book the size of this one could not possibly cover – or even allude to – all of the legal doctrines that are important to those who practice international entertainment law. What's more, the field of international entertainment law is rapidly changing. The material in this book is simply a snapshot of the ways things were, when this book was being written. As a result, this book should not be read for definitive knowledge about specific legal doctrines.

On the other hand, this book does illustrate the *processes* by which international legal issues are resolved in the entertainment industry; and there are several. Sometimes, issues are resolved by litigation between private parties in the national courts of one of them; other times, issues are resolved by litigation between nations in international forums agreed to by both of them. Sometimes, the law to be applied is that of a single nation (or even a single state), enacted by that nation's (or state's) own legislature; other times, the law to be applied is an international treaty, the provisions of which have been agreed to by several nations.

There are other processes as well, as you will read in this book. Often, entertainment lawyers must answer international questions quickly, on the basis of legal doctrines that do exist; and the task involves determining what those doctrines are. Other times, however – and especially today, as the entertainment industry is becoming more and more international in its scope – the question to be answered will not involve the straightforward application of existing legal doctrine. Rather, the question will involve the creation of new doctrines, or changes to old doctrines. On those occasions, the proper *process* to be used to seek that change will be a critical preliminary decision. For this reason, it important to take note of the *processes* reflected in these pages – perhaps more important than it is to take note of the specific doctrines.

*Chapter 1*

# ACQUISITION OF RIGHTS

---

## 1.1 CELEBRITY NAMES AND LIKENESSES

For a fairly small number of performers and other celebrities, considerable value attaches to uses of their names, likenesses, and other indicia of identity. In some cases (e.g., Michael Jackson, Madonna, The Artist Formerly Known as Prince), the international value of their identities may ultimately surpass that in the U.S. In some cases (e.g., Tom Cruise, Mel Gibson, Elton John) fame is truly global. However, the extent to which a famous personality may exploit and/or restrain others from exploiting indicia of his/her identity is not uniform throughout the world. The materials which follow illustrate the different ways in which legal systems deal with these issues, and the variety of results which can flow from these differences.

---

### 1.1.1 Right of Publicity

**Bi-Rite Enterprises, Inc. v. Bruce Miner Co.**
**757 F.2d 440 (1st Cir. 1985)**

Senior Judge Weigel:

This is an appeal from a preliminary injunction prohibiting distribution of posters depicting certain popular music performers.[1] [Fn.1 Defendants do not challenge the preliminary injunction's prohibition relating to distribution of posters depicting American performers.]

Plaintiffs Bi-Rite Enterprises Inc. (Bi-Rite), an Illinois corporation, and Artemis, Inc. (Artemis), a Connecticut corporation, are manufacturers and distributors of novelty merchandise. Their wares include posters of British popular music performers from whom they hold exclusive licenses.

There are also fourteen individual plaintiffs, all residents of Great Britain. Each is member of one or another of the popular musical groups known as Judas Priest, Duran Duran, and Iron Maiden. The groups license commercial exploitation of their names and likenesses through their United States merchandizing representative, the Great Southern Company, Inc., a Georgia corporation, which is not a party here.

The defendants, Bruce Miner and Bruce Miner Co., Inc., a Massachusetts corporation, are in the business of distributing posters of popular music performers. Neither the defendants nor the European manufacturers from whom they purchase posters hold licenses from the depicted performers. Defendants claim that the posters they distribute were made from publicity photographs legally purchased by the European manufacturers.

The preliminary injunction prohibits defendants from distributing posters depicting any of the performers from whom Bi-Rite or Artemis holds an exclusive license for posters. It also prohibits distribution of posters depicting the individual plaintiffs.

The sole question on appeal is whether, under Massachusetts law, rights relating to commercial exploitation of a person's name or likeness are governed by the law of the person's domicile or by that of the residence of the person's exclusive licensee or merchandizing representative. The law of Great Britain does not recognize a right to control commercial exploitation of personal names or likenesses. The law of the American jurisdictions here involved does recognize that right. The district court applied the law of the American jurisdictions.

We affirm.

I. American jurisdictions have recently recognized the right of well known individuals to control commercial exploitation of their names and likenesses. Called "the right of publicity," or the tort of "appropriation" of name or likeness, this right has been recognized in some form by virtually all states. As a commercial, rather than a personal right, it is fully assignable.

> [T]he effect . . . is to recognize or create an exclusive right in the individual plaintiff to a species of trade name, his own, and a kind of trade mark in his likeness. . . . Once protected by law, it is a right of value upon which the plaintiff can capitalize by selling licenses.

Great Britain does not recognize a right of publicity. Consequently, the choice between United States and British law is determinative in this case.

II. When a federal court exercises pendent jurisdiction over state law claims, as here, it must apply the substantive law of the state in which it sits. This includes the forum state's choice of law rules. Thus, we must determine what law the Massachusetts courts would apply.

As in most American jurisdictions, Massachusetts' choice of law rules are in transition. The state has turned away from the rigid, single-factor analysis associated with the first *Restatement of Conflict of Laws* (1934) in favor of the more flexible, multiple-factor, "interest analysis" or "most significant relationship" analysis exemplified by the *Restatement (Second) of Conflict of Laws* (1971). Under the older approach, courts determined which jurisdiction's law governed by categorizing an action (as a tort, contract, or property dispute, for example) and then looking to a single connecting factor (such as place of injury, place of agreement, or situs of property).[2] [Fn.2 The "right of publicity" does not fit neatly into any of the categories — Tort, Property, Contract, etc. — which provided the framework for traditional (First Restatement) choice of law analysis. The alleged infringement in the present action implicates elements of both Tort and Property law. Appellants' assertion that their rights derive from implied consent and trade custom invokes Contract principles as well.]

If Massachusetts still adhered to the single-factor mode of analysis of the first Restatement, categorizing this action would be critical. Indeed, the parties' briefs are largely dedicated to asserting that one categorization or another is appropriate.

However, Massachusetts' choice of law rules no longer rest on such a rigid system. Massachusetts' current approach is based on a set of overarching principles and considerations applicable to all choice of law questions. . . .

III. In light of Massachusetts' adoption of modern choice of law rules, we reject at the outset defendants' contention that a court need only consider the domicile of the person whose name or likeness is being exploited to determine the law governing this action. To focus solely on that domicile would disregard the development of Massachusetts law which now calls for the "more functional approach". . . . Under such an approach, domicile is significant only to the extent that it implicates interests that are cognizable under an "interest" or "most significant relationship" analysis.

The *Second Restatement of Conflict of Laws*, section 6(2) sets forth the perimeters for the kind of analysis the Massachusetts courts would employ:

> (2) When there is no [contrary statutory] directive, the factors relevant to the choice of applicable rule of law include:
> (a) the needs of the interstate and international systems,
> (b) the relevant policies of the forum,
> (c) the relevant policies of other interested states and the relative interests of those states in the determination of the particular issue,
> (d) the protection of justified expectations,
> (e) the basis policies underlying the particular field of law,
> (f) certainty, predictability and uniformity of result, and
> (g) ease in the determination and application of the law to be applied.

We begin our choice of law analysis with the first of the factors listed in section 6(2) of the Second Restatement – here, the needs of the international system. In the popular music industry, trade between Great Britain and the United States is pervasive and much prized. It is nurtured in part by the policy in both countries of affording the same commercial rights to foreigners as to national. Moreover, it might very well be unconstitutional for an American jurisdiction to extend lesser contractual rights to foreign performers in this country than to their American counterparts.

Defendants urge that the law of Great Britain should be applied to the American merchandising activities of British performers. To do so would extend lesser commercial rights to British than to American performers. A British performer could not enter into an exclusive licensing agreement with an American merchandiser while an American performer could. Such a result cannot be squared with the needs of the international system in this area.

Turning next to the relevant policies of the forum, it is clear that Massachusetts recognizes a right of publicity. However, since none of the plaintiffs is domiciled there, Massachusetts courts, in the interest of comity, would look to the laws of other jurisdictions to determine whether plaintiffs can validly claim a right of publicity. This calls for determining the jurisdictional law which Massachusetts would apply.

Making that determination calls, in turn, for consideration of the policy interests underlying the relevant rules of Illinois, Connecticut, Georgia and Great Britain — i.e., the four jurisdictions involved in this case.

Although Illinois, Connecticut and Georgia may differ in the extent to which they recognize a "right of publicity," they can be considered together for purposes of choice of law. They share the basic policy interests underlying the right of publicity as recognized in most American jurisdictions:

> The rationale for [protecting the right of publicity] is the straight-forward one of preventing unjust enrichment by the theft of good will. No social purpose is served by having the defendant get free some aspect of the plaintiff that would have market value and for which he would normally pay."

[As the United States Supreme Court said in *Zacchini v. Scripps-Howard Broadcasting*, discussing Ohio law:]

> Of course, [the] right of publicity here rests on more than a desire to compensate the performer for the time and effort invested in his act; the protection provides an economic incentive for him to make the investment required to produce a performance of interest to the public. This same consideration underlies the patent and copyright laws long enforced by this Court.

It is more difficult to ascertain the policy interests underlying Britain's refusal to recognize a right of publicity. Indeed, in the very case confirming that refusal, the wisdom of the rule was challenged by Lord Greer:

> I have no hesitation in saying that in my judgment the defendants in publishing the advertisement in question, without first obtaining Mr.. Tolley's consent, acted in a manner inconsistent with the decencies of life, and in doing so they were guilty of an act for which there ought to be a legal remedy.

Even though the policy interests underlying the British rule have not been fully articulated, the British refusal to recognize a right of publicity should be taken into account. In the area of publicity rights, as in the areas of trademark, patent, and copyright, the law must balance the competing goals, on the one hand, of facilitating public access to valuable images, inventions and ideas and, on the other, rewarding individual effort. In American law there are some areas on which the public interest is thought to be served best by allowing unrestricted competitive commerce in images and information. For purposes of choice of law analysis, it must be assumed that Britain's refusal to recognize a right of publicity represents a policy choice favoring unrestricted competition in the area of commercial exploitation of names and likenesses.

Even so, the differing policy choices behind American and British law do not necessarily call for application of British law in the present case. Recognizing American publicity rights for British performers does not restrict free commerce in Britain. That is to say, Britain's presumed interest in allowing its citizens unrestricted access to the names and likenesses of performers is not disserved by allowing those performers to restrict the merchandising of their names and likenesses in the United States. Nor does it follow that because Britain has not seen fit to provide direct economic incentives for performers to market their public images in England, there need be any proscription of allowing those performers such incentives in the United States. The British public is not harmed if the laws of the United States aggrandize British performers.

The next consideration listed in section 6(2) of the Second Restatement, protecting justifiable expectations, is somewhat problematic. On the one hand, American merchandisers justifiably expect that the performers with whom they have entered into exclusive merchandising contracts have the right to license their publicity rights. On the other hand, defendants argue that the posters they well are in fact authorized wares because they come from publicity photographs which the photographers sell to the European manufacturers of the posters. Under British law, photographers and their assignees enjoy copyright protection and justifiably expect to possess a broad range of rights with respect to the photographs. Defendants' argument merits some discussion.

Defendants claim that the posters they sell are made from publicity photographs taken at British "photosessions." According to defendants, these photosessions are customary in the British popular music industry. The photographers distribute the resultant photographs through syndicating agencies to newspapers, to magazines, and occasionally to poster manufacturers. While some photosessions are conducted on an express understanding that resulting pictures may only be used for specific purposes, such as newspaper publication, others, so-called "unrestricted photosessions," are conducted without any discussion of limitations. Thus, defendants claim, performers who agree to pose at unrestricted photosessions do so with the understanding that the photographers may use the resultant photographs however they choose.

The claim is too broad. To be sure, British performers who participate in unrestricted photosessions know or may reasonably be charged with knowledge, that, under British law, they retain no publicity rights in Great Britain. But nothing in the record justifies an assumption that any performers in this case intended to convey American publicity rights to the photographers. The relevant British law speaks only to uses in Great Britain. It does not purport to speak to uses in other nations.

In the case at bar, the law of the United States governs. It has long been established here, as the district court noted, that "by authorizing photographs, a performer does not, without more, license their commercial exploitation." The automatic legal consequences of posing for photographs in Britain cannot be construed to constitute a contractual undertaking with respect to American publicity rights.

The final considerations listed in section 6(2) of the Second Restatement are "certainty, predictability, and uniformity of result, and ease in the determination and application of the law to be applied." With respect to these considerations, the better decision is obvious. Any rule basing publicity rights on the nationality of the performer would give rise to unnecessary confusion. To require American producers and merchandisers of novelties to tailor their expectations and actions according to the nationality of the individuals depicted would be anomalous and unworkable. Such a rule would also create tremendous uncertainty for foreign performers, such as the individual plaintiffs, who seek to do business in this country.

V. In light of the foregoing considerations, we conclude that the district court correctly decided that, for Bi-Rite's claims, the law of Illinois governs, for those of Artemis, the law of Connecticut, and for those of the individual plaintiffs, the law of Georgia.

The judgment of the district court is AFFIRMED.

---

**Cairns v. Franklin Mint Company**
**292 F.3d 1139 (9th Cir. 2002)**

Pregerson, Circuit Judge.

Plaintiffs-Appellants are the trustees of the Diana Princess of Wales Memorial Fund ("the Fund") and the executors of the Estate of Diana, Princess of Wales ("the Estate"). We will refer to them collectively as "the Fund." The Fund brought several state and federal claims against Defendant-Appellee Franklin Mint. The Fund based these claims on Franklin Mint's use of the name and likeness of the late Princess

Diana on commercially sold jewelry, plates, and dolls, and in advertisements for these products. The Fund appeals three holdings by the District Court: (1) the District Court's denial of the Fund's motion to reinstate its dismissed post-mortem right of publicity claim under California Civil Code § 3344.1(a)(1); (2) the District Court's grant of summary judgment in favor of Franklin Mint on the Fund's Lanham Act claim for false endorsement under 15 United States Code § 1125(a)(1); and (3) the District Court's award of attorneys' fees to Franklin Mint. We . . . affirm.

*I. FACTUAL AND PROCEDURAL BACKGROUND*

Since 1981, when Princess Diana married Prince Charles, Franklin Mint has produced, advertised, and sold collectibles – jewelry, plates, and dolls – bearing her name and likeness. Similar products bearing Princess Diana's name and likeness were sold by other companies. Princess Diana neither authorized nor objected to any of these products.

The Fund was established in 1997 after Princess Diana's death to accept donations to be given to various charities with which Princess Diana was associated during her lifetime. The Estate exclusively authorized the Fund to use Princess Diana's name and likeness for this purpose. The Fund in turn authorized about twenty parties – but not Franklin Mint – to use the name and likeness of Princess Diana in conjunction with products sold in the United States. Franklin Mint continued to market unauthorized Diana-related products.

On May 18, 1998, the Fund brought suit against Franklin Mint in the United States District Court for the Central District of California. The complaint alleged violations of the Lanham Act for false endorsement and false advertisement under 15 United States Code § 1125(a)(1), and dilution of trademark under 15 United States Code § 1125(c)(1). The complaint also alleged violations of California's post-mortem right of publicity statute, California Civil Code § 990(a) (now California Civil Code § 3344.1(a)).[2] [[2] Both California Civil Code § 990(a), and California Civil Code § 3344.1(a), provide in part: "Any person who uses a deceased personality's name, voice, signature, photograph, or likeness, in any manner, on or in products, merchandise, or goods, or for purposes of advertising or selling, or soliciting purchases of, products, merchandise, goods, or services, without prior consent from the [decedent's successor or successors in interest], shall be liable for any damages sustained by the person or persons injured as a result thereof."] . . . .

On October 16, 1998, the District Court granted Franklin Mint's motion to dismiss the Fund's post-mortem right of publicity claim under California Civil Code § 990. *Cairns v. Franklin Mint Co.*, 24 F. Supp. 2d 1013, 1022 (C.D.Cal. 1998) ["*Cairns I*"]. The District Court reasoned that California's default personal property choice of law provision, California Civil Code § 946, applied to the Fund's post-mortem right of publicity claim and required application of the law of Great Britain, which does not recognize a post-mortem right of publicity. [3] [[3] California Civil Code § 946 states: "If there is no law to the contrary, in the place where personal property is situated, it is deemed to follow the person of its owner, and is governed by the law of his domicile."] . . . [W]e affirmed the District Court's dismissal of the Fund's post-mortem right of publicity claim and the denial of a preliminary injunction on the Fund's Lanham Act claims in an unpublished memorandum disposition. . . .

After the District Court dismissed the Fund's post-mortem right of publicity claim, the California Legislature renumbered the post-mortem right of publicity statute from § 990 to § 3344.1 and amended it to "apply to the adjudication of liability and the imposition of any damages or other remedies in cases in which the liability, damages, and other remedies arise from acts occurring directly in this state." Cal.Civ.Code § 3344.1(n). Based on this amendment, the Fund filed a motion to reinstate its dismissed post-mortem right of publicity claim. The Fund argued that § 3344.1(n) is a choice of law provision that requires application of California law, which recognizes a post-mortem right of publicity.

On June 22, 2000, the District Court denied the Fund's motion to reinstate its post-mortem right of publicity claim and motion for a preliminary injunction. *Cairns v. Franklin Mint Co.*, 120 F. Supp. 2d 880, 887 (C.D.Cal. 2000) ["*Cairns II*"]. The District Court concluded, based on the plain language of § 3344.1(n) and its legislative history, that this section is *not* a choice of law provision. The District Court further concluded that California's default personal property choice of law provision, California Civil Code § 946, continues to apply to the Fund's post-mortem right of publicity claim and requires application of the law of Great Britain, which does not recognize a post-mortem right of publicity.

On June 27, 2000, the District Court granted Franklin Mint's motion for summary judgment on the Fund's Lanham Act false endorsement claim. *Cairns v. Franklin Mint Co.*, 107 F.Supp.2d 1212, 1223 (C.D. Cal. 2000) ["*Cairns III*"]. The District Court concluded that Franklin Mint's use of Princess Diana's name and likeness did not implicate the source identification purpose of trademark protection. . . . The District Court also . . . concluded that there was no likelihood of consumer confusion as to the origin of Franklin Mint's Diana-related products.

On September 12, 2000, the District Court granted Franklin Mint's motion for attorneys' fees and awarded Franklin Mint $2,308,000 in attorneys' fees out of $3,124,121.85 requested. *Cairns v. Franklin Mint Co.*, 115 F.Supp. 2d 1185, 1190 (C.D.Cal. 2000) ["*Cairns IV*"].

The Fund timely appealed the District Court's denial of its motion to reinstate the post-mortem right of publicity claim and the District Court's grant of Franklin Mint's motion for summary judgment on the Lanham Act claim for false endorsement. Separately, the Fund timely appealed the District Court's award of attorneys' fees to Franklin Mint. The two appeals have been consolidated.

*II. POST-MORTEM RIGHT OF PUBLICITY CLAIM*

*A. Introduction*

California's post-mortem right of publicity statute, in both its former version, California Civil Code § 990(a), and its current version, California Civil Code § 3344.1(a), provides in part that "[a]ny person who uses a deceased personality's name, voice, signature, photograph, or likeness, in any manner, on or in products, merchandise, or goods, or for purposes of advertising or selling, or soliciting purchases of, products, merchandise, goods, or services, without prior consent from the [decedent's successor or successors in interest], shall be liable for any damages sustained by the person or persons injured as a result thereof." It further provides that "[t]he rights recognized under this section are [personal] property rights."

As enacted in 1984 and amended in 1988, California's post-mortem right of publicity statute did not contain a choice of law provision. The District Court concluded that California's default personal property choice of law provision in California Civil Code § 946 applied to the Fund's post-mortem right of publicity claim and required application of the law of the decedent's domicile.[5] [[5] California Civil Code § 946 states: "If there is no law to the contrary, in the place where personal property is situated, it is deemed to follow the person of its owner, and is governed by the law of his domicile." The Fund argues, and we assume *arguendo*, that its alleged post-mortem right of publicity would be "situated" in California.] The law of Great Britain, where Princess Diana was domiciled, does not recognize post-mortem right of publicity claims. *See Bi-Rite Enters. v. Bruce Miner Co.*, 757

F.2d 440, 442 (1st Cir. 1985) (citing *Tolley v. Fry*, 1 K.B. 467 (1930); J. Thomas McCarthy, *Rights of Publicity & Privacy*, § 6.21 (1998). Accordingly, the District Court dismissed the claim. On interlocutory appeal of this dismissal . . . , we affirmed by memorandum disposition.

Effective January 1, 2000, the Legislature renumbered California's post-mortem right of publicity statute from § 990 to § 3344.1 and amended it to "apply to the adjudication of liability and the imposition of any damages or other remedies in cases in which the liability, damages, and other remedies arise from acts occurring directly in this state." Cal.Civ.Code § 3344.1(n) . The former version of the statute contained no comparable provision. Following this amendment, the Fund moved to reinstate its post-mortem right of publicity claim, arguing that § 3344.1(n) is a choice of law provision that requires application of California law. The District Court denied the motion, concluding that § 3344.1(n) is not a choice of law provision. The District Court further concluded that California's default personal property choice of law provision in California Civil Code § 946 applies to the current version of the post-mortem right of publicity in § 3344.1 – as it did to the former version of that right in § 990 – and requires the application of the law of the decedent's domicile, Great Britain, which does not recognize a post-mortem right of publicity.

The Fund argues before us – as it did before the District Court – that § 3344.1(n) is a choice of law provision requiring application of California law to its post-mortem right of publicity claim. . . . We conclude that the plain language of § 3344.1(n), as well as its legislative history, supports the District Court's decision not to reinstate the Fund's post-mortem right of publicity claim.

*B. Plain Language of the Statute*

. . . Section 3344.1(n) limits the application of California's post-mortem right of publicity statute to "cases in which the liability, damages, and other remedies arise from acts occurring directly in this state." The District Court concluded that by the plain meaning of its language, this provision is not a choice of law provision, but "simply addresses the reach of the statute's coverage."

We agree. Section 3344.1(b) provides that the postmortem right of publicity is a (personal) property right. Section 3344.1(n) states that California's post-mortem right of publicity statute "shall apply to cases . . . aris[ing] from acts occurring directly in [California]." Section 3344.1(n) does *not* state that California's post-mortem right of publicity statute applies to such cases *regardless of the domicile* of the owner of the right. Section 946 provides that personal property is governed by the law of the domicile of its owner unless there is law to the contrary in the place where the personal property is situated, i.e., California. The statement in § 3344.1(n) that California's post-mortem right of publicity statute "shall apply to cases . . . aris[ing] from acts occurring directly in [California]" is compatible with the post-mortem right of publicity being governed by the law of the domicile of its owner, because the statute does not state by its plain language that such cases are *not* governed by the law of the domicile of the owner. Thus, there is no "law to the contrary" to prevent application of the default choice of law provision in § 946 to the post-mortem right of publicity statute in § 3344.1. Accordingly, unless the "literal application" of the statute will produce "a result demonstrably at odds with the intentions of its drafters," § 946 applies to § 3344.1, and the Fund's post-mortem right of publicity claim is foreclosed.

The Fund argues that "[t]here is nothing in [§ 3344.1] to suggest that a court should look to Cal. Civil Code § 946 . . . to determine whether the post-mortem right of publicity applies to a particular plaintiff or her heirs." Section 946, however, is a *default* choice of law provision that applies "[i]f there is no law to the contrary," and no explicit reference to this default provision should be expected in § 3344.1 – let alone required – for § 946 to apply.

*C. Legislative History*

The legislative history of § 3344.1 further supports our conclusion that § 3344.1(n) is not a choice of law provision. On January 20, 1999, Senator Burton introduced Senate Bill 209 seeking to amend the former version of the post-mortem right of publicity statute in § 990. The proposed amendment initially contained a subsection (o) that stated: "[A] plaintiff has standing to bring an action pursuant to this section if any of the acts giving rise to the action occurred in this state, *whether or not the plaintiff is a domiciliary of this state.*" The "domiciliary of this state" language was later deleted from the proposed amendment. The amendment was ultimately adopted without this language as § 3344.1(n), which reads as follows: "This section shall apply to the adjudication of liability and the imposition of any damages or other remedies in cases in which the liability, damages, and other remedies arise from acts occurring directly in this state." Cal.Civ.Code § 3344.1(n) .

The California Assembly Judiciary Committee Hearing of June 22, 1999 provides evidence that the Legislature did *not* intend § 3344.1(n), as adopted, to prevent application of § 946 to the post-mortem right of publicity. During that hearing, Senator Burton attempted to re-introduce the "domiciliary of this state" language. Assembly Member and Committee Vice-Chair Pacheco asked whether such an addition was necessary and whether there was "any law that says you have to be domiciled in the state at the time of death." Mark Lee, counsel for the Fund in this case before the District Court and present at the hearing on behalf of the Fund as a proponent of Senate Bill 209, answered that the District Court in *Cairns I* had "held that domicile was required."[6] [[6] Similarly, the Senate Rules Committee Report on Senate Bill No. 209, as amended March 3, 1999, states: SB 209 would state that "pursuant to the jurisdiction provided under Code of Civil Procedure 410.10, a plaintiff has standing to bring an action pursuant to this section if any of the acts giving rise to the action occurred in this state, *whether or not the decedent was a domiciliary of this state at the time of death.*" . . . The author [i.e., Senator Burton] asserts that *this clarification of law is necessary in light of a recent decision, Lord Simone Cairnes v. Franklin Mint.*] After further discussion, Senator Burton withdrew his proposed amendment to add the "domiciliary of the state" language to what became § 3344.1(n).

. . . Here, the Committee deleted the "domiciliary of this state" language and resisted Senator Burton's attempt to reinsert this language. The Legislature ultimately passed § 3344.1(n) without the "domiciliary of this state" language. . . . [T]his "rejection by the Legislature" of the "domiciliary of this state" language is "most persuasive to the conclusion that [§ 3344.1(n)] should not be construed to include the omitted ['domiciliary of this state' language]." The rejection of the "domiciliary of this state" language is made more persuasive by the California Assembly Judiciary Committee's insistence on deleting this language although the Committee was made aware that the District Court's decision in *Cairns I* required domicile in California in the absence of such language.

Taken together, the legislative history strongly indicates that the Legislature did *not* intend to statutorily overrule the District Court's requirement of California domicile in *Cairns I*. Thus, a "literal application" of § 3344.1(n) will not produce "a result demonstrably at odds with the intentions of its drafters." Accordingly, the Fund's post-mortem right of publicity claim must fail because the law of Princess Diana's domicile, Great Britain, governs and that law does not recognize a post-mortem right of publicity.

*III. FALSE ENDORSEMENT...*

The District Court granted Franklin Mint's motion for summary judgment on the Fund's Lanham Act claim for false endorsement because Franklin Mint's use of Princess Diana's name and likeness did not implicate the source-identification purpose of trademark protection, and because there was no likelihood of customer confusion as to the origin of Franklin Mint's Diana-related products. . . .

Under the law of false endorsement, likelihood of customer confusion is the determinative issue. Between 1981 and 1997, many products, including some that were largely indistinguishable from Franklin Mint products, bore the name and likeness of Princess Diana, who neither endorsed nor objected to any of these products. Consumers, therefore, had no reason to believe Franklin Mint's Diana-related products were endorsed by the Princess. This did not change when, following Princess Diana's death in 1997, the Fund endorsed approximately twenty products – but not Franklin Mint's – amidst a flood of *un*-endorsed Diana-related memorabilia. Under these circumstances, there was no likelihood of confusion as to the origin of Franklin Mint's Diana-related products. In addition, Franklin Mint is entitled to a "fair use" defense for its references to Princess Diana to describe its Diana-related products. Accordingly, the District Court did not err when it granted summary judgment in favor of Franklin Mint on this claim. . . .

*IV. ATTORNEYS' FEES*

The District Court awarded Franklin Mint $2,308,000 in attorneys' fees. We review such an award for an abuse of discretion, and, finding no abuse of discretion, we affirm. . . .

*V. CONCLUSION*

For the foregoing reasons, we affirm the District Court's denial of the Fund's motion to reinstate its post-mortem right of publicity claim. We also affirm the District Court's grant of Franklin Mint's motion for summary judgment on the Fund's false endorsement claim. We finally affirm the District Court's award of $2,308,000 in attorneys' fees to Franklin Mint.

---

**Note on British right of publicity law**

At the time the Princess Diana Estate's right of publicity claim was first dismissed, it could be said that British law did not recognize a right of publicity – something the Court of Appeals did say in its decision affirming that dismissal. That is no longer true, however.

In a case filed by British Formula One race car driver Eddie Irvine, the Chancery Division of the U.K. High Court of Justice held that the British law doctrine of "passing off" gives celebrities the right to bring "false endorsement" claims against those who use celebrity names and likenesses without authorization. *Irvine v. Talksport Limited,* [2002] EWHC 367 (Ch) [available at www.courtservice.gov.uk]. As a result, Irvine won his lawsuit against a British sports talk radio station that used Irvine's photograph, without his consent, in a brochure the station sent to advertising agencies to publicize changes to its programming format.

Nevertheless, the *Irvine* decision would not have affected the outcome of the Princess Diana case, for at least three reasons. First, the Chancery Division emphasized that its *Irvine* decision concerns "false endorsement" claims only, not unauthorized merchandising, while the Princess Diana Estate's right of publicity claims were based on unauthorized merchandising. Moreover, the Chancery Division decision dealt only with the claims of living celebrities; it did not discuss the more difficult issue of whether deceased celebrities have false endorsement rights as well. Finally, the Princess Diana Estate was permitted to assert a false endorsement claim under U.S. law, even before such a claim was recognized in British law; the Estate simply failed to prove the facts necessary to win that claim.

---

**Note on Ohio right of publicity statute**

Not all right of publicity statutes are as ambiguous as California's about who they benefit. Ohio's statute, for example, explicitly provides that its benefits are limited to *living* individuals "whose domicile or residence" was Ohio on or since November 22, 1999, and to *deceased* individuals who died on or since January 1, 1998 and "whose domicile or residence" was Ohio the day they died. Title 27 Ohio Revised Code Section 2741.03 (1999). Thus, Princess Diana's publicity rights are unprotected in Ohio – not because she was British, but rather because neither her domicile nor residence was in Ohio the day she died. On the other hand, the publicity rights of many deceased (and living) American celebrities are not protected in Ohio either, because they don't live there.

---

**Cuccioli v. Jekyll & Hyde Neue Metropol Bremen Theater Produktion GmbH & Co.**
**150 F. Supp. 2d 566 (S.D.N.Y. 2001)**

Lewis A. Kaplan, District Judge.

Plaintiff [Robert Cuccioli], the star of the New York production of the musical, *Jekyll & Hyde,* here sues the producer of the German production for violation of Sections 50 and 51 of the New York Civil Rights Law. He contends that the German producer is using his likeness on merchandise and other materials in violation of the statute. The matter is before the Court on cross motions for summary judgment. The two main issues at this stage are whether there is any genuine issue of material fact regarding the exercise of personal jurisdiction over the defendant and whether the New York Civil Rights Law has extraterritorial effect.

I

The following facts are undisputed. The plaintiff appeared in the eponymous role(s) in the Houston, off-Broadway, and Broadway productions of the musical *Jekyll & Hyde* from 1995 to 1999. The defendant, a German company, is in the business of theatrical productions and related endeavors. Its principal place of business is Bremen, Germany. Following negotiations in New York, Music Theatre International ("MTI"), Wildhorn Productions, Inc. ("WPI"), and Stage and Screen Music, Inc.("SSMI"), licensed the defendant to produce *Jekyll & Hyde* in Germany, Austria, and Switzerland.

This dispute dates back at least to 1998. On March 20, 1998, the defendant received a fax from MTI stating that "per my voice mail message, PACE[3] [n3 Pace Theatricals is one of various affiliates or successors that produced *Jekyll & Hyde* in New York] has signed off on the use of the title treatment for *Jekyll & Hyde.*" The parties disagree concerning whether this approved defendant's title treatment only or the logo as a whole. In any case, defendant's musical and art director wrote to the plaintiff in August 1998, enclosing samples of merchandise and stating that "our logo is a combination of the tour logo (red and black) and the Broadway logo. If you have a closer look at it, you will see that the face is yours! So I thought it a nice idea to get you some samples of it. . . ." So much for good intentions.

During the following month, plaintiff's management firm demanded that defendant cease and desist from this use of plaintiff's image. The parties agree that the defendant never obtained written consent from the plaintiff to use his likeness.

The German production of *Jekyll & Hyde* premiered on February 19, 1999, a month after plaintiff's final appearance in the Broadway production. In March 1999, defendant signed an agreement with Polydor Records, GmbH, to release a compact disc of its German-language cast recording of *Jekyll & Hyde*. The logo containing plaintiff's image appears on the CD itself, on the back of the package liner, and on pages of the liner that offer other merchandise featuring the disputed image. The parties agree that this CD made its way to New York consumers through at least one sale off defendant's web site, <www.jekyll-hyde.de>, and several sales through local record stores,[7] [n7 On July 28, 1999, a cast album CD was sold to a New York resident through defendant's web site, <www.jekyll-hyde.de> and in June and August 2000, plaintiff purchased CDs at record stores in New York] although there is no evidence that defendant was responsible for the CD reaching the local stores.

Plaintiff brought this action in March 2000, premising subject matter jurisdiction on diversity or, more properly, alienage. The amended complaint alleges use of the plaintiff's image in violation of New York Civil Rights Law Sections 50 and 51 and requests compensatory and exemplary damages as well as injunctive relief. . . .

On September 21, 2000, following discovery, plaintiff moved for summary judgment and to dismiss defendant's affirmative defenses. Defendant cross-moved for summary judgment dismissing the complaint on the ground that it fails to state a claim upon which relief may be granted. It argues that its use of plaintiff's likeness outside New York is not reached by the New York Civil Rights Law, that plaintiff cannot establish any injury from any use of his likeness in New York, and that the Court lacks jurisdiction over defendant's person. It seeks dismissal of plaintiff's prayer for an injunction on the ground of mootness.

II.

A. *Personal Jurisdiction*

[Judge Kaplan held that his court did have personal jurisdiction over the German company, because it transacted business in New York by negotiating the licensing agreement in New York, paying royalties to licensors in New York, and by agreeing (in the license agreement) to submit to the jurisdiction of New York courts.]

*B. Statute of Limitations*

Plaintiff moves also for summary judgment dismissing the statute of limitations defense. . . .

Plaintiff concedes that the statute of limitations on Section 51 claims is one year and that this action was commenced two years after defendant began to produce merchandise bearing the allegedly offending logo. He nevertheless argues that defendant's actions have been of a continuing nature and that the statute first began to run from the most recent abuse, thus saving the entirety of his claim. The argument is without merit.

Under New York law, a statute of limitations begins to run when a claim accrues. A tort claim accrues upon the occurrence of the last event necessary to give rise to a claim, generally at the time of injury. . . .

In view of these principles, plaintiff's concession that it did not sue until more than one year after the defendant's first use of the logo would appear to be fatal to his claim. But the matter is not quite so simple for two reasons.

First, each new edition of a work – such as a paperback edition of a work previously published only in hard cover – ordinarily is viewed as "a new publication upon which a separate cause of action may be based and for which the statute of limitations begins to run again." The same principle applies to merchandise bearing names or images allegedly violative of Section 51. . . . [T]he statute of limitations runs separately as to each new product distributed with a name or image, the use of which contravenes the statute. Hence, the statute began to run as to the CD of the German cast recording on the date that it first was placed on sale in violation of Section 51, and it began to run as to each other item of merchandise on the analogous date for each.

The second difficulty is implicit in what has been said already and is intertwined with defendant's principal argument – that plaintiff has no claim for the allegedly unconsented to use of his likeness outside the State of New York. As the statute of limitations begins to run upon the occurrence of the last event necessary to give rise to a claim, the date of first publication or distribution of a given article of merchandise triggers the statute only if that publication or distribution is actionable. Hence, if Section 51 gives rise to a claim only for use of plaintiff's likeness *in the State of New York,* then the last event necessary to give rise to a claim occurs – and the statute begins to run – only upon first publication or distribution in New York. Accordingly, the Court turns to that question.

*C. Effect of Section 51 With Respect to Out-of-State Uses*

Defendant seeks dismissal of so much of plaintiff's claim as relates to out-of-state uses of his likeness on the ground that Section 51 of the Civil Rights Law creates a cause of action in favor only of "any person whose name, portrait, picture, or voice is used *within this state* for advertising purposes or for the purposes of trade" without written consent as required by Section 50. Plaintiff disputes this conclusion, contending that the single publication rule permits a plaintiff injured in the manner claimed here to bring a single action and to recover therein damages for all injuries sustained, wherever the publication occurred. But plaintiff misses the point.

To be sure, the single publication rule usually is summarized as standing for the propositions that a plaintiff, as to any single publication, may bring only one action and may recover in that action "all damages suffered in all jurisdictions." But this summary does not do away with choice of law analysis. Plaintiff brought this action in a federal court in New York, thereby submitting himself to application of New York choice of law rules. New York applies its own substantive law to claims for violation of the right of publicity brought by New York domiciliaries such as plaintiff.

The inquiry does not end there. For application of New York law to comport with due process New York must have "a significant contact or significant aggregation of contacts" with the parties and transaction "creating state interests, such that choice of its law is neither arbitrary nor fundamentally unfair. Choice of New York law meets this standard. Plaintiff is a New York domiciliary, and the dispute arises from contracts that both plaintiff and defendant negotiated in New York. At least one of those contracts contains a New York choice-of-law provision. Defendant's agreements provide for on-going contacts between the defendant and New York. Moreover, just as New York, in its role as "financial capital of the world, serving as an international clearinghouse and market place for a plethora of international transactions," has an interest in resolving financial disputes related to it, New York has an interest in resolving disputes involving subsidiary rights to Broadway theater productions.

Having concluded that New York substantive law controls this dispute, the Court proceeds to its determination. In *Roberson v. Rochester Folding Box Co.,* the New York Court of Appeals broadly declared that there is no common law right of privacy in the State of New York and denied recovery to an infant plaintiff whose photograph had been distributed widely by the defendant in order to advertise its baking flour. The Legislature promptly adopted the statute here in question to overturn the holding of *Roberson,* albeit not its broad dictum, by creating a cause of action for the commercial or trade use of one's name or picture without one's consent. In doing so, however, it created a claim in favor only of one whose likeness had been used for prohibited purposes "within this state." In consequence, as New York courts uniformly have held, the substantive law of New York is that one may recover for trade or commercial use of one's likeness only to the extent that the use occurs in New York.

This conclusion has two implications here. The first is that out-of-state uses of plaintiff's likeness for trade or advertising purposes are not actionable under New York law. To the extent that plaintiff seeks damages based on such uses, his claim must be dismissed. Second, as the out-of-state uses are not actionable, they cannot trigger the running of the statute of limitations. Accordingly, the statute of limitations as to each type of merchandise on which plaintiff's likeness has appeared runs from the date on which it first was offered for sale in New York.

The merchandise that indisputably was sold by defendant in New York was the one CD purchased in July 1999 from defendant's web site. As that sale occurred less than one year before the commencement of this action, the claim with respect to that sale is timely unless the offering of the German language cast recordings via the Internet web site accessible from New York (a) began more than one year before the commencement of this action, and (b) was sufficient to trigger the running of the statute of limitations – in other words, was a use "within this state."

New York courts do not seem to have addressed the question whether items on a web site that can be viewed in New York are published or offered for sale to the public in New York. Perhaps the most useful analogy is to jurisdictional analysis of commercial torts such as trademark infringement because such a tort is committed within New York if infringing goods have been offered for sale in New York. There is consensus in the developing case law that whether a defendant has committed a tort in the state through its web site depends on how interactive the web site is. . . .

Defendant's web site was created and maintained in Germany in connection with the Bremen production of the show. The CD in question was of a German language cast recording, certainly an item of limited appeal in the United States. The web site itself was in German. The only suggestion that the merchandise, the web site, or the Bremen production was promoted in New York or, for that matter, elsewhere in the United States is plaintiff's unsupported assertion that there was a hyperlink from the New York production's web site to defendant's web site. Although such a hyperlink might be a factor suggesting an offer for sale in New York, plaintiff here alleges only that defendant's web site was "accessible" through that hyperlink, not that defendant was responsible for the connection. In these circumstances, the Court holds that the offering of merchandise containing the plaintiff's image on the German web site did not constitute a use of the image "within this state." Accordingly, it neither began the running of the statute of limitations nor gave rise to a broader cause of action.

III

For the foregoing reasons, plaintiff's motion for summary judgment dismissing the affirmative defenses is granted to the extent that the defense of lack of personal jurisdiction is dismissed. . . . Defendant's cross-motion for summary judgment dismissing the complaint is granted to the extent that the action, insofar as it seeks damages for allegedly unconsented to uses of plaintiff's likeness outside the State of New York, is granted.

---

**The Legal Protection Accorded to Personal Names**
Excerpted from
***The Recognition of Rights and the Use of Names in the Internet Domain Name System***
***Report of the Second WIPO Internet Domain Name Process* (2001)**



Personal names are rarely protected *as such* by the law. Their protection is usually a part of a broader legal principle or policy of which the misuse of personal names constitutes only one means of violation. Other means of violation include misuse of a person's likeness, image or voice.

Because of the diversity of interests affected by the treatment of personal names, the legal principles and policies that can be deployed to protect personal names are similarly diverse and vary, as might be expected, from country to country. These legal principles and policies include the right to publicity or the right to control the commercial use of one's identity, recognized in many States of the United States of America; the tort of unfair competition; the tort of passing-off (conceptually treated, in many cases, as part of the law of unfair competition), recognized generally in common-law countries; and the right to privacy.

It has not been possible to review in detail all the legal principles and policies that can be used for the protection of personal names in all of the countries of the world. Nevertheless, it is possible to identify two main interests that underlie particular approaches adopted in a number of countries to the protection of personal names against misuse:

(i) A commonly expressed public policy for the protection of personal names against misuse is economic. This economic policy, in turn, has two bases. The first of those bases is the prevention of unjust enrichment through the unauthorized commercial use of another's identity. As stated by Kalven and quoted by the Supreme Court of the United States of America, "The rationale for [protecting the right of publicity] is the straight-forward one of preventing unjust enrichment by the theft of good will. No social purpose is served by having the defendant get free some aspect of the plaintiff that would have market value and for which he would normally pay." The second basis of the economic interest underlying the protection of personal names against misuse is the prevention of deception and confusion on the part of consumers.

(ii) A social interest is also expressed as underlying legal principles protecting personal names against misuse. This interest is apparent in the right to privacy, or the qualified right to control exposure of oneself, where personal distress and anxiety are recognized as valid reasons to accord protection.

In a number of cases, both the economic and the social interests are recognized in the protection that law accords. Thus, in Switzerland, Article 29.2 of the Civil Code states that "Where a person assumes the name of another to the latter's prejudice, the latter can apply for an injunction to restrain the continuation of this assumption, and can in addition claim damages if the act is proved to be wrongful, and moral compensation if this is justified by the nature of the wrong suffered." And in Spain, Section 7.6 of the Law of May 5, 1982, provides that the unpermitted use of one's name, voice or likeness for *advertising or trade* purposes is an invasion of one's *personal* life.

The notoriety that attaches to certain persons can, in some countries, establish a basis for protection which is not available to ordinary persons. [For example, in Japan, on the basis of Article 709 of the Civil Code.] In other instances, notoriety can be a factor which can influence the extent of damages granted as a result of the wrongful use of the person's name, rather than a ground for establishing a separate form of protection from that available to non-famous persons.

In commerce, the protection that is recognized for personal names and other attributes of the personality is usually exploited through the vehicle of contract. Thus, by permitting, under contract (or license), another to use a person's name in association with products or services, the personal name becomes an asset.

The status of the personal name as a potential asset may be secured through the registration of a trademark (or service mark). Most national laws, and the Agreement on Trade-Related Aspects of Intellectual Property Rights (the TRIPS Agreement), explicitly recognize that personal names are eligible for registration as trademarks. While personal names are eligible for registration as trademarks, however, like any sign for which trademark registration is sought, they must be *distinctive in order to be valid trademarks. Distinctiveness can be inherent, or can* be acquired through use which causes consumers to identify the name with a particular source of goods or services.

While there are, as indicated in the preceding paragraphs, several different legal doctrines that apply on a widespread basis at the national level to protect personal names against misuse, there is no specific norm established at the international level for the protection of personal names. The absence of any such norm reflects the fact that there is a diversity of legal approaches to the protection of personal names at the national level.

---

### 1.1.2 Privacy

**Douglas v. Hello! Ltd.**
**United Kingdom Court of Appeal (Civil Division) (2000)**



*Lord Justice Brooke:*

On 22nd and 23rd November 2000 we heard an appeal by the defendants Hello! Ltd against an injunction granted by Hunt J on 21st November restraining them until trial or further order from publishing or further publishing photographs of the first and second claimants Michael Douglas and Catherine Zeta-Jones taken at their wedding at the Plaza Hotel New York on 18th-19th November 2000. . . .

We discharged the injunction at the end of the hearing of the appeal and said that we would give our reasons for allowing the appeal in due course.

The defendants are the proprietors of Hello! magazine. The third claimants Northern & Shell plc are the proprietors of OK! magazine. These two magazines are rivals in the same market. At the time we heard the appeal the most recent circulation figures from the Audit Bureau of Circulation ("ABC") showed that they were neck and neck, with Hello! showing an average weekly circulation of 458,663, and OK! lagging slightly behind at 455,162. Mr Ashford, who is the editorial director of OK!, has told the court that the ABC rating at the end of the ABC year has an enormous effect on the rates which magazines can charge advertisers over the next six months, so that the magazine which has the highest rating has a significant advantage over its rival(s). Mr Ashford added that the Douglas wedding, for which OK! had secured exclusive rights, was the last important feature before the end of the ABC year.

. . . [T]his is not the trial of the action. The court is not concerned to decide whether, as the claimants contend, Hello! has acted unlawfully. If at the trial it is held that Hello! has acted unlawfully, it is likely that it will have to pay the claimants very substantial sums of money, whether as damages or as a consequence of any account they may be ordered to make in relation to all the profits it has received as a result of its unlawful acts. Since it decided to proceed with the publication of Issue 639 of its magazine after we discharged the injunction, and after it had had the opportunity of reading all the evidence which the claimants placed before the court, it could have no possible excuse for its behaviour if it were held that it has acted unlawfully.

. . . Our sole concern is to decide whether in accordance with well established principles an injunction restraining this publication should be continued in force until trial, thereby in effect "killing" this weekly issue of Hello! . . . .

OK! bases its claim in the present action on the rights it secured under an agreement it made with Mr Douglas and Ms Zeta-Jones on 10th November 2000, eight days before the wedding. It undertook to pay a very large sum of money to each of them in respect of these rights, payable not later than one week before the wedding. OK! asserted that Hello! offered three times the eventual contract sum for rights to exclusive coverage, but that the couple trusted OK! to project only the images they wanted projected to the public. Hello! does not dispute that it tendered for the rights, although we were told that it did dispute that it had offered three times as much as OK!. At all events, this evidence shows that Hello! knew that exclusive rights were to be granted for coverage of the wedding, and that it did not secure them themselves.

The 10th November agreement, in summary, provided that the third claimants were granted exclusive rights for a nine-month period to publish colour photographs of the wedding taken by a photographer hired by Mr Douglas and Ms Zeta-Jones, and to publish an article, including a story and photographs, about the wedding. It was also granted similar rights for a similar period in respect of the consent to use Mr Douglas's and Ms Zeta-Jones's name, voice, signature, photograph or likeness in connection with the wedding. The couple retained wide rights of approval in relation to anything that was to be published and the identity of any other publications in which published material might appear. Mr Douglas and Ms Zeta-Jones undertook to use their best efforts to ensure that:

> "no other media (including but not limited to photographers, television crews or journalists) shall be permitted access to the Wedding, and that no guests or anyone else present at the Wedding (including staff at the venues) shall be allowed to take photographs."

If any infringing material was used by a third party, OK! undertook to pursue all necessary legal action to cause such infringement to cease, if requested to do so. The obligation to provide security rested with Mr Douglas and Ms Zeta-Jones. There was also a profit-sharing agreement in relation to the exploitation of the rights once OK! had recouped its original investment.

OK! adduced evidence to the effect that it had been widely reported in the international media before the event that there would be security at the wedding, and that no one would be allowed to photograph or videotape anything at the wedding or the wedding reception. It was also made clear in the media coverage that the news media (including the paparazzi tabloids) would not be permitted to gain access to the wedding or reception so that they could not take any photographs of the couple, or any of the members of their family, or the other wedding guests. Mr Ashford described a sophisticated large-scale operation, planned with military precision, to try to ensure that no other media reporting took place. . . .

. . . [C]onfidentiality agreements prohibited each service company and each vendor which signed them (including each of their respective employees) from keeping, disclosing, using or selling any "photograph, film, videotape, etc" which were obtained at the wedding reception. The agreements also specifically provided that any such disclosure would constitute a material breach of them, and might also constitute a breach of trust, breach of fiduciary duty and an invasion of privacy, which would cause irreparable harm to Michael and Catherine and that, therefore, they would have the right to seek and obtain an injunction to prevent any such disclosure. . . .

. . . [A]ll the guests who were invited to the wedding or the reception received with their invitation a separate written notice which stated: "We would appreciate no photography or video devices at the ceremony or reception." Moreover, in order for a guest to gain access to both the wedding ceremony and the wedding reception, he or she had to go through a secure entrance or a check point which was maintained by a professional security service, and by others. There was said to be a notice posted at the entrance which announced a similar message: "no photography or video devices at the ceremony or reception". Each guest who went into the wedding ceremony and into the ballroom at the Plaza Hotel where the wedding reception was held, was visually checked to make certain that he or she did not have any cameras, videotape machines or any other audio or video or recording devices and, where there was any suspicious circumstance, security personnel used high-tech equipment to make certain that no camera or videotape devices were smuggled into the wedding reception. Any guest who had, mistakenly, brought a camera or videotape machine with them had to turn it in or check it before entering, in order to be permitted to attend the wedding and/or the reception. . . .

They also said that during the wedding reception, the security personnel looked for anyone who appeared to have, or might have, a camera or videotape machine. Security personnel saw someone with a camera on about six occasions during the reception. They immediately confiscated the camera and took the film out of it, thereby exposing the film and destroying any photographs that might have been taken. They then either escorted the person out of the reception, or if a wedding guest was involved, detained the camera until the guest was ready to leave the reception. Although a large number of security staff were monitoring the reception for this purpose, none of them reported having seen anyone else taking photographs or doing any videotaping at the reception.

It was also said that there was no way of gaining access to the ballroom of the Plaza Hotel without going through the security check point. As a further security measure to try to keep uninvited people from crashing the wedding or reception, security passes were issued to the invited guests within 24 hours before the ceremony and each invited guest was given a specially made gold pin to wear. No one was allowed to enter the ballroom unless he or she was an invited guest or someone working at the wedding reception, and no one could see into the ballroom from outside, or take photographs or make a videotape from outside the ballroom, since there was no visual access. . . .

The wedding celebrations began at 7.30pm New York time (12.30am GMT) on the evening of Saturday 18th November. At 7.30pm on Monday evening, 20th November, Ms Zeta-Jones telephoned the third claimants' head of legal affairs in London. She sounded upset and told him that a magazine was about to publish unauthorised photographs taken at their wedding. An interim injunction was obtained from Buckley J, as I have said, on the telephone later that evening. Although we have not been furnished with the reasons he gave for granting the injunction, it appears that he was told that OK! had received information earlier that day from more than one source that photos were being offered for sale; that nine low resolution photos of the wedding had been faxed to OK! from Holland; that OK! had been told that the photos were by Phil Ramey, a well known Californian paparazzo; that copies of Hello! were already in the United Kingdom with a photo of the wedding on the front and would be distributed very shortly; that a distributor had told Mr Martin Townsend (of OK!) that copies were coming in through Stansted for delivery to a warehouse at Borehamwood; and that efforts, which were continuing, had been made to contact the editor of Hello! after a security guard who answered the phone at their premises had been unable to help. . . .

Because Ms Zeta-Jones and Mr Douglas trusted OK! to project only the images they wanted to be projected to the public, it was a condition in their agreement with OK! that they would vet the photographs of the wedding to be published by OK! before they were published. Mr Gill explained that the condition that photographs published by magazines such as OK! be carefully selected and approved and retouched before publication, was commonly demanded by celebrities because they were inevitably very anxious about controlling the images of them released to the public. Neither of them would wish to see unflattering, fuzzy photographs of them at their wedding made public. He asserted that the publication of these photographs had caused irreparable harm to them.

He added that his company had concluded about £750,000 worth of syndicate deals for the exclusive photographs, and that they had received numerous telephone calls and e-mails from licensees threatening to terminate the licence as a result of these unauthorised photos being published. . . .

It appears from the evidence adduced by Hello! that a company called Neneta Overseas Ltd, with an address in the British Virgin Islands, sold the exclusive UK rights in the nine photographs to which the claimants took exception to Hola SA for use in Hello! magazine, pursuant to an agreement it concluded with Mr Sanchez, the proprietor of Hello!, on Sunday 19th November. Mr Sanchez, for his part, has said that he did not commission these photos or finance them or agree a price for them in advance. One of his employees had agreed a price for them on the Sunday as soon as they had been delivered to him that day. He maintained that he merely owned the exclusive rights for publication in the United Kingdom, Spain and France and he denied that he had any agents representing him in the United States. Ms Cartwright, for her part, said that Hello! had no previous knowledge that these pictures were going to be taken until they were offered on the open market around the world on the Sunday. She explained that Hello! was then able to fit them in the magazine which was by then substantially ready.

Mr Moore, who is the circulation director of Hello!, said that the print order had been confirmed to the printers in Spain on the Friday, and that the first copies of the magazine traditionally arrived in this country at 7am on the Monday. This issue had been running later than usual. To the best of his knowledge the print run had started on the Sunday, and about a third of the total order had arrived at Stansted on a cargo plane at 4.50pm on the Monday.

OK! on the other hand adduced evidence from Mr Paul Anderson, its Photos Editor, who said that he had spoken on the telephone on the Monday with Phil Ramey . . . who had told him that it was Mr Sanchez who owned the photos, and that he was acting as Mr Sanchez's agent in the United States. Mr Anderson said that later that evening Mr Ramey told him that he was "pulling" the photos from all the US magazines to which he had distributed them, because it was clear that it was now not worth his while to distribute them in the United States.

Mr Anderson said that he believed the disputed photos had been taken by a small camera which was either a digital or an ordinary camera or video camera. Their appearance suggested that the photographer was trying to take the photographs covertly, and they may have been taken with two different types of equipment, either by an amateur photographer or by a professional photographer operating under difficult conditions.

The remainder of the evidence related to the damage which each side claimed that it would suffer if the injunction was, alternatively was not, continued. So far as Mr Douglas and Ms Zeta-Jones are concerned, this evidence was largely based on what Mr Maninder Gill told the court in his witness statement . . . . We were also shown a confidential statement of the reasons why the publication of each of these photographs was said to have caused them such damage.

OK!, for its part, relied on the evidence about the importance of the ABC rating. . . . This, Mr Ashford said, was even more important than usual because OK! was planning to float on the stock market next year, and the rating would be pivotal in attracting investors. He had anticipated that the circulation of the edition of OK! containing the wedding photographs would be double the usual circulation of the magazine. He believed that this would be no longer possible if Hello! was allowed to publish, because the appetites of non-regular readers would have been sated by seeing these photos. In addition, because of Hello!'s action OK! had been forced to publish an incomplete set of pictures a week earlier than they had planned. OK! was also concerned about the potential loss of the value of the syndication agreements they had secured.

Hello!, for its part, described its potential losses, if in effect it "lost" the whole of this issue (as would be inevitable for a weekly magazine if the injunction was continued) under three main headings: the loss of advertising revenue, the loss of readership income, and the damage to its relationship with the news trade.

As to the first, Ms Cartwright said that Hello! would have to refund to advertisers the costs they had paid for space in this issue. Two very important advertisers had placed time-sensitive advertisements in this issue, and in a fiercely competitive market she feared that if they let down any of their advertisers it was probable that they would decline to advertise for some time to come. OK! had been trying for some time to make inroads into Hello!'s advertisement sales, and if Issue 639 could not be put on sale, she feared that some advertisers might be so annoyed they would switch to OK! on a long term basis.

She was also very concerned about the potential loss of readership if Hello! did not appear that week. It was bought by about 456,000 people every week, a large proportion of whom were regular buyers, and it had a readership of 2.2 million readers every week. She said that any interruption in the publishing schedule could be extremely damaging to reader loyalty, and it could take a considerable time to regain lost readers, as they might feel let down and cheated by the non-appearance of Issue 639. Since Hello! had published regular features about the forthcoming wedding in earlier issues, readers would have been led to expect that the wedding itself would be covered in some way in the week after it took place.

So far as relationships with the news trade were concerned, she said that for 12 years Hello! had always been on sale in London on a Tuesday and in the rest of the country on a Wednesday, and the magazine had long-established relationships with 90 wholesale houses and 55,000 retailers. It occupied a premium position on the shelves because it had always been seen to be reliable and profitable, and Ms Cartwright feared that this position would be damaged (to the advantage of OK!) if it was perceived to be unreliable. She feared that if Issue 639 failed to appear, Hello! would suffer a damaging loss of confidence in the eyes of its partners in the news trade. . . .

So much for the evidence. I now turn to the question we had to decide, in the exercise of our own discretion (given that we do not know how the judge decided to exercise the discretion vested in him . . . ). If this matter goes forward and the claimants' case succeeds at trial, the bill which Hello! will have to pay is likely to be enormous, but this is a risk it decided to take, with its eyes open, after we discharged the injunction. We had to decide a very different matter, that is to say whether the court should continue the injunction which would prevent over half a million copies of Issue 639 from reaching its readers at all. It goes without saying that this is a case concerned with freedom of expression. Although the right to freedom of expression is not in every case the ace of trumps, it is a powerful card to which the courts of this country must always pay appropriate respect. . . .

On the facts of the present case, . . . there is clearly a serious issue to be tried in relation to the claims made by all three claimants. Although the evidence they adduced is often rather impersonal, and one might reasonably be sceptical about the efficiency of some of the security measures, given that no less than six different cameras were later found in the possession of people who had passed through the security checks, it appears that a real effort was made to inform everyone who entered the relevant parts of the hotel that the occasion had characteristics of confidentiality. In other words, people were being trusted to participate in this private occasion, in whatever role, on the strict understanding that they might not take photographic images of what they saw. There was also evidence to the effect that the images could not have been taken by someone from outside who was not bound by these obligations of confidence.

In those circumstances it would certainly be arguable, if the appropriate facts were established at trial, that "unauthorised" images were taken on this private occasion by someone in breach of his or her duty of confidence, and that they therefore constituted "confidential information" as to what was going on at the wedding and the wedding reception. . . .

I cannot, however, exclude the possibility that the trial judge might find, as Sedley LJ has suggested in . . . his judgment, that the photographer was an intruder with whom no relationship of trust or confidence had been established. In that event the court would have to explore the law relating to privacy when it is not bolstered by considerations of confidence.

In this context Article 10(2) [of the European Convention on Human Rights] provides a potential justification for denying the right to freedom of expression not only by restrictions that are necessary "for preventing the disclosure of information received in confidence", but also those that are necessary "for the protection of the reputation or rights of others". On the hypothesis I have suggested . . . above, the question would arise whether Mr Douglas and Ms Zeta-Jones had a right to privacy which English law would recognise.

It is well known that this court in Kaye v Robertson [1991] FSR 62 said in uncompromising terms that there was no tort of privacy known to English law. In contrast, both academic commentary and extra-judicial commentary by judges over the last ten years have suggested from time to time that a development of the present frontiers of a breach of confidence action could fill the gap in English law which is filled by privacy law in other developed countries. This commentary was given a boost recently by the decision of the European Commission on Human Rights in Earl Spencer and Countess Spencer v the United Kingdom 25 EHRR CD 105, and by the coming into force of the Human Rights Act 1998. . . .

It is well settled, then, that equity may intervene to prevent the publication of photographic images taken in breach of an obligation of confidence. In other words, if on some private occasion the prospective claimants make it clear, expressly or impliedly, that no photographic images are to be taken of them, then all those who are present will be bound by the obligations of confidence created by their knowledge (or imputed knowledge) of this restriction. English law, however, has not yet been willing to recognise that an obligation of confidence may be relied on to preclude such unwanted intrusion into people's privacy when those conditions do not exist.

That was the problem at the heart of Kaye v Robertson. A television celebrity was recovering from catastrophic injuries in a private room which formed part of a ward at a NHS hospital. There were notices at the entrance to the ward, and also on the door of the private room, asking visitors to see a member of staff before they visited Mr Kaye, and a list of the people who might be allowed to visit him was pinned up outside his room. Journalists from the first defendant's newspaper ignored all these notices. They claimed that Mr Kaye had consented to being interviewed (although the evidence showed that he was in no fit state to give any kind of informed consent), and they sought to publish this interview, together with a number of photographs they took during their unwelcome intrusion into his rooms. Among these photographs were some which showed substantial scars to Mr Kaye's head at the site where his severe head and brain injuries had been caused.

The action was not brought in confidence, and no cases derived from the law of confidence were cited to the court during the one-day hearing. In the course of his short judgment Bingham LJ said . . . that the case highlighted, yet again, the failure of both the common law of England and statute to protect the personal privacy of individual citizens in an effective way. . . .

. . . So far as privacy is concerned, the case of the first and second claimants is not a particularly strong one. They did not choose to have a private wedding, attended by a few members of their family and a few friends, in the normal sense of the words "private wedding". There is nothing in the court's papers to belie the suggestion at page 88 of the disputed Issue 639 of Hello! that they invited 250 guests, and the trappings of privacy in this context are identical with the trappings of confidentiality to which I have alluded earlier in this judgment. Although by clause 6 of their agreement with OK! they undertook to use their best efforts to ensure that their guests "shall not publish and/or broadcast ... or write any article about, or give any extended comment, report or interview to any media concerning the Wedding", there is no evidence before the court which shows that they took any steps to enforce that undertaking, so far as their guests were concerned.

. . . Either the claimants will establish at trial that this particular occasion successfully retained the necessary indicia of confidentiality, so far as the taking of photographic images is concerned, or they will not. I do not consider that their privacy-based case, as distinct from their confidentiality-based case, adds very much. I am satisfied, however, that on the present untested evidence the claimants are "likely to establish that publication should not be allowed" on confidentiality grounds. This is not, however, the end of the matter, as I must turn to other factors affecting the balance of convenience and the manner in which the court should exercise its equitable jurisdiction.

So far as Hello!'s case is concerned, it appears to me on the evidence that there is a substantial risk that if an injunction "killing" this weekly edition of Hello! were to turn out to have been wrongly granted, Hello! would suffer damages which it would be extremely difficult to quantify in money terms. Although I take into account Mr Myerson's emollient evidence in answer, there appears on first impression to be a good deal of force in Ms Cartwright's evidence to the effect that Hello! would be likely to suffer losses over and above the financial loss associated with killing this edition which it would be very difficult to compute in money terms.

So far as OK! is concerned, if it wins at the trial, it will be able to have recourse to the very powerful weapon, fashioned by equity, of requiring Hello! to account to it for all the profits it has made from the publication of Issue 639. Even if it prefers to pursue its remedy in damages, I cannot see anything in its evidence which would make it particularly difficult for experienced accountants to compute its financial losses. Before deciding to pay Mr Douglas and Ms Zeta-Jones sums of the magnitude set out in its agreement with them, OK! must have had a pretty good idea of the income stream it hoped to generate from the exploitation of the rights it was acquiring. Since Hello! did not publish Issue 639 until after it had seen OK!'s evidence in this court, it could not realistically maintain that the losses claimed by OK! were too remote or were otherwise unforeseeable. . . .

It therefore appears to me that the balance of convenience, as between OK! and Hello!, therefore favours Hello! because it might be very difficult for Hello! to compute its losses in money terms if Issue 639 was killed, whereas OK! did not appear to face the same difficulties if publication was allowed. There was no suggestion in the evidence that Hello! might be unable to pay the huge sums it might be held liable to pay (whether as damages or by way of an account of profits) if this action succeeded at trial.

As between these two parties, therefore, the balance of convenience appeared to favour leaving OK! to assert its legal rights at the trial of what is essentially a commercial dispute between two magazine enterprises which are not averse to exercising spoiling tactics against each other. . . .

The matter which gave me greater cause for hesitation was whether having decided that the balance of convenience favoured the withholding of injunctive relief so far as OK! was concerned, Mr Douglas and Ms Zeta-Jones were nevertheless entitled to the protection of an injunction. In the end I came to agree with the views expressed on this issue by Sedley LJ, to which I have nothing to add.

*Lord Justice Sedley:*

Let me first set out my conclusions: . . .

- The two first-named claimants have a legal right to respect for their privacy, which has been infringed.
- The circumstances of the infringements are such that the claimants should be left to their remedy in damages.

*Is there today a right of privacy in English law?*

The common law, and equity with it, grows by slow and uneven degrees. . . .

The courts have done what they can, using such legal tools as were to hand, to stop the more outrageous invasions of individuals' privacy; but they have felt unable to articulate their measures as a discrete principle of law. Nevertheless, we have reached a point at which it can be said with confidence that the law recognises and will appropriately protect a right of personal privacy.

The reasons are twofold. First, equity and the common law are today in a position to respond to an increasingly invasive social environment by affirming that everybody has a right to some private space. Secondly, and in any event, the Human Rights Act 1998 requires the courts of this country to give appropriate effect to the right to respect for private and family life set out in Article 8 of the European Convention on Human Rights and Fundamental Freedoms. The difficulty with the first proposition resides in the common law's perennial need (for the best of reasons, that of legal certainty) to appear not to be doing anything for the first time. The difficulty with the second lies in the word "appropriate". But the two sources of law now run in a single channel because, by virtue of s.2 and s.6 of the Act, the courts of this country must not only take into account jurisprudence of both the Commission and the European Court of Human Rights which points to a positive institutional obligation to respect privacy; they must themselves act compatibly with that and the other Convention rights. This, for reasons I now turn to, arguably gives the final impetus to the recognition of a right of privacy in English law.

The reason why it is material to this case is that on the present evidence it is possible that the photographer was an intruder with whom no relationship of trust had been established. If it was a guest or an employee, the received law of confidence is probably all that the claimants need. . . .

The Human Rights Act 1998

The Human Rights Act 1998 was brought into force on 2 October 2000. It requires every public authority, including the courts, to act consistently with the European Convention on Human Rights. . . .

[Section 12 of the Act . . . provides:]

12. Freedom of expression

(1) This section applies if a court is considering whether to grant any relief which, if granted, might affect the exercise of the Convention right to freedom of expression. . . .

(3) No such relief is to be granted so as to restrain publication before trial unless the court is satisfied that the applicant is likely to establish that publication should not be allowed.

(4) The court must have particular regard to the importance of the Convention right to freedom of expression and, where the proceedings relate to material which the respondent claims, or which appears to the court, to be journalistic, literary or artistic material (or to conduct connected with such material), to-

(a) the extent to which –

(i) the material has, or is about to, become available to the public; or

(ii) it is, or would be, in the public interest for the material to be published;

(b) any relevant privacy code. . . .

The Convention right in question is the right to freedom of expression:

Article 10 Freedom of expression

(1) Everyone has the right to freedom of expression. This right shall include freedom to hold opinions and to receive and impart information and ideas without interference by public authority and regardless of frontiers. . . .

(2) The exercise of these freedoms, since it carries with it duties and responsibilities, may be subject to such formalities, conditions, restrictions or penalties as are prescribed by law and are necessary in a democratic society . . . for the protection of the reputation or rights of others, for preventing the disclosure of information received in confidence, or for maintaining the authority and impartiality of the judiciary.

Two initial points need to be made about s. 12 of the Act. First, by subsection (4) it puts beyond question the direct applicability of at least one article of the Convention as between one private party to litigation and another . . . . The other point, well made by Mr Tugendhat, is that it is "the Convention right" to freedom of expression which both triggers the section (see s. 12(1)) and to which particular regard is to be had. That Convention right, when one turns to it, is qualified in favour of the reputation and rights of others and the protection of information received in confidence. In other words, you cannot have particular regard to Article 10 without having equally particular regard at the very least to Article 8:

> Article 8 Right to respect for private and family life
>
> (1) Everyone has the right to respect for his private and family life, his home and his correspondence.
>
> (2) There shall be no interference by a public authority with the exercise of this right except such as is in accordance with the law and is necessary in a democratic society in the interests of national security, public safety or the economic well-being of the country, for the prevention of disorder or crime, for the protection of health or morals, or for the protection of the rights and freedoms of others.

Mr Carr was disposed to accept this; so far as I can see he had no choice, although it is perhaps unexpected to find a claimant relying on s.12 against a publisher rather than vice versa. But he balked at what Mr Tugendhat submitted, and I agree, was the necessary extension of the subsection's logic. A newspaper, say, intends to publish an article about an individual who learns of it and fears, on tenable grounds, that it will put his life in danger. The newspaper, also on tenable grounds, considers his fear unrealistic. First of all, it seems to me inescapable that s. 12(4) makes the right to life, which is protected by Article 2 and implicitly recognised by Article 10(2), as relevant as the right of free expression to the court's decision; and in doing so it also makes Article 17 (which prohibits the abuse of rights) relevant. But this in turn has an impact on s. 12(3) which, though it does not replace the received test (or tests) for prior restraint, qualifies them by requiring a probability of success at trial. The gauging of this probability, by virtue of s. 12(4), will have to take into account the full range of relevant Convention rights.

How is the court to do this when the evidence – viz that there is and that there is not an appreciable risk to life – is no more than evenly balanced? A bland application of s. 12(3) could deny the claimant the court's temporary protection, even if the potential harm to him, should the risk eventuate, was of the gravest kind and that to the newspaper and the public, should publication be restrained, minimal; and a similarly bland application of s. 12(4), simply prioritising the freedom to publish over other Convention rights (save possibly freedom of religion: see s.13), might give the newspaper the edge even if the claimant's evidence were strong. I agree with Mr Tugendhat that this cannot have been Parliament's design. This is not only, as he submits, because of the inherent logic of the provision but because of the court's own obligation under s. 3 of the Act to construe all legislation so far as possible compatibly with the Convention rights, an obligation which must include the interpretation of the Human Rights Act itself. The European Court of Human Rights has always recognised the high importance of free media of communication in a democracy, but its jurisprudence does not – and could not consistently with the Convention itself – give Article 10(1) the presumptive priority which is given, for example, to the First Amendment in the jurisprudence of the United States' courts. Everything will ultimately depend on the proper balance between privacy and publicity in the situation facing the court.

For both reasons, and in agreement with . . . the judgment of Keene LJ and . . . the judgment of Brooke LJ, I accept that s. 12 is not to be interpreted and applied in the simplistic manner for which Mr Carr contends. It will be necessary for the court, in applying the test set out in s. 12(3), to bear in mind that by virtue of s. 12(1) and (4) the qualifications set out in Article 10(2) are as relevant as the right set out in Article 10(1). This means that, for example, the reputations and rights of others – not only but not least their Convention rights – are as material as the defendant's right of free expression. So is the prohibition on the use of one party's Convention rights to injure the Convention rights of others. Any other approach to s.12 would in my judgment violate s.3 of the Act. Correspondingly, as Mr Tugendhat submits, "likely" in s. 12(3) cannot be read as requiring simply an evaluation of the relative strengths of the parties' evidence. If at trial, for the reasons I have given, a minor but real risk to life, or a wholly unjustifiable invasion of privacy, is entitled to no less regard, by virtue of Article 10(2), than is accorded to the right to publish by Article 10(1), the consequent likelihood becomes material under s. 12(3). Neither element is a trump card. They will be articulated by the principles of legality and proportionality which, as always, constitute the mechanism by which the court reaches its conclusion on countervailing or qualified rights. . . . If freedom of expression is to be impeded, in other words, it must be on cogent grounds recognised by law.

Let me summarise. For reasons I have given, Mr Douglas and Ms Zeta-Jones have a powerful prima facie claim to redress for invasion of their privacy as a qualified right recognised and protected by English law. The case being one which affects the Convention right of freedom of expression, s.12 of the Human Rights Act requires the court to have regard to Article 10 (as, in its absence, would s.6). This, however, cannot, consistently with s.3 and Article 17, give the Article 10(1) right of free expression a presumptive priority over other rights. What it does is require the court to consider Article 10(2) along with 10(1), and by doing so to bring into the frame the conflicting right to respect for privacy. This right, contained in Article 8 and reflected in English law, is in turn qualified in both contexts by the right of others to free expression. The outcome, which self-evidently has to be the same under both articles, is determined principally by considerations of proportionality.

*The injunction*

In his opening argument Mr Carr, having submitted (acceptably for present purposes) that this case is a case of breach of confidence or nothing, sought to stifle that cause of action at birth by arguing that pictures such as the defendant was proposing to publish were not information at all. This had the makings of an own goal, since it might well have excluded Article 10 and with it s.12 from the defendants' own armoury. But it is plainly wrong. The offending photographs convey the simple information: "This is what the wedding and the happy couple looked like."

It is also as information, however, that the photographs invade the privacy of Mr Douglas and Ms Zeta-Jones: they tell the world things about the wedding and the couple which the claimants have not consented to. On the present evidence, whoever took the photographs probably had no right to be there; if they were lawfully there, they had no right to photograph anyone; and in either case they had no right to publicise the product of their intrusion. If it stopped there, this would have been an unanswerable case for a temporary injunction and no doubt in due course for a permanent one; perhaps the more unanswerable, not the less, for the celebrity of the two principal victims. Article 8, whether introduced indirectly through s. 12 or directly by virtue of s.6, will of course require the court to consider "the rights and freedoms of others", including the Article 10(1) right of Hello! And Article 10, by virtue of s.6 and s.12, will require the court, if the common law did not already do so, to have full regard to Hello!'s right to freedom of expression. But the circumstances in which the photographs must have been obtained would have robbed those rights and freedoms of substance for reasons which should by now be plain.

The facts, however, do not stop here. The first two claimants had sold most of the privacy they now seek to protect to the third claimant for a handsome sum. If all that had happened were that Hello! had got hold of OK's photographs, OK would have proprietary rights and remedies at law, but Mr Douglas and Ms Zeta-Jones would not, I think, have any claim for breach of the privacy with which they had already parted. The present case is not so stark, because they were careful by their contract to retain a right of veto over publication of OK's photographs in order to maintain the kind of image which is professionally and no doubt also personally important to them. This element of privacy remained theirs and Hello!'s photographs violated it.

Article 8, however, gives no absolute rights, any more than does the law of breach of confidence or privacy. Not only are there the qualifications under Article 8(2); what paragraph (1) requires is respect for, not inviolability of, private and family life. Taking it for the present that it is the state, represented by the court, which must accord that respect, what amounts to respect must depend on the full set of circumstances in which the intrusion has occurred. This intrusion was by uncontrolled photography for profit of a wedding which was to be the subject of controlled photography for profit.

Thus the major part of the claimants' privacy rights have become the subject of a commercial transaction: bluntly, they have been sold. For reasons more fully spelt out by Brooke LJ the frustration of such a transaction by unlawful means, if established, is in principle compensable in money, whether by way of an account of profits or damages. There is no reason in law why the cost to the wrongdoer should not be heavy enough to demonstrate that such activity is not worthwhile. The retained element of privacy, in the form of editorial control of OK's pictures, while real, is itself as much a commercial as a personal reservation. While it may be harder to translate into lost money or an account of profits, it can readily be translated into general damages of a significant amount.

Two caveats are necessary. I do not suggest for a moment that there is a bright line between the personal and the commercial and that everything on the commercial side, being about money, can be dealt with by an award of damages. Nor, equally, should it be thought that either Article 8 or our domestic law will never protect privacy which is being turned to commercial ends. Everything will depend on the infinite variety of facts thrown up case by case.

In the present case, and not without misgiving, I have concluded that although the first two claimants are likely to succeed at trial in establishing a breach of their privacy in which Hello! may be actionably implicated, the dominant feature of the case is that by far the greater part of that privacy has already been traded and falls to be protected, if at all, as a commodity in the hands of the third claimant. This can be done without the need of an injunction, particularly since there may not be adequate countervailing redress for the defendants if at trial they stave off the claim for interference with contractual relations. The retained element of the first two claimants' privacy is not in my judgment – though I confess it is a close thing - sufficient to tilt the balance of justice and convenience against such liberty as the defendants may establish, at law and under Article 10, to publish the illicitly taken photographs.

*Lord Justice Keene:*

. . . The claim is put in terms of breach of confidence in the Particulars of Claim, but it was said in argument by Mr. Tugendhat that the case has more to do with privacy that with confidentiality.

It is clear that there is no watertight division between the two concepts. Argyll v Argyll [1967] Ch. 302 was a classic case where the concept of confidentiality was applied so as, in effect, to protect the privacy of communications between a husband and wife. Moreover, breach of confidence is a developing area of the law, the boundaries of which are not immutable but may change to reflect changes in society, technology and business practice. I reject without hesitation the submission by Mr. Carr for the defendants that it cannot encompass photographs of an event. It is said that those photographs in the present case did not convey any information which had the quality of confidence, because the guests were not prevented from imparting the same information subsequently, whether in words, by drawings based on recollection or any other means. This argument is unsustainable. The photographs conveyed to the public information not otherwise truly obtainable, that is to say, what the event and its participants looked like. It is said that a picture is worth a thousand words. Were that not so, there would not be a market for magazines like Hello! and OK! The same result is not obtainable through the medium of words alone, nor by recollected drawings with their inevitable inaccuracy. There is no reason why these photographs inherently could not be the subject of a breach of confidence.

Since the coming into force of the Human Rights Act 1998, the courts as a public authority cannot act in a way which is incompatible with a Convention right: section 6(1). That arguably includes their activity in interpreting and developing the common law, even where no public authority is a party to the litigation. Whether this extends to creating a new cause of action between private persons and bodies is more controversial, since to do so would appear to circumvent the restrictions on proceedings contained in section 7(1) of the Act and on remedies in section 8(1). But it is unnecessary to determine that issue in these proceedings, where reliance is placed on breach of confidence, an established cause of action, the scope of which may now need to be approached in the light of the obligation on this court arising under section 6(1) of the Act. Already before the coming into force of the Act there have been persuasive dicta in Hellewell v Chief Constable of Derbyshire [1995] 1 WLR 804 and Attorney General v Guardian Newspapers (No 2) [1990] 1 AC 109, cited by Lord Justice Sedley in his judgment in these proceedings, to the effect that a pre-existing confidential relationship between the parties is not required for a breach of confidence suit. The nature of the subject matter or the circumstances of the defendant's activities may suffice in some instances to give rise to liability for breach of confidence. That approach must now be informed by the jurisprudence of the Convention in respect of Article 8. Whether the resulting liability is described as being for breach of confidence or for breach of a right to privacy may be little more than deciding what label is to be attached to the cause of action, but there would seem to be merit in recognising that the original concept of breach of confidence has in this particular category of cases now developed into something different from the commercial and employment relationships with which confidentiality is mainly concerned.

Because of these developments in the common law relating to confidence and the apparent obligation on English courts now to take account of the right to respect for private and family life under Article 8 when interpreting the common law, it seems unlikely that Kaye v Robertson (ante), which held that there was no actionable right of privacy in English law, would be decided the same way on that aspect today. It is noteworthy that no claim for breach of confidence was mounted in that case, and that Argyll v Argyll and Attorney General v Guardian Newspapers (No 2) do not seem to have been cited to the court. In the latter decision the House of Lords had made it clear that a duty of confidence could arise from the circumstances in which the information was obtained, so that the recipient was to be precluded from disclosing it to others. Consequently if the present case concerned a truly private occasion, where the persons involved made it clear that they intended it to remain private and undisclosed to the world, then I might well have concluded that in the current state of English law the claimants were likely to succeed at any eventual trial.

But any consideration of Article 8 rights must reflect the Convention jurisprudence which acknowledges different degrees of privacy. The European Court ruled in Dudgeon v United Kingdom [1982] 4 EHRR 149 that the more intimate the aspect of private life which is being interfered with, the more serious must be the reasons for interference before the latter can be legitimate: see p.165, para. 152. Personal sexuality, as in that case, is an extremely intimate aspect of a person's private life. A purely private wedding will have a lesser but still significant degree of privacy warranting protection, though subject to the considerations set out in Article 8(2). But if persons choose to lessen the degree of privacy attaching to an otherwise private occasion, then the balance to be struck between their rights and other considerations is likely to be affected.

In the present case, it is of considerable relevance that very widespread publicity was to be given in any event to the wedding very soon afterwards by way of photographs in OK! magazine. The occasion thereby lost much of its private nature. The claimants were by their security measures and by their agreements with the service companies seeking not so much to protect the privacy of the first two claimants but rather to control the form of publicity which ensued. This is apparent from the witness statement of Paul Ashford, Editorial Director of OK! magazine, who says that: "all guests were informed they should not bring cameras *because of the exclusive deal that had been entered with OK!*" para. 6. (emphasis added)

One does not need to assume that that was the sole purpose of the various security measures. It is enough that it was clearly a very important purpose. Indeed, it was made clear by Mr. Tugendhat in his submissions that what was complained of here was the loss of control over the photographs to be published, leading to damage to the image of the first and second claimants because of unflattering photographs.

It may be that a limited degree of privacy remains in such a situation and it could be that at trial the claimants would succeed in obtaining a permanent injunction. There must still be some doubt about that. But even if the claimants had passed that threshold of showing that it is likely that they would obtain an injunction at trial, this court in exercising its discretion at this interlocutory stage must still take account of the widespread publicity arranged by the claimant for this occasion. When that organised publicity is balanced against the impact on the defendants of an injunction restraining publication, I have no doubt that the scales come down in this case against prior restraint. This is a matter where any damage to the claimants can adequately be dealt with in monetary terms. In those circumstances I would allow this appeal and discharge the injunction.

Micheal Douglas Order: Appeal allowed; action to be transferred to the Chancery Division; Costs below to be the Appellants in the case; Costs of the appeal to be the appellants in any event; Question of whether there be an inquiry as to damages on cross-undertaking's to be reserved to trial judge.

---

**Note on subsequent proceedings in Douglas v. Hello! Ltd.**

The U.K. Court of Appeal decision you just read created British legal precedent by ruling that Michael Douglas and Catherine Zeta-Jones have a "right of privacy" under British law. On the other hand, because the Court of Appeal vacated the injunction (on the grounds that money damages would be an adequate remedy in this particular case, if the photos were published) Hello! was able to publish the photos after all, and it did, thus setting the stage for liability and damages phases of the case.

The liability part of the case was heard by Mr. Justice Lindsay. The trial took 20 courtroom days over six-week period in February and March 2003, and it resulted in a victory for Douglas, Zeta-Jones and OK! magazine. *Douglas v. Hello! Ltd.*, [2003] EWHC 786 (Ch) (available at http://www.courtservice.gov.uk/judgmentsfiles/j1700/douglas_v_Hello!.htm).

Much of Justice Lindsay's 80-page decision is devoted to a detailed recitation of the facts – one that reads much like a *New Yorker* magazine article. For what might have been a simple invasion of privacy case, the facts were unusually dramatic. They included surprisingly elaborate precautions taken by Douglas and Zeta-Jones in an ultimately unsuccessful effort to prevent unauthorized photos of their wedding. The facts also included surprisingly devious steps taken by Hello!, after the lawsuit was filed, to mislead the courts about the role the magazine played in having paparazzi sneak into the wedding, in order to shoot the photos Hello! eventually published.

Justice Lindsay's legal conclusions were surprising too, for two reasons: first, because they were so conservative; and second, because despite Justice Lindsay's conclusion that "that the case advanced by Hello! . . . was a false one," no consequences flowed from that. Instead, Justice Lindsay ruled in favor of Douglas, Zeta-Jones and OK! on their "breach of confidence" (and "Data Protection Act") claims, rejecting their other claims, including those for invasion of privacy and for exemplary and aggravated damages.

Justice Lindsay found that the wedding was "a valuable trade asset, a commodity the value of which depended, in part at least, upon its content at first being kept secret and then on its being made public in ways controlled by Miss Zeta-Jones and Mr. Douglas for the benefit of them and of [OK!]" For this reason, the Justice concluded, photos of the wedding were entitled to "confidentiality." Moreover, the paparazzo who took the unauthorized photos "knew (or at the very least ought to have known) that the Claimants reasonably expected the private character of the event and photographic representation of it to be protected."

Hello! knew too that OK! had an exclusive contract to publish wedding photos, and Hello! knew that "elaborate security procedures" had been taken "to protect the secrecy of the event." Nevertheless, Hello! "indicated to paparazzi in advance that [Hello!] would pay well for photographs and [Hello!] knew the reputation of the paparazzi for being able to intrude." These and other factors satisfied "all the elements of a successful case in breach of confidence."

In its own defense, Hello! argued that it had a right of "freedom of expression," based on the U.K.'s implementation of the Human Rights Convention in 1998 in the U.K. Human Rights Act. That Act does protect freedom of expression; but it also requires regard to be given to "any relevant privacy code." In the U.K., the Press Complaints Commission has adopted a code that requires respect for "private and family life," and prohibits journalists from obtaining "pictures through misrepresentation and subterfuge." In this case, Justice Lindsay found that the unauthorized wedding photos were "obtained by misrepresentation and subterfuge."

As a result, Hello!'s right to freedom of expression was "overborne" by the rights of Douglas, Zeta-Jones and OK! "under the law of confidence," the Justice concluded.

Surprisingly, Justice Lindsay did not base his ruling on the law of privacy, even though the Court of Appeals' earlier ruling in this case held that British law now recognizes such a right. Justice Lindsay declined to rely on the right of privacy because he concluded that Douglas and Zeta-Jones would not have been entitled to any greater recovery under privacy law than under breach of confidence law. Moreover, Justice Lindsay expressed the view that privacy law is "so broad" that "the subject is better left to Parliament."

Justice Lindsay's decision dealt only with liability, not damages. The amount of damages to be awarded was scheduled to be decided in a trial to be held in July 2003, after this book went to press.

Also left for later proceedings was the question of whether the photo agency that represented the paparazzo who took the unauthorized photos also would be held liable. The photos were taken by British-born but California-based photographer Rupert Thorpe, whose photo agent was California-based Philip Ramey. Ramey – himself a paparazzo of note – was the one who dealt with Hello! in negotiating a $188,000 fee for the photos and in transmitting the photos by computer from the United States to Hello!'s London office. Though Thorpe was not named as a defendant, Ramey was.

At first, it appeared that Ramey would avoid potential liability, because he was served in the United States. A lower court set aside service on him, on the grounds that nothing Ramey did was done in Britain, and thus British courts did not have jurisdiction over him. The Court of Appeal, however, ruled otherwise. It held that the allegation against Ramey was that he "agreed to obtain photos by unlawful means with a view to their unlawful publication," and thus it was alleged that participated in "unlawful" activities that took place in Britain. These allegations, the Court of Appeal held, were sufficient to give British courts jurisdiction over Ramey. But that decision came too late to include Ramey in the already-scheduled trial against Hello! *Douglas v. Hello! Ltd.*, [2003] EWCA Civ 139 available at http://www.courtservice.gov.uk/judgmentsfiles/j1553/douglas_v_Hello!.htm).

---

### 1.1.3 Internet Domain Names

**Protection of Personal Names Under the UDRP**
Excerpted from
***The Recognition of Rights and the Use of Names in the Internet Domain Name System***
***Report of the Second WIPO Internet Domain Name Process* (2001)**



As mentioned above, personal names may, in appropriate circumstances, be registered as trademarks and, in practice, many are. The protection of personal names as trademarks has provided a basis for the application of the Uniform Domain Name Dispute Resolution Policy (UDRP) to the protection of personal names against deliberate, bad faith registration as domain names in the gTLDs. While a few oppose this application of the UDRP, the clear weight of authority of many decisions is in favor of the application of the UDRP to the protection of personal names when they constitute trademarks. The present section of this Chapter outlines the main trends in this authority. Annex VI to this Report contains an indicative list of UDRP cases involving personal names that have been filed with the WIPO Arbitration and Mediation Center. [These are just some of the many celebrity domain names listed in Annex VI: juliaroberts.com, jimihendrix.com, tinaturner.net, sting.com, danmarino.com, madonna.com, isabelle-adjani.net, michaelfeinstein.com, bridgetjones.com, edwardvanhalen.com, nicholekidman.com, brucespringsteen.com, backstreeboys.com, venusandserenawilliams.com, barrydiller.org, celinedion.com, dustin-hoffman.com, hughhefner.com, ledzeppelin.com, mariah-carey.com, pinkfloyd.com, tom-cruise.com.]

It is recalled that the UDRP provides that three conditions must be satisfied in order to establish that a domain name registration is abusive and that the complainant is entitled to relief:

(i) the domain name is identical or confusingly similar to a trademark or service mark in which the complainant has rights;

(ii) the registrant of the domain name has no rights or legitimate interests in respect of the domain name; and

(iii) the domain name has been registered and is being used in bad faith.

The application of each of these conditions in the context of the protection of personal names is described in the ensuing paragraphs.

*Trademark or Service Mark Rights*

The first condition requires that in each case the complainant must demonstrate that the personal name in question is protected as a trademark or service mark, in which that complainant has rights.

There have been a number of cases in which a complainant has demonstrated that it meets this requirement by submitting evidence that the personal name in question is registered as a trademark. The UDRP, however, does not require that a complainant must hold rights specifically in a *registered* trademark or service mark. Instead, it provides only that there must be "a trademark or service mark in which the complainant has *rights*," without specifying how these rights are acquired. With this distinction in mind, many decisions under the UDRP have therefore determined that common law or unregistered trademark rights may be asserted by a complainant and will satisfy the first condition of the UDRP. In relation to personal names, in particular, numerous UDRP decisions have relied upon a complainant's demonstration that it holds such common law rights in the disputed name. In making these decisions, panels have given attention to a number of factors, including: (i) the distinctive character or notoriety of the name and the requirement that the domain name must be "identical or confusingly similar" to it, (ii) the relationship between this distinctive character and use of the name in connection with goods or services in commerce, and (iii) the location of the parties and the bearing that this may have on the acquisition of unregistered trademark rights.

Regarding the distinctiveness of the name, panels have emphasized in many cases that the particular complainant's personal name, in the relevant field of commerce, enjoys widespread notoriety and fame. "A claim based on an unregistered mark, including a personal name, requires that the claimant establish the distinctive character of the mark or name on which the claim is based." Panels have also focused this analysis of distinctive character in relation to the second element mentioned above, "whether or not the person in question is sufficiently famous in connection with the services offered by that complainant" in commerce. Using a personal name in association with certain goods or services can create distinctiveness and a secondary meaning in the name. With respect to similarity between the personal name in which trademark rights are held and the domain name registration, panels have found that small variations between the two (e.g., such as removing the space between the first and last names), just as in cases involving words or terms other than personal names, are legally insignificant, so long as the registered domain name is "confusingly similar" to the personal name.

The location of the parties can be significant for determining whether the complainant has trademark rights. Rule 15(a) of the Rules for Uniform Domain Name Dispute Resolution Policy (the "Rules of Procedure") provides that the panel shall decide a complaint on the basis, *inter alia*, of ". . . rules and principles of law that it deems applicable." The applicable law will depend on the facts of the case, including the location of the parties. This Rule has allowed panels the flexibility to deal with disputes between parties with different national affiliations and concerning activity on a global medium. It is also a feature that has enabled complainants to seek protection for their names under trademark law, although they have not registered their names as a trademark or service mark in every country of the world.

*The Registrant Has No Rights or Legitimate Interests in the Domain Name*

The second condition of the UDRP requires that there be no evidence that the domain name registrant has any rights or legitimate interests in the domain name that it has registered. Panels normally review the full record in a case to assess whether a respondent has any rights or interests in the domain name. Based on the distinctiveness of the personal name in question and certain facts indicating that (i) the domain name does not correspond to the respondent's own name, and (ii) the respondent has registered the names of many other celebrities, this determination in a number of cases has been almost self-evident. In other cases, however, a more probing analysis has been called for. For example, the panel in one case found that, while the respondent's use of the name in question, "sting," as a nickname on the Internet was *not* substantial enough to show any rights or legitimate interests in the domain name *sting.com*, the respondent's proven use was in fact relevant to the separate issue of bad faith. In another case, the panel disagreed with the respondent's argument that the domain name in question, *sade.com*, was being offered merely as a legitimate email service. Instead, the panel found that, by placing the domain name in the music section of its web site and having registered it under the contact, "The Sade Internet Fan Club," the respondent "has set out to deliberately associate this service with the Complainant." In a further case, the panel acknowledged that the respondent's contention was a serious one and that use of the domain name in question, *montyroberts.net*, was for legitimate non-commercial or fair use purposes. In balancing the rights of the complainant in its mark and the rights of the respondent to freely express its views about the complainant, however, the panel determined that:

> "the rights to express one's views is not the same as the right to use another's name to identify one's self as the source of those views. One may be perfectly free to express his or her views about the quality or characteristics of the reporting of the New York Times or Time Magazine. That does not, however, translate into a right to identify one's self as the New York Times or Time Magazine."

The panel found that, while the respondent's primary motive for establishing the web site might have been to criticize the complainant, this did "not insulate Respondent from the fact that it is directly and indirectly offering products for sale on its website, or at websites hyperlinked to its site."

*The Domain Name Has Been Registered and Is Being Used in Bad Faith*

The third condition that must be satisfied is evidence of bad faith. The UDRP sets forth four non-exhaustive examples of what may be considered "evidence of the registration and use of a domain name in bad faith." A review of the decisions concerning personal names indicates that each of these circumstances has been relied upon in one or more cases to support a determination that the registration and use of the domain name in dispute was in bad faith. Given the distinctive character of a number of the names in question and a consideration of other relevant facts, an underlying and consistent perception has been that the respondent, through the domain name registration, has clearly targeted the complainant's unique personal or professional name. Panels, however, have exercised caution in confirming that such parasitic practices relate to one of the illustrative bad faith factors listed in the UDRP or to a similar bad faith *commercial* exploitation of the complainant's name. Thus, in one case the panel ruled that, where the domain name was identical to the complainant's professional name but was connected to a *non-commercial* web site expressing criticism of the complainant (operated by a brother-in-law), the case involved alleged defamation and not infringement of a trademark right. Defamation, which goes to the reputation of an individual, does not have any necessary relationship to the commercial and infringing exploitation of a personal name used as a mark.

The UDRP has proven to be a useful tool for giving expression to the protection of personal names where trademark rights exist in those personal names, where the domain name holder has no right or legitimate interest and where there is evidence of bad faith in the registration and use of the domain name. However, it by no means affords comprehensive protection to personal names. For a start, the names of many persons, particularly ordinary persons, may have no distinctiveness attached to them, either inherently or as a result of use. Secondly, the names of political figures, religious leaders, scientists and historical persons may never have been used in commerce and, thus, are unlikely to have trademarks associated with them. Nevertheless, many sensitivities may attach to their use. . . .

*Recommendation*

It is clear that many sensitivities are offended by the unauthorized registration of personal names as domain names. It is clear also that UDRP does not provide solace for all those offended sensitivities, nor was it intended to do so, as originally designed. The result is that there are some perceived injustices. Persons who have gained eminence and respect, but who have not profited from their reputation in commerce, may not avail themselves of the UDRP to protect their personal names against parasitic registrations. The UDRP is thus perceived by some as implementing an excessively materialistic conception of contribution to society. Furthermore, persons whose names have become distinctive in countries that do not recognize unregistered trademark rights are unlikely to find consolation in the UDRP in respect of bad faith registration and use of their personal names as domain names in those countries.

Nevertheless, we believe that the views expressed by the majority of commentators against the modification of the UDRP to meet these perceived injustices are convincing at this stage of the evolution of the DNS and the UDRP.

The most cogent of the arguments against modification of the UDRP is, we believe, the lack of an international norm protecting personal names and the consequent diversity of legal approaches deployed to protect personal names at the national level. We consider that this diversity would place parties and panelists in an international procedure in an untenable position and would jeopardize the credibility and efficiency of the UDRP.

It is recommended that no modification be made to the UDRP to accommodate broader protection for personal names than that which currently exists in the UDRP.

In making this recommendation, we are conscious of the strength of feeling that the unauthorized, bad faith registration and use of personal names as domain names engenders. We believe, however, that the most appropriate way in which the strength of this feeling should be expressed is through the development of international norms that can provide clear guidance on the intentions and will of the international community.

---

**Bruce Springsteen v. Jeff Burgar and Bruce Springsteen Club**
**WIPO Arbitration and Mediation Center, Case No. D2000-1532 (25 Jan. 2001)**
**http://arbiter.wipo.int/domains/decisions/html/2000/d2000-1532.html**

Gordon D. Harris, Presiding Panelist
A. Michael Froomkin, Panelist

*1. The Parties*

The Complainant is Bruce Springsteen whose address is given as c/o Parcher, Hayes & Snyder, 500 Fifth Avenue, 38th Floor, New York, NY 10110, USA ("Bruce Springsteen").

The Respondent is Jeff Burgar and Bruce Springsteen Club of PO Box 2570, 4901 51st Avenue, High Prairie AB, TOG 1EO, Canada ("Mr. Burgar").

*2. The Domain Name and Registrar*

The domain name at issue is <brucespringsteen.com>. The Registar is Network Solutions Inc. of 505 Huntmar Park Drive, Herndon, Virginia VA 20170, USA.

*3. Procedural History*

Complaint was filed by email and hard copy on 7 November and 9 November 2000 respectively. The relevant notification procedures were then complied with.

Notification of the complaint was submitted to the Respondent on 21 November 2000, and a response by email and hard copy was received on 10 December and 20 December 2000 respectively.

The Respondent failed to state its preferred candidates for the three member Panel. This deficiency was notified on 13 December 2000 and rectified by a reply on 15 December 2000.

The Panel has been duly appointed and the Panelists have submitted a Statement of Acceptance and Declaration of Impartiality and Independence. The language of the proceeding is English.

*4. Factual Background*

The Complainant is the famous, almost legendary, recording artist and composer, Bruce Springsteen. Since the release of his first album in 1972 he has been at the top of his profession, selling millions of recordings throughout the world. As a result, his name is instantly recognisable in almost every part of the globe. There is no assertion made on behalf of Bruce Springsteen that his name has been registered as a trade mark but he rather relies upon common law rights acquired as a result of his fame and success.

The domain name at issue was registered by Mr. Burgar apparently on 26 November 1996 according to the Who-Is search at exhibit 1 to the complaint. . . .

It appears that the domain name at issue was registered under the name "Bruce Springsteen Club" with Mr.. Burgar identified as the administrative point of contact. . . .

*5. The Parties' Contentions*

Representatives of Bruce Springsteen have succinctly addressed the requirements under the UDRP [Uniform Domain Name Dispute Resolution Policy] and commented as follows.

In relation to the issue of "identical or substantially similar" marks, they have asserted the common law rights of Bruce Springsteen in his name and drawn analogy with previous cases, for example, the "Julia Roberts" case to support their contention.

In relation to the question of whether Mr. Burgar has any right or legitimate interest in the name, they indicate that no permission was given by Bruce Springsteen for the name to allow the domain name at issue to be used. They point out that Mr. Burgar has never been known as "Bruce Springsteen", and assert that the use of the name creates a misleading impression of association which is not based in fact.

In relation to the issue of bad faith, Mr. Springsteen's representatives point to the fact that Mr. Burgar is the owner of around 1,500 names, and that many of those names, including the domain name at issue, take the internet user to his own site, "celebrity1000.com". They therefore point to the fact that this constitutes bad faith under paragraphs 4(b)(ii) and (iv) of the UDRP.

They further assert that he has registered this domain name, and others, using a fictitious name. In this case the fictitious name is "Bruce Springsteen Club".

Bruce Springsteen's representatives rely heavily on authorities, and produce copies of a number of previous decisions and court cases which they believe to be relevant.

Mr. Burgar, on his own behalf, has produced a substantial response, far in excess of the guideline size for such responses set out in the WIPO rules. It is easy to understand his desire to make a point, but it does substantially increase the workload of the Panelists who have to wade through a large volume of material. For the purposes of this section, the Panel will refer only to that part of Mr. Burgar's submission which relates specifically to the three requirements under the UDRP.

In relation to the question of identicality of name, Mr. Burgar says that Bruce Springsteen's representatives have given no evidence of any common law rights. He points to the fact that the name has already been registered in a domain name, namely "brucespringsteen.net" and, that his use does not besmirch or denigrate the name of Bruce Springsteen to any extent.

He refers to other websites which feature the name in question, including, for example, "artistplace.com/brucespringsteen".

He also claims in relation to this heading that there has been and can be no confusion.

In relation to the question of rights or legitimate interests, he counters the statement of Mr. Springsteen's representatives by saying that there was no suggestion that permission is needed from Bruce Springsteen or anyone in relation to the registration of a domain name. He uses, for the first time, an analogy with magazines, indicating that the mere use of the name of a celebrity on the front page of a magazine does not mean that the magazine is claiming any kind of specific rights in relation to the name, but merely that it features an article about the individual in question. He asserts that the internet is of a similar nature. He refers to the habits of internet users, and the relative unlikelihood that they would be typing in the full domain name, namely "brucespringsteen.com", and that if they did so they would be sufficiently sophisticated users to understand that the disclaimer contained on his site indicates that it is not an "official" Bruce Springsteen site.

He avers that he does not operate this domain name for profit or gain, and indeed has made none, and that he is not misleadingly directing people to his site.

In relation to the question of bad faith, he says that there has been no evidence submitted that he intended to stop Bruce Springsteen from registering the domain name "brucespringsteen.com" himself. He points to the fact that the domain name "brucespringsteen.net" has been registered by Mr. Springsteen's record company for some years and that, presumably, that should have sufficed.

In relation to the question of fictitious names, he denies that he owns 1,500 celebrity names, and that any of them have been registered in a fictitious name pointing out that he personally is identified as the administrative contact in relation to all the domain names which he has registered.

In relation to paragraph 4(b)(iv) of the UDRP, he denies that he has "intentionally attempted to attract, for commercial gain, internet users to his website or other online location, by creating a likelihood of confusion with the Complainant's mark as to the source, sponsorship, affiliation or endorsement of his website". He points to the nature of the internet and the volume of sites available, to indicate that it is most unlikely that confusion could have occurred in the minds of an internet user. He asserts that confusion is a necessary factor in paragraph 4(b)(iv).

He repeats his analogy regarding magazines, and refers to the fact that he has over 200 "mini sites" accessible from his principal site, "www.celebrity1000.com".

He points out that he now has a working functioning website at the domain name in issue in these proceedings.

*6. Panel's Findings*

Under paragraph 4 of the UDRP, the Complainant's burden is to prove in relation to the complaint, that:-

(i) The domain name at issue is identical or confusingly similar to a trade mark or service mark in which the Complainant has rights;

(ii) The Respondent has no rights or legitimate interests in respect of the domain name; and

(iii) The domain name has been registered as being used in bad faith.

The Complainant must prove that each of these three elements are present in order to make out a successful case.

The first question to be considered is whether the domain name at issue is identical or confusingly similar to trade marks or service marks in which the Complainant has rights.

It is common ground that there is no registered trade mark in the name "Bruce Springsteen". In most jurisdictions where trade marks are filed it would be impossible to obtain a registration of a name of that nature. Accordingly, Mr. Springsteen must rely on common law rights to satisfy this element of the three part test.

It appears to be an established principle from cases such as Jeanette Winterson, Julia Roberts, and Sade that in the case of very well known celebrities, their names can acquire a distinctive secondary meaning giving rise to rights equating to unregistered trade marks, notwithstanding the non-registerability of the name itself. It should be noted that no evidence has been given of the name "Bruce Springsteen" having acquired a secondary meaning; in other words a recognition that the name should be associated with activities beyond the primary activities of Mr. Springsteen as a composer, performer and recorder of popular music.

In the view of this Panel, it is by no means clear from the UDRP that it was intended to protect proper names of this nature. As it is possible to decide the case on other grounds, however, the Panel will proceed on the assumption that the name Bruce Springsteen is protected under the policy; it then follows that the domain name at issue is identical to that name.

It is a clearly established principal that the suffix ".com" does not carry the domain name away from identicality or substantial similarity.

The second limb of the test requires the Complainant to show that the domain name owner has no rights or legitimate interests in respect of the domain name. The way in which the UDRP is written clearly requires the Complainant to demonstrate this, and the mere assertion that the Respondent has no such rights does not constitute proof, although the panel is free to make reasonable inferences. That said, a Respondent would be well advised to proffer some evidence to the contrary in the face of such an allegation. Paragraph 4(c) of the UDRP sets out specific circumstances to assist the Respondent in demonstrating that he or she has legitimate rights or legitimate interests in the domain name. The circumstances are stated to be non-exclusive, but are helpful in considering this issue.

Dealing with each in turn as follows:

(i) The first circumstance is that, before any notice of the dispute to the Respondent, the Respondent had shown demonstrable preparations to use the domain name in connection with a bona fide offering of goods or services.

In this case, there is no suggestion that the domain name <brucespringsteen.com> had in fact been used in this way prior to notification of the complaint. Instead, the domain name resolved to another website belonging to Mr. Burgar, namely "celebrity1000.com".

(ii) The second circumstance is that the Respondent has "been commonly known by the domain name, even if he has acquired no trade mark or service mark rights". This is much more problematic. Mr. Burgar would say that the domain name at issue was registered in the name of "Bruce Springsteen Club" and consequently that the proprietor of the domain name has "been commonly known by the domain name" as required in the UDRP. The question in this case involves the meaning of the words "commonly" and "known by".

(iii) It is hard to say that the mere use of the name "Bruce Springsteen Club" can give rise to an impression in the minds of internet users that the proprietor was effectively "known as" Bruce Springsteen. It is even more remote that it could be said that the proprietor was "commonly" recognised in that fashion. Accordingly the Panel finds that this circumstance in paragraph 4(c) is not met.

The third circumstance is that the Respondent is "making a legitimate non-commercial or fair use of the domain name, without intent for commercial gain to misleadingly divert customers or to tarnish the trade mark or service mark at issue".

There are a number of concepts contained within this "circumstance" which make it a complex issue to resolve. For example, at what point does use of a domain name become "commercial" or alternatively what amounts to "fair use" since those concepts appear to be in the alternative.

An internet search using the words "Bruce Springsteen" gives rise to literally thousands of hits. It is perfectly apparent to any internet user that not all of those hits are "official" or "authorised" sites. The user will browse from one search result to another to find the information and material which he or she is looking for in relation to a search item, in this case the celebrity singer Bruce Springsteen. It is therefore hard to see how it can be said that the registration of the domain name at issue can be "misleading" in its diversion of consumers to the "celebrity1000.com" website.

There have been examples in other cases of blatant attempts, for example, by the use of minor spelling discrepancies to entrap internet users onto sites which have absolutely no connection whatsoever with the name which is being used in its original or slightly altered form. In this case, the internet user, coming upon the "celebrity1000.com" website would perhaps be unsurprised to have arrived there via a search under the name "Bruce Springsteen". If the internet user wished to stay longer at the site he or she could do so, or otherwise they could clearly return to their search results to find more instructed material concerning Bruce Springsteen himself.

Accordingly, it is hard to infer from the conduct of the Respondent in this case an intent, for commercial gain, to misleadingly divert consumers. There is certainly no question of the common law rights of Mr. Springsteen being "tarnished" by association with the "celebrity1000.com" website. The Panelists' own search of that site indicates no links which would have that effect, for example connections to sites containing pornographic or other regrettable material.

Accordingly the Panel finds that Bruce Springsteen has not satisfied the second limb of the three part test in the UDRP.

Moving on to the question of bad faith, once again the UDRP contains helpful guidance as to how the Complainant may seek to demonstrate bad faith on the part of the Registrant. The four, non-exclusive, circumstances are set out in paragraph 4(b) of the UDRP, and can be dealt with as follows:-

(i) The first circumstance is that there is evidence that the Registrant obtained the domain name primarily for the purpose of selling, renting or otherwise transferring it to the Complainant or to a competitor. This can be dealt with swiftly. There is simply no evidence put forward by the Complainant that there has been any attempt by Mr. Burgar to sell the domain name, either directly or indirectly.

(ii) The second circumstance is that the Registrant obtained the domain name in order to prevent the owner of the trade mark or service mark from reflecting that mark in a corresponding domain name, provided that there has been a pattern of such conduct. In this case, Bruce Springsteen's representatives point to the many other celebrity domain names registered by Mr. Burgar as evidence that he has indulged in a pattern of this conduct.

However, Mr. Burgar is clearly experienced in the ways of the internet. When he registered the domain name at issue in 1996, he would have been well aware that if he had wanted to block the activities of Bruce Springsteen or his record company in order to extract a large payment, or for whatever other reason there may be in creating such a blockage, he could, at nominal cost, have also registered the domain names <brucespringsteen.net> and <brucespringsteen.org>. He did not do so, and indeed subsequently in 1998 Mr. Springsteen's record company registered the name <brucespringsteen.net> which has been used as the host site for the official Bruce Springsteen website since that time. It appears in the top five items in a search on the internet under the name "Bruce Springsteen".

It is trite to say that, by registering the domain name at issue, the Registrant has clearly prevented Bruce Springsteen from owning that name himself. However, that does not have the effect required in paragraph 4(b)(ii) of the UDRP. That paragraph indicates that the registration should have the effect of preventing the owner of a trade mark or service mark from reflecting the mark "in a corresponding domain name". In these circumstances what is meant by the word "corresponding"? Nothing that has been done by Mr. Burgar has prevented Bruce Springsteen's official website at <brucespringsteen.net> being registered and used in his direct interests. That is surely a "corresponding domain name" for these purposes, as the expression "corresponding domain name" clearly refers back to the words "trade mark or service mark" rather than the domain name at issue referred to in the first line of paragraph 4(b)(ii).

It is perhaps pertinent to observe that the so-called "official" site at <brucespringsteen.net> was registered in 1998. It seems unlikely that, at that time, the existence of the domain name at issue did not become apparent.

Whilst this is pure surmise, and consequently in no way relevant to the findings of the Panel, it might be thought that the alleged "blocking" effect of the domain name at issue might have given rise to a complaint at that time, if only in correspondence.

This Panel believes that previous Panels have all too readily concluded that the mere registration of the mark, and indeed other marks of a similar nature, is evidence of an attempt to prevent the legitimate owner of registered or common law trade mark rights from obtaining a "corresponding domain name". This is an issue which should be looked at more closely, and for the purposes of this complaint, the Panel finds that the "circumstance" in paragraph 4(b)(ii) does not arise for the purpose of demonstrating bad faith on the part of the Registrant.

(i) The third circumstance is that the Registrant has obtained the domain name "primarily for the purpose of disrupting the business of a competitor". This can be dealt with very swiftly as there is no suggestion that that is the case in the present complaint.

(ii) The fourth circumstance is that, by using the domain name, the Registrant has "intentionally attempted to attract, for commercial gain, internet users to his website or other online location, by creating a likelihood of confusion with the Complainant's mark as to the source, sponsorship, affiliation or endorsement of the website or location or of a product or a service on the website or location".

Once again, this sub-paragraph contains a number of concepts which render it complex to analyse and apply. However, the key issue appears to be the requirement that the use of the domain name must "create a likelihood of confusion with the Complainant's mark". As indicated above, a simple search under the name "Bruce Springsteen" on the internet gives rise to many thousands of hits. As also indicated above, even a relatively unsophisticated user would be clearly aware that not all of those hits would be directly associated in an official and authorised capacity with Bruce Springsteen himself, or his agents or record company. The nature of an internet search does not reveal the exact notation of the domain name. Accordingly, the search result may read "Bruce Springsteen - discography", but will not give the user the exact address. That only arises on a screen once the user has gone to that address. The relevance of this is that it is relatively unlikely that any user would seek to go straight to the internet and open the site <brucespringsteen.com> in the optimistic hope of reaching the official Bruce Springsteen website. If anyone sufficiently sophisticated in the use of the internet were to do that, they would very soon realise that the site they reached was not the official site, and consequently would move on, probably to conduct a fuller search.

Accordingly, it is hard to see that there is any likelihood of confusion can arise in these circumstances. The name of the Registrant is not shown in an internet search, accordingly the fact that the Registrant in this case is "Bruce Springsteen Club" would not have the effect of giving rise to the sort of confusion which might satisfy the test under paragraph 4(b)(iv).

The Panel therefore finds that none of the circumstances in paragraph 4(b) of the UDRP are met in this case.

Paragraph 4(b) makes it quite clear that the four "circumstances" are non-exclusive. In this case, the Complainant has urged the Panel to find bad faith on the grounds of the use of the "fictitious" name "Bruce Springsteen Club" as the Registrant. It may be that there is some element of bad faith in the conduct of Mr..

Burgar in registering in the name of "Bruce Springsteen Club". However, on reflection, the Panel does not believe that it is sufficient to satisfy the necessary burden under the UDRP.

Before moving onto the final decision, it is perhaps appropriate in a case of this complexity and profile, that the Panel should briefly consider the authorities which have been referred to, in particular by the Complainant.

Bruce Springsteen's representatives referred to the court decision in the "Northern Lights case" as evidence of the conduct and consequently the bad faith of Mr. Burgar. The written decision appended to the complaint is inconclusive, and contains no valid decisions on contested items of evidence such as the allegations that certain conversations took place which are denied by either party to the case in different circumstances. Accordingly, the Panel cannot read anything of significance into that decision.

There have been a number of cases concerning celebrity names, some of which were referred to in this case. Many of those decisions are flawed in some way or another.

The case of Jeannete Winterson -v- Mark Hogarth (WIPO case number D2000-0235) has been credited with establishing the principle that common law rights can arise in a proper name. The case is also noteable for an erroneous interpretation of the third requirement, namely the demonstration of bad faith. There is an indication in the case that the burden falls on the Registrant to demonstrate that the domain name at issue has been used in good faith. That is clearly not the case, and that confusion appears to have knocked on into other cases, for example the Julia Roberts case. The burden is clearly with the Complainant to demonstrate that bad faith has been shown.

In the case of Julia Fiona Roberts -v- Russell Boyd (WIPO case number D2000-0210) the question of "permission" arises. In relation to the question of "rights or legitimate interests" it is stated that "Respondent has no relationship with or permission from Complainant for the use of her name or mark". As indicated above, that is simply irrelevant. It is perfectly clear from general principles protecting registered and unregistered trade marks the world over, and indeed from the UDRP, that whilst permission might be conclusive against an allegation of infringement if it can be shown to have been granted, the absence of permission is not conclusive that an infringement has occurred, nor is it conclusive proof that the alleged infringer has no rights of his or her own.

Further, in the Julia Roberts case, there is a suggestion that the registration of the domain name <juliaroberts.com> "necessarily prevented the Complainant from using the disputed domain name". As indicated above, that is not sufficient to meet the criteria required under the URDP for the relevant circumstance in paragraph 4(b).

The case of Daniel C Mario Jnr -v- Video Images Productions (WIPO case number D2000-0598) contains a passage highlighted when annexed to the complaint in this case in the following terms:-

> "in fact, in light of the uniqueness of the name <danmarino.com>, which is virtually identical to the Complainant's personal name and common law trade mark, it would be extremely difficult to foresee any justifiable use that the Respondent could claim. On the contrary, selecting this name gives rise to the impression of an association with the Complainant which is not based in fact."

This Panel contends that that assertion is erroneous. For all the reasons set out above, the users of the internet do not expect all sites bearing the name of celebrities or famous historical figures or politicians, to be authorised or in some way connected with the figure themselves. The internet is an instrument for purveying information, comment, and opinion on a wide range of issues and topics. It is a valuable source of information in many fields, and any attempt to curtail its use should be strongly discouraged. Users fully expect domain names incorporating the names of well known figures in any walk of life to exist independently of any connection with the figure themselves, but having been placed there by admirers or critics as the case may be.

Accordingly, in all the circumstances the Panel does not believe that Bruce Springsteen has met the necessary criteria to sustain a complaint under the URRP.

*7. Decision*

In light of the foregoing, the Panel decides that although the domain name at issue is identical to the un-registered trade mark of the Complainant, the Registrant has demonstrated that he has some rights or legitimate interests in respect of the domain name, and the Complainant has failed to demonstrate that the domain name was registered and has been used in bad faith.

Accordingly, the Panel orders that the registration of the domain name be left as it stands.

*Richard W. Page, Dissenting Panelist, Dissent*

Paragraph 4(a)(i) of the UDRP requires a Complainant to show the existence of "a trade mark or service mark in which Complainant has rights." The majority has presumed (and should have concluded) that the personal name "Bruce Springsteen" has acquired distinctive secondary meaning giving rise to common law trademark rights in the "famous, almost legendary, recording artist and composer, Bruce Springsteen."

The majority notes that no evidence was presented to establish secondary meaning. Complainant alleges in paragraph 14 of the Complaint, without contradiction by the Respondent, that:

Complainant is an internationally renowned and critically acclaimed composer, lyricist, recording artist, singer, musician and performer. He has been a professional singer and musician since 1964. His first album, "Greetings from Asbury Park N.J." was released to the public in 1972. Since that time, millions of copies of his recordings have been sold throughout the world. He has received numerous awards recognizing the quality of his compositions and recordings, including multiple Grammies and an Oscar. As a result of the foregoing, Complainant's name has acquired secondary meaning, has come to be recognized by the general public as indicating an association with the Complainant, and is the source of enormous goodwill towards the Complainant.

Accordingly, Complainant has common law trademark rights in his name. See, e.g., Julia Fiona Roberts v. Russell Boyd,WIPO Case No. D2000-0210, May 29, 2000 ("Roberts")(Annex 3); Daniel C. Marino, Jr. v. Video Images Productions, WIPO Case No. D2000-0598, August 2, 2000 ("Marino")(Annex 4); Rita Rudner v. Internetco Corp., WIPO Case No. D2000-0581, August 3, 2000 ("Rudner")(Annex 5); Helen Folsade Adu, known as Sade v. Quantum Computer Services Inc., WIPO Case No. D2000-0794, Sep. 26, 2000 ("Sade")(Annex 6).

In addition, the majority later notes that "an internet search using the words 'Bruce Springsteen' gives rise to literally thousands of hits. Therefore, secondary meaning has been adequately shown.

Regardless of commentary that personal names (presumably without secondary meaning) are not protected, the language of paragraph 4(a)(i) does not exclude any specific type of common law trademarks from protection. The majority further concludes that the disputed domain name is identical with the common law mark. Therefore, Complainant has met the requirements of paragraph 4(a)(i).

Paragraph 4(a)(ii) requires a Complainant to show Respondent has no rights or legitimate interest in the disputed domain name. Although the way in which the UDRP is written requires the Complainant to demonstrate this, the logic of this burden of proof is questionable in that it requires the Complainant to prove the nonexistence of certain facts. In effect the assertion by Complainant that Respondent has no rights in the mark, through permission or consent of the Complainant or otherwise, is sufficient to shift the burden to Respondent.

Paragraphs 4(c)(i)-(iii) describe the nonexclusive circumstances which may be used to prove that Respondent has rights or legitimate interest in the disputed domain name. The majority bases its decision on a finding that Complainant has failed to disprove 4(c)(iii). This circumstance allows Respondent rights or legitimate interest upon a showing of noncommercial or fair use without misleading diversion of customers. Specifically, the majority finds that Respondent has not misleadingly diverted customers to Respondent's website www.celebrity1000.com.

The majority assumes that the internet user will search literally thousands of hits on "Bruce Springsteen" without going directly to <brucespringsteen.com> and without concluding that "brucespringsteen.com" resolves to a website sanctioned by Complainant. Apparently the Presiding Panelist conducted his independent search in this manner and concludes that a hypothetical internet user would search in the same manner. This is an insufficient basis to conclude that resolution of the domain name <brucespringsteen.com> into Respondent's website www.celebrity1000.com is not misleading.

The Dissenting Panelist concludes that the average internet user would not sift through thousands of hits searching for information on Bruce Springsteen. Instead, the internet user would devise shortcuts. One obvious shortcut is to go directly to <brucespringsteen.com> with the expectation that it would lead to the official website.

Respondent alludes to the phenomenon that "postponing the creation of other Tld's until the '.com' name space dominated the world just sort of happened." The dominance of the ".com" name space is reflected in the common usage of the phrase ".com" as being synonymous with commercial activity on the Internet. Given a vast array of information on the performer Bruce Springsteen, the internet user is more likely than not to associate <brucespringsteen.com> with commercial activity and with an official domain name, resolving to an official website. Therefore, the Dissenting Panelist concludes that that resolution of the domain name <brucespringsteen.com> into Respondent 's website www.celebrity1000.com is misleading.

Complainant has alleged that Respondent has no rights or legitimate interest in the disputed domain name, through permission, consent or otherwise. Respondent has not presented sufficient evidence that any of the circumstances in paragraph 4(c)(i)-(iii) is present. Therefore, Complainant has made the necessary showing under paragraph 4(a)(ii).

Paragraphs 4(b)(i)-(iv) describe the nonexclusive circumstances which may be used to prove that Respondent has registered and used the disputed domain name in bad faith. Complainant relies on paragraphs 4(b)(ii) and (iv) to demonstrate Respondent 's bad faith. Proving either of these two circumstances is sufficient. Paragraph 4(b)(iv) requires Complainant to prove that Respondent has intentionally attracted internet users to Respondent's website for commercial gain by creating a likelihood of confusion as to the source of the website.

The majority reiterates its analysis that internet users will not be confused by resolution of the <brucespringsteen.com> domain name to Respondent's website and have no expectation of finding an official website. The Dissenting Panelist has already concluded to the contrary.

The remaining element under paragraph 4(b)(iv) is to show that Respondent is engaged in a commercial undertaking. Respondent states in his Response that: "...given the hundreds of millions of dollars presently lost by companies such as Amazon and Infospace on the Internet, we are not ashamed to say, we do not have any commercial gain. We lose money." The test of a commercial undertaking is not that the enterprise turns a profit.

From Respondent's statements, the Dissenting Panelist infers that the activities of respondent are commercial. Therefore, the circumstances of paragraph 4(b)(iv) are met.

The Dissenting Panelist would rule that Complainant has met his burden and that the disputed domain name should be transferred.

---

## 1.2 PERSONAL REPUTATIONS

Just as national attitudes toward celebrity names and likenesses varies from country to country, so too does commitment to protection of personal reputation. For example, while the definitions of libel are basically the same in the U.S. and the U.K. – the unprivileged publication of a false factual statement which tends to damage the reputation of another – the U.K. tilts far more toward plaintiffs than the U.S., as the *Telnikoff* case illustrates.

These disparities are of major concern to companies that distribute their products internationally or license them to third parties for overseas distribution (especially if the licensor has warranted and represented that the products in question do not violate any third party rights).

Such questions also take on importance when a producer or publisher seeks "errors and omissions" insurance to protect itself against libel claims (as well as claims for other non-physical torts such as infringements of rights of privacy, publicity and trademark). At least in theory, the producer or publisher – as well as the producer or publisher's attorney – are required to use their best efforts to assure the carrier that the project or product is not subject to attack in the areas covered. This may present serious problems in the area of libel.

---

**Telnikoff v. Matusevitch**
**702 A.2d 230 (Md. 1997)**

Opinion by Eldridge, J.

The issue presented in this certified question case is whether a particular English libel judgment, under the circumstances presented, is contrary to the public policy of Maryland so that it should be denied recognition under principles of comity.

I. Vladimir Matusevitch, now a Maryland resident, was born to parents of Belarusan Jewish descent in New York City in 1936. In 1940, Matusevitch moved to Russia where he remained until 1968 when he defected to Norway and received political asylum. Between 1969 and 1992, Matusevitch worked in several countries as a journalist for Radio Free Europe/Radio Liberty (RFE/RL), a publicly-funded

American corporation that broadcasts to listeners in Eastern Europe and countries formerly under Soviet control. Matusevitch presently works at RFE/RL's corporate headquarters in the District of Columbia.

Vladimir Telnikoff, an English citizen, was born in Leningrad in 1937 and remained there until 1971, when he emigrated to Israel. The following year, Telnikoff began working as a freelance writer and broadcaster for the British Broadcasting Corporation (BBC) in London. In 1983, Telnikoff became employed as a journalist at RFE/RL in Munich, Germany.

On February 13, 1984, an article written by Telnikoff was published in the London *Daily Telegraph*, headed "Selecting the Right Wavelength to Tune in to Russia." The article stated in pertinent part as follows:

> "But still, after three decades of gradually becoming aware of the significance of Russian language broadcasting, I believe [the BBC's] general concept has never been set right. It continues to reflect the fatal confusion of the West, which has yet to clarify to itself whether it is threatened by Russia or by Communism. We fail to understand that Communism is as alien to the religious and national aspirations of the Russian people as those of any other nation.
>
> "This confusion further manifests itself in the policy of recruitment for the Russian Service. While other services are staffed almost exclusively from those who share the ethnic origin of the people to whom they broadcast, the Russian Service is recruited almost entirely from Russian-speaking national minorities of the Soviet empire, and has something like 10 per cent of those who associate themselves ethnically, spiritually or religiously with Russian people. However high the standards and integrity of that majority there is no more logic in this than having a Greek service which is 90 per cent recruited from the Greek-speaking Turkish community of Cyprus.
>
> "When broadcasting to other East European countries, we recognize them to be enslaved from outside, and better able to withstand alien, Russian, Communism through our assertion of their own national spirit and traditions. However, this approach leaves room for flirting with Euro-communism or 'socialism with a human (non-Russian) face' as a desirable further alternative, and well suits the Left in the West.
>
> "Resisting the ideological advance of Communism by encouraging anti-Russian feelings is of less obvious value with a Russian audience. Making 'Russian' synonymous with 'Communist' alienates the sympathetic Russian listeners. It stirs up social resentment in others against the Russians. Making those word synonymous also makes sympathy for Russian into support for the Communist system."

In response, a letter written by Matusevitch, entitled "Qualifications for Broadcasting to Russia," was published in the *Daily Telegraph* on February 18, 1984. It was as follows:

> "Sir — Having read 'Selecting the Right Wavelength to Tune in to Russia' (Feb 13) I was shocked, particularly by the part on alleged inadequacies of the BBC's Russian Service recruitment policies.
>
> "Mr. Vladimir Telnikoff says: 'While other services are staffed almost exclusively from those who share the ethnic origin of the people to whom they broadcast, the Russian Service is recruited almost entirely from Russian-speaking national minorities of the Soviet empire.'
>
> "Mr. Telnikoff must certainly be aware that the majority of new emigres from Russia are people who grew up, studied and worked in Russia, who have Russian as their mother tongue and have only one culture — Russian.

"People with Jewish blood in their veins were never allowed by the Soviet authorities to feel themselves equal with people of the same language, culture and way of life. Insulted and humiliated by this paranoiac situation, desperate victims of these Soviet racialist (anti-Semitic) policies took the opportunity to emigrate.

"Now the BBC's Russian Service, as well as other similar services of other Western stations broadcasting to Russia, who are interested in new staff members (natives), employ those people in accordance with common democratic procedures, interested in their professional qualifications and not in the blood of the applicants.

"Mr. Telnikoff demands that in the interest of more effective broadcasts the management of the BBC's Russian Service should switch from *professional testing* to a *blood* test.

"Mr. Telnikoff is stressing his racialist recipe by claiming that no matter how high the standards and integrity 'of ethnically alien' people Russian staff might be, they should be dismissed.

"I am certain the *Daily Telegraph* would reject any article with similar suggestions of lack of racial purity of the writer in any normal section of the British media.

"One could expect that the spreading of racialist views would be unacceptable in a British newspaper."

After Matusevitch refused to apologize for his February 18th letter, Telnikoff filed a libel action against Matusevitch in the High Court of Justice, Queen's Bench Division, in London. . . .

At the May 22nd trial, Telnikoff argued that the "natural and ordinary" meaning of the words contained in Matusevitch's letter implied that Telnikoff advocated (1) the use of blood-testing as part of the recruitment policy in the BBC Russian Services, (2) the dismissal of employees of the BBC Russian Service on racial grounds, and (3) racial discrimination and anti-semitic behavior. Matusevitch denied that the letter was defamatory and defended on the ground that the letter constituted "fair comment" on a matter of public interest.[2] [Fn.2 Under English law, "fair comment" is an affirmative defense under which a defendant must prove that the alleged libel was "comment," and that the "comment" was objectively "fair" or that it could honestly have been said by an honest person. . . . Matusevitch claimed that his letter was "fair comment" upon a matter of public interest because of "the view expressed by the Plaintiff as to the necessary qualifications for broadcasting to Russia and in particular the alleged inadequacies of the recruitment process of the BBC Russian Service."] Matusevitch did not, however, assert truth as a defense.[3] [Fn3 A second affirmative defense under English law is "justification" or "truth." Defamatory words are presumed false, and thus the defendant carries the burden of proving the "truth" of the alleged defamatory words. Because a defendant who pleads but fails to prove truth as a defense may be liable for aggravated damages, Matusevitch chose not to plead truth as a defense.] In reply to Matusevitch's "fair comment" defense, Telnikoff asserted that Matusevitch "had been actuated by express malice."[4] [Fn4 "Express malice," in the sense of ill-will, spite, or an intent to injure, will under English law, defeat a defense of "fair comment."]

At the conclusion of the trial, the High Court of Justice granted Matusevitch's motion for a judgment as a matter of law. Holding that a "reasonable jury" would find that the alleged libel was "comment," the court explained:

"Read in the context of the rest of the letter, I think that [Matusevitch] was doing no more than to make the comments that, if [Telnikoff's] views as stated in his article were given effect to, then the logical outcome would be that the

BBC would, when interviewing applicants to join the Russian Service, concentrate on the ethnic origins of the applicant rather than their expertise as broadcasters. I think it is clear that [Matusevitch] was using the suggestion of a blood test in a metaphorical sense and in no way suggesting that [Telnikoff] in his article had actually demanded that a blood sample should be taken from anyone. . . . Mr. Telnikoff had not demanded in his article that any existing staff should actually be dismissed; but by claiming that 90% of the existing staff were unsuitable for the service, I think it is comment rather than a bare statement of fact to state, as the defendant did in his letter, that Mr. Telnikoff was suggesting that those unsuitable staff should be dismissed."

The High Court went on to rule that Matusevitch's comment was objectively "fair," consisted of "a matter of public interest," and that there was no showing of express malice.

The Court of Appeal affirmed the High Court's judgment on May 16, 1990. Telnikoff appealed to the House of Lords which, on November 14, 1991, affirmed in part, reversed in part and remanded the case. While affirming the rulings below with regard to malice, the House of Lords set aside the holdings below that Matusevitch's letter was "pure comment." Lord Keith of Kinkel for the House of Lords reasoned that, in determining whether the letter was comment or fact, the jury should examine the letter by itself and not in context with Telnikoff's article. Accordingly, the House of Lords remanded the case to the High Court of Justice for a jury to decide "whether paragraphs 6 and 7 of [Matusevitch's] letter consisted of pure comment or whether they contained defamatory statements of fact." On remand, the High Court of Justice instructed the jury on this issue at a trial commencing March 10, 1992. The jury returned a 240,000 pound verdict in favor of Telnikoff, finding that Matusevitch's letter conveyed:

"1. That [Telnikoff] had made statements inciting racial hatred and/or racial discrimination; [and] 2. That [Telnikoff] was a racialist and /or anti-semite and/or a supporter and/or proponent of doctrines of racial superiority or racial purity."

Subsequently, a judgment was entered into Telnikoff's favor for the amount of the jury's verdict.

Telnikoff unsuccessfully attempted to have his judgment enforced against Matusevitch in the United States. On April 20, 1994, Matusevitch commenced the present action by filing a complaint in the United States District Court for the District of Maryland, seeking a declaratory judgment that the English judgment was "repugnant" to the First and Fourteenth Amendments to the United States Constitution, to Article 40 of the Maryland Declaration of the Rights, and to Maryland common law and Maryland public policy. Telnikoff counterclaimed, seeking enforcement of his English judgment in Maryland. Upon stipulation by the parties, the case was transferred to the United States District Court for the District of Columbia.

On January 27, 1995, the United States District Court for the District of Columbia entered judgment for Matusevitch, holding that the cause of action underlying the English libel judgment was "repugnant to the public policy of the State" within the meaning of Maryland's Uniform Foreign-Money Judgments Recognition Act, Maryland Code (1974, 1995 Repl. Vol.), § 10-704(b)(2) of the Courts and Judicial Proceedings Article, and that recognition of the foreign judgment under principles of comity "would be repugnant to the public policies of the State of Maryland and the United States." *Matusevitch v. Telnikoff*, 877 F. Supp. 1, 3, 4 (D.D.C. 1995). Alternatively, the United States District Court held that recognition and enforcement of the English judgment would violate the First and Fourteenth Amendments to the United States Constitution, *id.* at 4-6.

Telnikoff appealed to the United States Court of Appeals for the District of Columbia Circuit. After hearing oral argument, the United States Court of Appeals certified, pursuant to the Uniform Certification of Questions of Law Act, Code (1974, 1995 Repl. Vol., 1996 Supp.), §§ 12-601 through 12-609 of the Courts and Judicial Proceedings Article, the following question to this Court: "Would recognition of Telnikoff's foreign judgment be repugnant to the public policy of Maryland?"

We shall answer the question in the affirmative.

II. Telnikoff argues that the English libel judgment is entitled to recognition under principles of "comity." Matusevitch, on the other hand, asserts that the English judgment is repugnant to the public policy of the United States and of Maryland and, therefore, should be denied recognition.

The recognition of foreign judgments is governed by principles of comity. . . .

The United States Supreme Court discussed the meaning of comity in *Hilton v. Guyot, supra,* 159 U.S. at 163-164, 16 S. Ct. at 143, 40 L. Ed. at 108, where Justice Gray wrote for the Court:

> "No law has any effect, of its own force, beyond the limits of the sovereignty from which its authority is derived. The extent to which the law of one nation, as put in force within its territory, whether by executive order, by legislative act, or by judicial decree, shall be allowed to operate within the dominion of another nation, depends upon what our greatest jurists have been content to call 'the comity of nations.' Although the phrase has been often criticised, no satisfactory substitute has been suggested.
>
> "'Comity,' in the legal sense, is neither a matter of absolute obligation, on the one hand, nor mere courtesy and good will, upon the other. But it is the recognition which one nation allows within its territory to the legislative, executive or judicial acts of another nation, having due regard both to international duty and convenience, and to the rights of its own citizens or of other persons who are under the protection of its laws.". . .

Although foreign judgments are entitled to a degree of deference and respect under the doctrine of comity, courts will nonetheless deny recognition and enforcement to those foreign judgments which are inconsistent with the public policies of the forum state. . . .

The principles underlying comity, including the public policy exception, have been codified in the Maryland Uniform Foreign-Money Judgments Recognition Act, Code (1974, 1995 Repl. Vol.), §§ 10-701 et seq. of the Courts and Judicial Proceedings Article. . . .

Section 10-704(b)(2) of the Act specifically states that a "foreign judgment need not be recognized if" the "cause of action on which the judgment is based is repugnant to the public policy of the State . . . ."

III. The question before us is whether Telnikoff's English libel judgment is based upon principles which are so contrary to Maryland's public policy concerning freedom of the press and defamation actions that recognition of the judgment should be denied.

A. In resolving this public policy issue, it is important to emphasize what is *not* before this Court. The certified question does not ask us to decide whether the Free Press Clause of the First Amendment or Article 40 of the Maryland Declaration of Rights directly precludes Maryland recognition or enforcement of the English judgment, and we do not decide those issues. . . .

While we shall rest our decision in this case upon the non-constitutional ground of Maryland public policy, nonetheless, in ascertaining that public policy, it is appropriate to examine and rely upon the history, policies, and requirements of the First Amendment and Article 40 of the Declaration of Rights. In determining non-constitutional principles of law, courts often rely upon the policies and requirements reflected in constitutional provisions. . . .

Consequently, it is appropriate to examine some of the history, policies, and requirements of the free press clauses of the First Amendment and Article 40 of the Declaration of Rights, as well as the present relationship between those provisions and defamation actions in Maryland.

B. American and Maryland history reflects a public policy in favor of a much broader and more protective freedom of the press than ever provided for under English law. . . .

D. The contrast between English standards governing defamation actions and the present Maryland standards is striking. For the most part, English defamation actions are governed by principles which are unchanged from the earlier common law period. . . .

Thus, under English defamation law, it is unnecessary for the plaintiff to establish fault, either in the form of conscious wrongdoing or negligence. The state of mind or conduct of the defendant is irrelevant. . . .

Moreover, under English law, defamatory statements are presumed to be false unless a defendant proves them to be true. . . . In addition, a defendant risks punitive damages if he pleads truth but fails to prove it. . . . .

In England, a qualified privilege can be overcome without establishing that the defendant actually knew that the publication was false or acted with reckless disregard of whether it was false or not. It can be overcome by proof of "spite or ill-will or some other wrong or improper motive." Peter F. Carter-Ruck, *Libel and Slander*, 137 (1973). English law authorizes punitive or exemplary damages under numerous circumstances in defamation actions; unlike Maryland law, they are not limited to cases in which there was actual knowledge of the falsehood or reckless disregard as to truth or falsity. *Id.* at 172-173. Furthermore, as one scholar has pointed out, *id.* at 172, "in practice only one sum is awarded and it is impossible to tell to what extent the damages awarded in any particular case were intended to be compensatory and to what extent exemplary or punitive. The very high damages awarded in recent years in actions against newspapers can only be explained on the basis that the sums awarded reflect the juries' opinion of the defendants' conduct."

English defamation law presumes that a statement is one of fact, and the burden is on the defendant to prove "fair comment." . . .

Proof of malice, in the sense of ill-will, spite, etc., "will vitiate fair comment as a defense event though in all other respects the comment fulfils the qualifications which the law stipulates." *Id.* at 126. In addition, "the malice of one defendant will destroy the defence for all the defendants and each defendant is not entitled to have his case considered separately." *Id.* at 127. Moreover, as the opinion of the House of Lords in the present controversy shows, a statement is not evaluated in the context of the publication to which it responds. *Matusevitch v. Telnikoff* [1991] 4 All Eng. 817, 822-826. Context appears to be eliminated from a court's determination of whether a statement is considered fact or comment.

Finally, English defamation law flatly rejects the principles set forth in *New York Times Co. v. Sullivan, supra*, and *Gertz v. Robert Welch, Inc., supra.* The basic rules are the same regardless of whether the plaintiff is a public official, public figure, or a private person, regardless of whether the alleged defamatory statement involves a matter of public concern, and regardless of the defendant's status. As

Professor Smolla has observed (Rodney A. Smolla, *Law of Defamation*, *supra*, at 1.03[3]), "British law recognizes no special protection for defamation actions arising from critiques of public figures or public officials, routinely imposing large damages awards in cases involving what American courts would characterize as core political discourse."

E. A comparison of English and present Maryland defamation law does not simply disclose a difference in one or two legal principles. . . . Instead, present Maryland defamation law is totally different from English defamation law in virtually every significant respect. Moreover, the differences are rooted in historic and fundamental public policy differences concerning freedom of the press and speech.

The stark contrast between English and Maryland law is clearly illustrated by the underlying litigation between Telnikoff and Matusevitch. Telnikoff, an employee of the publicly funded Radio Free Europe/Radio Liberty, was undisputably a public official or public figure. In this country, he would have had to prove, by clear and convincing evidence, that Matusevitch's letter contained false statements of fact and that Matusevitch acted maliciously in the sense that he knew of the falsity or acted with reckless disregard of whether the statements were false or not. The English courts, however, held that there was no evidence supporting Telnikoff's allegations that Matusevitch acted with actual malice, either under the *New York Times Co. v. Sullivan* definition or in the sense of ill-will, spite or intent to injure. Despite the absence of actual malice under any definition, Telnikoff was allowed to recover. He was not even required to prove negligence, which is the minimum a purely private defamation plaintiff must establish to recover under Maryland law.

In addition, Telnikoff was not required to prove that Matusevitch's letter contained a false statement of fact, which would have been required under present Maryland law. Instead, falsity was presumed, and the defendant had the risky choice of whether to attempt to prove truth. Furthermore, Telnikoff did not have to establish that the alleged defamation even contained defamatory statements of fact; the burden was upon the defendant to establish that the alleged defamatory language amounted to comment and not statements of fact.

Finally, contrary to the decisions of the Supreme Court and this Court, Matusevitch's letter was not examined in context but in isolation. It must be remembered that Telnikoff began the public debate with his published article, and Matusevitch's letter constituted his rebuttal. . . .

The principles governing defamation actions under English law, which were applied to Telnikoff's libel suit, are so contrary to Maryland defamation law, and to the policy of freedom of the press underlying Maryland law, that Telnikoff's judgment should be denied recognition under principles of comity. In the language of the Uniform Foreign-Money Judgments Recognition Act, § 10-704(b)(2) of the Courts and Judicial Proceedings Article, Telnikoff's English "cause of action on which the judgment is based is repugnant to the public policy of the State. . . ."

The only American case which the two parties have called to our attention, which is directly on point, reached a similar conclusion. In *Bachchan v. India Abroad Publications*, 154 Misc. 2d 228, 585 N.Y.S.2d 661 (1992), an Indian national brought a libel action in the High Court of Justice in London against the New York operator of a news service which transmitted stories exclusively to India. The suit was based upon an article, written by a London reporter and transmitted by the defendant to India, in which the plaintiff's name was used in connection with an international scandal. After a jury assessed 40,000 pounds in damages against the defendant, the plaintiff sought to enforce the judgment against the defendant in New

York. The defendant opposed recognition of the judgment on the ground that the judgment was "repugnant to public policy" of New York as embodied in the First Amendment to the United States Constitution and the free speech and press guarantees of the New York Constitution. . . .

Moreover, recognition of English defamation judgments could well lead to wholesale circumvention of fundamental public policy in Maryland and the rest of the country. With respect to the sharp differences between English and American defamation law, Professor Smolla has observed (Rodney A. Smolla, *Law of Defamation*, *supra*, at § 1.03[3]):

"This striking disparity between American and British libel law has led to a curious recent phenomenon, a sort of balance of trade deficit in libel litigation: Prominent persons who receive bad press in publications distributed primarily in the United States now often choose to file their libel suits in England. London has become an international libel capital. Plaintiffs with the wherewithal to do so now often choose to file suit in Britain in order to exploit Britain's strict libel laws, even when the plaintiffs and the publication have little connection to that country."

"At the heart of the First Amendment," as well as Article 40 of the Maryland Declaration of Rights and Maryland public policy, "is the recognition of the fundamental importance of the free flow of ideas and opinions on matters of public interest and concern." *Hustler Magazine v. Falwell*, *supra*, 485 U.S. at 50, 108 S. Ct. at 879, 99 L. Ed. 2d at 48. The importance of that free flow of ideas and opinions on matters of public concern precludes Maryland recognition of Telnikoff's English libel judgment. . . .

Dissenting Opinion by Chasanow, J.

. . . I believe Maryland public policy should not prevent enforcement of this English libel judgment. . . .

Matusevitch's letter was determined to be libelous by a jury; the proceedings were fair and carefully reviewed by the House of Lords, the highest court in England. There is no grave injustice in this internal English litigation. . . .

. . . Our interest in international good will, comity, and res judicata fostered by recognition of foreign judgments must be weighed against our minimal interest in giving the benefits of our local libel public policy to residents of another country who defame foreign public figures in foreign publications and who have no reasonable expectation that they will be protected by the Maryland Constitution. Unless there is some United States interest that should be protected, there is no good reason to offend a friendly nation like England by refusing to recognize a purely local libel judgment for a purely local defamation. In the instant case, there is no United States interest that might necessitate non-recognition or non-enforcement of the English defamation judgment. . . .

Here, Plaintiff and Defendant were both Russian emigres living in England. If England wishes to protect its public figures from even non-negligent libel by private citizens, it should be able to do so. There should be no need for Maryland public policy to give protection to an English resident who libels an English public figure in England. . . .

There should be no question about the need for First Amendment protection for a United States news wire service and that enforcement of the judgment in *Bachchan* would chill the free press rights of the New York newspaper wire service. There is a huge difference between giving First Amendment protection to a United States news wire service and giving First Amendment protection (or Article 40 protection) to all English libel defendants. It is unwarranted to simply refuse, on the basis of freedom of the press and Maryland public policy, to enforce all English libel judgments. England has an interest in protecting its residents, including its own public officials and public figures, from even unintentionally false and defamatory statements damaging to their reputation. It should not violate our public policy to recognize that interest as long as it does not endanger our interest in the free dissemination of information by our media and those people shielded by our Constitution. Our national interest might necessitate non-recognition of an English libel judgment if it was a judgment against a United States publication that was circulated abroad, or even perhaps a defamation judgment obtained in a foreign country by a United States public figure who cannot sue for merely negligent or unintended defamation under our Constitutions and public policy. Each case should be examined on its own facts to see if the United States freedom of the press is implicated or if the free speech rights of people entitled to the protection of our First Amendment are implicated.

Public policy should not require us to give First Amendment protection or Article 40 protection to English residents who defame other English residents in publications distributed only in England. Failure to make our constitutional provisions relating to defamation applicable to wholly internal English defamation would not seem to violate fundamental notions of what is decent and just and should not undermine public confidence in the administration of law. The Court does little or no analysis of the global public policy considerations and seems inclined to make Maryland libel law applicable to the rest of the world by providing a safe haven for foreign libel judgment debtors.

---

## 1.3 TITLES AND COMPANY NAMES

Trademarks are the subject of international treaties; however, like copyright (as you will read in the following section), trademark protection is at bottom a matter of national statute. If services are to be rendered, or goods distributed, outside of the U.S., the trademark proprietor needs to be sure that its trade- or sevice-mark is protected. This is especially crucial if one is planning to do business on the Internet. Other countries do not necessarily follow the U.S. principle that the establishment of a mark through use in commerce is the key to protection; in many countries, the first to file is the owner of the mark. As the following case shows, however, there are exceptional situations in which the trademark statute of one country can be applied to events occurring in another country.

---

### Les Ballets Trockadero De Monte Carlo, Inc. v. Trevino
### 945 F. Supp. 563 (S.D.N.Y. 1996)

John G. Koeltl, United States District Judge

The plaintiff "Les Ballets Trockadero de Monte Carlo, Inc." is an all male satirical ballet troupe. It seeks a preliminary injunction enjoining the defendants from directly or indirectly using the name "Les Ballets Torokka de Russia," or the words "Trocks," "Trock," "Trockettes," "Trockadero," "Torokka," "Torokkadero," or "Trocadero" (or similar variations of any such word) in conjunction with the words "Ballet," "Ballets," or any other words identifying a dance company or dance troupe, or using any other mark, words, or names confusingly similar to the plaintiff's, including the use thereof in any advertising or promotional material, whether printed, verbal, broadcast, electronically or otherwise. The plaintiff alleges that the defendants have been unlawfully infringing its registered service marks and promoting their dance troupe in a way that is confusingly similar to the plaintiff's, all in violation of the Lanham Act. The plaintiff argues that the defendants are likely to continue their infringing activities unless enjoined and that the plaintiff will be irreparably injured.

For the reasons stated below, the motion for a preliminary injunction is granted.

I. . . . The plaintiff, Les Ballets Trockadero de Monte Carlo, Inc. (the "Trocks"), is an all male satirical ballet troupe founded in 1974 in New York as a not-for-profit corporation. The Trocks have performed for more than twenty years in the United States and abroad. The plaintiff has obtained federal service mark protection from the United States Patent and Trademark Office for the names "Les Ballets Trockadero de Monte Carlo," "Trocks," and "Trockadero." Japan represents the Trocks' largest market from which it derives approximately eighty percent of its annual revenues. The Trocks stage approximately forty performances every summer in Japan. For many years, ZAK Corporation, a Japanese company owned and operated by Kyoichi Miyazaki ("Zak"), has produced the Trocks' tours in Japan. In return for payments of approximately $660,000 per year, Zak has the exclusive right to promote the Trocks in Japan, and the Trocks can only perform in Japan through engagements obtained for it by Zak. Zak also established and derives income from the Trocks' official Japanese fan club, Club Trockadero, which has over one thousand members. On January 25, 1994, ZAK Corporation filed an application in Japan to register the mark "Trockadero de Monte Carlo Ballets Dan."

In May, 1995, Zak formed defendant International Promotion for Music ("IPM") as a New York corporation with Zak as the President, sole director, and sole shareholder. According to Suguru Saito, the Vice President of IPM, Zak established IPM in order to extend his business operations and to create a New York presence. In late 1995, IPM retained defendant Victor Trevino, a former Trocks ballet dancer, to help organize an all male satirical ballet company that would compete with the Trocks and to be IPM's artistic director for all its ventures. Trevino recruited the individual defendant dancers, negotiated their contracts, organized music for the performances, retained a photographer, ordered the costumes and sets, and selected the ballets to be performed. During early 1996, Zak, Trevino, and Saito considered names for the new ballet company and ultimately selected Les Ballets Torokka de Russia (the "Torokka"). According to Zak, IPM is the sole owner of defendant Torokka, which was created in order to provide an additional source of income through the scheduling of a winter tour. Although the defendants contend that in April, 1996, Zak applied to register the mark "Les Ballet Torokka de Russia" in Japan, the plaintiff maintains that Zak instead applied for the mark "Torokkadero Sia Ballets Dan" or Torokkadero (Trockadero) Theater Ballet Company.

The defendants made plans for a Torokka winter 1996-1997 tour in Japan. During the Trocks' Japanese tour in July and August 1996, flyers were distributed at the Trocks' performances and inserts were placed in the Trocks' programs that promoted the defendants' planned tour as a "Trockadero Winter Version" and "Trockadero's Winter Company." In letters to the Trocks during that period, Zak disclaimed responsibility for these actions and informed the Trocks that he was having trouble obtaining bookings for them in 1997. On August 19, 1996, the plaintiff's counsel sent the defendants a cease and desist letter, and on August 30, 1996, the plaintiff commenced this action. . . .

III.A. As a threshold issue, the defendants argue that this action should be dismissed because the proceeding should take place in Japan under Japanese law. However, "Congress in prescribing standards of conduct for American citizens may project the impact of its laws beyond the territorial boundaries of the United States." Steele v. Bulova Watch Co., 344 U.S. 280, 282, 97 L. Ed. 319, 73 S. Ct. 252 (1952). The Lanham Act may be applied to activities outside the United States. See id. at 285-87 (applying the Lanham Act to conduct in Mexico). In Vanity Fair Mills, Inc. v. T. Eaton Co., 234 F.2d 633, 633, 641-42 (2d Cir.), cert. denied, 352 U.S. 871, 1 L. Ed. 2d 76, 77 S. Ct. 96 (1956), the Court of Appeals for the Second Circuit articulated the factors to be considered in determining the extraterritorial application of the Lanham Act: (1) whether the defendant's conduct has a substantial effect on United States commerce; (2) whether the defendant is a United States citizen; and (3) whether there is no conflict with trademark rights established under foreign law. See id. at 642. . . .

As to the first factor, the plaintiff has demonstrated that the defendants' conduct has a substantial effect on United States commerce. . . .

The defendants have engaged in conduct in the United States designed to further their infringing activities: Zak has formed defendant IPM, a New York corporation, in order to extend his business operations, to create a New York presence, and to organize the Torokka in the United States, and those activities have been assisted by the individual defendants; defendant Trevino used "Les Ballet Torokka de Russia" letterhead to correspond with dancers across the United States; and defendant Trevino recruited the defendant dancers, negotiated their contracts, organized music for the performances, retained a photographer, ordered the costumes and sets, selected the ballets to be performed, and reserved rehearsal space in the United States.

Moreover, as a result of the defendants' infringing activities, the effects on United States commerce include dilution and damage to the plaintiff's U.S. registered marks and reputation, as well as damage to the Trocks' prospective business and licensing negotiations in a market from which it derives eighty percent of its income.

The second Vanity Fair factor, the existence of an American defendant, is also satisfied. The individual defendants are all citizens of the United States, and defendant IPM is incorporated in New York state.

The third Vanity Fair factor, no conflict with the trademark rights under foreign law, also supports the exercise of extraterritorial application of the Lanham Act in this case. Protecting the plaintiff's rights in its marks by preventing the defendants from infringing those rights by using confusingly similar marks in Japan would not conflict with Japanese law. The plaintiff has persuasively demonstrated the likelihood that, under Japanese law, the defendants, as well as Zak and ZAK Corporation, do not have protectable rights under Japanese law to any of the marks at issue in this case.

The plaintiff's expert on Japanese trademark law, Kazuko Matsuo, explains without contradiction that, under Japanese trademark law, registration of marks provides protection. But before registration is granted and recorded in the Patent Office in Japan, an applicant has no legal rights in the mark other than rights it may have in an unregistered mark, and none are created by filing an application. Although Zak and/or ZAK Corporation has filed applications for the registration of various marks in Japan, those applications are being contested, and it is undisputed that neither Zak nor ZAK Corporation holds a registration on any of the marks at issue in this case. Indeed, the plaintiff has persuasively shown that it is likely to be able to prevent Zak and/or ZAK Corporation from obtaining a valid registration on any of the marks at issue because the plaintiff's mark is a well-known mark in Japan and, under Japanese law, would take precedence over any application filed by Zak or ZAK Corporation for similar marks. Mr. Matsuo explains that unregistered trademarks and service marks are protected under Japanese Unfair Competition Prevention Law where there is proof of (1) the well-known nature of the mark; (2) the similarity of the defendant's mark; and (3) the likelihood of confusion. The owner of a well-known mark can institute invalidation proceedings against the owner of a registered mark if it can demonstrate that it was the first to use and continue to use the mark. Although Japan has adopted the "first to file" rule for competing applications, a party cannot successfully register its mark if it is similar to another party's registered mark or well-known unregistered mark.

The plaintiff's uncontradicted evidence supports the conclusion that the plaintiff's marks are well known in Japan and therefore that ZAK Corporation holds no protectable rights in any relevant marks. Mr. Matsuo testifies that, based on his review of performances, promotional materials, and newspaper and magazine articles, the plaintiff's marks "Les Ballets Trockadero de Monte Carlo," "Trockadero," and "Trocks" have become so well-known in Japan that the plaintiff is entitled to protection under Japanese Unfair Competition Prevention Law and can prevent others from using confusingly similar marks. His testimony is also supported by evidence that the Trocks' largest following is in Japan, that it derives approximately eighty percent of its annual revenues from its Japanese tours, and that its fan club in Japan, Club Trockadero, has over a thousand members.

An injunction in this case will not conflict with rights granted under Japanese law.

Accordingly, each of the three Vanity Fair factors supports the exercise of extraterritorial application of the Lanham Act in this case.

B. . . . In Polaroid Corp. v. Polarad Elecs. Corp., 287 F.2d 492 (2d Cir.), cert. denied, 368 U.S. 820, 7 L. Ed. 2d 25, 82 S. Ct. 36 (1961), the Court of Appeals for the Second Circuit set forth eight factors that courts are to consider when determining whether a likelihood of confusion exists. . . .

Analysis of the Polaroid factors demonstrates a plain likelihood of confusion. . .

There is some degree of similarity between the English-language version of the defendants' name "Les Ballet Torokka de Russia" and the plaintiff's marks "Les Ballets Trockadero de Monte Carlo," "Trockadero," and "Trocks." The plaintiff has presented evidence that some of the friends and relatives of the defendant dancers have commented on the similarity of the names and asked whether there is a connection between them. Moreover, the similarities between the Trocks and the Torokka extend beyond their names. The Torokka is being presented in the marketplace as similar to the Trocks. The Torokka contains seven former members of the Trocks who previously toured in Japan. All the ballets that the Torokka plan to perform in Japan have been part of the Trocks repertoire at some point in time. The Torokka will also use some of the same choreography.

The defendants also promoted the Torokka to the Japanese public in such a way as to capitalize on the similarity. The Torokka promotional materials distributed at actual Trocks performances and elsewhere specifically stated that the Torokka is a winter version of the Trocks. . . .

The plaintiff has presented evidence of actual confusion in both the United States and Japan. . . .

. . . The plaintiff persuasively argues that although consumers of all male satirical ballet are likely to be somewhat more sophisticated about that service than the average consumer, the relevant consumers in this case are likely to purchase the defendants' service without careful advance scrutiny for several reasons. The Torokka is partly comprised of former Trocks dancers, the Trocks' fans are being targeted for sales of the infringing service, there is a strong similarity between the plaintiff's and the defendants' marks, and the defendants have actually used the plaintiff's marks in advertising and promotional materials. Moreover, even consumers who distinguish between the Trocks and the Torokka are not likely to realize that the origin of the two troupes is different. . . .

IV. For the foregoing reasons, the defendants, their officers, agents, servants, employees, and attorneys, acting as such, and those persons acting in concert or participation with them who receive actual notice of this order, are enjoined during the pendency of this action from directly or indirectly using the name "Les Ballets Torokka de Russia," or the words "Trocks," "Trock," "Trockettes," "Trockadero," "Torokka," "Torokkadero," or "Trocadero" (or similar variations of any such word) in conjunction with the words "Ballet," "Ballets," or any other words identifying a dance company or dance troupe, or using any other mark, words, or names confusingly similar to Les Ballet Trockadero de Monte Carlo, Inc., including the use thereof in any advertising or promotional material, whether printed, verbal, broadcast, electronically or otherwise.

. . .________________

**Mecklermedia Corp. v. D.C. Congress Gesellschaft mbH**
**U.K. High Court of Justice, Chancery Division**
**[1998] 1 All E.R. 148, 1997 WL 1104749**



Jacob J.:

This is an application by the defendants D.C. Congress GmbH (DC) for an order setting aside the writ on the grounds that this court does not have jurisdiction to hear and determine the claim made against them under the provisions of the Civil Jurisdiction and Judgments Act 1982. Alternatively DC seek an order staying this action or declining jurisdiction on the grounds that the Landgericht Munchen I is first seized of a related action in which DC is plaintiff and a corporation called Messe Berlin GmbH is defendant. Further or alternatively DC seek an order striking out the claim under the provisions of the Ord. 18, r. 19 or the inherent jurisdiction of the court.

The plaintiffs allege that DC commit the English tort of passing off. The relief sought is in relation to the activities of DC in and from Germany said to lead to that tort being committed. It is said that the plaintiffs have a goodwill in England and Wales, that DC are making a misrepresentation within the jurisdiction and that that misrepresentation has caused and will cause the plaintiffs damage within the jurisdiction – the trinity of elements constituting passing off.

It is convenient to consider the strength of this claim first, for if DC can show that the claim has no prospect of success it should be struck out on purely English law principles. Further, it is common ground that the strength of the claim is relevant to jurisdiction under the relevant provisions of the Brussels Convention which apply by virtue of the Act. In particular it is common ground that a higher standard than that for a strike out is required: it is for the plaintiff to satisfy the court that there is "a serious question which calls for trial for its proper determination". . . . Clearly a foreign (even an E.U.) defendant should not be brought before our courts unless there is a serious question to be tried.

I turn to the first element of the trinity. The first plaintiffs, Mecklermedia Corporation, are incorporated in Delaware. The second plaintiffs, Mecklermedia Ltd, are their English subsidiary. The second plaintiffs have, since 1994, been involved in the organisation of three trade shows in the United Kingdom. These were called "Internet World and Document Delivery World" (1994), and "Internet World International" (1995-96). It is said that these trade shows were widely advertised and attended. The trade shows were organised in conjunction with a licensee company. It is said that it was specifically agreed that all goodwill in the name "Internet World" should vest in the first plaintiff whom I will henceforth call Mecklermedia.

Mecklermedia have, since 1993, published in the United States a magazine called Internet World. This is claimed to have some circulation within the United Kingdom, but this must be essentially of the "spillover" variety. In the Autumn of 1996 an English version of the magazine was launched under the same name. It is published by VNU Business Publications but claims association (correctly) with the United States magazine by saying: "Internet World is already the most popular Internet magazine in the U.S. Now Internet World is to be published in the U.K. by the people who bring you Personal Computer World."

The first edition was given away free with Personal Computer World and there was no dispute but that that magazine has a substantial U.K. circulation. It is claimed that VNU publish the English edition under licence from Mecklermedia and that it is specifically agreed by VNU that the goodwill in the name "Internet World" should belong to Mecklermedia.

Finally it is claimed that Mecklermedia owns two web sites having the addresses "http://www.internetworld.com" and "http://www.iworld.com". It is said that anyone "visiting" these sites would see prominent use of the name "Internet World" and promotion of the plaintiffs' trade shows and magazines. Not much information is given about these sites (for instance their date of establishment and the number of English visitors) and I do not place reliance on them.

The upshot of these activities is said to be that the plaintiffs own an "extensive goodwill" in England. I certainly think that the plaintiffs have established that there is a "serious question" that they do own such a goodwill. The most prominent activity has been the trade shows here. I do not see how they can have done other than create goodwill. It was suggested that the second plaintiffs may not own any part of that goodwill (by virtue of the provisions of the licence) but I do not think that matters for present purposes: one or other of the plaintiffs or both are entitled to it. It is a goodwill which at least extends to the holding of trade shows.

The other two activities said to contribute to goodwill are much less significant for several reasons. The spillover from the United States magazine and the web site names is, on the present evidence, too shadowy. And the United Kingdom magazine is too late to be relevant to the question of whether the plaintiffs had a United Kingdom goodwill at the relevant time, namely July 1996 when DC started the activities complained of.

By way of attack on the claimed goodwill DC suggest that "Internet World" is descriptive, so descriptive that goodwill cannot exist in the name. This sits ill with its contention that in Germany it has a valid registered mark consisting of that name. Moreover, it uses the name as a trade mark, complete with the symbol ® on brochures sent to this country. True it is that in Germany the name is in a foreign language, but that contention is of little weight having regard to the fact that most (if not all) of those likely to be interested will speak English because English is the main language of the internet. Moreover a German would not have to know much English to understand the two words: "internet" is an international word and "world" is far from an obscure English word.

. . . I think here the words are to some degree descriptive though not wholly so. "Internet World" is not so descriptive that people familiar with past trade shows under that name would not expect further "Internet World" trade shows to be run by the same people who used that name in the past. On the contrary I think, prima facie, they would.

The next element of the trinity is misrepresentation. DC have organised their own trade shows, also calling them "Internet World". The shows have been in Dusseldorf (November 26-28, 1996) and Vienna (February 11-13, 1997). To promote these shows, DC, based in Germany, have prepared an English language letter and brochure and sent them out to prospective visitors and exhibitors. I have no information about other language promotional material, but I expect there is at least a German brochure. It is clear from what DC have done that they do not regard their shows as purely national affairs – they seek business internationally, including from here. DC have also established a German web site under the domain name "http://www.internetworld.de".

So far as this country is concerned, DC specifically put onto their database the names and addresses of people and companies who appeared in the plaintiffs' "Internet World" trade show catalogue in London. DC openly so admitted in a fax of August 12, 1996. Actually the fax is a little ambiguous (it speaks of the "congress visitors"). I was told (and there seems to be no dispute) that the trade show brochure contained a list of exhibitors and those visitors who had booked their tickets in advance. So DC have deliberately targeted those particularly interested in the plaintiffs' shows. Moreover DC have asked the Overseas Department of the Department of Trade and Industry to promote their "Internet World" exhibitions. They are clearly drumming up business from the United Kingdom.

I think there is certainly a serious question to be tried as to whether what they have been doing would mislead the interested public here. It is true that DC use the name "dc conferences" in small type. I cannot see how that would help those who spotted that use. The show here was organised with a local company and I rather think that quite a number of recipients of the defendants' material would expect the two shows advertised to be connected with the plaintiffs by much the same sort of arrangement. True it is that evidence of misrepresentation at this stage does not include evidence from deceived or confused persons (I disregard the thin evidence that the second plaintiff's managing director has received calls from confused customers as too vague). But I do not think that matters. After all the names are the same and I am entitled to form my own view of the matter.

What about the third element of the trinity, damage? [DC'S counsel] says none has been proved. Now in some cases one does indeed need separate proof of damage. This is particularly so, for example, if the fields of activity of the parties are wildly different (*e.g.*, . . . [a] nightclub and chips). But in other cases the court is entitled to infer damage, including particularly damage by way of dilution of the plaintiff's goodwill. Here I think the natural inference is that Mecklermedia's goodwill in England will be damaged by the use of the same name by DC. To a significant extent Mecklermedia's reputation in this country is in the hands of DC – people here will think there is a trading connection between the German and Austrian fairs and the Mecklermedia's fairs.

It is to be noted that all the activities of DC take place in Germany and Austria – none take place within the territorial jurisdiction of this court. But I cannot think that matters so far as the English law of passing off is concerned. To do acts here which lead to damage of goodwill by misleading the public here is plainly passing off. To do those same acts from abroad will not avoid liability. Whether the court can assume jurisdiction (in the sense of become seized of an action) over a defendant abroad, is another matter. That depends upon the extent to which the court has the power to make a person abroad party to an action. The Brussels Convention regulates that power for members of the Convention.

I therefore think that there is a serious question to be tried. That disposes of the strike out application and gets the plaintiffs over the first hurdle to justify service out of the jurisdiction. I now turn to the remaining points, which concern the Brussels Convention.

[The Court then upheld out-of-jurisdiction service of process under the applicable provisions of the Brussels Convention.]

In this case the deception alleged is in England. On that reasoning there are close connecting factors with England. . . .

It is submitted that it would be better if all questions were decided by a single court and that multiple litigation should be avoided. That as a generality is of course always true, but on the other hand when an enterprise wants to use a mark or word throughout the world (and that may include an internet address or domain name) it must take into account that in some places, if not others, there may be confusion. Here it is clear DC knew that Mecklermedia used the name "Internet World" and I do not think it is surprising that it is met with actions in places where confusion is considered likely.

So I decline to set aside service.

---

**Note on Brussels Convention**

UK jurisdiction over the German defendant in the *Mecklermedia* case was facilitated by the EC Convention on Jurisdiction and the Enforcement of Judgments in Civil and Commercial Matters, commonly referred to as the "Brussels Convention." (EU Official Journal C27, 26/01/1998)(available in Westlaw database "EU-ALL").

Adopted in 1968, the Brussels Convention contains provisions similar to state "long-arm" jurisdiction statutes and the "Full Faith and Credit Clause" of the United States Constitution. Thus, under Section 3 of Article 5 of the Convention, a domiciliary of one member state can be sued in the courts of another member state "in matters of tort, delict or quasidelict, in the courts for the place in which the harmful event occurred." Pursuant to Article 26, "[a] judgment given in a Contracting State shall be recognized in the other Contracting States without any special procedure being required." However, Article 27 permits a Contracting Party to refuse to enforce a judgment if, *inter alia*, the judgment is contrary to the Contracting Party's public policy, if the defendant was not properly served and thereby defaulted, or if the judgment is contrary to a previous judgment involving the same parties rendered in the Contracting Party in which enforcement is sought. These exceptions are similar to those found in United States law, as you read in the *Telnikoff* case earlier in this chapter.

The European Commission has since issued Council Regulation (EC) No. 44/2001 of 22 December 2000 (Document 301R0044) (available at http://europa.eu.int/eur-lex/en/lif/dat/2001/en_301R0044.html), which essentially restates the principles set forth above, one notable change being that a judgment must be "manifestly" contrary to public policy to be rejected on that ground. (Article 34, Sec. 1.)

Since the Brussels Convention is among members of the European Community, the United States of course is not a signatory. (That may explain why Mecklermedia – an American company – chose to file suit in the United Kingdom – rather than in the United States – against a German company on account of things that occurred in

Germany in Austria.) Many other countries of the world too are not signatories to the Brussels Convention, even though their nationals are engaged in significant international business transactions.

As a result, in 2001, a Diplomatic Conference was held at the Hague to consider a proposed "Hague Convention" which would have expanded the applicability of the principles of the Brussels Convention to signatory nations on a global basis. However, due to the opposition of a number of countries including the United States, the Hague Convention has not yet been adopted. (For a discussion of the proposed convention, see the report of the International Trademark Association at http://www.inta.org/europe/hague.shtml.)

---

## 1.4 LITERARY, DRAMATIC, MUSICAL AND ARTISTIC WORKS

The ability to control the exploitation of the work on which an entertainment product or project is based is critically important in the entertainment industries. Although there is an extensive network of copyright and copyright-related international treaties (e.g., the Berne Convention, the Universal Copyright Convention, the so-called "TRIPS" provisions of the 1994 Uruguay Round of the General Agreement on Tariffs and Trade which establishs minimum protections and procedures with respect to the trade-related aspects of intellectual property rights), copyright protection – like trademark protection – is nonetheless a matter of national statute. Nevertheless, a global overview is required.

For example, while U.S. copyright law recognizes the concept of "work for hire," under which the employer is deemed the "author" of a work, and therefore has complete rights to deal with the work as it will, other countries do not recognize this doctrine, and refuse to apply the contract law of the jurisdiction in which the "work for hire" agreement is sited, so that U.S. directors, writers, performers, and musicians may well have the ability to prevent the exploitation of their works in foreign countries if they can convince the courts of those countries that a particular use violates their "moral rights."

Of course, the outcome of any particular case is often dependent upon the forum in which it is heard. This makes the question of which court has "jurisdiction" a very important one. As you will read below, U.S. courts will accept jurisdiction over allegedly infringing activities that take place outside the United States, but only if a sufficiently significant act occurs in the U.S. as part of the process through which the infringing activity occurs.

### 1.4.1 Requirements for Obtaining International Protection

#### U.S. Copyright Act § 104

Subject matter of copyright: National origin

(a) Unpublished Works.—The works specified by sections 102 and 103 [i.e., all works protected by the Copyright Act], while unpublished, are subject to protection under this title without regard to the nationality or domicile of the author.

(b) Published Works.—The works specified by sections 102 and 103, when published, are subject to protection under this title if—

(1) on the date of first publication, one or more of the authors is a national or domiciliary of the United States, or is a national, domiciliary, or sovereign authority of a treaty party, or is a stateless person, wherever that person may be domiciled; or

(2) the work is first published in the United States or in a foreign nation that, on the date of first publication, is a treaty party; or

(3) the work is a sound recording that was first fixed in a treaty party; or

(4) the work is a pictorial, graphic, or sculptural work that is incorporated in a building or other structure, or an architectural work that is embodied in a building and the building or structure is located in the United States or a treaty party; or

(5) the work is first published by the United Nations or any of its specialized agencies, or by the Organization of American States; or

(6) the work comes within the scope of a Presidential proclamation. Whenever the President finds that a particular foreign nation extends, to works by authors who are nationals or domiciliaries of the United States or to works that are first published in the United States, copyright protection on substantially the same basis as that on which the foreign nation extends protection to works of its own nationals and domiciliaries and works first published in that nation, the President may by proclamation extend protection under this title to works of which one or more of the authors is, on the date of first publication, a national, domiciliary, or sovereign authority of that nation, or which was first published in that nation. The President may revise, suspend, or revoke any such proclamation or impose any conditions or limitations on protection under a proclamation.

For purposes of paragraph (2), a work that is published in the United States or a treaty party within 30 days after publication in a foreign nation that is not a treaty party shall be considered to be first published in the United States or such treaty party, as the case may be.

(c) Effect of Berne Convention.—No right or interest in a work eligible for protection under this title may be claimed by virtue of, or in reliance upon, the provisions of the Berne Convention, or the adherence of the United States thereto. Any rights in a work eligible for protection under this title that derive from this title, other Federal or State statutes, or the common law, shall not be expanded or reduced by virtue of, or in reliance upon, the provisions of the Berne Convention, or the adherence of the United States thereto.

(d) Effect of Phonograms Treaties.—Notwithstanding the provisions of subsection (b), no works other than sound recordings shall be eligible for protection under this title solely by virtue of the adherence of the United States to the Geneva Phonograms Convention or the WIPO Performances and Phonograms Treaty.

---

**Bong v. Alfred S. Campbell Art Company**
**214 U.S. 236 (1909)**

Mr. Justice McKenna delivered the opinion of the court.

This is an action under the copyright statutes to recover penalties and forfeitures for the infringement of a copyright of a painting.

The complaint shows the following facts: Plaintiff . . . was a citizen and subject of the German Empire and resident of the city of Berlin, that nation being one which permits to citizens of the United States the benefit of copyright on substantially the same basis as its own citizens. It is a party to an international agreement which provides for reciprocity in the granting of copyright, by the terms of which agreement the United States may at its pleasure become a party, the existence of which condition has been determined by the President of the United States by proclamation duly made.

April 15, 1892, 27 Stat. 1021. The defendant is a New Jersey corporation doing business in New York under the laws of the latter State.

In 1899 one Daniel Hernandez painted and designed a painting called "Dolce far niente," he then being a citizen and subject of Spain, which nation permits the benefit of copyright to citizens of the United States on substantially the same basis as its own citizens, as has been determined by the proclamation of the President of the United States. July 10, 1895, 29 Stat. 871. Prior to November 8, 1902, plaintiff became the sole proprietor of said painting by due assignment pursuant to law. About said date plaintiff applied for a copyright, in conformity with the laws of the United States respecting copyrights, before the publication of the painting or any copy thereof. Plaintiff inscribed, and has kept inscribed, upon a visible portion of the painting the words "Copyright by Rich Bong," and also upon every copy thereof. By reason of the premises, it is alleged, plaintiff became and was entitled for the term of twenty-eight years to the sole liberty of printing, reprinting, publishing and vending the painting. A violation of the copyright by defendant is alleged by printing, exposing for sale and selling copies of the painting under the name of "Sunbeam," by Hernandez, and that defendant has in its possession over 1,000 copies. By reason of the premises, it is alleged [that under §4965 of the then-current copyright law] as amended by the act of March 2, 1891, defendant has [infringed plaintiff's copyright in the painting by Hernandez]. . . .

Defendant answered, admitting that it was a corporation as alleged, and was doing business in New York. It denied, either absolutely or upon information and belief, all other allegations.

The court directed a verdict for the defendant, counsel for the plaintiff having stated in his opening, as it is admitted, that he would offer no evidence to establish the citizenship of Hernandez, and would not controvert the statement made by the defense that he was a citizen of Peru (it was alleged in the complaint that he was a citizen of Spain), as to which country the President had issued no copyright proclamation. It is also admitted that plaintiff never owned the "physical painting." There was introduced in evidence a conveyance of the right to enter the painting for copyright protection in America and the exclusive right of reproduction. . . .

The ruling of the District Court, and that of the Court of Appeals sustaining it, were based on the ground that Hernandez, being a citizen of Peru and not having the right of copyright in the United States, could convey no right to plaintiff. Plaintiff attacks this ruling and contends that the act of March 3, 1891, "confers copyright where the person applying for the same as proprietor or assign of the author or proprietor is a subject of a country with which we have copyright relations, whether the author be a subject of one of those countries or not."

Whatever strength there is in the contention must turn upon the words of the statute conferring the copyright. Section 4952 of the [then-current copyright act], as amended by the act of March 3, 1891, reads as follows: "The author, inventor, designer or proprietor of any book, map, chart, . . . painting . . . and the executors, administrators and assigns of any such person shall, upon complying with the provisions of this chapter, have the sole liberty of printing, reprinting, publishing, completing, copying, executing, finishing and vending the same," etc.

Other sections prescribe the proceedings to be taken to secure copyright, and §13 provides as follows: "That this act shall only apply to a citizen or subject of a foreign state or nation when such foreign state or nation permits to citizens of the United States of America the benefit of copyright on substantially the same basis as its own citizens, or when such foreign state or nation is a party to an international agreement which provides for reciprocity in the granting of copyright, by the terms of which agreement the United States of America may at its pleasure become a party to such agreement. The existence of either of the conditions aforesaid shall be determined by the President of the United States by proclamation made, from time to time, as the purposes of this act may require."

Plaintiff urges that he is "the 'assign' of the author and proprietor of the painting . . . and being himself a 'citizen or subject of a foreign nation' with which we have copyright relations," the condition of the statute is satisfied, and his copyright is valid, though Hernandez was not such citizen or subject. In other words, though the author of a painting has not the right to copyright, his assignee has if he is a citizen or subject of a foreign state with which we have copyright relations, these being, it is contended, the conditions expressed in §13. Counsel's argument in support of this contention is able, but we are saved from a detailed consideration of it by the decision of this court in American Tobacco Company v. Werckmeister. In that case we said that "the purpose of the copyright law is not so much the protection and control of the visible thing, as to secure a monopoly, having a limited time, of the right to publish the production, which is the result of the inventor's thought." In considering who was entitled to such right under the statute we defined the word "assigns," as used in the statute. We said: "It seems clear that the word 'assigns' in this section is not used as descriptive of the character of the estate which the 'author, inventor, designer or proprietor' may acquire under the statutes, for the 'assigns' of any such person, as well as the persons themselves, may, 'upon complying with the provisions of this chapter, have the sole liberty of printing, publishing and vending the same.' This would seem to demonstrate the intention of Congress to vest in 'assigns,' before copyright, the same privilege of subsequently acquiring complete statutory copyright as the original author, inventor, dealer or proprietor," and there was an explicit definition of the right transferred as follows: "While it is true that the property in copyright in this country is the creature of the statute, the nature and character of the property grows out of the recognition of the separate ownership of the right of copying from that which inheres in the mere physical control of the thing itself, and the statute must be read in the light of the intention of Congress to protect these intangible rights as a reward of the inventive genius that has produced the work." In other words, an assignee within the meaning of the statute is one who receives a transfer, not necessarily of the painting but of the right to multiply copies of it. And such right does not depend alone upon the statute, as contended by plaintiff, but is a right derived from the painter and secured by the statute to the assignee of the painter's right. Of this the opinion leaves no doubt, for it is further said: "We think every consideration of the nature of the property and the things to be accomplished support the conclusion that this statute means to give to the assignees of the original owner of the *right to copyright* an article [italics ours], the right to take out the copyright secured by the statute independently of the ownership of the article itself." The same idea was repeated when the court came to consider whether the exhibition of the painting, which was the subject matter of the case, in the Royal Gallery, constituted a general publication which deprived the painter, as the owner of the copyright, of the benefit of the statutory provision. It was said: "Considering this feature of the case, it is well to remember that the property of the author or painter in his intellectual creation is absolute until he voluntarily parts with the same." And the painter had the right of copyright, he being a subject of Great Britain, that country having copyright relations with the United States. His assignee, Werckmeister, was also a citizen of a country having copyright relations with us. But it was the right of the painter which was made prominent in the case and determined its decision.

It was not an abstract right the court passed on, one that arose simply from ownership of the painting. It was the right given by the statute, and which, when transferred, constituted the person to whom it was transferred an assignee under the statute and of the rights which the statute conferred on the assignor. "It is the physical thing created, or the right of printing, publishing, copying, etc., which is within the statutory protection." It is this right of multiplication of copies that is asserted in the case at bar, and it is not necessary to consider what right plaintiff might have had under the common law "before he sought his Federal copyright and published the painting."

It is next contended that Hernandez, as a subject of Peru, was entitled to a statutory copyright in his own right, because, as it is further contended, Peru belongs to the Montevideo International Union. This contention is based on the words of §13 which gives the right of copyright to a citizen or subject of a foreign state or nation when such state or nation "is a party to an international agreement which provides for reciprocity in the granting of copyright, by the terms of which agreement the United States of America may, at its pleasure, become a party to such agreement." If this were all there were in the statute, the contention of the plaintiff might have some foundation. The statute, however, provides that the existence of such condition "shall be determined by the President of the United States by proclamation, made from time to time, as the purposes" of the "act may require." It is insisted, however, that this provision is directory and a right is conferred independent of the action of the President, his proclamation being only a convenient mode of proving the fact. We cannot concur in this view. . . .

It is admitted that the decision of the State Department is adverse to the contention, and, it is asserted by defendant and not denied by plaintiff, that the Librarian of Congress has always construed the statutes as denying to citizens of Peru copyright protection. We think, besides, the statute is clear and makes the President's proclamation a condition of the right. And there was reason for it. The statute contemplated a reciprocity of rights, and what officer is better able to determine the conditions upon which they might depend than the President?

On the record, we think there was no error in directing a verdict on the opening statement of counsel. . . .

Judgment affirmed.

---

The next two cases illustrate the "requirements for protection" principle from a European perspective. In order to understand those cases, you first must know something about the Berne Convention, the Rome Convention, European Community law, and German copyright law. The following, very short discussion of those matters is excerpted from a decision of the Court of Justice of the European Communities in the case of *Collins v. Imtrat Handelsgesellschaft MbH*, [1993] 3 CMLR 773.

*International conventions . . .*

The Berne Convention [for the protection of literary and artistic works] constitutes a Union among the countries to which it applies for the protection of the rights of authors in their literary and artistic works (Article 1). The Convention, to which the 12 member-States and the United States have adhered, protects literary and artistic works in all the countries of the Union (Article 2(6)) and authors who are nationals of one of the countries of the Union (Article 3(1)(a)).

Pursuant to Article 5(1) of the Convention:

> Authors shall enjoy, in respect of works for which they are protected under this Convention, in countries of the Union other than the country of origin, the rights which their respective laws do now or may hereafter grant to their nationals, as well as the rights specially granted by this Convention.

Article 11(1) of the Convention provides as follows:

> Authors of dramatic, dramatico-musical and musical works shall enjoy the exclusive right of authorising: (i) the public performance of their works, including such public performance by any means or process; (ii) any communication to the public of the performance of their works.

Th[e Rome] Convention [for the protection of performers, producers of phonograms and broadcasting organisations] has the object, inter alia, of protecting the rights (so-called neighbouring rights) of performers, i.e. actors, singers, musicians, dancers and other persons who perform, sing, recite, declaim, play or execute in any other way literary or artistic works. Eight member-States, including Germany and the United Kingdom, have acceded to this Convention, but the United States has not.

Article 4 of the Convention provides for the application of the national treatment rule to artists who are nationals of the Contracting States, provided that the performance takes place in one of those States (a) or that the phonogram has a connection with one of them (b).

Article 7(1) of the Convention provides as follows:

> The protection provided for performers by this Convention shall include the possibility of preventing: . . .
>
> (b) the fixation, without their consent, of their unfixed performance;
>
> (c) the reproduction, without their consent, of a fixation of the unfixed performance:
>
> (i) if the original fixation itself was made without their consent.

*Community law*

In addition to Article 7 EEC, with which the question referred to the Court is concerned, the existence of the following measures, which are subsequent to the main actions, should be noted:

– The Council Resolution of 14 May 1992 on increased protection for copyright and neighbouring rights ([1992] OJ C 138/1), noting that the member-States undertake 'to become parties, if they have not already done so, to the Paris Act of the Berne Convention and the Rome Convention before 1 January 1995 and to ensure compliance with them in their internal legal systems.'

– Council Council Directive 92/100 of 19 January 1992 on rental right and lending right and on certain rights related to copyright in the field of intellectual property, ([1992] OJ L346/61), which gives artists the exclusive right to authorise or prohibit recordings of their performances (Article 6(1)), the reproduction of recordings of their performances (Article 7(1), and an exclusive right to distribute them (Article 9).

*National law*

In Germany copyright and related rights are governed by the Copyright Act (Urheberrechtsgesetz, 'UrhG.' [1965] IBGBI 1273))

(a) *Copyright proper*

Section 120(1) UrhG provides that 'German nationals shall enjoy the protection attaching to copyright for all their works, irrespective of whether they have been published or not and wherever publication may have taken place.' In defining the rights of foreign authors, section121 UrhG takes account of, inter alia, the place of publication of the work and the fact that the author is either a national of a State which has adhered to the Berne Convention or another international treaty, or a national of a State offering equivalent protection to German nationals.

(b) *Related rights of performing artists*

Pursuant to section 75 UrhG, 'a performance by a performing artist may be recorded on a sound or visual support only with his consent. The visual or sound supports may be reproduced only with his consent.' Section 96(1) UrhG provides in turn that 'copies obtained by means of a process of reproduction in a manner contrary to the right shall not be broadcast or used in transmissions to the public.'

Section 125 UrhG clarifies the ambit of the artist's protection by making a distinction according to nationality. Artists of German nationality have the full protection granted by sections 73 to 84 UrhG 'for all their performances irrespective of the place of performance.'

The protection given to foreign artists is defined by section 125(2) to (6) UrhG as follows:

> (2) Foreign nationals shall enjoy such protection for all their performances if the place of performance is within the ambit of this Act, without prejudice to subsections (3) and (4).
>
> (3) If performances by foreign nationals are lawfully recorded on visual or sound supports and if those recordings have been published, the foreign nationals shall enjoy, in relation to such visual or sound supports, the protection granted by sections 75, sentence 2, 76(2) and 77 where publication of the visual or sound supports takes place within the ambit of this Act, unless the said supports are published outside that territory more than 30 years before publication within the ambit of this Act.
>
> (4) In the case of the lawful radio or television broadcasting of performances of foreign nationals, they shall enjoy protection against the recording of the broadcast on visual or sound supports (section 75, sentence 1) and the repetition of sound or television broadcasts (section 76(1)), as well as the protection given by section 77, if the radio or television transmission was broadcast within the ambit of this Act.
>
> (5) In addition, foreign nationals shall enjoy the protection arising from treaties ...
>
> (6) Foreign nationals shall enjoy the protection provided for by sections 74, 75, sentence 1, and 83 for all their performances even where the conditions referred to by subsections 2 to 5 are not fulfilled.

---

**Re Copyright in an Unauthorized U.S. Recording**
**[1993] ECC 428, Regional Court of Appeal, Cologne (1991)**

Spatgens, Schneider and Fox, Judges

The plaintiff cannot require the defendant to desist from marketing the records [in issue] containing recordings of one of his concerts, given in New Orleans, USA, in 1981.

The plaintiff, who is a U.S. citizen and is claiming performing rights protection as a performing artist, has no rights under German copyright law which go beyond the minimum protection for foreign nationals under section 125(6)of the Copyright Act.

Section 125(2) of the Copyright Act cannot provide a basis for the plaintiff's injunction application, since the performance for which protection is sought took place in the USA, in New Orleans.

Section 125(5) of the Copyright Act, under which foreign nationals are to be given protection in accordance with any treaties in force, also does not apply in the present case. It has already been pointed out correctly by the Landgericht . . . that the Rome Convention of 26 October 1961 does not apply in the plaintiff's favour, and he no longer seeks to challenge this matter. As the plaintiff also no longer disputes, the agreement between Germany and the USA on the mutual protection of copyright of 15 January 1892 likewise provides no support for the injunction application. That is so, apart from anything else, because the agreement does not apply to recordings which (as in the present case) were made after the Copyright Act came into force (on 1 January 1956).

Accordingly, it is only section 125(6) of the Copyright Act which might provide a basis for the plaintiff's claims under copyright law. But this provision too, with the rights for foreign artists which it specifies, does not lead to the prohibition of the marketing of the compact disc in issue.

. . . German copyright law already grants foreign artists a considerable degree of protection for their artists in Germany by acceding to international conventions or by concluding reciprocal agreements (which at the same time grant German artists an increased level of protection abroad). If other countries (like the USA in the present case) do not make use of that opportunity, the gap cannot be filled by an extension of the sphere of application of section 125(6). Otherwise there would be no point in the incentive, deliberately created by the scheme of sections 121 and 125 in the interests of protecting German claimants abroad, for other states to act in accordance with the opportunity provided for in section 125(5) of the Act.

But the plaintiff's injunction application likewise cannot be supported on the basis of section 125(6), in conjunction with section 83, of the Copyright Act.

It is questionable in the first place whether sections 125(6) and 83 of the Act do cover the marketing of the compact disc [here in issue] at all. Section 83 gives the artist the right to prevent a distortion or other mistreatment of his performance which is calculated to endanger his reputation or his prestige as a performing artist. . . . But . . . the plaintiff has not made a sufficiently convincing case that there has been a distortion or mistreatment within the meaning of section 83(1).

It is not sufficient for these purposes that the plaintiff claims that he regards any recording of a live concert not authorised by him as being such a mistreatment because he does not regard such live recordings as guaranteeing the best possible version of his performance. As already explained, the plaintiff is not protected against the distribution of duplicate copies of secret recordings solely on the basis of copyright provisions. Therefore he cannot obtain that protection either on the round that he regards such a form of exploitation as a mistreatment for the purposes of section 83(1). Furthermore, in the context of section 83(1) it is the performing artist's interest in the integrity of his interpretation of a work that is protected, which in this case means the plaintiff's interest in a communication of his performance at the concert of 1981 that is not false, but not his interest in an imaginary best possible interpretation of the works in issue here. If any unauthorised recording of the artist's performance were to constitute a mistreatment under section 83(1), as the plaintiff is ultimately arguing, there would have been no need for the additional provision of section 75(1).

But even so, no circumstances are evident which convincingly demonstrate a mistreatment or distortion within the meaning of section 83. This Court, like the Landgericht, is willing to assume on the basis of the aural test which it carried out that the compact disc in issue here is a record which is of poor quality even by the standards of live recordings. . . . But not every technical defect establishes the existence of a distortion or mistreatment under section 83(1). What is required is that the plaintiff's performance has been factually changed in a manner which affects his interests or that there is a risk that the listener will ascribe the defects not to an inadequate recording technique but to a deficient artistic performance on the plaintiff's part. That cannot be assumed in the present case. . . .

But it is also impossible to assume that there was a distortion or other mistreatment within the meaning of section 83(1) of the Copyright Act on the ground that there is at least a risk that persons hearing the compact disc will ascribe the alleged defects not to an inadequate recording technique but to a deficient artistic performance by the plaintiff. Although the defects in the compact disc established by the court at the test hearing in the appeal proceedings made it clear that there were technical defects in the recording, it has not been shown with sufficient certainty that listeners will attribute the defects to the plaintiff as being due to a faulty artistic performance. The legend on the sleeve of the compact disc informs the listener not only that the disc contains a recording of a live concert in 1981 which was not authorised by the plaintiff, but also that the disc is a live recording made 'from the audience' which conveys 'a realistic impression of the concert atmosphere without its being possible to avoid some impairment of quality as compared with a studio recording.' But the defects in the compact disc established by the court at the test hearing appear to be such as one would expect from poor recording technique. There is therefore nothing to indicate sufficiently clearly that if the listener does not enjoy the recording he will, despite the 'warning' on the sleeve of the disc, attribute it not to the poor quality of the recording but to the bad performance of the plaintiff and his group, and as a result may no longer buy recordings by the plaintiff in the future. . . .

Accordingly, if the injunction application is not justified on any legal basis, the further application for the confiscation of the discs must also fail for that reason.

Application dismissed with costs.

---

**Collins v. Imtrat Handelsgesellschaft MbH**
**[1993] 3 CMLR 773, Court of Justice of the European Communities**

Presiding, Due C.J.; Mancini, Moitinho de Almeida and Edward PPC.; Joliet, Schockweiler, Grevisse, Zuleeg and Murray JJ.; Mr. Francis Jacobs, Advocate General. . . .

*Facts of the Cases*

*Case C-92/92 [The Phil Collins case]*

In 1983 Phil Collins, a singer and composer of British nationality, gave a concert in the United States which was recorded without his consent. The recording was distributed in Germany by Imtrat Handelsgesellschaft mbH ('Imtrat') in the form of a compact disc entitled 'Phil Collins–Live USA.' The singer brought a summary action before the Regional Court, Munich I, for an injunction restraining Imtrat from marketing the disc and for the seizure of copies which had not been distributed. . . .

*Case C-326/92 [The Cliff Richard case]*

EMI Electrola GmbH ('EMI Electrola') owns the exclusive right to exploit in Germany recordings made by the British singer Cliff Richard in Great Britain in 1958 and 1959.

EMI Electrola contends that Patricia Im- und Export Verwaltungsgesellshcaft ('Patricia') marketed, in breach of its exclusive rights, phonograms containing recordings by Cliff Richard. It is said that the contested phonograms were originally produced in Germany for a Danish company. They are said to have been exported to Denmark and then reimported to Germany. . . .

*Opinion*

Two German courts have requested preliminary rulings on the questions whether copyright and related rights fall within the ambit of the EEC Treaty and whether a member-State which allows its own nationals to oppose the unauthorised reproduction of their musical performances must grant identical protection to nationals of other member-States, in accordance with the prohibition of discrimination on grounds of nationality laid down in Article 7 EEC.

*Case C-92/92 [The Phil Collins case]*

The plaintiff in Case C-92/92 is Phil Collins, a singer and composer of British nationality. The defendant – Imtrat Handelsgesellschaft mbH ('Imtrat') – is a producer of phonograms. In 1983 Mr. Collins gave a concert in California which was recorded without his consent. Reproductions of the recording were sold in Germany by Imtrat on compact disc under the title 'Live and Alive.' Mr. Collins applied to the Landgericht Munchen I for an injunction restraining Imtrat from marketing such recordings in Germany and requiring it to deliver copies in its possession to a court bailiff.

It appears that if Mr. Collins were a German national his application would undoubtedly have succeeded. Section 75 of the Gesetz uber Urheberrecht und verwandte Schutzrechte (Law on copyright and related rights, hereafter 'Urheberrechtsgesetz') provides that a performing artist's performance may not be recorded without his consent and recordings may not be reproduced without his consent. Section 125(1) of the Urheberrechtsgesetz provides that German nationals enjoy the protection ofsection 75, amongst other provisions, for all their performances regardless of the place of performance. However, foreign nationals have less extensive rights under the Urheberrechtsgesetz. Under section 125(2) they enjoy protection in respect of performances which take place in Germany, and under section 125(5) they enjoy protection in accordance with international treaties. The Landgericht Munchen I refers to the Rome Convention of 26 October 1961 for the Protection of Performers, Producers of Phonograms and Broadcasting Organisations, but deduces from its terms that Germany is required to grant foreign performing artists the same treatment as its own nationals only in respect of performances that take place within the territory of a Contracting State; since the United States has not acceded to the Rome Convention, section 125(5) of the Urheberrechtsgesetz is of no avail to Mr. Collins in the circumstances of the present case. However, Mr. Collins argued that he was entitled to the same treatment as a German national by virtue of Article 7 EEC. The Landgericht Munchen I therefore decided to refer the following questions to the Court:

[The Advocate General repeated the questions, and continued:]

*Case C-326/92 [The Cliff Richard case]*

The plaintiff and respondent in Case C-326/92 – EMI Electrola GmbH ('EMI Electrola') – produces and distributes phonograms. It owns the exclusive right to exploit in Germany recordings of certain works performed by Cliff Richard, a singer of British nationality. The defendants and appellants are Patricia Im- und

Export Verwaltungsgesellschaft mbH ('Patricia'), a company which distributes phonograms, and Mr. L. E. Kraul, its managing director. EMI Electrola applied for an injunction restraining Patricia and Mr. Kraul (together with other persons) from infringing its exclusive rights in recordings of certain performances by Cliff Richard. The recordings were first published in the United Kingdom in 1958 and 1959, apparently by a British phonogram producer to which Cliff Richard had assigned his performer's rights in the recordings. That company subsequently assigned the rights to EMI Electrola.

The Landgericht granted EMI Electrola's application and that decision was confirmed on appeal. Patricia and Mr. Kraul appealed on a point of law to the Bundesgerichtshof, which considers that, under German law, EMI Electrola would be entitled to an injunction if Cliff Richard were of German nationality but is not so entitled because he is British. It is not entirely clear from the order for reference how or why the Bundesgerichtshof arrived at the view that German law provides for such a difference of treatment. The reason appears to be that the performances in question took place before 21 October 1966, on which date the Rome Convention came into force in Germany, and that Germany is only required to grant 'national treatment' to foreign performers, under the Rome Convention, in respect of performances that take place after that date

It is in any event common ground that a difference in treatment, depending on the nationality of the performer, exists in German law. The Bundesgerichtshof therefore referred the following questions to the Court:

[The Advocate General repeated the questions, and continued:]

*The issues raised by the two cases*

Both cases raise essentially the same issues: (a) whether it is compatible with Community law, in particular Article 7 EEC, for a member-State to grant more extensive protection in respect of performances by its own nationals than in respect of performances by nationals of other member-States and (b) if such a difference in treatment is not compatible with Community law, whether the relevant provisions of Community law produce direct effect, in the sense that a performer who has the nationality of another member-State is entitled to claim, in proceedings against a person who markets unauthorised recordings of his performances, the same rights as a national of the member-State in question.

I note in passing that, although both the national courts refer to copyright, the cases are in fact concerned not with copyright in the strict sense but with certain related rights known as performers' rights.

The prohibition of discrimination on grounds of nationality is the single most important principle of Community law. It is the leitmotiv of the EEC Treaty. It is laid down in general terms in Article 7 of the Treaty, the first paragraph of which provides:

> Within the scope of application of this Treaty, and without prejudice to any special provisions contained therein, any discrimination on grounds of nationality shall be prohibited.

... There cannot be any doubt that Article 7, either alone or in conjunction with other provisions of the Treaty, has the effect that nationals of a member-State are entitled to pursue any legitimate form of economic activity in another member-State on the same terms as the latter State's own nationals. ...

Certainly there can be no doubt about the economic importance of the performing artist's exclusive right to authorise the reproduction and distribution of recordings embodying his performance. The exercise of that right is essential to the commercial exploitation of a performance. The sale of unauthorised recordings damages the performing artist in two ways: first, because he earns no royalties on such recordings, the sale of which must inevitably reduce the demand for his authorised recordings, since the spending power of even the most avid record collector is finite; secondly, because he loses the power to control the quality of the recordings, which may, if technically inferior, adversely affect his reputation. The latter point was argued forcefully, but to no avail, by the 'world-famous Austrian conductor' who was unable to prevent the sale of unauthorised recordings in the Zauberflote case referred to above.

Performers' rights also play a role in the field of consumer protection: the consumer doubtless assumes that recordings made by well-known, living performers are not released without the performer's authorisation and that such persons would not jeopardise their reputation by authorising the distribution of low-quality recordings; that limited guarantee of quality is lost entirely if recordings may be distributed without the performer's consent. It may thus be seen that performers' rights operate in much the same way as trade marks, the economic significance of which was recognised by the Court in the Hag II case.

The defendants in both the present cases advance a number of arguments purporting to show that the contested German legislation is not contrary to the prohibition of discrimination on grounds of nationality. I shall briefly summarise the main arguments and state why, in my view, none of them is convincing.

Both defendants contend that the discrimination lies outside the scope of application of the Treaty. Imtrat reaches that conclusion on the grounds that the performance in question took place outside the territory of a member-State and that the existence of intellectual property rights is a matter for national law by virtue of Article 222 EEC. That cannot be correct. The place where the original performance took place is irrelevant; what matters is that Phil Collins and his licensees are denied protection, in an overtly discriminatory manner, when they attempt to exploit–or prevent others from exploiting–the performance in a member-State. . . .

It is contended on behalf of Patricia and Mr. Kraul that the absence of Community legislation harmonising the laws of member-States on copyright and related rights removes such matters from the scope of the Treaty entirely. That argument is of course doomed to failure. The application of the principle of non-discrimination is not dependent on the harmonisation of national law; on the contrary, it is precisely in areas where harmonisation has not been achieved that the principle of national treatment assumes special importance. . . .

The only argument advanced by either of the defendants that has some plausibility is the one based on the Rome Convention, on which great reliance is placed by Imtrat. According to that argument, all questions concerning the level of protection to be granted to foreign performers are to be resolved in the context of the Rome Convention, which has established a delicate balance based on considerations of reciprocity. The connecting factor, under the Rome Convention, is not nationality–which would be unworkable because many performances are given by groups of performers who may have different nationalities–but place of performance. Imtrat points out further that both Germany and the United Kingdom were bound by the Rome Convention before they became mutually bound by the EEC Treaty (presumably on 1 January 1973, when the United Kingdom acceded to the Communities) and argues that the Rome Convention should therefore take precedence over the EEC Treaty by virtue of Article 234 of the latter. Imtrat suggests that dire consequences would ensue if Article 7 of the Treaty were applied in the field of copyright and related rights: authors from other member-States would, for example, be able to claim in Germany the long term of protection (70 years after the author's death) provided for in German law, whereas under Article

7(8) of the Berne Convention Germany is not required to grant them a longer term of protection than the term fixed in the country of origin of the work.

In response to those arguments the following points may be made. First, even if the Rome Convention had been concluded before the EEC Treaty, Article 234 of the latter would not give precedence to the Convention as regards relations between member-States. Article 234 is concerned solely with relations between member-States and non-member-States.

Secondly, there is in any event no conflict between Community law and the Rome Convention. That Convention merely lays down a minimum standard of protection and does not prevent the Contracting States from granting more extensive protection to their own nationals or to nationals of other States. . . .

The Rome Convention does not prevent Germany from granting performers more extensive protection than the minimum provided for in the Convention. However, Article 7 of the Treaty requires that, if more extensive protection is granted to German performers, the same level of protection should be available to nationals of other member-States. . . .

*The direct effect of Article 7(1)*

I turn now to the issue of direct effect. In my view, it is clear from the considerations set out above that the Treaty provisions which prohibit discrimination must be capable of being invoked by performers in the circumstances of the present cases.

. . . [N]ational courts are under a duty to disapply national provisions that are contrary to Article 7. It is equally clear that that duty arises not only in proceedings against the State but also in litigation between individuals.

*A factual difference between Case C-92/92 and Case C-326/92*

A final issue that remains to be explored is whether any significance attaches to an obvious factual difference between Case C-92/92 and Case C-326/92: in the former case the performer, Phil Collins, has remained the proprietor of the performer's rights and has granted an exclusive licence to a producer of phonograms to exploit those rights in Germany; in the latter case the performer, Cliff Richard, has assigned his rights to a British company, which has reassigned them to a German company. I am satisfied that that difference is not relevant to the issue of discrimination. Although in Case C-326/92 the direct victim of the discriminatory German legislation is a German company, the indirect victim will, on the assumption that royalties are paid to the performer by EMI Electrola, be Cliff Richard himself. Even in the case of an outright assignment without any provision for the payment of royalties, it would be wrong in principle to discriminate on the basis of the nationality of the performer and original right-holder. If such discrimination were permitted, it would mean that the exclusive right granted to a German performer would be an assignable asset, potentially of considerable value, while a British performer's exclusive right would have virtually no assignable value, since it would be extinguished on assignment. Thus the indirect victim of the discrimination would always be the performer himself. It would in any case be illogical, in the circumstances of the present cases, to distinguish between a performer's right which has been the subject of an exclusive licence and a performer's right which has been the subject of an assignment.

*Conclusion*

I am therefore of the opinion that the questions referred to the Court by the Landgericht Munchen I in Case C-92/92 and the Bundesgerichtshof in Case C-326/92 should be answered as follows:

By virtue of Article 7(1) of the Treaty, the courts of a member-State must allow performing artists who are nationals of other member-States to oppose the unauthorised reproduction of their performances on the same terms as the nationals of the first member-State. . . .

*Order*

On those grounds, the Court, in answer to the questions referred to it by the Regional Court, Munich I, by order of 4 March 1992, and by the Federal Supreme Court by order of 30 April 1992,

Hereby rules:

1. Copyright and related rights are within the scope of application of the Treaty within the meaning of Article 7(1); the general principle of non-discrimination laid down by that Article is consequently applicable to those rights.

2. Article 7(1) EEC must be interpreted as meaning that it prevents the law of a member-State from refusing authors and performing artists of other member-States and their successors in title the right, which is granted by the same law to nationals, to prohibit the marketing in national territory of a phonogram made without their consent, if the performance in question was given outside national territory.

3. Article 7(1) EEC must be interpreted as meaning that the principle of non-discrimination which it lays down can be relied upon directly before the national court by an author or artist of a member-State or his successor in title in order to seek the protection given to national authors and artists.

---

### 1.4.2 Obligations of Those Who Seek International Protection

International treaties give literary, dramatic, musical and artistic works from one country the right to protection in other countries (as you read in the preceding section). Those same treaties also impose obligations on adhering countries. Indeed, one country's "right" to have its works protected in other countries derives from the "obligation" of other countries to provide that protection. Over the course of the last decade or so, the United States and other countries have adhered to new treaties – or have newly adhered to old treaties – and therefore have been confronted by this obligation.

As you will read in the materials that follow, in some cases, countries have readily complied with their obligations, even when those obligations have required radical changes in their existing law. In other cases, they have complied with their obligations after being pressured to so. And in at least one case, they have resisted compliance, despite being pressured to do so.

---

### Note on U.S. Restoration of Foreign Copyrights

In 1993, the United States Congress did something simple, though surprising. It created a new section of the Copyright Act – section 104A – that restored the U.S. copyrights of certain foreign works, if those works went into the public domain in the U.S. for certain reasons. Once restored, those copyrights give their owners virtually all of the same rights their owners would have enjoyed, had those works not gone into the public domain at all. This simple statement of what Congress did masks many complexities and ambiguities that are of practical importance in applying the new section. But even this simple statement makes it apparent just how significant and dramatic this new section is, within the larger fabric of American copyright law.

*Why U.S. restored copyrights*

In two words, Congress restored copyrights because of "international trade." That is, in connection with international trade negotiations, other countries insisted that the U.S. copyrights to certain of their works be restored; and in order for the U.S. to get concessions that were desired from those countries, the U.S. agreed to their copyright restoration demands.

*NAFTA restoration*

Congress did this the first time in 1993 as part of the North American Free Trade Agreement (NAFTA) with Mexico and Canada. A small part of the NAFTA Implementation Act added a then-new section 104A to the Copyright Act, and that section provided for the restoration of the copyrights to certain Mexican and Canadian movies.

While conceptually significant, this first version of section 104A was of relatively little practical significance to the North American entertainment industry, because it only restored the copyrights to Mexican and Canadian movies (not other types of works), if those movies had gone into the public domain in the U.S. because they were published without notice between 1978 and March 1, 1989, and only if the owners of the copyrights to those movies filed written statements with the Copyright Office during a specified one-year period. The NAFTA version of section 104A resulted in the restoration of the copyrights to only 345 movies, all or virtually all of which were from Mexico. (A list of titles of those movies was published by the Copyright Office in *Copyright Restoration of Certain Motion Pictures*, 60 Federal Register 8252 (1995).)

Though NAFTA-restoration was of little practical consequence, it showed Congress what it could do and gave it taste for doing it.

*GATT restoration*

The NAFTA version of section 104A was replaced in just a year with what can be called the "GATT" version of section 104A, or more accurately the "Uruguay Round Agreements Act" version. The Uruguay Round negotiations resulted in an annex to GATT known as "TRIPs" which is short for "Agreement on Trade-Related Aspects of Intellectual Property Rights." TRIPs was added to GATT largely at the behest of the United States, Europe and Japan; and it made adequate and effective protection for intellectual property, including copyrights, an obligation of membership in the new World Trade Organization.

Congress rewrote section 104A of the Copyright Act in 1994, by significantly broadening its copyright-restoring effects, in order to satisfy obligations imposed on the U.S. by TRIPs. This is how it worked. TRIPs requires all World Trade Organization members (of which the U.S. is one) to comply with most articles of the Berne Convention, including Article 18 which requires all Berne Union members to provide copyright protection for works from all other Berne countries. This Article 18 obligation is imposed on new Berne members as soon as they adhere to Berne, and thus it requires new members to provide retroactive protection to foreign works (so long as they have not yet fallen into the public domain in their country of origin when the new member joined). Old members are required to provide retroactive protection for works from newly-adhering countries too, so this retroactive-protection obligation is reciprocal.

The United States has been a Berne member since March 1989, so the U.S. was obligated to comply with Berne's retroactive-protection requirement for almost six years before Congress enacted a version of section 104A that actually provides such protection. Congress was not simply asleep at the switch for those six years. At the time the U.S. joined Berne in 1989, Congress was under the impression that then-existing law satisfied Berne obligations, even though the Berne Implementation Act specifically said that retroactive protection would not be provided to foreign works.

The reason that Congress thought – in 1989 – that retroactive protection was not necessary is this. Berne Article 18 contains a paragraph – Article 18(2) – that says that if a foreign work is in the public domain in another country because its copyright in that country *expired*, it is not necessary for that country to grant retroactive protection to that work. As you read in the preceding section of this book, American copyright law provides – and has long provided – copyright protection for all unpublished foreign works. [Copyright Act §104(a)] Since all published works start out as unpublished works, this means that the U.S. provided copyright protection to all foreign works for at least the period between the time they were created and the time they were published. Thus, when the U.S. joined Berne in 1989, it took the position that any foreign works that were in the public domain in the U.S. were works whose copyrights had simply "expired" when they were published; and therefore, the U.S. did not have to grant retroactive protection to such works, because of Article 18(2).

If this interpretation of Berne Article 18 seems a stretch, or even tortured, others thought so too – especially because the U.S. also took the position that Article 18 required other Berne countries to give retroactive protection to U.S. works even though the U.S. was not required to give retroactive protection to theirs! Russia and Thailand reportedly rejected the U.S. position out of hand, and it seems safe to suppose that other countries would have as well. This then is the reason that after six years of Berne membership, the U.S. finally amended the Copyright Act to provide retroactive protection for certain works.

*Why foreign works only*

Congress decided to make retroactive protection available only for foreign works and not for American works, because Berne and therefore TRIPs only require countries to provide retroactive protection for foreign works (and NAFTA only required restoration of the copyrights to Mexican and Canadian movies).

This of course means that Congress has treated foreigners more favorably than Americans. This is likely to strike most American copyright owners – especially those whose works are in the public domain – as a counterintuitive thing for the United States Congress to do. But if, someday, Congress decides to restore copyright to public domain works of American origin, it will have done so for political reasons, not because Berne or TRIPs require it.

*Eligible works*

Thusfar, works whose copyrights were restored have been referred to as "foreign" works, but only for convenience. In fact, not all foreign works had their copyrights restored. The test for determining which were is a multi-step test involving inquiry into at least three things: the identity of the work's "source country"; whether the work was still protected by copyright in its source country; and the reason the work went into the public domain in the United States in the first place.

*Eligible source country*

To have its copyright restored, a foreign work's "source country" must be a member of Berne or the WTO, or must be a country as to which the President issues a proclamation. [Copyright Act §104A(h)(3)&(6)]

A work's "source country" is the country of author's (or rightholder's) nationality or domicile, and (if the work has been published) the country where it was first published. [Copyright Act §104A(h)(8)] (A "rightholder" is the person who "first fixes a sound recording with authorization" or who acquires the rights to a sound recording from such a person. [Copyright Act §104A(h)(7)])

Thus, to have its copyright restored, a work must have an author (or rightholder) whose nationality or domicile is a member of Berne or the WTO, or must be a country as to which the President issues a proclamation; and if the work has been published, it must have been published in such a country as well.

*Still protected by copyright in source country*

To have its copyright restored, a foreign work also must still be protected by copyright in its source country. [Copyright Act §104A(h)(6)(B)]

*In public domain in U.S. for designated reason*

To have its copyright restored, a foreign work must have gone into the public domain in the U.S. for one of three reasons:

(1) because the copyright owner failed to comply with formalities once imposed by U.S. copyright law, including a failure to renew, a lack of proper notice, or failure to comply with domestic manufacturing requirements;

(2) because the work is a pre-February 15, 1972 sound recording (and thus did not receive copyright protection, because U.S. law did not protect sound recordings until that date); or

(3) because the work was first published in a country with which the United States did not then have a copyright treaty (or reciprocal proclamations). [Copyright Act §104A(h)(6)(C)]

*Effects of restoration*

The most important provisions of section 104A – as well as the lengthiest and most complex – are those that deal with the consequences of copyright restoration on the continued exploitation of those works that once were in the public domain in the U.S. but now are protected again. These consequences will be felt by two separate classes of people and companies: (1) by those who did *not* exploit restored works while they were in the public domain, but who do exploit them (or would like to) after their copyrights are restored; and (2) by those who *did* exploit restored works while they were in the public domain and continue to do so (or would like to) after their copyrights are restored.

*On those who did not exploit restored works while they were in the public domain*

The rights of the owner of a restored copyright as against those who did not exploit the work while it was in the public domain are easy to describe. An unauthorized use of the work (of a kind that amounts to copyright infringement) by any such person or company after its copyright was restored amounts to copyright infringement; and all of the remedies provided by the Copyright Act are available to the owner of a restored copyright, just as though the work had never been in the public domain. [Copyright Act §104A(d)(1)]

*On those who did exploit restored works while they were in the public domain*

The rights of the owner of a restored copyright as against those who did exploit the work while it was in the public domain are more difficult to describe and are subject to some formalities and limitations.

A person or company who did exploit a restored work while it was in the public domain is referred to as a "reliance party." This term is a term of art, and is given a very specific definition by section 104A. [Copyright Act §104A(h)(4)] In plain English (which is only a paraphrase of the more precise language actually used in section 104A), a "reliance party" is one who: has engaged in an act that would have infringed the copyright to a particular work, but did so before the work's copyright was restored, and then continued to do so after its copyright was restored; has made or acquired copies or phonorecords of a public domain work; or is a successor, assignee or licensee of someone who created a derivative work that was based on a restored work (before its copyright was restored). Getting the definition of "reliance party" right is important, because reliance parties are given certain rights (that others are not given) to continue using restored works, despite the restoration of the copyrights to such works.

The rights that reliance parties are given (that others are not) are of two types. With respect to restored works themselves, reliance parties are given the right to continue exploiting such works for a period of time. And with respect to derivative works based on restored works, reliance parties are given the right to continue exploiting those derivative works forever under certain conditions. The details are important, but beyond the scope of this Note.

The important thing to take from this Note is that copyright restoration for foreign public domain works was a good idea. Because of it, American copyright owners can reasonably expect that their copyrights will be retroactively protected in other countries that would not have done so otherwise. This ought to be particularly valuable to the motion picture business, because without retroactive protection, pre-1955 movies (now on video) may not have been protected in many countries of the world simply because the United States did not have copyright treaties with many countries before we adhered to the Universal Copyright Convention in that year.

It also was valuable to the music business, for the reasons exlained in the following Note.

(The constitutionality of copyright restoration has been challenged in *Golan v. Ashcroft*, Civ. No. 01-B-1854 (D.Colo.), filed Sept. 19, 2001. The Government's motion to dismiss that case was pending, as this book went to press. The pleadings in that case are available at http://eon.law.harvard.edu/openlaw/golanvashcroft/)

---

### Note on Japan's Retroactive Protection for Foreign Recordings

Jay Berman used to be chairman of the Recording Industry Association of America, so it was his job to get intense about issues affecting the record business; and one day in 1996, he was. "I am extremely disappointed," he began, "with Japan's failure to implement its obligations by denying the full term of retroactive protection to pre-1971 U.S. sound recordings."

Those who are old enough, or who follow music law closely enough, may have detected an anomaly in Mr. Berman's complaint about Japan's refusal to protect pre-1971 U.S. recordings. After all, the U.S. itself didn't begin protecting U.S. sound recordings until February 15, 1972 – and still doesn't protect recordings made before that date. How then, some might ask, did the RIAA have standing to complain about Japan's failure to protect pre-'71 recordings?

The answer to this question is buried in an international trade agreement known as the "Agreement on Trade Related Aspects of Intellectual Property Rights" – commonly referred to as "TRIPs." As a result of Article 14 of TRIPs, members of the World Trade Organization are supposed to provide protection against the unauthorized duplication of recordings from other countries for 50 years, retroactively if necessary, beginning in 1996. So record companies – including, of course, RIAA members – were looking forward to getting protection in all WTO countries for recordings first made as long ago as 1946. Japan is a member of the WTO. And according to Mr. Berman, the need for 50-year retroactive protection is "particularly significant in Japan where unauthorized compilations of rock and roll classics are a big business, against which the legitimate U.S. record companies cannot compete."

The Japanese, however, did not read TRIPs the way Mr. Berman and many others did. Instead, the Japanese thought that TRIPs authorized them to limit protection to foreign recordings made since 1971, not before. And that is what Japan indicated at first it would do, not more.

Japan was not alone in believing that it could limit protection for foreign recordings to those made since 1971. Christopher Heath, of the prestigious Max-Planck Institute in Munich, thought so too. "Japan seems to be correct in its interpretation of the law," he then wrote, "at least according to general international standards." (Christopher Heath, "All her Troubles Seemed so Far Away: EU v. Japan before the WTO," 18 EIPR 677 (Dec. 1996))

But the RIAA had the government of the United States on its side, and in 1996 the U.S. Trade Representative initiated dispute proceedings against Japan before the WTO. In fact, Mr. Berman's swipe at the Japanese was contained in a press release issued by the RIAA to announce the WTO proceeding.

Moreover, the U.S. wasn't the only country that took issue with Japan's position. Japan had intended to deny retroactive protection to all pre-1971 recordings from other countries, including those from European nations. So in 1996, the European Union initiated WTO proceedings of its own against Japan.

In response to the U.S. and EU proceedings, Japan changed its mind. Within months, Japan amended its copyright law to retroactively protect foreign recordings for 50 years. And the U.S. Trade Representative notified the WTO that a "mutually satisfactory solution had been reached." This change in Japanese law means that American and other non-Japanese recordings made since 1947 are now protected in Japan, and they will remain protected there for 50 years from the year they were first recorded.

Mr. Berman was pleased. "Record companies and performers owe a huge debt of gratitude to ambassadors [Charlene] Bareshefsky [who was then the United States Trade Representative] and [former USTR Mickey] Kantor for their tireless efforts to ensure that American recordings and performances are adequately protected in foreign markets," the RIAA chairman said. "The amendment to Japanese legislation will put an end to the current trade in pre-1971 unauthorized recordings that is presently costing U.S. record companies a half-billion [dollars] annually."

Mr. Berman was right about the gratitude that American record companies and artists owed to Ambassadors Bareshefsky and Kantor. Getting Japan to change its law was a significant diplomatic triumph. Embedded within that triumph, however, are some noteworthy anomalies and ironies.

To appreciate these anomalies and ironies, it is first necessary to appreciate how TRIPs goes about requiring WTO members to protect recordings for 50 years, retroactively if necessary.

The 50-year part of this requirement is done in a straightforward way. Paragraphs 1 and 2 of Article 14 of TRIPs require WTO countries to have laws that give performers and record companies the right to prevent the unauthorized reproduction of their recordings. Paragraph 5 of Article 14 then provides that the term of this protection must be at least 50 years from the end of the calendar year in which the recording was made.

The retroactive protection requirement is done only indirectly. TRIPs itself says nothing about retroactivity. Instead, Paragraph 6 of Article 14 provides that ". . . Article 18 of the Berne Convention . . . shall . . . apply . . ." to the rights of performers and record companies. The Berne Convention is an entirely separate agreement (one whose woeful lack of effective enforcement mechanisms is what made TRIPs necessary in the first place). Article 18 is what makes Berne – and thus TRIPs – retroactive. It does so by making Berne applicable "to all works which . . .

have not fallen into the public domain in the country of origin through the expiry of the term of protection."

In other words, as you read in the preceding Note, when a new country joins Berne, countries that already are members of Berne must protect all works from the new member whose copyrights have not yet expired in that country. And the new member must protect all works from countries that already are Berne members whose copyrights in those countries have not yet expired. Note, however, that retroactive protection does not have to be given to works whose copyrights had already expired in their countries of origin, before the new country joined Berne.

Likewise, under TRIPs, retroactive protection does not have to be given to recordings whose copyrights had already expired in their countries of origin before 1996 when TRIPs became effective. Herein lies the source of one enormous – and potentially embarrassing – irony: although Japan granted protection to American recordings made since 1947, the United States protects only those Japanese recordings made since 1962!

It is ironic, for several reasons, that Japan provides retroactive protection to American recordings for 15 years more than the U.S. provides retroactive protection to Japanese recordings. First, of course, it is ironic because U.S. pressure was instrumental in Japan's decision to grant protection to foreign recordings, retroactive for 50 years, even though Japan may not have been legally required to do so. Second, it is ironic because the RIAA declared Japan's original position to be "totally unacceptable," partially because that position would have permitted other countries to "randomly select[] a date other than the called for January 1946, from which to begin protection" – something which at first glance it appears the U.S. did with respect to Japanese recordings. And third, it is ironic because the 15-year gap is solely the result of an accident of Japanese and American copyright history which has nothing to do with either country's policies about granting legal protection to foreign recordings.

In order to see why the United States grants retroactive protection to Japanese recordings made only since 1962, while Japan granted retroactive protection to U.S. recordings made since 1947, it is necessary to look at both U.S. and Japanese copyright law. It's the interaction of these two separate laws that produces this ironic result.

The United States responded to its obligations under TRIPs by amending section 104A of the Copyright Act to grant retroactive protection to foreign works that satisfied certain requirements (as you read above). Two of these requirements are key, with respect to Japanese recordings.

First, the foreign work must have been in the public domain in the U.S. for one of three specific reasons. If the foreign work is a recording, that reason can be that it was first released (anywhere in the world) before February 15, 1972 (and thus was in the public domain in the U.S. because the U.S. did not protect recordings before that date). [Copyright Act §104A(h)(6)(C)(ii)] Thus, pre-February 15, 1972 Japanese recordings qualify for retroactive protection in the U.S., insofar as this requirement is concerned.

Second, the foreign work must "not [be] in the public domain in its source country through expiration of [its] term of protection." [Copyright Act §104A(h)(6)(B)] The U.S. and other countries were authorized to impose this requirement by Article 18 of the Berne Convention and thus by TRIPs; and the United States did so. In order to determine whether a Japanese recording is in the public domain in its "source country" – that is, in Japan – it is of course necessary to look at Japanese copyright law. This is where the part of the accident of history occurred.

Japan began protecting Japanese recordings back in 1934, but foreign recordings have been protected in Japan only since 1971. At first, and for many years, Japan protected recordings for 30 years. In 1992, protection for recordings was lengthened to 50 years, but existing recordings got the benefit of the 50-year term only if they were still protected in 1992. Since recordings made in 1961 or earlier went into the public domain in Japan 30 years later, in 1991 or earlier, pre-1962 recordings did not get the benefit of the 50-year term and remained in the public domain in Japan.

Since pre-1962 Japanese recordings were already in the public domain in Japan when the United States granted retroactive protection to foreign works, those Japanese recordings did not satisfy one of the requirements for retroactive protection in the U.S., and they didn't get it. Pre-1962 Japanese recordings remain in the public domain in the U.S. as well.

Pre-February 15, 1972 American recordings do not suffer the same fate in Japan, however. Even though these recordings are still in the public domain in the U.S., they are now protected in Japan (so long as they were made since 1947) because of the other part of the accident of history. The other part is this: pre-February 15, 1972 American recordings are in the public domain in the U.S. because they never have been protected by copyright at all – not because they once were protected and that protection has expired. The distinction is critical, because Berne and thus TRIPs permit countries to deny retroactive protection to foreign works whose copyrights have expired in their country of origin; but Berne and TRIPs do not permit countries to deny retroactive protection to foreign works that are in the public domain in their countries of origin because they were never protected there.

Thus, even if Japanese law were to contain a provision that denies retroactive protection to foreign recordings that are in public domain in their countries of origin because their copyrights expired – as U.S. law does – such a provision would not deprive pre-February 15, 1972 American recordings of retroactive protection in Japan, because those recordings did not have their copyrights expire in the U.S. They never had copyright in the U.S. in the first place.

It's unlikely that Japan will ever have a practical reason to complain about U.S. treatment of pre-1962 Japanese recordings. As the U.S. Trade Representative pointed out when announcing the settlement with Japan, American recordings from the pre-1971 era include those by Duke Ellington, John Coltrane, Elvis Presley, Chuck Berry, Little Richard, Johnny Cash, Patsy Cline, Bob Dylan, the Beach Boys and Otis Redding. It has been estimated that 6 million unauthorized recordings by these and other non-Japanese artists have been made and sold in Japan each year. The number of pre-1962 Japanese recordings made and sold in the U.S. without authorization has not been estimated; but the number is almost certainly tiny.

Moreover, Japan has little reason to complain, even on principle. This is so because of one further and final anomaly. It is true that Japan now provides more protection to American recordings than the United States provides to Japanese recordings. But it also is true that the United States now provides more protection to Japanese recordings (back to 1962) than it does to American recordings (which are protected only back to February 15, 1972)!

---

**United States Section 110(5) of the US Copyright Act**
**World Trade Oganization – Report of the Panel**
**WT/DS160/R (WTO 2000)**

*I. Introduction*

On 26 January 1999, the European Communities and their member States (hereafter referred to as the European Communities) requested consultations with the United States under Article 4 of the Understanding on Rules and Procedures Governing the Settlement of Disputes ("DSU") and Article 64.1 of the Agreement on Trade-Related Aspects of Intellectual Property Rights ("TRIPS Agreement") regarding Section 110(5) of the United States Copyright Act as amended by the "Fairness in Music Licensing Act" enacted on 27 October 1998.

The European Communities and the United States held consultations . . . , but failed to reach a mutually satisfactory solution. . . .

*II. Factual Aspects*

The dispute concerns Section 110(5) of the US Copyright Act of 1976, as amended by the Fairness in Music Licensing Act of 1998 ("the 1998 Amendment"), which entered into force on 26 January 1999. The provisions of Section 110(5) place limitations on the exclusive rights provided to owners of copyright in Section 106 of the Copyright Act in respect of certain performances and displays.

The relevant parts of the current text of Section 106 read as follows:

"§ 106. Exclusive rights in copyrighted works

Subject to sections 107 through 120, the owner of copyright under this title has the exclusive rights to do and to authorize any of the following: . . .

(4) in the case of literary, musical, dramatic, and choreographic works, pantomimes, and motion pictures and other audiovisual works, to perform the copyrighted work publicly. . . .

The relevant parts of the current text of Section 110(5) read as follows:

"§ 110. Limitations on exclusive rights: Exemption of certain performances and displays

Notwithstanding the provisions of section 106, the following are not infringements of copyright: . . .

(5)(A) except as provided in subparagraph (B), communication of a transmission embodying a performance or display of a work by the public reception of the transmission on a single receiving apparatus of a kind commonly used in private homes, unless

(i) a direct charge is made to see or hear the transmission; or

(ii) the transmission thus received is further transmitted to the public;

(B) communication by an establishment of a transmission or retransmission embodying a performance or display of a nondramatic musical work intended to be received by the general public, originated by a radio or television broadcast station licensed as such by the Federal Communications Commission, or, if an audiovisual transmission, by a cable system or satellite carrier, if—

(i) in the case of an establishment other than a food service or drinking establishment, either the establishment in which the communication occurs has less than 2,000 gross square feet of space (excluding space used for customer parking and for no other purpose), or the establishment in which the communication occurs has 2,000 or more gross square feet of space (excluding space used for customer parking and for no other purpose) and—

(I) if the performance is by audio means only, the performance is communicated by means of a total of not more than 6 loudspeakers, of which not more than 4 loudspeakers are located in any 1 room or adjoining outdoor space; or

(II) if the performance or display is by audiovisual means, any visual portion of the performance or display is communicated by means of a total of not more than 4 audiovisual devices, of which not more than 1 audiovisual device is located in any 1 room, and no such audiovisual device has a diagonal screen size greater than 55 inches, and any audio portion of the performance or display is communicated by means of a total of not more than 6 loudspeakers, of which not more than 4 loudspeakers are located in any 1 room or adjoining outdoor space;

(ii) in the case of a food service or drinking establishment, either the establishment in which the communication occurs has less than 3,750 gross square feet of space (excluding space used for customer parking and for no other purpose), or the establishment in which the communication occurs has 3,750 gross square feet of space or more (excluding space used for customer parking and for no other purpose) and—

(I) if the performance is by audio means only, the performance is communicated by means of a total of not more than 6 loudspeakers, of which not more than 4 loudspeakers are located in any 1 room or adjoining outdoor space; or

(II) if the performance or display is by audiovisual means, any visual portion of the performance or display is communicated by means of a total of not more than 4 audiovisual devices, of which not more than one audiovisual device is located in any 1 room, and no such audiovisual device has a diagonal screen size greater than 55 inches, and any audio portion of the performance or display is communicated by means of a total of not more than 6 loudspeakers, of which not more than 4 loudspeakers are located in any 1 room or adjoining outdoor space;

(iii) no direct charge is made to see or hear the transmission or retransmission;

(iv) the transmission or retransmission is not further transmitted beyond the establishment where it is received; and

(v) the transmission or retransmission is licensed by the copyright owner of the work so publicly performed or displayed. . . ."

Subparagraph (A) of Section 110(5) essentially reproduces the text of the original "homestyle" exemption contained in Section 110(5) of the Copyright Act of 1976. When Section 110(5) was amended in 1998, the homestyle exemption was moved to a new subparagraph (A) and the words "except as provided in subparagraph (B)" were added to the beginning of the text.

A House Report (1976) accompanying the Copyright Act of 1976 explained that in its original form Section 110(5) "applies to performances and displays of all types of works, and its purpose is to exempt from copyright liability anyone who merely turns on, in a public place, an ordinary radio or television receiving apparatus of a kind commonly sold to members of the public for private use." "The basic rationale of this clause is that the secondary use of the transmission by turning on an ordinary receiver in public is so remote and minimal that no further liability should be imposed." "[The clause] would impose liability where the proprietor has a commercial 'sound system' installed or converts a standard home receiving apparatus (by augmenting it with sophisticated or extensive amplification equipment) into the equivalent of a commercial sound system." A subsequent Conference Report (1976) elaborated on the rationale by noting that the intent was to exempt a small commercial establishment "which was not of sufficient size to justify, as a practical matter, a subscription to a commercial background music service."

The factors to consider in applying the exemption are largely based on the facts of a case decided by the United States Supreme Court immediately prior to the passage of the 1976 Copyright Act. In *Aiken*, the Court held that an owner of a small fast food restaurant was not liable for playing music by means of a radio with outlets to four speakers in the ceiling; the size of the shop was 1,055 square feet (98 $m^2$), of which 620 square feet (56 $m^2$) were open to the public. The House Report (1976) describes the factual situation in *Aiken* as representing the "outer limit of the exemption" contained in the original Section 110(5). This exemption became known as the "homestyle" exemption.

As indicated in the first quotation in the preceding paragraph, the homestyle exemption was originally intended to apply to performances of all types of works. However, given that the present subparagraph (B) applies to "a performance or display of a nondramatic musical work," the parties agree . . . that the effect of the introductory phrase "except as provided in subparagraph (B)," that was added to the text in subparagraph (A), is that it narrows down the application of subparagraph (A) to works other than "nondramatic musical works."

The Panel notes that it is the common understanding of the parties that the expression "nondramatic musical works" in subparagraph (B) excludes from its application the communication of music that is part of an opera, operetta, musical or other similar dramatic work when performed in a dramatic context. All other musical works are covered by that expression, including individual songs taken from dramatic works when performed outside of any dramatic context. Subparagraph (B) would, therefore, apply for example to an individual song taken from a musical and played on the radio. Consequently, the operation of subparagraph (A) is limited to such musical works as are not covered by subparagraph (B), for example a communication of a broadcast of a dramatic rendition of the music written for an opera.

The 1998 Amendment has added a new subparagraph (B) to Section 110(5), to which we, for the sake of brevity, hereinafter refer to as a "business" exemption. It exempts, under certain conditions, communication by an establishment of a transmission or retransmission embodying a performance or display of a nondramatic musical work intended to be received by the general public, originated by a radio or television broadcast station licensed as such by the Federal Communications Commission, or, if an audiovisual transmission, by a cable system or satellite carrier.

The beneficiaries of the business exemption are divided into two categories: establishments other than food service or drinking establishments ("retail establishments"), and food service and drinking establishments. In each category, establishments under a certain size limit are exempted, regardless of the type of equipment they use. The size limits are 2,000 gross square feet (186 $m^2$) for retail establishments and 3,750 gross square feet (348 $m^2$) for restaurants.

In its study of November 1995 prepared for the Senate Judiciary Committee, the Congressional Research Service ("CRS") estimated that 16 per cent of eating establishments, 13.5 per cent of drinking establishments and 18 per cent of retail establishments were below the area of the restaurant ran by Mr. Aiken, i.e. 1,055 square feet. Furthermore, the CRS estimated that 65.2 per cent of eating establishments and 71.8 per cent of drinking establishments would have fallen at that time under a 3,500 square feet limit, and that 27 per cent of retail establishments would have fallen under a 1,500 square feet limit.

In 1999, Dun & Bradstreet, Inc. ("D&B") was requested on behalf of the American Society of Composers, Authors and Publishers (ASCAP) to update the CRS study based on 1998 data and the criteria in the 1998 Amendment. In this study, the D&B estimated that 70 per cent of eating establishments and 73 per cent of drinking establishments fell under the 3,750 square feet limit, and that 45 per cent of retail establishments fell under the 2,000 square feet limit.

The studies conducted by the National Restaurant Association (NRA) concerning its membership indicate that 36 per cent of table service restaurant members (those with sit-down waiter service) and 95 per cent of quick service restaurant members are less than 3,750 square feet. . . .

Section 110(5) does not apply to the use of recorded music, such as CDs or cassette tapes, or to live performances of music.

Holders of copyright in musical works (composers, lyricists and music publishers) normally entrust the licensing of nondramatic public performance of their works to collective management organizations ("CMOs" or performing rights organizations). The three main CMOs in the United States in this area are ASCAP, the Broadcast Music, Inc. (BMI) and SESAC, Inc. CMOs license the public performance of musical works to users of music, such as retail establishments and restaurants, on behalf of the individual right holders they represent, collect licence fees from such users, and distribute revenues as royalties to the respective right holders. They normally enter into reciprocal arrangements with the CMOs of other countries to license the works of the right holders represented by them. Revenues are distributed to individual right holders through the CMOs that represent the right holders in question. The above-mentioned three US CMOs license nondramatic public performances of musical works, including nondramatic renditions of "dramatic" musical works.

*III. Findings and Recommendations Requested by the Parties*

The European Communities alleges that the exemptions provided in subparagraphs (A) and (B) of Section 110(5) of the US Copyright Act are in violation of the United States' obligations under the TRIPS Agreement. In particular, it alleges that these US measures are incompatible with Article 9.1 of the TRIPS Agreement together with Articles 11(1)(ii) and 11*bis*(1)(iii) of the Berne Convention (1971) and that they cannot be justified under any express or implied exception or limitation permissible under the Berne Convention (1971) or the TRIPS Agreement. In the view of the EC, these measures cause prejudice to the legitimate rights of copyright owners, thus nullifying and impairing the rights of the European Communities.

The European Communities requests the Panel to find that the United States has violated its obligations under Article 9.1 of the TRIPS Agreement together with Articles 11*bis*(1)(iii) and 11(1)(ii) of the Berne Convention (1971) and to recommend that the United States bring its domestic legislation into conformity with its obligations under the TRIPS Agreement.

The United States contends that Section 110(5) of the US Copyright Act is fully consistent with its obligations under the TRIPS Agreement. The Agreement, incorporating the substantive provisions of the Berne Convention (1971), allows Members to place minor limitations on the exclusive rights of copyright owners. Article 13 of the TRIPS Agreement provides the standard by which to judge the appropriateness of such limitations or exceptions. The exemptions embodied in Section 110(5) fall within the Article 13 standard.

The United States requests the Panel to find that both subparagraphs (A) and (B) of Section 110(5) of the US Copyright Act meet the standard of Article 13 of the TRIPS Agreement and the substantive obligations of the Berne Convention (1971). Accordingly, the United States requests the Panel to dismiss the claims of the European Communities in this dispute. . . .

*VI. Findings . . .*

*D. Substantive aspects of the dispute*

*1. General considerations about the exclusive rights concerned and limitations thereto*

*(a) Exclusive rights implicated by the EC claims*

Articles 913 of Section 1 of Part II of the TRIPS Agreement entitled "Copyright and Related Rights" deal with the substantive standards of copyright protection. Article 9.1 of the TRIPS Agreement obliges WTO Members to comply with Articles 121 of the Berne Convention (1971) (with the exception of Article 6*bis* on moral rights and the rights derived therefrom) and the Appendix thereto. The European Communities alleges that subparagraphs (A) and (B) of Section 110(5) are inconsistent primarily with Article 11*bis*(1)(iii) but also with Article 11(1)(ii) of the Berne Convention (1971) as incorporated into the TRIPS Agreement.

We note that through their incorporation, the substantive rules of the Berne Convention (1971), including the provisions of its Articles 11*bis*(1)(iii) and 11(1)(ii), have become part of the TRIPS Agreement and as provisions of that Agreement have to be read as applying to WTO Members.

*(i) Article 11bis of the Berne Convention (1971)*

The provision of particular relevance for this dispute is Article 11*bis*(1)(iii). Article 11*bis*(1) provides:

"Authors of literary and artistic works shall enjoy the exclusive right of authorizing:

(i) the broadcasting of their works or the communication thereof to the public by any other means of wireless diffusion of signs, sounds or images;

(ii) any communication to the public by wire or by re-broadcasting of the broadcast of the work, when this communication is made by an organization other than the original one;

(iii) the public communication by loudspeaker or any other analogous instrument transmitting, by signs, sounds or images, the broadcast of the work."

Subparagraph (iii) provides an exclusive right to authorize the public communication of the broadcast of the work by loudspeaker, on a television screen, or by other similar means. Such communication involves a new public performance of a work contained in a broadcast, which requires a licence from the right holder. For the purposes of this dispute, the claims raised by the European Communities under Article 11*bis*(1) are limited to subparagraph (iii).

*(ii) Article 11 of the Berne Convention (1971)*

Of relevance to this dispute are also the exclusive rights conferred by Article 11(1)(ii) of the Berne Convention (1971). Article 11(1) provides:

"Authors of dramatic, dramatico-musical and musical works shall enjoy the exclusive right of authorizing:

(i) the public performance of their works, including such public performance by any means or process;

(ii) any communication to the public of the performance of their works."

As in the case of Article 11*bis*(1) of the Berne Convention (1971), which concerns broadcasting to the public and communication of a broadcast to the public, the exclusive rights conferred by Article 11 cover *public* performance; private performance does not require authorization. Public performance includes performance by any means or process, such as performance by means of recordings (e.g., CDs, cassettes and videos). It also includes communication to the public of a performance of the work. The claims raised by the European Communities under Article 11(1) of the Berne Convention (1971) are limited to its subparagraph (ii).

Regarding the relationship between Articles 11 and 11*bis*, we note that the rights conferred in Article 11(1)(ii) concern the communication to the public of performances of works in general. Article 11*bis*(1)(iii) is a specific rule conferring exclusive rights concerning the public communication by loudspeaker or any other analogous instrument transmitting, by signs, sounds or images, the broadcast of a work.

As noted above, the United States acknowledges that subparagraphs (A) and (B) of Section 110(5) implicate Articles 11*bis*(1)(iii) and 11(1)(ii) of the Berne Convention (1971). Consequently, the core question before this Panel is which of the exceptions under the TRIPS Agreement invoked are relevant to this dispute and whether the conditions for their invocation are met so as to justify the exemptions under subparagraphs (A) and (B) of Section 110(5) of the US Copyright Act.

*(b) Limitations and exceptions*

A major issue in this dispute is the interpretation and application to the facts of this case of Article 13 of the TRIPS Agreement. The US defense is firmly based upon it. . . .

Article 13 of the TRIPS Agreement, entitled "Limitations and Exceptions," is the general exception clause applicable to exclusive rights of the holders of copyright. It provides:

"Members shall confine limitations or exceptions to exclusive rights to certain special cases which do not conflict with a normal exploitation of the work and do not unreasonably prejudice the legitimate interests of the right holder." . . .

As we noted above, the US view is that Article 13 of the TRIPS Agreement clarifies and articulates the scope of the minor exceptions doctrine, which is applicable under the TRIPS Agreement. . . .

We note that, in addition to the explicit provisions on permissible limitations and exceptions to the exclusive rights embodied in the text of the Berne Convention (1971), the reports of successive revision conferences of that Convention refer to "implied exceptions" allowing member countries to provide limitations and exceptions to certain rights. The so-called "minor reservations" or "minor exceptions" doctrine is being referred to in respect of the right of public performance and certain other exclusive rights. Under that doctrine, Berne Union members may provide minor exceptions to the rights provided, *inter alia*, under Articles 11*bis* and 11 of the Berne Convention (1971). . . .

. . . We note that the parties and third parties have brought to our attention several examples from various countries of limitations in national laws based on the minor exceptions doctrine. [Fn: For example, Australia exempts public performance by wireless apparatus at premises of, *inter alia*, hotels or guest houses. Belgium exempts a work's communication to the public in a place accessible to the public where the aim of the communication is not the work itself, and exempts the performance of a work during a public examination where the purpose is the assessment of the performer. Finland exempts public performance in connection with religious services and education. Finland and Denmark provide for exceptions where a work's performance is not the main feature of the event, provided that no fee is charged and the event is not for profit. New Zealand exempts public performance of musical works at educational establishments. The Philippines exempts public performances for charitable and educational purposes. A similar exception applies in India, where also performances at amateur clubs or societies are exempted. Canadian law provides for exceptions with respect to different exclusive rights for educational, religious or charitable purposes, and also at conventions and fairs. South Africa exempts public performances in the context of demonstrations of radio or television receivers and recording equipment by dealers of or clients for such equipment. Brazil allows free use of works in commercial establishments for the purpose of demonstration to customers in establishments that market equipment that makes such use possible.] . . . .

Having concluded that the minor exceptions doctrine forms part of the "context" of, at least, Articles 11*bis* and 11 of the Berne Convention . . . , we next address the second step of our analysis outlined above. This second step deals with the question whether or not the minor exceptions doctrine has been incorporated into the TRIPS Agreement, by virtue of its Article 9.1, together with Articles 1-21 of the Berne Convention (1971) as part of the Berne *acquis*.

We note that the express wording of Article 9.1 of the TRIPS Agreement neither establishes nor excludes such incorporation into the Agreement of the minor exceptions doctrine as it applies to Articles 11, 11*bis*, 11*ter*, 13 and 14 of the Berne Convention (1971). . . .

Thus we conclude that, in the absence of any express exclusion in Article 9.1 of the TRIPS Agreement, the incorporation of Articles 11 and 11*bis* of the Berne Convention (1971) into the Agreement includes the entire *acquis* of these provisions, including the possibility of providing minor exceptions to the respective exclusive rights. . . .

[I]t is sufficient that a limitation or an exception to the exclusive rights provided under Article 11*bis*(1) of the Berne Convention (1971) as incorporated into the TRIPS Agreement meets the three conditions contained in its Article 13 to be permissible. If these three conditions are met, a government may choose between different options for limiting the right in question, including use free of charge and without an authorization by the right holder. . . .

In our view, Section 110(5) of the US Copyright Act contains exceptions that allow use of protected works without an authorization by the right holder and without charge. Whether these exceptions meet the United States' obligations under the TRIPS Agreement has to be examined by applying Article 13 of the TRIPS Agreement. . . .

*Summary of limitations and exceptions*

In the light of the foregoing analysis, we conclude that the context of Articles 11 and 11*bis* of the Berne Convention (1971) comprises . . . the possibility of providing minor exceptions to the exclusive rights in question. This minor exceptions doctrine has been incorporated into the TRIPS Agreement, by virtue of its Article 9.1, together with these provisions of the Berne Convention (1971). Therefore, the doctrine is relevant as forming part of the context of Articles 11(1)(ii) and 11*bis*(1)(iii) of the Berne Convention (1971) as incorporated into the TRIPS Agreement. . . .

We conclude that Article 13 of the TRIPS Agreement applies to Articles 11*bis*(1)(iii) and 11(1)(ii) of the Berne Convention (1971) as incorporated into the TRIPS Agreement . . . .

We now proceed to applying the three conditions contained in Article 13 of the TRIPS Agreement to the exemptions contained in Section 110(5) of the US Copyright Act in relation to Articles 11*bis*(1)(iii) and 11(1)(ii) of the Berne Convention (1971) as incorporated into the TRIPS Agreement.

*2. The three criteria test under Article 13 of the TRIPS Agreement*

Article 13 of the TRIPS Agreement requires that limitations and exceptions to exclusive rights (1) be confined to certain special cases, (2) do not conflict with a normal exploitation of the work, and (3) do not unreasonably prejudice the legitimate interests of the right holder. . . .

*(b) "Certain special cases"* . . .

In our view, the first condition of Article 13 requires that a limitation or exception in national legislation should be clearly defined and should be narrow in its scope and reach. . . .

In the case at hand, in order to determine whether subparagraphs (B) and (A) of Section 110(5) are confined to "certain special cases," we first examine whether the exceptions have been clearly defined. Second, we ascertain whether the exemptions are narrow in scope, *inter alia*, with respect to their reach. In that respect, we take into account what percentage of eating and drinking establishments and retail establishments may benefit from the business exemption under subparagraph (B), and in turn what percentage of establishments may take advantage of the homestyle exemption under subparagraph (A). . . .

*(ii) The business exemption of subparagraph (B)*

The factual information presented to us indicates that a substantial majority of eating and drinking establishments and close to half of retail establishments are covered by the exemption contained in subparagraph (B) of Section 110(5) of the US Copyright Act. Therefore, we conclude that the exemption does not qualify as a "certain special case" in the meaning of the first condition of Article 13. . . .

*(iii) The homestyle exemption of subparagraph (A)*

We believe that from a quantitative perspective the reach of subparagraph (A) in respect of potential users is limited to a comparably small percentage of all eating, drinking and retail establishments in the United States. . . .

. . . In our view, the term "homestyle equipment" expresses the degree of clarity in definition required under Article 13's first condition. . . .

We have noted the common view of the parties that the addition of the introductory phrase "except as provided in subparagraph (B)" to the homestyle exemption in the 1998 Amendment should be understood . . . as limiting the coverage of the exemption to works other than "nondramatic" musical works. As regards musical works, the currently applicable version of the homestyle exemption is thus understood to apply to the communication of music that is part of an opera, operetta, musical or other similar dramatic work when performed in a dramatic context. All other musical works are covered by the expression "nondramatic" musical works, including individual songs taken from dramatic works when performed outside any dramatic context. Subparagraph (B) would, therefore, apply for example to an individual song taken from a musical and played on the radio. Consequently, given the common view of the parties, the operation of subparagraph (A) is limited to such musical works as are not covered by subparagraph (B), for example a communication of a broadcast of a dramatic rendition of the music written for an opera, operetta, musical or other similar works. . . .

In practice, this means that most if not virtually all music played on the radio or television is covered by subparagraph (B). Subparagraph (A) covers, in accordance with the common understanding of the parties, dramatic renditions of operas, operettas, musicals and other similar dramatic works. We consider that limiting the application of subparagraph (A) to the public communication of transmissions embodying such works, gives its provisions a quite narrow scope of application in practice. . . .

Taking into account the specific limits imposed in subparagraph (A) and its legislative history, as well as in its considerably narrow application in the subsequent court practice on the beneficiaries of the exemption, permissible equipment and categories of works, we are of the view that the homestyle exemption in subparagraph (A) of Section 110(5) as amended in 1998 is well-defined and limited in its scope and reach. We, therefore, conclude that the exemption is confined to certain special cases within the meaning of the first condition of Article 13 of the TRIPS Agreement. . . .

*(c) "Not conflict with a normal exploitation of the work"* . . .

*(ii) The business exemption of subparagraph (B)* . . .

Right holders of musical works would expect to be in a position to authorize the use of broadcasts of radio and television music by many of the establishments covered by the exemption and, as appropriate, receive compensation for the use of their works. Consequently, we cannot but conclude that an exemption of such scope as subparagraph (B) conflicts with the "normal exploitation" of the work in relation to the exclusive rights conferred by Articles 11*bis*(1)(iii) and 11(1)(ii) of the Berne Convention (1971).

In the light of these considerations, we conclude that the business exemption embodied in subparagraph (B) conflicts with a normal exploitation of the work within the meaning of the second condition of Article 13.

*(iii) The homestyle exemption of subparagraph (A) . . .*

We recall that it is the common understanding of the parties that the operation of subparagraph (A) is limited, as regards musical works, to the public communication of transmissions embodying dramatic renditions of "dramatic" musical works, such as operas, operettas, musicals and other similar dramatic works. Consequently, performances of, e.g., individual songs from a dramatic musical work outside a dramatic context would constitute a rendition of a nondramatic work and fall within the purview of subparagraph (B).

It is our understanding that the parties agree that the right holders do not normally license or attempt to license the public communication of transmissions embodying dramatic renditions of "dramatic" musical works in the sense of Article 11*bis*(1)(iii) and/or 11(1)(ii). We have not been provided with information about any existing licensing practices concerning the communication to the public of broadcasts of performances of dramatic works (e.g., operas, operettas, musicals) by eating, drinking or retail establishments in the United States or any other country. In this respect, we fail to see how the homestyle exemption, as limited to works other than nondramatic musical works in its revised form, could acquire economic or practical importance of any considerable dimension for the right holders of musical works.

Therefore, we conclude that the homestyle exemption contained in subparagraph (A) of Section 110(5) does not conflict with a normal exploitation of works within the meaning of the second condition of Article 13.

*(d) "Not unreasonably prejudice the legitimate interests of the right holder" . . .*

*(ii) The business exemption of subparagraph (B) . . .*

The United States estimates that the maximum annual loss to EC right holders of distributions from the largest US collecting society, ASCAP, as a result of the Section 110(5) exemption, is in the range of $294,113 to $586,332. Applying the same analysis, it estimates that the loss from the second largest society, BMI, is $122,000. . . .

The European Communities estimates that the annual loss to all right holders amounts to $53.65 million. . . .

. . . [T]he ultimate burden of proof concerning whether all of the conditions of Article 13 are met lies with the United States as the Member invoking the exception. In the light of our analysis of the prejudice caused by the exemption, including its actual and potential effects, we are of the view that the United States has not demonstrated that the business exemption does not unreasonably prejudice the legitimate interests of the right holder.

Accordingly, we conclude that the business exemption of subparagraph (B) of Section 110(5) does not meet the requirements of the third condition of Article 13 of the TRIPS Agreement.

*(iii) The homestyle exemption of subparagraph (A) . . .*

. . . [A]s regards the exemption as amended in 1998 to exclude from its scope nondramatic musical works, the European Communities has not explicitly claimed that the exemption would currently cause any prejudice to right holders.

In the light of the considerations above, we conclude that the homestyle exemption contained in subparagraph (A) of Section 110(5) does not cause unreasonable prejudice to the legitimate interests of the right holders within the meaning of the third condition of Article 13.

*VII. Conclusions and Recommendations*

. . . [T]he Panel concludes that:

(a) Subparagraph (A) of Section 110(5) of the US Copyright Act meets the requirements of Article 13 of the TRIPS Agreement and is thus consistent with Articles 11*bis*(1)(iii) and 11(1)(ii) of the Berne Convention (1971) as incorporated into the TRIPS Agreement by Article 9.1 of that Agreement.

(b) Subparagraph (B) of Section 110(5) of the US Copyright Act does not meet the requirements of Article 13 of the TRIPS Agreement and is thus inconsistent with Articles 11*bis*(1)(iii) and 11(1)(ii) of the Berne Convention (1971) as incorporated into the TRIPS Agreement by Article 9.1 of that Agreement.

The Panel *recommends* that the Dispute Settlement Body request the United States to bring subparagraph (B) of Section 110(5) into conformity with its obligations under the TRIPS Agreement.

---

**Note on the aftermath of the WTO Panel Report**

The WTO Panel Report was the equivalent of a trial court decision. The United States could have appealed to a WTO Appellate Body, but chose not to. Instead, the United States informed the WTO that it would implement the Panel's recommendation that "the United States . . . bring subparagraph (B) of Section 110(5) into conformity with its obligations under the TRIPS Agreement." The only way to do that, of course, would be to repeal the Fairness in Music Licensing Act. And that is something only Congress has the power to do; it cannot be done by the U.S. Trade Representative nor by anyone else in the Executive Branch of the government.

The Panel Report was issued in June 2000, just months before the end of the then-current session of Congress, and just months before the 2000 Presidential election. As a result, repealing the Fairness in Music Licensing Act was not a high priority for anyone in Congress (and for some it wasn't a priority at all). As a result, the United States advised the WTO that it would need a "reasonable period of time" within which to implement that Panel's recommendation. Because the United States and the European Communities were not able to agree on how long a time would be "reasonable," that issue was referred to arbitration (as permitted by WTO procedural rules).

The European Communities argued that the Panel's recommendation should be implemented by May 27, 2001, which was 10 months from the date of adoption of the Panel Report. Ten months was sufficient, the E.C. said, because doing so merely "requires a 'repeal' of Section 110(5)(B) of the Copyright Act, as well as a 'modest adaptation' to Section 110(5)(A) of that Act."

The United States, on the other hand, argued that it needed "at least 15 months" from the adoption of the Panel Report, but added that it would be "even more prudent" to give it until the adjournment of the next session of Congress which might have occurred as late as December 31, 2001. The U.S. justified its request by explaining the multi-step legislative process that is required to enact legislation, and by noting that because the United States had recently elected a new President, Congress would be spending its first few months getting organized and confirming President George Bush's appointments. As a result, the U.S. explained that the process of repealing the Fairness in Music Licensing Act was unlikely to begin until March or April 2001.

The WTO Dispute Settlement Understanding provides that although "particular circumstances" may require shorter or longer times, 15 months from the adoption of a Panel Report is a "guideline" for arbitrators to consider when deciding how much time is "reasonable" for the implementation of recommendations.

Arbitrator Julio Lacarte-Muro agreed with the European Communities that "that the period of time proposed by the United States . . . is not justified by the 'particular circumstances' of this case." On the other hand, the Arbitrator agreed with the United States that "Given that the Congressional schedule for 2001 begins, at the earliest, in January, a 'reasonable period of time' of 10 months, ending on 27 May 2001, does not seem sufficient in the particular circumstances of this case."

The Arbitrator therefore concluded that "that the 'reasonable period of time' for the United States to implement the recommendations and rulings of the [Panel] in this case is 12 months from the date of adoption of the Panel Report by the DSB on 27 July 2000. The 'reasonable period of time' will thus expire on 27 July 2001." *United States – Section 110(5) of the US Copyright Act, Arbitration under Article 21.3(c) of the Understanding on Rules and Procedures Governing the Settlement of Disputes*, WT/DS160/12 (15 January 2001)

Just a few days before the July 27, 2001, deadline, the E.C. agreed to extend the deadline until December 31, 2001 (the date the U.S. had originally requested in arbitration).

In the meantime, however, the case proceeded to the next stage. That stage required a determination of "the nature and level of the benefits [that otherwise would have been received by E.C. publishers and songwriters] which are being nullified or impaired" by the Fairness in Music Licensing Act. The E.C. and the U.S. could not agree on an amount. The E.C. contended that its music publishers and songwriters are losing almost $25.5 million a year in royalties, while the U.S. contended they are losing only $773,000 a year or less.

Since the U.S. and the E.C. could not agree, that issue too was submitted to arbitration. A panel of three arbitrators decided that the Fairness in Music Licensing Act is costing European songwriters and music publishers $1.1 million a year in lost royalties. While that amount was more than the U.S. estimate, it was less than one-twentieth of the E.C. estimate. In this respect, then, it can be said that the United States "won" that round of the case.

There were several reasons the U.S. and the E.C. were so far apart on how much damage the Fairness in Music Licensing Act is doing to E.C. publishers and songwriters.

- The E.C. and U.S. had different views about whether the damage should be measured by the amount of royalties that *all* U.S. restaurants, bars and retail stores should have been paying (the E.C.'s position), or only by those royalties that would have been paid by restaurants, bars and stores that ASCAP and BMI *would have licensed* (the U.S.'s position) if the Fairness in Music Licensing Act had not been passed.
- They also disagreed about whether the damage should be measured by the royalties that would have been *collected* by ASCAP and BMI on behalf of E.C. publishers and songwriters (the E.C.'s position), or only the amount that would have been *distributed* by ASCAP and BMI to E.C. publishers (or their U.S. subpublishers) and songwriters (the U.S.'s position).

- They could not agree on whether the amount should be calculated by taking, as a starting point, the number of restaurants, bars and stores that are improperly exempted from paying public performance royalties by the Fairness in Music Licensing Act (the E.C.'s position), or whether the starting point should be the amount of royalties that were actually paid by ASCAP and BMI to E.C. publishers and songwriters before the Fairness in Music Licensing Act became law (the U.S.'s position).
- Finally, because the arbitrators could not obtain all of the exact data necessary for making their calculations, estimates had to be made in some areas; and the U.S. and E.C. were unable to agree on the proper figures for some of those estimates.

The arbitrators – Mr. Ian F. Sheppard, Mrs. Margaret Lian, and Mr. David Vivas-Eugui – agreed with the United States on most of these issues.

While the arbitrators agreed with the E.C. that *all* U.S. users of music *should* be licensed and *should* pay licensing fees, the arbitrators noted that in actual practice, E.C. publishers and songwriters rely on ASCAP and BMI to collect their public performance royalties; and ASCAP and BMI do not in fact attempt to license all restaurants, bars and stores, because the cost of licensing some would exceed the fees that could be collected from them. The arbitrators therefore decided that damages should be measured by reference to licenses that ASCAP and BMI actually would have issued if the Fairness in Music Licensing Act had not been passed.

The arbitrators determined that the E.C.'s damages should be determined by reference to the amount of *distributions* that ASCAP and BMI would have made to E.C. publishers and songwriters, rather than the license fees ASCAP and BMI would have collected from restaurants, bars and stores. This was so, the arbitrators explained, because the amounts actually lost by E.C. publishers and songwriters are those they would have received, after ASCAP and BMI deducted their own collection and administrative costs.

The arbitrators determined that they should start with the amounts paid to E.C. publishers and songwriters by ASCAP and BMI before the Fairness in Music Licensing Act became law, rather than with the number of restaurants, bars and stores that are improperly exempted by the Act. They reached this conclusion, because even before the Act was passed in 1998, some restaurants, bars and stores were exempt under the old "home style receiver" exemption; and the arbitrators decided that amounts lost by E.C. publishers and songwriters under that exemption were not at issue in this case.

To calculate the amount lost by E.C. publishers and songwriters as a result of the Fairness in Music Licensing Act, the arbitrators:

- took the amount ASCAP and BMI distributed to E.C. publishers and songwriters annually, before the Act was passed (an amount the decision does not reveal, because it was considered to be confidential);
- determined how much of that amount was attributable to license fees paid by restaurants, bars and stores, by multiplying the total amount paid by 18.45% which is the percentage of total domestic receipts attributable to the "general licensing" category (by ASCAP), and then multiplying that by 50% which is the estimated percentage of "general licensing" fees attributable to restaurants, bars and stores; and
- determined how much of that amount was attributable to radio and television play (rather than, say, live performances or the use of CD players), by multiplying that amount by an undisclosed percentage (because the percentage was considered confidential).

These calculations led the arbitrators to conclude that before the Fairness in Music Licensing Act was passed, E.C. publishers and songwriters received $1.55 million a year on account of radio and television play of their compositions by restaurants, bars and stores in the U.S. The arbitrators then:

- determined that 58.5% of this $1.55 million – or $0.91 million – was paid by restaurants, bars and stores that became exempt because of the Act; and the arbitrators
- adjusted this $0.91 million to take into account "the evolution of the market" from 1998 until the arbitration began in July 2001; they did so
- by increasing the $0.91 million by the percentage of growth in the U.S. gross domestic product for 1998, 1999, 2000 and the first six months of 2001 (i.e., 5.6%, 5.5%, 6.5% and 1.7%).

These calculations yielded the $1.1 million figure the arbitrators decided was the amount per year E.C. publishers and songwriters have lost, as a result of the public performance fee exemptions that the Fairness in Music Licensing Act has improperly given to restaurants, bars and stores. *United States – Section 110(5) of the US Copyright Act – Recourse to Arbitration under Article 25 of the DSU*, WT/DS160/ARB25/1 (Nov. 9, 2001).

The December 31, 2001 deadline came and went, and Congress did nothing to repeal the Fairness in Music Licensing Act. However, the arbitrators' decision that E.C. publishers and songwriters have suffered damage of $1.1 million a year since 1998 did *not* lead to a "judgment" that the E.C. could collect from the U.S. Instead, under WTO rules, the E.C. became eligible to suspend "obligations" it owes the U.S. under the WTO agreement.

"Suspension of obligations" is a polite way of describing the initiation of a trade war. The WTO Dispute Settlement Understanding provides that "the general principle is that the complaining party" – in this case, the E.C. – "should first seek to suspend . . . obligations in the same sector(s) as that in which the panel . . . found a violation. . . ." This "general" principle would authorize the E.C. to impose tariffs on, say, American-made copyrighted goods imported by Europe.

The WTO Dispute Settlement Understanding contains an "alternate" principle as well. The alternate principle would have authorized the E.C. "to suspend . . . obligations in other sectors." It would, for example, permit the E.C. to impose tariffs on other types of goods (having nothing to do with copyright) manufactured in the United States and exported to Europe.

For a while, there was reason to suppose that the E.C. might take advantage of the "alternate" principle – to impose tariffs on non-copyrighted goods – for reasons buried in the U.S. legislative and political process.

When originally enacted, the Fairness in Music Licensing Act was approved by a majority of the members of both the House and the Senate, and it was signed (rather than vetoed) by President Bill Clinton – even though all were told in advance that the Act probably would be found to violate TRIPs, just as it actually was.

While this means that blame for the Act can fairly be spread around, a bigger share should go to Representative James Sensenbrenner Jr. The Act's original enactment was spearheaded by Representative Sensenbrenner, and in January 2001, he became Chairman of the House Judiciary Committee – the very committee that would have jurisdiction over legislation to repeal the Fairness in Music Licensing Act. In the wake of the WTO's original ruling that the Act violates TRIPs, an unidentified Sensenbrenner "spokeswoman" told the *Hollywood Reporter* that the Fairness in Music Licensing Act "is U.S. law, and allowing an international body to say, 'You will change the law,' is not a good precedent to set." (*Hollywood Reporter*, Nov. 10-12, 2001, pg. 8) Sensenbrenner also reportedly wrote to the

United States Trade Representative, protesting the government's decision not to appeal the WTO ruling, arguing that despite the WTO ruling, the Act is consistent with U.S. obligations as a WTO member, in his opinion.

It therefore seems likely that Representative Sensenbrenner is the person most responsible for Congress' failure even to consider repealing the Fairness in Music Licensing Act.

Representative Sensenbrenner, a Republican, represents a district in Wisconsin. The state of Wisconsin is home to a huge number of manufacturers, including, for example, Harley-Davidson, Inc., the manufacturer of Harley-Davidson motorcycles. In the year 2000, Harley-Davidson shipped 19,870 motorcycles to Europe (just over 10% of all its shipments that year). How perfectly ironic it would have been if the E.C. chose to impose tariffs on Harley-Davidson motorcycles and other Wisconsin-made goods. If the E.C. chose to do that, Representative Sensenbrenner might have understood why compliance with international law – as determined by an international body that the U.S. has used to good advantage in other disputes – is in fact a good precedent to set.

Alas, that was not to be, though for a while, it looked as though the E.C. would not impose tariffs on American made goods of any type.

On December 19, 2001 – less than two weeks before the extended deadline for U.S. compliance with the WTO Panel's recommendations – the EU announced that it and the United States had agreed on a "temporary solution" of their dispute over the Fairness in Music Licensing Act. According to an EU press release, "the agreement came during a meeting between EU Trade Commissioner Pascal Lamy and . . . US Trade Representative Robert Zoellick." The release reported that "We have agreed on a process that will result in a US financial contribution to support projects and activities for the benefit of European music creators," though the release reported that the United States remains obliged to bring its copyright legislation into line with its WTO obligations.

The release said that the U.S. Trade Representative would propose that the Bush Administration seek authorization and funding from Congress to enable it to contribute to the financing of projects and activities for the benefit of European music creators. "Once the authorization is granted," the release said, "the EU and the US will be in a position to finalise an arrangement, which will be in place for three years." *EU and US agree on temporary solution in music copyright dispute*, Press Release (dated Dec. 19, 2001).

But December 31, 2001 came and went without any Congressional activity to repeal the Act or to fund the settlement. On January 7, 2002, the EU notified the WTO that the U.S. had failed to meet its deadline, and – despite its December 19, 2001 press release announcing a settlement – the EU informed the WTO that "no mutually acceptable arrangement has yet been made."

At the same time, the EU indicated what remedies it had chosen to pursue. It requested authorization "to suspend its obligations under the TRIPS Agreement in order to permit the levying of a special fee from US nationals in connection with border measures concerning *copyright[ed]* goods." [Emphasis added.] The EU noted that a WTO arbitration panel had found that the Fairness in Music Licensing Act had cost EU songwriters and music publishers $1.1 million per year in lost public performance royalties. Therefore, the EU promised to "fix the amount of the special fee . . . so as to ensure that the level of affected US benefits will not exceed the level of EC benefits nullified or impaired as a result of the WTO-inconsistent provisions of the US Copyright Act." That was just a polite way of telling the U.S. that if the EU does impose "special fees" – that is, "tariffs" – on copyrighted goods from the United States, those "special fees" will amount to as much as $1.1 million per year. *United States – Section 110(5) of the US Copyright Act: Recourse by the European Communities to Article 22.2 of the DSU*, WT/DS160/19 (WTO 7 January 2002)

The United States replied almost immediately. On January 17, 2002, it sent a missive of its own to the WTO, objecting "to the level of suspension of obligations proposed by the European Communities" on January 7th. What's more, the United States claimed that certain necessary "principles and procedures" had "not been followed." The U.S. therefore demanded that "the matter . . . be referred to arbitration." *Request by the United States for Arbitration under Article 22.6 of the DSU*, WT/DS160/20 (WTO 18 January 2002)

Just four days after the United States' demand for arbitration, a further development occurred, suggesting that the settlement was not dead after all, and that the public record during 2002 merely reflects the diplomacy that is necessary to keep it alive. This is what happened. On January 22, 2002, the U.S. sent the WTO a "status report" in which it assured the WTO that "the European Communities and the United States have been engaged in productive discussions with a view to resolving the dispute," and "Those discussions are continuing." *Status Report by the United States*, WT/DS160/18 (WTO 22 January 2002)

The WTO nevertheless appointed three arbitrators, in response to the United States' request. *Recourse by the United States to Article 22.6 of the DSU*, WT/DS160/21 (WTO 19 February 2002). Just one week later, the EC and the U.S. sent the arbitrators a joint communication saying, "The EC and the US would like to inform you that they are engaged in constructive discussions with a view to finding a solution to this dispute. Therefore, the EC and the US would respectfully request the Arbitrator to suspend the arbitration proceeding." The arbitrator therefore suspended the arbitration. *Recourse by the United States to Article 22.6 of the DSU*, WT/DS160/22 (WTO 1 March 2002).

That is where the case stands, as this book goes to press. To satisfy the United States' obligations under the settlement, Congress has appropriated, for payment to the E.C., what is now $3.3 million ($1.1 million a year for three years). Eventually, it must repeal the Fairness in Music Licensing Act too. Representative Sensenbrenner is not a member of the House Appropriations Committee (let alone its Chair), so appropriating the needed $3.3 million in settlement funds was possible. On the other hand, since repeal of the Act will have to be blessed by the Judiciary Committee, that's unlikely to happen until Sensenbrenner retires, is defeated for re-election, or Democrats retake control of the House.

---

### 1.4.3 Applicable Law

**Turner Entertainment Co. v. Huston**
**Court of Appeal of Versailles France (1994)**

. . .

I

1. The cinematographic work entitled "Asphalt Jungle" was produced in 1950 in the United States by the Metro Goldwyn Mayer (MGM) company, a division of Loew's Inc. The film was shot in black and white by the late John Huston, a movie director of American nationality, at the time bound by a contract of employment to Loew's Inc., and co-author of the screenplay with Ben Maddow, bound to the same company by a contract as a salaried writer.

2. On 2nd May 1950, Loew's Inc. obtained from the U.S. Copyright Office a certificate of registration of its rights to the film. This registration was duly renewed in 1977. On 26th September 1986 the benefit of this registration was transferred to the Turner Entertainment Co. by virtue of a merger with MGM, including transfer of the ownership of MGM's movie library and connected rights.

3. The Turner company had the movie colorized, an operation which on 20th June 1988 resulted in registration of a copyright application, and it enabled the Fifth French Television Channel (La Cinq) to announce that it would broadcast this colorized version at 8:30 p.m. on 26th June 1988.

4. The broadcast was objected to by John Huston's heirs, Angelica, Daniel and Walter Huston, who were subsequently joined by Mr Ben Maddow, the Societe des Auteurs et Compositeurs Dramatiques (SACD), the Societe des Realisateurs de Films (SRF), the Syndicat Frangais des Artistes Interpretes (SFA), the Federation Europeenne des Relisateurs de l'Audiovisuel (FERA), the Syndicat Frangais des Realisateurs de Television CGT and the Syndicat National des Techniciens de la Production Cinematographique et de Television. They opposed the broadcast because they deemed it a violation of the author's moral right, aggravated in their opinion by the fact that John Huston had opposed colorization of his works during his life.

5. The dispute thus arising with La Cinq and the Turner Entertainment Co. (TEC) resulted in France in the following decisions:

a) An order in summary proceedings on 24th June 1988, confirmed by a judgment of the Court of Appeal of Paris on 25th June 1988, which suspended the broadcast of the colorized film as being likely to cause unacceptable and irreparable damage;

b) On 23rd November 1988 the Court of First Instance of Paris judged as follows:

"Declares the action of Messrs and Mrs Huston and Mr Ben Maddow and the voluntary intervention of TEC admissible insofar as they are limited to the television broadcasting of the colorized version of the film entitled 'Asphalt Jungle'; Declares the claims of the secondary voluntary intervenors admissible; Formally takes cognizance of the fact that Societe d'Exploitation de la Cinquieme Chaine has abandoned its plans for broadcasting the colorized version of the film entitled 'Asphalt Jungle'; As necessary forbids it from broadcasting this version on television; Dismisses all other claims; Dismisses the claim of the TEC company."

In admitting the claim, this judgment referred in substance to the Universal Copyright Convention signed in Geneva on 6th September 1952, ratified by the United States, to deduce that this convention provides citizens of member States in France with the benefit of the Law of 11th March 1957, notably Section 6, which provides that the moral right is attached to the person and is perpetual, inalienable and imprescribable. Thus it distinguished between this moral right and the economic rights held by the Turner company to the work, notably under contracts signed with John Huston and Ben Maddow.

Finally, it held that John Huston and Ben Maddow, by their art, had imbued their work with an original and personal character and that, because Huston's renown is based on the interplay of black and white, creating an atmosphere, the said atmosphere would be jeopardized by colorization.

c) The Court of Appeal of Paris, appealed to by the Turner company, judged as follows on 6th July 1989:

"States that the author of the film entitled 'Asphalt Jungle' is the Turner company and that the heirs of John Huston as well as Ben Maddow have no moral right to this work shot in black and white; Notes that the colorized version of the said film is an adaptation, under U.S. law, for which the Turner company obtained a registration certificate on 20th June 1988; States that the principle of colorization could not be criticized by the heirs of John Huston and by Ben Maddow, even if they could claim a moral right to the black and white film; Accordingly, reversing the judgment, Dismisses the claims of the heirs of John Huston and Ben Maddow and judges admissible but unfounded the interventions of the six legal entities supporting their claims; Authorizes the Fifth Channel to broadcast the colorized version of the film entitled 'Asphalt Jungle,' formally recognizing the cognizance petitioned for."

The judgment further provided for various warning notices intended for television viewers, with respect to the possibility of using the color control device and respect for the memory of John Huston.

In reversing the judgment against which the appeal was brought, the Court of Appeal of Paris settled the conflict of laws in favor of U.S. law, the law of the first publication of the work having, according to said court, granted the status of author solely to Loew's, which cannot be defeated by the Berne Convention, effective from 1st March 1989, which is an instrument to harmonize relations between the member countries and is not competent to affect acquired rights or the effect of contracts between producer and director. Moreover, it dismissed the exception according to which the French conception of international law was violated and held that the copyright granted to the "derivative work" transferred in 1988 to the Turner company made it impossible for Messrs and Mrs Huston and Mr Maddow to raise it if they had a moral right to claim.

6. Messrs and Mrs Huston and Mr Maddow and the intervenors appealed against this judgment of the Court of Appeal of Paris to the Cour de Cassation.

In a ruling dated 28th May 1991, the Supreme Court reversed and cancelled every provision of the judgment of the Court of Appeal for violation of Section 1.2 of Law 64-689 of 8th July 1964 and Section 6 of the Law of 11th March 1957, stating: "According to the first of these texts, the integrity of a literary or art work cannot be affected in France, regardless of the State in whose territory the said work was made public for the first time. The person who is its author, by its creation alone, enjoys the moral right stipulated in his favor by the second of the aforesaid texts; these are laws of mandatory application."

II

1. The Turner Entertainment Co. duly referred the case to the Court of Appeal of Versailles, appointed as Court of Remand, and petitioned it to reverse the judgment of the Court of First Instance of Paris, to judge that the claims of Messrs and Mrs Huston are inadmissible or that they have in any case no grounds to claim the moral right to which they refer and therefore to dismiss their case and all other intervenors. It also claims as follows:

In support of its argument of inadmissibility, that Messrs and Mrs Huston cannot claim the status of foreign author, which is reserved for the Turner company under the laws applicable at the place of creation and the agreements governed by them; that they are therefore not entitled to claim French law, under the Geneva Convention, in order to protect themselves and exercise rights which they have not acquired;

That it is in any event the recognized holder of the patrimonial rights of the authors and that it was therefore entitled to introduce the colorized version by applying a technique which does not alter the essence of the work.

2. Messrs and Mrs Huston and Mr Maddow petitioned the Court of Remand to confirm the judgment of the Court of First Instance of Paris, further petitioning the court to add that the broadcasting of the colorized version of the film entitled

"Asphalt Jungle" has violated their moral right and thus to order the Turner company to pay them FRF 1,000,000 by way of damages and costs and a further FRF 100,000 under Section 700 of the New Code of Civil Procedure; thus:

They oppose that French law alone is competent to determine the status of author, as pointed out by the Cour de Cassation in a decision which stresses the importance of moral right and results in dismissal of the law applicable to the agreement between director and producer; and that their claim is therefore admissible;

That black and white is the form of expression in which the authors and especially John Huston have delivered their esthetic conception to the public; that colorization therefore alters the very essence of the work, of which it is no "adaptation" at all but a "transformation" or "modification"; that, moreover, John Huston was formally opposed to this during his life.

3. Societe des Auteurs et Compositeurs Dramatiques (SACD) intervened voluntarily and joined itself to the submissions of Messrs and Mrs Huston, whose claims it supports in application of Section 3.1 of its bylaws and Section 65, paragraph 2 of the Law of 11th March 1957 and Section 38 of the Law of 3rd July 1985.

4. Societe des Realisateurs de Films (SRF), Syndicat Francais des Artistes Interpretes (SFA), Federation Europeenne des Realisateurs de I'Audiovisuel (FERA), Syndicat Francais des Realisateurs de Television CGT and Syndicat National des Techniciens de la Production Cinematographique et de Television pleaded the same and claimed FRF 10,000 from the Turner company by virtue of Section 700 of the New Code of Civil Procedure. . . .

6. Maitre Pierrel ex-officio petitioned the court to declare his appeal admissible and well-founded, to take formal cognizance of the fact that La Cinq, in accordance with the judgment of the Court of Appeal of Paris on 6th July 1989, broadcast the film accompanied by the ordered notices, to reverse the referred judgment of the Court of First Instance of Paris and, judging again, to judge that Messrs and Mrs Huston and Mr Maddow do not have status as the film's authors and that they cannot claim in France the benefit of the moral right, to judge secondarily that colorization is in principle a legal adaptation and does not violate any moral right, to dismiss the claims of the opponents and to order Messrs and Mrs Huston and Mr Maddow to pay them FRF 30,000 by virtue of Section 700 of the New Code of Civil Procedure. He thus reiterated the arguments already produced by the Turner company, stressing that John Huston could not be unaware of the fact that he did not have the status of an author by virtue of the law governing the contracts signed with the producer.

7. The Turner Entertainment Co. maintained its initial claims, notably on the inadmissibility of the opponents' claims in submissions in answer to which it maintains:

That it is the constant rule in private international law that the situation is governed by the law of the place where it occurs; that, therefore, the status of author of an art work is the status recognized in the country where the work has been created, i.e. in this case the United States of America; that this means Loew's Inc., to which the rights have been transferred;

That the Court of Remand is not bound by the judgment of the Cour de Cassation, criticized by an authorized doctrine;

That, in fact, the Law of 8th July 1964, incorporated as Section L 111-4 in the Code of Intellectual Property, does not apply in that it assumes that the foreign State does not provide French works with adequate and effective protection, which is not the case in the United States; that the second paragraph of Section 1 of this law, which alone is referred to in the judgment of the Cour de Cassation, is not severable;

That, lastly, the Geneva Convention does not govern the formation of rights and the pre-existing status of author, for which it only organizes protection;

That, secondarily, the Cour de Cassation has not pronounced itself on the violation of the moral right alleged to result from the colorization and that this violation has not been shown.

8. SACD opposed in replication the submissions produced ex-officio by Me Pierrel and maintained its claims as an intervenor.

9. In their turn, Messrs and Mrs Huston and Mr Maddow replicated as follows:

That the Cour de Cassation found for a solution which alone enables the authors to exercise their moral right in France; that this position complies with Section 14 bis 2 of the Berne Convention, which provides for application of the law of the country of protection in designating the holder of the rights to a cinematographic work;

That U.S. law only protects economic rights, wherefore the Law of 8th July 1964 remains applicable for lack of reciprocal agreements on moral right;

That, contrary to the submissions of the Turner company, colorization violates the moral right retained.

They furthermore petitioned the court to take cognizance of the violation of the authors' moral right by La Cinq's broadcasting of the "colorized" film and to order Me Pierrel ex-officio to pay them one million francs in damages and costs on this ground.

10. In its rejoinder, the Turner Entertainment Co. petitioned the court again to judge that Messrs and Mrs Huston and Mr Maddow cannot claim the benefit of the Berne Convention and Law of 8th July 1985, which have no retroactive application, to dismiss application of the Law of 8th July 1964 because of the protection afforded by U.S. law for every attribute of copyright; to judge

That colorization is by its nature an adaptation in the meaning of the law and to grant it the benefit of its earlier submissions;

That ratification by the United States of the Berne Convention postdates the disputed situation by a considerable time;

That, contrary to the ground produced by Messrs and Mrs Huston and Mr Maddow, U.S. caselaw sanctions violation of the integrity or authorship of a work, which excludes application of the Law of 8th July 1964;

That the Law of 3rd July 1985 cannot be claimed whereas it is not disputed that the Turner company is the holder of the patrimonial rights, including the right to adapt the work and therefore to introduce a colorized version.

11. The closing order was pronounced on 17th February 1994.

III . . .

3. The Turner company first opposes to Messrs and Mrs Huston and Mr Maddow and the intervenors that U.S. law should be applied to determine who has the status of the film's author; it designates the producer, i.e. Loew's Inc., which obtained the copyright on 2nd May 1950 and whose rights, renewed on 2nd May 1977, were transferred to the Turner company; the action of Messrs and Mrs Huston and Mr Maddow to protect rights which they have not acquired is therefore not admissible.

4. But the judges in first instance correctly stressed the "very different conceptions" of U.S. and French laws, the first focusing exclusively on the protection of economic rights without referring to the creative act underlying the inalienable moral right recognized by French law, viz. Section 6 of the Law of 11th

March 1957, at the time applicable, which provides that "the author enjoys the right to respect for his name, his status, his work this right is attached to his person it is perpetual, inalienable and imprescribable it is transmitted after death to the author's heirs."

John Huston and Ben Maddow, of whom it is not disputed that the first is the co-author of the screenplay and the director of the film entitled "Asphalt Jungle" and the second the co-author of the same film, as already referred to under (I-1), are in fact its authors, having created it, and whereas they are therefore, in the meaning of the aforesaid law, vested with the corresponding moral right, which is part of public law and therefore mandatorily protected.

5. Section 1 of Law No 64-689 of 8th July 1964 on the application of the principle of reciprocity with respect to copyright provides as follows:

"Subject to the provisions of the international conventions to which France is a party, in the event that it is noted, after consultation of the Minister of Foreign Affairs, that a State does not provide adequate and effective protection for works disclosed for the first time in France, irrespective of the form thereof, works disclosed for the first time in the territory of the said State shall not benefit from the copyright protection recognized by French law. However, the integrity or authorship of such works may not be violated. In the case provided for in paragraph 1 heretofore, royalties shall be paid to organizations of general interest designated by decree."

The defect in protection thus likely to affect the foreign work on the conditions governing reciprocity, as laid out in paragraph 1, can only concern its economic aspects, i.e., the patrimonial rights attached thereto, in that it is limited by the general mandatory rule providing for respect of an author's moral right as proclaimed without reservation in paragraph 2.

6. It follows that the moral rights attached to the person of the creators of the work entitled "Asphalt Jungle" could not be transferred and, therefore, the judges in first instance correctly ruled that Messrs and Mrs Huston and Ben Maddow were entitled to claim recognition and protection thereof in France.

7. However, the Turner company, which it is not disputed is the holder of the author's economic rights, maintains that these rights include the right to adapt the work and therefore to colorize the film entitled "Asphalt Jungle," arguing that it cannot be maintained that this denatures the work; Me Pierrel, ex-officio, follows the same argument, submitting that the colorized version of the film is merely an adaptation of the original black-and-white version which is left intact and is therefore not affected.

8. However, "colorization" is a technique based on the use of computer and laser and it makes it possible, after transferring the original black-and-white tape onto a videographic media, to give color to a film which did not originally have color; the application of this process is in no event to be considered an adaptation, defined as "an original work both in its expression and in its composition," even if it borrows formal elements from the pre-existing work; colorization, far from meeting these criteria, in fact merely consists in modifying the work by adding an element thus far not part of the creator's aesthetic conception.

9. The judges in first instance in the present case have precisely pointed out that the aesthetic conception which earned John Huston his great fame is based on the interplay of black and white, which enabled him to create an atmosphere according to which he directed the actor and selected the backdrops; moreover, he expressed himself clearly about his film entitled "The Maltese Falcon" when stating, "I wanted to shoot it in black and white like a sculptor chooses to work in clay, to pour his work in bronze, to sculpt in marble."

In 1950, while color film technique was already widespread and another option was available, the film entitled "Asphalt Jungle" was shot in black and white, following a deliberate aesthetic choice, according to a process which its authors considered best suited to the character of the work.

10. Therefore, the film's colorization without authorization and control by the authors or their heirs amounted to violation of the creative activity of its makers, even if it should satisfy the expectations of a certain public for commercially obvious reasons; the use of this process without the agreement of Messrs and Mrs Huston and Ben Maddow infringed the moral right of the authors as mandatorily protected under French law; Messrs and Mrs Huston and Ben Maddow have therefore good grounds to petition the court for reparation of their prejudice at the hands of the Turner company, and they will therefore be allotted FRF 400,000 by way of damages and costs for the damage done; moreover, the judges in first instance correctly recognized their right to demand that La Cinq SA be forbidden to broadcast the modified version of the film entitled "Asphalt Jungle."

11. It is constant that, contrary to the act required by the Court of First Instance, La Cinq SA broadcast the colorized version of the film entitled "Asphalt Jungle" further to a judgment by the Court of Appeal of Paris, quashed by the Cour de Cassation on the conditions reiterated under (I-5); this broadcasting is also a direct and definite violation of the moral right whose protection was demanded by Messrs and Mrs Huston and Ben Maddow, who are also wellfounded to demand reparation on this head; the Court has the elements needed to allot them the sum of FRF 200,000 by reversing the referred judgment on the pronounced cognizance. . . .

. . .[T]he . . . consideration of equity prompts the allotment, in application of the said Section 700 of the New Code of Civil Procedure, of FRF 60,000 to Messrs and Mrs Huston and Ben Maddow and FRF 2,000 each to SRF, SFA, FERA, Syndicat Francais des Realisateurs de Television CGT and Syndicat National des Techniciens de la Production Cinematographique et de Television.

On these grounds:

The Court, judging publicly, after hearing all parties and in last instance as Court of Remand; Pursuant to the closing order pronounced on 17th February 1994;

1. Declares that the Turner Entertainment Co. was entitled to petition the Court of Referral;

2. Declares admissible the interventions, before the same court, of Societe des Auteurs et Compositeurs Dramatiques (SACD), Societe des Realisateurs de Films (SRF), Syndicat Francais des Artistes Interpretes (SFA), Federation Europeenne des Realisateurs de I'Audiovisuel (FERA), Syndicat Frangcis des Realisateurs de Television CGT and Syndicat National des Techniciens de la Production Cinematographique et de Television; . . .

4. Confirms the judgment pronounced on 23rd November 1988 by the Court of First Instance of Paris, subject to the cognizance and the provisions dismissing application of Section 700 of the New Code of Civil Procedure in favor of Messrs and Mrs Huston and Ben Maddow and the secondary intervenors;

Judging again and adding:

5. States that the colorization of the film entitled "Asphalt Jungle" by the Turner Entertainment Co. and its broadcasting by La Cinq SA in this version, contrary to the will of the authors or their heirs, has violated their moral right;

6. Orders the Turner Entertainment Co. to pay Messrs and Mrs Huston and Ben Maddow Four Hundred Thousand French Francs (FRF 400,000) by way of damages and costs;

7. Orders Maitre Pierrel, ex-officio as court-appointed liquidator of Societe d'Exploitation de la Cinquieme Chaine (La Cinq SA) to pay them Two Hundred Thousand French Francs (FRF 200,000) in damages and costs; . . .

9. Orders it jointly and severally with the Turner Entertainment Co. to pay Messrs and Mrs Huston and Ben Maddow Sixty Thousand French Francs (FRF 60,000) under the same Section 700 of the New Code of Civil Procedure and to pay Two Thousand (FRF 2,000) to each of the intervenors referred to under (2), except SACD, which has lodged no claim in this respect;

10. Orders it further, jointly and severally with the Turner Entertainment Co., to bear the full cost of the appeal. . . .

This Judgment was pronounced and signed by: Mr Thavaud, President [and] Mrs Clem, District Registrar

---

**Itar-Tass Russian News Agency v. Russian Kurier, Inc.**
**153 F.3d 82 (2nd Cir. 1998)**

Jon O. Newman, Circuit Judge:

This appeal primarily presents issues concerning the choice of law in international copyright cases and the substantive meaning of Russian copyright law as to the respective rights of newspaper reporters and newspaper publishers. The conflicts issue is which country's law applies to issues of copyright ownership and to issues of infringement. The primary substantive issue under Russian copyright law is whether a newspaper publishing company has an interest sufficient to give it standing to sue for copying the text of individual articles appearing in its newspapers, or whether complaint about such copying may be made only by the reporters who authored the articles. Defendants-appellants Russian Kurier, Inc. ("Kurier") and Oleg Pogrebnoy (collectively "the Kurier defendants") appeal from the March 25, 1997, judgment of the District Court for the Southern District of New York (John G. Koeltl, Judge) enjoining them from copying articles that have appeared or will appear in publications of the plaintiffs-appellees, mainly Russian newspapers and a Russian news agency, and awarding the appellees substantial damages for copyright infringement.

On the conflicts issue, we conclude that, with respect to the Russian plaintiffs, Russian law determines the ownership and essential nature of the copyrights alleged to have been infringed and that United States law determines whether those copyrights have been infringed in the United States and, if so, what remedies are available. We also conclude that Russian law, which explicitly excludes newspapers from a work-for-hire doctrine, vests exclusive ownership interests in newspaper articles in the journalists who wrote the articles, not in the newspaper employers who compile their writings. We further conclude that to the extent that Russian law accords newspaper publishers an interest distinct from the copyright of the newspaper reporters, the publishers' interest, like the usual ownership interest in a compilation, extends to the publishers' original selection and arrangement of the articles, and does not entitle the publishers to damages for copying the texts of articles contained in a newspaper compilation. We therefore reverse the judgment to the extent that it granted the newspapers relief for copying the texts of the articles. However, because one non-newspaper plaintiff-appellee is entitled to some injunctive relief and damages and other plaintiffs-appellees may be entitled to some, perhaps considerable, relief, we also remand for further consideration of this lawsuit.

*Background*

The lawsuit concerns Kurier, a Russian language weekly newspaper with a circulation in the New York area of about 20,000. It is published in New York City by defendant Kurier. Defendant Pogrebnoy is president and sole shareholder of Kurier and editor-in-chief of Kurier. The plaintiffs include corporations that publish, daily or weekly, major Russian language newspapers in Russia and Russian language magazines in Russia or Israel; Itar-Tass Russian News Agency ("Itar-Tass"), formerly known as the Telegraph Agency of the Soviet Union (TASS), a wire service and news gathering company centered in Moscow, functioning similarly to the Associated Press; and the Union of Journalists of Russia ("UJR"), the professional writers union of accredited print and broadcast journalists of the Russian Federation.

The Kurier defendants do not dispute that Kurier has copied about 500 articles that first appeared in the plaintiffs' publications or were distributed by Itar-Tass. The copied material, though extensive, was a small percentage of the total number of articles published in Kurier. The Kurier defendants also do not dispute how the copying occurred: articles from the plaintiffs' publications, sometimes containing headlines, pictures, bylines, and graphics, in addition to text, were cut out, pasted on layout sheets, and sent to Kurier's printer for photographic reproduction and printing in the pages of Kurier.

Most significantly, the Kurier defendants also do not dispute that, with one exception, they had not obtained permission from any of the plaintiffs to copy the articles that appeared in Kurier. Pogrebnoy claimed at trial to have received permission from the publisher of one newspaper, but his claim was rejected by the District Court at trial. Pogrebnoy also claimed that he had obtained permission from the authors of six of the copied articles. The District Court made no finding as to whether this testimony was credible, since authors' permission was not pertinent to the District Court's view of the legal issues.

*Preliminary injunction ruling.* After a hearing in May 1995, the District Court issued a preliminary injunction, prohibiting the Kurier defendants from copying the "works" of four plaintiff news organizations. Since the Court's analysis framed the key issue that would be considered at trial and is raised on appeal, the Court's opinion and the Russian statutory provisions relied on need to be explained.

Preliminarily, the Court ruled that the request for a preliminary injunction concerned articles published after March 13, 1995, the date that Russia acceded to the Berne Convention. The Court then ruled that the copied works were "Berne Convention works," 17 U.S.C. § 101, and that the plaintiffs' rights were to be determined according to Russian copyright law.

The Court noted that under Russian copyright law authors of newspaper articles retain the copyright in their articles unless there has been a contractual assignment to their employer or some specific provision of law provides that the author's rights vest in the employer. Since the defendants alleged no claim of a contractual assignment, the Court next considered the provision of the 1993 Russian Federation Law on Copyright and Neighboring Rights ("Russian Copyright Law") (World Intellectual Property Organization (WIPO) translation) concerning what the United States Copyrights Act calls "works made for hire," 17 U.S.C. § 201(b). See Russian Copyright Law, Art. 14(2). That provision gives employers the exclusive right to "exploit" the "service-related work" produced by employees in the scope of their employment, absent some contractual arrangement. However, the Court noted, Article 14(4) specifies that subsection 2 does not apply to various categories of works, including newspapers. Accepting the view of plaintiffs' expert, Professor Vratislav Pechota, Judge Koeltl therefore ruled that the Russian version of the work-for-hire doctrine in Article 14(2), though exempting newspapers, applies to press agencies, like Itar-Tass.

Turning to the rights of the newspapers, Judge Koeltl relied on Article 11, captioned "Copyright of Compiler of Collections and Other Works." This Article contains two sub-sections. Article 11(1) specifies the rights of compilers generally:

The author of a collection or any other composite work (compiler) shall enjoy copyright in the selection or arrangement of subject matter that he has made insofar as that selection or arrangement is the result of a creative effort of compilation.

The compiler shall enjoy copyright subject to respect for the rights of the authors of each work included in the composite work.

Each of the authors of the works included in the composite work shall have the right to exploit his own work independently of the composite work unless the author's contract provides otherwise. . . . .

Article 11(2), the interpretation of which is critical to this appeal, specifies the rights of compilers of those works that are excluded from the work-for-hire provision of Article 14(2):

The exclusive right to exploit encyclopedias, encyclopedic dictionaries, collections of scientific works – published in either one or several installments – newspapers, reviews and other periodical publications shall belong to the editor thereof. The editor shall have the right to mention his name or to demand such mention whenever the said publications are exploited.

The authors of the works included in the said publications shall retain the exclusive rights to exploit their works independently of the publication of the whole work. Art. 11(2).

In another translation of the Russian Copyright Law, which was in evidence at the trial, the last phrase of Article 11(2) was rendered "independently from the publication as a whole." Russian Copyright Law, Art. 11(2) (Newton Davis translation). Because the parties' experts focused on the phrase "as a whole" in the Davis translation of Article 11(2), we will rely on the Davis translation for the rendering of this key phrase of Article 11(2), but all other references to the Russian Copyright Law will be to the WIPO translation.

The District Court acknowledged, as the plaintiffs' expert had stated, that considerable scholarly debate existed in Russia as to the nature of a publisher's right "in a work as a whole." Judge Koeltl accepted Professor Pechota's view that the newspaper could prevent infringing activity "sufficient to interfere with the publisher's interest in the integrity of the work." Without endeavoring to determine what extent of copying would "interfere with" the "integrity of the work," Judge Koeltl concluded that a preliminary injunction was warranted because what Kurier had copied was "the creative effort of the newspapers in the compilation of articles including numerous articles for the same issues, together with headlines and photographs." The Court's preliminary injunction opinion left it unclear whether at trial the plaintiffs could obtain damages only for copying the newspapers' creative efforts as a compiler, such as the selection and arrangement of articles, the creation of headlines, and the layout of text and graphics, or also for copying the text of individual articles.

*Expert testimony at trial.* At trial, this unresolved issue was the focus of conflicting expert testimony. The plaintiffs' expert witness at trial was Michael Newcity, coordinator for the Center for Slavic, Eurasian and East European Studies at Duke University and an adjunct member of the faculty at the Duke University Law School. He opined that Article 11(2) gave the newspapers rights to redress copying not only of the publication "as a whole," but also of individual articles. He acknowledged that the reporters retained copyrights in the articles that they authored, but stated that Article 11(2) created a regime of parallel exclusive rights in both the newspaper publisher and the reporter. He rejected the contention that exclusive rights could not exist in two parties, pointing out that co-authors shared exclusive rights to their joint work.

Newcity offered two considerations in support of his position. First, he cited the predecessor of Article 11(2), Article 485 of the Russian Civil Code of 1964. That provision was similar to Article 11(2), with one change that became the subject of major disagreement among the expert witnesses. Article 485 had given compilers, including newspaper publishers, the right to exploit their works "as a whole." The 1993 revision deleted "as a whole" from the first paragraph of the predecessor of Article 11(2), where it had modified the scope of the compiler's right, and moved the phrase to the second paragraph of revised Article 11(2), where it modifies the reserved right of the authors of articles within a compilation to exploit their works "independently of the publication as a whole."

Though Newcity opined that even under Article 485, reprinting of "one or two or three, at most," articles from a newspaper would have constituted infringement of the copyright "as a whole," he rested his reading of Article 11(2) significantly on the fact that the 1993 revision dropped the phrase "as a whole" from the paragraph that specified the publisher's right. This deletion, he contended, eliminated whatever ambiguity might have existed in the first paragraph of Article 485.

Second, Newcity referred to an opinion of the Judicial Chamber for Informational Disputes of the President of the Russian Federation ("Informational Disputes Chamber"), issued on June 8, 1995. That opinion had been sought by the editor-in-chief of one of the plaintiffs in this litigation, Moskovskie Novosti (Moscow News), who specifically called the tribunal's attention to the pending litigation between Russian media organizations and the publisher of Kurier. The Informational Disputes Chamber stated, in response to one of the questions put to it, "In the event of a violation of its rights, including the improper printing of one or two articles, the publisher [of a newspaper] has the right to petition a court for defense of its rights."

Defendants' experts presented a very different view of the rights of newspapers. Professor Peter B. Maggs of the University of Illinois, Urbana-Champaign, College of Law, testifying by deposition, pointed out that Article 11(2) gives authors the exclusive rights to their articles and accords newspaper publishers only the "exclusive rights to the publication as a whole, because that's the only thing not reserved to the authors." He opined that a newspaper's right to use of the compiled work "as a whole" would be infringed by the copying of an entire issue of a newspaper and probably by copying a substantial part of one issue, but not by the copying of a few articles, since the copyright in the articles belongs to the reporters. He also disagreed with Newcity's contention that exclusive rights to individual articles belonged simultaneously to both the newspaper and the reporter. Exclusive rights, he maintained, cannot be held by two people, except in the case of co-authors, who have jointly held rights against the world.

The defendants' first expert witness at trial was Michael Solton, who has worked in Moscow and Washington as an associate of the Steptoe & Johnson law firm. Under Article 11, he testified, authors retain exclusive rights to their articles in compilations, the compiler acquires a copyright in the selection and creative arrangement of materials in the compilation, and a newspaper publisher typically acquires the limited rights of the compiler by assignment from the compiler. The publisher, he said, does not acquire any rights to the individual articles. Solton declined to attach any significance to the decision issued by the Informational Disputes Chamber because, he explained, the bylaws of that body accord it authority only over limited matters concerning the mass media and explicitly preclude it from adjudicating matters that Russian law refers to courts of the Russian Federation, such as copyright law.

The defendants' second expert trial witness was Svetlana Rozina, a partner of the Lex International law firm, who has consulted for the Russian government. She wrote the first draft of what became the 1993 revision of the Russian Copyright Law. She also testified that authors of works in compilations retain the exclusive right to their works, and that publishers of compilations do not have any rights to individual articles. Turning to the change in the placement of the phrase "as a whole" from Article 11(1) to Article 11(2), she explained that no substantive change was intended; the shift was made "for the purpose of Russian grammar." She also agreed with Solton that the Informational Disputes Chamber renders advice on matters concerning freedom of mass information and lacks the competence to adjudicate issues of copyright law.

*Trial ruling.* The District Court resolved the dispute among the experts by accepting Newcity's interpretation of Russian copyright law. As he had previously ruled in granting the preliminary injunction, Judge Koeltl recognized that newspapers acquire no rights to individual articles by virtue of Article 14 since the Russian version of the work-for-hire doctrine is inapplicable to newspapers. Nevertheless, Judge Koeltl accepted Newcity's view of Article 11, relying on both the movement of the phrase "as a whole" from the first paragraph of Article 11(2) to the second paragraph of Article 11(2), and the opinion of the Informational Disputes Chamber. He also reasoned that publishers have "the real economic incentive to prevent wholesale unauthorized copying," and that, in the absence of assignments of rights to individual articles, widespread copying would occur if publishers could not prevent Kurier's infringements.

The District Court estimated Kurier's profits during the relevant years at $2 million and found that 25 percent of these profits were attributable to the copied articles. The Court therefore awarded the plaintiffs $500,000 in actual damages against Kurier and Pogrebnoy. The Court also ruled that the plaintiffs were entitled to statutory damages with respect to 28 articles for which the plaintiffs had obtained United States copyright registrations. The Court found that the registered articles had originally appeared in 15 different publications and concluded that the plaintiffs were entitled to 15 awards of statutory damages. The Court found the violations willful, see 17 U.S.C. §504(c)(1), and set each statutory award at $2,700. However, to avoid duplicative recovery, the Court ruled that the actual and statutory damages could not be aggregated and afforded the plaintiffs their choice of whether to receive statutory damages (offsetting the statutory award from the actual damages award) or actual damages. The Court awarded $3,934 in total damages against defendant Linco Printing, which prints Kurier; this sum comprised actual damages of $1,017, reduced to $934 to avoid partial duplication with statutory damages, plus $3,000 in statutory damages.

*Discussion*

*I. Choice of Law*

The threshold issue concerns the choice of law for resolution of this dispute. That issue was not initially considered by the parties, all of whom turned directly to Russian law for resolution of the case. Believing that the conflicts issue merited consideration, we requested supplemental briefs from the parties and appointed Professor William F. Patry as Amicus Curiae. Prof. Patry has submitted an extremely helpful brief on the choice of law issue.

Choice of law issues in international copyright cases have been largely ignored in the reported decisions and dealt with rather cursorily by most commentators.

Examples pertinent to the pending appeal are those decisions involving a work created by the employee of a foreign corporation. Several courts have applied the United States work-for-hire doctrine, see 17 U.S.C. § 201(b), without explicit consideration of the conflicts issue. See, e.g., Aldon Accessories Ltd. v. Spiegel, Inc., 738 F.2d 548, 551-53 (2d Cir. 1984) (U.S. law applied to determine if statuettes crafted abroad were works for hire); Dae Han Video Productions, Inc. v. Kuk Dong Oriental Food, Inc., 1990 U.S. Dist. LEXIS 18329, 19 U.S.P.Q.2D (BNA) 1294 (D. Md. 1990) (U.S. law applied to determine if scripts written abroad were works for hire); P & D International v. Halsey Publishing Co., 672 F. Supp. 1429, 1435-36 (S.D. Fla. 1987) (U.S. work for hire law assumed to apply). Other courts have applied foreign law. See Frink America, Inc. v. Champion Road Machinery Ltd., 961 F. Supp. 398 (N.D.N.Y. 1997) (Canadian copyright law applied on issue of ownership); Greenwich Film Productions v. DRG Records Inc., 1992 U.S. Dist. LEXIS 14770, 1992 WL 279, at *357 (S.D.N.Y. 1992) (French law applied to determine ownership of right to musical work commissioned in France for French film); Dae Han Video Production Inc. v. Dong San Chun, 1990 U.S. Dist. LEXIS 18496, 17 U.S.P.Q.2D (BNA) 1306, 1310 n.6 (E.D. Va. 1990) (foreign law relied on to determine that alleged licensor lacks rights); see also Autoskill, Inc. v. National Educational Support Systems, Inc., 994 F.2d 1476, 1489 n.16 (10th Cir. 1993) (U.S. work for hire law applied where claim that contrary Canadian law should apply was belatedly raised and for that reason not considered); Pepe (U.K.) Ltd. v. Grupo Pepe Ltda., 1992 U.S. Dist. LEXIS 17144, 24 U.S.P.Q.2D (BNA) 1354, 1356 (S.D. Fla. 1992) (congruent foreign and U.S. law both applied). In none of these cases, however, was the issue of choice of law explicitly adjudicated. The conflicts issue was identified but ruled not necessary to be resolved in Greenwich Film Productions S.A. v. D.R.G. Records, Inc., 1992 U.S. Dist. LEXIS 14770, 25 U.S.P.Q.2D (BNA) 1435, 1437-38 (S.D.N.Y. 1992).

The Nimmer treatise briefly (and perhaps optimistically) suggests that conflicts issues "have rarely proved troublesome in the law of copyright." See Nimmer on Copyright § 17.05 (1998) ("Nimmer") (footnote omitted). Relying on the "national treatment" principle of the Berne Convention and the Universal Copyright Convention ("U.C.C."), Nimmer asserts, correctly in our view, that "an author who is a national of one of the member states of either Berne or the U.C.C., or one who first publishes his work in any such member state, is entitled to the same copyright protection in each other member state as such other state accords to its own nationals." Id. (footnotes omitted). Nimmer then somewhat overstates the national treatment principle: "The applicable law is the copyright law of the state in which the infringement occurred, not that of the state of which the author is a national, or in which the work is first published." Id. (footnote omitted). The difficulty with this broad statement is that it subsumes under the phrase "applicable law" the law concerning two distinct issues ownership and substantive rights, i.e., scope of protection. Another commentator has also broadly stated the principle of national treatment, but described its application in a way that does not necessarily cover issues of ownership. "The principle of national treatment also means that both the question of whether the right exists and the question of the scope of the right are to be answered in accordance with the law of the country where the protection is claimed." S.M. Stewart, International Copyright and Neighboring Rights § 3.17 (2d ed. 1989). We agree with the view of the Amicus that the Convention's principle of national treatment simply assures that if the law of the country of infringement applies to the scope of substantive copyright protection, that law will be applied uniformly to foreign and domestic authors. See Murray v. British Broadcasting Corp., 906 F. Supp. 858 (S.D.N.Y. 1995), aff'd, 81 F.3d 287 (1996).

*Source of conflicts rules.* Our analysis of the conflicts issue begins with consideration of the source of law for selecting a conflicts rule. Though Nimmer turns directly to the Berne Convention and the U.C.C., we think that step moves too quickly past the Berne Convention Implementation Act of 1988, Pub L. 100-568, 102 Stat. 2853, 17 U.S.C.A. § 101 note. Section 4(a)(3) of the Act amends Title 17 to provide: "No right or interest in a work eligible for protection under this title may be claimed by virtue of . . . the provisions of the Berne Convention . . . . Any rights in a work eligible for protection under this title that derive from this title . . . shall not be expanded or reduced by virtue of . . . the provisions of the Berne Convention." 17 U.S.C. § 104(c).

We start our analysis with the Copyrights Act itself, which contains no provision relevant to the pending case concerning conflicts issues.[10] [n10 The recently added provision concerning copyright in "restored works," those that are in the public domain because of noncompliance with formalities of United States copyright law, contains an explicit subsection vesting ownership of a restored work "in the author or initial rightholder of the work as determined by the law of the *source country* of the work." 17 U.S.C. § 104A(b) (emphasis added); see id. § 104A(h)(8) (defining "source country"). This provision could be interpreted to be an example of the general conflicts approach we take in this opinion to copyright ownership issues, or an exception to some different approach. See Jane C. Ginsburg, Ownership of Electronic Rights and the Private International Law of Copyright, 22 Colum.-VLA J.L. & Arts 165, 171 (1998). We agree with Prof. Ginsburg and with the amicus, Prof. Patry, that section 104A(b) should not be understood to state an exception to any otherwise applicable conflicts rule.] We therefore fill the interstices of the Act by developing federal common law on the conflicts issue. In doing so, we are entitled to consider and apply principles of private international law, which are "'part of our law.'"

The choice of law applicable to the pending case is not necessarily the same for all issues. See Restatement (Second) of Conflict of Laws § 222 ("The courts have long recognized that they are not bound to decide all issues under the local law of a single state."). We consider first the law applicable to the issue of copyright ownership.

*Conflicts rule for issues of ownership.* Copyright is a form of property, and the usual rule is that the interests of the parties in property are determined by the law of the state with "the most significant relationship" to the property and the parties. The Restatement recognizes the applicability of this principle to intangibles such as "a literary idea." Since the works at issue were created by Russian nationals and first published in Russia, Russian law is the appropriate source of law to determine issues of ownership of rights. That is the well-reasoned conclusion of the Amicus Curiae, Prof. Patry, and the parties in their supplemental briefs are in agreement on this point. In terms of the United States Copyrights Act and its reference to the Berne Convention, Russia is the "country of origin" of these works, see 17 U.S.C. §101 (definition of "country of origin" of Berne Convention work); Berne Convention, Art. 5(4), although "country of origin" might not always be the appropriate country for purposes of choice of law concerning ownership.[11] [n11 In deciding that the law of the country of origin determines the ownership of copyright, we consider only initial ownership, and have no occasion to consider choice of law issues concerning assignments of rights. ]

To whatever extent we look to the Berne Convention itself as guidance in the development of federal common law on the conflicts issue, we find nothing to alter our conclusion. The Convention does not purport to settle issues of ownership, with one exception not relevant to this case.[12] [n12 The Berne Convention expressly provides that "ownership of copyright in a cinematographic work shall be a matter for legislation in the country where protection is claimed." Berne Convention, Art. 14bis(2)(a). With respect to other works, this provision could be understood to have any of three meanings. First, it could carry a negative implication that for other works, ownership is not to be determined by legislation in the country where protection is claimed. Second, it could be thought of as an explicit assertion for films of a general principle already applicable to other works. Third, it could be a specific provision for films that was adopted without an intention to imply anything about other works. In the absence of any indication that either the first or second meanings were intended, we prefer the third understanding.] See Jane C. Ginsburg, Ownership of Electronic Rights and the Private International Law of Copyright, 22 Colum.-VLA J.L. & Arts 165, 167-68 (1998) (The Berne Convention "provides that the law of the country where protection is claimed defines what rights are protected, the scope of the protection, and the available remedies; the treaty does not supply a choice of law rule for determining ownership.").

Selection of Russian law to determine copyright ownership is, however, subject to one procedural qualification. Under United States law, an owner (including one determined according to foreign law) may sue for infringement in a United States court only if it meets the standing test of 17 U.S.C. § 501(b), which accords standing only to the legal or beneficial owner of an "exclusive right."

*Conflicts rule for infringement issues.* On infringement issues, the governing conflicts principle is usually lex loci delicti, the doctrine generally applicable to torts. We have implicitly adopted that approach to infringement claims, applying United States copyright law to a work that was unprotected in its country of origin. See Hasbro Bradley, Inc. v. Sparkle Toys, Inc., 780 F.2d 189, 192-93 (2d Cir. 1985). In the pending case, the place of the tort is plainly the United States. To whatever extent lex loci delicti is to be considered only one part of a broader "interest" approach, United States law would still apply to infringement issues, since not only is this country the place of the tort, but also the defendant is a United States corporation.

The division of issues, for conflicts purposes, between ownership and infringement issues will not always be as easily made as the above discussion implies. If the issue is the relatively straightforward one of which of two contending parties owns a copyright, the issue is unquestionably an ownership issue, and the law of the country with the closest relationship to the work will apply to settle the ownership dispute. But in some cases, including the pending one, the issue is not simply who owns the copyright but also what is the nature of the ownership interest. Yet as a court considers the nature of an ownership interest, there is some risk that it will too readily shift the inquiry over to the issue of whether an alleged copy has infringed the asserted copyright. Whether a copy infringes depends in part on the scope of the interest of the copyright owner. Nevertheless, though the issues are related, the nature of a copyright interest is an issue distinct from the issue of whether the copyright has been infringed,. The pending case is one that requires consideration not simply of who owns an interest, but, as to the newspapers, the nature of the interest that is owned.

*II. Determination of Ownership Rights Under Russian Law*

Since United States law permits suit only by owners of "an exclusive right under a copyright," 17 U.S.C. § 501(b), we must first determine whether any of the plaintiffs own an exclusive right. That issue of ownership, as we have indicated, is to be determined by Russian law. . . .

Under Article 14 of the Russian Copyright Law, Itar-Tass is the owner of the copyright interests in the articles written by its employees. However, Article 14(4) excludes newspapers from the Russian version of the work-for-hire doctrine. The newspaper plaintiffs, therefore, must locate their ownership rights, if any, in some other source of law. They rely on Article 11. The District Court upheld their position, apparently recognizing in the newspaper publishers "exclusive" rights to the articles, even though, by virtue of Article 11(2), the reporters also retained "exclusive" rights to these articles.

Having considered all of the views presented by the expert witnesses, we conclude that the defendants' experts are far more persuasive as to the meaning of Article 11. . . . As the defendants' experts testified, Article 11 lets authors of newspaper articles sue for infringement of their rights in the text of their articles, and lets newspaper publishers sue for wholesale copying of all of the newspaper or for copying any portions of the newspaper that embody their selection, arrangement, and presentation of articles (including headlines) copying that infringes their ownership interest in the compilation. . . .

Nor can the District Court's conclusion be supported by its observation that extensive copying of newspapers will ensue unless newspapers are permitted to secure redress for the copying of individual articles. In the first place, copying of articles may always be prevented at the behest of the authors of the articles or their assignees. Second, the newspapers may well be entitled to prevent copying of the protectable elements of their compilations. Lastly, even if authors lack sufficient economic incentive to bring individual suits, as the District Court apprehended, Russian copyright law authorizes the creation of organizations "for the collective administration of the economic rights of authors . . . in cases where the individual exercise thereof is hampered by difficulties of a practical nature." Russian Copyright Law, Art. 44(1). Indeed, UJR, the reporters' organization, may well be able in this litigation to protect the rights of the reporters whose articles were copied by Kurier.

*Relief.* Our disagreement with the District Court's interpretation of Article 11 does not mean, however, that the defendants may continue copying with impunity. In the first place, Itar-Tass, as a press agency, is within the scope of Article 14, and, unlike the excluded newspapers, enjoys the benefit of the Russian version of the work-for-hire doctrine. Itar-Tass is therefore entitled to injunctive relief to prevent unauthorized copying of its articles and to damages for such copying, and the judgment is affirmed as to this plaintiff.

Furthermore, the newspaper plaintiffs, though not entitled to relief for the copying of the text of the articles they published, may well be entitled to injunctive relief and damages if they can show that Kurier infringed the publishers' ownership interests in the newspaper compilations. Because the District Court upheld the newspapers' right to relief for copying the text of the articles, it had no occasion to consider what relief the newspapers might be entitled to by reason of Kurier's copying of the newspapers' creative efforts in the selection, arrangement, or display of the articles. Since Kurier's photocopying reproduced not only the text of articles but also headlines and graphic materials as they originally appeared in the plaintiffs' publication, it is likely that on remand the newspaper plaintiffs will be able to obtain some form of injunctive relief and some damages. On these infringement issues, as we have indicated, United States law will apply.

Finally, there remains for consideration what relief, if any, might be awarded to UJR, acting on behalf of any of its members whose articles have been copied. In its opinion granting the newspapers a preliminary injunction, the District Court noted that the plaintiffs had not "established the union's organizational standing to sue to enforce the rights of its members," an issue the Court expected would be considered later in the lawsuit. In its ruling on the merits, the District Court ruled that the UJR had standing to sue on behalf of its members. However, the Court noted that UJR sought only injunctive relief and then ruled that since UJR declined to furnish a list of its members, the Court was unable to frame an injunction that would be narrowly tailored and sufficient to give the defendants notice of its scope.

In view of our conclusion that the newspaper plaintiffs may not secure relief for the copying of the text of any articles as such, it will now become appropriate for the District Court on remand to revisit the issue of whether relief might be fashioned in favor of UJR on behalf of the authors. Despite UJR's unwillingness to disclose its entire membership list, it might be possible to frame some form of injunctive relief that affords protection for those author-members that UJR is willing to identify. And UJR should now be given an opportunity to amend its prayer for relief to state whatever claim it might have to collect damages for the benefit of its member-authors whose rights have been infringed. Finally, the District Court should consider the appropriateness and feasibility of giving some form of notice (perhaps at the defendants' expense) that is calculated to alert the authors of the infringed articles to their right to intervene in this lawsuit. Such notice might, for example, be addressed generally to the group of reporters currently employed at each of the plaintiff newspapers.

In view of the reckless conduct of the defendants in the flagrant copying that infringed the rights of Itar-Tass, the rights of the authors, and very likely some aspects of the limited protectable rights of the newspapers, we will leave the injunction in force until such time as the District Court has had an opportunity, on remand, to modify the injunction consistent with this opinion and with such further rulings as the District Court may make in light of this opinion.

*Conclusion*

Accordingly, we affirm the judgment to the extent that it granted relief to Itar-Tass, we reverse to the extent that the judgment granted relief to the other plaintiffs, and we remand for further proceedings. No costs.

---

**Note on special provisions concerning ownership of movie copyrights**

The 1991 decision of the French Supreme Court in the "Asphalt Jungle" colorization case – holding the French rather than U.S. law determines who owns the authors' moral rights in France – was surprising to at least some observers in the United States. An American company, after all, produced the movie in the United States; and both John Huston and Ben Maddow were Americans. Indeed, in 1950, when "Asphalt Jungle" was produced, neither the movie nor any of those involved in its production had any connection with France, and none of them had any reason to suppose that French law would ever control ownership of any of the rights necessary to exploit the movie anywhere in the world.

The case was filed Huston's heirs and by Maddow in 1988, *before* the United States joined the Berne Convention. From 1956 to March 1989, copyright relations between the United States and France were governed by the Universal Copyright Convention ("UCC"). And in 1950, when "Asphalt Jungle" was produced, copyright relations between the two countries were governed by a bilateral treaty dating back to 1891. Neither the UCC nor the 1891 bilateral treaty contained provisions suggesting that the ownership of rights in an American work would be determined by applying French rather than American law.

In March 1989, however, the United States joined the Berne Convention – a multinational copyright treaty to which France has adhered since 1887 – and thus the Berne Convention has governed copyright relations between the United States and France since that time. If the United States had become a member of the Berne Convention *before* "Asphalt Jungle" was produced, the ultimate result in the case would have been less surprising. This is so, because the Berne Convention contains a "Special Provision" concerning the ownership of the copyright in a "cinematographic work" (i.e., a movie). Article 14*bis*, paragraph (2)(a), provides: "Ownership of copyright in a cinematographic work shall be a matter for legislation *in the country where protection is claimed.*" (Emphasis added.) Legislation in France provides that *moral* rights in all works, cinematographic works included, belong to the "author" as determined by French law; and moral rights may not be transferred (though economic rights may be).

The Berne Convention is not the only law that contains "special provisions" concerning copyright ownership for specific types of works. As noted by Judge Newman in the *Itar-Tass v. Russian Kurier* case and in the Note on U.S. Restoration of Foreign Copyrights (above), the United States Copyright Act itself contains one such special provision. Titled "Copyright in restored works," section 104A(b) of the U.S. Copyright Act provides: "Ownership of restored copyright. A restored work vests initially in the author or initial rightholder of the work *as determined by the law of the source country of the work.*" (Emphasis added.) This means, for example, that if the copyright to a French movie went into the public domain in the United States (for any of several reasons), and that copyright was restored in the U.S. by section 104A, the owner of the restored copyright would be the "author" of the movie as determined by the *law of France*, without regard to who the "author" of the movie would have been under United States law.

---

### 1.4.4 Proper Court and Available Remedies

**Subafilms, Ltd. v. MGM-Pathe Communications Co.**
**24 F.3d 1088 (9th Cir. 1994)**

D.W. Nelson, Circuit Judge:

In this case, we consider the "vexing question" of whether a claim for infringement can be brought under the Copyright Act, 17 U.S.C. § 101 *et seq.* (1988), when the assertedly infringing conduct consists solely of the authorization within the territorial boundaries of the United States of acts that occur entirely abroad. We hold that such allegations do not state a claim for relief under the copyright laws of the United States.

*Factual and Procedural Background*

In 1966, the musical group The Beatles, through Subafilms, Ltd., entered into a joint venture with the Hearst Corporation to produce the animated motion picture entitled "Yellow Submarine" (the "Picture"). Over the next year, Hearst, acting on behalf of the joint venture (the "Producer"), negotiated an agreement with United Artists Corporation ("UA") to distribute and finance the film. Separate distribution and financing agreements were entered into in May, 1967. Pursuant to these agreements, UA distributed the Picture in theaters beginning in 1968 and later on television.

In the early 1980s, with the advent of the home video market, UA entered into several licensing agreements to distribute a number of its films on videocassette. Although one company expressed interest in the Picture, UA refused to license

"Yellow Submarine" because of uncertainty over whether home video rights had been granted by the 1967 agreements. Subsequently, in 1987, UA's successor company, MGM/UA Communications Co. ("MGM/UA"), over the Producer's objections, authorized its subsidiary MGM/UA Home Video, Inc. to distribute the Picture for the domestic home video market, and, pursuant to an earlier licensing agreement, notified Warner Bros., Inc. ("Warner") that the Picture had been cleared for international videocassette distribution. Warner, through its wholly owned subsidiary, Warner Home Video, Inc., in turn entered into agreements with third parties for distribution of the Picture on videocassette around the world.

In 1988, Subafilms and Hearst ("Appellees") brought suit against MGM/UA, Warner, and their respective subsidiaries (collectively the "Distributors" or "Appellants"), contending that the videocassette distribution of the Picture, both foreign and domestic, constituted copyright infringement and a breach of the 1967 agreements. The case was tried before a retired California Superior Court Judge acting as a special master. The special master found for Appellees on both claims, and against the Distributors on their counterclaim for fraud and reformation. Except for the award of prejudgment interest, which it reversed, the district court adopted all of the special master's factual findings and legal conclusions. Appellees were awarded $ 2,228,000.00 in compensatory damages, split evenly between the foreign and domestic home video distributions. In addition, Appellees received attorneys' fees and a permanent injunction that prohibited the Distributors from engaging in, or authorizing, any home video use of the Picture.

A panel of this circuit, in an unpublished disposition, affirmed the district court's judgment on the ground that both the domestic and foreign distribution of the Picture constituted infringement under the Copyright Act. With respect to the foreign distribution of the Picture, the panel concluded that it was bound by this court's prior decision in *Peter Starr Prod. Co. v. Twin Continental Films, Inc.*, 783 F.2d 1440 (9th Cir. 1986), which it held to stand for the proposition that, although "'infringing actions that take place entirely outside the United States are not actionable' [under the Copyright Act, an] 'act of infringement within the United States' [properly is] alleged where the illegal *authorization* of international exhibitions *takes place in the United States.*" Because the Distributors had admitted that the initial authorization to distribute the Picture internationally occurred within the United States, the panel affirmed the district court's holding with respect to liability for extraterritorial home video distribution of the Picture.

We granted Appellants' petition for rehearing en banc to consider whether the panel's interpretation of *Peter Starr* conflicted with our subsequent decision in *Lewis Galoob Toys, Inc. v. Nintendo of Am., Inc.*, 964 F.2d 965 (9th Cir. 1992), *cert. denied,* 123 L. Ed. 2d 149, 113 S. Ct. 1582 (1993), which held that there could be no liability for authorizing a party to engage in an infringing act when the authorized "party's use of the work would not violate the Copyright Act." Because we conclude that there can be no liability under the United States copyright laws for authorizing an act that *itself* could not constitute infringement of rights secured by those laws, and that wholly extraterritorial acts of infringement are not cognizable under the Copyright Act, we overrule *Peter Starr* insofar as it held that allegations of an authorization within the United States of infringing acts that take place entirely abroad state a claim for infringement under the Act. Accordingly, we vacate the panel's decision in part and return the case to the panel for further proceedings.

*Discussion*

*I. The Mere Authorization of Extraterritorial Acts of Infringement does not State a Claim under the Copyright Act*

As the panel in this case correctly concluded, *Peter Starr* held that the authorization within the United States of entirely extraterritorial acts stated a cause of action under the "plain language" of the Copyright Act. . . .

The *Peter Starr* court accepted, as does this court, that the acts *authorized* from within the United States themselves could not have constituted infringement under the Copyright Act because "in general, United States copyright laws do not have extraterritorial effect," and therefore, "infringing actions that take place entirely outside the United States are not actionable." The central premise of the *Peter Starr* court, then, was that a party could be held liable as an "infringer" under section 501 of the Act merely for authorizing a third party to engage in acts that, had they been committed *within* the United States, would have violated the exclusive rights granted to a copyright holder by section 106.

Since *Peter Starr,* however, we have recognized that, when a party authorizes an activity *not* proscribed by one of the five section 106 clauses, the authorizing party cannot be held liable as an infringer. . . .

The apparent premise of *Lewis Galoob* was that the addition of the words "to authorize" in the Copyright Act was not meant to create a new form of liability for "authorization" that was divorced completely from the legal consequences of authorized conduct, but was intended to invoke the preexisting doctrine of contributory infringement. We agree. . . .

Appellees . . . argue that liability in this case is appropriate because . . . the conduct authorized in this case was precisely that prohibited by section 106, and is only uncognizable because it occurred outside the United States. Moreover, they contend that the conduct authorized in this case would have been prohibited under the copyright laws of virtually every nation.

Even assuming *arguendo* that the acts authorized in this case would have been illegal abroad, we do not believe the distinction offered by Appellees is a relevant one. Because the copyright laws do not apply extraterritorially, each of the rights conferred under the five section 106 categories must be read as extending "no farther than the [United States'] borders." In light of our above conclusion that the "authorization" right refers to the doctrine of contributory infringement, which requires that the authorized act *itself* could violate one of the exclusive rights listed in section 106(1)-(5), we believe that "it is simply not possible to draw a principled distinction" between an act that does not violate a copyright because it is not the type of conduct proscribed by section 106, and one that does not violate section 106 because the illicit act occurs overseas. In both cases, the authorized conduct could not violate the exclusive rights guaranteed by section 106. In both cases, therefore, there can be no liability for "authorizing" such conduct.

. . . Accordingly, accepting that wholly extraterritorial acts of infringement cannot support a claim under the Copyright Act, we believe that the *Peter Starr* court, and thus the panel in this case, erred in concluding that the mere authorization of such acts supports a claim for infringement under the Act.

*II. The Extraterritoriality of the Copyright Act*

Appellees additionally contend that, if liability for "authorizing" acts of infringement depends on finding that the authorized acts themselves are cognizable under the Copyright Act, this court should find that the United States copyright laws *do extend* to extraterritorial acts of infringement when such acts "result in adverse effects within the United States." Appellees buttress this argument with the contention that failure to apply the copyright laws extraterritorially in this case will have a disastrous effect on the American film industry, and that other remedies, such as suits in foreign jurisdictions or the application of foreign copyright laws by American courts, are not realistic alternatives.

We are not persuaded by Appellees' parade of horribles.[10] [n10 As Appellants note, breach of contract remedies (such as those pursued in this case) remain available. Moreover, at least one court has recognized that actions under the copyright laws of other nations may be brought in United States courts. *See London Film Prods. Ltd. v. Intercontinental Communications, Inc.*, 580 F. Supp. 47, 48-50 (S.D.N.Y. 1984). *See generally* 2 Goldstein, *supra,* § 16.3, at 683 ("Subject to jurisdictional requirements, a copyright owner may sue an infringer in United States courts even though the only alleged infringement occurred in another country."). *But see ITSI,* 785 F. Supp. at 866 (discerning, despite *London Film,* "no clear authority for exercising such jurisdiction" and stating that "American courts should be reluctant to enter the bramble bush of ascertaining and applying foreign law without an urgent reason to do so"). Finally, although we note that the difficulty of protecting American films abroad is a significant international trade problem, the United States Congress, in acceding to the Berne Convention, has expressed the view that it is through increasing the protection afforded by *foreign* copyright laws that domestic industries that depend on copyright can best secure adequate protection.] More fundamentally, however, we are unwilling to overturn over eighty years of consistent jurisprudence on the extraterritorial reach of the copyright laws without further guidance from Congress. . . .

*Conclusion*

We hold that the mere authorization of acts of infringement that are not cognizable under the United States copyright laws because they occur entirely outside of the United States does not state a claim for infringement under the Copyright Act. *Peter Starr* is overruled insofar as it held to the contrary. Accordingly, we vacate Part III of the panel's disposition, in which it concluded that the international distribution of the film constituted a violation of the United States copyright laws. We also vacate that portion of the disposition that affirmed the damage award based on foreign distribution of the film and the panel's affirmance of the award of attorneys' fees. Finally, we vacate the district court's grant of injunctive relief insofar as it was based on the premise that the Distributors had violated the United States copyright laws through authorization of the foreign distribution of the Picture on videocassettes.

The cause is remanded to the panel for further proceedings consistent with the mandate of this court.

---

**Los Angeles News Service v. Reuters Television International, Limited**
**149 F.3d 987 (9th Cir. 1998)**

William W. Schwarzer, Senior District Judge:

On this appeal we must decide whether, under the Copyright Act, a plaintiff may recover actual damages accruing from the unauthorized exploitation abroad of copyrighted work infringed in the United States. . . .

*Background*

Los Angeles News (LANS) is an independent news organization which produces video and audio tape recordings of newsworthy events and licenses them for profit. During the April 1992 riots following the Rodney King verdict, LANS covered the events at Florence Avenue and Normandie Boulevard in Los Angeles from its helicopter, producing two videotapes: "The Beating of Reginald Denny" and "Beating of Man in White Panel Truck" (the works). LANS copyrighted these works and licensed them to National Broadcasting Company, Inc. (NBC), which used them on the *Today* show with the logo of KCOP, a Los Angeles station not affiliated with NBC, superimposed (known in the trade as the downstream). Under the agreement, LANS retained ownership of the works and the right to license them.

. . .

The Reuters defendants (Reuters Television International, Ltd., Reuters America Holdings, Inc., and Reuters America, Inc., collectively Reuters) are television news agencies that gather and provide audiovisual and other news material to their subscribers for an annual fee. Visnews International (USA), Ltd. (Visnews), a joint venture of Reuters Television Limited, NBC and the British Broadcasting Company, had a news supply agreement with NBC News Overseas. When NBC broadcast the *Today* show featuring the LANS footage to its affiliates, it simultaneously transmitted the show via fiber link to Visnews in New York. Visnews made a videotape copy of the works as broadcast and transmitted it to subscribers in Europe and Africa. It also transmitted copies of the videotape to the New York office of the European Broadcasting Union (EBU), which in turn made a videotape copy and transmitted it via satellite to Reuters' London branch, which provided copies to its subscribers.

LANS brought this action for copyright infringement against the Reuters defendants and Visnews. Defendants moved for summary judgment on several grounds. So far as relevant to this appeal, they contended that (1) extraterritorial infringement does not violate American copyright law. . . . The district court granted defendants' motion with respect to extraterritorial infringement. . . . Following a bench trial on the remaining issues, the district court found that Visnews had infringed by making one copy of each videotape and contributing to the making by EBU of one copy of each tape, LANS failed to prove the infringement was willful, and defendants failed to prove that it was innocent. The court entered judgment for LANS for $ 60,000 in statutory damages based on the four domestic infringements by Visnews. . . .

LANS appeals from the ruling barring extraterritorial damages. . . .

*Discussion . . .*

It is settled that the Copyright Act does not apply extraterritorially. *Subafilms, Ltd. v. MGM-Pathe Communications Co.*, 24 F.3d 1088, 1094 (9th Cir. 1994) (en banc). For the Act to apply, "at least one alleged infringement must be completed entirely within the United States." *Allarcom Pay Television Ltd. v. General Instrument Corp.*, 69 F.3d 381, 387 (9th Cir. 1995). The district court found that "any damages arising extraterritorially are the result of extraterritorial infringement." Relying on *Allarcom*, the court held that "the transmissions from Visnews and [EBU] did not violate the Copyright Act. . . . Therefore, Defendants are not liable . . . for damages arising extraterritorially." We review the district court's grant of partial summary judgment de novo.

The district court's ruling was premised on the assumption that LANS's claim was based on the transmissions from Visnews and EBU to Reuters. However, it also held that Visnews completed acts of infringement in the United States when it copied the works in New York and then transmitted them to EBU which also copied them in New York. Each act of copying constituted a completed act of infringement. *See* 17 U.S.C. § 106(1). It was only after these domestic acts of infringement had been completed that Visnews and EBU transmitted the works abroad.

This case then presents a situation different from that in *Subafilms* and *Allarcom*. In *Subafilms*, the allegedly infringing conduct consisted solely of authorization given within the United States for foreign distribution of infringing videocassettes. Similarly, in *Allarcom*, the alleged infringement consisted either of authorization given in the United States for infringement in Canada or broadcasts of copyright material from the United States into Canada, with the infringement not completed until the signals were received in Canada.

The issue before us which the *Subafilms* court did not resolve is whether LANS "may recover damages for international distribution of the [works] based on the theory that an act of direct infringement, in the form of a reproduction of the . . . [works], took place in the United States." While this circuit has not heretofore addressed the issue, the Second Circuit has done so in a line of cases beginning with *Sheldon v. Metro-Goldwyn Pictures Corp.*, 106 F.2d 45, 52 (2d Cir. 1939), *aff'd*, 309 U.S. 390, 84 L. Ed. 825, 60 S. Ct. 681 (1940). In *Sheldon* the court held, in an opinion by Judge Learned Hand, that plaintiff could recover the profits from exhibiting a motion picture abroad where the infringing copy had been made in the United States. . . .

LANS urges us to adopt the Second Circuit's rule because the unauthorized copying of its works in the United States enabled further exploitation abroad. While the extraterritorial damages resulted from Reuters's overseas dissemination of the works received by satellite transmissions from Visnews and EBU, those transmissions were made possible by the infringing acts of copying in New York. The satellite transmissions, thus, were merely a means of shipping the unlicensed footage abroad for further dissemination.

The *Subafilms* court's concerns are inapplicable to the present case. The Second Circuit rule would not permit application of American law to "acts of infringement that take place entirely abroad." Nor would a copyright holder be entitled to recover extraterritorial damages unless the damages flowed from extraterritorial exploitation of an infringing act that occurred in the United States. In *Subafilms*, the court reasoned that liability based solely on the authorization of infringing acts "would produce the untenable anomaly, inconsistent with the general principles of third party liability, that a party could be held liable as an infringer for violating the 'authorization' right when the party that it authorized could not be considered an infringer under the Copyright Act." Under the Second Circuit's rule, by contrast, a party becomes liable for extraterritorial damages only when an act of infringement occurs within the United States, subjecting it to liability as an infringer (or a contributory infringer) under the Copyright Act.

Defendants' argument that adoption of the Second Circuit rule would permit plaintiffs to circumvent the statute of limitation by recovering damages for distribution abroad occurring many years after the infringing act in the United States is without merit. An action must be "commenced within three years after the claim accrued." 17 U.S.C. § 507(b). A claim accrues when an act of infringement occurs, not when consequent damage is suffered. A plaintiff's right to damages is limited to those suffered during the statutory period for bringing claims, regardless of where they may have been incurred.

We therefore hold that LANS is entitled to recover damages flowing from exploitation abroad of the domestic acts of infringement committed by defendants...

---

**Boosey & Hawkes Music Publishers, Ltd. v. Walt Disney Co.**
**145 F.3d 481 (2nd Cir. 1998)**

Leval, Circuit Judge:

Boosey & Hawkes Music Publishers Ltd., an English corporation and the assignee of Igor Stravinsky's copyrights for "The Rite of Spring," brought this action alleging that the Walt Disney Company's foreign distribution in video cassette and laser disc format ("video format") of the film "Fantasia," featuring Stravinsky's work, infringed Boosey's rights. In 1939 Stravinsky licensed Disney's distribution of The Rite of Spring in the motion picture. Boosey, which acquired Stravinsky's copyright in 1947, contends that the license does not authorize distribution in video format. . . .

*I. Background*

During 1938, Disney sought Stravinsky's authorization to use The Rite of Spring (sometimes referred to as the "work" or the "composition") throughout the world in a motion picture. Because under United States law the work was in the public domain, Disney needed no authorization to record or distribute it in this country, but permission was required for distribution in countries where Stravinsky enjoyed copyright protection. In January 1939 the parties executed an agreement (the "1939 Agreement") giving Disney rights to use the work in a motion picture in consideration of a fee to Stravinsky of $6000.

The 1939 Agreement provided that

> In consideration of the sum of Six Thousand ($6,000) Dollars, receipt of which is hereby acknowledged, [Stravinsky] does hereby give and grant unto Walt Disney Enterprises, a California corporation . . . the nonexclusive, irrevocable right, license, privilege and authority to record in any manner, medium or form, and to license the performance of, the musical composition hereinbelow set out . . .

Under "type of use" in P3, the Agreement specified that

> The music of said musical composition may be used in one motion picture throughout the length thereof or through such portion or portions thereof as the Purchaser shall desire. The said music may be used in whole or in part and may be adapted, changed, added to or subtracted from, all as shall appear desirable to the Purchaser in its uncontrolled discretion. . . . The title "Rites of Spring" or "Le Sacre de Printemps", or any other title, may be used as the title of said motion picture and the name of [Stravinsky] may be announced in or in connection with said motion picture.

The Agreement went on to specify in P4 that Disney's license to the work "is limited to the use of the musical composition in synchronism or timed-relation with the motion picture."

Paragraph Five of the Agreement provided that

> The right to record the musical composition as covered by this agreement is conditioned upon the performance of the musical work in theatres having valid licenses from the American Society of Composers, Authors and Publishers, or any other performing rights society having jurisdiction in the territory in which the said musical composition is performed.

We refer to this clause, which is of importance to the litigation, as "the ASCAP Condition."

Finally, P 7 of the Agreement provided that "the licensor reserves to himself all rights and uses in and to the said musical composition not herein specifically granted" (the "reservation clause").

Disney released Fantasia, starring Mickey Mouse, in 1940. The film contains no dialogue. It matches a pantomime of animated beasts and fantastic creatures to passages of great classical music, creating what critics celebrated as a "partnership between fine music and animated film." The soundtrack uses compositions of Bach, Beethoven, Dukas, Schubert, Tchaikovsky, and Stravinsky, all performed by the Philadelphia Orchestra under the direction of Leopold Stokowski. As it appears in the film soundtrack, The Rite of Spring was shortened from its original 34 minutes to about 22.5; sections of the score were cut, while other sections were reordered.

For more than five decades Disney exhibited The Rite of Spring in Fantasia under the 1939 license. The film has been re-released for theatrical distribution at least seven times since 1940, and although Fantasia has never appeared on television in its entirety, excerpts including portions of The Rite of Spring have been televised occasionally over the years. Neither Stravinsky nor Boosey has ever previously objected to any of the distributions.

In 1991 Disney first released Fantasia in video format. The video has been sold in foreign countries, as well as in the United States. To date, the Fantasia video release has generated more than $ 360 million in gross revenue for Disney.

Boosey brought this action in February 1993. The complaint sought (1) a declaration that the 1939 Agreement did not include a grant of rights to Disney to use the Stravinsky work in video format; (2) damages for copyright infringement in at least 18 foreign countries. . . .

. . . In determining that the license did not cover the distribution of a video format, the district court found that while the broad language of the license gave Disney "the right to record [the work] on video tape and laser disc," the ASCAP Condition "prevents Disney from distributing video tapes or laser discs directly to consumers." The court therefore concluded that Disney's video format sales exceeded the scope of the license.

However, as noted, the district court invoked forum non conveniens to dismiss all of Boosey's claims of copyright infringement because they involved the application of foreign law. . . .

The decision below thus declared Disney an infringer, but granted Boosey no relief, leaving it to sue in the various countries under whose copyright laws it claims infringement. This appeal followed.

*II. Discussion*

. . . Disney challenges the summary judgment which declared that the 1939 Agreement does not authorize video distribution of The Rite of Spring. Boosey appeals . . . the dismissal for forum non conveniens. . . .

*b. Foreign Copyright Claims*

Invoking the doctrine of forum non conveniens, the district court dismissed Boosey's second cause of action, which sought damages for copyright infringement deriving from Disney's sales of videocassettes of Fantasia in at least eighteen foreign countries. The court below concluded that these claims should be tried "in each of the nations whose copyright laws are invoked." Boosey appeals, seeking remand to the district court for trial. . . .

The district court failed to consider whether there were alternative fora capable of adjudicating Boosey's copyright claims. It made no determination whether Disney was subject to jurisdiction in the various countries where the court anticipated that trial would occur and did not condition dismissal on Disney's consent to jurisdiction in those nations. . . .

The private interests of the litigants favor conducting the litigation in New York where the plaintiff brought suit. Disney does not allege that a New York forum is inconvenient. The necessary evidence and witnesses are available and ready for presentation. A trial here promises to begin and end sooner than elsewhere, and would allow the parties to sort out their rights and obligations in a single proceeding. This is not a circumstance where the plaintiff's choice of forum is motivated by harassment. Indeed, it seems rather more likely that Disney's motion seeks to split the suit into 18 parts in 18 nations, complicate the suit, delay it, and render it more expensive.

In dismissing the cases, the court relied on the "public interests". . . . It reasoned that the trial would require extensive application of foreign copyright and antitrust jurisprudence, bodies of law involving strong national interests best litigated "in their respective countries." The court concluded as well that these necessary inquiries into foreign law would place an undue burden on our judicial system."

While reluctance to apply foreign law is a valid factor favoring dismissal . . ., standing alone it does not justify dismissal. Numerous countervailing considerations suggest that New York venue is proper: defendant is a U.S. corporation, the 1939 agreement was substantially negotiated and signed in New York, and the agreement is governed by New York law. The plaintiff has chosen New York and the trial is ready to proceed here. Everything before us suggests that trial would be more "easy, expeditious and inexpensive" in the district court than dispersed to 18 foreign nations. We therefore vacate the dismissal of the foreign copyright claims and remand for trial. . . .

*Conclusion*

The grants of summary judgment in Boosey's favor declaring that Disney's foreign video format marketing exceeded the terms of the license, and in Disney's favor dismissing Boosey's claim for breach of contract are vacated. The dismissal of the action by reason of forum non conveniens is reversed. . . .

---

**Roth v. Garcia Marquez**
**942 F.2d 617 (9th Cir. 1991)**

Circuit Judge Dorothy Nelson:

This case revolves around Richard Roth's and Richard Roth Productions' ("Roth") attempt to secure the movie rights to Gabriel Garcia Marquez' novel *Love in the Time of Cholera.* Roth appeals the district court's dismissal of his complaint for failure to state a claim and its denial of leave to amend. In addition, Garcia Marquez and agent Carmen Balcells appeal the district court's denial of their motion to dismiss for lack of personal jurisdiction. While none of these three issues is easily resolved, we initially affirm the district court's finding of personal jurisdiction. We also affirm the district court's dismissal for failure to state a claim and its denial of leave to amend. In sum, we are unwilling to grant through litigation what negotiation could not achieve.

*I. Factual and Procedural Background*

Appellant Richard Roth is a movie producer who lives in California and carries out his projects through Richard Roth Productions. Gabriel Garcia Marquez, an internationally renowned author who won the Nobel Prize for Literature in 1982, has written numerous bestselling novels. The film rights to his work *Love in the Time of Cholera* ("*Cholera*") are at issue in the present litigation. Garcia Marquez has resided in Mexico City for the last sixteen years. Carmen Balcells is the president of a literary agency headquartered in Barcelona, Spain. A resident of Barcelona, Balcells has been Garcia Marquez' literary agent for more than 25 years.

In late 1986, Roth contacted Garcia Marquez in Mexico City to express his interest in making a film based on Cholera. Roth flew to Havana, Cuba, to meet Garcia Marquez on this matter. Garcia Marquez told Roth that he would consider selling film rights under the following three conditions: 1) Roth would agree to pay him a large sum of money (later Balcells specified the sum of five million dollars); 2) Roth would agree to use a Latin American director; and 3) Roth would shoot the film in Colombia. Garcia Marquez later authorized Balcells to pursue negotiations with Roth.

Negotiations dragged on with disputes both about the price for the option and the identity of the possible director. Roth traveled a number of times to Barcelona and Mexico City to meet with Balcells and Garcia Marquez, and repeated calls, letters, and faxes passed between the parties. The only meetings that occurred in the United States were in May 1988, when Balcells traveled to California to attend an American Booksellers Association convention and met with Roth on the side, and in November 1988, when Garcia Marquez visited Los Angeles for four days at the social invitation of a friend. He met with Roth and agreed that Roth could shoot the film in Brazil, not Colombia, but he remained firm on the other two terms.

On November 17, 1988, the same day that Roth and Garcia Marquez met, Alan Schwartz, Roth's representative, faxed a letter to Balcells in Barcelona. The letter offered Garcia Marquez $200,000 for the grant of an option of two years on the film rights, the right to extend the option for another year for an additional $100,000, these monies to be applied against $1,250,000 to be paid when the option was exercised, $400,000 more on the release of the video, $350,000 more on the release of television showing, and 5% of the net profits of the film. On January 19, 1989, Schwartz telecopied another letter, which changed the first sum of $200,000 for the option to $400,000. The letter, which is the crux of this litigation, stated that the first paragraph of the November 17, 1988, letter was changed to the following:

> (a) A payment of $400,000 for an option of two years to acquire the motion picture and allied rights to this novel. The option shall commence upon signature by Gabriel Garcia Marquez to the formal agreement and the return of said signed agreement to me or Richard Roth, at which time the option payment shall be made to you as agent for Gabriel Garcia Marquez.

The letter also stated: "On behalf of Richard Roth and myself I am very happy to confirm the final agreement between Richard and Gabriel Garcia Marquez . . ." and "Please convey to Garcia Marquez the excitement Richard and I feel in being able finally to get this project moving." Balcells countersigned the letter and faxed back the following the next day: "Thank you for today's fax and I am happy that this deal is finally concluded. I had no time to tell Gabo [Marquez] about this conclusion. In any case, I am returning your letter duly signed. I shall await the formal agreement at your earliest convenience."

That same day, Roth wrote independently to Balcells thanking her "so much for concluding the deal" and telling her he was "putting the best champagne on ice so we can celebrate and drink it together."

In late February Schwartz transmitted the 25-page formal agreement to Balcells. Balcells objected to a number of points, particularly the omission of clauses about a Latin American director and the site of the shooting. Balcells communicated these objections, and weeks of renewed negotiations failed to produce an agreement. Garcia Marquez never signed the formal agreement, and the money was never paid him.

For personal jurisdiction analysis, Garcia Marquez lives in Mexico City and has never resided in California. He has visited the state four times for a total of twenty days. He met with Roth once in California, but entered the state for a social purpose. He has never owned property in the state, nor has he ever conducted business on a regular basis or authorized any resident of the state to do so on his behalf. He has maintained a checking account, not his principal one, in Los Angeles since 1988 for the purposes of having an account in dollars for certain transactions occurring outside of California.

Balcells lives in Barcelona. She has never lived in California, though she has visited twice. On one of those occasions, she met with Roth, though she was in the state for a convention. She has never owned property in California, has no office or telephone number there, and has never conducted business on a regular basis or authorized any resident of the state to do so for her.

In December 1989, Roth filed a complaint in district court seeking declaratory relief to determine the status of his rights to produce the film. Appellees filed a motion to dismiss, alleging both that the court lacked personal jurisdiction over each defendant and that because appellees had not entered into a binding contract, the complaint failed to state a claim upon which relief could be granted. The district court denied the motion to dismiss for lack of personal jurisdiction, but it granted the motion to dismiss for failure to state a claim. The district court also denied Roth's motion for leave to amend the complaint. Both sides now appeal the unfavorable ruling(s) against them.

*II. Personal Jurisdiction*

Appellees cross-appeal the district court's denial of their motion to dismiss for lack of personal jurisdiction. Neither Balcells nor Garcia Marquez may be haled into court, they contend, without offending due process.

We review de novo the denial of a motion to dismiss for lack of personal jurisdiction where the underlying facts are undisputed.

The California long-arm statute provides that jurisdiction may be exercised over nonresident defendants "on any basis not inconsistent with the Constitution of this state or of the United States." Cal.Civ.Proc.Code §410.10. Since California's jurisdictional statute is coextensive with federal due process requirements, the jurisdictional inquiries under state law and federal due process merge into one analysis. The due process clause prohibits the exercise of jurisdiction over nonresident defendants unless those defendants have "minimum contacts" with the forum state so that the exercise of jurisdiction "does not offend traditional notions of fair play and substantial justice." *International Shoe Co. v. Washington*, 326 U.S. 310 (1945)

We have interpreted *International Shoe* and its progeny as allowing jurisdiction by California courts over a nonresident defendant if he has enough continuous contacts with California to subject him to the court's general jurisdiction or if the specific cause of action arises out of a defendant's more limited contacts with the state so that California may exercise limited or specific jurisdiction over him. Appellants concede that there is no general jurisdiction over appellees; the question, then, turns on whether the contacts in this case enable California to exercise limited jurisdiction over Balcells and Garcia Marquez. A three-part test has been articulated for limited jurisdiction: 1) the nonresident defendant must have purposefully availed himself of the privilege of conducting activities in the forum by some affirmative act or conduct; 2) plaintiff's claim must arise out of or result from the defendant's forum-related activities; and 3) exercise of jurisdiction must be reasonable.

*A. Purposeful Availment*

As we explained in *Sinatra*:

> Purposeful availment analysis examines whether the defendant's contacts with the forum are attributable to his own actions or are solely the actions of the plaintiff. In order to have purposefully availed oneself of conducting activities in the forum, the defendant must have performed some type of affirmative conduct which allows or promotes the transaction of business within the forum state.

The Supreme Court has explained: "The purposeful availment requirement ensures that a defendant will not be haled into a jurisdiction solely as a result of random, fortuitous, or attenuated contacts, or of the unilateral activity of another party or third person." *Burger King v. Rudzewicz*, 471 U.S. 462 (1985).

It is important to distinguish contract from tort actions. For example, we have stated in a tort case that "within the rubric of 'purposeful availment' the Court has allowed the exercise of jurisdiction over a defendant whose only 'contact' with the forum state is the 'purposeful direction' of a foreign act having effect in the forum state."

In the contract context, however, *Burger King* specifically noted that the existence of a contract with a resident of the forum state is insufficient by itself to create personal jurisdiction over the nonresident. *Burger King* stated that "with respect to interstate contractual obligations, we have emphasized that parties who 'reach out beyond one state and create continuing relationships and obligations with citizens of another state' are subject to regulation and sanctions in the other State for the consequences of their activities."

Appellees argue that because Roth initiated all the contacts and because he was the one who "reached out" to effect the contract, they should not be subject to California law. There was no solicitation of business by appellees, they maintain, that resulted in contract negotiations or the transaction of business. We have explained that "the purposeful availment analysis turns upon whether the defendant's contacts are attributable to 'actions by the defendant himself,' or conversely to the unilateral activity of another party."

Here, it seems clear that the predominant efforts were made by the appellant, not the appellees. Roth traveled to Havana, Barcelona, and Mexico City in his peripatetic effort to secure the movie rights. Garcia Marquez and Balcells were in Los Angeles for other purposes when each met individually with Roth. While we concede that negotiations did take place at that time, it should be borne in mind that "temporary physical presence" in the forum does not suffice to confer personal jurisdiction. Further, Roth and his agents placed over 100 calls and sent numerous faxes to the two appellees. "When a California business seeks out purchasers in other states . . . [and] deals with them by out-of-state agents or by interstate mail and telephone, it is not entitled to force the customer to come to California to defend an action on the contract."

Roth also contends that the phone lines were used in the other direction, i.e., appellees made calls and returned letters and faxes to him. As this court held in *Shute*, "[M]any transactions take place solely by mail or wire across state lines, obviating the need for physical presence. . . . Thus, the Court has held that the physical absence of the defendant and the transaction from the forum cannot defeat the exercise of personal jurisdiction." However, "both this court and the courts of California have concluded that ordinarily 'use of the mails, telephone, or other international communications simply do not qualify as purposeful activity invoking the benefits and protection of the [forum] state.'"

There are two facts, then, that marginally work in appellees' favor: their minimal physical presence in the forum and the fact that it was appellant who made the sedulous efforts of solicitation. While this is a very close call, a final and broader issue appears to swing the first prong for Roth, namely the future consequences of the contract. The *Burger King* Court, in finding jurisdiction, emphasized that the Michigan franchisee defendant had entered into a relationship that "envisioned continuing and wide-reaching contacts with Burger King in Florida [the forum]."

The point here is simply that the contract concerned a film, most of the work for which would have been performed in California. Though the shooting most likely would have taken place in Brazil, all of the editing, production work, and advertising would have occurred in California. This is not an instance where the contract was a one-shot deal that was merely negotiated and signed by one party in the forum; on the contrary, most of the future of the contract would have centered on the forum. The checks that Roth would have sent Garcia Marquez, which appellees attempt to minimize, would have depended upon activities in California and the United States. In looking at the "economic reality," it seems that the contract's subject would have continuing and extensive involvement with the forum.

Though neither side decisively triumphs under this analysis, it appears that there was enough purposeful availment here to compel a finding of jurisdiction on this prong.

*B. Arising Out of Forum-Related Activities*

There is no dispute on this second prong, as appellees concede that appellant's claim arises out of the January 19 letter, which was negotiated and executed by a party who was in the forum at the time, namely Roth in Los Angeles.

*C. Reasonableness*

The third prong asks whether the exercise of jurisdiction would be reasonable. We have set forth a congeries of factors to be considered in determining whether the exercise of jurisdiction over a nonresident defendant satisfies the reasonableness test: 1) the extent of the defendant's purposeful interjection into the forum state's affairs; 2) the burden on the defendant; 3) conflicts of law between the forum and defendant's home jurisdiction; 4) the forum's interest in adjudicating the dispute; 5) the most efficient judicial resolution of the dispute; 6) the plaintiff's interest in convenient and effective relief; and 7) the existence of an alternative forum. Since none of these factors is dispositive, we must balance the seven.

*1. Extent of Purposeful Interjection*

In light of the first prong of purposeful availment, analysis of this first factor in the third prong would be redundant. As we have concluded, albeit narrowly, that appellees purposefully availed themselves of the privilege of conducting activities in California, there is no need to analyze this first factor separately.

*2. Burdens on Defendant*

Appellees argue that because they are residents of foreign countries and speak different languages than English, requiring them to come defend a suit in California would impose a great burden. They cite *Asahi Metal Industry Co. v. Superior Court of California*, 480 U.S. 102 (1987), for the proposition that a court should give "significant weight" to the "unique burdens" placed on a defendant that must defend in a foreign court. Appellant rejoins that "modern advances in communications and transportation have significantly reduced the burden of litigating in another country." Yet *Sinatra* specifically noted that "the continuing contacts between the Clinic's United States-based agent and California translate into less of a litigation burden than if the Clinic maintained no physical presence or agent within the United States." Here, neither appellee has an agent or office in the United States.

Roth argues that it would be no more burdensome for appellees to litigate here than for him to litigate in Mexico or Spain, and "this court 'must examine the burden on the defendant in light of the corresponding burden on the plaintiff.'" This seems to be in conflict with language from FDIC, which states that "[t]he primary concern is for the defendant's burden." At bottom, because Roth had no problems in his globe-trotting endeavors to persuade Balcells and Garcia Marquez to sell the film rights to him, he should not complain that litigation outside the United States would be particularly onerous for him. Appellees have shown no similar propensity for travel. Although this factor cuts in favor of appellees, "unless such inconvenience is so great as to constitute a deprivation of due process, it will not overcome clear justifications for the exercise of jurisdiction." An examination of the other factors is thus required.

3. *Extent of Conflict With Sovereignty of Foreign State*

Appellees point the court to the language of *Asahi*: "Great care and reserve should be exercised when extending our notions of personal jurisdiction into the international field." In addition, "a foreign nation presents a higher sovereignty barrier than another state within the United States." Nonetheless, "[t]he factor of conflict with the sovereignty of the defendant's state is not dispositive because, if given controlling weight, it would always prevent suit against a foreign national in a United States court." The *Sinatra* court found that the scales tipped for the plaintiff on this issue, but much of that was again based on the fact that the defendant had an agent in the United States, unlike appellees. In fact, Sinatra even distinguished FDIC on the grounds that there the defendant maintained no officer or affiliate in the United States. This factor, then, must line up on appellees' side.

4. *Forum State's Interest in Adjudication*

Appellees argue that California has little interest in the outcome of a private contractual dispute. They distinguish torts, for which there is a strong public interest in redress of wrongs. Appellees even go so far as to say that assumption of jurisdiction where minimal contacts exist might have an adverse effect on commerce, since foreigners would be loathe to enter into contracts with Californians that might result in their being haled into foreign courts. Appellant states simply that any state has an interest in providing an effective means of redress for residents who have negotiated and executed contracts within the state. Of course, appellees remonstrate that their whole point is that this contract was neither negotiated for the most part nor executed in California.

*Sinatra* intones the bromide that California has a greater interest in protecting her residents than nonresidents who wish to sue in her courts. On the other hand, the preceding sentence's reference to a "strong interest" is in the tort context. There is little case law in the contracts context in this circuit. One other case that appellees note is *Floyd J. Harkness Co. v. Amezcua*, 60 Cal.App.3d 687, 693 (1976), where the state appellate court held that jurisdiction over a Mexican defendant was unreasonable because the forum state had little interest in the outcome of a dispute over performance under a contract.

In sum, this factor seems to be a toss-up, with perhaps a slight edge going to appellees.

5. *Most Efficient Judicial Resolution*

This category, too, holds no edge for either party. Appellees live outside the United States, while appellant lives in California. Witnesses to the meetings in Mexico City, Havana, and Barcelona obviously live in foreign countries, while Roth's agents live in California. Though the film would be financed in California and would employ other Californians, these persons' testimony would not be relevant to whether a contract was formed; they would not be witnesses in this trial. Other cases in this circuit provide no guidance because of differing fact patterns. This factor is a push.

6. *Convenience and Effectiveness of Relief for Plaintiff*

Appellees dare not argue that it would be more convenient for Roth to litigate outside the United States. Nevertheless, they posit that because Roth was willing and able to pursue Balcells and Garcia Marquez by flying to different countries, he cannot now complain that it would be too inconvenient for him to return to the site of his solicitations in order to seek by litigation what he failed to achieve by negotiation. Both *Shute* and *Sinatra* stated that it would be more inconvenient for those plaintiffs to try cases outside the forum, but no doctorate in astrophysics is required to deduce that trying a case where one lives is almost always a plaintiff's preference. Both of the aforementioned cases can be distinguished from the present on the grounds that Sinatra never went to Switzerland to talk to the Clinic and the Shutes never traveled to Florida. Here, Roth did display an ability to meet and work in foreign countries. In all, this factor goes to Roth, but not as decisively as in other cases.

*7. Availability of an Alternative Forum*

Alternative fora are Spain, where Balcells lives, and Mexico, where Garcia Marquez resides. While neither is decidedly a worse place than California to try the case, neither is demonstrably better. We have held that the plaintiff "bears the burden of proving the unavailability of an alternative forum." In *FDIC* the court held that "although [plaintiff] has argued that California would be a more convenient forum, it has not met its burden of proving that it would be precluded from suing [defendant] outside of California." Here, Roth has not shown that he could not litigate in Spain or Mexico. Doubtless he would prefer not to, but that is not the test. Chalk this one up for appellees.

*8. Balancing the Seven Factors*

Of the seven factors, then, the following two favor appellant: purposeful interjection and convenience for plaintiff. The following three tilt toward appellees: burden on defendant, conflict with sovereignty of another state, and availability of an alternative forum. Finally, two factors do not favor either side: forum state's interest and efficient judicial resolution. This is, in sum, an extremely close question.

*D. Weighing the Three Prongs*

Appellant has narrowly satisfied the first prong, namely that appellees purposefully availed themselves of the privilege of conducting activities in the forum. He has also passed the second prong in that the claim arises out of appellees' forum-related activities. Garcia Marquez and Balcells, on the other hand, can make a strong argument on the third prong, namely that the exercise of jurisdiction may be unreasonable. Their difficulty, though, is in surmounting the following standard: "Once purposeful availment has been established, the forum's exercise of jurisdiction is presumptively reasonable. To rebut that presumption, a defendant 'must present a compelling case' that the exercise of jurisdiction would, in fact, be unreasonable." Appellees may be able to show that the exercise of jurisdiction might be unreasonable, but the closeness of the question manifests that they cannot do so in a compelling fashion. Because in the end appellees' showing does not surmount their hurdle, we find that personal jurisdiction does exist. We affirm the district court's denial of appellees' motion to dismiss.

[However, the Ninth Circuit went on to affirm the district court's dismissal of the case on the substantive ground that no contract existed between the parties as a result of the January 19 letter.]

---

**Rano v. Sipa Press, Inc.**
**987 F.2d 580 (9th Cir. 1993)**

Brunetti, Circuit Judge:

*Overview*

This appeal from a dismissal for lack of personal jurisdiction and grant of summary judgment in a copyright infringement suit turns on issues of federal preemption of state law in the copyright field and the termination of copyright licenses. For the reasons stated below, we affirm in part, reverse in part, and remand.

*Facts and Proceedings Below*

The parties to this appeal include: Plaintiff-Appellant Kip Rano, a professional photographer and citizen of Great Britain who resides and has his principal place of business in California; and Defendants-Appellees Sipa Press, a French corporation, Sipa Press, Inc., a Delaware subsidiary corporation, and Sipa, Inc., a New York subsidiary corporation (collectively Sipa), and Goskin Sipahioglu, President and one of three owners of Sipa Press. Sipa is a photograph distribution syndicate.

In France, on or before 1978, the parties entered into an oral copyright license agreement whereby Rano granted to Sipa a non-exclusive license of unspecified duration to reproduce, distribute, sell, and authorize others to reproduce, distribute, and sell his photographs. In return, Sipa agreed to store and develop the negatives and to pay fifty percent of the net royalties generated from its sales and distributions.

The relationship went smoothly for about eight years. Pursuant to agreement, Rano submitted several thousand of his photographs to Sipa, which Sipa distributed and paid royalties for. In March of 1986, however, Rano sent a letter to Sipahioglu informing him that he was changing agencies and that he would no longer be sending his negatives to Sipa. He gave as his reasons Sipa's failure to timely pay royalties, low sales, poor photography assignments, and unwillingness to reimburse certain expenses. Starting in July of 1986, Rano made several requests that Sipa return all of the negatives he had sent to them. Finally, on March 12, 1987, Rano informed Sipahioglu that he "did not authorize Sipa to sell any more of [his] photographs."

In July of 1989, Rano sued Sipa and Sipahioglu alleging that Sipa infringed his copyright by: (1) failing to credit him for a photograph of the Duchess of York, the former Sara Ferguson; (2) failing to pay certain royalties; (3) continuing to distribute some of his photographs after he demanded their return and after he had attempted to terminate their licensing agreement; (4) failing to return some of his photographs upon demand; and (5) placing defective copyright notices on slide mounts for his photographs. Rano also alleged state breach of contract, intentional interference with economic relationship, and malicious conversion claims. As a remedy for the copyright infringement claims, Rano sought an injunction against Sipa's further use of his photographs, the delivery of the photographs for impoundment, a declaratory judgment as to the rights to his photographs, compensatory and punitive damages, and costs of the suit and attorney's fees.

The district court dismissed Rano's pendent claims for malicious conversion and intentional interference with economic relationship and granted defendant Sipahioglu's motion to dismiss for lack of personal jurisdiction. After reviewing the affidavits and memoranda submitted by the parties and conducting a hearing, the district court granted Sipa's motion for summary judgment, holding that all but one of Rano's copyright infringement claims did not constitute copyright claims under the Copyright Act, but were merely breach of contract claims. The one claim that did allege copyright infringement – failure to affix a proper copyright notice – was, as a matter of law, meritless because the notice Sipa did provide was adequate to protect his copyright. The district court dismissed the remaining pendent state claims for lack of subject matter jurisdiction.

*Discussion*

I. *Jurisdiction in the District Court.*

The district court had subject matter jurisdiction over Rano's action under 28 U.S.C. § 1338(a) because the suit "arises under" federal copyright law.[1] [n1 Although Rano is not a citizen of the United States, his work is protected under the Copyright Act. A work is subject to copyright if on the date of first publication the author was a national of a foreign nation that is a party to a copyright treaty to which the United States is also a party. 17 U.S.C. § 104(b)(1).] . . .

In this case, Rano is seeking remedies under several sections of the Copyright Act: 17 U.S.C. §§502 (injunctive relief), 503 (impoundment), 504 (damages and profits), and 505 (attorney's fees and costs). Thus, federal jurisdiction is proper. . . .

IV. *Allegations of Copyright Infringement.*

Rano alleges infringement of two of the rights granted to him, as creator of the photographs, by the Copyright Act: the right to reproduce the copyrighted work in copies and the right to distribute copies of the work to the public by sale or other transfer of ownership. See 17 U.S.C. § 106(1) and (3). Rano concedes that, under normal circumstances, his licensing agreement with Sipa would provide Sipa with a valid defense against his copyright infringement claim. Rano argues, however, that although he and Sipa did at one time have a copyright agreement, he terminated the agreement with Sipa. He claims that the termination deprived Sipa of its right to use the negatives Rano already had sent to Sipa, and that Sipa's subsequent use of Rano's negatives constituted copyright infringement.

It is undisputed that the licensing agreement did not contain any provision, either express or implied, regarding its duration. Rano relies on two theories to prove that he properly terminated the agreement. First, Rano argues that California law provides for termination at will of a contract of unspecified duration. Thus, when he wrote Sipahioglu on March 12, 1987, and informed him of his intent to use a different photograph distributor, he terminated their licensing agreement. Second, Rano argues that California law provides for the termination of a contract upon the material breach of the contract by the other party, and that Sipa's alleged actions constituted material breaches of the licensing agreement, permitting him to terminate the agreement.

Sipa counters that the express provision in the Copyright Act regarding termination rights, 17 U.S.C. §203, preempts state law and prevents Rano from terminating their license agreement until thirty-five years have elapsed. Thus, Sipa claims, its alleged acts of reproducing and distributing Rano's photographs remained licensed at all times and did not constitute copyright infringement.

*A. Termination at Will.*

Under California contract law, agreements of non-specified duration are terminable at the will of either party. *Zimco Restaurants, Inc. v. Bartenders and Culinary Workers' Union, Local 340,* 165 Cal. App. 2d 235, 331 P.2d 789, 792-92 (Cal. Ct. App. 1958); *but cf. Foley v. Interactive Data Corp.,* 47 Cal. 3d 654, 765 P.2d 373, 385-86, 254 Cal. Rptr. 211 (Cal. 1988) (noting that this general rule increasingly has given way to courts' willingness to "gap fill" a reasonable duration). Rano argues that the non-exclusive licensing agreement was a contract of non-specified duration, and as such was terminable at will. He further argues that he exercised his right to terminate the contract.

However, application of this principle of California contract law here would directly conflict with federal copyright law. Under section 203 of the Copyright Act, licensing agreements are not terminable at will from the moment of creation; instead, they are terminable at the will of the author only during a five year period beginning at the end of thirty-five years from the date of execution of the license (unless they explicitly specify an earlier termination date). 17 U.S.C. §203 (a). Since California law and federal law are in direct conflict, federal law must control.

Section 203 applies to non-exclusive, as well as exclusive, licenses executed by the author on or after January 1, 1978. 17 U.S.C. § 203(a). Rano asserts that Section 203 is inapplicable because the licensing agreement was oral and thus not executed. We disagree. Not only was the agreement evidenced by several letters signed by both parties, but it also was successfully operative for approximately eight years. Thus, the agreement was executed and is within the purview of Section 203 and is not terminable at will.

Contrary to Rano's allegation, holding that Section 203 preempts California's termination at will rule of contract construction would not mean that Sipa, and other licensees, would be able to breach the licensing agreement with impunity. Under well-settled copyright law, Rano would be able to claim copyright infringement if Sipa exceeded the scope of the licensing agreement, breached a covenant or condition, or breached the agreement in such a substantial and material way as to justify rescission. Moreover, he could sue in state court under a breach of contract theory.

*B. Termination for Material Breach.*

Rano argues that Sipa materially breached the licensing agreement and that the breach gave him the right to terminate the agreement. Although licensing agreements are not terminable at will, under federal and state law a material breach of a licensing agreement gives rise to a right of rescission which allows the nonbreaching party to terminate the agreement. After the agreement is terminated, any further distribution would constitute copyright infringement.

Here, it is clear that Rano attempted to rescind the agreement. The question is whether he had the right to rescind. A breach will justify rescission of a licensing agreement only when it is "of so material and substantial a nature that [it] affects the very essence of the contract and serves to defeat the object of the parties . . . . [The breach must constitute] a total failure in the performance of the contract."

Rano has not provided evidence sufficient to withstand summary judgment on this issue. Rano points to a number of acts that he contends constitutes a material breach, but only those acts preceding Rano's purported termination on March 12, 1987 are relevant. These acts include Sipa's alleged failure to pay royalties, failure to return negatives, and failure to credit for the Sara Ferguson photograph. The first two breaches claimed by Rano, upon which he relies most heavily, are not supported by the record. Sipa actually paid Rano 99.99% of the royalties due him up to approximately the time Rano sought to terminate the licensing agreement, excluding royalties due for photos published in the United States from 1985 to 1986. Of the latter, Sipa paid 86.85% of the royalties due. As to the second alleged breach, nothing in the letters evidencing the oral contract between the parties provided for a return of Rano's negatives on demand. Rano merely points to a letter from Sipa stating that the negatives would be filed at its offices and "could be returned if necessary, although [Sipa] would want to keep them for a while." Finally, Rano provides no evidence to support his claim that he was due credit for the photograph of Sara Ferguson. Sipa provided evidence that the photograph was taken by another journalist; the duty was on Rano to show there was a genuine issue as to this fact.

Even if we found Rano's allegations had merit, however, we could not conclude that Sipa materially breached the licensing agreement in light of the fact that the parties' enjoyed a harmonious eight-year relationship (in which Rano received royalties and credit for his work). "After considerable performance, a slight breach which does not go 'to the root' of the contract will not justify termination."

V. *Failure To Affix a Proper Copyright Notice.*

Rano argues Sipa affixed an improper copyright notice on the negatives it distributed to various publications. In the case before us. . . , Sipa failed to affix the year of publication on a number of photographs. Such an omission [before March 1989, when the notice requirement was deleted from U.S. copyright law] generally deprive[d] a work of copyright protection. *See* 17 U.S.C. § 405. Although Sipa alleges a number of possible defenses, because of the factual nature of these issues, we are unable as a matter of law to find that there is no material issue of fact as to whether the notice was adequate. Accordingly, we reverse the district court's grant of summary judgment as to this issue.

VI. *Personal Jurisdiction Over Sipahioglu. . . .*

*B. Analysis.*

The district court dismissed the claim against Sipahioglu because it found it lacked personal jurisdiction over him. Sipahioglu is a citizen of Turkey and a long-time resident of France. His ties to California include three short visits to California in the last seven years, totaling six days. None of Sipahioglu's visits to California involved Rano or his photographs.

There is no applicable federal statute governing personal jurisdiction in this matter, hence the law of the state in which the district court sits California applies. California has adopted a typical "long-arm" statute, rendering jurisdiction coextensive with the outer limits of due process.

A state may assert either general or specific jurisdiction over a nonresident defendant. If the defendant's activities in the state are "substantial" or "continuous and systematic," general jurisdiction may be asserted even if the claim is unrelated to the defendant's activities. Rano does not argue that Sipa is subject to general jurisdiction; instead, Rano relies on specific jurisdiction.

Under specific jurisdiction, a court may assert jurisdiction for a cause of action that arises out of the defendant's forum-related activities. . . . [W]e established a three-part test for determining when a court can exercise specific jurisdiction: (1) the defendant must perform an act or consummate a transaction within the forum, purposefully availing himself of the privilege of conducting activities in the forum and invoking the benefits and protections of its laws; (2) the claim must arise out of or result from the defendant's forum-related activities; (3) exercise of jurisdiction must be reasonable. Rano must show that all three prongs are satisfied for us to assert personal jurisdiction.

Rano contends that Sipahioglu caused and profited from Sipa's grant of licenses of Rano's photographs to magazine publications that he knew would be distributed in California. This is enough, Rano argues, to satisfy the "purposeful availment" and "arising out of" requirements. . . .

We disagree. Sipahioglu could not have foreseen Rano's fortuitous move from Europe to California. Further, there is no evidence that Sipahioglu invoked any of the benefits or protections of California's laws. Rano's argument, if accepted, would render Sipahioglu, and other foreign owners of art who sell their products to publications, amenable to personal jurisdiction in every state in which their art eventually is displayed. We have held that litigation against an alien defendant requires a higher jurisdictional barrier than litigation against a citizen from a sister state.

We find that Rano has not satisfied the burden of establishing personal jurisdiction over Sipahioglu; hence we affirm the district court's dismissal of the claims against Sipahioglu. . . .

*Conclusion*

We affirm the district court's grant of summary judgment in favor of Sipa on the issue of copyright infringement as to Rano's claims based on material breach.

We reverse the district court's grant of summary judgment in favor of Sipa as to Rano's claim for improper copyright notice and remand for further proceedings consistent with this opinion.

We affirm the district court's dismissal of Goskin Sipahioglu for lack of personal jurisdiction.

# *Chapter 2*

# EMPLOYMENT OF TALENT

## 2.1 IMMIGRATION

All countries of the world attempt to control the flow of foreigners into their territories. Short-term, money-spending tourists may be welcomed with only a few formalities. But job-seeking foreigners are almost always confronted with significant administrative hurdles. The reason for this is that countries usually have fewer desirable jobs than residents who need work, and local workers view foreign job seekers as undesired competitors. This is just as true in the entertainment industry as it is in others.

Nevertheless, most countries will allow certain foreigners to work, under circumstances designed to minimize, if not eliminate, the impact on job opportunities for local residents. In order to work legally, even temporarily, foreigners must obtain work permits (not to be confused with United States "green cards" which authorize permanent U.S. residency as well as the right to work).

The process of getting a work permit is intended to be administrative, rather than adversarial. If a foreigner is eligible, a work permit will be issued simply in response to a properly prepared application. If a foreigner is not eligible, a work permit will be denied, even in the face of aggressive litigation.

The question in all cases is whether the foreigner has the personal characteristics that are necessary to qualify for a permit for the type of work he or she would like to do, under the law of the country where the foreigner would like to do it. The particular personal characteristics that are necessary depend on the type of work the foreigner would like to do. Those characteristics are different for lawyers than they are for entertainers, of course. They also are different for entertainers than for athletes. And (in the United States, at least) they even are different for entertainers who perform *individually* than they are for those who perform with *groups*.

The materials that follow include two application forms: the form used to apply for work permits for "sportspeople and entertainers" in the United Kingdom; and the form used to apply for work permits for "nonimmigrant workers" of all kinds, including "artists, athletes and entertainers," in the United States. (In U.S. parlance, a "nonimmigrant" is someone who intends to stay in the United States only temporarily, though "temporarily" may last for years; while an "immigrant" is someone who intends to stay in the U.S. permanently.)

The United Kingdom's Work Permits Office has prepared plain-English instructions explaining how its "sportspeople and entertainers" application form should be prepared; and the following materials include an edited version of those instructions as well. The only (accurate) "instructions" that exist for preparing the U.S. application form for artists, entertainers and athletes are the Immigration and Nationality Act itself and INS regulations; and the following materials include excerpts from both.

---

### 2.1.1 British Law Concerning Foreign Performers

To help organize your thoughts as you read these British materials, think about *who* should submit a work permit application, *how* it should be filled out, and *what supporting materials* should be submitted with it, if a work permit were being sought for:

*Actress and entourage*

A. An Academy-Award winning American actress who has been offered the leading role in a play to be staged in a theater in London.
B. The American actress's young child.
C. The American actress's long-time personal assistant.
D. A caretaker, who has been employed by the actress to care for her child ever since the child was born.

*Band and entourage*

E. An Grammy-Award winning American band that has received an offer from a concert promoter to do a summer-long European tour that includes a dozen concerts in England, Wales and Scotland.
F. The band's equipment manager who is responsible for packing, transporting and caring for the band's musical instruments and stage costumes.
G. The band's personal manager who arranges the band's transportation and accomodations, and who is the band's business contact with the concert promoter.
H. An American solo performer who is to be the opening act for the Grammy-Award winning band referred to above, who recently recorded his or her very first album and has not yet won an Grammy or any award.

*Athlete and entourage*

I. A German or Latin American soccer player, who once received a Golden Ball award as the best player in a FIFA championship match, who has received an offer to play for Manchester United in Britain's Premier League.
J. The player's German or Latin American personal assistant.
K. The player's German or Latin American agent.
L. The player's German or Latin American girl friend.

---

## Work permit application: for sportspeople and entertainers

- *If you are applying to extend a work permit, please use form WP3X.*
- *Please read the Sportspeople and Entertainers notes before you fill in this form.*
- *Please type or print the form in block capitals*

**Use from 01/11/2001-1/03/2002**

Is this application for: an individual? ☐ ***start at Question 1*** or a group? ☐ ***go straight to Question 14***

### Details of the person

1. Surname/family name
2. Surname/family name at birth (if different)
3. First names
4. Stage name (if applicable)
5. Sex ☐ Male ☐ Female
6. Date of birth — day / month / year
7. Nationality
8. Passport number *(if known)*
9. Government issuing the passport
10. Is this person currently in the UK or Ireland? ☐ No; go to Question 12 ☐ Yes; in what capacity?
11. Address in UK or Ireland
12. Has the person previously held a UK work permit? ☐ No; go to Question 14 ☐ Yes, please give details below
13. Worker or work permit reference number (if known)

WP3 Page 1 of 9 over →

## Details of the employer in Great Britain

14. Full name of employer in Great Britain [ ]

15. Type of business [ ]

16. Address in Great Britain (including postcode) [ ]

Phone number [ ]

Fax number [ ]

E-mail address [ ]

17. Name of contact in your organisation who is dealing with this application. Please give their address if this is different from that in question 16. [Title ]

18. Position in organisation [ ]

19. Has your organisation made a work permit application in the last five years?

[ ] Yes; go to Question 20

[ ] No *Please send us information about your company (see paragraph 4 of the Sportspeople & Entertainers (notes))*

## Details of employment

20. Are you applying for a multiple entry work permit?
(See paragraphs 29-34 of Sportspeople & Entertainers (notes) for more details.)

[ ] No

[ ] Yes

21. Job title or name of group:

[ ]

22. For groups, has the group worked in Great Britain before? [ ] No [ ] Yes; please provide group reference number (if known)

[ ]

## Details of employment (continued)

23. Are the group currently in the UK or Ireland?
   - [ ] No; go to Question 24
   - [ ] Yes; in what capacity?

24. For individuals, please provide a full job description. For groups, please explain what they do e.g. music, theatre, circus troupe.

25. Have you offered the person or group a contract?
   - [ ] Yes; please attach a copy signed by both parties
   - [ ] No; please explain below why there is no contract

26. Do you have written confirmation of the venue(s)?
   - [ ] Yes; please attach copies
   - [ ] No; please explain below why there are no venue confirmations

27. Over what period will this work take place?

   From: day month year

   To: day month year

28. When will the person or the first member of the group arrive in the UK? day month year

29. How much will the person or group be paid? (excluding expenses) £ per day / week / month / performance or in total

30 How much will be paid as expenses or other payments? (attach details) £ per day / week / month / performance or in total

Where you, the employer named in the application, are not providing the payments and other expenses above please attach full details, including evidence to confirm the source of payment.

## Reasons for employing the person or group

31. Please give details and send supporting evidence to show what you have done to recruit a 'resident worker' or if you have not carried out a recruitment search, say why the person is uniquely qualified for the

32. Please give specific details why you did not recruit each 'resident worker', including those you did not shortlist.

## Skills and experience

33. Please enclose evidence to show that the person/group is an established entertainer, cultural artist or sportsperson as requested in the Sportspeople & Entertainers (notes). If you are not able to do so please give reasons below.

34. Please describe employment/major engagements, including any in the UK, in the last two years which demonstrate that the person/group have been maintaining their international reputation.

| Dates | | Name and address of employer | Type of work and locations |
|---|---|---|---|
| From | To | | |
| | | | |

*For entertainment groups continue on page 5.*
*For individual entertainers now go to page 7.*
*For sportspeople now go to the declarations on page 8.*

WP3

## Details of group members

**Please print clearly in capitals - this information will be printed on the work permit.**

- If there are up to 19 members in the group, we will issue a work permit for each person.
- If there are 20 or more people in a group travelling together we will send a letter of permission for the group to the employer or representative and notify the port of entry.
- If any group members need an entry visa please give details of the relevant visa issuing office(s) at the bottom of the page.

| | Surname/family name on passport (in alphabetical order) | First names | Date of birth D M Y | Sex M/F | Nationality | Passport number *(if known)* | Issuing Government | Job title | If travelling separately *(tick)* | If currently in the UK *(tick)* |
|---|---|---|---|---|---|---|---|---|---|---|
| 1. | | | | | | | | | | |
| 2. | | | | | | | | | | |
| 3. | | | | | | | | | | |
| 4. | | | | | | | | | | |
| 5. | | | | | | | | | | |
| 6. | | | | | | | | | | |
| 7. | | | | | | | | | | |
| 8. | | | | | | | | | | |
| 9. | | | | | | | | | | |
| 10. | | | | | | | | | | |
| 11. | | | | | | | | | | |
| 12. | | | | | | | | | | |
| 13. | | | | | | | | | | |
| 14. | | | | | | | | | | |
| 15. | | | | | | | | | | |
| 16. | | | | | | | | | | |
| 17. | | | | | | | | | | |
| 18. | | | | | | | | | | |
| 19. | | | | | | | | | | |
| 20. | | | | | | | | | | |

- For groups of 20 or more, please give details of when the main part of the group will arrive in the UK, if known (if not, please supply when known):

Date ______ Time ______ Airport and terminal/seaport ______

Flight number ______ Visa issuing office (where appropriate) ______



over—

## Details of group members (continued)

| Surname/family name on passport *(in alphabetical order)* | First names | Date of birth | Sex M/F | Nationality | Passport number *(if known)* | Issuing Government | Job title | If travelling separately | If currently in the UK |
|---|---|---|---|---|---|---|---|---|---|
| | | D M Y | | | | | | *(tick)* | *(tick)* |
| 21. | | | | | | | | | |
| 22. | | | | | | | | | |
| 23. | | | | | | | | | |
| 24. | | | | | | | | | |
| 25. | | | | | | | | | |
| 26. | | | | | | | | | |
| 27. | | | | | | | | | |
| 28. | | | | | | | | | |
| 29. | | | | | | | | | |
| 30. | | | | | | | | | |
| 31. | | | | | | | | | |
| 32. | | | | | | | | | |
| 33. | | | | | | | | | |
| 34. | | | | | | | | | |
| 35. | | | | | | | | | |
| 36. | | | | | | | | | |
| 37. | | | | | | | | | |
| 38. | | | | | | | | | |
| 39. | | | | | | | | | |
| 40. | | | | | | | | | |
| 41. | | | | | | | | | |
| 42. | | | | | | | | | |
| 43. | | | | | | | | | |
| 44. | | | | | | | | | |
| 45. | | | | | | | | | |

## Details of engagements in Great Britain

**If there is not enough room, please copy this sheet before you fill it in.**

| Dates of work | | Name, and address of venue |
|---|---|---|
| From | To | |

## Employer declaration

This declaration must be signed by the employer in Great Britain. However, if you have no employee in Great Britain it may be signed by a solicitor.

- I am authorised to make this application on behalf of the employer named in this application.
- The details given in this application are true and complete to the best of my knowledge and belief. I understand that if knowingly I fail to provide any relevant information or I provide information which is false or misleading the matter may be referred to the appropriate authorities.
- The employer named in this application knows of no suitable 'resident worker' who will be displaced or excluded as a result of us employing the person who is the subject of this application.
- The employer named in this application agrees to comply with UK legislation and any requirements for registration or licensing necessary for the employment which is subject to this application.
- The employer named in this application agrees to comply with the terms and conditions governing the issue of work permits as determined by the Secretary of State for the Home Department.
- I understand that the Secretary of State for the Home Department may carry out checks on compliance.

Your signature | | Date | |

Name (CAPITALS please) | Title |

Position | |

For and on behalf of (the employer in Great Britain) | |

## Other details

Date by which you require the permit | day | Month | year |

We will make every effort to meet your requirements within our published Service and Standards.

Please return this form to:

**Work Permits (UK)**
**Immigration and Nationality Directorate**
**Home Office**
**Level 5, Moorfoot**
**Sheffield**
**S1 4PQ**

For sports/entertainments enquiries please phone: 0114 259 3710

For general work permit enquiries please phone: 0114 259 4074

Data Protection Act 1998: the information given in this form will be processed only for the purpose of administering work permit applications in line with the Department's notification to the Data Protection Commissioner.

## Representative declaration

If you are an external representative dealing with this application on behalf of the employer, please complete the details below.

Name of representative company

Address (including postcode)

Name of contact if different from below — Title

Phone number

Fax number

E-mail address

This declaration must be signed by the representative

- I have been appointed by the employer to make this application.
- I confirm that all the facts relating to this application have been given to me by the employer or on their behalf and to the best of my knowledge and belief are true and complete.
- I confirm that the employer has seen and signed the completed application.
- Once the application is decided I will provide the employer with all correspondence from you relating to your decision.

Signed — Date

Name (CAPITALS please) — Title

Position

For and on behalf of (the representative)



**Please note the HMSO Copyright Unit cannot deal with queries about work permits or applications. All enquiries about work permits should be made to us (see Other details section on Page 8 of this form).**

WP3 Page 9 of 9

**Guidance notes for employers on how to apply for a sportspeople and entertainers work permit**

Work Permits (UK) Home Office (2001)



Published in Great Britain by the Home Office, Moorfoot, Sheffield S1 4PQ



*Eligibility to apply for a work permit*

1. Information you supply on the application form will be assessed against the criteria described in this document. Please use form WP3 when applying for first work permits, multiple entry work permits and for changes of employment or use WP3X for extensions to existing work permits. . . .

2. For the purposes of these guidance notes a 'resident worker' is a person who is an European Economic Area (EEA) national . . . or has settled status within the meaning of the Immigration Act 1971.

3. You can make a work permit application if you are an employer based in this country and you need to employ a person to work in England, Scotland or Wales. In some cases, in the entertainment industry, the person's agent may be the employer. You should make a work permit application for a named person to do a specific job for the British employer. The person cannot transfer a work permit to a different job or to work for a different employer.

4. You should be an established employer in the sports or entertainment industry. In addition, if you have not made a work permit application in the past five years you should send documents that show that you are a British based employer. . . .

*Contracts for work*

5. A copy of the employment contract outlining the terms and conditions of the employment and signed by both parties should normally be provided.

6. Venue contracts or letters of confirmation of an offer of employment in this country should also be provided.

*Conditions of employment*

7. The pay and other conditions of employment should be at least equal to those normally given to a 'resident worker' doing this kind of work.

(a) The employment must meet all UK legislation including the National Minimum Wage (NMW) and the Working Time Regulations (WTR). Also the application must comply with any requirements for registration or licensing necessary for the employment. . . .

(b) You will normally be expected to operate PAYE and class 1 National Insurance (NI) Contributions. Payments made via an overseas service company or a third party whose main involvement with the worker is to hire the worker's services to others will not normally be appropriate because we expect a direct contract of employment between the person and their employer, a company based in this country. If the person's contract of employment will stay with their overseas company, you will need to make sure the arrangements for their tax and National Insurance payments are acceptable to the appropriate UK authorities. . . .

*General criteria*

8. We only issue work permits for established sportspeople, entertainers, cultural artists and some technical/support people, whose employment will not displace or exclude 'resident workers' (see paragraphs 11 to 14).

9. The criteria for work permit applications for sportspeople are agreed following consultation with the appropriate governing bodies. To find out which criteria apply to a particular sport, please contact the relevant governing body or the Sportspeople & Entertainments Team. . . .

*Skills and experience of the person or group*

10. The skills and experience of people who may qualify are described below.

*(a) Sportspeople*

People who are internationally established at the highest level in their sport, and whose employment will make a significant contribution to the development of that particular sport in this country at the highest level. Coaches must also be suitably qualified at the highest level.

You will need to show that the person is currently internationally established at the highest level. Please provide evidence of their skill level and achievements. For coaches please send copies of the qualifications to coach and evidence of any coaching experience they have. You should also provide a copy of their health and safety qualifications where this does not form part of the main coaching qualification.

*(b) Entertainers*

People who have performed at the highest level and have established a reputation in their profession; and people/groups who are engaged to perform or do work which only they can do.

Please provide relevant past publicity material or press reviews with the source clearly identified. For groups, publicity material should clearly explain the status of each member of that group. Printed programme, record, compact disc or audio cassette material or their covers are also acceptable. If they are not in English please send a translation. If you are using the e-mail application form, you can scan in this information as an attachment if appropriate. However, Work Permits (UK) reserves the right to request originals if they deem it necessary.

Biographical articles in magazines or the press about groups or individuals are not acceptable.

*Unit companies*

A unit company is a large group of entertainers who have performed together before and have toured overseas as part of an established production before entering the UK. A group formed specifically for a British tour will not be classed as a unit company. Unit companies will normally be groups such as orchestras, ballet corps and theatre productions. Pop/music groups are not classed as unit companies.

You should supply publicity material on the unit company as a whole; this should include a letter from the unit company, on letter-headed notepaper, which names all the members. You should also provide evidence to show that the unit company has performed previously, this may include relevant past publicity material, printed programmes or press reviews with the source clearly identified.

*(c) Cultural Artists*

People who are skilled in foreign arts that are rare or unavailable in this country and can make a contribution to the arts, cultural relations and cultural awareness.

Please provide relevant past publicity material or press reviews with the source clearly identified. For groups, publicity material should clearly explain the status of each member of that group. Printed programme, record, compact disc or audio cassette material or their covers are also acceptable. If they are not in English please send a translation. If you are using the e-mail application form, you can scan in this information as an attachment if appropriate. However, Work Permits (UK) reserves the right to request originals if they deem it necessary.

Biographical articles in magazines or the press about groups or individuals are not acceptable.

If exceptionally, you are unable to provide press or publicity material as evidence of a cultural artist's status, you must, either provide a letter of verification from their home country's Ministry of Culture; or where agreed by Work Permits (UK), the artist must attend an interview with their nearest British Embassy, High Commission, or Consulate.

*(d) Technical / support people*

People whose work is directly related to the employment of an entertainer, cultural artist, sportsperson or a dramatic production. The person should have proven technical or other specialist skills.

It is not normally necessary to provide material to demonstrate the skills and experience of non-performers.

*Availability of suitably qualified 'resident workers'*

11. In some sports, we recognise that there are likely to be shortages of 'resident workers' who are skilled at the highest level. We have agreed with the governing bodies and players' representatives that work permit applications for these posts do not need to be supported by evidence of the availability of 'resident workers.' This information is made available to employers in the sport through the governing bodies and players' representatives.

12. For some employment, where an established entertainer who is to perform in their own right or where they are a cultural artist, the question of whether a 'resident worker' could do the job will not be appropriate.

13. In other cases you will need to show why you cannot fill the post with a 'resident worker.' This would include applications for residencies where the length of time required is for three months or more and people/groups are performing at the same venue or series of venues for the whole period. The people/group will not normally be well known nor unique and usually perform at venues where the audience would go to listen to music rather than specifically go to see that artist/group. You should give details of your recruitment methods and give reasons why you did not employ a suitably qualified 'resident worker.'

14. The recruitment methods you use, including advertising, should be appropriate to the job and represent a genuine attempt to recruit a suitably qualified person. Where these conditions are not met an application may be refused and the employer may be asked to carry out a further recruitment exercise before it is considered again.

*Recruitment Search*

15. Where advertising is appropriate (see paragraphs 11 to 13), you should have advertised the job in the most appropriate medium that provides the best way of reaching suitably qualified 'resident workers.' This will normally be national newspapers or professional journals. The publications or other media you use should be readily available throughout the EEA. Where, within the publication, you choose to have it displayed, and how prominently, should reflect the level and nature of the post.

16. Advertisements should normally give details of the post, the qualifications and experience needed and an indication of the salary or salary range. You should allow four weeks from the date the advertisement appears to receive applications. To make sure that the results of your advertising reflect the current availability of the skills you need, you should place the advertisement within the six months before you apply to us for the work permit. . . .

*Details of responses to all recruitment methods*

23. You also need to give us details of the responses you received to all advertising or other recruitment methods you used. This should include the total number of people who responded, the number you short-listed for interview and full reasons why you did not employ each 'resident worker.'

*Length of permits*

24. Sportspeople are issued with work permits in line with the length of contract up to a maximum of five years.

25. Work permits for entertainers are issued only on a short term basis to cover the period of contracted work or the period of engagement.

26. Multiple entry work permits can be issued for a minimum of six months and a maximum of two years for individuals and for a minimum of six months and a maximum of 12 months for a group.

27. In the case of an entertainer on a short term engagement, if you foresee that the artist or group may need to extend the period to perform extra dates for you, you should indicate this in your initial application. You should send us confirmation and details of the additional employment as soon as you have it.

*Types of applications*

28. For a first work permit, you should use a postal or e-mail WP3 form.

*Multiple entry work permits*

29. This type of permit allows workers who are based overseas to enter the country for short periods of time on a regular basis to work, rather than obtaining a permit each time they enter the country to work.

30. This type of permit can be applied for under any category of the sportspeople and entertainers arrangements.

31. Multiple entry work permits can be issued for a minimum of six months and up to two years for individuals and for a minimum of six months and a maximum of 12 months for a group. .

32. The applications for this type of permit must be made whilst the person(s) is/are out of the country.

33. If you want to apply for a multiple entry work permit you should fill in a WP3 form. You cannot apply for an extension; a fresh application must be submitted on a WP3 form if a further period is required. This also applies to any change of employment.

34. The employee will not be allowed to undertake supplementary employment whilst on this type of permit. Any additional promotional activities required to support the main work for which the work permit is required will be allowed under this category.

*Extension applications*

35. If you want to extend a work permit you should fill in form WP3X and say why and for how much longer you need to employ the person or group. . . .

*How do I apply for work permits for a group?*

54. You only need to complete one WP3 form. Please list on the form the details of each member of the group who needs a work permit.

55. The procedure followed depends on the number of members in the group:

(a) if there are up to 19 members in the group we will issue a work permit for each member;

(b) for groups of 20 or more members travelling together, we will not issue a work permit for each member, but we will send a letter of permission to you the employer or your representative instead.

(c) if members of a group are travelling separately we will issue individual work permits.

(d) if a multiple entry work permit has been issued, any new or additional member(s) would need to apply for a work permit separately on a WP3 form.

56. We will send a copy of the group list and exact arrival details to the Immigration Office at the port of entry (we will need to contact you later for the date, time and place of arrival if you do not have these details when you apply).

57. On completion of the engagements the entertainers or artists are expected to return abroad.

*When should I apply?*

58. You should apply when you have found the person that you want to employ but no more than six months before you want to bring them into the country. . . .

65. Some people may need an entry visa for the UK as well as a work permit. The husbands, wives and children of people who hold work permits need entry clearance in all cases, whatever their nationality. If the person needs a visa and entry clearance they must apply to their nearest British Diplomatic Post abroad. . . .

*Where do I send the application form?*

77. Please post the completed application to us at:

Work Permits (UK)
Immigration and Nationality Directorate
Home Office
Level 5, Moorfoot
Sheffield
S1 4PQ

Or you can e-mail your application (and scanned attachments) to us at office.forms@dfee.gov.uk.

*Where will Work Permits (UK) send the permit and any other letters?*

78. We will send all letters to the employer named on the application form, unless you are using a solicitor or other representative. In these cases we will send the permit and all letters to them.

*How do I get further advice on making an application?*

79. If you want advice about completing an application form or clarification of these guidance notes please contact the Sportspeople and Entertainments team who will consider your application.

Phone: 0114 259 3710
Fax: 0114 259 4987
E-mail: ents.workpermits@dfes.gsi.gov.uk

Write to us at:

Sportspeople and Entertainments Team
Work Permits (UK)
Immigration and Nationality Directorate
Home Office
Level 5, Moorfoot
Sheffield
S1 4PQ

Please Note: All of Work Permit (UK)'s e-mail addresses may change before these guidance notes expire. See our website: www.workpermits.gov.uk for further details. . . .

*How do I appeal against a decision?*

81. The decision letter we send to you will explain the terms under which we have approved the application. If we cannot approve your application the letter will

explain why and, if appropriate, give details of how to appeal against the decision.

. . .

---

### 2.1.2 United States Law Concerning Foreign Performers

To help organize your thoughts as read these U.S. immigration materials, think about *who* should submit a work permit application, *how* it should be filled out, and *what supporting materials* should be submitted with it, if a work permit were being sought for:

*Actress and entourage*

A. An Academy-Award winning British actress who has been offered the leading role in a play to be staged in a theater in New York City.
B. The British actress's young child.
C. The British actress's long-time personal assistant.
D. A caretaker, who has been employed by the actress to care for her child ever since the child was born.

*Band and entourage*

E. An Grammy-Award winning British band that has received an offer from a concert promoter to do a summer-long American tour that includes a dozen concerts in New York, Illinois and California.
F. The band's equipment manager who is responsible for packing, transporting and caring for the band's musical instruments and stage costumes.
G. The band's personal manager who arranges the band's transportation and accomodations, and who is the band's business contact with the concert promoter.
H. A British solo performer who is to be the opening act for the Grammy-Award winning band referred to above, who recently recorded his or her very first album and has not yet won an Grammy or any award.

*Athlete and entourage*

I. A German or Latin American soccer player, who once received a Golden Ball award as the best player in a FIFA championship match, who has received an offer to play for Major League Soccer's Los Angeles Galaxy.
J. The player's German or Latin American personal assistant.
K. The player's German or Latin American agent.
L. The player's German or Latin American girl friend.

---

U.S. Department of Justice
Immigration and Naturalization Service

OMB No. 1115-0168
Petition for a Nonimmigrant Worker

**START HERE - Please Type or Print**

**Part 1. Information about the employer filing this petition.**
If the employer is an individual, use the top name line. Organizations should use the second line.

Family Name | Given Name | Middle Initial

Company or Organization Name

**Address - Attn:**

Street Number and Name | Apt. #

City | State or Province

Country | Zip/Postal Code

IRS Tax #

**Part 2. Information about this Petition.**
(See instructions to determine the fee)

1. **Requested Nonimmigrant classification:**
(write classification symbol at right)
2. **Basis for Classification** (check one)
   a. ☐ New employment
   b. ☐ Continuation of previously approved employment without change
   c. ☐ Change in previously approved employment
   d. ☐ New concurrent employment
3. **Prior Petition.** If you checked other than "New Employment" in item 2 (above) give the most recent prior petition numbers for the worker(s):
4. **Requested Action:** (check one)
   a. ☐ Notify the office in Part 4 so the person(s) can obtain a visa or be admitted (NOTE: a petition is not required for an E-1, E-2, or R visa)
   b. ☐ Change the person(s)' status and extend their stay since they are all now in the U.S. in another status (see instructions for limitations). This is available only where you check "New Employment" in item 2, above.
   c. ☐ Extend or amend the stay of the person(s) since they now hold this status.
5. **Total number of workers in petition:**
(See instructions for where more than one worker can be included)

**Part 3. Information about the person(s) you are filing for.**
Complete the blocks below. Use the continuation sheet to name each person included in this petition.

If an entertainment group, give their group name.

Family Name | Given Name | Middle Initial

Date of Birth (Month/Day/Year) | Country of Birth

Social Security # | A #

If in the United States, complete the following:

Date of Arrival (Month/Day/Year) | I-94 #

Current Nonimmigrant Status | Expires (Month/Day/Year)

**FOR INS USE ONLY**

Returned | Receipt

Resubmitted

Reloc Sent

Reloc Rec'd

Interviewed
☐ Petitioner
☐ Beneficiary

Class:
# of Workers:
Priority Number:
Validity Dates: From
To

☐ **Classification Approved**
☐ Consulate/POE/PFI Notified
At:
☐ Extension Granted
☐ COS/Extension Granted

**Partial Approval (explain)**

**Action Block**

**To be Completed by Attorney or Representative, if any**
☐ Fill in box if G-28 is attached to represent the applicant.

VOLAG#

ATTY State License #

Form I-129 (Rev. 12/11/91)N

*Continued on back.*

**Part 4. Processing Information**

a. If the person named in Part 3 is outside the U.S. or a requested extension of stay or change of status cannot be granted, give the U.S. consulate or inspection facility you want to be notified if this petition is approved.

Type of Office (check one): ☐ Consulate ☐ Pre-flight inspection ☐ Port of Entry

Office Address (City) U.S. State or Foreign Country

Person's Foreign Address

b. Does each person in this petition have a valid passport?
☐ Not required to have passport ☐ No - explain on separate paper ☐ Yes

c. Are you filing any other petitions with this one? ☐ No ☐ Yes - How many? ______

d. Are applications for replacement/Initial I-94's being filed with this petition? ☐ No ☐ Yes - How many? ______

e. Are applications by dependents being filed with this petition? ☐ No ☐ Yes - How many? ______

f. Is any person in this petition in exclusion or deportation proceedings? ☐ No ☐ Yes - explain on separate paper

g. Have you ever filed an immigrant petition for any person in this petition? ☐ No ☐ Yes - explain on separate paper

h. If you indicated you were filing a new petition in Part 2, within the past seven years has any person in this petition:

1) ever been given the classification you are now requesting? ☐ No ☐ Yes - explain on separate paper

2) ever been denied the classification you are now requesting? ☐ No ☐ Yes - explain on separate paper

i. If you are filing for an entertainment group, has any person in this petition not been with the group for at least 1 year?
☐ No ☐ Yes - explain on separate paper

**Part 5. Basic information about the proposed employment and employer.**
Attach the supplement relating to the classification you are requesting.

Job Title | Nontechnical Description of Job

Address where the person(s) will work if different from the address in Part 1.

Is this a full-time position? ☐ No - Hours per week ☐ Yes | Wages per week or per year

Other Compensation (Explain) | Value per week or per year | Dates of intended employment From: To:

Type of petitioner - check one ☐ U.S. citizen or permanent resident ☐ Organization ☐ Other - explain on separate paper

Type of business | Year established

Current number of employees | Gross Annual Income | Net Annual Income

**Part 6. Signature.**
Read the information on penalties in the instructions before completing this section.

I certify, under penalty of perjury under the laws of the United States of America, that this petition, and the evidence submitted with it, is all true and correct. If filing this on behalf of an organization, I certify that I am empowered to do so by that organization. If this petition is to extend a prior petition, I certify that the proposed employment is under the same terms and conditions as in the prior approved petition. I authorize the release of any information from my records, or from petitioning organization's records, which the Immigration and Naturalization Service needs to determine eligibility for the benefit being sought.

Signature and title | Print Name | Date

**Please note:** If you do not completely fill out this form and the required supplement, or fail to submit required documents listed in the instructions, then the person(s) filed for may not be found eligible for the requested benefit, and this petition may be denied.

**Part 7. Signature of person preparing form if other than above.**

I declare that I prepared this application at the request of the above person and it is based on all information of which I have knowledge.

Signature | Print Name | Date

Firm Name and Address

OMB No. 1115-0168

**U.S. Department of Justice**
Immigration and Naturalization Service

**O and P Classification**
Supplement to Form I-129

Name of person or organization filing petition:

Name of person or group or total number of workers you are filing for:

Classification sought (check one):

☐ O-1 Alien of extraordinary ability in sciences, art, education, or business
☐ P-2 Artist or entertainer for reciprocal exchange program
☐ P-2S Essential Support Personnel for P-2

Explain the nature of the event

Describe the duties to be performed

If filing for O-2 or P support alien, dates of alien's prior experience with the O-1 or P alien.

Have you obtained the required written consultation(s)? ☐ Yes - attached ☐ No - Copy of request attached
If not, give the following information about the organization(s) to which you have sent a duplicate of this petition.

O-1 Extraordinary ability

Name of recognized peer group — Phone #
Address — Date sent

O-1 Extraordinary achievement in motion pictures or television

Name of labor organization — Phone #
Address — Date sent
Name of management organization — Phone #
Address — Date sent

O-2 or P alien

Name of labor organization — Phone #
Address — Date sent

Form I-129 Supplement O/P/Q/R (12/11/91) N

## U.S. Immigration and Nationality Act

*Section 101 [8 U.S.C. §1101]*

(a)(15) The term "immigrant" means every alien except an alien who is within one of the following classes of nonimmigrant aliens . . .

(O) an alien who:

(i) has extraordinary ability in the sciences, arts, education, business, or athletics which has been demonstrated by sustained national or international acclaim or, with regard to motion picture and television productions a demonstrated record of extraordinary achievement, and whose achievements have been recognized in the field through extensive documentation, and seeks to enter the United States to continue work in the area of extraordinary ability; or

(ii) (I) seeks to enter the United States temporarily and solely for the purpose of accompanying and assisting in the artistic or athletic performance by an alien who is admitted under clause (i) for a specific event or events,

(II) is an integral part of such actual performance,

(III) (a) has critical skills and experience with such alien which are not of a general nature and which cannot be performed by other individuals, or

(b) in the case of a motion picture or television production, has skills and experience with such alien which are not of a general nature and which are critical either based on a pre-existing long-standing working relationship or, with respect to the specific production, because significant production (including pre- and post-production work) will take place both inside and outside the United States and the continuing participation of the alien is essential to the successful completion of the production, and

(IV) has a foreign residence which the alien has no intention of abandoning; or

(iii) is the alien spouse or child of an alien described in clause (i) or (ii) and is accompanying, or following to join, the alien;

(P) an alien having a foreign residence which the alien has no intention of abandoning who:

(i) (a) is described in section 214(c)(4)(A) (relating to athletes), or

(b) is described in section 214(c)(4)(B) (relating to entertainment groups);

(ii) (I) performs as an artist or entertainer, individually or as part of a group, or is an integral part of the performance of such a group, and

(II) seeks to enter the United States temporarily and solely for the purpose of performing as such an artist or entertainer or with such a group under a reciprocal exchange program which is between an organization or organizations in the United States and an organization or organizations in one or more foreign states and which provides for the temporary exchange of artists and entertainers;

(iii) (I) performs as an artist or entertainer, individually or as part of a group, or is an integral part of the performance of such a group, and

(II) seeks to enter the United States temporarily and solely to perform, teach, or coach as such an artist or entertainer or with such a group under a commercial or noncommercial program that is culturally unique; or

(iv) is the spouse or child of an alien described in clause (i), (ii), or (iii) and is accompanying, or following to join, the alien;

*Section 214 [8 U.S.C. §1184]*

(a)(2)

(A) The period of authorized status as a nonimmigrant described in section 101(a)(15)(O) shall be for such period as the Attorney General may specify in order to provide for the event (or events) for which the nonimmigrant is admitted.

(B) The period of authorized status as a nonimmigrant described in section 101(a)(15)(P) shall be for such period as the Attorney General may specify in order to provide for the competition, event, or performance for which the nonimmigrant is admitted. In the case of nonimmigrants admitted as individual athletes under section 101(a)(15)(P), the period of authorized status may be for an initial period (not to exceed 5 years) during which the nonimmigrant will perform as an athlete and such period may be extended by the Attorney General for an additional period of up to 5 years. . . .

(c)(3) The Attorney General shall approve a petition-

(A) with respect to a nonimmigrant described in section 101(a)(15)(O)(i) only after consultation in accordance with paragraph (6) or, with respect to aliens seeking entry for a motion picture or television production, after consultation with the appropriate union representing the alien's occupational peers and a management organization in the area of the alien's ability, or

(B) with respect to a nonimmigrant described in section 101(a)(15)(O)(ii) after consultation in accordance with paragraph (6) or, in the case of such an alien seeking entry for a motion picture or television production, after consultation with such a labor organization and a management organization in the area of the alien's ability.

In the case of an alien seeking entry for a motion picture or television production, (i) any opinion under the previous sentence shall only be advisory, (ii) any such opinion that recommends denial must be in writing, (iii) in making the decision the Attorney General shall consider the exigencies and scheduling of the production, and (iv) the Attorney General shall append to the decision any such opinion. The Attorney General shall provide by regulation for the waiver of the consultation requirement under subparagraph (A) in the case of aliens who have been admitted as nonimmigrants under section 101(a)(15)(O)(i) because of extraordinary ability in the arts and who seek readmission to perform similar services within 2 years after the date of a consultation under such subparagraph. Not later than 5 days after the date such a waiver is provided, the Attorney General shall forward a copy of the petition and all supporting documentation to the national office of an appropriate labor organization.

(4)(A) For purposes of section 101(a)(15)(P)(i)(a) , an alien is described in this subparagraph if the alien

(i) performs as an athlete, individually or as part of a group or team, at an internationally recognized level of performance, and

(ii) seeks to enter the United States temporarily and solely for the purpose of performing as such an athlete with respect to a specific athletic competition.

(B)(i) For purposes of section 101(a)(15)(P)(i)(b), an alien is described in this subparagraph if the alien-

(I) performs with or is an integral and essential part of the performance of an entertainment group that has (except as provided in clause (ii)) been recognized internationally as being outstanding in the discipline for a sustained and substantial period of time,

(II) in the case of a performer or entertainer, except as provided in clause (iii), has had a sustained and substantial relationship with that group (ordinarily for at least one year) and provides functions integral to the performance of the group, and

(III) seeks to enter the United States temporarily and solely for the purpose of performing as such a performer or entertainer or as an integral and essential part of a performance.

(ii) In the case of an entertainment group that is recognized nationally as being outstanding in its discipline for a sustained and substantial period of time, the Attorney General may, in consideration of special circumstances, waive the international recognition requirement of clause (i)(I).

(iii) (I) The one-year relationship requirement of clause (i)(II) shall not apply to 25 percent of the performers and entertainers in a group.

(II) The Attorney General may waive such one-year relationship requirement for an alien who because of illness or unanticipated and exigent circumstances replaces an essential member of the group and for an alien who augments the group by performing a critical role.

(iv) The requirements of subclauses (I) and (II) of clause (i) shall not apply to alien circus personnel who perform as part of a circus or circus group or who constitute an integral and essential part of the performance of such circus or circus group, but only if such personnel are entering the United States to join a circus that has been recognized nationally as outstanding for a sustained and substantial period of time or as part of such a circus.

(C) A person may petition the Attorney General for classification of an alien as a nonimmigrant under section 101(a)(15)(P) .

(D) The Attorney General shall approve petitions under this subsection with respect to nonimmigrants described in clause (i) or (iii) of section 101(a)(15)(P) only after consultation in accordance with paragraph (6).

(E) The Attorney General shall approve petitions under this subsection for nonimmigrants described in section 101(a)(15)(P)(ii) only after consultation with labor organizations representing artists and entertainers in the United States.

(5)(A) In the case of an alien who is provided nonimmigrant status under section 101(a)(15)(H)(i)(b) or 101(a)(15)(H)(ii)(b) and who is dismissed from employment by the employer before the end of the period of authorized admission, the employer shall be liable for the reasonable costs of return transportation of the alien abroad.

(B) In the case of an alien who is admitted to the United States in nonimmigrant status under section 101(a)(15)(O) or 101(a)(15)(P) and whose employment terminates for reasons other than voluntary resignation, the employer whose offer of employment formed the basis of such nonimmigrant status and the petitioner are jointly and severally liable for the reasonable cost of return transportation of the alien abroad. The petitioner shall provide assurance satisfactory to the Attorney General that the reasonable cost of that transportation will be provided.

(6)(A) (i) To meet the consultation requirement of paragraph (3)(A) in the case of a petition for a nonimmigrant described in section 101(a)(15)(O)(i) (other than with respect to aliens seeking entry for a motion picture or television production), the petitioner shall submit with the petition an advisory opinion from a peer group (or other person or persons of its choosing, which may include a labor organization) with expertise in the specific field involved.

(ii) To meet the consultation requirement of paragraph (3)(B) in the case of a petition for a nonimmigrant described in section 101(a)(15)(O)(ii) (other than with respect to aliens seeking entry for a motion picture or television production), the petitioner shall submit with the petition an advisory opinion from a labor organization with expertise in the skill area involved.

(iii) To meet the consultation requirement of paragraph (4)(D) in the case of a petition for a nonimmigrant described in section 101(a)(15)(P)(i) or 101(a)(15)(P)(iii), the petitioner shall submit with the petition an advisory opinion from a labor organization with expertise in the specific field of athletics or entertainment involved.

(B) To meet the consultation requirements of subparagraph (A), unless the petitioner submits with the petition an advisory opinion from an appropriate labor organization, the Attorney General shall forward a copy of the petition and all supporting documentation to the national office of an appropriate labor organization within 5 days of the date of receipt of the petition. If there is a collective bargaining representative of an employer's employees in the occupational classification for which the alien is being sought, that representative shall be the appropriate labor organization.

(C) In those cases in which a petitioner described in subparagraph (A) establishes that an appropriate peer group (including a labor organization) does not exist, the Attorney General shall adjudicate the petition without requiring an advisory opinion.

(D) Any person or organization receiving a copy of a petition described in subparagraph (A) and supporting documents shall have no more than 15 days following the date of receipt of such documents within which to submit a written advisory opinion or comment or to provide a letter of no objection. Once the 15-day period has expired and the petitioner has had an opportunity, where appropriate, to supply rebuttal evidence, the Attorney General shall adjudicate such petition in no more than 14 days. The Attorney General may shorten any specified time period for emergency reasons if no unreasonable burden would be thus imposed on any participant in the process.

(E) (i) The Attorney General shall establish by regulation expedited consultation procedures in the case of nonimmigrant artists or entertainers described in section 101(a)(15)(O) or 101(a)(15)(P) to accommodate the exigencies and scheduling of a given production or event.

(ii) The Attorney General shall establish by regulation expedited consultation procedures in the case of nonimmigrant athletes described in section 101(a)(15)(O)(i) or 101(a)(15)(P)(i) in the case of emergency circumstances (including trades during a season).

(F) No consultation required under this subsection by the Attorney General with a nongovernmental entity shall be construed as permitting the Attorney General to delegate any authority under this subsection to such an entity. The Attorney General shall give such weight to advisory opinions provided under this section as the Attorney General determines, in his sole discretion, to be appropriate.

(7) If a petition is filed and denied under this subsection, the Attorney General shall notify the petitioner of the determination and the reasons for the denial and of the process by which the petitioner may appeal the determination.

---

**Title 8 of Code of Federal Regulations**
**8 CFR: Subchapter B – Immigration Regulations**

*Sec. 214.2(o) Aliens of extraordinary ability or achievement. . . .*

(2) *Filing of petitions.*

(i) General. . . [A] petitioner seeking to classify an alien as an O-1 or O-2 nonimmigrant shall file a petition on Form I-129, Petition for a Nonimmigrant Worker, with the Service Center which has jurisdiction in the area where the alien will work. . . . An O-1 or O-2 petition may only be filed by a United States employer, a United States agent, or a foreign employer through a United States agent. . . . An O alien may not petition for himself or herself.

(ii) Evidence *required to accompany a petition.* Petitions for O aliens shall be accompanied by the following:

(A) The evidence specified in the particular section for the classification;

(B) Copies of any written contracts between the petitioner and the alien beneficiary or, if there is no written contract, a summary of the terms of the oral agreement under which the alien will be employed;

(C) An explanation of the nature of the events or activities, the beginning and ending dates for the events or activities, and a copy of any itinerary for the events or activities; and

(D) A written advisory opinion(s) from the appropriate consulting entity or entities.

(iii) *Form of documentation.* The evidence submitted with an O petition shall conform to the following:

(A) Affidavits, contracts, awards, and similar documentation must reflect the nature of the alien's achievement and be executed by an officer or responsible person employed by the institution, firm, establishment, or organization where the work was performed.

(B) Affidavits written by present or former employers or recognized experts certifying to the recognition and extraordinary ability, or in the case of a motion picture or television production, the extraordinary achievement of the alien, shall specifically describe the alien's recognition and ability or achievement in factual terms and set forth the expertise of the affiant and the manner in which the affiant acquired such information. . . .

(iv) *Other filing situations. . . .*

(G) *Traded professional O-1 athletes.* In the case of a professional O-1 athlete who is traded fron one organization to another organization, employment authorization for the player will automatically continue for a period of 30 days after acquisition by the new organization, within which time the new organization is expected to file a new Form I-129. If a new Form I-129 is not filed within 30 days, employment authorization will cease. If a new Form I -129 is filed within 30 days, the professional athlete shall be deemed to be in valid O-1 status, and employment shall continue to be authorized, until the petition is adjudicated. If the new petition is denied, employment authorization will cease.

(3) *Petition for alien of extraordinary ability or achievement (O-1). . . .*

(ii) *Definitions. As used in this paragraph, the term:*

*Arts* includes any field of creative activity or endeavor such as, but not limited to, fine arts, visual arts, culinary arts, and performing arts. Aliens engaged in the field of arts include not only the principal creators and performers but other essential persons such as, but not limited to, directors, set designers, lighting designers, sound designers, choreographers, choreologists, conductors, orchestrators, coaches, arrangers, musical supervisors, costume designers, makeup artists, flight masters, stage technicians, and animal trainers. . . .

*Extraordinary ability in the field of arts means distinction.* Distinction means a high level of achievement in the field of arts evidenced by a degree of skill and recognition substantially above that ordinarily encountered to the extent that a person described as prominent is renowned, leading, or well-known in the field of arts.

*Extraordinary ability in the field of . . . athletics* means a level of expertise indicating that the person is one of the small percentage who have arisen to the very top of the field of endeavor.

*Extraordinary achievement with respect to motion picture and television productions,* as commonly defined in the industry, means a very high level of accomplishment in the motion picture or television industry evidenced by a degree of skill and recognition significantly above that ordinarily encountered to the extent that the person is recognized as outstanding, notable, or leading in the motion picture or television field. . .
.

(iii) *Evidentiary criteria for an O-1 alien of extraordinary ability in the fields of . . . athletics.* An alien of extraordinary ability in the fields of . . . athletics must demonstrate sustained national or international acclaim and recognition for achievements in the field of expertise by providing evidence of:

(A) Receipt of a major, internationally recognized award, such as the Nobel Prize; or

(B) At least three of the following forms of documentation:

((1)) Documentation of the alien's receipt of nationally or internationally recognized prizes or awards for excellence in the field of endeavor;

((2)) Documentation of the alien's membership in associations in the field for which classification is sought, which require outstanding achievements of their members, as judged by recognized national or international experts in their disciplines or fields;

((3)) Published material in professional or major trade publications or major media about the alien, relating to the alien's work in the field for which classification is sought, which shall include the title, date, and author of such published material, and any necessary translation; . . .

((7)) Evidence that the alien has been employed in a critical or essential capacity for organizations and establishments that have a distinguished reputation;

((8)) Evidence that the alien has either commanded a high salary or will command a high salary or other remuneration for services, evidenced by contracts or other reliable evidence.

(C) If the criteria in paragraph (o)(3)(iii) of this section do not readily apply to the beneficiary's occupation, the petitioner may submit comparable evidence in order to establish the beneficiary's eligibility.

(iv) *Evidentiary criteria for an O-1 alien of extraordinary ability in the arts.* To qualify as an alien of extraordinary ability in the field of arts, the alien must be recognized as being prominent in his or her field of endeavor as demonstrated by the following:

(A) Evidence that the alien has been nominated for, or has been the recipient of, significant national or international awards or prizes in the particular field such as an Academy Award, an Emmy, a Grammy, or a Director's Guild Award; or

(B) At least three of the following forms of documentation:

((1)) Evidence that the alien has performed, and will perform, services as a lead or starring participant in productions or events which have a distinguished reputation as evidenced by critical reviews, advertisements, publicity releases, publications contracts, or endorsements;

((2)) Evidence that the alien has achieved national or international recognition for achievements evidenced by critical reviews or other published materials by or about the individual in major newspapers, trade journals, magazines, or other publications;

((3)) Evidence that the alien has performed, and will perform, in a lead, starring, or critical role for organizations and establishments that have a distinguished reputation evidenced by articles in newspapers, trade journals, publications, or testimonials;

((4)) Evidence that the alien has a record of major commercial or critically acclaimed successes as evidenced by such indicators as title, rating, standing in the field, box office receipts, motion picture or television ratings, and other occupational achievements reported in trade journals, major newspapers, or other publications;

((5)) Evidence that the alien has received significant recognition for achievements from organizations, critics, government agencies, or other recognized experts in the field in which the alien is engaged. Such testimonials must be in a form which clearly indicates the author's authority, expertise, and knowledge of the alien's achievements; or

((6)) Evidence that the alien has either commanded a high salary or will command a high salary or other substantial remuneration for services in relation to others in the field, as evidenced by contracts or other reliable evidence; or

(C) If the criteria in paragraph (o)(3)(iv) of this section do not readily apply to the beneficiary's occupation, the petitioner may submit comparable evidence in order to establish the beneficiary's eligibility.

(v) *Evidentiary criteria for an alien of extraordinary achievement in the motion picture or television industry.* To qualify as an alien of extraordinary achievement in the motion picture or television industry, the alien must be recognized as having a demonstrated record of extraordinary achievement as evidenced by the following:

(A) Evidence that the alien has been nominated for, or has been the recipient of, significant national or international awards or prizes in the particular field such as an Academy Award, an Emmy, a Grammy, or a Director's Guild Award; or

(B) At least three of the following forms of documentation:

((1)) Evidence that the alien has performed, and will perform, services as a lead or starring participant in productions or events which have a distinguished reputation as evidenced by critical reviews, advertisements, publicity releases, publications contracts, or endorsements;

((2)) Evidence that the alien has achieved national or international recognition for achievements evidenced by critical reviews or other published materials by or about the individual in major newspapers, trade journals, magazines, or other publications;

((3)) Evidence that the alien has performed, and will perform, in a lead, starring, or critical role for organizations and establishments that have a distinguished reputation evidenced by articles in newspapers, trade journals, publications, or testimonials;

((4)) Evidence that the alien has a record of major commercial or critically acclaimed successes as evidenced by such indicators as title, rating, standing in the field, box office receipts, motion picture or television ratings, and other occupational achievements reported in trade journals, major newspapers, or other publications;

((5)) Evidence that the alien has received significant recognition for achievements from organizations, critics, government agencies, or other recognized experts in the field in which the alien is engaged. Such testimonials must be in a form which clearly indicates the author's authority, expertise, and knowledge of the alien's achievements; or

((6)) Evidence that the alien has either commanded a high salary or will command a high salary or other substantial remuneration for services in relation to others in the field, as evidenced by contracts or other reliable evidence.

(4) *Petition for an O-2 accompanying alien.*

(i) *General.* An O-2 accompanying alien provides essential support to an O-1 artist or athlete. . . . Although the O-2 alien must obtain his or her own classification, this classification does not entitle him or her to work separate and apart from the O-1 alien to whom he or she provides support.

An O-2 alien must be petitioned for in conjunction with the services of the O-1 alien.

(ii) *Evidentiary criteria for qualifying as an O-2 accompanying alien.*

(A) *Alien accompanying an O-1 artist or athlete of extraordinary ability.* To qualify as an O-2 accompanying alien, the alien must be coming to the United States to assist in the performance of the O-1 alien, be an integral part of the actual performance, and have critical skills and experience with the O-1 alien which are not of a general nature and which are not possessed by a U.S. worker.

(B) *Alien accompanying an O-1 alien of extraordinary achievement.* To qualify as an O-2 alien accompanying an O-1 alien involved in a motion picture or television production, the alien must have skills and experience with the O-1 alien which are not of a general nature and which are critical based on a pre-existing longstanding working relationship or, with respect to the specific production, because significant production (including pre- and post-production work) will take place both inside and outside the United States and the continuing participation of the alien is essential to the successful completion of the production.

(C) The evidence shall establish the current essentiality, critical skills, and experience of the O-2 alien with the O-1 alien and that the alien has substantial experience performing the critical skills and essential support services for the O-1 alien. In the case of a specific motion picture or television production, the evidence shall establish that significant production has taken place outside the United States, and will take place inside the United States, and that the continuing participation of the alien is essential to the successful completion of the production.

(5) *Consultation.*

(i) *General.*

(A) Consultation with an appropriate U.S. peer group (which could include a person or persons with expertise in the field), labor and/or management organization regarding the nature of the work to be done and the alien's qualifications is mandatory before a petition for an O-1 or O-2 classification can be approved.

(B) . . . [E]vidence of consultation shall be in the form of a written advisory opinion from a peer group (which could include a person or persons with expertise in the field), labor and/or management organization with expertise in the specific field involved.

(C) . . . [T]he petitioner shall obtain a written advisory opinion from a peer group (which could include a person or persons with expertise in the field), labor, and/or management organization with expertise in the specific field involved. The advisory opinion shall be submitted along with the petition when the petition is filed. If the advisory opinion is not favorable to the petitioner, the advisory opinion must set forth a specific statement of facts which supports the conclusion reached in the opinion. Advisory opinions must be submitted in writing and must be signed by an authorized official of the group or organization.

(D) . . . [W]ritten evidence of consultation shall be included in the record in every approved O petition. Consultations are advisory and are not binding on the Service. . . .

(ii) *Consultation requirements for an O-1 alien of extraordinary ability.*

(A) *Content.* Consultation with a peer group in the area of the alien's ability (which may include a labor organization), or a person or persons with expertise in the area of the alien's ability, is required in an O-1 petition for an alien of extraordinary ability. . . .

(iii) *Consultation requirements for an O-1 alien of extraordinary achievement.* In the case of an alien of extraordinary achievement who will be working on a motion picture or television production, consultation shall be made with the appropriate union representing the alien's occupational peers and a management organization in the area of the alien's ability. . . .

(iv) *Consultation requirements for an O-2 accompanying alien.* Consultation with a labor organization with expertise in the skill area involved is required for an O-2 alien accompanying an O-1 alien of extraordinary ability. In the case of an O-2 alien seeking entry for a motion picture or television production, consultation with a labor organization and a management organization in the area of the alien's ability is required. . . . If the alien will accompany an O-1 alien involved in a motion picture or television production, the advisory opinion should address the alien's skills and experience with the O-1 alien and whether the alien has a pre-existing longstanding working relationship with the O-1 alien, or whether significant production will take place in the United States and abroad and if the continuing participation of the alien is essential to the successful completion of the production. A consulting organization may also submit a letter of no objection in lieu of the above if it has no objection to the approval of the petition. . . .

(6) *Approval and validity of petition.*

(i) *Approval.* The Director shall consider all of the evidence submitted and such other evidence as may be independently required to assist in the adjudication. The Director shall notify the petitioner of the approval of the petition on Form I-797, Notice of Action. . . .

(iii) *Validity.*

(A) *O-1 petition.* An approved petition for an alien classified under section 101(a)(15)(O)(i) of the Act shall be valid for a period of time determined by the Director to be necessary to accomplish the event or activity, not to exceed 3 years.

(B) *O-2 petition.* An approved petition for an alien classified under section 101(a)(15)(O)(ii) of the Act shall be valid for a period of time determined to be necessary to assist the O-1 alien to accomplish the event or activity, not to exceed 3 years. . . .

(11) *Extension of visa petition validity.* The petitioner shall file a request to extend the validity of the original petition under section 101(a)(15)(O) of the Act on Form I-129, Petition for a Nonimmigrant Worker, in order to continue or complete the same activities or events specified in the original petition. Supporting documents are not required unless requested by the Director. A petition extension may be filed only if the validity of the original petition has not expired.

(12) *Extension of stay.*

(i) *Extension procedure.* The petitioner shall request extension of the alien's stay to continue or complete the same event or activity by filing Form I-129, accompanied by a statement explaining the reasons for the extension. The petitioner must also request a petition extension. . . .

(ii) *Extension period.* An extension of stay may be authorized in increments of up to 1 year for an O-1 or O-2 beneficiary to continue or complete the same event or activity for which he or she was admitted plus an additional 10 days to allow the beneficiary to get his or her personal affairs in order. . . .

*Sec. 214.2(p) Artists, athletes, and entertainers . . . .*

(2) *Filing of petitions*

(i) *General.* A P-1 petition for an athlete or entertainment group shall be filed by a United States employer, a United States sponsoring organization, a United States agent, or a foreign employer through a United States agent. . . . A P-2 petition for an artist or entertainer in a reciprocal exchange program shall be filed by the United States labor organization which negotiated the reciprocal exchange agreement, the sponsoring organization, or a United States employer. A P-3 petition for an artist or entertainer in a culturally unique program shall be filed by the sponsoring organization or a United States employer. . . . [T]he petitioner shall file a P petition on Form I-129, Petition for Nonimmigrant Worker, with the Service Center which has jurisdiction in the area where the alien will work. . . .

(ii) *Evidence required to accompany a petition for a P nonimmigrant.* Petitions for P nonimmigrant aliens shall be accompanied by the following:

(A) The evidence specified in the specific section of this part for the classification;

(B) Copies of any written contracts between the petitioner and the alien beneficiary or, if there is no written contract, a summary of the terms of the oral agreement under which the alien(s) will be employed;

(C) An explanation of the nature of the events or activities, the beginning and ending dates for the events or activities, and a copy of any itinerary for the events or activities; and

(D) A written consultation from a labor organization.

(iii) *Form of documentation.* The evidence submitted with a P petition should conform to the following:

(A) Affidavits, contracts, awards, and similar documentation must reflect the nature of the alien's achievement and be executed by an officer or responsible person employed by the institution, establishment, or organization where the work was performed.

(B) Affidavits written by present or former employers or recognized experts certifying to the recognition and extraordinary ability, or, in the case of a motion picture or television production, the extraordinary achievement of the alien, which shall specifically describe the alien's recognition and ability or achievement in factual terms. The affidavit must also set forth the expertise of the affiant and the manner in which the affiant acquired such information. . . .

(iv) *Other filing situations . . . .*

(C) *Change of employer . . .*

(2) *Traded professional P-1 athletes.* In the case of a professional P-1 athlete who is traded from one organization to another organization, employment authorization for the player will automatically continue for a period of 30 days after acquisition by the new organization, within which time the new organization is expected to file a new Form I-129 for P-1 nonimmigrant classification. If a new Form I-129 is not filed within 30 days, employment authorization will cease. If a new Form I-129 is filed within 30 days, the professional athlete shall be deemed to be in valid P-1 status, and employment shall continue to be authorized,

until the petition is adjudicated. If the new petition is denied, employment authorization will cease. . . .

(3) *Definitions.* As used in this paragraph, the term:

*Arts* includes fields of creative activity or endeavor such as, but not limited to, fine arts, visual arts, and performing arts.

*Competition, event, or performance* means an activity such as an athletic competition, athletic season, tournament, tour, exhibit, project, entertainment event, or engagement. Such activity could include short vacations, promotional appearances for the petitioning employer relating to the competition, event, or performance, and stopovers which are incidental and/or related to the activity. An athletic competition or entertainment event could include an entire season of performances. A group of related activities will also be considered an event. In the case of a P-2 petition, the event may be the duration of the reciprocal exchange agreement. In the case of a P-1 athlete, the event may be the duration of the alien's contract.

*Contract* means the written agreement between the petitioner and the beneficiary(ies) that explains the terms and conditions of employment. The contract shall describe the services to be performed, and specify the wages, hours of work, working conditions, and any fringe benefits.

*Culturally unique* means a style of artistic expression, methodology, or medium which is unique to a particular country, nation, society, class, ethnicity, religion, tribe, or other group of persons.

*Essential support alien* means a highly skilled, essential person determined by the Director to be an integral part of the performance of a P-1, P-2, or P-3 alien because he or she performs support services which cannot be readily performed by a United States worker and which are essential to the successful performance of services by the P-1, P-2, or P-3 alien. Such alien must have appropriate qualifications to perform the services, critical knowledge of the specific services to be performed, and experience in providing such support to the P-1, P-2, or P-3 alien.

*Group* means two or more persons established as one entity or unit to perform or to provide a service.

*Internationally recognized* means having a high level of achievement in a field evidenced by a degree of skill and recognition substantially above that ordinarily encountered, to the extent that such achievement is renowned, leading, or well-known in more than one country.

*Member of a group* means a person who is actually performing the entertainment services. . . .

*Team* means two or more persons organized to perform together as a competitive unit in a competitive event.

(4) *Petition for an internationally recognized athlete or member of an internationally recognized entertainment group (P-1)*

(i) *Types of classification.*

(A) *P-1 classification as an athlete in an individual capacity.* A P-1 classification may be granted to an alien who is an internationally recognized athlete based on his or her own reputation and achievements as an individual. The alien must be coming to the United States to perform services which require an internationally recognized athlete.

(B) *P-1 classification as a member of an entertainment group or an athletic team.* An entertainment group or athletic team consists of two or more persons who function as a unit. The entertainment group or athletic team as a unit must be internationally recognized as outstanding in the discipline and must be coming to perform services which require an internationally recognized entertainment group or athletic team. A person who is a member of an internationally recognized entertainment group or athletic team may be granted P-1 classification based on that relationship, but may not perform services separate and apart from the entertainment group or athletic team. An entertainment group must have been established for a minimum of 1 year, and 75 percent of the members of the group must have been performing entertainment services for the group for a minimum of 1 year.

(ii) *Criteria and documentary requirements for P-1 athletes*

(A) *General.* A P-1 athlete must have an internationally recognized reputation as an international athlete or he or she must be a member of a foreign team that is internationally recognized. The athlete or team must be coming to the United States to participate in an athletic competition which has a distinguished reputation and which requires participation of an athlete or athletic team that has an international reputation.

(B) *Evidentiary requirements for an internationally recognized athlete or athletic team.* A petition for an athletic team must be accompanied by evidence that the team as a unit has achieved international recognition in the sport. Each member of the team is accorded P-1 classification based on the international reputation of the team. A petition for an athlete who will compete individually or as a member of a U.S. team must be accompanied by evidence that the athlete has achieved international recognition in the sport based on his or her reputation. A petition for a P-1 athlete or athletic team shall include:

((1)) A tendered contract with a major United States sports league or team, or a tendered contract in an individual sport commensurate with international recognition in that sport, if such contracts are normally executed in the sport, and

((2)) Documentation of at least two of the following:

((i)) Evidence of having participated to a significant extent in a prior season with a major United States sports league;

((ii)) Evidence of having participated in international competition with a national team;

((iii)) Evidence of having participated to a significant extent in a prior season for a U.S. college or university in intercollegiate competition;

((iv)) A written statement from an official of a major U.S. sports league or an official of the governing body of the sport which details how the alien or team is internationally recognized;

((v)) A written statement from a member of the sports media or a recognized expert in the sport which details how the alien or team is internationally recognized;

((vi)) Evidence that the individual or team is ranked if the sport has international rankings; or

((vii)) Evidence that the alien or team has received a significant honor or award in the sport.

(iii) *Criteria and documentary requirements for members of an internationally recognized entertainment group*

(A) *General.* A P-1 classification shall be accorded to an entertainment group to perform as a unit based on the international reputation of the group. Individual entertainers shall not be accorded P-1 classification to perform separate and apart from a group. . . . [I]t must be established that the group has been internationally recognized as outstanding in the discipline for a sustained and substantial period of time. Seventy-five percent of the members of the group must have had a sustained and substantial relationship with the group for at least 1 year and must provide functions integral to the group's performance.

(B) *Evidentiary criteria for members of internationally recognized entertainment groups.* A petition for P-1 classification for the members of an entertainment group shall be accompanied by:

((1)) Evidence that the group has been established and performing regularly for a period of at least 1 year;

((2)) A statement from the petitioner listing each member of the group and the exact dates for which each member has been employed on a regular basis by the group; and

((3)) Evidence that the group has been internationally recognized in the discipline for a sustained and substantial period of time. This may be demonstrated by the submission of evidence of the group's nomination or receipt of significant international awards or prizes for outstanding achievement in its field or by three of the following different types of documentation:

((i)) Evidence that the group has performed, and will perform, as a starring or leading entertainment group in productions or events which have a distinguished reputation as evidenced by critical reviews, advertisements, publicity releases, publications, contracts, or endorsements;

((ii)) Evidence that the group has achieved international recognition and acclaim for outstanding achievement in its field as evidenced by reviews in major newspapers, trade journals, magazines, or other published material;

((iii)) Evidence that the group has performed, and will perform, services as a leading or starring group for organizations and establishments that have a distinguished reputation evidenced by articles in newspapers, trade journals, publications, or testimonials;

((iv)) Evidence that the group has a record of major commercial or critically acclaimed successes, as evidenced by such indicators as ratings; standing in the field; box office receipts; record, cassette, or video sales; and other achievements in the field as reported in trade journals, major newspapers, or other publications;

((v)) Evidence that the group has achieved significant recognition for achievements from organizations, critics, government agencies, or other recognized experts in the field. Such testimonials must be in a form that clearly indicates the author's authority, expertise, and knowledge of the alien's achievements; or ((vi)) Evidence that the group has either commanded a high salary or will command a high salary or other substantial remuneration for services comparable to others similarly situated in the field as evidenced by contracts or other reliable evidence. . . .

(iv) *P-1 classification as an essential support alien.*

(A) *General.* An essential support alien as defined in paragraph (p)(3) of this section may be granted P-1 classification based on a support relationship with an individual P-1 athlete, P-1 athletic team, or a P-1 entertainment group.

(B) Evidentiary *criteria for a P-1 essential support petition.* A petition for P-1 essential support personnel must be accompanied by:

((1)) A consultation from a labor organization with expertise in the area of the alien's skill;

((2)) A statement describing the alien(s) prior essentiality, critical skills, and experience with the principal alien(s); and

((3)) A copy of the written contract or a summary of the terms of the oral agreement between the alien(s) and the employer.

(5) *Petition for an artist or entertainer under a reciprocal exchange program (P-2)*

(i) *General.*

(A) A P-2 classification shall be accorded to artists or entertainers, individually or as a group, who will be performing under a reciprocal exchange program which is between an organization or organizations in the United States, which may include a management organization, and an organization or organizations in one or more foreign states and which provides for the temporary exchange of artists and entertainers, or groups of artists and entertainers.

(B) The exchange of artists or entertainers shall be similar in terms of caliber of artists or entertainers, terms and conditions of employment, such as length of employment, and numbers of artists or entertainers involved in the exchange. However, this requirement does not preclude an individual for group exchange.

(C) An alien who is an essential support person as defined in paragraph (p)(3) of this section may be accorded P-2 classification based on a support relationship to a P-2 artist or entertainer under a reciprocal exchange program.

(ii) *Evidentiary requirements for petition involving a reciprocal exchange program.* A petition for P-2 classification shall be accompanied by:

(A) A copy of the formal reciprocal exchange agreement between the U.S. organization or organizations which sponsor the aliens and an organization or organizations in a foreign country which will receive the U.S. artist or entertainers;

(B) A statement from the sponsoring organization describing the reciprocal exchange of U.S. artists or entertainers as it relates to the specific petition for which P-2 classification is being sought;

(C) Evidence that an appropriate labor organization in the United States was involved in negotiating, or has concurred with, the reciprocal exchange of U.S. and foreign artists or entertainers; and

(D) Evidence that the aliens for whom P-2 classification is being sought and the U.S. artists or entertainers subject to the reciprocal exchange agreement are artists or entertainers with comparable skills, and that the terms and conditions of employment are similar.

(iii) *P-2 classification as an essential support alien.*

(A) *General.* An essential support alien as defined in paragraph (p)(3) of this section may be granted P-2 classification based on a support relationship with a P-2 entertainer or P-2 entertainment group.

(B) Evidentiary *criteria for a P-2 essential support petition.* A petition for P-2 essential support personnel must be accompanied by:

((1)) A consultation from a labor organization with expertise in the area of the alien's skill;

((2)) A statement describing the alien(s) prior essentiality, critical skills, and experience with the principal alien(s); and

((3)) A copy of the written contract or a summary of the terms of the oral agreement between the alien(s) and the employer.

(6) *Petition for an artist or entertainer under a culturally unique program*

(i) *General.*

(A) A P-3 classification may be accorded to artists or entertainers, individually or as a group, coming to the United States for the purpose of developing, interpreting, representing, coaching, or teaching a unique or traditional ethnic, folk, cultural, musical, theatrical, or artistic performance or presentation.

(B) The artist or entertainer must be coming to the United States to participate in a cultural event or events which will further the understanding or development of his or her art form. The program may be of a commercial or noncommercial nature.

(ii) *Evidentiary criteria for a petition involving a culturally unique program.* A petition for P-3 classification shall be accompanied by:

(A) Affidavits, testimonials, or letters from recognized experts attesting to the authenticity of the alien's or the group's skills in performing, presenting, coaching, or teaching the unique or traditional art form and giving the credentials of the expert, including the basis of his or her knowledge of the alien's or group's skill, or

(B) Documentation that the performance of the alien or group is culturally unique, as evidenced by reviews in newspapers, journals, or other published materials; and

(C) Evidence that all of the performances or presentations will be culturally unique events.

(iii) *P-3 classification as an essential support alien.*

(A) *General.* An essential support alien as defined in paragraph (p)(3) of this section may be granted P-3 classification based on a support relationship with a P-3 entertainer or P-3 entertainment group.

(B) Evidentiary criteria for a P-3 essential support petition. A petition for P-3 essential support personnel must be accompanied by:

((1)) A consultation from a labor organization with expertise in the area of the alien's skill;

((2)) A statement describing the alien(s) prior essentiality, critical skills and experience with the principal alien(s); and

((3)) A copy of the written contract or a summary of the terms of the oral agreement between the alien(s) and the employer.

(7) *Consultation*

(i) *General.*

(A) Consultation with an appropriate labor organization regarding the nature of the work to be done and the alien's qualifications is mandatory before a petition for P-1, P-2, or P-3 classification can be approved.

(B) Except as provided in paragraph (p)(7)(i)(E) of this section, evidence of consultation shall be a written advisory opinion from an appropriate labor organization.

(C) Except as provided in paragraph (p)(7)(i)(E) of this section, the petitioner shall obtain a written advisory opinion from an appropriate labor organization. The advisory opinion shall be submitted along with the petition when the petition is filed. . . .

(D) . . .[W]ritten evidence of consultation shall be included in the record of every approved petition. Consultations are advisory and are not binding on the Service. . . .

(ii) *Consultation requirements for P-1 athletes and entertainment groups.* Consultation with a labor organization that has expertise in the area of the alien's sport or entertainment field is required in the case of a P-1 petition.

. . .

(iv) *Consultation requirements for P-2 alien in a reciprocal exchange program.* In P-2 petitions where an artist or entertainer is coming to the United States under a reciprocal exchange program, consultation with the appropriate labor organization is required to verify the existence of a viable exchange program. The advisory opinion from the labor organization shall comment on the bona fides of the reciprocal exchange program and specify whether the exchange meets the requirements of paragraph (p)(5) of this section. If the advisory opinion is not favorable to the petitioner, it must also set forth a specific statement of facts which support the conclusion reached in the opinion.

(v) *Consultation requirements for P-3 in a culturally unique program.* Consultation with an appropriate labor organization is required for P-3 petitions involving aliens in culturally unique programs. . . .

(vi) *Consultation requirements for essential support aliens.* Written consultation on petitions for P-1, P-2, or P-3 essential support aliens must be made with a labor organization with expertise in the skill area involved.

. . .

(8) *Approval and validity of petition*

(i) *Approval.* The Director shall consider all the evidence submitted and such other evidence as he or she may independently require to assist in his or her adjudication. The Director shall notify the petitioner of the approval of the petition on Form I-797, Notice of Action. . . .

(iii) *Validity.* The approval period of a P petition shall conform to the limits prescribed as follows:

(A) *P-1 petition for athletes.* An approved petition for an individual athlete classified under section 101(a)(15)(P)(i) of the Act shall be valid for a period up to 5 years. An approved petition for an athletic team classified under section 101(a)(15)(P)(i) of the Act shall be valid for a period of time determined by the Director to complete the competition or event for which the alien team is being admitted, not to exceed 1 year.

(B) *P-1 petition for an entertainment group.* An approved petition for an entertainment group classified under section 101(a)(15)(P)(i) of the Act shall be valid for a period of time determined by the Director to be necessary to complete the performance or event for which the group is being admitted, not to exceed 1 year.

(C) *P-2 and P-3 petitions for artists or entertainers.* An approved petition for an artist or entertainer under section 101(a)(15)(P)(ii) or (iii) of the Act shall be valid for a period of time determined by the Director to be necessary to complete the event, activity, or performance for which the P-2 or P-3 alien is admitted, not to exceed 1 year. . . .

(E) *Essential support aliens.* Petitions for essential support personnel to P-1, P-2, and P-3 aliens shall be valid for a period of time determined by the Director to be necessary to complete the event, activity, or performance for which the P-1, P-2, or P-3 alien is admitted, not to exceed 1 year. . . .

(14) *Extension of stay*

(i) *Extension procedure.* The petitioner shall request extension of the alien's stay to continue or complete the same event or activity by filing Form I-129, accompanied by a statement explaining the reasons for the extension. . . .

(ii) *Extension periods*

(A) *P-1 individual athlete.* An extension of stay for a P-1 individual athlete and his or her essential support personnel may be authorized for a period up to 5 years for a total period of stay not to exceed 10 years.

(B) *Other P-1, P-2, and P-3 aliens.* An extension of stay may be authorized in increments of 1 year for P-1 athletic teams, entertainment groups, aliens in reciprocal exchange programs, aliens in culturally unique programs, and their essential support personnel to continue or complete the same event or activity for which they were admitted.

---

**Muni v. Immigration and Naturalization Service**
**891 F.Supp. 440 (N.D.Ill. 1995)**

James B. Moran, Chief Judge, U.S. District Court

Plaintiff Craig Muni brings this action against the Immigration and Naturalization Service (INS or the Service) and its commissioner, Doris Meissner, challenging the Service's denial of his visa petition. In June or July 1993 Muni, a player in the National Hockey League (NHL), petitioned the INS for an immigrant visa, claiming that he was a worker with extraordinary ability . . . under . . . the Immigration and Naturalization Act. The director of the INS' Northern Service Center denied his petition, and the Administrative Appeals Unit (AAU) affirmed. Muni now appeals that decision to this court. Both parties have moved for summary judgment. For the reasons set forth below, Muni's motion is granted and the INS' motion is denied.

*Facts*

Muni was born in Canada on July 19, 1962 and is a Canadian citizen. In 1980, he was drafted by the Toronto Maple Leafs, an NHL team, and he began his career as a defenseman for that team in the 1981-82 season. In October 1986 he was traded to the Edmonton Oilers, where he stayed for seven years. In the 1986-87, 1987-88, and 1989-90 seasons, the Oilers won the Stanley Cup, the NHL's championship trophy. At that time Muni was a regular player and had one of the best plus-minus ratios[5] on the team. [n5 The plus-minus ratio is not really a ratio; it is the number of goals scored by a player's team while he is on the ice minus the number of goals scored against the team when the player is on the ice. The plus-minus ratio is a standard measure of a defensive player's ability: the higher the number, the better the player.] In the 1988-89 season he had the fourth best plus-minus ratio in the entire NHL. A poll taken by Goal magazine (an NHL publication) rated him the "most underrated defenseman" in the League in 1990, and in 1991 Hockey Digest named him one of the top ten hitting defensemen.

In March 1993 Muni was traded to the Chicago Blackhawks. He now plays for the Buffalo Sabres, whom he joined in October 1993. Muni presently earns $550,000 per year; in the 1992-93 season, when his petition was filed, his annual salary was $400,000. The average salary for an NHL defenseman in 1992-93 was $387,914.

In addition to salary information, Muni submitted to the INS numerous magazine and newspaper articles purporting to establish his stature in the hockey world. He also submitted affidavits from eight veteran NHL players stating that he is highly regarded by other players and is one of the best defensemen in hockey. Finally, Muni alleged that other NHL players of comparable ability – Steve Smith, Rob Brown, and Brent Sutter – have received immigrant visas. . . .

The director of the INS' Northern Service Center denied Muni's petition. She found that there was no evidence that Muni's salary is high compared with what other NHL players receive; that he failed to explain the reputation, significance, or selection criteria of the awards from Hockey Digest and Goal; that the newspaper articles established only his improvement as a player after joining the Oilers, his contributions to the Oilers' Stanley Cup victories, and the fact that he is remembered for playing while sutures on his face were leaking; and that the affidavits showed that Muni was an excellent, hard-hitting defenseman. The director concluded that

> while [Muni] appears to enjoy a noteworthy career as a professional hockey player, there is no evidence that [he] has been selected to all-star teams or received official recognitions as an extraordinary hockey player. The evidence submitted does not establish that [he] is one of the few who have risen to the very top of his field of endeavor.

The AAU affirmed. In addition to reiterating the arguments made by the regional director in her initial decision, the AAU found that Muni had not established his role in the Oilers' Stanley Cup victories; that his extended membership in the NHL was not sufficient in itself to establish extraordinary ability; and that he had not presented enough evidence comparing the experience, abilities, and salaries of players who have already received immigrant visas with his own qualifications. The AAU rejected Muni's argument that anyone who plays in the NHL for an extended period of time has extraordinary ability. Instead, because Muni was not "within the small percentage at the very top of the players in the NHL," the AAU concluded that he was not an alien of extraordinary ability and affirmed the director's decision to deny his petition.

*Discussion*

. . .[T]he only issue before this court is whether the INS properly concluded that Muni is not an alien of extraordinary ability. . . .

*A. Definition of Extraordinary Ability*

As an initial matter, we reject Muni's contention that we should treat the definition of extraordinary ability as a question of statutory construction subject to de novo review. It is well established that "[a] court reviewing an agency's interpretation of a statute must first look to the statute in question: if the statute addresses the precise question at issue and its meaning is clear, the text controls. But if 'the court determines Congress has not directly addressed the precise question at issue,' then 'the question for the court is whether the agency's answer is based on a permissible construction of the statute.'" [The Immigration and Naturalization Act] does not address the precise question at issue here: how to define extraordinary ability. Therefore, the INS definition of that term is binding unless it is unreasonable.

The INS regulations . . . define extraordinary ability as "a level of expertise indicating that the individual is one of that small percentage who have risen to the very top of the field of endeavor."...

Under the INS' view, membership on a major league team does not by itself qualify an athlete as one having extraordinary ability, though it may help to establish that the athlete meets several of the criteria listed. In the INS' words, "Not all athletes, particularly those new to major league competition, would be able to meet [the sustained national or international acclaim] standard. A blanket rule for all major league athletes would contravene Congress' intent to reserve this category to 'that small percentage of individuals who have risen to the very top of their field of endeavor.'" As further clarification, the regulations explain as follows:

> (3) Initial evidence. A petition for an alien of extraordinary ability must be accompanied by evidence that the alien has sustained national or international acclaim and that his or her achievements have been recognized in the field of expertise. Such evidence shall include evidence of a one-time achievement (that is, a major, internationally recognized award), or at least three of the following: [one of which is]...
>
> (iii) Published material about the alien in professional or major trade publications or other major media, relating to the alien's work in the field for which classification is sought. . . .

We agree with prior decisions in this district holding that the INS' definition of extraordinary ability is a permissible interpretation . . . and therefore is controlling here. But our conclusion that the INS' definition is binding does not mean that the Service correctly applied the definition to the facts of Muni's case, and that is the central question posed by the motions for summary judgment.

*B. Application of the Definition to the Facts*

In reviewing the denial of a visa petition we must defer to the decision of the INS unless it constituted an abuse of discretion. . . . We find that the INS abused its discretion here because it failed to consider several facts that supported Muni's petition and failed to explain why the facts it did consider were insufficient to establish Muni's extraordinary ability.

*1. Individual Facts*

First, the INS found that Muni's role in the Oilers' three Stanley Cup victories had not been established. This conclusion overlooks some rather obvious facts. As Muni points out, there is a direct correlation between a team's performance and its players' performances, and the correlation is even stronger where key players are concerned. The facts that Muni was a starting defenseman for the Oilers and had one of the team's top plus-minus ratios strongly suggest that he was a key player.[8] [n8 We take judicial notice of the fact that a team's best players are usually those in its starting lineup. Even if this was not the case here, other evidence establishes that Muni was one of the team's leaders in plus-minus ratios, which indicates that he was indeed one of the team's best defensemen.] Thus the team's performance reflects his individual ability. The INS seems to believe that being a good player on a great team does not establish one's ability, but it offers no explanation why we should accept such a counterintuitive belief.

Second, the INS discounted the awards Muni received, saying that he had not shown what was necessary to qualify for the awards or what significance they have. We disagree. We think the awards – best hitting defenseman, most underrated defenseman – are rather self-explanatory, and the publications – the official NHL magazine and the largest hockey magazine – are certainly significant and reputable. The INS had no legitimate basis for refusing to consider the awards as evidence of Muni's ability.

Third, the INS did not adequately address evidence that Muni commands a high salary. The evidence showed that he made more than the average NHL defenseman in 1992-93 and that his pay increased by $150,000 for the 1993-94 and 1994-95 seasons. Thus his salary is well above average. Moreover, since a few very highly paid players can skew the average salary upward, it is reasonable to assume that a player making even the average salary is making more than most other players.[9] [n9 In other words, the median salary would probably be a more useful figure for the INS to consider.] Yet the INS stated that because Muni's salary "is well below the top salaries earned in the NHL . . . it has not been established that [his] salary is high in relation to that of other professional hockey players" This statement contains two errors: ignorance of the simple math explained above and an assumption (which we reject below) that a player must be one of the League's superstars to be considered to have extraordinary ability.

Fourth, the INS gave short shrift to the articles Muni submitted to support his petition. These articles do not establish that Muni is one of the stars of the NHL, but that is not the applicable standard. Under the INS' own regulations, all Muni need show is that there is "published material about [him] in professional or major trade publications or other major media, relating to [his] work in the field for which classification is sought." The articles Muni submitted, which appeared in various newspapers and hockey magazines, clearly fit this requirement; even the INS admits that some of the articles "discuss [Muni's] hitting ability and his record as a defenseman." Yet the INS did not explain why the articles did not qualify as proof of Muni's ability.

Finally, the INS completely ignored the eight affidavits Muni submitted.[10] [n10 The AAU did not even mention these affidavits in its decision. The director's prior decision at least acknowledged that the affidavits characterized Muni as an excellent and hard-hitting defenseman. But the director made no effort to explain why these affidavits were insufficient to help establish Muni as a player of exceptional ability; she merely pointed out that he had not been selected to an all-star team or received official recognition as an extraordinary player. As explained below, this is not the correct standard.] Those affidavits, sworn to by veteran NHL players of considerable renown,[11] [n11 Affiants include hockey greats Basil McRae, Bernie Nichols, Jeremy Roenick, and Chris Chelios.] describe Muni as "an excellent defenseman," "one of the best defenseman in professional hockey," "a prominent hockey player in the NHL with great skating and defensive abilities," "one of the better defenders in the game," and "one of the premier defensemen in the NHL." The INS' failure even to consider these affidavits is clear evidence that it did not adequately evaluate the facts before it. The affidavits establish that Muni is, at minimum, an above-average player whose peers – the world's best hockey players – respect his athletic abilities. Better evidence of an alien's extraordinary ability would be difficult to find, yet the INS did not even mention it in its decision.

*2. Totality of the Evidence*

In sum, Muni presented evidence that he is an NHL veteran who was a starting player on the League's best team for several years, has a reputation among his peers as an excellent defenseman, earns a salary well above average for a defenseman, and has been recognized in major media publications. As previously noted, [an INS regulation] requires an alien to show that he has sustained national or international acclaim and recognition in his field. Such evidence must include "evidence of a one-time achievement (that is, a major, internationally recognized award)" or evidence that falls into at least three of the ten categories set forth in . . . the regulations. The Oilers' Stanley Cup victories while Muni was a key player arguably are evidence of a major, internationally recognized award that establishes Muni's international acclaim and recognition in his field. But even if sustained membership on the championship team is not enough, Muni's evidence still fits into five of the ten categories. While the satisfaction of the three-category production requirement does not mandate a finding that the petitioner has sustained national or international acclaim and recognition in his field, it is certainly a start, and the INS made no attempt to explain why Muni's evidence did not meet the acclaim and recognition standard. Thus, it has not only failed to explain why it does not accept some of the individual facts Muni presents, it has also failed to explain why the sum of those facts and others is insufficient to warrant granting his petition. We deem such arbitrary decisionmaking an abuse of discretion.

We think there is a deeper problem here than the INS' failure to give fair consideration to all the evidence Muni presented in support of his petition. The Service also misapplied its own definition of extraordinary ability. It apparently was under the impression that only all-stars or the League's highest-paid players have extraordinary ability. That is an overly grudging interpretation of its own regulation, which defines an athlete of extraordinary ability as "one of that small percentage who have risen to the very top of the field of endeavor." There was considerable evidence before the INS that Muni is a very good professional hockey player – and therefore one of those at the top of his field – yet the INS disregarded that evidence.

*Conclusion*

We conclude that the INS' denial of Muni's petition was an abuse of discretion. Muni's motion for summary judgment is granted and the INS' motion is denied. The case is remanded for further proceedings consistent with this opinion.

---

**Grimson v. Immigration and Naturalization Service**
**934 F. Supp. 965 (N.D.Ill. 1996)**

Robert W. Gettleman, United States District Judge

This case, much like the National Hockey League playoffs and the Energizer Bunny, just keeps going and going and going. Plaintiff Allan Stuart Grimson, a citizen of Canada, has filed a complaint for declaratory and injunctive relief . . . , seeking to overturn defendant Immigration and Naturalization Service's ("INS") denial of his visa petition. Both parties have moved for summary judgment . . . . For the reasons set forth below, plaintiff's motion is granted, defendant's cross-motion is denied, and the decision of the INS is reversed.

*Procedural History*

This is the third time that this case has reached this district court. Plaintiff is a professional hockey player. He has played in the "professional leagues" since the 1982-83 season when he began playing for the Regina, Saskatchewan team in the now defunct World Hockey League. He has been playing in the NHL since the 1989 season. He is currently a member of the Detroit Red Wings, one of the better teams in the league.

Plaintiff initially filed a visa petition with defendant INS on January 20, 1993, seeking classification as a priority worker of extraordinary ability. . . . The petition was denied by the Director of the INS Northern Service Center on the ground that plaintiff had failed to demonstrate that he was a player of extraordinary ability as defined by the INS. Plaintiff appealed to the Administrative Appeals Unit ("AAU"), contending that he had achieved sustained national and international acclaim as a professional hockey player, and that the Northern Service Center had recently classified four other hockey players of comparable ability as aliens of extraordinary ability.

The AAU affirmed the denial of plaintiff's petition, holding that, "while the record indicates that the petitioner had played several seasons with an NHL team, it has not been established that the petitioner has achieved the sustained national or international acclaim required for classification as an alien with extraordinary ability, that he is one of the small percentage who have risen to the very top of his field of endeavor, or that his entry into the United States would substantially benefit prospectively the United States."

Plaintiff then filed an action in this court . . . for declaratory and injunctive relief with respect to the INS's denial of his visa petition. Judge Kocoras, to whom that case was assigned, remanded it back to the INS for further evidentiary proceedings, concluding that remand would allow plaintiff to take into consideration the INS's statutory interpretation of extraordinary ability when submitting further documentary evidence. Of particular note is Judge Kocoras's conclusion rejecting the INS's argument that it need not compare plaintiff's petition to those of other hockey players who had been granted visas, concluding that such position "not only lacked merit but borders on the specious." Judge Kocoras concluded that how the INS treated others in the field, particularly those alleged to possess no greater skill than petitioner, was highly relevant under the statutory scheme.

Plaintiff's petition was again denied by the Director of the Northern Service Center, which denial was again affirmed by the AAU. Plaintiff then filed the present action seeking declaratory and injunctive relief. On March 23, 1995, this court issued a memorandum opinion and order again remanding the case to the INS for further evidentiary proceedings. This court specifically directed plaintiff to submit and defendant to consider evidence regarding the necessity of a player with plaintiff's style of play and abilities, and evidence comparing his skill, salary level and other abilities to those of comparable players in the NHL, players who fulfill the same role for their respective teams. In addition, the court directed defendant to consider plaintiff's argument that a sustained career in the NHL demonstrates extraordinary ability.

Consistent with this court's instruction, on remand plaintiff submitted evidence of his current salary and contract with the Detroit Red Wings, a table from the Hockey News showing the 1996 players' salaries, newspaper and magazine articles about plaintiff, and an affidavit from Darren Pang, former renown NHL goaltender and current television broadcaster and NHL analyst for ESPN. Pang is a recognized expert on NHL hockey. Pang's affidavit lists all the "enforcers" in the league and their current salaries. It also sets forth the necessity for an enforcer, and indicates that most teams carry two such players on their rosters. Finally, Pang's affidavit indicates that plaintiff is currently the third rated and third highest paid enforcer in the NHL (the other two being paid more because of their goal scoring ability), and that plaintiff was rated the fifth best enforcer in 1993 when he filed his original petition. . . .

*Discussion*

As in plaintiff's previous case, this case turns on the interpretation of "extraordinary ability". . . .

The statute itself does not define extraordinary ability; however, the regulations promulgated by the INS define the term as "a level of expertise indicating that the individual is one of that small percentage who has risen to the very top of the field of endeavor." A petition for relief under this section must be accompanied by evidence that the alien has "sustained national or international acclaim and that his or her achievements have been recognized in the field of expertise." The regulations set forth various types of evidence that may be submitted to meet this evidentiary burden, including the documentation of memberships and associations which require outstanding achievements, major media publications relating to the alien's work in the field at issue, and evidence that the alien has commanded a large salary in relation to others in the field.

On remand from this court, the Director again completely rejected all plaintiff's evidence and denied his petition. First, . . . the Director determined that evidence relating to plaintiff's career after January 12, 1993 (the day plaintiff filed petition) would not be considered because it could not establish eligibility at the time of filing the petition.

Next, the Director rejected plaintiff's argument that a sustained career in professional hockey and four years in the NHL should be considered as evidence of extraordinary ability. The Director determined that plaintiff had failed to present evidence that four years in the NHL as an enforcer qualified as a sustained career. The Director then rejected those portions of Pang's affidavit in which he attested that plaintiff's $300,000 salary in 1993 ranked hint among the highest paid enforcers, and that plaintiff was considered among the top five enforcers in the league at that time. The basis for rejecting this evidence was that the affidavit contained no backup information for what the Director determined to be conclusory statements. The affidavit, however, indicates Mr. Pang's background and extensive knowledge of the NHL. He clearly states that he is familiar with plaintiff and the other enforcers in the league, and gives a basis for his opinions. He further states that if called to testify, he would testify that in his opinion in 1993 plaintiff was one of the top five enforcers in the league, and was so considered among his peers.

It is apparent to this court that at the heart of defendant's refusal to grant plaintiff a visa (as it has to other comparable NHL players) is its distaste for the role he plays on a hockey team. As stated in the Director's decision, "the service has never argued that the role of enforcer is not prevalent in the NHL. The necessity of such a role appears to be debatable. The service does argue that the sport itself has never condoned the kind of activity that petitioner is known for, as evidenced by the number of penalty minutes he is charged." The decision further states, "At the time the petition was filed, the petitioner's main claim to fame was that he held the record for the most penalty minutes in a game. The amount of penalties the petitioner amasses is indicative of the amount of fighting he does but quantity does not equate to extraordinary ability." Despite this language, however, the only evidence presented to the Director was that plaintiff was the fifth best enforcer in the league at the time he filed his petition. The decision to simply ignore this evidence was an abuse of discretion.

Moreover, it is apparent from the above quoted language that the Director simply rejects the notion that an enforcer can have extraordinary ability limited to the role that he plays on a hockey team. Indeed, as set forth in defendant's memorandum in support of his cross-motion for summary judgment, defendant's position remains that because plaintiff engages in conduct which is "disfavored," his abilities cannot properly be considered as a factor supportive of his claim to be an athlete of extraordinary ability. This court disagrees. The only evidence that was presented to the Director indicates that the role of an enforcer is necessary to the success of an NHL hockey team. The fact that a player is penalized for fighting does not mean that it is not both a necessary and accepted element of the game. Indeed, if it was not a necessary and accepted element of the game, the league would simply ban fighting altogether. Moreover, plaintiff presented evidence that his role as an enforcer entails much more than fighting. Pang's affidavit indicates that the role of an enforcer is to fight when necessary, but also to protect the team stars from being roughed up by the opposing team. An enforcer also serves as a deterrent to fighting, depending upon the reputation of the team's enforcer.

The fact remains that plaintiff has presented evidence sufficient to demonstrate that he is currently among the top three players in the world at what he does, and in 1993, when he filed his petition, he was among the top five players in the world. It goes without saying that there are countless players attempting to replace him every day. Yet, in 1993 he was, and remains today, among the best in the world. He has reached the very top of his field of endeavor. There is virtually no evidence in the record (let alone substantial evidence) to support defendant's finding that plaintiff is not among the best in the world, or that he is not an athlete of extraordinary ability.

The court concludes that the decision to reject plaintiff's role and unquestioned ability as an enforcer was without rational explanation, and that there was not substantial evidence for the factual finding that plaintiff is not at the top of his field of endeavor. Accordingly, plaintiff's motion for summary judgment is granted, defendant's cross-motion is denied, and defendant is ordered to issue plaintiff the visa he seeks.

*Conclusion*

For the reasons set forth above, plaintiff's motion for summary judgment is granted, defendant's cross-motion is denied and defendant is ordered to issue a visa to plaintiff.

---

**Note on nonimmigrant vs. immigrant status**

The foregoing materials all concern the requirements that must be satisfied for "nonimmigrant" artists, athletes and entertainers to be eligible for work permits authorizing them to perform in the United States *temporarily*.

As you will read below, in the materials that follow in the section on "Talent Guild Jurisdiction Over Foreign Performers," at least one U.S. entertainment union has negotiated a collective bargaining agreement with employers that prohibits those employers from hiring foreign performers – even temporarily – without the union's consent. If the union does consent, it will support the employer's application to the INS for a work permit for the foreign performer. If the union does not consent, however, the employer is barred from hiring the foreign performer, even if the performer satisfies the legal requirements for a work permit and gets one from the INS. As you read the "Talent Guild Jurisdiction . . ." materials, consider whether the union's conditions for consenting to the employment of foreign performers are the same as the work permit requirements in the Immigration and Nationality Act and INS Regulations, or whether instead the union's requirements are more difficult for a foreign performer to satisfy.

Before beginning the materials on "Talent Guild Jurisdiction," one further point needs to be made with respect to United States immigration law. Many foreign artists, entertainers and athletes seek and obtain authorization to live and work in the United States *permanently* (rather than just temporarily). They seek, in other words, to become "immigrants" rather than "nonimmigrant aliens." The work permits discussed above – O and P permits – are by definition "nonimmigrant alien" permits authorizing temporary work only. The sections of U.S. law most often used by artists, entertainers and athletes to seek permanent residency (including the right to work permanently) are the following.

---

## U.S. Immigration and Nationality Act
## Section 203 [8 U.S.C. §1153]

(b) . . . Aliens subject to [quotas] for employment-based immigrants in a fiscal year shall be allotted visas as follows:

(1) . . . Visas shall first be made available . . . to qualified immigrants who are . . . :

(A) *Aliens with extraordinary ability.* - An alien is described in this subparagraph if –

(i) the alien has extraordinary ability in the . . . arts . . . or athletics which has been demonstrated by sustained national or international acclaim and whose achievements have been recognized in the field through extensive documentation,

(ii) the alien seeks to enter the United States to continue work in the area of extraordinary ability, and

(iii) the alien's entry into the United States will substantially benefit prospectively the United States. . . .

(2) Aliens . . . of exceptional ability. –

(A) . . .Visas shall be made available . . . to qualified immigrants who . . . because of their exceptional ability in the . . . arts . . . will substantially benefit prospectively the . . . cultural . . . interests, or welfare of the United States, and whose services in the . . . arts . . . are sought by an employer in the United States.

(B) (i) . . . the Attorney General may, when the Attorney General deems it to be in the national interest, waive the requirements of subparagraph (A) that an alien's services in the . . . arts . . . be sought by an employer in the United States.

---

## Title 8 of Code of Federal Regulations
## Part 204 – Immigrant Petitions

*Sec. 204.5 Petitions for employment-based immigrants*

(h) *Aliens with extraordinary ability* –

(1) An alien, or any person on behalf of the alien, may file an I-140 visa petition for classification under section 203(b)(1)(A) of the Act as an alien of extraordinary ability in the . . . arts . . . or athletics.

(2) Definition. As used in this section: Extraordinary ability means a level of expertise indicating that the individual is one of that small percentage who have risen to the very top of the field of endeavor.

(3) Initial evidence. A petition for an alien of extraordinary ability must be accompanied by evidence that the alien has sustained national or international acclaim and that his or her achievements have been recognized in the field of expertise. Such evidence shall include evidence of a one-time achievement (that is, a major, internationally recognized award), or at least three of the following:

(i) Documentation of the alien's receipt of lesser nationally or internationally recognized prizes or awards for excellence in the field of endeavor; . . .

(iii) Published material about the alien in . . . major trade publications or other major media, relating to the alien's work in the field for which classification is sought. . . .

(v) Evidence of the alien's . . . artistic, [or] athletic . . . contributions of major significance in the field; . . . her major media;

(vii) Evidence of the display of the alien's work in the field at artistic exhibitions or showcases; . . .

(ix) Evidence that the alien has commanded a high salary or other significantly high remuneration for services, in relation to others in the field; or

(x) Evidence of commercial successes in the performing arts, as shown by box office receipts or record, cassette, compact disk, or video sales.. . .

(5) No offer of employment required. Neither an offer for employment in the United States nor a labor certification is required for this classification; however, the petition must be accompanied by clear evidence that the alien is coming to the United States to continue work in the area of expertise. Such evidence may include letter(s) from prospective employer(s), evidence of prearranged commitments such as contracts, or a statement from the beneficiary detailing plans on how he or she intends to continue his or her work in the United States. . . .

(k) Aliens of exceptional ability.

(1) Any United States employer may file a petition on Form I-140 for classification of an alien under section 203(b)(2) of the Act as an . . . alien of exceptional ability in the . . . arts. . . . If an alien is claiming exceptional ability in the . . . arts . . . and is seeking an exemption from the requirement of a job offer in the United States pursuant to section 203(b)(2)(B) of the Act, then the alien, or anyone in the alien's behalf, may be the petitioner.

(2) Definitions. As used in this section: . . . Exceptional ability in the . . . arts . . . means a degree of expertise significantly above that ordinarily encountered in the . . . arts . . . .

(3) Initial evidence. The petition must be accompanied by documentation showing that the alien is . . . an alien of exceptional ability in . . . the arts . . . .

(ii) To show that the alien is an alien of exceptional ability in the . . . arts . . . , the petition must be accompanied by at least three of the following: . . .

(D) Evidence that the alien has commanded a salary, or other remuneration for services, which demonstrates exceptional ability; . . .

(4) Labor certification . . .

(i) General. Every petition under this classification must be accompanied by an individual labor certification from the Department of Labor. . . . The job offer portion of the individual labor certification . . . must demonstrate that the job requires . . . an alien of exceptional ability.

(ii) Exemption from job offer. The director may exempt the requirement of a job offer, and thus of a labor certification, for aliens of exceptional ability in the . . . arts . . . if exemption would be in the national interest. To apply for the exemption, the petitioner must submit . . . evidence to support the claim that such exemption would be in the national interest.

---

**Note on consequences of permanent residency**

The decision to seek a permanent residency visa is not one that should be taken lightly. For artists, entertainers and athletes who intend to continue residing in their home countries most of the time, there is a potential downside to becoming a permanent resident of the United States, even though having a permanent residency visa would enable them to remain in the U.S. as long as they like, to go and return as often as they like, and to work for as many different employers as they like. The downside concerns the tax implications of becoming a permanent resident of the U.S. – a subject considered in the final section of this chapter.

---

## 2.2 TALENT GUILD JURISDICTION

### 2.2.1 Over Foreign Performers

**National Labor Relations Board v. Actors' Equity Association**
**644 F.2d 939 (2nd Cir. 1981)**

Mansfield, Circuit Judge

The National Labor Relations Board (NLRB) and Intervenor, Yul Brynner, petition this court for enforcement of the Board's order dated February 19, 1980, requiring Actors' Equity Association (Equity), a theater actors' union, to cease violating §§ 8(b)(1)(A) and 8(b)(2) of the National Labor Relations Act by charging non-uniform dues that unjustifiably discriminate against aliens who belong to the union and are in this country temporarily to perform in stage productions. The order also mandates repayment of all past overcharges from April 6, 1976, to the present. We agree with the NLRB's finding that the assessment of non-uniform dues against aliens without any reasonable basis violates the Act, and find no fault in the Board's choice of remedy.... Accordingly, we grant the Board's petition for enforcement.

Actors' Equity is an employees' association that has entered into collective bargaining agreements on behalf of stage actors with various theater organizations in New York and throughout the United States and Canada. Its bargaining agreements universally contain a "union security clause" providing that the employer will hire only union members to act in its productions.

Equity has for many years attempted to regulate participation by foreign actors in American theater performances. This regulation has taken several forms. First, since 1964 Equity has participated in an agreement with the United States Department of Labor and the Immigration and Naturalization Service to the effect that the Labor Department would seek Equity's advice on aliens' applications for visas under [a section of the Immigration and Naturalization Act] which permits resident aliens to obtain jobs in the United States only if they are rendering exceptional or temporary service in jobs which no unemployed Americans are capable of performing. Second, Equity has agreed with New York theater employers' organization the Council of Stock Theatres (COST), League of Resident Theatres (LORT), and the League of New York Theatres and Producers (Producers) that members of those organizations (the primary employers of aliens in the United States) will not hire non-resident aliens without Equity's consent.[1] [n1. Equity's agreements with COST and LORT wholly prohibit employment of non-resident aliens without Equity's prior consent. Its agreement with Producers provides that a producer may not apply to the Immigration and Naturalization Service for admission of an alien actor unless Equity and Producers both approve the application, and that differences of opinion between Equity and Producers will be resolved by arbitration.]

Finally, Equity has imposed a separate dues schedule on non-resident aliens. Citizens of the United States and Canada who belong to Actors Equity, as well as aliens who reside here with the intention of making this country their permanent residence, pay dues according to a sliding scale ranging from $42 per year for an actor earning no more than $2,500 per year to a maximum of $400 for an actor earning more than $30,000 per year. Once a so-called "resident member" makes more than $1,400 per year his dues will never exceed 3% of gross income, with a $400 per year limit. Non-resident aliens who are allowed to perform in the United States, on the other hand, must pay 5% of their stage income as dues, with no ceiling. Yul Brynner, the Intervenor, is a Swiss citizen and resident of France who was admitted into the United States to play the King of Siam in *The King and I*, a revival of a play in which he starred some years ago. If he had been a U.S. citizen or resident, his dues to Actor's Equity for the first year of the play's run would have been $400; under the separate schedule for non-resident aliens, he was required to pay $45,000.

Charges were filed with the Board on October 8, 1976, alleging that the union was violating §§ 8(b)(1)(A) and 8(b)(2) of the Act through employment of its discriminatory dues schedule. Noting that those provisions prohibit discrimination against employees except as provided by § 8(a)(3), which allows unions and employers to enter union security agreements, the charging party relied on the second proviso to § 8(a)(3), which states that employees who belong to a union having in effect a union security agreement may be required as a condition of membership only to "tender the periodic dues and the initiation fees uniformly required as a condition of acquiring or retaining membership."

The administrative law judge, and later the Board, agreed that the separate dues structure unlawfully discriminated against aliens by violating the union's duty to charge uniform dues or to demonstrate a reasonable justification for the non-uniformity. While it declined to impose a per se rule that any discrimination in dues charged to aliens was unacceptable under the Act, it nevertheless found such discrimination presumptively invalid, and declared that absent some justification for the non-uniformity it must be found illegal. It then rejected the justifications claimed by Equity that the higher dues structure was necessary (1) to limit the number of alien actors in the United States, (2) to prevent reprisals from British Equity, Britain's "friendly adversary" correlative of Actors' Equity, and (3) to counterbalance British Equity's power to exclude as many American actors as it wants simply by telling the British Labor Board whom it wants excluded. . . .[T]he Administrative Law Judge ordered Equity to desist from imposing a discriminatory dues schedule and ordered repayment of all amounts collected after April 6, 1976 (six months before the complaint was filed in this case) in excess of what non-resident aliens would have paid if treated like residents or citizens.

Equity first contends that the Board has no jurisdiction over the rights of aliens because the NLRA is aimed at protecting American workers only and that non-resident aliens therefore have no cognizable rights under the Act. We disagree. Nothing in the terms or construction of the NLRA limits the meaning of the word "employees" to American citizens or permanent residents. The provisions in question here do not specify "American-citizen" employees as opposed to non-resident aliens. They merely proscribe discriminatory treatment of individuals or groups of employees who belong to unions, without regard to the employees' nationality or residence. For instance, Equity does not deny that Canadian citizens and resident aliens have rights as union members under the NLRA. It would be unthinkable to allow Equity to demand union membership and payment of dues by alien members performing in the United States while denying them rights associated with union membership.[2] [n2. . . . [O]ur opinion [does not] bear on the union's power to limit the number of aliens who perform on American stages by impeding their entry into the United States or into the union.]

Having recognized that aliens possess equal rights as union members, we have no difficulty concluding that the union's two-tiered dues structure discriminates against non-residents by failing to impose uniform dues without some legitimate basis for the discrimination. Equity attempts to justify its dues discrimination on three grounds. First, it argues that the 5% dues rate protects employment opportunities for members by limiting alien membership in American productions. Second, it suggests that the rule protects Americans from hostile or retaliatory actions on the part of British Equity, which now reciprocally charges American theater actors 5% dues.[3] [n3. Though British Equity serves both theatrical and film actors, unlike American Equity it does not impose differential dues on American movie actors, just as no American union imposes higher dues on British film actors.] Third, and relatedly, it says that the rule (or at least the power to have the rule) provides a needed counterweight to British Equity's influence over alien admissions in England.

We find no merit in these asserted justifications. There is no substantial evidence that the 5% dues assessment, either because of parity between American and foreign pay scales or for some other reason, would inhibit foreign actors from participating in America's comparatively lucrative theater productions. On the contrary, past statements by Equity indicate that the 5% dues rate was adopted primarily as a revenue-producing measure. Moreover, Equity's power to exclude aliens derives from an entirely different source, its agreements with COST, LORT, and Producers. In the face of these agreements, which give Equity effective authority to decide which aliens to admit and which to exclude, the 5% dues rate has no significant exclusionary force.

Similarly, the asserted justification that the higher dues are necessary to protect American actors from retaliatory action on the part of British Equity, which imposes a reciprocal 5% dues rate, lacks rationality. The fairness of discriminatory acts under American labor law does not depend on what is practiced under British labor law. The 5% American dues levy seems more likely to provoke hostility than to eliminate it. Nor has it had much influence upon British Equity's decision-making, since it has been in existence for about 50 years and British Equity's retaliatory 5% dues rate has existed almost that long.[4] [n4. Equity places much emphasis on the statement by British Equity's General Secretary that British Equity would not necessarily feel bound to eliminate its 5% dues rate if the Board's enforcement petition is granted. Even assuming that British Equity would impose a non-reciprocal dues assessment on Americans after this case, this argument merely proves that British Equity acts independently of American Equity, shedding doubt on Equity's protests that its dues rates somehow affect British Equity's rates.] Finally, on a narrower level, concerns about British Equity could hardly be relevant as a justification for charging higher dues to Brynner, who is a Swiss citizen and French resident and has never been either a citizen or a resident of Great Britain. . . .

---

**Actors' Equity Association Production Contract**

*Rule 3. Aliens*

(A) *Employment of Non-resident Aliens.* Non-resident aliens may be employed only if approved through the following procedures, and the Producer agrees not to take any action (i.e., make contractual commitments with aliens, import a show or cast into the United States, or make application to the United States Immigration, and Naturalization Service or any other government agency) unless Equity has given such approval in writing or there has been an arbitration award pursuant to this Rule and Rule 4, ARBITRATION. As a further part of the application procedures, the Producer agrees not to advertise, and will endeavor not to publicize the engagement of any Alien Actor or Unit Company until written approval for such employment has been given by Equity.

(1) *Application Required.* A written application for such approval must first be submitted by the Producer to Equity, accompanied by whatever information the Producer thinks relevant.

(2) Following receipt of such application, which shall be accompanied by all *materials* specified herein, Equity's Alien Committee shall have 15 business days in which to render its decision.

(3) *Right to Appeal.* In the event the Producer is dissatisfied with the Equity Alien Committee's decision, Producer may appeal and present the case to the Equity Council at its next meeting, at which time the Council will render its decision, or Producer may go directly to arbitration under provisions of Rule 4. In the event the Producer appeals to Equity's Council and is dissatisfied with the Council's decision, the matter may be submitted directly to arbitration.

(4) In the event of arbitration, the Arbitrator shall, within one week's time, render a decision which shall be final, and binding on both Parties. The Arbitrator shall reach a decision based on the criteria set forth in Rule 3(B) below.

(5) Unless the Producer complies with the conditions or procedures set forth above, the Producer's request for employment of non-resident alien(s) will be automatically denied.

(6) In arriving at his decision, the arbitrator shall use the criteria for qualifying described in B. below.

(B) To qualify for employment under terms of this agreement, non-resident aliens must meet all the requirements of any one of the following three categories:

(1) *Star.* The application to Equity must include at least the following documentation:

(a) Documents testifying to the current widespread acclaim, and international recognition accorded to the alien, receipt of internationally recognized prizes, or awards for excellence;

(b) Documents showing that the alien's work experience during the past year did, and the alien's intended work in the United States will, require exceptional ability;

(c) Published material by or about the alien such as critical reviews in major newspapers, periodicals, and trade journals;

(d) Documentary evidence of earnings commensurate with the claimed level of renown;

(e) Playbills, and other materials reflecting "star" billings;

(f) Documents attesting to the outstanding reputation of theatres, and other establishments in which the alien has appeared or is scheduled to appear; and/or documents attesting to the outstanding reputation of repertory companies or other organizations with which the alien has performed during the past year in a leading or starring capacity.

(2) *Actor Providing Unique Services*. The application to Equity must include at least the following documentation:

(a) That the Actor whose services are sought will be providing unique services which cannot be performed by any current member of Equity, and that there is no citizen of the United States or resident alien domiciled in the U.S. capable of performing such services;

(b) That a diligent search has been made within the United States to find such an Actor.

(3) *Unit Company*. The application to Equity must include at least the following documentation:

(a) That the Unit Company is a repertory organization which will perform at least two full productions from its repertoire for a limited engagement not to exceed 20 weeks in any one city and that it be specified in advance to Equity that the Unit Company will give an equal number of performances in each city or town of each of the two or more productions to be presented in the United States;

(b) That it is of internationally recognized status and considered to be of the highest artistic standard and reputation;

(c) That it has established its identity over a period of at least 10 years;

(d) That the productions intended to be presented are regularly on its production schedule;

(e) That the Unit Company shall have a cast complement in which at least 80% of the members appeared in at least eight performances in the repertory production(s) in a repertory season at one of its repertory theatres. (Examples of companies which may qualify as Unit Companies are: *the Royal Shakespeare Company, the British National Theatre, the Comedie Francaise and the Jean-Louis Barrault Company*.)

(C) In the event the determination is made, pursuant to paragraph (A) above, that a non-resident alien or a Unit Company and its non-resident alien members satisfy the criteria set forth herein, Equity will support the Producer's application to the Immigration and Naturalization Service for the temporary admission and employment of said alien(s). Application on behalf of the same non-resident alien or Unit Company and its non-resident alien members for subsequent productions shall follow the procedures detailed herein.

(D) Companies and Plays of Special Character. Companies and Plays first presented outside the United States which do not fall within the categories described in paragraph (B) above, may be allowed to perform in the United States under terms and conditions to be determined by Equity. Applications under this paragraph shall be made to Equity in a form satisfactory to Equity and the determination of whether such a company or Play of special character shall be allowed to be performed in the United States and under what terms and conditions, shall be entirely within the discretion of the Council of Actors' Equity Association, such determination to be final and binding.

(E) Additional Provisions Relating to Non-resident Aliens.

(1) No Actor may be replaced by a non-resident alien.

(2) Non-resident aliens may not be employed under Chorus contracts except in Unit Companies.

(3) Split-Week tours and National tours where the majority of engagements are one week or less may not employ non-resident aliens in any capacity under any circumstance.

(4) A non-resident alien who has been employed hereunder shall not be permitted again to rehearse or perform in the United States under this Rule until a period of one year has elapsed from the date of said alien's last employment hereunder.

(5) Each Unit Company, or company or Play of special character as defined in paragraphs (B) and (D) above shall be required to hire a resident Stage Manager qualified in accordance with Rule 68, STAGE MANAGERS. Such Stage Manager shall be hired no later than the first day of rehearsal or performance, whichever comes first, after the company arrives in the United States and shall remain employed until the final performance in the United States.

(6) A Unit Company accepted by Equity must perform an Actors' Fund Benefit as required by Rule 6, BENEFITS.

(7) When an alien Actor is employed in any company other than a Unit Company, an Actor other than an alien Actor will be engaged solely as Understudy to the alien Actor or in another job function which is in addition to the complement required under this Agreement for both Point of Organization and touring productions except that for Pre-point of Organization tryouts, such Actor shall be required commencing with the sixth week after the first paid public performance.

(F) Notwithstanding any of the above provisions, it is the purpose of this rule that a balance be maintained so that in each country where English is spoken, the number of non-resident aliens from each such country admitted to perform under this Rule shall not exceed the number of United States citizens employed in the theatre in such foreign country. It is understood that while absolute equality in numbers is not capable of attainment, it is nevertheless the intention of this Rule that failure to adhere to this precept violates the letter and spirit of this Rule.

(1) In order to implement the purpose stated in (F) above, the League of American Theatres and Producers and Actors' Equity Association will exercise their best efforts to foster reciprocal exchange of Unit Companies. Toward this end, the parties agree to meet quarterly to review the status of such exchanges.

(2) Further, to implement the purpose stated in (F) above, the Producer who licenses a play under the Production Contract to be performed in a country where English is spoken will use best efforts to place in the Agreement with the foreign Producer a provision that either two Actors or 15% of the cast, whichever is greater, engaged in the foreign production will be United States Citizens.

---

**Arbitration between
Don Gregory, Mike Merrick & Dome Productions
and Actors' Equity Association
re "My Fair Lady" (1980)**

Before Daniel G. Collins, Arbitrator

The issue here is whether under Rule 3 B1 and/or B2 of the Production contract Cheryl Kennedy may be employed for the part of Eliza Doolittle in a proposed production of MY FAIR LADY. . . .

Producers Don Gregory and Mike Merrick contend as follows: Cheryl Kennedy is a Star within the meaning of Rule 3 Bl. In addition, the part of Eliza Doolittle requires unique services within the meaning of Rule 3 B2, which she, but no Equity member or other person within the United States, is capable of performing.

Equity responds that Kennedy does not meet a number of the express "Star" criteria set forth in Rule 3 Bl, and that the role of Eliza Doolittle does not require unique services within the meaning of Rule 3 B2. Equity notes that this last point was affirmed by this very Arbitrator in a 1975 proceeding with respect to the 1976 Broadway revival of MY FAIR LADY.

The Arbitrator has carefully reviewed the documentation presented by the Producers in support of the claim under Rule 3 B1. While that documentation indicates that Kennedy has achieved considerable success and acclaim on the English musical stage, there is simply no showing that she has received "international recognition" or has received "internationally recognized prizes or awards for excellence," as expressly required by Rule 3 Bl (a). Since in order to be eligible, an actor must meet all of the stated requirements of the "Star" category, the Arbitrator need not, therefore, consider the degree to which Kennedy satisfies the other 3 B1 requirements. The Arbitrator finds that Cheryl Kennedy is not eligible under Rule 3 B1.

Whether the role of Eliza Doolittle poses unique requirements which no resident of the United States can satisfy was an extremely difficult question when it was first brought to arbitration in 1975. In addressing that question then, this Arbitrator noted that the part was "extremely demanding and required a variety of talents," and that the producers there had made a painstaking search for a resident actress qualified for the part. Nevertheless he noted that American actresses had played the role for substantial periods during the original Broadway run, and he was of the opinion that the part was not "inherently demanding of skills unpossessed by American actors." In holding that the English actress then proposed was ineligible under the predecessor Production Contract's (H)(ii) language, i.e. "unemployed persons capable of performing such service or labor cannot be found in this country," the Arbitrator noted that the issue was not whether the actress proposed was the best available in the producer and director's opinions, but whether there was anything inherent in the part which would preclude a resident from successfully playing it.

Many of the arguments advanced in the present proceeding are similar to those made earlier. What is new here, though, in terms of evidence bearing on this issue, is the experience with the 1976 Broadway revival, in which following this Arbitrator's rejection of the then producers claimed need to employ an English actress in the role of Eliza Doolittle, the role was played by an American. That actress was, in fact, one of those American actresses who, the producers had asserted in the arbitration proceeding, satisfied some important requirements for the role, but was deficient in terms of accent and the ability to make the stage transition from Cockney flower girl to Queen's English lady.

The 1976 production was widely reviewed. Almost without exception, the critics found the portrayal of Eliza Doolittle lacking linguistically and/or in a convincing, comprehensible role transition: Clive Barnes, writing in "The New York Times," spoke of a "not quite convincing . . . transformation from cabbage leaf to daffodil." "Time" magazine speculated that "perhaps it is difficult for an American actress to comprehend either . . . flower girl or lady." "Variety" remarked that "She's obviously not to the Cockney rhythm born. . ." John Simon, in "The New Leader," stated that "she had neither the true guttersnipe querulousness of the Cockney flower vendor, nor the grandeur of Higgin's Galatea – a duchess more real than a real one – although she managed the requisite accents fairly well for an American." In this connection it should be noted that intensive dialect coaching was provided for that production.

In addition, Jerry Adler testified in the present proceeding that he had been associated with nine productions of MY FAIR LADY, both on Broadway – he was the director of the 1976 revival – and in road companies, and that the only artistic or financial successes among them had been when an English actress had played Eliza Doolittle. He stated his firm belief that the unusual combination of qualities required for the part – good singing voice, stage stature, conventional acting, ability, and both the accent for and understanding of the transition from flower girl to lady – made it unlikely in the extreme that any American actress could master the role. Adler added that he knew of no English actresses with a "green card" who would be suitable now for a Broadway production.

Rex Harrison would return to his role as Henry Higgins in the proposed production. . . . Harrison stated that he personally had auditioned fifteen resident finalists for the role of Eliza Doolittle, without success. Harrison spoke of his and the director and producer's unrealized hope to find a "green carded" linguistic genius who could have the manner and speech of the Cockney plus a perfect copy of Higgins' perfect English, not to mention a singer who could hit and hold a top "g." Harrison opinioned that "no American actress with an American background can successfully play this part." As to Cheryl Kennedy, Harrison stated that she "is Cockney; her mother and father, musicians, are Cockneys; she has been taught to speak English correctly but has no difficulty whatsoever reverting to the accent she heard when she was growing up. She sings beautifully; she is an actress of natural fire and ability; she is tall; she is 32, the age we want; she also has charisma, a rare commodity. . . ." The Producers testified concerning their efforts to find a resident actress for the part. They stated that they had made a nationwide search, had held auditions in Los Angeles and New York for 51 actresses, including one English actress who had become an American citizen and other actresses with green cards; and had asked one prospect to obtain dialect coaching, but this had not make her any more suitable for the part.

The evidence establishes that the Producers have made diligent search within the meaning of Rule 3 B2(b). The question then is whether Cheryl Kennedy would provide unique services within the meaning of 3 B2(a).

The art of acting by definition involves character portrayal, and role transition, using speech and song, not infrequently with dialect. Given the range and traditions of the American acting profession, there is something like a rebuttable presumption that its members can competently play any role in a production on the American stage. While producers thus have a heavy burden in Rule 3 B2 proceedings, that burden is not impossible – the very existence of the Rule suggests the possibility that a role may make such extraordinary demands that even the most exhaustive national search will. not produce an appropriate actor.

In the 1975 proceeding the presumption that resident actors could perform the role in question was reinforced by the fact that American actresses had played Eliza

Doolittle for substantial periods of time in the original Broadway production. While the producers in that proceeding introduced expert opinion testimony to the contrary, the Arbitrator did not believe that it offset the foregoing considerations.

Here Equity's Alien Committee and its Council have again fully considered the issue and again have determined that unique services are not involved. In a sense the Producers have here an even heavier burden of proof, since added to the 1975 considerations, is this Arbitrator's prior Opinion and the fact that an American actress played Eliza Doolittle in the 1976 Broadway revival.

At the same time there is now considerably more to be said on the Producers' side. First, if there ever was any doubt that American critics, and presumably the public, would demand authenticity in the portrayal of Eliza Doolittle, that doubt has been dispelled by the 1976 experience. Second, despite all of the resources of the original production that were available to the 1976 Broadway revival, and despite the concerted effort to provide coaching as to the linguistic and class considerations in the part of Eliza Doolittle, the critics with considerable unanimity saw major deficiencies in those aspects of the portrayal. Furthermore, the critical comments suggested, and in some cases expressed, disbelief that any American actress could successfully play the role. Third, there is now additional, important opinion evidence, in the form of a statement by Rex Harrison, who surely is qualified to address the subject, that the part cannot be successfully played by anyone but an English actress.

Equity responds that the 1976 production was criticized on a variety of grounds, and that the portrayal of Eliza Doolittle received mixed, not uniformly negative, reviews. Furthermore, Equity argues, Harrison, for whom it has the utmost respect and affection, is intimately involved in the proposed production, and contractually enjoys artistic approval rights.

Equity's points are important. Nevertheless, a persuasive rebuttal is to be found in the testimony of Jerry Adler. While Adler is not to be director of the proposed production, he has been associated with nine productions of MY FAIR LADY, including the major ones. He was emphatic that productions have only been successful artistically or financially when an Eliza Doolittle was played by an English actress.

This is not an easy question. On balance, however, the Arbitrator finds that the Producers here have met their heavy burden of demonstrating that in the role of Eliza Doolittle Cheryl Kennedy would provide unique services within the meaning of Rule 3 B2 (a).

For the foregoing reasons the Arbitrator finds that while Cheryl Kennedy is not eligible for the part of Eliza Doolittle in the proposed production of MY FAIR LADY pursuant to Rule 3 B1, she is eligible pursuant to Rule 3 B2.

---

**Arbitration between**
**Cameron Mackintosh and Actors' Equity Association**
**re "Miss Saigon" (1991)**

Before Daniel G. Collins, Permanent Arbitrator

This proceeding involves a dispute concerning the application of Rule 3(A) and (B) of the Agreement and Rules Governing Employment under the Production Contract effective for the period 1990 to 1992 (the "Production Contract") between Actors' Equity Association and the League of American Theatres and Producers, Inc., to which Cameron Mackintosh, the Producer of the forthcoming Broadway production of the musical play MISS SAIGON, is a party. . . .

*The Issue*

The . . . issue [is] whether Lea Salonga shall be permitted under Rule 3(B) (1) or (2) of the Production Contract to play the part of Kim in the Producer's Broadway production of the musical play MISS SAIGON.

*The Background of the Dispute*

Cameron Mackintosh is the Producer of the forthcoming Broadway production of MISS SAIGON. He is also the producer of the current London production of MISS SAIGON, which opened in September 1989. Lea Salonga, a national of the Philippines, opened in the principal role of Kim, one of several leading roles, in the London production. Subsequently, in response to the extraordinary vocal demands of the part, Salonga was regularly assigned to only four of the eight weekly performances of the play, in rotation with Monique Wilson, who does three performances, and Jenine Desiderio, who does one.

In August of 1990 a dispute arose between the Producer and Equity concerning the appearance of British Actor Jonathan Pryce in the leading role of the Engineer in MISS SAIGON, a part in which he opened in the London production. The dispute broadly addressed the question of opportunities for Asian Americans on Broadway, but focused initially on Equity's contention that the part of the Engineer, an Eurasian in the play, should be played in the Broadway production by an Asian American actor. Ultimately that dispute was resolved–Mr. Pryce, a Caucasian, was permitted to play, as a "Star" under Rule 3(B)(1). Thereafter in a negotiated "Statement of Mutual Understanding" dated September 25, 1990 and signed by the Producer and Alan Eisenberg, Equity's Executive Secretary (the "Statement of Understanding"), the parties made commitments and established procedures to serve the goal of theatrical opportunities for Asian American actors, while recognizing the Producer's creative responsibilities. In this connection the Statement of Understanding provided in part as follows:

> The tragic love story told in MISS SAIGON is meaningful only within the context of illustrating the cultural differences between East and West. The majority of the roles in the production are racially specific. Mr. Mackintosh has acknowledged the racially specific roles should be played by Actors of the appropriate race wherever it is possible, and he and the entire creative team have reiterated their commitment to cast accordingly. Equity agrees to cooperate with the Production by way of advice and consultation.
>
> Mr. Mackintosh and the creative team acknowledge that Equity has acted in good faith in reaffirming its long-standing policy of seeking increased employment opportunities for its minority members and its conviction that roles where race is germane should be cast in such a manner. Equity has expressed its belief to Mr. Mackintosh and the creative team that there is a substantial pool of talent from which roles where race is germane can be cast accordingly. In turn, Equity acknowledges that Mr. Mackintosh and the creative team have represented in good faith their concern that due to the very specific performance requirements of MISS SAAGON, particularly in relation to the vocal demands required to perform the six major Principal roles, Mr. Mackintosh and his creative team believe it may not always be possible to achieve the goal of racially specific casting.

As to the part of Kim, the Statement of Understanding provided as follows:

> Equity acknowledges the artistic integrity of the Producer, Authors, and creative team of MISS SAIGON. Equity further recognizes that the creative team has conducted an extensive worldwide search for the London

and potential New York productions. The documentary evidence received by Equity from the Producer indicates that the search commenced two years ago in June 1988, and initially concentrated upon finding Asian Actors to play the role of Kim. Commencing in December 1989, their efforts were solely focused upon casting the Broadway production, with continued emphasis on the role of Kim, as well as for all of the other male and female Asian roles. The casting search, however, was not intended to find candidates to create the role of the Engineer, although it was intended to find understudies for the original Broadway company. The creative team has represented that its casting efforts to date have been motivated by the principles of artistic excellence and equal opportunity for all, and Equity acknowledges that this representation has been made in good faith.

The creative team has also confirmed its commitment to seek Asian American artists to appear in MISS SAIGON. Open auditions will be conducted on a regular basis is the future in order to insure that every Asian American Actor is given an opportunity to audition. In addition to publication in the customary trade papers, advertisements will be placed in leading Asian American newspapers announcing these auditions. The Producer will contact performing arts schools and universities to notify them of such auditions. The Producer will provide casting information to Equity, and Equity will distribute that information to theatres across the country. Jointly, Equity and the Production will solicit the cooperation of the Asian American community at large to insure that the "word is spread" concerning these auditions.

Prior to the final selection of the cast for the Broadway production, further open auditions will be held for ethnic minority performers in New York and in Los Angeles. These auditions will be advertised as widely as possible, bearing in mind that the final casting deadline for the original cast is the beginning of October.

With respect to the role of Kim, Mr. Mackintosh has confirmed that is has never been his intention to seek permission for Lea Salonga to appear in the Broadway production. It has always been his intention to find a new Asian Actor for Broadway. His experience has shown that the requirements of the role of Kim are so demanding that it will be necessary to cast two Actors to perform on an alternating basis. At present, the eight candidates under consideration for the role of Kim are Asian and it is hoped that future auditions may provide additional Asian American candidates. Equity acknowledges the extensive search to date for the role of Kim, and takes into account that two of these eight candidates are Asian Actors who are not American citizens. If no Asian American Actors can be found, Equity agrees to the hiring of no more than two non-American Asian Actors to originate the role of Kim and the alternate on Broadway. The maximum employment period for any such non-American Asian Actor hired shall be twelve months, plus a one-time option to extend for an additional six months, if necessary. However, if none of the candidates proves to have the specific qualities necessary to originate this major role on Broadway, Mr. Mackintosh must reserve the right to request permission for Miss Salonga to appear.

Following the execution of the Statement of Understanding the Producer made further efforts to find Asian Americans for the part of Kim. However, on December 4, 1990 the Producer in writing asked Equity for permission for Lea Salonga to play that part in the Broadway production. Initially the request appears to have been based solely on the "unique services" provision in Rule 3(B) (2); later the request was expanded to assert that Salonga was a "Star" within the meaning of Rule 3(B)(1), and also was entitled to perform pursuant to the Statement of Understanding. Equity's Alien Committee denied the Producer's request, and that decision was affirmed by Equity's Council. The Producer then initiated thus arbitration proceeding.

The parties submitted voluminous testimonial and documentary evidence in support of their respective positions. The Arbitrator will not attempt to recite that evidence here, but will refer to it insofar as he deems it relevant. . . .

*The Parties' Positions*

The Producer argues as follows: Lea Salonga is, as the documentation establishes, a "Star" of international renown and distinction within the meaning of Rule 3(B)(1). She also will under Rule 3(B)(2) provide "unique services" which cannot be performed by any resident American or American domiciled alien actress.

Equity responds as follows: Salonga, while an accomplished musical actress, is not a Star as that term is used in Rule 3(B)(1) – industry practice and arbitration decisions under the Production Contract recognize that Star status involves more than critical acclaim in one play, and that the receipt of an Olivier, or the receipt in New York of a Tony, does not in itself establish a performer as a Star of international renown and distinction. Salonga's theatrical credentials and achievements simply do not compare with those of the foreign actors admitted in the last five or ten years under Rule 3(B)(1), or the American actors permitted to play as Stars in Great Britain. Furthermore, her credentials and achievements compare unfavorably even to those of American and British actors who have participated in exchanges agreed by American Equity and British Equity. As to Salonga's achievements in the Phillipines, the Presidential Medal of Merit awarded to her in June 1990 appears simply to reflect her Olivier award, and her other prizes and her work in the Phillipines must be viewed in the context of that nation's fledgling and not yet fully professional theatre. As to Salonga's alleged uniqueness, the Producer understandably wants an actor of proven ability to open on Broadway in the role of Kim. However, the test under Rule 3(B)(2) is not whether a foreign actor is the best performer for a part, but whether she is the only performer capable of giving a professional performance in the part. Here there are two non-American Asian actors, Monique Wilson and Jenine Desiderio, who have been performing regularly in the London production, and the Producer plans there to utilize an Asian American actor, Meera Popkin, as a regular alternate. Furthermore, the Producer has indicated that Xam Cheng, an Asian American, will be the alternate in the Broadway production, and that Melanie Tojio, also an Asian American, will be the Broadway understudy. The Producer has also indicated that it hopes eventually to use Jatnie Rivera, a non-American Asian, as an alternate in London.

The Producer responds as follows: It is inappropriate to refer to exchanges, which constitute accommodations by parties who have no need or desire to pursue the issue of Star status. As to foreign actors recently admitted by Equity as Stars, Sting, in particular, possessed almost no theatrical credentials. In contrast Salonga has more than ten years stage experience and an Olivier. On the issue of unique services, there is no real or reasonable alternative but for Salonga to open as the originator of the role of Kim on Broadway. The London production will continue and no thought has been given to Monique Wilson's coming to New York. Desiderio has not demonstrated that she can meet the physical and vocal demands of regular rotation. Popkin's only professional experience was as an understudy in the national tour of STARLIGHT EXPRESS. Rivera has no professional experience. Cheng has no professional, only college theatrical experience. Tojio has stage experience only as a dancer. Equity in rebuttal, cites a host of actors and actresses who have made very successful Broadway debuts in major parts.

*Discussion*

The Producer, in a letter to Equity dated December 7, 1990, and again at the outset of the hearing before the Arbitrator, appeared to take the position that in addition to Rule 3(B)(1) and 3(B)(2), there was a separate basis for admitting Salonga as one of the two non-American Asian actors who could be employed to originate the role of Kim and the alternate if no Asian American actors could be found for those positions. Testimony presented by both parties at the hearing established, however, that there had been no such agreement; on the contrary the understanding was that if none of the Asian American and non-American Asian candidates for the part of Kim proved to be adequate, then the Producer could request permission to use Salonga, but that in order to be admitted she would have to satisfy the requirements of Rule 3(B) (1) or 3(B) (2).

That is not to say, though, that the Statement of Understanding has no relevance for this proceeding. It certainly does. It recognized that Kim is a racially specific part. It attests to the extraordinary world-wide search that the Producer had undertaken to find Asian actors to play the role of Kim, and it committed the Producer, with Equity's assistance, to a further search to fill that and other racially specific parts. Also, it gave permission to the Producer to use nonAmerican Asian actors, other than Salonga, as the originator and alternate in the part of Kim if suitable Asian American candidates could not be found. Finally, it indicated that the Producer's two-year search had, as of September 25, 1990, produced only eight candidates, two of whom were non-American Asians.

The Producer initially sought permission for Salonga to play Kim in the Broadway production under the "unique services" provision in Rule 3(B)(2). The Arbitrator will therefore address this issue at the outset.

The Arbitrator is very mindful of the dearth of employment opportunities, and opportunities for career progression for American actors, and that these problems have been compounded for minority actors, including in particular Asian Americans. He also believes that there may be pressures on a producer of a successfully mounted London production to utilize the starring members of the London cast in a Broadway opening, rather than attempting to find qualified American actors. Furthermore, the concepts of "unique" and "best" to some extent overlap, and in all good faith a creative director may not see any distinction in these respects as to the work of a performing artist. Nevertheless, the Production Contract in Rule 3(B) (2) recognizes that there may be unique services that can be supplied only by a foreign artist. The question here is whether the services Lea Salonga would provide fall into this category.

In considering whether Salonga's services in the Broadway production of MISS SAIGON would be unique, account must be taken of several salient, and undisputed facts. First, the parties agree that the part of Kim is an Asian racially specific part. Second, for a variety of reasons the pool of Asian American and non-American Asian actors who have professional experience on the British or American stage is very limited. Third, the part of Kim poses extraordinary vocal, and physical demands – not only must Kim have a range of two octaves, but she must sing in thirteen numbers, in eight of which she is a principal singer. The difficulty of performing the part, according to Musical Supervisor David Caddick, is compounded by the fact that the actor playing Kim must appear to be less than twenty years old, and actors of such a young age are not vocally developed enough to perform such a role day after day. This was confirmed by medical advice to the Producer that Salonga was straining her vocal chords by constant performances, which was why the part had to be rotated in London and will be rotated in New York. Fourth, the part of Kim, according to London Director Nicholas Hytner, requires considerable acting ability and emotional suitability since it moves from a position of vulnerability and naivette to bitter emotional experience. Only Salonga and Wilson, both of whom are non-American Asians, have any significant professional acting experience. All of that experience, with the exception of their respective performances in the London production of MISS SAIGON, has been in the Philippines. Salonga opened in London and played the part of Kim, for which Wilson was the understudy, until the vocal and physical demands of that part required rotation, primarily with Wilson. Desiderio has appeared in the London production, but that is her first stage experience. The Producer, Director Hytner and London Musical Supervisor Caddick all testified that in their opinion Salonga, who has "created" and put a definitive stamp on the part of Kim will, for that reason and others, provide services in the Broadway opening that neither Wilson nor Desiderio can provide. However, the Arbitrator does not believe that the question of whether Wilson or Desiderio is capable professionally of being the originator in the Broadway production, has any bearing on the Producer's application to use Salonga under Rule 3(B)(2). That Rule defines unique services only in terms of services that cannot be performed by a member of Equity or a United States citizen or resident alien. Wilson and Desiderio fall into none of these categories. Furthermore there is nothing in the Statement of Understanding that changes the definition of uniqueness as it applies to Salonga. On the contrary, prior to entering into the Statement of Understanding the Producer was free under the Production Contract to pursue a claim that Salonga should be permitted to perform in the Broadway production pursuant to Rule 3(B)(2), and in the Statement of Understanding the Producer "reserved" that night.

The Arbitrator is persuaded then that despite the unprecedented and documented search for an actor to play the part of Kim in the Broadway production, there is no Equity member, United States citizen or resident alien who has, in addition to the vocal and physical capacity to perform the part, any significant professional experience on the musical stage, no less any experience in opening in a major Broadway production. On this point the search has produced only three Asian American actors who have the potential to perform the part of Kim: Meera Popkin, Kam Cheng and Melanie Tojio. Cheng and Tojio have no professional stage experience; Popkin has only appeared as an understudy in the national company of one musical play. Of course there have been, as Equity cites, many instances in which professional debuts have turned into Broadway triumphs. However, while any Broadway producer is free to cast a complete novice in a major part, the Arbitrator does not believe Rule 3(B)(2) can reasonably read as requiring a producer to do so. On this point, the Arbitrator understands a premise of Rule 3(B) (2) to be that the American acting profession is rich in professionally experienced talent suitable for most if not all theatrical roles. It must then be a rare instance in which there is not such experienced talent—but this is that rare case.

For the foregoing reasons the Arbitrator finds that Lea Salonga will provide unique service within the meaning of Rule 3 (B)(2) and therefore shall be permitted to play the part of Kim in the Producer's Broadway production of the musical play MISS SAIGON. This conclusion makes it unnecessary to address the Producer's application under Rule 3(B)(1).

---

### 2.2.2 Over Performances Abroad

. . . U.S. producers have been increasingly involved in producing theatrical and television motion pictures outside of the United States. This increase in foreign production has raised a number of questions regarding the geographical scope of the collective bargaining agreements between U.S. producers and the various guilds representing directors, actors and writers. [Excerpted from *Geographical Issues Raised by the DGA, WGA and SAG Agreements* by William F. Cole, UCLA Entertainment Law Symposium Syllabus (1987). Reprinted with author's permission.]

---

**Directors Guild of America Basic Agreement**

*Section 17-201 Geographical Application of this BA*

The provisions of this BA shall apply to work on motion pictures based in the United States and performed in the United States (including its territories and dependencies) and Canada; provided, however, that the provisions of this BA shall also apply to work performed by any Employee employed by the Employer in the United States, to direct, or to be a UPM or an Assistant Director or Technical Coordinator on a motion picture based outside the United States (including its territories and dependencies). If the Director is so employed in the United States, as defined, for photographing of principal photography on a motion picture produced by Employer, then a First Assistant Director shall also be sent. However, no such First Assistant Director need be sent to any foreign production where an applicable foreign labor restriction, quota, or law prohibits such an assignment or where such assignment would result in a loss of foreign production subsidy. The Employer shall give the Guild prompt written notice where a First Assistant Director cannot be taken due to any of the foregoing conditions.

Notwithstanding the foregoing if the Employee whose services are utilized is a permanent resident of the United States but is temporarily resident abroad and the negotiations are carried out in the United States by the Employee's attorney, agent or other representative (including the Guild) in the United States, such agreement for the services of the Employee shall be within the scope and coverage of this BA. The foregoing test of coverage shall be met as long as the representative, agent or attorney of the Director is in the United States when the agreement is negotiated even if it is negotiated by telephone with, or mailed or cabled to a representative of the Employer who is not within the United States during all or any part of said negotiation. Any Employee who is transported from the United States for purposes of employment outside the United States is also covered by this BA.

---

**Writers Guild of America Theatrical and Television Basic Agreement**

*Article 5: Geographical Application of this Basic Agreement*

Notwithstanding anything to the contrary contained herein, this Basic Agreement shall apply to writers only in the specific instances set forth below regardless of where the contract of employment or acquisition, as the case may be, is signed:

A. As to a writer or professional writer who lives in the United States, if a deal is made in the United States to employ such writer to render his services or if an acquisition deal is made in the United States with such professional writer, and if at the time such deal is made such writer or professional writer is present in the United States, regardless of where the services are rendered; provided further however that if such writer or professional writer is a permanent resident of the United States but is temporarily abroad, and if the deal is made by his/her agent, attorney or other representative (including the Guild acting on the writer's behalf) who is in the United States at the time the deal is made, such deal shall be within the scope and coverage of this paragraph A., even if such deal is made by such representative in communication by telephone, mail or cable with a representative of the Company, whether such representative of the Company is in the United States or abroad.

B. As to a writer or professional writer who lives in the United States and is transported abroad by Company, if a deal is made to such writer to render his/her services or if an acquisition deal is made with such professional writer while the writer or professional writer is abroad as a result of being so transported.

C. As to an employee whose writing services are required or requested by the Company to be performed and are performed in the United States under the supervision and direction of the Company.

D. "A writer or professional writer who lives in the United States," as such phrase is used in Paragraphs A. and B. above, does not include either of the following:

1. A person who lives outside the United States (other than for a temporary visit) even though he may at any given time be temporarily in the United States; or

2. A person who lives outside of the United States (other than for a temporary visit) whether or not he has retained his domicile in the United States.

E. A "deal is made" within the meaning of both Paragraphs A. and B. above when agreement is reached by the Company and the writer as to the money terms.

---

**In the Matter of the Arbitration between**
**Directors Guild of America, Inc. and Cannon Group, Inc.,**
**Relating to "America 3000"**
**Directors Guild of America – Producers Arbitration Tribunal**
**Case No. 2608 (1989)**

Sol Rosenthal, Arbitrator

. . . Cannon . . . is signatory to the DGA Basic Agreement of 1984 ("BA") . . . .

On or about September 14, 1984 Cannon and Write Ink, Direct Inc. ("WIDI") entered into an agreement in which Cannon promised to borrow and WIDI promised to lend David Engelbach's services to direct a theatrical motion picture entitled . . . "America 3000" (the "Picture").

Under the terms of the loanout agreement and the BA, David Engelbach directed the Picture. He was transported outside the United States on or about January 21, 1985, to begin preparation for the Picture. . . .

The . . . issue concerns the Company's failure to employ a First Assistant Director on the Picture. . . .

Cannon at no time notified the DGA that a First Assistant Director could not be taken to Israel due to any of the conditions referred to in Section 17-201, nor did the Company submit any evidence to that effect.

The Company argues that it reasonably believed that it was not required to transport a First Assistant Director from the United States when one was readily qualified and available to render services in Israel. However, the Company has not explained the basis of this belief. It seems clear that Cannon has violated the provisions of Section 17-201 by failing to employ a DGA First Assistant Director on the Picture.

The remaining question is what damages should be awarded for this failure to employ a First Assistant Director. . . .

. . . Cannon should be liable for the full amount which a First Assistant Director would have received in compensation and benefits had he or she been assigned to the Picture. This amount is $43,828.24. . . .

---

**In the Matter of the Arbitration Between**
**Directors Guild of America, Inc., and Twentieth Century-Fox Film Corp., Relating to "Bad Medicine"**
**Directors Guild of America – Producers Arbitration Tribunal**
**Case No. 01776 (1986)**

Hermione K. Brown, Arbitrator

This proceeding was brought by the Directors Guild of America, Inc. ("DGA") on behalf of Jeffrey Ganz and his loanout corporation (collectively "Ganz") against Twentieth Century-Fox Film Corporation ("Fox"). . . .

Ganz was engaged by Fox as co-producer on a feature motion picture entitled "Bad Medicine" to be filmed entirely in Spain. While in Spain, Ganz performed as director of some second unit photography. . . .

The undisputed fact is that Ganz was employed in the United States as a co-producer to work with the director, Harvey Miller. There was no written deal memo or other employment agreement for his services as second unit director. While in Spain during production of the picture, Ganz rendered services as second unit director for several days, the exact number of which is in dispute. In mid-March 1985, the unit production manager, Sam Manners, who supervised the production for Fox, reported to Steve Kravit, Fox's Senior Vice President, Business Affairs, that Ganz had directed a second unit for two days. Correspondence and telephone conversations occurred thereafter between Mr. Kravit and Ganz's business manager, Cathryn Jaymes, as a consequence of which, Fox agreed to and did pay Ganz $6,208.00. It was stipulated that no health and welfare or pension payments based thereon were made. There is a sharp dispute in the testimony with respect to whether Ganz was expected to render second unit directing services prior to his departure from the United States for the location in Spain, or whether, as Fox insists, it was only after he was in Spain that he volunteered to perform such services. Fox's position is that because the services were not negotiated for in the United States, they do not come within the jurisdiction of DGA under paragraph 17-201 of the BA quoted above, and because he volunteered his services, he was really not entitled to any compensation whatsoever. However, since second unit directing was within the budget, Fox was willing to pay the $6,208.00. Fox's further position is that Ganz worked at most two days in second unit directing, while Ganz stated that he rendered such services for five days.

While Ganz's testimony is not as specific as one would wish, he stated that on several occasions, at which executives of Fox, as well as the executive producers of the picture, were present, second unit directing was discussed with him, and in each instance it was assumed that he would be rendering such services. Mr. Kravit denies that there were any discussions between representatives of Fox and Ganz or his business manager on the subject, but Mr. Kravit was not present at all of the production meetings, and no other executives involved with the picture were called as witnesses. Moreover, although Mr. Kravit testified that Mr. Manners had stated at a pre-production meeting in Los Angeles that he could find a second unit director in London or Spain, there is no evidence that he ever attempted to do so.

In light of the foregoing, the arbitrator finds that DGA has established that Ganz was employed as a second unit director, at least inferentially, in the United States. Moreover, even if the subject of Ganz's rendition of services as second unit director first arose in March 1985 during the course of filming in Spain, the negotiations for his compensation at least were conducted by his business manager in the United States. This, again, would bring his employment within the scope of-paragraph 17-201.

Therefore, Ganz is entitled to compensation for five days work, plus three days preparation time, as provided in paragraph 4-102 of the BA, at the rate of $1,552.00 per day, or a total of $12,416.00. Since he has already been paid $6,208.00, he is entitled to receive an additional $6,208.00.

Since Ganz's services are subject to the BA, Fox is also obligated to pay employer contributions to the DGA Pension and Health and Welfare Plans equal to 12% of the total compensation specified above, or $1,489.92. . . .

---

**In the Matter of the Arbitration between**
**Directors Guild of America, Inc., and Warner Bros., Inc.,**
**Relating to "Club Paradise"**
**Directors Guild of America – Producers Arbitration Tribunal**
**Case No. 01882 (1986)**

Murray L. Schwartz, Sole Arbitrator

. . . The basic facts are undisputed. Warner employed DGA member Harold Ramis to direct, and Michael Shamberg to serve as executive producer of, the theatrical motion picture, "Club Paradise." Both Ramis and Shamberg were employed in the United States. Subsequent to their employment, Warner decided to film Club Paradise in Jamaica, with planning and preproduction work to be performed in England. Warner Ltd., which, like Warner, is a subsidiary of Warner Communications, Inc., was to be the producing company.

Warner Ltd. hired the crew, including Pat Clayton as First Assistant Director, in England. From February 25, 1985 to March 19, 1985, Clayton worked in England; from March 20 to 26 he worked in Jamaica; from March 27 to April 1 in England. The entire crew and all the equipment for their production proceeded to Jamaica where principal photography took place from April 2 to July 6. There were an additional four days of principal photography in the United States with a U.S. crew and U.S. First Assistant Director. Post-production work took place in the United States in mid-July. . . .

It is undisputed that British law made it impossible for Warner to employ a DGA represented First Assistant Director for the preproduction work in England. It is also undisputed that there was no such legal prohibition governing the photography done in Jamaica, and that no foreign subsidy would have been lost by Warner had it employed a DGA-represented First

Assistant Director in Jamaica. DGA therefore claims that Warner violated Paragraph 17-201 because it did not hire a DGA-represented First Assistant Director in Jamaica, but retained Clayton in that position. . . . In its October 7, 1985 Notice of Claim, DGA sought monetary damages, at the appropriate First Assistant Director scale, for 15 days preparation ($5,727), 10 weeks photography and production fee ($27,230), completion of assignment pay ($2,358), unworked holiday pay ($1,090), vacation pay ($1,310), and contributions to the Employer Pension, Health and Welfare Plans, Directors Guild-Producers Training Plan and DGA Contract Administration contributions and Employee Pension Plan Contributions ($5,460.75), together with fees and costs in this arbitration. Warner denies any liability.

I.

The substantive issue turns on the interpretation of Paragraph 17-201. DGA contends that, if the Director has been employed in the United States, a DGA-represented First Assistant Director must be sent whenever any phase of the production of a theatrical motion picture takes place in a foreign country in which there is no prohibition, such as a foreign labor law restriction, or loss of a foreign subsidy. Warner argues that its collective bargaining agreement with the British Association of Cinematograph and Television and allied Technicians (ACTT) constituted such a prohibition since that agreement required the continuation of Clayton in Jamaica in the First Assistant Director Position. Warner further argues that Paragraph 17-201 permits it not to send a DGA-represented First Assistant Director to a country where there are no restrictions when the production is based in a country which has such restrictions, at least where, as in the circumstances of the production of the film "Club Paradise," preproduction planning, selection of equipment and employment of crew for the principal photography takes place in that country.

A. Warner's first argument finds little support in the language of Paragraph 17-201 or the evidence in this record. At most, Warner was committed by its ACTT collective bargaining agreement to continue Clayton's employment in Jamaica. However, the exception in Paragraph 17-201 applies only where an "applicable foreign labor restriction, quota, or law prohibits such an assignment." It seems clear that voluntary collective bargaining agreements are not within the scope of "restrictions, quotas, or laws," words that imply governmental statutory or regulatory constraints, not voluntary contractual obligations. To interpret Paragraph 17-201 as Warner urges would mean that DGA has conceded that the requirements of its collective bargaining agreement are to be subordinate to those of any foreign labor organization with which a Basic Agreement signatory chose to negotiate. The language of Paragraph 17-201 does not support such an interpretation.

B. Warner's second argument raises a different issue of interpretation, whether Paragraph 17-201, which clearly excused Warner from employing a DGA-represented First Assistant Director in England, also excused Warner from employing a DGA-represented First Assistant Director in Jamaica. Essentially, Warner urges that if a foreign production is "based" in a country that has an applicable labor restriction, that restriction is applicable to any part of the production, even if it takes place in a country that does not have its own applicable labor restriction.[2] [Fn.2 DGA does not concede that the production of Club Paradise was based in Great Britain, pointing to the employment of Ramis and Shamberg in the United States, some prephotography preparation in the United States, all post-production in the United States, and financing and distribution of the film by Warner. From these incidents of production DGA argues that the motion picture production was based in the United States. The record, however, clearly supports the conclusion that Warner, Ltd., a British company, was the producer and that the principal aspects of the production – preproduction and principal photography – were performed outside the United States. Whatever else Club Paradise might have been, it was not a U.S.-based motion picture.] Specifically, Warner states that the purpose of the adoption of Paragraph 17-201 in 1968 was to assist U.S. Directors of foreign productions by assuring that DGA-represented First Assistant Directors would be employed on the production. To interpret Paragraph 17-201 so as to result in handicapping the Director, as by requiring the replacement of a First Assistant Director who had worked throughout the preproduction phase, would run counter to the purpose of Paragraph 17-201. In support of this interpretation, Warner relies upon the language of Paragraph 17-201, the negotiating history of the provision when it was adopted in the 1968 Basic Agreement, industry practice in its application, and the allegedly undesirable if not chaotic results a contrary interpretation would produce.

*Language of Paragraph 17-201*: Warner's interpretative position is that the phrase "foreign production" embodies the foreign labor law restriction, that is, Club Paradise was a foreign production as to which there was an applicable labor restriction; that restriction became an integral part of the production of Club Paradise and remained with it when the production moved to Jamaica. . . .

Assessment of this interpretative argument can best be made after Warner's other, supporting arguments are evaluated.

*Collective bargaining history*: The evidence as to collective bargaining history is scant. Paragraph 17-201 first appeared in the 1986 Basic Agreement with the Association of Motion Picture and Television Producers. . . .

[Because that history was inconclusive,] it is hazardous to place heavy reliance upon the bargaining history to illuminate Paragraph 17-201. . . .

*Industry practice*: Warner claims that its interpretation has been generally understood to be correct both by producers and by DGA. . . .

[But that] Industry practice is too uncertain a foundation for a firm conclusion about the interpretation of Paragraph 17-201.

*Hardship and impossibility*: Warner's most powerful argument has to do with the disruption caused by replacement of the (non-DGA) preproduction First Assistant Director by a different (DGA) First Assistant Director for principal photography. In support of its claim of serious disruption, Warner points to: the statement of Club Paradise's Director Ramis that, "[replacing] our English Assistant Director with an American Assistant Director would have been a severe handicap to the production when we moved to Jamaica for principal photography"; the relation to the Director and unique role of the First Assistant Director; the impossibility in at least some circumstances of "replacing" the First Assistant Director; and the disruption and cost of bringing in a new First Assistant Director, who has had no previous contact with planning, site selection, equipment, crew or presumably any other phase of preproduction.

There is much force in these arguments. There is no reason not to accept Ramis' statement that the production would have been handicapped had Clayton been replaced for principal photography in Jamaica; certainly there would have been additional costs of time and money. So too, the Basic Agreement does treat the Director-First Assistant Director relationship specially, *see* Paragraph 7-204 (right of Director to select and replace First Assistant Director), and the Job description of the First Assistant Director is clearly spelled out in the Basic Agreement, *see* Paragraphs 1-303, 13-208. Further, there may well be circumstances in which the labor organization in the country with the labor restriction requires, under its collective bargaining agreement with the producer, employment of the designated member of that organization through the preproduction and production process, making replacement a breach of that agreement. It is highly likely that in general replacement will introduce inefficiency at the minimum.

Warner asserts that a decision for DGA in this case would mean that "a picture [can] be prepared in Great Britain only if all the principal photography were to take place in Great Britain . . . ." and "the ability of a signatory company to base a production in a foreign country (such as England) and to shoot any of the principal photography for that production in most other countries in the world . . . would be greatly restricted." Whether these far-reaching consequences will follow from an interpretation of the Basic Agreement that the signatory company must replace the foreign First Assistant Director or add a DGA-represented one for work performed in countries with no labor restrictions is, to say the least, speculative. That uneconomic consequences for the producer are likely to follow in most cases is less debatable, although, as shown by the four days of principal photography shot in the United States on Club Paradise, even this result will not always follow.

These consequences are, however, not uncommon for companies whose operations are conducted across national boundaries; they often represent the "costs of doing business" in a multinational way. With respect to the disadvantage to the Director occasioned by the replacement of the preproduction First Assistant Director, it is unnecessary to point out that Directors and First Assistant Directors are both represented by DGA, which presumably takes account of conflicts between the two groups in negotiating and enforcing the collective bargaining agreement.

Thus, Warner's most effective argument in support of its interpretation of Paragraph 17201 is that of the likely disruption resulting from DGA's view of that Paragraph. Nevertheless, despite the force of this argument, the language of Paragraph 17-201 and its context do not permit the interpretation Warner seeks.

In the filming of Club Paradise, there were three possible sources of labor law, the United States, England and Jamaica. None prohibited Warner's employment of a DGA-represented First Assistant Director in Jamaica. All that was prohibited was the employment of a DGA represented First Assistant Director in England. To read Paragraph 17-201 as Warner proposes would accord to English law (the "applicable" foreign labor restriction) an unwarranted and unintended extra-territorial effect.

. . . English labor law does not apply to restrict the employment of a DGA-represented First Assistant Director in Jamaica. Accordingly, the "applicable foreign restriction" of Paragraph 17-201 did not apply to the principal photography in Jamaica. Paragraph 17-201 thus required Warner to send a DGA-represented First Assistant Director to Jamaica during the filming of the principal photography of Club Paradise.

II.

The issue of damages remains. . . .

Warner has strongly urged that it was bound by its agreement with the British labor organization ACTT to continue Clayton as First Assistant Director in Jamaica. The conclusion of this Opinion is that Warner was obligated to employ a DGA-represented First Assistant Director in Jamaica. Whether DGA's suggestion that the agreement with ACTT would not have prevented Warner from employing the British First Assistant Director in Jamaica "in addition to" the employment of a DGA-represented First Assistant Director, is feasible or desirable, it is clear that Warner had two independent obligations – one under its ACTT agreement and the other under the 1984 DGA Basic Agreement. Thus, there is no basis to conclude that full satisfaction of one obligation should also satisfy the other. Warner is not entitled to deduct from the award to DGA that which it paid Clayton under its agreement with him and ACTT. Accordingly, DGA is entitled to recover the full amount set forth in its Notice of Claim. . . .

---

**In the Matter of the Arbitration between**
**Writers Guild of America, West, Inc. and Warner Bros. Inc.**
**Relating to "The Witches"**
**Writers Guild of American, West, Inc. – Producers Arbitration Tribunal**
**Case No. 89-CR-29 (1989)**

Sol Rosenthal, Arbirator

. . . This case involves a credit dispute as to whether Company may use as the top line of a one-sheet for the advertising campaign for the theatrical motion picture "The Witches" ("the Picture") the following wording: "FROM THE IMAGINATION OF JIM HENSON AND DIRECTOR NICHOLAS ROEG."

The facts, which are undisputed, may be summarized as follows: Warner is signatory to the 1988 WGA Theatrical and Television Basic Agreement ("MBA"). During the term of the MBA, Warner, through its subsidiary Lorimar Film Entertainment, produced the Picture. It was stipulated by the parties that Warner stands in the shoes of the employer of the writer, Allan Scott. In September 1988, the writing credit on the Picture became final. The writing credit was determined to be: Screenplay by Allan Scott Based on the book by Roald Dahl.

On or about September 29, 1989, Warner sent, and the WGA received, a copy of a one-sheet to be used in the advertising campaign for the Picture with the top line reading "FROM THE IMAGINATION OF JIM HENSON AND DIRECTOR NICHOLAS ROEG." The WGA immediately notified Warner that the advertisement in question was disapproved and not in compliance with the MBA.

The Guild contends that the top line of the proposed one-sheet, by omitting the name of the credited screenwriter, denigrates the writer credit, causes confusion as to the identity of the screenwriter, and is misleading. . . .

There is a threshold question about the jurisdiction of the WGA in this matter. The Company contends that the WGA has no jurisdiction over credit matters or otherwise, since the screenwriter, Allan Scott, resides in England and most of the work which he did on the Picture was done in England. Thus, under Article 5 of the MBA, the MBA would not apply and the WGA would have no jurisdiction over the credits. However, the Guild emphasizes that the Writer's Agreement provided as follows: "This agreement is subject to all of the terms and provisions of the Writers Guild of America 1985 Theatrical and Television Basic Agreement . . ."

It further provided that the "provisions of the MBA shall govern the determination of credit to be accorded to Writer for the work and all material written hereunder." It should also be noted that the writing credits were submitted by Warner to the WGA for determination and the advertisements were submitted by Warner to the WGA for approval. Company nevertheless contends that the provisions of the Writer's Agreement could not bring that agreement within the jurisdiction of the WGA and that the Company's submission of credits and advertisements to the WGA was done in accordance with Warner's past practice even on films where there was no WGA jurisdiction, but did not confer jurisdiction. on the Guild. Warner further argues that even if the MBA was incorporated by reference in the Writer's Agreement, then the geographical limitations of Article 5 of the MBA were also incorporated and those geographical limitations would mean that the Writer's Agreement was not covered by the MBA.

Article 9 of the MBA provides in relevant part as follows:

> "The terms of this Basic Agreement are minimum terms; nothing herein contained shall prevent any writer from negotiating and contracting with any Company for better terms for the benefit of such writer than are here

provided, excepting only credits for screen authorship, which may be given only pursuant to the terms and in the manner prescribed in Article 8."

I agree with the position of the WGA with respect to the jurisdictional issue. The Company and the writer have incorporated by reference in the Writer's Agreement all the terms of the MBA. They have the right to do this under Article 9 of the MBA which allows the writer to negotiate and contract with a company for better terms for the benefit of the writer than are provided in the MBA. By incorporating all the terms and provisions of the MBA, the parties incorporated all the provisions regarding credit and credit enforcement. Further, the Writer's Agreement specifically incorporated provisions regarding determination of writing credits pursuant to the MBA. Warner argues that even though the parties may have incorporated all the provisions of the MBA, they also incorporated the provisions of Article 5 limiting geographical application, and thus this agreement would be taken out of the MBA, since the writer resided and worked in England. I do not believe this argument has merit. If Warner's position were upheld, this would clearly undermine the intent of the parties in incorporating the credit provisions of the MBA. In short, the MBA applies, and the WGA has jurisdiction.

I now turn to a consideration of the merits of the one-sheet advertisement in question, specifically the top line reading "FROM THE IMAGINATION OF JIM HENSON AND DIRECTOR NICHOLAS ROEG." . . .

. . . [T]he advertisement in question is permissible under the MBA.

---

**In the Matter of the Arbitration between**
**Directors Guild of America, Inc. and Columbia Pictures Industries, Inc.,**
**Relating to "Deceptions"**
**Case No. 01799 (1986)**

Joseph F. Gentile, Arbitrator

*Statement of the Matter*

On June 17, 1985, the DIRECTORS GUILD OF AMERICA, INC. ("DGA" or "Guild) filed a "Notice of Claim and Arbitration Claim" . . . with COLUMBIA PICTURES INDUSTRIES ("Columbia"). . . . In the Claim, the Guild . . . made certain claims on behalf of Robert Chenault ("RC"), who had been employed as the Director on the motion picture DECEPTIONS through RC's loanout company, Hightide, Inc.

Though the evidence record was somewhat confusing, the best reconstruction of the relationship between Columbia and the producer of DECEPTIONS, Colgems, Ltd., was that Colgems, Ltd., was producing DECEPTIONS pursuant to a financing, production and distribution agreement with Columbia. In any event, the Parties stipulated at the hearing that if the Arbitrator found the employment of RC fell within the geographical scope of the BA pursuant to Section 17-201, Columbia would be responsible under the BA for certain contractual obligations if so determined by the Arbitrator.

. . . In this response, Columbia, took the position . . . that RC was employed outside the geographical jurisdiction of the BA; thus, the BA's terms and conditions were neither applicable nor relevant. . . .

The issue . . . was . . . whether the employment of RC as the Director of the television motion picture DECEPTIONS was covered by the BA or whether this employment was outside the geographical scope of the BA. . . .

*Factual and Procedural Summary*

The essential factual context for this Claim was not in sharp dispute, but there were disagreements as to the content, tone and "understandings" of various conversations between the percipient witnesses. The real disagreement, however, rested on the interpretation and application of the BA and, more particularly, Section 17-201, as it related to the factual situation.

Colgems, Ltd. was producing DECEPTIONS for Columbia in Great Britain. The Director was Mel Shavelson ("MS"), who had been employed by Columbia and loaned to Colgems, Ltd. MS was terminated in or around February, 1985.

MS was replaced by the Director of Photography and this replacement created a problem with the DGA pursuant to Section 7-1401 of the BA; thus, to resolve this matter, another person to fill the Director's position was needed immediately.

RC was working in London as a Producer on the post-production of another Columbia motion picture, JENNY'S WAR. RC was employed by Columbia Pictures Television and transported to London for this work.

It was during this time frame that RC was contacted by the Producer of DECEPTIONS and a discussion followed as to the idea of RC directing DECEPTIONS.

Following the above contact, a number of telephone conversations took place between various persons directly and indirectly involved with the production of DECEPTIONS. These conversations involved persons from the Guild, Colgems, Ltd., Columbia, RC and RC's agent.

As already noted, the content and tone of certain of these conversations were in dispute; there was certainly a disagreement as to whether an "agreement" or "understanding" was ultimately reached as to the employment terms attendant to RC's directorial responsibilities and, if there was an "agreement" or "understanding" as to the terms of employment, the scope of any "agreement" or "understanding" vis-a-vis the BA was in dispute.

From the above conversations and the surrounding circumstances, certain conclusions were drawn with respect to the "intent" and perceptions of those involved as to the terms of RC's deal to direct DECEPTIONS:

1) the exigency created by the absence of a Director for DECEPTIONS caused all concerned to move quickly without the benefit of a memoralized deal;

2) RC did indeed direct DECEPTIONS for Colgems, Ltd. pursuant to an apparent "oral deal";

3) RC desired to have no problems with the DGA concerning his employment as the Director on DECEPTIONS and RC further perceived, and honestly so, that this employment would be covered by the BA as to those matters which appeared in the Claim;

4) Columbia did not desire to have any more problems with the DGA over the production of DECEPTIONS; thus, it was the desire and expressed "intent" of Columbia that such problems would be avoided if all negotiations as to RC's deal to direct DECEPTIONS would take place in England; and

5) Columbia, on behalf of Colgems, Ltd., filed a "deal memorandum" with the Guild to cover RC's employment in the United States in connection with the principal photography shot on April 1 and April 2, 1985, in the United States regarding DECEPTIONS.

As to the first two conclusions, the evidence record was clear and without contradiction in its support. The evidence record was in conflict on three pivotal matters: (1) the physical location of the "actual" negotiations which culminated in the employment of RC as the Director of DECEPTIONS (England or the United States); (2) the persons involved in the "negotiations" of RC's initial "oral deal" to direct DECEPTIONS and (3) the specific terms of the "oral deal," particularly, whether there was a firm and enforceable commitment that RC would be covered by the BA on such subjects as those presented in the Claim.

The Guild argued that the negotiations effectively took place in the United States, and, more specifically, in Los Angeles, California, and that one of the terms of the "agreement" or "understanding" which brought about RC's employment as the Director of DECEPTIONS was that RC would be covered by the BA.

Columbia contended the reverse, namely, that the "actual" negotiations to employ RC on DECEPTIONS took place in England between RC and Colgems, Ltd., and that there was neither an "agreement" nor "understanding" to bring RC's employment within the ambit of the BA. On the contrary, Columbia argued, the "intent" was not to have RC's employment covered by the BA. . . .

*Discussion*

A reasonable reading of Section 17-201 clearly demonstrates that the Parties to the BA carefully considered the geographical scope of the Agreement and its applicability to motion pictures produced outside of the United States by signatory Employers.

The "proviso" to the general, geographical statement extends the BA's coverage to work outside the United States; however, . . . this extension is conditioned on the presence of three keys. These must be viewed in the context of the facts and circumstances established and proven in this case.

DECEPTIONS was based "outside the United States." RC was employed by Colgems, Ltd. "to direct" DECEPTIONS. However, RC was not "employed by the Employer in the United States." Thus, the Arbitrator must look to the next contractual guideline, the "notwithstanding clause. "

The "notwithstanding clause" provides a "two pronged" test to determine whether the initial oral deal worked out for RC's employment as the Director of DECEPTIONS will be within the scope and coverage of the BA. If both elements of the test are established, the "notwithstanding clause" mandates ("shall") coverage. In meeting the test, the Parties further provided insight into what it takes to "meet" the test.

The two prongs of the test which must be met are as follows:

1) "if the Employee whose services are utilized is a permanent resident of the United States but is temporarily resident abroad

*AND*

2) "the negotiations are carried out in the United States by the Employee's attorney, agent or other representative (including the Guild) in the United States. . ."

With respect to RC, the first element of the test was established. As to the second element, there was a disagreement. The Guild argued that the negotiations for RC's services on DECEPTIONS were conducted in the United States and Columbia contended that they were not.

Though certain conversations regarding RC.'s employment did take place in the United States, this evidence record indicated that the arrangements for RC's employment and the successful completion of negotiations for his services on DECEPTIONS did take place in England. Though there may now exist a disagreement as to the "terms" of the deal which was cut between Colgems, Ltd. and RC, the evidence record strongly supported the conclusion that negotiations took place in England, any arguments to the contrary notwithstanding.

Therefore, the second prong of the two pronged coverage test was not met in RC's case.

The "notwithstanding clause" provides, however, another element in that portion of the clause which addresses and describes how the "test of coverage shall be met." That element is this: "Any Employee who is transported from the United States for purposes of employment outside the United States is also covered by this BA."

The evidence record established that RC was employed by Columbia in the United States to perform work outside the United States and that RC was transported from the United States for the purpose of working on a production in England; that production was JENNY'S WAR.

The Guild argued that the above provision should be controlling in RC's situation even though such transportation was for another television motion picture production; Columbia disagreed. The basis for Columbia's disagreement was the failure of RC to meet the "Employee" definition. RC was employed by Columbia as a Producer; thus, Columbia argued that RC did not fall within the BA's definitions of employees recognized as covered by the BA and as found in Section 1-300.

Having considered this evidence record, the Arbitrator would agree with Columbia that RC's employment as a Producer to work on JENNY'S WAR in England did not allow a contractual "bootstrap" which would place RC's current work as a Director on DECEPTIONS within the scope of the just quoted language from the "notwithstanding clause" of Section 17-201.

The next aspect of this case which must be addressed is whether the initial "oral deal" which resulted in RC's employment as the Director on DECEPTIONS provided for the coverage of the BA and, if it did, is such a commitment enforceable in the instant forum.

The plague or affliction of an "oral deal" is the absence of express, written language to reflect the mutual "understandings" and "terms" of an agreement of employment. Each side draws from the oral discussions a set of perceptions, perspectives, explanations, expectations and "intent" of what was discussed. Each side may honestly hold to these as being the "essence" or "thrust" of a deal. The calamity of such situations is when, as in the instant situation, the principal parties acknowledge that a subject was discussed only to find disagreement and an apparent no meeting of the minds.

Reasonable persons will disagree as to whether this evidence record demonstrates an enforceable oral "understanding" to have RC's employment as the Director of DECEPTIONS covered by the BA; however, this Arbitrator can not find in this evidence record a mutually agreed to "understanding" to provide coverage under the BA.

Absent such a finding, the next aspect, namely the enforceabiliy of such an "understanding" in this forum is moot.

The last major concern which must be addressed is the subsequent involvement of RC as the Director of DECEPTIONS in connection with the principal photography shot on April 1 and April 2, 1985. A "deal memorandum" was prepared with respect to this work.

The question which must be asked is whether this "deal memorandum" and the work it covered change the above conclusions as to RC's coverage under the BA for his work in England. Having already concluded that DECEPTIONS was based outside the United States and that RC was employed outside the United States, the Arbitrator would agree with Columbia that these few days of work in the United States at the end of principal photography should not act to apply the BA retroactively. The Arbitrator would find this "new employment" as there was no indication in this evidence record that RC's initial "oral deal" even contemplated this short addendum to the production of DECEPTIONS within the United States.

*Award*

Based on the evidence record, it is the AWARD of this Arbitrator that: The employment of RC as the Director of the television motion picture DECEPTIONS was outside the geographical scope of the BA and thus not covered by the BA.

---

**In the Matter of Arbitration Between Writers Guild of America West, Inc., and Universal City Studios, Inc. Relating to "Kentucky Derby" Case No. 87-CO-264 (1988)**

Robert D. Steinberg, Arbitrator

*Issue*

The parties are in agreement that the fundamental issue pertains to the applicability of the 1981 and 1985 Theatrical and Television Basic Agreements (hereinafter, MBA) and the issue is framed accordingly:

Did the writing services performed herein by Elliott Baker fall within the geographical jurisdiction of the MBA as set forth by Article 5 such that pension and health fund contributions are due and payable on his behalf in accordance with Article 17?

*Award*

After complete review of the evidence record and the well-stated argument of counsel, upon due deliberation and for the reasons set forth hereinafter, the duly selected neutral arbitrator hereby renders the following award:

The writing services performed by Elliott Baker did *not* fall within the jurisdiction of the MBA as set forth by Article 5. . . .

*Background*

Virtually all of the essential facts are stipulated to or are not in dispute. Elliott Baker (Baker) is a professional writer within the meaning of the MBA and in December 1984 he entered into a writing contact (through his loan-out company) with Universal whereby he was to prepare a "bible" and two two-hour teleplays for the sum of $225,000. He fulfilled his contractual obligation by writing a bible and teleplay for the four-hour miniseries "Kentucky Derby" which was produced by Universal for the ABC Network.

Baker's services on the project were rendered between mid-December 1984 and mid-June 1985. During this period he was in the United States, according to his estimate, for a total of 30 days. While Baker was and is a United States citizen, he was a resident of Great Britain from March 1982 through November 1985 and he neither lived nor maintained a residence in the United States during that period of time. His driver's license was issued in Great Britain in 1976.

Universal is a signatory to the MBA and the pension and health fund provisions of the MBA were incorporated by reference into Baker's writing agreement. Universal made several pension and health payments to the funds administered by the Guild on Baker's behalf and Baker was otherwise fully remunerated. Universal failed to make the balance of pension and health fund payments when ABC refused to reimburse it for such contributions and it thereafter claimed a credit for the contributions it had previously paid. When Baker received his year-end fund statement for 1986 he learned of the non-payment, as it were, and the issue became joined.

*Summary of Party Positions*

*Guild*

Baker spent 75 days on the "Kentucky Derby" project, 30 days (or 40%) were spent performing writing services in the United States. "Writing services" encompasses more than putting the written word on paper. It encompasses necessary research and story conferences to analyze dialogue, discuss characters, and perform revisions. At all times he performed in the United States it was at the request and under the direction of Universal. All the necessary elements as set forth in MBA Article [5.C] were met to bring the specific contract for writing services under the geographical jurisdiction of the MBA.

The relevant portions of Article 5 have remained virtually unchanged since 1963 when there were separate film and television agreements. While language has been consolidated, while incidental language has been added and/or modified and while the Guild has not been successful in achieving MBA coverage for all writers irrespective of where a contract was executed or where services were to be performed, the applicable Article [5.C] language has remained in effect and continues to apply to nonresident writers performing writing services in the United States under the authority and control of a signatory producer.

Universal understood the MBA to apply to its contract with Baker. There were seven references to the MBA in that contract, including the preeminence of more advantageous MBA terms, and it specifically dovetailed pension and health contributions as per the MBA. Universal proceeded to make such payments in the understanding that the MBA applied. Universal has failed to evidence a contrary intent. Reference to England in the unexecuted writers agreement was Respondent's unilateral assertion and the reason why Baker did not pay California tax on his "Kentucky Derby" income is that he was not residing in California. . . .

*Universal*

The arbitrator would enjoy jurisdiction only if the MBA applies and the MBA could only apply if the conditions of Article 5 pertain to the dispute. Since Baker did not live in the United States at the time he performed writing services for "Kentucky Derby, neither Article [5.A] or [5.B], as interpreted by [5.D], applies. Article [5.C] should not be interpreted to mean that Baker's services are covered by the MBA. This would be contrary to the historic intent of the parties and the intent of Baker and Universal as expressed in their writer's contract.

It was unnecessary for Baker to perform his writing services in the United States and it was the expressed intent of his agent and Universal that his writing would be performed in Great Britain. When California income tax was withheld, Baker objected. None of the facts indicate a contrary intent.

The essence of Baker's writing services were performed in Great Britain. He only revised his bible and made some pencil changes in his teleplay during business in the United States. He was present in the United States for only 29 days within the six month period he worked on this project, and most of this time was for meetings. This United States presence was not sufficient to make him a "writer who lives in the United States" under Article [5.D]. The fact that Universal paid for his travel is neither probative of his being a resident or that he was writing under the direction and control of Universal. Article [5.C] language is suggestive that a master-servant relationship exists and that was not the case with "Kentucky Derby.

Article [5.D.1] suggests that temporary presence in the United States does not satisfy the MBA's residency requirements. For consistency, partial work on a bible or teleplay in the United States should not satisfy the requirements of Article [5.C] If partial performance was intended to give the Guild jurisdiction under the MBA, the parties could have clearly stated that intent. They properly did not. The Union's proposals over the years to broaden the scope of MBA jurisdiction, wherein it would cover nonresident writers, were rejected. In the only other arbitration of Article [5.C], Arbitrator Maxwell in the *First Asian Films* grievance, held six days work in the United States by a Tokyo resident writer was insufficient.

The MBA contemplates that for Article [5.C] to apply all writing services must be performed in the United States and under the supervision and direction of an employer. Brief visits for story meetings and research is insufficient. Bargaining unit status is not a percentage affair: "You're either in or you're out."

*Analysis*

Both parties would agree that the MBA cannot be partially applicable, covering whatever portion of writing services were actually performed in the United States. The MBA either applies or it does not apply to all of the writing services performed. Because Grievant was living in Great Britain and was a nonresident at the time he contracted with and performed relevant writing services for Universal, the MBA, and its health and pension provisions, would apply only if Article [5.C] can be interpreted in favor of the Guild. That provision requires two conditions be met: (1) That writing services are "required or requested by the company" to be performed in the United States. (2) that writing services are performed in the United States under the supervision and direction of the Company.

Whatever work Baker performed in the United States on the "Kentucky Derby" project was performed at the request or requirement of Universal. Producer's agents wanted him or required him to conduct research, attend meetings and revise the bible in conjunction with his meetings with the producer in Los Angeles. Universal paid for Baker's travel expenses while he was in the United States. This was necessary work and all that Universal contested was whether a majority of that work could be considered "writing services." That term, as well as "under the supervision and direction," are both in dispute and need to be defined before determining how much, if less than all, writing services need to performed in the United States by a nonresident writer so as to make the MBA applicable.

In the most narrow sense, writing services could be limited to the written literary product, either an original or final draft thereof. It would disallow all preparatory work and intermediate drafting. Such an interpretation is overly restrictive. In the least, all elements for which a professional writer would be compensated under the MBA should be considered as writing services under that Agreement. While pre-writing research may not be sufficient on its own to constitute writer services, where that is a contemporaneous part of the literary contribution, adding to the legitimacy of the final script, it is difficult to ignore.

Meetings and discussions with producers when character ideas and the script outline is discussed and approved, and where revisions are made, would appear to be writing services. Where merely two meetings are held to discuss a story, a writer would . . . be entitled to minimum compensation for a story. The more intensive the meetings or discussions, resulting in written notations and script reviews, the more the meetings become an essential aspect of the "pen to paper" exercise. The extensive rewriting of the bible that Baker engaged in while in Los Angeles, resulting in a revision to two thirds of the product, must be considered to constitute writing services.

That Baker's writing services were performed "under the supervision and direction" of Universal would also have to be found in favor of the Guild. Absent contractual definition, one turns to ordinary meaning of language. Webster's defines "direction" as containing the elements of guidance and management, the establishment of mood, tempo or intensity and setting a course of conduct or action. When joined with "supervision," the expressions include authoritative instructions or inspection. It means one body overseeing and controlling the scope and nature of a product as a producer would essentially guide and ultimately control the content and direction of a literary effort.

Contrary to the position of Universal, it would be irrelevant if the substance of Baker's writing was performed outside the *immediate* supervision of the producer's agents. The parties' loan-out contract recognizes the ultimate direction and control of Universal as *respondeat superior*. The writer and producer engaged in literary discussions from before the bible's first draft until the revision of the teleplay. Such meetings led to the initial approach and to significant revisions of the literary material. Universal gave meaningful direction and was in ultimate control. That is sufficient to satisfy Article [5.C] of the MBA and Article 5 would apply if it were determined that Baker's writing services were sufficiently performed in the United States.

Absent a clear and unambiguous expression in Baker's writing contract with Universal that the MBA was applicable in all instances, and there is no claim to that effect, the MBA's applicability is limited by its expression of geographical scope. While Baker, through his agent, and Universal intended various MBA provisions to apply, such as pension and health fund contributions and the applicability of minimum terms, incorporating these provisions by reference in the writer agreement, that agreement is silent on the applicability of the MBA's enforcement provisions.

It cannot be inferred that the parties intended the MBA to apply in all cases. While the parties could have stated that writing services would be considered as being performed in the United States for the applicability of jurisdiction, the draft contract evidences what may be considered a contrary intent by the reference to "Services Being Rendered in England." While this phrase was inserted perhaps for no reason other than saving Baker income taxes, as testified to by Universal's then agent, it was there at the request of Baker's attorney.

This is virtually a case of first impression, and there are little or no external factors to assist in interpreting Article [5.C]. While Arbitrator Maxwell referenced Article [5.C] in his *First Asian Films* award, that case also involved the interpretation of Article [5.A] and [5.B] and most of the discussion was directed at those sections. That case could not be of guidance as it appears the foreign writer therein spent only six days in the United States within a literary effort that encompassed four months.

Bargaining history also fails to explain what the parties meant by "writing services . . . performed in the United States. . . ." While the Guild has failed in its efforts to have the MBA apply to nonresident writers as well as resident writers, [5.C] has been in effect in some fashion since 1963. While it obviously cannot be interpreted to apply to nonresident writers performing writing services outside the United States and should not be interpreted to apply to de minimis writing services performed in the United States by nonresident writers, it does not mean, as argued by Universal, that Article [5.C] can apply only where all writing services are performed in the United States (under the supervision and direction of an employer). While the parties to the MBA could arguably have stated that partial performance would satisfy the jurisdictional requirements of the MBA, they perhaps more assuredly would have stated that all writing services had to be performed in the United States if that were their intent. By their silence in this area, the parties must have intended that the rule of reason apply.

Neither minimum performance nor complete performance should be inferred as both extremes could easily frustrate one party's benefit of the bargain. It would be just as innane and illogical to find a nonresident writer who spent 114 out of 120 writing days in the United States not protected by the MBA as it would be to apply the jurisdiction of the MBA to a nonresident writer spending only 6 of 120 working days in the United States.

A rational approach, doing justice to the parties' intent of covering United States resident writers and United States writing, is to apply a doctrine of substantial performance so that if Baker's writing services for "Kentucky Derby" were substantially performed in the United States the MBA should apply. If the major portion of writing services, measured by both time and intensity, were performed outside of the United States, then it should not be concluded that they fall within the jurisdictional scope of the MBA. The substance of Baker's writing services for "Kentucky Derby" was performed abroad.

By measuring time spent alone, Baker spent no more than 30 days of 75 days he was working on the project in the United States. The quality of that time was diminished by the fact that about half his time was spent in research and in meetings which resulted only in the making of "pencil changes" to the teleplay. Only the two weeks where Baker and the producers met in Los Angeles in the mornings and where Baker rewrote his bible in the afternoons can be considered intensive, quality writing time.

In contrast, while in Great Britain, Baker spent part of his time between December 14, 1984 and January 20, 1985 writing the bible for "Kentucky Derby," while also spending time completing his "Lace" project for ABC. After the bible was revised in Los Angeles he testified he spent 3 1/2 intensive weeks in writing the first draft of the four-hour teleplay. After visiting Churchill Downs and meeting with the producers in New York City, he spent another two weeks in Great Britain writing "night and day" completing his final draft. This totals about 7 1/2 - 8 weeks of intensive writing. If just time alone were considered, the writing time favored Great Britain by a 60/40 ratio, but in intensive, creative writing time, it favored Great Britain by at least three to one.

It was the Guild's burden to prove that Baker's writing services were substantially performed in the United States so that the MBA would apply. To the contrary, it appears that a substantial majority of his writing time and effort occurred in Great Britain and since Baker was a nonresident writer living in England the MBA does not apply. . . . Accordingly, the grievance for the claim herein must be denied.

---

**Screen Actors Guild Theatrical Motion Pictures and Television Basic Contract**

*Paragraph 1.B. Scope of Agreement*

(1) When Producer has its base of production in the United States or any commonwealth, territory or possession of the United States, the Basic Contract shall apply . . . .

(2) When Producer has its base of production as provided in (1) above and goes on location in Canada, the Basic Contract . . . shall apply to all performers hired by Producer at such location.

(3) When Producer employs a performer in the United States and transports him anywhere outside the United States for a motion picture, the terms of the Basic Agreement shall apply. If a performer whose services are utilized is a permanent resident of the United States but is temporarily resident abroad and the negotiations are carried out in the United States by the performer's attorney, agent or other representative (including the Union) in the United States, such agreement for the services of the performer shall be within the scope and coverage of this Agrement. The foregoing test of coverage shall be met as long as the representative, agent or

attorney of the performer is in the United States when the agreement is negotiated even if it is negotiated by telephone with or mailed or cabled to a representative of the Producer who is not within the United States during all or any part of said negotiation.

---

**American Federation of Musicians**
**Basic Theatrical Picture [and Television Film] Agreement[s]**

*Article 1: Scope of Agreement*

This Agreement shall be applicable to [musicians] . . . employed by the Producer in the State of California or elsewhere in the United States and Canada and whose services are rendered in connection with the production of theatrical motion pictures [and television motion pictures] . . . .

*Article 3: Scoring in the United States and Canada*

All theatrical motion pictures [and television motion pictures] produced by the Producer in the United States or Canada, if scored, shall be scored in the United States or Canada.

---

**Potential Union Discipline Against Union Members Who Agree to Work on Foreign Projects for Non-Union Signatory Companies or for Signator Companies which are Treating the Employment as Non-Covered Work**

Excerpted from
***Geographical Issues Raised by the DGA, WGA and SAG Agreements***
**by William L. Cole**
UCLA Entertainment Law Symposium Syllabus (1987)
Reprinted with the author's permission.

The foregoing . . . focuses upon the obligations of producers which are signatories to the DGA, WGA and SAG Basic Agreements. Naturally, when a non-signatory company is involved, none of these Guilds can maintain a contractual action against the company in order to preclude it from employing Guild members under terms and conditions different from those set forth in the collective bargaining agreements. The primary vehicle which the Guilds use to prevent non-signatory producers from taking advantage of this fact is the threat of union discipline against members who work for non-signatory companies. . . .

Each of the Guilds maintains a work rule requiring that *members* of the union refrain from working for non-signatory companies under certain conditions and prohibiting members from working for signatory companies under terms and conditions less favorable than those contained in the applicable Guild agreement. Thus, for example, Article IX Section B.5 of the Constitution and By-laws of the Directors Guild of America, Inc., provides:

> "No Guild member shall accept employment from an employer who is not a signatory to a Basic Agreement or a substitute agreement with the Guild."

While this prohibition is broadly stated and would appear to prohibit members of the DGA from working for *any* non-signatory company, regardless of where the production is to take place, it has not been enforced in that manner. Rather, in at least one DGA disciplinary proceeding of which the author is aware, the Guild took the position that it applies its work rule in a manner which is consistent with the geographical scope clause of the Basic Agreement. Thus, the rule is interpreted such that it would not prohibit a member of the Guild from working for a non-signatory company (or, presumably, for a signatory company on a foreign production based outside the United States) if the employment would otherwise fall outside of the geographical scope clause of the Basic Agreement.

Since reported decisions of disciplinary proceedings are not readily available, we cannot be certain of the enforcement positions taking by the Screen Actors Guild and the Writers Guild under their work rules. However, based upon the fact that American actors often work[ed] on a non-union basis for foreign companies on foreign films [before May 2002] without any apparent adverse action by SAG, it would appear that at least [before May 2002] that union [took] a similar position to that of the DGA. [SAG, however changed its position as of May 2002, as the following item indicates.]

Before leaving the area of union discipline, it should also be pointed out that such discipline may be imposed only on *members* of the union. Under the National Labor Relations Act, employees have the right to refuse to become formal members of a labor organization and can, instead, choose to be "financial core" members. A financial core member pays the same initiation fees and dues as a union member but is not subject to the union's internal rules. [*Pattern Makers' League v. NLRB*, 473 U.S. 95 (1985)] Unions are prohibited by the National Labor Relations Act from attempted to prohibit employers from employing such financial core members as long as they continue to tender their dues.

---

**Screen Actors Guild Constitution and By-Laws**

*Rules and Regulations: Rule 1*

No member shall work as a performer or make an agreement to work as a performer for any producer who has not executed a basic minimum agreement with the Guild which is in full force and effect.

*From the Screen Actors Guild website (http://www.sag.org/rule_one/)*

Rule One is one of the founding principles and strengths of our union: we stand together as actors and do not work without a Guild contract.

Up until now, Rule One has been enforced on productions shot in the United States.

SAG is expanding its protections globally, as the DGA and WGA have done, in order to better serve the needs of members in this rapidly changing, global entertainment economy.

To ensure that the protections of the Guild follow our performers wherever they may work, Rule One will be enforced globally as of May 1, 2002.

---

## 2.3 TAXATION OF FOREIGN PERFORMERS

International tax law is very complex – so complex in fact that any general statement about it is likely to be misleading or even wrong in many circumstances. In order to make statements more accurate, it would be necessary to insert adjectives, adverbs, provisos and exceptions. But once that's done, those statements would be difficult to understand, and of little use in a book like this one.

On the other hand, saying nothing at all about international tax in a book about international entertainment law would be misleading as well. Everyone in the enterainment industry who earns income abroad, and every company that employs anyone from abroad, is likely to affected by international tax law. Even scheduling (of such things as movie film shoots and stage play runs) may be affected by tax laws, because (for reasons explained below) performers may suffer expensive tax consequences if they remain too long in a country other than their own.

While it is not necessary for all international entertainment lawyers to have tax law expertise, it is necessary for them to be aware of tax issues, so that experts can be retained when and where necessary. The materials that follow are designed to make you aware (though not expert).

---

Three distinct types of income commonly earned by those in the entertainment industry may be subject to international taxation: compensation for personal services; royalties for the use of protected rights; and profits from the sale of entertainment and artistic products. These three types of income are taxed differently from one another, so the proper classification of an entertainer's international income is significant, as the following case reveals.

---

**Boulez v. Commissioner of Internal Revenue**
**83 T.C. 584, 1984 U.S. Tax Ct. LEXIS 23 (1984)**

Korner, Judge.

Respondent [the Commissioner of Internal Revenue] determined a deficiency in petitioner's individual income tax for the calendar year 1975 in the amount of $20,685.61. After concessions, the sole issue which we are called upon to decide is whether certain payments received by petitioner in the year 1975 constitute "royalties," within the meaning of the applicable income tax treaty between the Federal Republic of Germany and the United States, and are therefore exempt from tax by the United States, or whether said payments constitute compensation for personal services within the meaning of that treaty, and are therefore taxable by the United States. . . .

*Findings of Fact*

The petitioner, Pierre Boulez, resided in Paris, France, at the time the petition was filed in this case. Petitioner is a citizen of France, and during the calendar year 1975 was a resident of the Federal Republic of Germany (hereinafter [Germany]). For the taxable year 1975, petitioner was a nonresident alien of the United States for Federal income tax purposes, and he timely filed a Federal nonresident alien income tax return for that year with the Office of International Operations of respondent.

At all times relevant to this case, petitioner was a world-renowned music director and orchestra conductor. On February 19, 1969, petitioner entered into a contract with CBS Records, a division of CBS United Kingdom, Ltd., which is a subsidiary of CBS, Inc., a U.S. corporation. Said contract was modified as of

September 13, 1971, and March 14, 1974, and, as so modified, was in effect during the year 1975. Under date of May 1, 1972, with the consent of CBS Records, the contract was assigned by petitioner to Beacon Concerts, Ltd., of London England, which acted as petitioner's agent and undertook to provide his services to CBS Records under the terms of the basic contract, as amended.

As relevant and material herein, the contract between petitioner and CBS Records, as in effect in the year 1975, provided in part as follows:

> 1. We [CBS Records] hereby agree to engage and you [the petitioner] agree to render your services exclusively for us as a producer and/or performer for the recording of musical and/or literary compositions for the purpose of making phonograph records. It is understood and agreed that such engagement by us shall include your services as a producer and/or performer with the New York Philharmonic for the recording of musical and/or literary compositions for the purposes of making phonograph records. . . .
>
> 3.(a) During the first two contract years of this agreement you will perform for the recording of satisfactory master recording[s] sufficient in number to constitute two (2) 12 inch long playing 33 1/3 rpm recordings, or their equivalent, and we will record your performances; and during each contract year commencing September 13, 1971, you will perform for the recording of satisfactory master recordings sufficient in number to constitute three (3) twelve inch long-playing 33 1/3 rpm recordings, or their equivalent, and we will record your performances. Additional master recordings will be performed by you and recorded by us at our election. . . .
>
> 4. During the period of this Agreement you will not for any reason whatsoever give or sell your services under your own or any assumed name or anonymously to any other person firm or corporation but nothing herein contained shall preclude you [from] giving or selling your services for films personal appearances and broadcasting (whether or not accompanied by television) provided such services are not reproduced as records for sale to the public and you undertake to have this proviso included in any contract for such services. You will not during the period of five years after the expiration of the term of this Agreement give or sell your services for the purpose of making or assisting in the making of records of any of the compositions or works which you shall have performed under this Agreement. You acknowledge that your services are unique and extraordinary and that we shall be entitled to equitable relief to enforce the provision of this paragraph 4.
>
> 5. All master recordings recorded hereunder and all matrices and phonograph records manufactured therefrom, together with the performances embodied thereon, shall be entirely our [CBS Records] property, free from any claims whatsoever by you [petitioner] or any person deriving any rights or interests from you. Without limiting the generality of the foregoing, we (including other divisions of our company) and/or our subsidiaries, affiliates and licensees shall have the unlimited right, from time to time, to manufacture, by any method now or hereafter known, phonograph records and other reproductions, on any mediums or devices now or hereafter known, of the master recordings made hereunder, and to sell transfer or otherwise deal in the same throughout the world under any trademark, trade names and labels or to refrain from such manufacture, sale and dealing; . . .

> 6. We hereby agree to pay the accompaniment costs and studio charges in connection with the master recordings made hereunder. . . .
>
> 13. If, by reason of illness, injury, accident or refusal to work, you fail to perform for us in accordance with the provisions of this agreement, . . . we shall have the option without liability to suspend the application of paragraph 2 and/or paragraph 7 (including the payment of any royalties) of this agreement for the duration of any such contingency by giving you written notice thereof.

Under paragraph 7a of the contract, it was provided "For your services rendered hereunder and for the rights granted to us herein we will pay you the following royalties." There then followed an elaborate formula by which the petitioner was to be paid, based upon a percentage of the retail price derived by CBS Records from the sale of its phonograph records produced under the contract, with said percentage varying depending upon various factors, including, inter alia, whether the musical composition involved was in the public domain, whether the performance conducted by petitioner was made with the New York Philharmonic Orchestra, whether sales were made by direct sales or mail order through what was termed a "Club Operation," whether the record involved was a "re-issue," etc. In all cases, however, the payments or "royalties" which petitioner was to be entitled to receive were dependent upon future sales of recordings by CBS Records.

Pursuant to the February 19, 1969, contract with CBS Records, as amended, petitioner conducted various performances with the Cleveland Orchestra, the New York Philharmonic, and others in the recording of musical compositions for CBS Records. None of these recordings were from "live" performances (i.e., performances before an audience). They were all private performances arranged solely for purposes of recording. CBS, Inc., was responsible for and exercised control over the setting up of the recording session, employing and paying the members of the orchestra, providing and arranging the equipment and engineers and technicians needed to capture and electronically process the sounds rendered by the orchestra, and for compiling and editing the sounds to make master recordings, matrices, and phonograph records.

Petitioner exercised control over the manner in which the orchestra transposed into aural form the underlying musical composition which was the subject of each recording. He determined the placement of the musicians and the volume of aural sound to be rendered by the various musical instruments making up the orchestra. In conducting the orchestra, petitioner exercised his individual artistic talents of interpreting the musical work. Such interpretation, which is the function of the conductor, differs from conductor to conductor and is unique to each conductor's recording of a particular work.

Applications for the copyrights of all the master recordings, matrices, and phonograph records embodying the sound recordings of the musical compositions conducted by petitioner pursuant to the contract were filed by CBS, Inc., and all registrations thereof were issued by the U.S. Copyright Office registered in the name of CBS, Inc.

As the result of performances conducted by petitioner under the terms of the contract, CBS, Inc., paid to Beacon Concerts, Ltd., as petitioner's agent, the sum of $39,461.47 in the year 1975. Beacon Concerts, Ltd., in turn, paid such sum to petitioner in 1976. In his 1975 U.S. nonresident alien income tax return, petitioner disclosed the receipt of such amount, but excluded it as not being subject to U.S. income taxation. Petitioner reported the identical amount in his 1976 income tax return filed with Germany as includable income subject to the German income tax, and petitioner paid German income tax thereon.

Upon audit of petitioner's 1975 U.S. income tax return, respondent determined, inter alia, that the entire amount of $39,461 was taxable to petitioner by the United States. Because of an apparent conflict between respondent and Germany concerning the proper taxation of this income under the existing income tax treaty between the United States and Germany, competent authority proceedings, pursuant to the provisions of the treaty, were instituted at the request of petitioner and were conducted by [the German] Ministry of Finance and respondent's Office of International Operations in an effort to resolve the issues arising under said income tax treaty.

The competent authorities of the two nations were unable to reach agreement on the correct treatment for income tax purposes of the income here involved. The position of Germany was that these payments constituted "royalties," within the meaning of article VIII of the treaty, and therefore were taxable exclusively by Germany. Respondent, on the other hand, took the position that said income was income from performance of personal services in the United States by petitioner, and therefore was taxable by the United States under the provisions of article X of said treaty, except that respondent here concedes that, of the total amount of $39,461.47, the amount of $9,000 was income from sources without the United States and was not subject to taxation by respondent, thus leaving the net amount of $30,461 in issue.[2] [n2 Petitioner concedes that, for U.S. income tax purposes, the payment of "royalties" by CBS, Inc., to Beacon Concerts, Ltd., in 1975 is to be treated as being paid directly to petitioner. . . .]

*Ultimate Finding of Fact*

The payments of CBS, Inc., to petitioner in 1975 were payments as compensation for personal services rendered by petitioner.

*Opinion*

Petitioner contends that the payments to him in 1975 by CBS, Inc., were not taxable by the United States, because they were "royalties" within the meaning of the applicable treaty between the United States and Germany. Respondent, as noted above, contends that the payments in question were taxable to petitioner by the United States because they represented compensation for personal services performed in the United States by petitioner. The parties are in agreement that the outcome of this dispute is governed by the effective income tax treaty between the United States and Germany.

Under date of July 22, 1954, there was executed a "Convention Between the United States of America and the Federal Republic of Germany for the Avoidance of Double Taxation with Respect to Taxes on Income," 5 U.S.T. (part 3) 2768, T.I.A.S. No. 3133. As amended by a Protocol, dated September 17, 1965, 16 U.S.T. (part 2) 1875, T.I.A.S. No. 5920, this convention (hereinafter the treaty) was in effect during the year 1975, and undertook to govern, in stated respects, the income taxation of natural and juridical persons resident in either of the two nations, whose affairs might bring into play the taxing laws of both nations. Petitioner, a resident of Germany, was a person within the coverage of the treaty. The relevant portions of the treaty provide, in part:

Article II

> (2) In the application of the provisions of this Convention by one of the contracting States any term not otherwise defined shall, unless the context otherwise requires, have the meaning which the term has under its own applicable laws. . . .

Article VIII

(1) Royalties derived by a natural person resident in the Federal Republic or by a German company shall be exempt from tax by the United States. . .

.

(3) The term "royalties", as used in this Article,

(a) means any royalties, rentals or other amounts paid as consideration for the use of, or the right to use, copyrights, artistic or scientific works (including motion picture films, or films or tapes for radio or television broadcasting), patents, designs, plans, secret processes or formulae, trademarks, or other like property or rights, or for industrial, commercial or scientific equipment, or for knowledge, experience or skill (know-how) and

(b) shall include gains derived from the alienation of any right or property giving rise to such royalties. . . .

Article X

(2) Compensation for labor or personal services (including compensation derived from the practice of a liberal profession and the rendition of services as a director) performed in the United States by a natural person resident in the Federal Republic shall be exempt from tax by the United States if – [3] [n3 The treaty then enumerates several conditions which must be fulfilled before the exemption from tax by the United States is effective. The parties are in agreement that the exceptions do not apply in the present case, so that the payments in question, if held to be income from personal services, are taxable by the United States to petitioner.]

Acknowledging that the provisions of the treaty take precedence over any conflicting provisions of the Internal Revenue Code of 1954, we must decide whether the payments received by petitioner in 1975 from CBS, Inc., constituted royalties or income from personal services within the meaning of that treaty. This issue, in turn, involves two facets:

(1) Did petitioner intend and purport to license or convey to CBS Records, and did the latter agree to pay for, a property interest in the recordings he was engaged to make, which would give rise to royalties?

(2) If so, did petitioner have a property interest in the recordings which he was capable of licensing or selling?

The first of the above questions is purely factual, depends upon the intention of the parties, and is to be determined by an examination of the record as a whole, including the terms of the contract entered into between petitioner and CBS Records, together with any other relevant and material evidence.

The second question – whether petitioner had a property interest which he could license or sell – is a question of law. The treaty is not explicit, and we have found no cases or other authorities which would give us an interpretation of the treaty on this point. We are therefore remitted to U.S. law for the purpose of determining this question.

We will examine each of these questions in turn.

*1. The Factual Question*

By the contract entered into between petitioner and CBS Records in 1969, as amended, did the parties agree that petitioner was licensing or conveying to CBS Records a property interest in the recordings which he was retained to make, and in return for which he was to receive "royalties?" Petitioner claims that this is the case, and he bears the burden of proof to establish it.

The contract between the parties is by no means clear. On the one hand, the contract consistently refers to the compensation which petitioner is to be entitled to receive as "royalties," and such payments are tied directly to the proceeds which CBS Records was to receive from sales of recordings which petitioner was to make. Both these factors suggest that the parties had a royalty arrangement, rather than a compensation arrangement, in mind in entering into the contract. We bear in mind, however, that the labels which the parties affix to a transaction are not necessarily determinative of their true nature, and the fact that a party's remuneration under the contract is based on a percentage of future sales of the product created does not prove that a licensing or sale of property was intended, rather than compensation for services.

On the other hand, the contract between petitioner and CBS Records is replete with language indicating that what was intended here was a contract for personal services. Thus, paragraph 1 (quoted in our findings of fact) clearly states that CBS Records was engaging petitioner "to render your services exclusively for us as a producer and/or performer. . . It is understood and agreed that such engagement by us shall include your services as a producer and/or performer." Paragraph 3 of the contract then requires petitioner to "perform" in the making of a certain number of recordings in each year. Most importantly, in the context of the present question, paragraph 4 of the contract (quoted in our findings) makes it clear that CBS considered petitioner's services to be the essence of the contract: petitioner agreed not to perform for others with respect to similar recordings during the term of the contract, and for a period of 5 years thereafter, and he was required to "acknowledge that your services are unique and extraordinary and that we shall be entitled to equitable relief to enforce the provision of this paragraph 4."

Under paragraph 5 of the contract (quoted *supra*), it was agreed that the recordings, once made, should be entirely the property of CBS Records, "free from any claims whatsoever by you or any person deriving any rights or interests from you." Significantly, nowhere in the contract is there any language of conveyance of any alleged property right in the recordings by petitioner to CBS Records, nor any language indicating a licensing of any such purported right, other than the designation of petitioner's remuneration as being "royalties." The word "copyright" itself is never mentioned. Finally, under paragraph 13 of the contract, CBS Records was entitled to suspend or terminate its payments to petitioner "if, by reason of illness, injury, accident or refusal to work, you fail to perform for us in accordance with the provisions of this agreement."

Considered as a whole, therefore, and acknowledging that the contract is not perfectly clear on this point, we conclude that the weight of the evidence is that the parties intended a contract for personal services, rather than one involving the sale or licensing of any property rights which petitioner might have in the recordings which were to be made in the future.

*2. The Legal Question*

Before a person can derive income from royalties, it is fundamental that he must have an ownership interest in the property whose licensing or sale gives rise to the income. . . .

In its definition of royalties, . . . in article VIII(3)(a) [of the treaty], "royalties" are defined to mean "amounts paid as consideration for the use of, or *the right to use*, copyrights, artistic or scientific works. . . *or other like property or rights*," and article VIII(3)(b) also states that the term "royalties" "shall include gains derived from the alienation of *any right or property* giving rise to such royalties." (Emphasis supplied.)

It is clear, then, that the existence of a property right in the payee is fundamental for the purpose of determining whether royalty income exists, and this is equally true under our domestic law as well as under the treaty.

Did the petitioner have any property rights in the recordings which he made for CBS Records, which he could either license or sell and which would give rise to royalty income here? We think not.

As noted in our findings, the basic contract between petitioner and CBS Records was executed in 1969. At that time, petitioner had no copyrightable property interest in the recordings which he made for CBS Records under the Copyright Act of 1909 as amended, and petitioner concedes that this was so.

Petitioner contends, however, that the Copyright Act of 1909 was amended by the Sound Recording Amendment of 1971, and by virtue of this amendment, petitioner then acquired copyrightable property interests in the recordings which he thereafter made for CBS Records.

We think that petitioner is correct, in that the Sound Recording Amendment of 1971, did amend the Copyright Act of 1909 so as to create, for the first time, copyrightable property interests in a musical director or performer such as petitioner who was making sound recordings of musical works, a property right which had not existed theretofore. In discussing the changes made by the Second Recording Amendment of 1971, and the new property rights therein created in both record producers such as CBS Records and performers such as petitioner, the legislative history contains the following significant statement: "As in the case of motion pictures, the bill does not fix the authorship, or the resulting ownership, of sound recordings, but leaves these matters to the employment relationship and bargaining among the interests involved." H. Rept. 92-487 (1971), 1971 U.S. Code Cong. & Adm. News 1566, 1570.

In spite of this change in the law in 1971, however, petitioner's contractual relationship with CBS Records went on as before. Neither the amendment to that contract of 1971, nor the further amendment in 1974, made any reference to the change of the copyright laws, nor modified the basic contract in any respect which would be pertinent to the instant question. We conclude, therefore, that the parties saw no need to modify their contract because they understood that even after the Sound Recording Amendment of 1971, petitioner still had no licensable or transferable property rights in the recordings which he made for CBS Records, and we think this was correct.

The Copyright Act of 1909, even after its amendment by the Sound Recording Amendment of 1971, describes the person having a copyrightable interest in property as the "author or proprietor" and further provides that "the word 'author' shall include an employer in the case of works made for hire." The above is a statutory enactment of the long-recognized rule that where a person is employed for the specific purpose of creating a work, including a copyrightable item, the fruits of his labor, carried out in accordance with the employment, are the property of his employer. The rule creates a rebuttable presumption to this effect, which can be overcome by express contractual provisions between the employee and the employer, reserving to the former the copyrightable interest.

Here, the petitioner, a musical conductor of world-wide reputation, was employed to make recordings for CBS Records, and in doing so, was to exercise his peculiar and unique skills in accordance with his experience, talent, and best judgment. In these circumstances, we do not think that petitioner was an "employee" in the common law sense, but rather was an independent contractor, with the same relationship to CBS Records as a lawyer, an engineer, or an architect would have to his client, or a doctor to his patient. This, however, provides no grounds for distinction, since the "works for hire" rule applies to independent contractors just as it does to conventional employees.

In the instant case, the application of the "works for hire" rule means that petitioner had no copyrightable property interest in the recordings which he created for CBS Records, even after 1971. Petitioner was engaged for the specific purpose of making the recordings in question; his contract with CBS Records reserved no property rights in the recordings to him, and indeed made it specific that all such rights, whatever they were, were to reside in CBS Records. Under these circumstances, we do not think that petitioner has overcome the statutory presumption of the "works for hire" rule, nor that he has shown that he had any property interest in the recordings, either before 1971 or thereafter, which he could either license or sell to CBS Records so as to produce royalty income within the meaning of the treaty. This conclusion, in turn, reinforces our belief, which we have found as a fact, that the contract between petitioner and CBS Records was one for the performance of personal services.

It follows that respondent was correct in taxing this income to petitioner under the provisions of article X of the treaty.

---

**Note on tax treaties**

As you read in the foregoing case, Pierre Boulez had already reported his income from CBS Records on his German income tax return and had "paid German income tax thereon." As a result of the U.S. Tax Court's decision, Boulez also had to pay United States income tax on that very same income. This tax dilemma confronts all of those who receive personal service income to perform internationally. They may be taxed twice or even three times on the very same income: once by the country where the income is earned; a second time by the country where they reside; and a third time by the country of their citizenship, if they reside in one country but are citizens of another. Boulez for example was a French citizen who resided in Germany and performed in the U.S.

The *Boulez* case does not indicate whether he was taxed by France (as well by Germany and the U.S.). France may not assert a right to tax the foreign income of its nonresident citizens. But the United States *does* tax the *worldwide* income of its citizens *and residents*. (More below about the taxation of resident aliens.)

Moreover, as a general rule, the United States and other countries impose tax on personal service income earned within their borders, even if it is earned by nonresident aliens. As a result, if a Canadian citizen – such as an orchestra conductor, actor or athlete – earns income performing in, say, the United States, the U.S. will want to tax that income and so will Canada. Worse yet, if a British citizen who resides in Canada earns income performing in the U.S., all three countries may want to tax that income. If all three countries did, the tax imposed might wipe out or even exceed the amount of income earned!

This dilemma has not gone unnoticed by countries and their taxpayers. As you read in the *Boulez* case, countries have entered into tax treaties with one another. In addition to exempting certain types of income (like royalties) from local taxation, tax treaties also contain provisions designed to avoid double and triple taxation of personal service income. They do this in one of two ways:

- by *exempting* (in other words, not taxing) the locally-earned personal service income of nonresidents; or
- by allowing a *credit* for the amount of the tax that is paid on personal service income earned in other tax-treaty countries against the tax that would otherwise be paid on that income in the country of taxpayer's residence or citizenship.

The United States has tax treaties with more than 50 countries. In addition to Germany (the treaty that was the subject of the *Boulez* case), these countries include Australia, Canada, Ireland and the United Kingdom. (These four countries are simply examples, and are mentioned for non-tax reasons that will become apparent in Chapter 3.)

Tax treaties usually exempt the locally-earned personal service income of certain nonresidents, but not all of them. Only some of those who work in the entertainment business are eligible for this exemption, because these treaties usually permit countries to tax the locally-earned income of nonresidents who are "artistes or athletes" such as actors, stage performers, singers and athletes. That is why the Canadian taxing authorities thought that they could tax the income of Tom Cheek, a United States citizen and resident who is known to professional baseball fans as the play-by-play announcer for the Toronto Blue Jays.

---

**Cheek and Her Majesty the Queen**
**Tax Court of Canada (2002)**
**Case No. 1999-1113(IT)G**

The Honourable Judge M.A. Mogan

The Appellant [Thomas "Tom" F. Cheek] has appealed from income tax assessments for the years 1993, 1994, 1995 and 1996. In each of those years, the Appellant was resident in the United States of America and was not resident in Canada. In those years, the Appellant came to Canada frequently to provide on radio a play-by-play description of all home games played by the Toronto Blue Jays, a professional baseball team playing in the American League. In the Toronto sports community, the Appellant is often identified as "the voice of the Blue Jays" but he does not think of himself that way.

The Appellant filed income tax returns in Canada for each of the years under appeal. In those returns, the Appellant reported the amounts of income earned in Canada from his radio broadcasts of Blue Jays home games, but he then deducted those same amounts under subparagraph 110(1)(*f*)(i) of the *Income Tax Act* on the assumption that such amounts were exempt from tax in Canada because of a provision contained in the *Canada-U.S. Income Tax Convention (1980)*. By notices of assessment, the Minister of National Revenue disallowed the deduction of the amounts claimed under paragraph 110(1)(*f*) in each of the years 1993, 1994, 1995 and 1996. The Appellant has appealed from those assessments claiming that his income earned in Canada from broadcasting Blue Jays home games is exempt from tax in Canada because of Articles XIV and XVI of the *Canada-U.S. Income Tax Convention (1980)* which I shall hereafter refer to as "the *Convention*." The principal issue in this case is the interpretation of Article XVI of the *Convention*.

A person who is not resident in Canada may be taxable on income earned in Canada if that person is employed or carries on business in Canada. Subsection 2(3) of the *Income Tax Act* states:

> 2(3) Where a person who is not taxable . . . [as a resident]
> (*a*) was employed in Canada,
> (*b*) carried on a business in Canada, or
> (*c*) disposed of a taxable Canadian property,
>
> . . . an income tax shall be paid . . . on the person's taxable income earned in Canada. . . .

Under the above provision, the Appellant reported as income those amounts which he regarded as earned in Canada through his sale of reporting and promotional services with respect to the Toronto Blue Jays. He then deducted those same amounts under subparagraph 110(1)(*f*)(i) which states:

> 110(1) For the purpose of computing the taxable income of a taxpayer for a taxation year, there may be deducted . . .
>
> (*f*) . . . any amount that is
>
> (i) . . . exempt from income tax in Canada because of a provision contained in a tax convention or agreement with another country. . . .

In the pleadings, the Respondent has admitted that the Appellant was not resident in Canada at any material time and that he was resident in the U.S.A. at all material times. Therefore, the Appellant's liability for income tax in Canada is determined by the *Convention* because, when there is any inconsistency between the provisions of the *Convention* and the provisions of the *Income Tax Act*, the provisions of the *Convention* prevail to the extent of the inconsistency. The relevant Articles of the *Convention* are XIV and XVI as follows:

> *Article XIV — Independent Personal Services*
>
> Income derived by an individual who is a resident of a Contracting State in respect of independent personal services may be taxed in that State. Such income may also be taxed in the other Contracting State if the individual has or had a fixed base regularly available to him in that other State but only to the extent that the income is attributable to the fixed base.
>
> *Article XVI — Artistes and Athletes*
>
> Notwithstanding the provisions of Articles XIV (Independent Personal Services) and XV (Dependent Personal Services), income derived by a resident of a Contracting State as an entertainer, such as a theatre, motion picture, radio or television artiste, or a musician, or as an athlete, from his personal activities as such exercised in the other Contracting State, may be taxed in that other State, except where the amount of the gross receipts derived by such entertainer or athlete, including expenses reimbursed to him or borne on his behalf, from such activities do not exceed fifteen thousand dollars ($15,000) in the currency of that other State for the calendar year concerned.

The Appellant claims that he is taxable only in the U.S.A. under Article XIV with respect to his baseball broadcasting income because he did not have at any material time "a fixed base regularly available to him" in Canada. When the assessments under appeal were first issued, the Minister of National Revenue relied on two basic propositions. First, the Appellant was taxable in Canada under Article XIV because his income earned in Canada was attributable to a fixed base in Canada (i.e. the SkyDome in Toronto) which was regularly available to him. And second, the Appellant was taxable in Canada under Article XVI because his income earned in Canada was derived "as an entertainer, such as a theatre, motion picture, radio or television artiste."

Six weeks before the commencement of trial, counsel for the Respondent informed the Court and opposing counsel that the Respondent would not rely on Article XIV of the *Convention*. Accordingly, the parties at trial argued only the application of Article XVI of the *Convention*. If the Respondent is successful under Article XVI, there is a subsidiary question concerning the amount of income which the Appellant derives from his services in Canada. To summarize, the principal question is whether the Appellant is "an entertainer, such as a theatre, motion picture, radio or television artiste" within the meaning of Article XVI of the *Convention*.

*Evidence*

At trial, the Appellant testified describing his long experience as a radio broadcaster and the services he performs in connection with the broadcast of Blue Jays games. The Appellant was born in Pensacola, Florida in 1939. He joined the U.S. Air Force in 1956 at the age of 17. He stayed in the U.S.A.F. for three years specializing in communications – assigned to the Strategic Air Command – using a teletype to send and receive messages. Upon his discharge from the U.S.A.F., he worked for an engineering firm in 1959-60 in upstate New York. In 1961-62, he attended the Cambridge School of Broadcasting in Boston. Upon completing his courses, he applied for jobs at small radio stations.

In 1962, the Appellant was hired for the summer as the "swing" announcer at radio station WEAV in Plattsburg, N.Y. He broadcast news, sports and music from 9:00 a.m. until noon and from 3:00 to 6:00 p.m. At the end of his summer job, he was hired by radio station WJOY at Burlington, Vermont in the fall of 1962 to broadcast news and sports and to sell radio advertising. He described this job as more selling than broadcasting. It was in this job, however, that the Appellant started to spend his evenings following basketball and hockey games at gymnasiums and rinks around Burlington.

In 1964, he moved to a radio station at Rutland, Vermont where he was on his own (unsupervised) from 6:00 to 9:00 a.m. broadcasting news, sports, weather, music, time checks and personal comments. The teletype machine was hooked up to United Press International ("UPI") as a news service and the Appellant described part of his job as "rip and read." He would rip the incoming material from UPI off the machine and read it directly to the radio audience without any prior opportunity to scan the written word. At Rutland, he started to cover local high school and college sports by going to the site; plugging in; and then broadcasting.

In 1965, the Appellant was back at WJOY in Burlington holding different jobs as sports director and broadcaster, program director, staff announcer and selling advertising. At various times, he also did the morning show and driving home show. In 1968, he joined the television group that is now Channel 22 in Burlington but the job lasted only eight months. In 1969, he went to radio station WCAX in Burlington which later became WBVT. He stayed there until 1976 as sales manager and later sports director. When his selling day ended, he went to his preferred avocation of broadcasting local sports events. In Rutland, he had done radio broadcasts of some Boston Red Sox home games and later (around 1973), while still at WBVT, he started doing radio broadcasts of some Montreal Expos home games.

The Appellant's big break came (while still at WBVT) when he was asked to do the radio side of those Montreal Expos games which were televised. He was the standby broadcaster for about 20 to 40 games in Montreal per season. He practised broadcasting into a tape which he would then play back and critique in his car while driving home to Burlington from Montreal. It was around 1976 when the Appellant heard that major league baseball was coming to Toronto. At the end of the 1976 baseball season, he was interviewed to discuss the possibility of his broadcasting on radio the Blue Jays games. He was given the job.

At that time, the Appellant and his wife and their children (son 10, daughter 7 and son 5) were living in Burlington, Vermont. When he accepted the opportunity to broadcast the Blue Jays games in the winter 1976-77, he and his wife sold their home in Burlington, Vermont; they purchased a home in Burlington, Ontario; and they moved to Canada. He recalls arriving in Canada in February 1977 just in time to unpack and then head south to Florida for spring training. The Appellant and his wife lived in Ontario as landed immigrants from 1977 until 1992 while their three children were growing up attending Ontario schools. By 1992, the three children were 25, 22 and 20 years of age and were leaving home (or had left) for post-high school education and employment in the U.S.A. The Appellant and his wife concluded that it was no longer necessary to maintain a home year round in Canada.

The Appellant was born in Florida and, in 1992, his mother was a senior citizen living there. It was fairly easy for the Appellant and his wife to decide in 1992 that they would sell their home in Ontario; and purchase a home in Florida near Dunedin where the Blue Jays did their spring training. They moved their domestic dwelling from Ontario to Florida in 1992 and, at that time, the Appellant ceased being resident in Canada. The first year under appeal is 1993 and that is the first year since the Appellant started broadcasting Blue Jays games when he was not at any time resident in Canada.

The Appellant's job is to broadcast on radio every game which the Blue Jays play: at home or away in the regular season, any and all post-season games in the playoffs, and all pre-season games during spring training. As I recall the Appellant's evidence, he has participated in the radio broadcast of every game which the Blue Jays have played since they entered the American League in 1977. He is a man of endurance. The Appellant described a typical workday if the Blue Jays were playing an evening game staring at 7:00 p.m. He would get up early and go on his computer to the web sights of the Blue Jays and the team they were playing that day to pick up any recent information concerning changes in the player roster, whether a regular player was sidelined with an injury, whether a new player was brought up from a farm team, etc. He might print any information which he regarded as particularly relevant. He would use the internet to scan the sports pages of daily newspapers for any significant event in games played the previous day.

He arrives at the ballpark about 4:00 p.m. and meets with the engineer to select radio clips from prior games which might be significant on that particular day. The manager of the Blue Jays usually has a scrum with the media on game day at 4:30 p.m. and the Appellant would always attend that scrum. He would visit the clubhouse of each team, the dugouts, the batting cages and speak with various players. He would eat a very light supper and be in the broadcast booth at 6:30 p.m. for the pre-game show. The Appellant works with Jerry Howarth. They take turns doing the play-by-play and colour commentary and have been working together for about 20 years. It was suggested to the Appellant in cross-examination that he was known as "the voice of the Blue Jays" but he said that he has never ever identified himself or regarded himself as the voice of the team. It is a fact, however, that the Appellant has been involved in the broadcast of every game which the Blue Jays have played since they entered the American League in 1977.

A typical baseball game consumes about three hours. Therefore, if an evening game started at 7:00 p.m., the Appellant would come off the air about 10:00 p.m. or shortly after, having been in the broadcast booth since 6:30 p.m. According to the Appellant, in the course of an average three-hour baseball game, there are only 16 to 18 minutes when there is actual "motion" on the field such as (i) a pitcher delivering a pitch from the mound; (ii) a base runner attempting to steal a base; or (iii) a batter hitting a particular pitch thereby causing the ball, the batter, any base runner and all fielders to be in motion. Because of the limited time when there is motion on the field, there is a substantial amount of "down time" in every baseball broadcast.

The challenge facing the professional broadcaster of baseball games is to hold the attention and interest of the radio audience during the down time when there is no motion on the field. The Appellant and his partner attempt to meet this challenge with their knowledge of the game and its rules, their experience, their knowledge of current and historical statistics, biographical information on players, team managers, coaches, and other prominent persons connected with the game, and historical information on each team. The Appellant stated that, during the regular season, he spends about five or six non-broadcasting hours each day doing research and accumulating current and historical information on the game and its people so that he will have interesting material at his finger tips for the down time in each game broadcast.

A significant amount of the Appellant's research each day is facilitated by the volume of material published by major league baseball. Exhibit A-1 is eight pages of "Media Information" published by the Blue Jays every game day. Every other team publishes the same kind of information on their game days. For a particular game, the Appellant will review Exhibit A-1 and the corresponding document from the Blue Jays' opponent in that game. Similarly, each team publishes an "Official Guide" for the season (like Exhibits A-3 and A-4) containing a substantial volume of team information. And finally, major league baseball publishes every day during the regular season up-to-date statistics on all teams and players. Some of that information is in Exhibit A-5. The Appellant himself keeps a box score of each game so that he will know what has happened inning-by-inning. Exhibit A-8 is his box score of a game between the Blue Jays and the Cleveland Indians.

Each party called an expert witness to support its respective position. I find that the evidence of the expert witnesses is not very helpful but will comment later in these reasons on the evidence of the Respondent's expert.

*Analysis*

The principal issue requires me to interpret Article XVI of the *Convention* and apply it to the facts. I will repeat from Article XVI only those words which are most relevant for the purpose of this appeal:

> . . . income derived by a resident of a Contracting State as an entertainer, such as a theatre, motion picture, radio or television artiste, or a musician, or as an athlete, from his personal activities as such exercised in the other Contracting State, may be taxed in that other State. . . .

The Appellant as resident in the U.S.A. is "a resident of a Contracting State." Also, the Appellant's broadcasts in Toronto of all home games of the Blue Jays are "personal activities . . . exercised in the other Contracting State." The basic question is whether the Appellant's income earned in Canada is derived "as an entertainer, such as a theatre, motion picture, radio or television artiste."

There is no doubt that professional sports in itself is entertainment. A particular league (baseball, hockey or football) will organize a schedule requiring all teams in the league to play an equal number of games. People will purchase tickets for the right to attend and watch and be entertained by the playing of the games. For those people who are not able to attend a game, a sponsor (frequently a corporation producing a consumer product like beer or gasoline) will pay for the right to describe on radio or to show on television the playing of the game. Is the presentation of the game in a stadium or arena or on radio or on television so inherently entertaining that all persons connected with the presentation of the game are "entertainers"?

A baseball fan who turns on the radio to listen to a Blue Jays game is entertained but who is the entertainer? Is it the players on the field? Is it the broadcaster like the Appellant who describes the play and whose objective is to hold the attention of the radio audience? Or is it both? If the Appellant is entertaining because of his knowledge and the skills he uses to hold the attention of the radio audience, is he in the words of Article XVI "an entertainer, such as a theatre, motion picture, radio or television artiste"? Can the Appellant be entertaining on the radio without being a "radio artiste" within the meaning of Article XVI?

Having regard to the pleadings, the Appellant claims that he is a sports broadcast journalist. The Respondent claims that the Appellant earned income in Canada as an entertainer and, in particular, as a radio artiste.

It seems to me that there are four basic ways in which a true baseball fan (probably a male!) may follow his favourite team. First, he may attend and watch a particular game. Second, if he cannot attend, he may watch the game on television so that he will see what the camera shows. Third, if he cannot watch on television, he may listen to the game on radio so that he will hear what the broadcaster describes. And fourth, if he cannot listen on radio, he will soon after the game learn whether his favourite team won or lost by reading the sports pages of a daily newspaper or by listening to a sports broadcaster on radio or television or by going on the internet.

There is a significant difference between the first three ways of following a favourite team (attending a game, watching on television or listening on radio) and the fourth way of learning the result after the event. There is a real quality of entertainment in the first three ways because the true baseball fan follows the game as it is played; he participates in the anticipation and tension of each pitch and in the thrill of any resulting action like a base hit, a homerun, a strike out or a double play. That quality of entertainment is not present when the fan learns the result after the game is completed because he is then like any other person reading the paper or listening to the news in order to know about an event which has already happened.

It is, therefore, somewhat misleading for the Appellant to describe himself as a sports broadcast journalist because the "broadcast" element of his particular work (a play-by-play description of a game as it is played) brings him within the entertainment area of professional baseball whereas some other sports broadcast journalist may appear on a radio or television morning show to report and comment on games played the previous day. Although the Appellant's broadcast activities bring him within the entertainment area of professional baseball, I am not persuaded that the Appellant is "an entertainer, such as a . . . radio . . . artiste" within the meaning of Article XVI of the *Convention*. For the reasons which follow, I will allow the appeals.

Upon examining the structure of Article XVI, I conclude that "artiste" is a noun and that adjoining words like "theatre, radio, television and motion picture" are adjectives. Accordingly, the Appellant can be brought within Article XVI only if he is a "radio artiste" because the other adjectives do not apply to him. For me, it is significant that the persons who drafted the *Convention* used the word "artiste" when they might have used some other word. Counsel for both parties provided definitions of "artiste" from prominent dictionaries as follows:

(a) an artist, esp. an actor, singer, dancer, or other public performer. *Random House Webster's Unabridged Dictionary* (Second edition, Random House, New York, 1999);

(b) a professional performer, esp. a singer or dancer. *Concise Oxford Dictionary* (Ninth Edition, Clarendon Press, Oxford, 1995)

(c) a professional person in any of the performing arts; a person very skilled in his work; often humorous or facetious. *Webster's New World Dictionary* (Second College Edition, Simon and Schuster, New York, 1980)

(d) a public performer who appeals to the aesthetic faculties, as a professional singer, dancer, etc.; also one who makes a 'fine art' of his employment, as an artistic cook, hairdresser, etc. *Oxford English Dictionary* (2nd ed. 1989)

All dictionaries referred to above define "artiste" in relation to the performing arts, like a singer or dancer. The performing arts would also include dramatic acting whether on a live stage (theatre) or in the movies (motion picture). There is no evidence that the Appellant is a singer or dancer or actor. Indeed, I would conclude from his evidence and his biography that he does not perform in any of those areas. He is by training, experience and reputation a radio broadcaster. When the Appellant was examined in chief, he stated that what happens on the field dictates what he has to say on radio. Under cross-examination, he stated that he regards himself as a reporter and, until something happens on the field, he has nothing to report.

I think of the Appellant as primarily a reporter. He is reporting live on radio what is happening in a baseball game. He cannot himself change or cause anyone else to change what happens on the field. Only the players can determine what happens on the field. The Appellant primarily is reporting what the players are doing as they do it. In terms of entertainment, it is the players who are the entertainers. Fans purchase tickets and attend games to see baseball played by highly skilled players. Other fans watch televised games for the same reason. Other fans listen to games on radio in order to know how the performance of those same highly skilled players affects a game play-by-play. It is the players who are "performing" as professional athletes.

Having regard to the dictionary definitions of "artiste," a radio artiste is a person who by some skillful and creative performance (for example, singing or acting or interviewing third parties) can attract an audience to hear that person herself or himself. In the golden age of radio (i.e. before television), Jack Benny, Fred Allen, Bing Crosby and Ma Perkins were radio artistes. In recent times, Peter Gzowski was a radio artiste because he used extraordinary interview skills to draw out individuals (public persons and very private persons) in a way which made their individual endeavours interesting to people all across Canada. Radio audiences listened to people like Jack Benny, Bing Crosby and Peter Gzowski just to hear them perform; not to hear them describe how someone else was performing. The persons drafting the *Convention* had some purpose in using the word "artiste" by preference over any other word, and in connection with words like "theatre," "motion picture," "radio" and "television," each of which can be a medium for the performing arts. . . .

I now turn to another set of extrinsic materials, other international taxation conventions and general models thereof, in order to help illustrate and illuminate the intentions of the parties to the *Canada-U.S. Income Tax Convention (1980)*. . . .

Of high persuasive value in terms of defining the parameters of the *Canada-United States Income Tax Convention (1980)* is the O.E.C.D. *Model Double Taxation Convention on Income and Capita.* As noted by the Court of Appeal, it served as the basis for the *Canada-United States Income Tax Convention (1980)* and also has world-wide recognition as a basic document of reference in the negotiation, application and interpretation of multi-lateral or bi-lateral tax conventions.

Following the guidance of the Supreme Court, counsel put before me the O.E.C.D. *Model Tax Convention on Income and on Capital* updated to April 2000. In particular, Article 17 of the O.E.C.D. *Model Convention* states:

> *Article 17: Artistes and Sportsmen*
>
> 1. . . . income derived by a resident of a Contracting State as an entertainer, such as a theatre, motion picture, radio or television artiste, or a musician, or as a sportsman from his personal activities as such exercised in the other Contracting State, may be taxed in that other State.

The O.E.C.D. Commentary on Article 17 of the O.E.C.D. *Model Convention* includes the following passage:

> 3. Paragraph 1 refers to artistes and sportsmen. It is not possible to give a precise definition of "artiste," but paragraph 1 includes examples of

> persons who would be regarded as such. These examples should not be considered as exhaustive. On the one hand, the term "artiste" clearly includes the stage performer, film actor, actor (including for instance a former sportsman) in a television commercial. The Article may also apply to income received from activities which involve a political, social, religious or charitable nature, if an entertainment character is present. On the other hand, it does not extend to a visiting conference speaker or to administrative or support staff (e.g. cameramen for a film, producers, film directors, choreographers, technical staff, road crew for a pop group etc.). In between there is a grey area where it is necessary to review the overall balance of the activities of the person concerned.

Respondent's counsel relies on the above passage to argue that any U.S. resident whose primary activity in Canada is to broadcast on radio is a radio artiste. It is obvious that the Appellant is not a "behind the scenes" man like a producer or sound engineer. Also, broadcasting is not a negligible part of what he does to earn his income in Canada. My concern is that if I disregard the content of what the Appellant broadcasts into a radio microphone, then I am not giving effect to the choice of the word "artiste" in Article XVI.

If I were to accept the Respondent's argument, any television "news anchor" like Lloyd Robertson or Peter Mansbridge in contemporary Canada would be a television artiste. I regard any one of those prominent news anchors as a highly competent journalist but not as a television artiste. Peter Gzowski as a radio personality may have been in the grey area between journalism and the performing arts but, in my view, he was a radio artiste because of the creative way in which he used his interview skills to shape the program. For the television news anchor, it is current events which shape the program. An artiste must have creative talent.

I do not find the evidence of the expert witnesses helpful but will comment briefly on the evidence of Tom Hedrick, called as an expert on behalf of the Respondent. . . . Mr. Hedrick has had a long career as a play-by-play radio broadcaster of football games including seven years with the Kansas City Chiefs, three Super Bowls for CBS and nine Cotton Bowls. Mr. Hedrick was asked to express his opinion on the question: What is the role of a major league baseball play-by-play broadcaster?

In Mr. Hedrick's opinion, the top radio announcer of a major league team has three basic skills. First, he must be able to describe the plays accurately. Second, he must be able to "fill in the blanks" because baseball is a slow-moving game. He must be able to fill the "down time" with stories, anecdotes, statistics and strategy. He has an obligation to entertain the audience and keep the broadcast lively, especially when the home team (i.e. Blue Jays) is losing. And third, he must be a salesman for the home team, getting the audience involved in the game and selling the fans on the idea of coming out to a home game (i.e. SkyDome) to watch a particular player.

I have no reason to challenge the opinion of Mr. Hedrick but his answer to the stated question seems to reinforce the view which the Appellant has of himself. The Appellant regards himself as a sports broadcast journalist. There is no perfect analogy but, if I think in terms of newspaper journalism, the Appellant is like a combined reporter and columnist with respect to Mr. Hedrick's first two basic skills. The political reporter describes accurately what is happening at city hall or in the legislature or on parliament hill just as the Appellant describes accurately the play on the field. The op-ed political columnist draws on his knowledge, experience and daily contact with politicians to comment on and express opinions on the political machinations of the day just as the Appellant draws on his knowledge, experience and daily contact with players and managers to fill the "down time" when there is no motion on the field. I see the Appellant as a journalist and not as a performing artist.

The headings used in any document may be helpful when construing that document. The heading for Article XVI is "Artistes and Athletes" and the heading for Article 17 of the O.E.C.D. *Model Convention* is "Artistes and Sportsmen." The Appellant is not performing as an athlete or sportsman when he comes to Canada to broadcast on radio the Blue Jays home games. It is obvious that athletes and sportsmen "perform" in their chosen athletic avocation; and their performance is inherently entertaining. The baseball fan who turns on the radio to hear a particular Blue Jays game wants to know how the Blue Jays athletes are performing on the field. The Appellant may be able to hold the attention and interest of the fan with his "down time" commentary but he is not the reason why the fan turns on the radio.

The Appellant is not a radio artiste. He is a very skillful and experienced radio journalist. The appeals are allowed, with costs. . . .

*Judgment*

The appeals from assessments of tax made under the *Income Tax Act* for the 1993, 1994, 1995 and 1996 taxation years are allowed, with costs, and the assessments are referred back to the Minister of National Revenue for reconsideration and reassessment on the basis that the Appellant is exempt from income tax in Canada under Article XVI of the *Canada-United States Income Tax Convention, 1980* because the Appellant is not a radio artiste.

---

**Notes on international taxation of athletes and entertainers**

The Cheek case seems to suggest that members of U.S.-based American League teams who play against the Blue Jays in Toronto may have to pay income tax in Canada on a portion of their baseball salaries, even though Cheek himself did not. This is so, because baseball players are "athletes," and they earn a portion of their salaries for playing services they render in Canada.

The paragraph of Article XVI of the Canadian-U.S. Income Tax Convention quoted in the Cheek decision – read by itself – would permit Canada to tax that portion of the players' salaries attributable to the games they play in Toronto, so long as that portion exceeds $15,000 in Canadian dollars, or about $9,500 in U.S. dollars. The New York Yankees played the Blue Jays in Toronto 10 times during the 2002 regular season. Those 10 games were about 6.2% of all 162 regular season games. Thus, every Yankee earned more than $9,500 (in U.S. dollars) for games played in Canada, because the minimum Major League Baseball salary was $200,000 (for the 2000 season); and 6.2% x $200,000 = $12,400.

However, Article XVI also provides – in a paragraph that wasn't relevant to Cheek's case and thus was not quoted by the court – that "The provisions of this Article shall not apply to the income of an athlete in respect of an employment with a team which participates in a league with regularly schedule games in both Contracting States." In other words, Article XVI does not authorize Canada to tax the income of U.S. citizens and residents who play for American League teams that are based in the U.S., because the American League regularly schedules games in both Canada and the U.S.

On the other hand, even though Article XVI – the "Artistes and Athletes" article – does not apply to U.S.-based American League players, those players are "subject to the rules of Article XV" – an article that permits Canada to tax the Canadian personal service income of employees who are U.S. citizens and residents.

(Treasury Department Technical Explanation of the Convention between the United States of America and Canada with Respect to Taxes on Income and on Capital, Article XVI.) Fortunately for professional baseball players, Article XV authorizes Canada to tax the Canadian "derived" income of Americans only if they are in Canada for more than 183 days in one year. U.S.-based American League players are not required to be in Canada for more than 183 days a year; and thus neither Article XVI nor Article XV authorizes Canada to tax their income.

If this seems a bit complicated, consider it this way:

Article XIV of the Canada-U.S. tax treaty permits Canada to tax the Canadian income of U.S. residents who are independent contractors, if they have a fixed base in Canada. Cheek apparently was an independent contractor for the Blue Jays, rather than an employee. But he did not have a fixed base in Canada, so Article XIV did not authorize Canada to tax his Canadian income. Article XIV would not allow Canada to tax the Canadian income of U.S.-resident American League baseball players either, because they too are "employees" rather than "independent contractors."

Article XV of the treaty permits Canada to tax the Canadian income of U.S. residents who are employees – if: (1) their income is more than $10,000 a year, and (2)(a) they are in Canada 183 days (or more) a year, or (2)(b) their employer is Canadian (or has an establishment in Canada). Cheek earned more than $10,000 a year but probably was not in Canada 183 days a year, and he probably was not an employee of the Blue Jays. Thus, Article XV did not authorize Canada to tax Cheek's Canadian income. Article XV would not allow Canada to tax the Canadian income of U.S.-resident American League baseball players either, because even though they are "employees," they are not in Canada 183 days a year, and (unless they play for the Blue Jays) their employer is not Canadian (and does not have an establishment in Canada). On the other hand, if they play for the Blue Jays, Article XV does appear to authorize Canada to tax their Canadian income, even if they are U.S. residents rather than Canadian residents. On this issue, however, consider the impact of Article XVI of the treaty.

Article XVI of the treaty permits Canada to tax the Canadian income of "artistes," musicians and athletes, even if their income would not be taxed under Articles XIV or XV. This is why Cheek's case turned on whether he was an "artiste" under Article XVI, and why the court's conclusion that he was not an "artiste" meant that Canada could not tax his Canadian income.

Consider once again the Canadian tax situation of U.S.-resident players who are members of the New York Yankees. Their Canadian income is not taxable by Canada under Article XIV, because they are not independent contractors. Their Canadian income is not taxable by Canada under Article XV, because they are not in Canada 183 days a year and are not employed by a Canadian company. Their Canadian income also is not taxable by Canada under Article XVI, even though they are "athletes," because the American League regularly schedules games in both Canada and the U.S.

This brings us back to the Canadian income of U.S.-resident players who are members of the Blue Jays. Their Canadian income appears to be taxable by Canada, because they are employed by a Canadian company. Is it, however, exempted from Canadian taxation by Article XVI, because the American League regularly schedules games in both Canada and the U.S.? Or does the "regularly scheduled games" provision of Article XVI exempt only income that otherwise would have been taxed under Article XVI but not income that is taxable under Article XV?

Finally, if U.S.-resident professional golfers, tennis players or boxers earn more than $15,000 a year in Canada, may Canada tax that income under Article XIV or XVI?

---

If the Canadian Tax Court had decided that Tom Cheek was an "artiste," Canada would have taxed the same income that Cheek paid taxes on in the United States, just the way the United States taxed the same income that Pierre Boulez paid taxes on in Germany. To avoid this kind of double taxation, performers need to be able to exclude foreign-earned personal service income from their taxable income in their *home* countries, or they will need to be able to claim a *credit* against their home country taxes for taxes paid in the country where their services were performed.

U.S. tax law does permit some U.S. citizens and residents – those who are "living abroad" – to exclude income earned in other countries. (Internal Revenue Code §911.) But the maximum amount that may be excluded is just $80,000 (for 2002), so it doesn't provide much protection against double taxation to high income entertainers and athletes.

For this reason, *credits* for income taxes paid in other countries are more important to entertainers and athletes than *exemptions*. If performers receive credit against their own country's tax for the *full* amount of tax they are required to pay in other countries, that credit would be sufficient to avoid double taxation entirely. The United States, however, limits the amount of the credit that may be claimed to the amount the entertainer would have paid on that income in the U.S. (Internal Revenue Code §904.) Thus, if tax rates are higher in the country where services are performed than they are in the U.S. – as they are, for example, in Canada – the U.S. credit will be less than the taxes actually paid in the other country. When this is likely to happen, performers seek "tax indemnity" clauses in their employment contracts – clauses that require their employers to pay them additional compensation to make up for the extra tax they will be paying in the country where their services will be performed.

---

Citizens of countries other than the United States may become tax "residents" of the U.S. without any conscious effort on their part, even while they remain citizens and residents of their home countries. This is so, because foreignors may become U.S. "residents" for tax purposes – without obtaining or even seeking permanent residency visas ("green cards") – if they are physically present in the U.S. for a certain number of days per year. The exact number is determined by a formula in the Internal Revenue Code. Since the United States taxes the worldwide income of residents, careful schedule planning may be necessary for entertainers and athletes who come to the U.S. to perform, so they don't inadvertently become U.S. tax residents. Here is the formula.

---

**United States Internal Revenue Code §7701(b)**
**26 U.S.C. §7701(b)**

Definition of resident alien . . .
(1) In general . . .
(A) Resident alien
An alien individual shall be treated as a resident of the United States with respect to any calendar year if . . . :
(ii) Substantial presence test
Such individual meets the substantial presence test of paragraph (3). . .
(3) Substantial presence test
(A) In general
Except as otherwise provided in this paragraph, an individual meets the substantial presence test of this paragraph with respect to any calendar year (hereinafter in this subsection referred to as the "current year") if –
(i) Such individual was present in the United States on at least 31 days during the calendar year, and
(ii) the sum of the number of days on which such individual was present in the United States during the current year and the 2 preceding calendar years (when multiplied by the applicable multiplier determined under the following table) equals or exceeds 183 days:

| In the case of days in: | The applicable multiplier is: |
|---|---|
| Current year | 1 |
| 1st preceding year | 1/3 |
| 2nd preceding year | 1/6 |

(B) Exception where individual is present in the United States during less than one-half of current year and closer connection to foreign country is established
An individual shall not be treated as meeting the substantial presence test of this paragraph with respect to any current year if –
(i) such individual is present in the United States on fewer than 183 days during the current year, and
(ii) it is established that for the current year such individual has a tax home . . . in a foreign country and has a closer connection to such foreign country than to the United States. . . .
(5) Exempt individual defined
For purposes of this subsection –
(A) In general
An individual is an exempt individual for any day if, for such day, such individual is – . . .
(iv) a professional athlete who is temporarily in the United States to compete in a charitable sports event. . . .

**Hypothetical illustrating the U.S. tax "residency" formula**

Here is a hypothetical that illustrates how the Internal Revenue Code §7701(b) formula works:

Paula Player is a professional golfer. She is an Australian citizen and resident, but during the year 2000, she was in the United States for a total of 126 days, participating in prize-money golf tournaments.

During the year 2001, Player was in the United States for a total of 120 days, again participating in prize-money golf tournaments.

In 2002, she was in the United States for a total of 123 days. Once again, she participated in prize-money golf tournaments; but during 2002, she also played in a 3-day charity golf tournament.

Given these facts, Player will *not* be treated as a tax resident of the U.S. for the year 2002, because she was not in the U.S. for 183 days or more, as calculated using the Internal Revenue Code §7701(b) formula.

| In the case of days in: | Number of days in U.S. | The applicable multiplier is: | The number of "tax" days is: |
|---|---|---|---|
| 2002 | 123 | 1 *for 120 days* | 120 |
| | | 0 *for 3 days of charity golf* | 0 |
| 2001 | 120 | 1/3 | 40 |
| 2000 | 126 | 1/6 | 21 |
| | | Total tax days | 181 |

Note, however, that *if* Player had spent 3 days in 2002 resting by a swimming pool, instead of playing in a charity golf event, her total number of "tax" days in the U.S. that year would have been 123 (rather than 120). In that event, her total tax days in the U.S. would have been 184 (rather than 181); and she would have been considered a U.S. tax "resident" – even though she is a resident of Australia for all other purposes – unless she could establish that for 2002, she had a tax home in Australia and had a closer connection to Australia than she had to the United States.

This is important, because if she were considered a U.S. tax "resident," her *worldwide* income for 2002 would have been taxable in the U.S., including whatever income she earned in Australia.

# Chapter 3

# FINANCE

---

The international market is crucial to the success of the American film industry and highly significant to the television industry as well. More than half of the revenues generated by U.S. theatrical films are derived from foreign markets, and while less significant than is the case with theatrical films, revenues derived by American television producers from foreign sales are nonetheless significant too.

For independent producers (and, increasingly, for the major studios as well) production financing is usually based upon *pre-sales* and *split rights* deals in which foreign distributors commit themselves to specific payments in order to acquire licenses (in the case of pre-sales) or equity participation (in the case of split rights) in specific films (usually coupled with an arrangement in which domestic distribution rights are acquired by a U.S. major under a so-called "negative pickup" agreement).

Recognizing the significance of these arrangements, the U.S. government has instituted a Film Production Guarantee Program through the Export-Import Bank, under which lenders can obtain partial guarantees for loans to small- to medium-budget independent producers of projects aimed at the international market.

Foreign governments and producers have long chafed at American dominance of audiovisual markets, and they have responded by offering tax incentives and direct production subsidies for local productions (as well as by erecting barriers in such forms as quotas establishing minimum screen and/or broadcast time for locally-produced fare, as is discussed in Chapter 5).

In addition, many countries have instituted training programs, and development subsidies to new writers and directors, in order to broaden and deepen the pool of qualified local personnel in film and television production. There also has emerged a worldwide network of co-production treaties, which enable foreign countries to combine their individual tax incentives and subsidies with those of other foreign countries to back higher-budget productions which can (at least in theory) compete with U.S. productions for wider audiences

Such initiatives have enabled Canada to develop a thriving production capacity. The U.K. has been able to maintain and improve its production capacity. Australia, New Zealand, and Ireland have a significance in film production far in excess of their relative population weights. The dominance of foreign markets by U.S. films and television has been reduced. In France, for example, the share of box office revenues going to French films was 43% in the first seven months of 2001; a few years ago, it was under 10%. However, seen from the viewpoint of U.S. guilds and unions – especially in the production centers of Southern California, New York, North Carolina, Texas, Florida and Chicago – these achievements have been accomplished with "runaway productions."

This chapter looks at the legal aspects of these developments. As you will see, the following materials focus on the international financing of motion picture production. It does, because although most types of entertainment are *marketed* internationally, the movie business – more than any other – also *finances* the creation of its productions internationally.

---

## 3.1 PRE-SALE FINANCING

### Overview of Independent Film Production Lending
### Export-Import Bank of the United States (2001)

Unlike the production of major studio films, independent film production relies heavily on bank financing. This may be supplemented by equity contributed by investors and by foreign government economic incentives. Bank production loans rely primarily on payment of foreign distribution contracts concluded prior to the loan due date for their repayment. These distribution contracts give distributors the right to exploit the film (in various media) in their geographic territory for a fixed period of time. Such contracts stipulate a *minimum guaranteed amount* that the distributor agrees to pay *unconditionally* for the distribution rights. While there may be a down payment, most of the amount becomes due when the film negative is made available to the distributor, usually by delivery to a bonded laboratory in its country.

Producers use sales agents to obtain these distribution contracts, and then assign the contracts to the lender as collateral for repayment of the production loan. When the lender's determination of the collateral value of contracts already concluded is sufficient, the lender may commit to finance the film. In determining the collateral value, many lenders value contracts with distributors in developed countries at (or near) the *minimum guaranteed amounts* (less any down payments), while valuing contracts with distributors in developing countries at deep discounts to their *minimum guaranteed amounts*, or granting them no collateral value at all.

In many cases, the amount of the loan required (including reserves for interest accruals) will be greater than the collateral value of existing contracts. Despite this collateral "gap," lenders will often commit to the loan based on a sufficiently high estimate of *minimum guaranteed amounts* related to expected contract sales of unsold geographic territories. (Foreign sales agents are instrumental in providing these estimates.) Lenders charge an additional "gap finance fee" (e.g., 10% flat on the amount of the "gap") for assuming the risk that additional contracts may not materialize or cumulate to an amount necessary to close the collateral gap. Once the film is completed and delivered, the distributors are obligated to pay the balances due on their contracts. As a result of assignment of these contracts, payments will be made directly to the lender to repay the loan.

The three major risks involved in this specialized form of lending are:

- *Performance risk*: The risk that the film will not be completed on time or within budget and delivered to the distributors is usually assumed by a special entity known as a *completion guarantor*, which provides a completion guarantee for a fee based on the loan amount. The completion guarantor approves the budget, handles disbursements, and in case of potential delays or overruns, has the option of terminating production and paying off the loan, or paying the additional costs (including interest for completion delays) out-of-pocket.

- *Marketing risk*: The risk that the gap will not be filled prior to the loan due date by concluding contracts of sufficient value on the unsold territories is usually borne by the lender. The lender may lay off some of this risk by purchasing specialized insurance, if available, although we require the lender to retain at least one-half of this risk for its own account (Minimum Lender Retention) in order to maintain prudent lending practices.
- *Credit risk*: The risks that distributors will not pay the balances on their contracts once the film is made available to them due to commercial causes (e.g., bankruptcy or liquidity problems) or political events (e.g., inability to obtain U.S. dollars for payment) are risks that we are assume under our [Export-Import Bank] Film Production Guarantee. . . .

---

**Note on International Motion Picture Pre-Sale Financing Documents**

The process by which the production of motion pictures is financed internationally is complicated. It requires a tangled web of contracts among many separate companies. This note offers a brief explanation of these various contracts, illustrated by charts that show the relationships between the parties to each contract, as well as each contract's relationship with others that make up the entire package. Though this note explains the process step-by-step, in actual practice most of the necessary contracts must be agreed to – or at least signed – simultaneously. Since each party's consent is usually contingent upon the consent of the others, the process is far more dynamic (and dramatic) than this note can reveal.

As the Export-Import Bank reported (in the excerpt above), the central feature of independent movie financing is a bank loan. Figure 1 illustrates this by showing a "Producer" (that is, a movie production company) borrowing money from a "Lender" (usually a bank). The Lender provides the Producer with the "Cash" the Producer needs to produce its movie, in accordance with a schedule set forth in a "Loan Agreement" signed by both. (Unlike home and auto loans which are funded in full at the time they are made, movie production loans are funded in installments over time, while the movie is being produced and as production costs must be paid.)

Figure 1

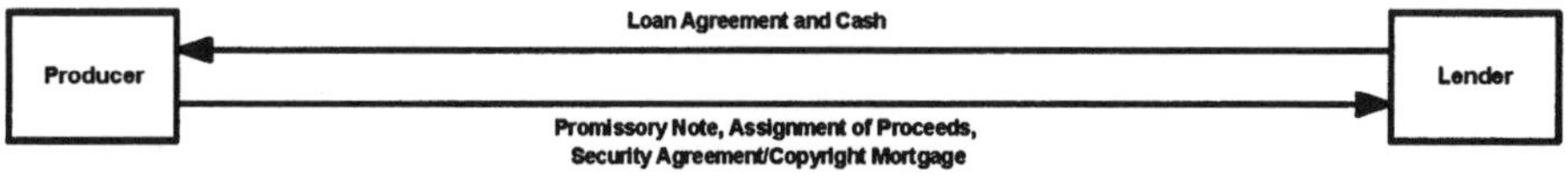

Producer

Loan Agreement and Cash

Promissory Note, Assignment of Proceeds,
Security Agreement/Copyright Mortgage

Lender

In return for the Lender's cash, the Producer provides the Lender with a "Promissory Note" – a short document by which the Producer promises to repay the amount loaned by a certain date along with interest at a specified rate.

While the Producer's promise to repay is of course necessary, it is not by itself sufficient. Banks need to have collateral for their loans. That collateral is the money the Producer will be entitled to receive from movie distributors, when the movie is completed. Thus, the Producer also provides the Lender with an "Assignment of Proceeds" – a document by which the Producer transfers to the Lender the Producer's right to receive money from distributors, when that money becomes due. The "Assignment of Proceeds" is, in other words, the document that instructs distributors to pay directly to the Lender whatever money those distributors would have paid to the Producer if the Producer had used its own money to finance the movie rather than money borrowed from the Lender.

The Producer also provides the Lender with a document known as a "Security Agreement" or a "Copyright Mortgage," so that if the Producer goes bankrupt before the loan is repaid, the Lender will have a legal right to be fully repaid *before* the Producer's other creditors may claim any money that may be due from distributors. (The proper use of this document is so important to Lenders that it is discussed in detail below.)

Since the Lender's collateral is the money that will be paid by distributors when the movie is completed, the Producer must enter into distribution agreements with at least some distributors, before the loan is made. Distribution agreements entered into *before* a movie is made are referred to as "Pre-Sale Agreements" (signifying that distribution rights were sold prior to the movie's completion). In their dealings with distributors, Producers are often represented by sales agents (the way authors are represented by literary agents). Sales agents are people who know distributors in many countries, who are experienced in negotiating Pre-Sale Agreements, and who are good at making sales.

Figure 2 illustrates Pre-Sale Agreements between a Producer and several Distributors. Each of these agreements authorizes a Distributor to distribute the Producer's movie in the Distributor's own country (or in a territory that includes several countries). Most important – for film finance purposes – each of these Pre-Sale Agreements requires the Distributor to pay an agreed-upon amount of money when the movie is completed and ready for distribution.

Figure 2

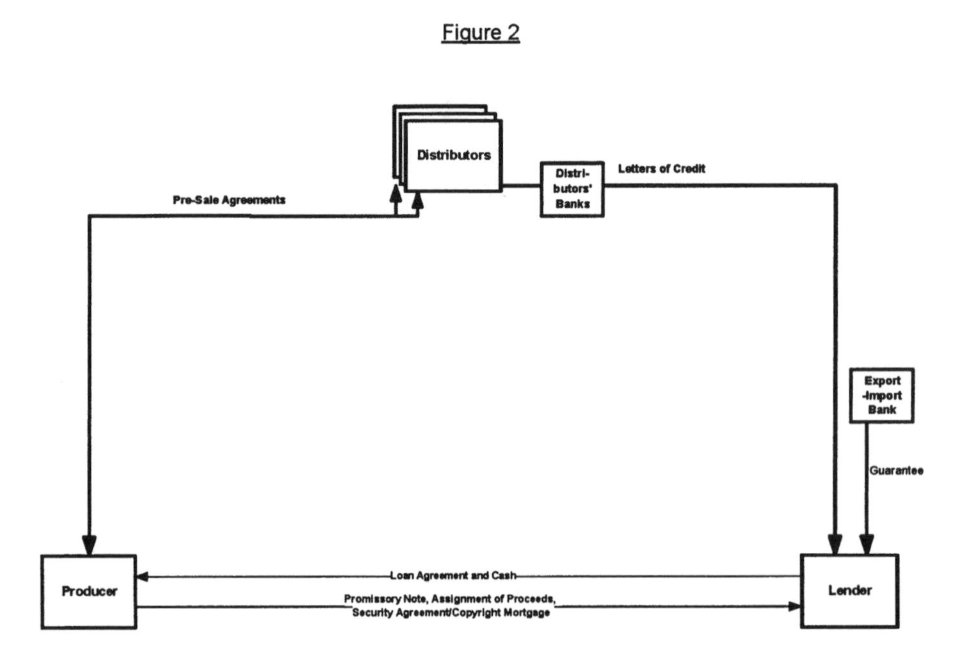

Producers' banks are sometimes unwilling to accept, as collateral, the contractual payment obligations of some Distributors, because some Distributors are not sufficiently credit-worthy. In those cases, Distributors may get Letters of Credit from their own banks. Letters of credit are guarantees by banks to pay money their customers are obligated to pay, if their customers fail to do so. In the motion picture finance business, this would mean that a Distributor's own bank would guarantee the Distributor's payment obligation, by issuing a letter of credit to the Producer's bank.

Some Distributors are unable to obtain Letters of Credit (or are unwilling do so, because they are not free). Until recently, that meant that the Producer's bank would not count distribution agreements with those Distributors as loan collateral at all. In 2001, however, the Export-Import Bank of the United States instituted a new Film Production Guarantee Program designed to fill that kind of collateral gap. (The Export-Import Bank program is described in the item that follows this Note.)

The chart entitled "The Going Rate" shows the amount of money a Producer might receive for the distribution rights to a theatrical film in each of more than 40 countries of the world. (The United States and Canada are not in "The Going Rate." On average, for an American movie, distribution rights for the U.S. and Canada together are likely to bring the Producer *roughly* the same amount as the rest of the world combined.)

Pre-Sale Agreements require Distributors to pay agreed-upon amounts when the Producer's movie is completed. If the movie is not completed, however, or is not completed by an agreed-upon date, Distributors are not obligated to pay anyone at all – not even the Lender. Nor will a Letter of Credit or an Export-Import Bank guarantee entitle the Lender to be repaid, if the movie isn't completed on time.

Thus, in order for the Lender to have real collateral, someone has to guaranty that the movie is finished on time. That responsibility is assumed by a Completion Bond Company. In return for a "premium" paid by the Producer, Completion Bond Companies agree that if a Producer doesn't complete the movie for any reason, the Completion Bond Company will do so itself at its own expense, or it will repay the Lender the amount owed by the Producer.

Completion Bond Companies (of which there are only a small number) employ people with significant experience in actual motion picture production. Before they enter into a "Completion Agreement" with a Producer or issue a "Completion Bond" to a Lender – illustrated in Figure 3 – they review the movie's budget and shooting schedule, and everything else that could affect the movie's on-time completition, to be certain the Producer's plans are realistic. Moreover, if the movie falls behind schedule, the "Completion Agreement" gives the Completion Bond Company the right to take over production in order to get the movie completed by the date required by the Pre-Sale Agreements.

If the Completion Bond Company has to spend its own money to get the movie finished, it is entitled to recoup the amount it spent, from whatever money the movie may earn from its distribution (just the way the Lender is entitled to be repaid the amount it loaned to the Producer). The Completion Agreement between the Producer and the Completion Bond Company so provides (just the way the Promissory Note and the Loan Agreement provide that the Lender is entitled to be repaid).

Completion Bond Companies are small, and have more expertise than capital. So a Completion Bond Company's promise to finish making a movie at its own expense, or to repay the Lender, may not give a Lender much comfort. (A Producer's failure to complete a movie could cost a Completition Bond Company

**The Going Rate**
**Estimated prices for all rights to theatrical films in various overseas territories**
**by Hy Hollinger**
**with the assistance of William Shields and Rob Aft**


| BUDGET | $750,000 to $1 million | $1 million to $3 million | $3 million to $6 million | $6 million to $12 million |
|---|---|---|---|---|
| **EUROPE** | | | | |
| France | $40 K - $75 K | $75 K - $150 K | $150 K - $300 K | $350 K - $1 M |
| Germany/Austria | $25 K - $50 K | $50 K - $200 K | $200 K - $600 K | $600 K - $1 M |
| Greece | $5 K - $10 K | $10 K - $15 K | $15 K - $25 K | $25 K - $50 K |
| Italy | $35K - $70 K | $70 K - $150 K | $150 K - $350 K | $350 K - $800 K |
| Netherlands | $25 K - $50 K | $50 K - $75 K | $75 K - $150 K | $150 K - $400 K |
| Portugal | $5 K - $15 K | $15 K - $30 K | $30 K - $60 K | $60 K - $90 K |
| Scandinavia | $25 K - $50 K | $50 K - $100 K | $100 K - $200 K | $200 K - $400 K |
| Spain | $40K - $90 K | $90 K - $175 K | $175 K - $400 K | $400 K - $800 K |
| United Kingdom | $50 K - $90 K | $90 K - $175 K | $175 K - $250 K | $250 K - $550 K |
| **ASIA/PACIFIC RIM** | | | | |
| Australia/ New Zealand | $20 K - $40 K | $ 40K - $75 K | $75 K - $100 K | $100 K - $350 K |
| Hong Kong | $10 K - $20 K | $20 K - $35 K | $35 K - $60 K | $60 K - $150 K |
| Indonesia | $5 K - $10 K | $10 K - $20 K | $20 K - $50 K | $50 K - $125 K |
| Japan | $50 K - $100 K | $100 K - $200 K | $200 K - $600 K | $600 K - $1.3 M |
| Malaysia | $5 K - $10 K | $10 K - $35 K | $35 K - $70 K | $70 K - $100 K |
| Philipines | $5 K - $15 K | $15 K - $30 K | $30 K - $50 K | $50 K - $90 K |
| Singapore | $10 K - $15 K | $15 K - $30 K | $30 K - $50 K | $50 K - $90 K |
| South Korea | $35 K - $75 K | $75 K - $150 K | $150 K - $300 K | $300 K - $550 K |
| Taiwan | $15 K - $40 K | $40 K - $100 K | $100 K - $175 K | $175 K - $300 K |
| **LATIN AMERICA** | | | | |
| Argentina/Paraguay/ Uruguay | $5 K - $10 K | $10 K - $20 K | $20 K - $40 K | $40 K - $75 K |
| Bolivia/Peru/Ecuador | $5 K - $10 K | $10 K - $20 K | $20 K - $50 K | $50 K - $75 K |
| Brazil | $15 K - $30 K | $30 K - $70 K | $70 K - $100 K | $100 K - $200 K |
| Chile | $5 K - $15 K | $15 K - $25 K | $25 K - $50 K | $50 K - $75 K |
| Colombia | $5 K - $10 K | $10 K - $20 K | $20 K - $40 K | $40 K - $75 K |
| Mexico | $25 K - $50 K | $50 K - $100 K | $100 K - $250 K | $250 K - $450 K |
| Venezuela | $5 K - $10 K | $10 K - $20 K | $20 K - $40 K | $40 K - $80 K |
| **EASTERN EUROPE** | | | | |
| Czech Republic/ Slovakia | $10 K - $20 K | $20 K - $35 K | $35 K - $80 K | $80 K - $120 K |
| Former Yugoslavia | $2 K - $10 K | $10 K - $15 K | $15 K - $25 K | $25 K - $50 K |
| Hungary | $10 K - $20 K | $20 K - $40 K | $40 K - $80 K | $80 K - $140 K |
| Poland | $5 K - $15 K | $15 K - $35 K | $35 K - $75 K | $75 K - $125 K |
| Russia | $10 K - $20 K | $20 K - $50 K | $50 K - $80 K | $80 K - $150 K |
| **OTHER** | | | | |
| China | $10 K - $20 K | $20 K - $40 K | $40 K - $60 K | $60 K - $150 K |
| India | $10 K - $15 K | $15 K - $30 K | $30 K - $60 K | $60 K - $125 K |
| Israel | $10 K - $15 K | $15 K - $25 K | $25 K - $40 K | $40 K - $70 K |
| Middle East | $10 K - $20 K | $20 K - $40 K | $40 K - $80 K | $80 K - $150 K |
| Pakistan | $4 K - $10 K | $10 K - $15 K | $15 K - $30 K | $30 K - $40 K |
| South Africa | $10 K - $20 K | $20 K - $30 K | $30 K - $50 K | $50 K - $100 K |
| Turkey | $10 K - $20 K | $20 K - $40 K | $40 K - $80 K | $80 K - $150 K |
| TOTALS | $571 K to $1.165 M | $1.165 M to $2.415 M | $2.415 M to $5.15 M | $5.15 M to $10.545 M |

more than $10 million; and bond companies issue bonds on several movies at once.) For this reason, Completion Bond Companies are backed by "Underwriters" – large insurance companies that can afford to pay claims of tens of millions of dollars.

An Underwriter could simply guaranty the obligations of a Completion Bond Company, and pay Lenders if the bond company could not. But Lenders have preferred to simplify the process by having contractual relationships with Underwriters directly. This is done with a "Cut-Through Endorsement" (also illustrated on Figure 3), which is simply a document by which the Underwriter assumes a direct obligation to repay the Lender, if the movie isn't completed on time.

Figure 3

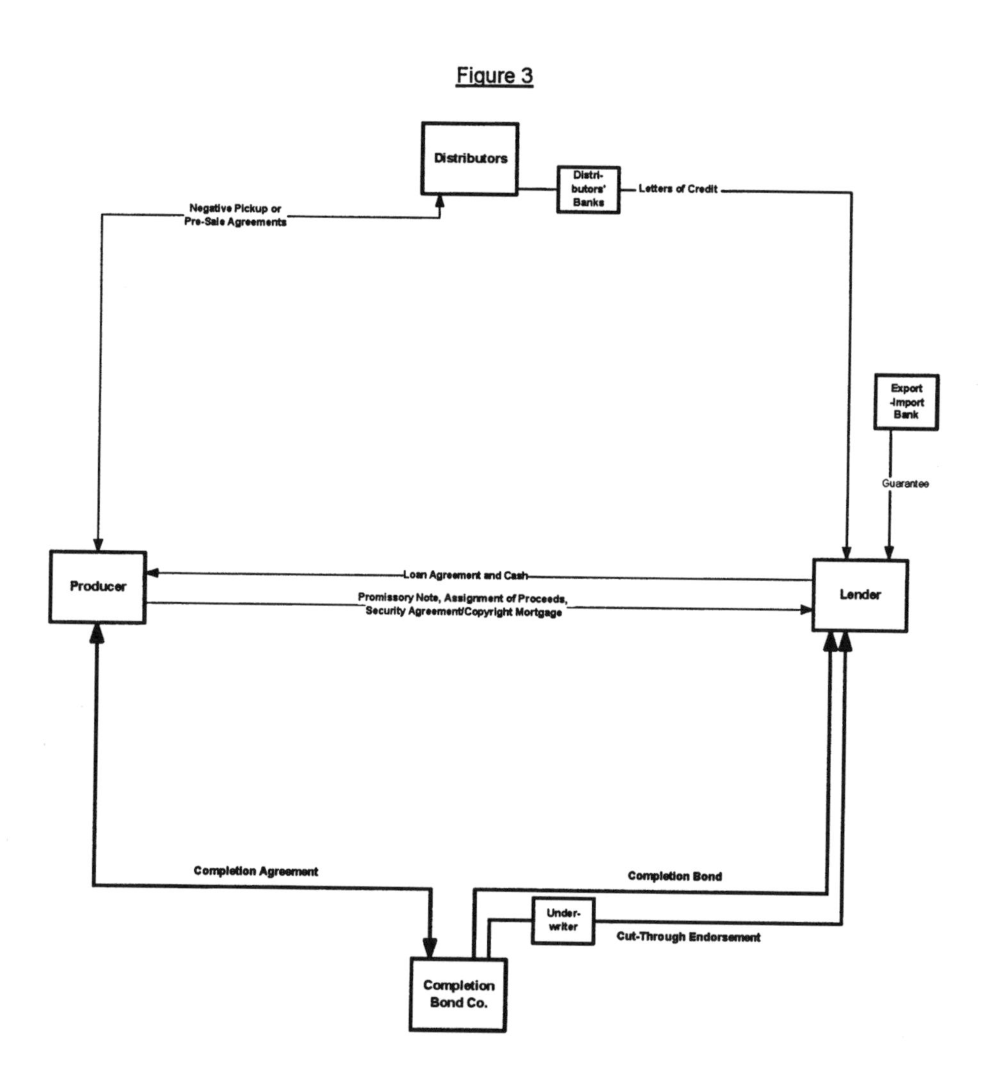

By now you have noticed that the package of financing documents already includes several sets of two-party agreements, and that three separate parties – the Lender, the Completion Bond Company and the Producer – are or may be entitled to payment from the movie's Distributors. The order in which they get paid is: Lender first, until the full amount of its loan to the Producer, plus interest, is repaid; Completion Bond Company second, if it had to spend money to get the movie finished, until the amount it spent plus interest is repaid; and Producer third, after the Lender and the Completion Bond Company are repaid.

The rights and obligations of all of the parties should be described identically in all of their two-party agreements. But just to be certain that they are – and that any discrepancies are corrected – another contract is entered into and signed by all of the parties. This multi-party contract is called an "Inter-Party Agreement," and it is illustrated in Figure 4.

Figure 4

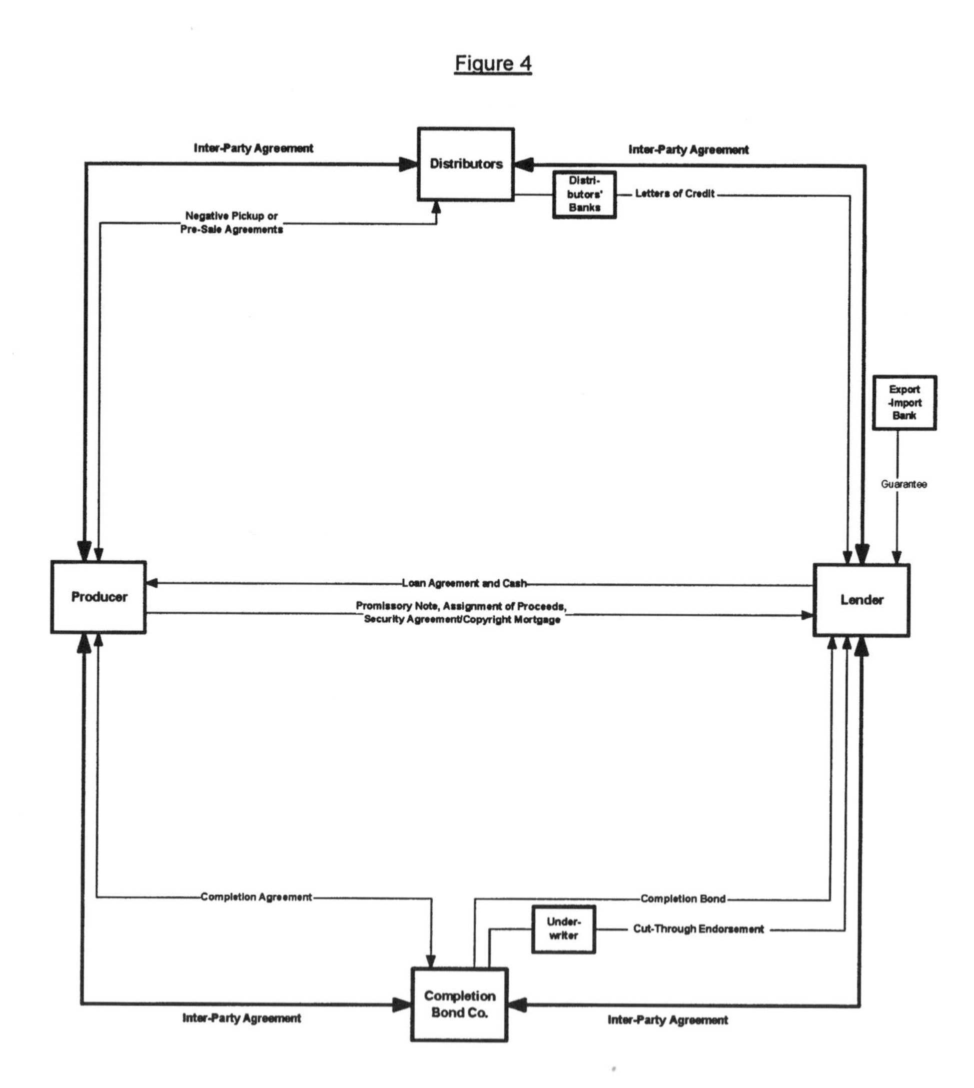

In the Inter-Party Agreement, the Distributors are formally notified that the Producer has assigned its right to receive payments to the Lender; and the Distributors agree to make those payments directly to the Lender until it has been repaid. Likewise, the Distributors are notified that the Completion Bond Company will be entitled to payments, if it is required to spend money getting the movie finished; and the Distributors agree to pay the Completion Bond Company, under those circumstances.

The Inter-Party Agreement also contains provisions by which the Completion Bond Company acknowledges that the Lender is entitled to be repaid first, and the Producer acknowledges that the Completion Bond Company is entitled to be repaid second, if it spends money getting the movie finished. The Lender and Completion Bond Company both agree that when they have been repaid, they will notify the Distributors so the Distributors may begin paying the Producer.

In short, the Inter-Party Agreement is a document that restates the rights and obligations of the parties – especially those rights and obligations between those who do not otherwise have two-party agreements between them.

Outside of the entertainment industry, it sometimes is said that "possession is 9/10s of the law." As you saw in Chapter 1, and will see again in Chapter 6, that is not so in the entertainment industry. In the entertainment industry, intangible legal rights are 9/10s – or more – of the law, and possession is rarely of legal significance. In the area of film finance, however, possession of a movie's negative (and the other physical elements that are used to make prints) is of practical significance – and therefore of legal significance as well.

As a movie is being shot, the undeveloped film is sent to a Film Laboratory to be processed; and when the movie is completed and edited, the lab makes prints for delivery to the Distributors. A dispute among the Producer, the Distributors, the Lenders and the Completion Bond Company – or just any two of them – could result in conflicting demands on the Film Laboratory for copies of prints (or possession of the negative). Of course, any exhibition, broadcast or sale of the movie, by a party not entitled to do so, would infringe its copyright. But infringements only give rise to expensive lawsuits. It's better, therefore, that the Film Laboratory be given clear instructions concerning *whose* demands it should follow. And that's what is done in the "Pledgeholder Agreement" illustrated in Figure 5.

The Pledgeholder Agreement provides that the Film Laboratory is to allow the Producer to have access to the negative, and is to make prints for delivery to the Distributors, *unless* the Lender notifies the Lab that the Producer has breached the Loan Agreement. If the Lender does notify the Lab that the Producer has breached, then the Lab is directed to follow the Lender's instructions and to provide the Distributors with the prints they are entitled to receive, but to ignore the demands of the Producer. Once the Lender is repaid, the Inter-Party Agreement authorizes the Lab to follow the instructions of the Producer and to continue to provide the Distributors with prints they are entitled to receive.

Earlier in this Note (in connection with its explanation of Figure 1), reference was made to the possibility that the Producer may go bankrupt before the Lender is fully repaid. If that were to happen, the Producer would owe money to many people and companies. But the Lender would want to have the legal right to be *fully* repaid *before* the Producer's other creditors are paid any money that may be due from Distributors. The Lender, in other words, would want to have priority, and in order to get that priority, the Lender would have to be a "secured party."

Figure 5

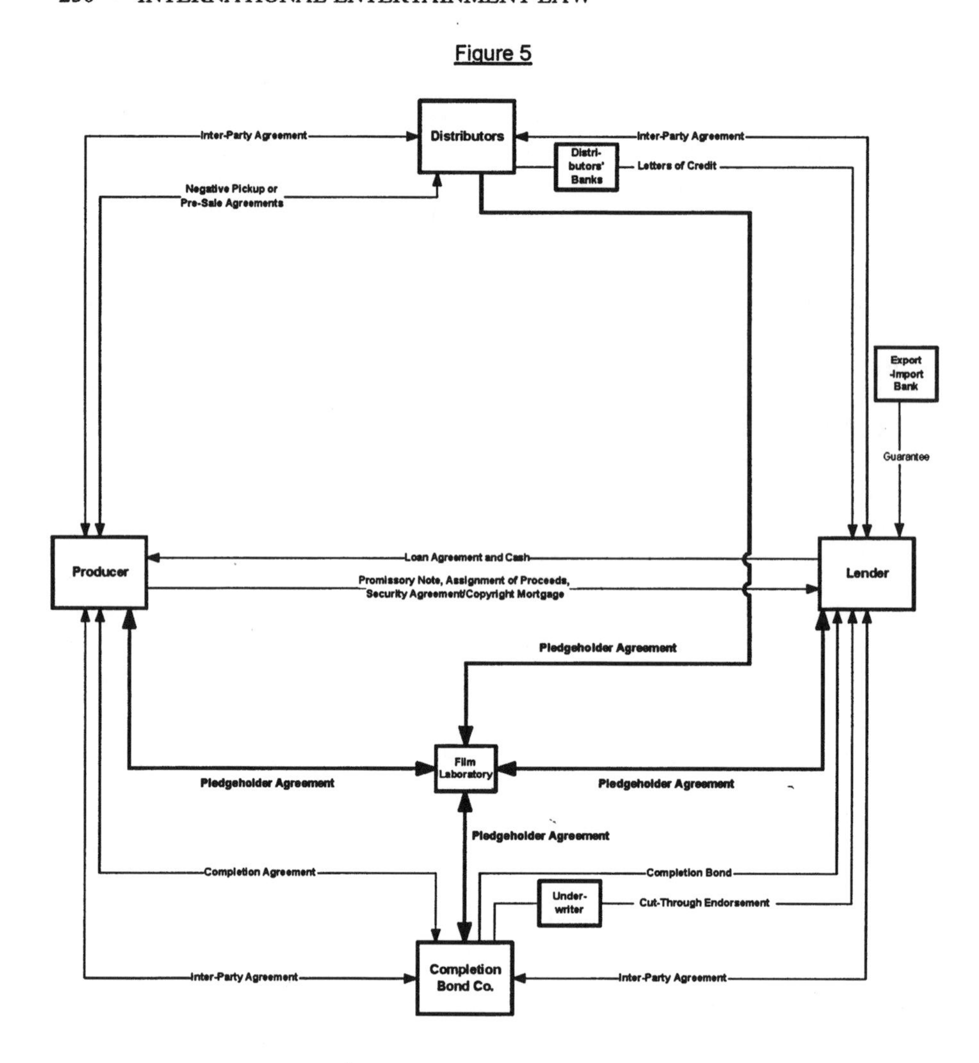


There is in fact, and in law, a way that Lenders may become secured parties and get the priority they desire. Indeed, if there weren't a way for Lenders to get priority, movie production loans simply wouldn't be made by banks. The procedures that Lenders must follow in order to become secured parties, and thus get the priority they require, is reviewed in some detail in the materials that begin with the *Peregrine Entertainment* case below. Those procedures are illustrated in Figure 6.

The Producer (or the Lender, acting on the Producer's behalf) must file a "Copyright Registration" certificate with the United States Copyright Office; and the Lender must record a "Security Agreement" or "Copyright Mortgage" in that Office as well. The Lender also should file a "Financing Statement" with the Secretary of State of the state in which the Producer has its headquarters. As you will read below, the benefits of filing a Financing Statement are unclear; but since the cost of doing so is minimal, cautious Lenders (and Lenders advised by cautious lawyers) will do so anyway. Finally, for reasons explored below, Lenders also should file a Security Agreement or Copyright Mortgage in the copyright (or commercial law) offices of other countries where the movie is being distributed.

Figure 6

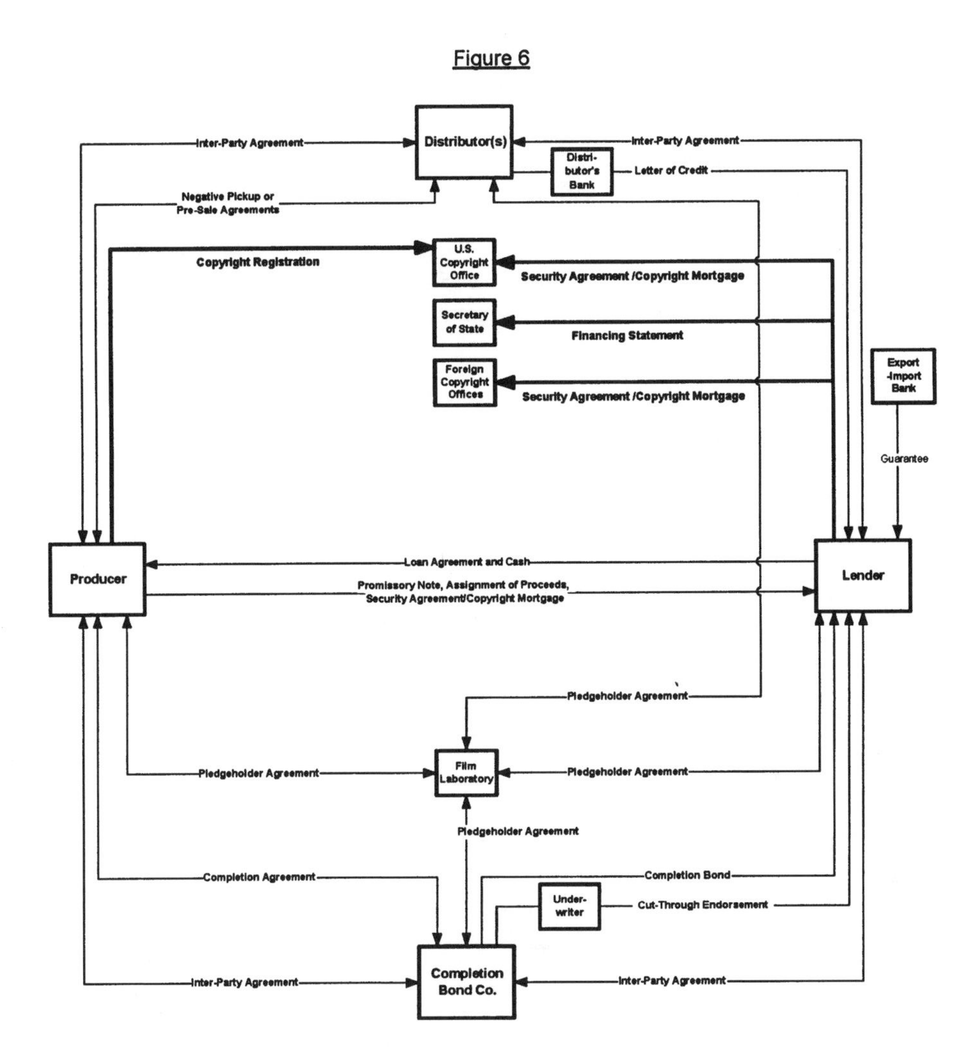


Finally, if the movie was written by a WGA member, directed by a DGA member, or featured actors who are members of SAG, residuals may become payable to those Guild members (as provided in their collective bargaining agreements). In that case, the Guilds may require the Producer to sign Security Agreements (or Copyright Mortgages) giving their members a priority – over the claims of the Producer and most of its other creditors – for the payment of those residuals. Those documents, and where the Guilds file them, are illustrated in Figure 7.

Two of the Producer's other creditors will insist on having priority over the Guilds: the Lender and the Completion Bond Company. Without that priority, the Lender will not agree to loan money to the Producer, and the Completion Bond Company will not agree to bond the Producer's movie. Since the movie could not be made – and Guild members would not be employed – without the loan and the bond, the Guilds will agree that their priority is subordinate to the priorities of the Lender and the Completion Bond Company. The Guilds will agree, in other words, that the Lender and Completion Bond Company are entitled to be repaid in full, before Guild members are entitled to their residuals. This agreement is documented by "Subordination and Assumption Agreements" which also are illustrated in Figure 7.

Figure 7

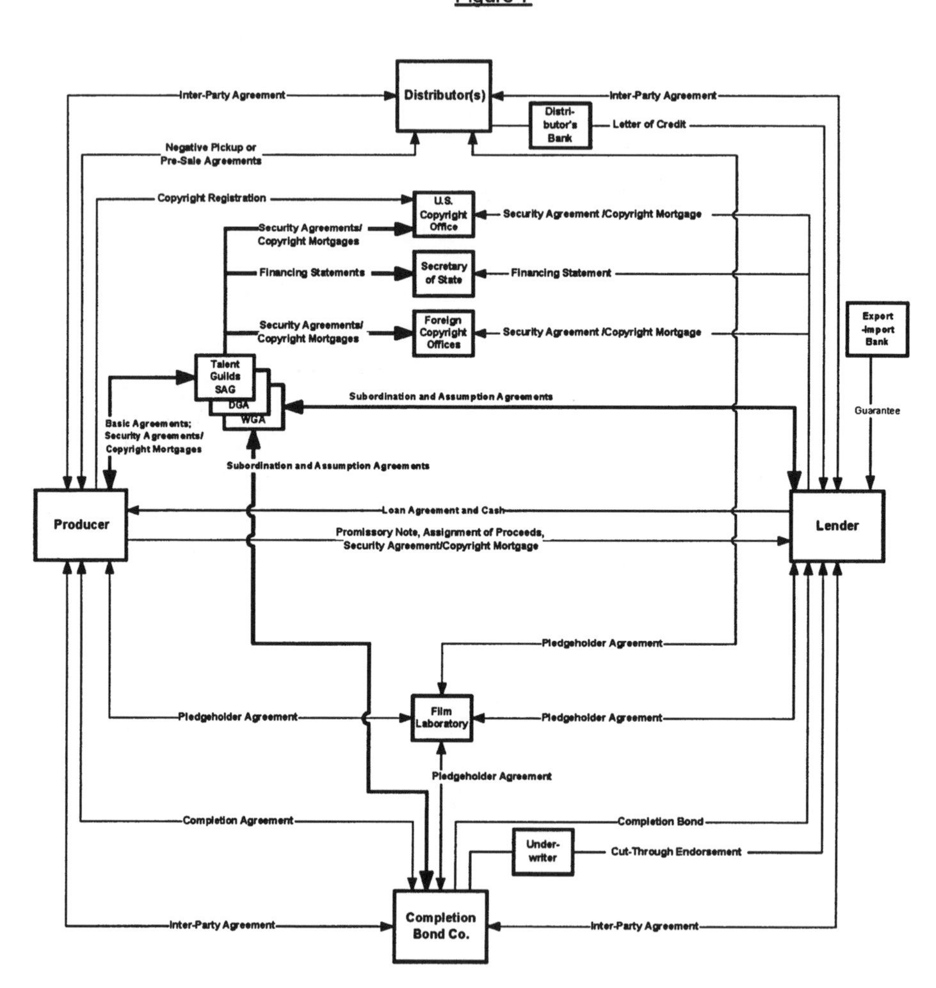

A complete picture of this "tangled web" of agreements is illustrated in Figure 8.

Figure 8

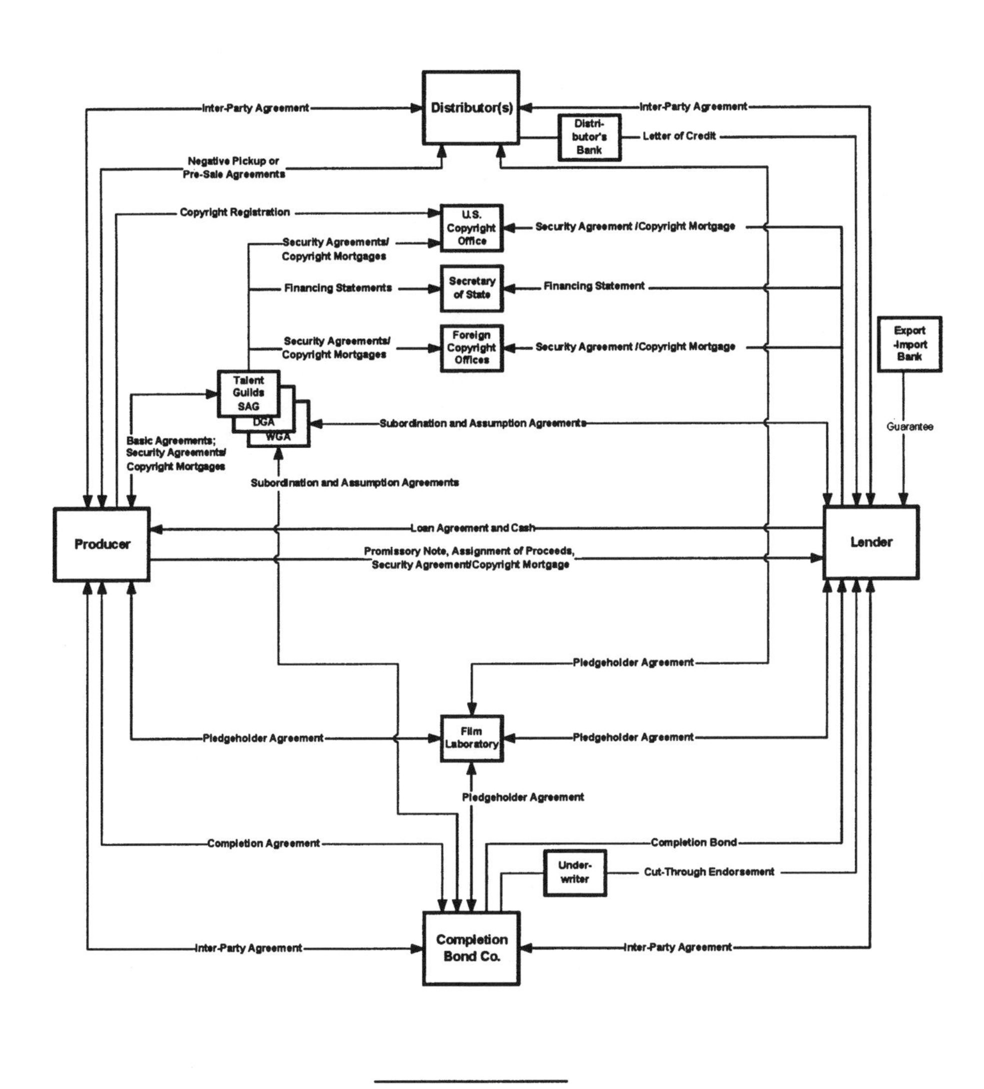

**Export-Import Bank of the United States**
**Film Production Guarantee Program (2001)**

*Why We Support Independent Film Production*

Our Film Production Guarantee Program is designed to support the financing of independent film production – a natural fit between our capabilities (assuming the credit risk of foreign buyers) and our mission (supporting U.S. jobs through exports).

*Our Capabilities:* Independent film production lending relies primarily on foreign (and occasionally, U.S.) distribution contracts, executed prior to, or during, the production period, as the sole source of repayment. We typically assume foreign credit risk related to export sales through insurance and guarantees. Our Film Production Guarantee assumes a portion of the payment risks associated with distribution contracts, thus encouraging the lender financing of independent films.

*Our Mission:* By supporting more independent film production, our Film Production Guarantees support the entertainment jobs maintained and created by the independent film sector:

According to one report, the independent film industry directly creates or maintains about 150,000 U.S. jobs annually with a combined payroll of $2.5 billion. Furthermore, according to a survey conducted by KPMG Peat Marwick, AFMA member companies generated over $2.3 billion in foreign sales in 1998.

The Film Production Guarantee Program also provides limited benefits in countering foreign government economic incentives designed to lure U.S. film production abroad ("runaway production"). Our guarantee is only available if at least half of the costs of production relate to U.S. content. [Most film production expenditures relate to personal services, such as acting, producing, directing and filming. To the extent that such services are performed by U.S. citizens or by permanent U.S. residents, they are deemed U.S. content for purposes of meeting the 50% U.S. content eligibility requirement.]

In some cases, taking advantage of foreign incentives might mean that the film would not meet our U.S. content requirements. In such cases, the producer would need to weigh the advantages of our Guarantee against the advantages of the foreign incentives. . . .

*Benefits for Producers*

- *Improved Access to Lender Finance*: Through our Film Production Guarantee, we assume a portion of the credit risks relating to your distribution contracts, thereby encouraging lenders to:
  - Finance films that they might otherwise refrain from financing due to concerns about receiving payment from overseas distributors or concerns about their exposure with certain distributors or geographic areas;
  - Commit to finance films sooner, rather than waiting for additional distribution contracts to be executed; and
  - Increase overall lending to the independent film sector, since the U.S. Government is effectively guaranteeing a portion of their exposure to international distributors.
- *Affordability*: We charge a flat 0.5% fee on the amount of the loan commitment. To the extent that our Guarantee effectively enhances the overall value of the initial basket of distribution contracts at the time of loan commitment, the Guarantee may save you money in "gap" financing fees. If the amount of the "gap" is reduced by only ½ of 1% of the total loan amount as a result of enhancement, the Guarantee can essential pay for itself.

*Benefits for Lenders*

- *Protect Yourself Against Credit Risk*: Our Film Production Guarantee effectively protects you against defaults by foreign (and U.S.) distributors, whether the cause of the default is due to commercial reasons (such as bankruptcy and liquidity problems) or political events (including inability of a foreign distributor to legally obtain U.S. dollars to make payment). Our Guarantee effectively covers up to 90% of nonpayment risk, depending upon our risk classification of the distributor.

    Under our Guarantee coverage, we *effectively* assume distributor credit risk. The amount that we assume with respect to individual distribution contracts depends upon our risk classification of the distributor as:

    - "Primary" distributors generally are those in developed countries. In this case we apply no discount and thus provide effective coverage of 100% x 90% = 90% (The "90%" multiplier relates to the fact that, in case of default by the borrower, the amount of our Guarantee is for 90% of the lesser of: (1) the sum of the discounted amounts due under the distribution contract collateral, or (2) the outstanding balance due under the loan);
    - "Secondary" distributors generally are those in developing countries, for which we are in possession of favorable credit information. In this case we apply a 35% discount and thus provide effective coverage of 65% x 90% = 58.5%; and
    - "Tertiary" distributors generally are those in developing countries, for which we have insufficient or adverse credit information. In this case we effectively provide no coverage – i.e., we completely discount the amounts due under contracts with "tertiary" distributors.

- *Exceed Exposure Limits, Leverage Your Capital*: Our Guarantee is backed by the full faith and credit of the U.S. Government. To the extent that we effectively assume a portion of the repayment risk on distribution contracts securing your loan, you are replacing distributor risk with U.S. Government risk. This may allow you to exceed (internal or external) exposure limits with respect to particular distributors, countries or geographic areas.
- *Reduce the "Gap" Element in Your Loans*: To the extent our Guarantee enhances the valuation of collateral backing your loan, you may be able to increase your valuation of the collateral, thereby reducing the need for "gap" finance. (Gap usually refers to the shortfall in collateral value as compared to the loan commitment amount.) In particular, we effectively cover 58.5% of the credit risks of our *secondary* distributor risk class. If you normally (without our Guarantee) value receivables from such distributors at a lesser amount, our Guarantee should enhance the value of this class of collateral. For illustration, we provide [the following] example of the benefits of collateral enhancement.

*Guarantee Fee v. Gap Fee Example:*

| | | |
|---|---|---|
| Loan Commitment: | $4,000,000 | |
| Our Guarantee Fee: | $ 20,000 | ($4,000,000 x 0.5%) |
| Distribution Contracts: | $3,492,000 | |

| | Face Amount | Lender Valuation | Percent Covered by Guarantee | Amount Covered by Guarantee |
|---|---|---|---|---|
| Primary contracts | $3,000,000 | 100% = $3,000,000 | 90% | $2,700,000 |
| Secondary contracts | $342,000 | 0% = 0 | 58.5% | $200,000 |
| Tertiary contracts | $150,000 | 0% = 0 | 0% | $0 |

*Case 1: No Guarantee*

| | | |
|---|---|---|
| Total Collateral Value ($3,000,000 + 0 + 0) | = | $3,000,000 |
| Gap Amount ($4,000,000 - $3,000,000) | = | $1,000,000 |
| Gap Fee @ 10% (assumed) | = | $ 100,000 |

*Case 2: With Guarantee*

| | | |
|---|---|---|
| Total Collateral Value ($3,000,000 + 200,000) | = | $3,200,000 |
| Gap Amount ($4,000,000 - $3,200,000) | = | $ 800,000 |
| Gap Fee @ 10% (assumed) | = | $ 80,000 |

Reduction in Gap Fee [$100,000 - $80,000] ($20,000) completely offsets our Guarantee Fee ($20,000) . . .

- *Letters-of-Credit*: In addition to straight production financing, our Guarantee documentation also allows for acquisition financing [by distributors, from producers] via letters-of-credit [provided by distribors' banks to producers' banks].
- *No Minimum or Maximum Loan Amount*: We place no minimum or maximum on the amounts of the loans we guarantee, although loans in excess of $15 million will take longer to process and will come under greater scrutiny as to why U.S. Government support is needed.
- *No Limit on Overseas Filming*: We do not restrict where filming takes place, but require that at least half of the budgeted expenditures of production qualify as U.S. content.

  Most film production expenditures relate to personal services, such as acting, producing, directing and filming. To the extent that such services are performed by U.S. citizens or by permanent U.S. residents, they are deemed U.S. content for purposes of meeting the 50% U.S. content eligibility requirement.
- *Flexible Payment Terms*: Our Guarantees provide lenders with the flexibility to extend the loan's due date up to a maximum of 240 days without our prior approval, but charge an additional fee for such extensions.
- *No Restrictions on Use of Foreign Government Incentives*: So long as the film meets our U.S. content requirements, we have no restrictions on taking advantage of foreign government financial incentives, such as production credits and tax incentives.
- *No Restriction on Gap Financing*: We place no restrictions on the use of "gap" financing, by which we mean the practice of making a loan commitment where the full commitment amount is greater than the value of the initial collateral. Our Guarantee coverage is limited to 90% of that portion of any loss that is

fully supported by our valuation of the collateral (i.e., the lesser of 90% of the outstanding balance or the Coverage Base Amount). Our requirement of Minimum Lender Retention, however, is designed to limit the imprudent use of "gap" financing.

- *Affordability*: We charge a flat 0.5% of the amount of your loan commitment, regardless of term. To the extent that our Guarantee allows you to increase your valuation of the collateral, thereby decreasing any "gap" amount, your borrower may be able to save on fees related to "gap" finance.
- *Quick Turnaround*: We anticipate a fairly rapid turnaround on requests for Guarantees on individual film production loans.
- *Flexible U.S. Content Definition*: In order to qualify as U.S. content for meeting our 50% minimum requirement, expenditures for personal services, such as acting, set building, filming, directing, *must* be performed by U.S. citizens or permanent legal residents. However, expenditures certain "key talent" that does not meet the U.S. citizen/resident requirement may still qualify as U.S. content, provided that the amounts are subject to U.S. federal income tax.

*Key Features*

- *Eligible Lenders:* Guaranteed lenders:
  - Must be financially viable and able to perform;
  - Must have substantial experience in lending secured primarily by international distribution contracts for the purpose of film and/or television programming production. Experience of management obtained at lenders other than the applicant can count towards this requirement;
  - Should have a distinct division or business unit set up primarily for the financing of film and/or television programming production; and
  - Can be U.S. or foreign, but must have at least a U.S. presence.

  We evaluate lenders' eligibility on the basis of information submitted in the *Lender Profile*.
- *Eligible Films*: Films must be:
  - *Feature-length theatrical motion pictures* (i.e., episodic television programs or non-feature length motion pictures do not qualify) intended for exploitation worldwide through various motion picture distributors.
  - *Independent in nature*, which means:
    - Not produced by a Major Studio ("Major Studio" means a so-called "major" (as such term is commonly understood in the Los Angeles, California motion picture and television industry) producer or distributor of motion pictures and/or television programs or any other Person who directly or indirectly controls, is controlled by, or is under common control with such "major" producer or distributor.):
    - For which less than 50% of the Production Budget is being furnished or guaranteed, directly or indirectly, by a Major Studio;
    - For which less than 50% of the aggregate receivables are due from Major Studios (so long as the 50% limit is not violated, the borrower can enter into contracts with Major Studios or distributors owned or controlled by Major Studios);
  - *Meet our U.S. Content Requirements*: At least 50% of the budgeted production expenditures should qualify as U.S. content.

    U.S. Content is defined as:
    - All budgeted expenditures for the purchase or rental of products, materials, supplies and other goods which are of U.S. origin and manufacture;

- All budgeted expenditures for personal services (such as services of writers, directors, cast, producers, special effects personnel, administrative personnel, animators, cameramen, consultants, attorneys or accountants):
  - To the extent such services are to be performed by an individual who is a U.S. citizen or lawful permanent resident, or
  - In the case of key talent (i.e., lead actor, director, writer, music composer or director of photography) services performed by an individual who is not a U.S. citizen or lawful permanent resident, to the extent such expenditures when paid to such individual are subject to U.S. federal income taxation; and
- All budgeted expenditures for services other than personal services (such as insurance, completion guarantee, transportation and payroll services) payable to a Person (excluding natural persons) legally organized and domiciled in the U.S.

There is no restriction on the geographic (U.S. or overseas) location of film production or the duration of film production in any particular site. The borrower must fill out a *U.S. Content Certificate*. Provided that the film meets our U.S. content requirements, there are no restrictions limiting the borrower from taking advantage of foreign government incentives, such as production credits and tax incentives.

- *Export-Oriented*: At least 50% of the value of the film receivables are derived from the licensing and distribution of the film in territories outside the United States.

- *Eligible Borrowers* are single purpose, bankruptcy-remote entities organized to produce a single film.
- *Type of Financing:* We will consider both:
  - Direct disbursements loans involving a completion guarantee; and
  - Film acquisition loans where the lender issues a letter-of-credit on behalf of the borrower for the benefit of a licensor or supplier of the borrower.
- *Coverage Base Schedule/Coverage Base Amount:* The Coverage Base Schedule (Annex A to the Loan Authorization Agreement) is a document that lists all of the film's distribution contracts, the "eligible" receivable amount of each contract and the discount factor (Applicable Percentages) that we have agreed to apply in calculating the Coverage Base Amount.
  - *Eligible Receivables* arise from distribution contracts:
    - That are payable in the U. S. in U.S. Dollars;
    - In which the lender has a perfected first priority lien; and
    - For which the payment that is due (or which will become due) is not subject to any condition except delivery of the film and/or passage of time, less all taxes and any allowances, credits and offsets required, allowed or permitted to be deducted.

    Receivables that do not meet the above qualifications are "ineligible" and not used in determining the Coverage Base Amount (see next section). Receivables that will become due after the distributor picks-up the negative, will generally be excluded from the Coverage Base Amount.
  - *Applicable Percentages* are the discount factors applied to the Eligible Receivables of any distribution contract. In general we determine the Applicable Percentage for receivables for a particular distributor when

executing the Coverage Base Schedule:

  - *Primary* distributors generally are those in developed countries. The Applicable Percentage is 100% (i.e., no discount);
  - *Secondary* distributors generally are those in developing countries, for which we are in possession of favorable credit information. The Applicable Percentage is 65% (i.e., 35% discount); and
  - *Tertiary* distributors generally are those in developing countries, for which we have insufficient or adverse credit information. The Applicable Percentage is 0% (i.e., 100% discount).

- *Modified Coverage Base Schedules:* From time-to-time the Coverage Base Schedule is updated to add new contracts that have been executed with respect to a film and/or to show changes in the receivable amounts.
- *Coverage Base Amount:* Whereas in traditional asset-based lending, the lender uses a borrowing base to control disbursements and ensure that the outstanding loan balance is fully supported by the collateral, the Collateral Base Schedule serves neither of these purposes. On the contrary, the primary purpose of the Collateral Base Schedule is to calculate the Collateral Base Amount, which helps determine our principal liability under the Guarantee. This amount is simply the discounted value of the Eligible Receivable Amounts using the relevant Applicable Percentages. The Collateral Base Amount (and our Guarantee liability) grows as new contracts are executed and added to (new versions of) the Collateral Base Schedule.

- *Amount Guaranteed:* Our principal liability under the Guarantee will usually be 90% of the Coverage Base Amount, but never more than 90% of the outstanding loan balance. Our interest liability is the unpaid interest on the principal liability amount calculated at the normal interest rate (excluding any penalty rate) to the date we pay your claim. In general, our principal liability is 90% of the lesser of the following:
  - Loan commitment amount – this puts an absolute limit on our exposure;
  - The outstanding principal balance on the claim date – i.e., our maximum coverage of a loss is 90%; or
  - Coverage Base Amount -- if the outstanding loan balance exceeds the Coverage Base Amount (i.e., the collateral is insufficient to support the full amount outstanding), our principal liability is limited to 90% of the Coverage Base Amount.
- *Gap Financing*: We place no restrictions on the usage of "gap" financing techniques, since our Guarantee does not cover outstanding loan balances in excess of the Coverage Base Amount. For example, if the borrower defaults on a $1 million loan that has a $500,000 outstanding unpaid balance and a Collateral Base Amount at the time of default of $300,000, we would pay a claim of 90% of the $300,000, plus covered interest, but would not pay any claim related to the $200,000 excess of the outstanding balance over the Coverage Base Amount.
- *Minimum Lender Retention (MLR)* is the amount that we require the lender to remain at-risk with respect to the loan amount outstanding.
  - If the outstanding loan balance is less than or equal to the Collateral Base Amount (i.e., the amount outstanding is completely supported by the collateral), the MLR is 10% of the outstanding loan balance.
  - If the outstanding loan balance exceeds the Collateral Base Amount (i.e., there is insufficient collateral to completely support the amount

outstanding), the MLR is:

  - 10% of the Coverage Base Amount (i.e., the portion of the Coverage Base Amount not covered by our Guarantee), plus
  - 50% of the excess of the loan balance over the Coverage Base Amount (i.e., one- half of the collateral "gap").

- *Maturity Date Extensions:* You can extend the loan maturity date without our approval, so long as:
  - The total extensions cannot exceed 240 days;
  - You pay the additional Facility Fee; and
  - Extensions exceeding 120 days in the aggregate must be related to delivery date extensions requested by the Completion Guarantor and the Completion Guarantor must be obligated to pay the interest accruing during such extensions.
- *Facility Fee:* Our compensation for providing a Guarantee is 0.5% of the Loan Commitment Amount and is payable up-front. If the loan maturity date is extended or the Commitment Amount is increased, additional Facility Fee is due as follows:
  - Maturity date extension: 0.5% x Commitment Amount x Extension Period (as a fraction of a year)
  - Commitment Amount Increase: 0.5% x Amount of Increase
- *Participations:* You may participate, transfer, assign, or sell your interests in the loan to other lenders provided that you remain responsible for your obligations under the Program, including the filing of claims and remaining at-risk for the Minimum Lender Retention.
- *Amount Limitations:* There are no minimum or maximum sized loan facilities, although requests for Guarantees of loan commitments in excess of $15 million will take longer to process and be subject to greater scrutiny as to the need for U.S. Government support. At this time, there are no aggregate limits on Program activity or individual lender activity under the Program.
- *Claims:* Only the guaranteed lender can file a claim. This must be done no earlier than 30 days after date of default and no later than 120 days after date of default. Claim documentation required includes such items as copies of:
  - Written demand on the borrower and all distributors still owing;
  - All loan documents including all lien perfection filings;
  - Evidence that film was delivered to each distributor still owing;
  - Certification that you have complied with all lender obligations;
  - Executed copies of each contract with a balance owing;
  - Records of disbursements and application of payments;
  - Certification of retention the Minimum Lender Retention.

  We may request that you execute an Assignment Agreement to us as a condition of claim payment. In general, we pay properly-documented claims within 30 days of receipt.
- *Recoveries:* Should there be any recoveries from any source, we receive 90% (and you receive 10%) of recoveries (net of any recovery expenses) until we have fully recovered our claim payment. After being made whole with respect to our claim payment, any excess recoveries revert to the lender. . . .

---

**In re Peregrine Entertainment, Ltd.**
**116 Bankr 194 (C.D.Cal. 1990)**

Alex Kozinski, United States Circuit Judge [stting by designation]

This appeal from a decision of the bankruptcy court raises an issue never before confronted by a federal court in a published opinion: Is a security interest in a copyright perfected by an appropriate filing with the United States Copyright Office or by a UCC-1 financing statement filed with the relevant secretary of state?

I

National Peregrine, Inc. (NPI) is a Chapter 11 debtor in possession whose principal assets are a library of copyrights, distribution rights and licenses to approximately 145 films, and accounts receivable arising from the licensing of these films to various programmers. NPI claims to have an outright assignment of some of the copyrights; as for the others, NPI claims it has an exclusive license to distribute in a certain territory, or for a certain period of time.

In June 1985, Capitol Federal Savings and Loan Association of Denver (Cap Fed) extended to . . . NPI . . . a six million dollar line of credit secured by what is now NPI's film library. Both the security agreement and the UCC-1 financing statements filed by Cap Fed describe the collateral as "all inventory consisting of films and all accounts, contract rights, chattel paper, general intangibles, instruments, equipment, and documents related to such inventory, now owned or hereafter acquired by the Debtor." Although Cap Fed filed its UCC-1 financing statements in California, Colorado and Utah, it did not record its security interest in the United States Copyright Office.

NPI filed a voluntary petition for bankruptcy on January 30, 1989. On April 6, 1989, NPI filed an amended complaint against Cap Fed, contending that the bank's security interest in the copyrights to the films in NPI's library and in the accounts receivable generated by their distribution were unperfected because Cap Fed failed to record its security interest with the Copyright Office. NPI claimed that, as a debtor in possession, it had a judicial lien on all assets in the bankruptcy estate, including the copyrights and receivables. Armed with this lien, it sought to avoid, recover and preserve Cap Fed's supposedly unperfected security interest for the benefit of the estate.

The parties filed cross-motions for partial summary judgment on the question of whether Cap Fed had a valid security interest in the NPI film library. The bankruptcy court held for Cap Fed. NPI appeals.

II

*A. Where to File*

The Copyright Act provides that "any transfer of copyright ownership or other document pertaining to a copyright" may be recorded in the United States Copyright Office. A "transfer" under the Act includes any "mortgage" or "hypothecation of a copyright," whether "in whole or in part" and "by any means of conveyance or by operation of law." The terms "mortgage" and "hypothecation" include a pledge of property as security or collateral for a debt. . . .

It is clear from the preceding that an agreement granting a creditor a security interest in a copyright may be recorded in the Copyright Office. Likewise, because a copyright entitles the holder to receive all income derived from the display of the creative work, an agreement creating a security interest in the receivables generated by a copyright may also be recorded in the Copyright Office. Thus, Cap Fed's security interest *could* have been recorded in the Copyright Office; the parties seem to agree on this much.

The question is, does the UCC provide a parallel method of perfecting a security interest in a copyright? One can answer this question by reference to either federal or state law; both inquiries lead to the same conclusion.

1. Even in the absence of express language, federal regulation will preempt state law if it is so pervasive as to indicate that "Congress left no room for supplementary state regulation," or if "the federal interest is so dominant that the federal system will be assumed to preclude enforcement of state laws on the same subject." Here, the comprehensive scope of the federal Copyright Act's recording provisions, along with the unique federal interests they implicate, support the view that federal law preempts state methods of perfecting security interests in copyrights and related accounts receivable.

The federal copyright laws ensure "predictability and certainty of copyright ownership," "promote national uniformity" and "avoid the practical difficulties of determining and enforcing an author's rights under the differing laws and in the separate courts of the various States."[T]he Copyright Act establishes a uniform method for recording security interests in copyrights. A secured creditor need only file in the Copyright Office in order to give "all persons constructive notice of the facts stated in the recorded document." Likewise, an interested third party need only search the indices maintained by the Copyright Office to determine whether a particular copyright is encumbered. . . .

If state methods of perfection were valid, a third party (such as a potential purchaser of the copyright) who wanted to learn of any encumbrances thereon would have to check not merely the indices of the U.S. Copyright Office, but also the indices of any relevant secretary of state. Because copyrights are incorporeal – they have no fixed situs – a number of state authorities could be relevant. Thus, interested third parties could never be entirely sure that all relevant jurisdictions have been searched. This possibility, together with the expense and delay of conducting searches in a variety of jurisdictions, could hinder the purchase and sale of copyrights, frustrating Congress's policy that copyrights be readily transferable in commerce. . . .

Moreover, . . . the Copyright Act establishes its own scheme for determining priority between conflicting transferees, one that differs in certain respects from that of Article Nine. . . .

Because the Copyright Act and Article Nine create different priority schemes, there will be occasions when different results will be reached depending on which scheme was employed. The availability of filing under the UCC would thus undermine the priority scheme established by Congress with respect to copyrights. This type of direct interference with the operation of federal law weighs heavily in favor of preemption. . . .

2. State law leads to the same conclusion. Article Nine of the Uniform Commercial Code establishes a comprehensive scheme for the regulation of security interests in personal property and fixtures. . . .

For most items of personal property, Article Nine provides that security interests must be perfected by filing with the office of the secretary of state in which the debtor is located. Such filing, however, is not "necessary or effective to perfect a security interest in property subject to . . . . [a] statute or treaty of the United States which provides for a national or international registration . . . . or which specifies a place of filing different from that specified in [Article Nine] for filing of the security interest."

When a national system for recording security interests exists, the Code treats compliance with that system as "equivalent to the filing of a financing statement under [Article Nine,] and a security interest in property subject to the statute or treaty can be perfected only by compliance therewith . . . ."

As discussed above, section 205(a) of the Copyright Act clearly does establish a national system for recording transfers of copyright interests, and it specifies a place of filing different from that provided in Article Nine. Recording in the Copyright Office gives nationwide, constructive notice to third parties of the recorded encumbrance. . . .

The court therefore concludes that the Copyright Act provides for national registration and "specifies a place of filing different from that specified in [Article Nine] for filing of the security interest." Recording in the U.S. Copyright Office, rather than filing a financing statement under Article Nine, is the proper method for perfecting a security interest in a copyright. . . .

*B. Effect of Failing to Record with the Copyright Office*

Having concluded that Cap Fed should have, but did not, record its security interest with the Copyright Office, the court must next determine whether NPI as a debtor in possession can subordinate Cap Fed's interest and recover it for the benefit of the bankruptcy estate. . . .

NPI may . . . avoid Cap Fed's interest and preserve it for the benefit of the bankruptcy estate.

*Conclusion*

The judgment of the bankruptcy court is reversed. The case is ordered remanded for a determination of which movies in NPI's library are the subject of valid copyrights. The court shall then determine the status of Cap Fed's security interest in the movies and the debtor's other property. To the extent that interest is unperfected, the court shall permit NPI to exercise its avoidance powers under the Bankruptcy Code.

---

**In re AEG Acquisition Corp.**
**127 Bankr. 34 (C.D.Cal.Bankr.Ct. 1991)**

Samuel L. Bufford, United States Bankruptcy Judge

*I. Introduction*

This preference and fraudulent conveyance action presents the issue of whether the contract between the parties, relating to distribution rights in three motion picture films, is an option contract or a conditional sales contract. If it is a conditional sales contract, the Court must determine whether the creditor has duly perfected its security interest in the three films at issue.

The Court finds that the agreement is a conditional sales contract, and that the creditor has duly perfected its interest in only one of the three films. The Court further finds that the two foreign films must be registered as a condition of perfecting a security interest in them. . . .

*II. Facts*

AEG Acquisition Corp. ("AEG") is a Chapter 11 debtor whose principal asset is a library of copyrights, distribution rights and licenses to more than 100 motion picture films.

In 1987 Atlantic Entertainment Group, Inc. ("Atlantic"), predecessor to the debtor, entered into three distribution agreements with Zenith Productions, Ltd. ("Zenith"). These distribution agreements relate to three motion pictures entitled "Patty Hearst," "For Queen and Country," and "The Wolves of Willoughby Chase." Zenith delivered the films to Atlantic in 1987.

Atlantic failed to pay the guaranteed minimum advances under the original agreements. . . .

[Subsequent] . . . negotiations resulted in a . . . Restructuring Agreement dated February 7, 1989 ("the Agreement"). . . .

The Agreement provided for AEG to reacquire the distribution rights to the three motion pictures for $6 million. . . .

AEG also gave Zenith a security agreement that granted a security interest in the motion pictures, and a UCC-1 financing statement, which Zenith filed in California, Indiana and New York. Zenith additionally recorded a copyright mortgage for each of the films with the United States Copyright Office on March 29, 1989. Shortly thereafter, on April 12, 1989, Zenith filed a certificate of copyright registration with respect to "Patty Hearst". Zenith claims that it was unnecessary to register the other two films, because they are foreign works exempt from registration pursuant to the "Berne Convention Act."

AEG made two payments to Zenith under the agreement: $250,000 on April 12 and $1.81 million on May 10, 1989. On July 28, 1989 AEG filed its chapter 11 petition. AEG subsequently filed this adversary proceeding to recover the $2,060,000 from Zenith as both preferences and fraudulent transfers pursuant to Bankruptcy Code §§ 547 and 548. . . .

*III. Analysis*

*A. Preferential Transfer*

AEG seeks to recover, as avoidable preferential transfers, the April and May payments to Zenith by AEG. Bankruptcy Code § 547(b) authorizes the avoidance of a preferential transfer. The elements of a preferential transfer are:

(1) a transfer of an interest of the debtor in property;
(2) to or for the benefit of a creditor;
(3) For or on account of an antecedent debt owed by the debtor before such transfer was made;
(4) made while the debtor was insolvent;
(5) made (A) on or within 90 days before the date of the filing of the petition; or (B) between 90 days and one year before the date of the filing of the petition, if such creditor at the time of such transfer was an insider; and
(6) that enables the creditor to receive more than the creditor would receive if (A) the case were a case under chapter 7; (B) the transfer had not been made; and (C) such creditor received payment of such debt to the extent permitted by the Bankruptcy Code.

Zenith . . . contends that it is secured, at least to the extent of the payments, and would have received as much under Chapter 7 as it has received from AEG. . . .

*3. Perfection*

Because the Agreement is a conditional sales contract, it is necessary to determine whether Zenith has a perfected security interest in each of the three films.[4] [n4 Zenith argues that its security interest is not limited to the copyright in the three films, but extends also to the prints of the films, contract and distribution rights, and to accounts relating thereto. The Court has not been made aware of any such interests that are not integral to the copyrights themselves. . . . ] The Debtor's hypothetical lien creditor status entitles it to prevail over the holder of an unperfected security interest under Bankruptcy Code § 544(a). The Court finds that Zenith perfected its interest in "Patty Hearst," but not in the two foreign works, "For Queen and Country" and "The Wolves of Willoughby Chase."

A security interest in a film is perfected under the United States Copyright Act, and not under the Uniform Commercial Code. *In re Peregrine Entertainment, Ltd.* The Copyright Act preempts the UCC for security interests in films. Thus Zenith's filing of its UCC-1 gave it no assistance in perfecting its security interest in these motion pictures.

Perfection of a security interest in a motion picture, as in any copyright, requires two steps: the film must be registered with the United States Copyright Office, and the security interest must be recorded in the same office. Registration of a copyright is accomplished by the submission of an application to the copyright office together with a nominal filing fee and one or two copies of the work to be copyrighted.

Recordation of a security interest is also accomplished through the Copyright Office. The Copyright Act states, "any transfer of copyright ownership or other document pertaining to a copyright" may be recorded in the United States Copyright Office. Section 205(c) further provides that recordation acts as constructive notice of the facts stated in the document if the document specifies the work and if registration has been made for the work. The first to execute in compliance with § 205(c) prevails when conflicting transfers arise. The filing of a copyright mortgage with the United States Copyright Office constitutes perfection of the security interest as long as an underlying registration is also filed with the Office.

*a. "Patty Hearst"*

It is undisputed that Zenith registered the film "Patty Hearst" on April 12, 1989, which was more than 90 days before the filing of this bankruptcy case. Zenith recorded its mortgage on March 29, 1989, 14 days prior to the registration.[8] [n8 Neither party has raised the issue of whether recordation of a copyright mortgage is valid if it is recorded before the registration of the underlying copyright. The Court notes that the recordation statute is modeled on real property recording acts, and that it is a "race-notice" type of statute. A mortgage on real property that is recorded outside of the chain of title would not be effective. The Court does not address this issue for copyrights.] Zenith's security interest in "Patty Hearst" was thus perfected at the time of the bankruptcy filing, and outside the 90-day preference period.

AEG has not attacked this registration and recordation as a preference to an insider. Thus the Court assumes that Zenith's security interest in "Patty Hearst" is valid.

*b. Foreign films. . .*

Zenith argues that the two foreign films are governed by the "Berne Convention Act," and that registration of the underlying works is not a prerequisite to perfection of its security interests. Presumably Zenith intends to refer to the Berne Convention for the Protection of Literary and Artistic Works (Paris Text, 1971) ("Berne Convention"). The Court disagrees and concludes that registration is required to perfect a security interest in a foreign film.

One of the principal substantive provisions of the Berne Convention is its provision that authors enjoy the same protection in any member country as the nationals of that country. The Convention provides certain rights superior to national law, however, which notably include the right to copyright protection without complying with any formalities. If this provision were applicable without restriction in the United States, Zenith might prevail in its argument that registration is not required as a condition for the perfection of a security interest in a foreign work.

Article VI of the United States Constitution provides: "This Constitution, and the Laws of the United States which shall be made in Pursuance thereof; and all Treaties made, or which shall be made, under the Authority of the United States, shall be the supreme Law of the Land . . . ." It is presumably under this constitutional provision that Zenith argues that the Berne Convention excuses it from registering its copyrights in the foreign films as a condition of perfecting its security interests. However, United States law on treaties is more complex.

Some treaties are self-executing, under United States treaty law, and some are not. A self-executing treaty creates rights for the nationals of a country that is a party to the convention without the need for any implementing domestic legislation. A treaty that is not self-executing, on the other hand, requires implementing domestic legislation to create rights thereunder for the citizens of the state party to the treaty. Whether a particular treaty is self-executing or not normally turns on the domestic law of the particular state party, and may vary from one state party to another.

At the time that it ratified the Berne Convention, the United States Senate determined that the treaty should not be self-executing in the United States, and Congress enacted implementing legislation to give it effect in the United States. Thus the Berne Convention creates rights in United States law only to the extent that it is implemented through domestic legislation. The language of the convention alone does not excuse Zenith from complying with United States law to preserve its rights as a secured creditor in the foreign films here at issue, except to the extent that internal United States law so provides.

Section 411 is specific in providing rights under the Berne Convention without further compliance with United States law. It permits "actions of infringement of copyright in Berne Convention works" without registration. United States copyright law provides no other Berne Convention exemption, however, from complying with the registration provisions. Thus Zenith is required to comply with domestic United States law to perfect its security interest in these films. Additionally, section 205, which deals specifically with transfers, does not distinguish between foreign and domestic works. Since Zenith did not register the underlying foreign films, third parties were not put on notice of the copyright mortgages for the foreign films, and Zenith's interests remained unperfected. . . .

---

**In re AEG Acquisition Corp.**
**161 Bankr. 50 (BAP 9th Cir. 1993)**

Jones, Bankruptcy Judge: . . .

. . . *Improper Perfection of Foreign Films*

The trial court determined that Zenith had failed to perfect its security interests in the foreign Films because the Films had not been registered with the United States Copyright Office. Zenith argues that the court erred because, under the Berne Convention for the Protection of Literary and Artistic Works (Paris Text 1971) ("Berne Convention"), registration is a prohibited formality.

Under United States law, recording a document in the Copyright Office gives all persons constructive notice of the information contained in the document only if the document identifies the work to which it relates and the work is registered. The Berne Convention provides that authors of foreign works enjoy the same protections of any member country as do nationals of that country. In addition, authors of Berne Convention works are entitled to copyright protections without complying with formalities.

Zenith argues that requiring registration is a "formality" which may not be imposed on a Berne Convention work. Zenith points out that registration is not a prerequisite to the bringing of an infringement action for a Berne Convention work, while it is a prerequisite for a work not covered by the Berne Convention. Zenith asserts that registration as a prerequisite to perfecting a security interest in a foreign film is a similarly prohibited formality.

As the trial court here noted, however, United States law provides no other exemptions for Berne Convention works. Moreover, 17 U.S.C. § 205, which deals with recordation of transfers of copyrights, makes no distinction between foreign and domestic works. We therefore hold that Zenith's failure to register the two foreign Films before AEG filed bankruptcy defeats its attempt to perfect its security interest in the copyrights. . . .

Based upon the foregoing, we affirm the trial court's decision.

---

**In re World Auxiliary Power Company**
**303 F.3d 1120 (9th Cir. 2002)**

Kleinfeld, Circuit Judge:

In this case we decide whether federal or state law governs priority of security interests in unregistered copyrights.

*FACTS*

Basically, this is a bankruptcy contest over unregistered copyrights between a bank that got a security interest in the copyrights from the owners and perfected it under state law, and a company that bought the copyrights from the bankruptcy trustees after the copyright owners went bankrupt. These simple facts are all that matters to the outcome of this case, although the details are complex. . . .

The bank perfected its security interest in the collateral, including the copyrights, pursuant to California's version of Article 9 of the Uniform Commercial Code, by filing UCC-1 financing statements with the California Secretary of State. The bank also took possession of the . . . copyrighted materials. But the copyrights still weren't registered with the United States Copyright Office, and the bank did not record any document showing the transfer of a security interest with the Copyright Office.

Subsequently, the three debtor companies filed simultaneous but separate bankruptcy proceedings. Their copyrights were among their major assets. Aerocon Engineering, one of their creditors (and the appellant in this case), wanted the copyrights. . . .

Meanwhile, [the bank] won relief from the bankruptcy court's automatic stay and, based on its security interest, foreclosed on the copyrights. . . .

Aerocon brought an adversary proceeding . . . against [the bank] . . . to avoid [the bank's] security interest and to recover the copyrights . . . . The bankruptcy court . . . granted summary judgment to [the bank] on all of Aerocon's claims on the ground that the bank had perfected its security interest in the copyrights under California's version of Article 9 of the Uniform Commercial Code. Aerocon appealed . . . to the district court, which affirmed the bankruptcy court. Aerocon appeals from the district court's order.

*ANALYSIS*

. . . Whether Aerocon . . . would take priority turns on whether federal or state law governs the perfection of security interests in unregistered copyrights. The bank did everything necessary to perfect its security interest under state law, so if state law governs, the bank has priority and wins. The bank did nothing, however, to perfect its interest under federal law, so if federal law governs, Aerocon . . . arguably has priority, although the parties dispute whether Aerocon might face additional legal hurdles.

We are assisted in deciding this case by two opinions, neither of which controls, but both of which are thoughtful and scholarly. The first is the bankruptcy court's published opinion in this case which we affirm largely for the reasons the bankruptcy judge gave. The second is a published district court opinion, *National Peregrine, Inc. v. Capitol Federal Savings & Loan Association (In re Peregrine Entertainment, Ltd.)*, the holdings of which we adopt but, like the bankruptcy court, distinguish and limit. . . .

Aerocon argues that the Copyright Act's recordation and priority scheme exclusively controls perfection and priority of security interests in copyrights. . . .

Under the U.C.C. . . . , there can be no question that, when a copyright has been registered, a security interest can be perfected only by recording the transfer in the Copyright Office. . . . As the district court held in *Peregrine*, . . . [f]or registered copyrights, the only proper place to file is the Copyright Office. We adopt *Peregrine's* holding to this effect.

However, the question posed by this case is whether the U.C.C. steps back [i.e., makes itself inapplicable] as to unregistered copyrights. We, like the bankruptcy court in this case, conclude that it does not. . . . [T]here's no way for a secured creditor to perfect a security interest in unregistered copyrights by recording in the Copyright Office . . . because unregistered copyrights don't have a registered name and number, [so] under the Copyright Act there isn't any place to file anything regarding unregistered copyrights that makes any legal difference. So, as a matter of state law, the U.C.C. doesn't step back in deference to federal law, but governs perfection and priority of security interests in unregistered copyrights itself. . . .

Aerocon argues, relying on *Peregrine*, that Congress intended to occupy the field of security interests in copyrights. Aerocon also argues that the U.C.C. actually conflicts with the Copyright Act's text and purpose. . . .

*Peregrine* reasoned that creditors could get conflicting results under the U.C.C. and the Copyright Act, because each provides a different priority scheme. That's true only for registered copyrights. The Copyright Act wouldn't provide a conflicting answer as to unregistered copyrights because it wouldn't provide any answer at all. *Peregrine's* holding applies to registered copyrights, and we adopt it, but as the bankruptcy court reasoned in the case at bar, it does not apply to unregistered copyrights.

We accordingly reject two other lower court opinions, *Zenith Productions, Ltd. v. AEG Acquisition Corp. (In re AEG Acquisition Corp.)* and [another case] that extended *Peregrine's* holding to unregistered copyrights. No circuit court has come to that erroneous conclusion. In both cases, the courts held that security interests in unregistered copyrights may not be perfected under the U.C.C.; perfection could be obtained only by registering the copyrights and recording the security interest with the Copyright Office. We reject these opinions because they miss the point made by the bankruptcy judge in this case, and discussed above, that *Peregrine's* analysis doesn't work if it's applied to security interests in unregistered copyrights. Moreover, such extensions of *Peregrine* to unregistered copyrights would make registration of copyright a necessary prerequisite of perfecting a security interest in a copyright. The implication of requiring registration as a condition of perfection is that Congress intended to make unregistered copyrights practically useless as collateral, an inference the text and purpose of the Copyright Act do not warrant.

. . . Nowhere does the Copyright Act explicitly condition the use of copyrights as collateral on their registration. Second, the Copyright Act contemplates that most copyrights will not be registered. Since copyright is created every time people set pen to paper, or fingers to keyboard, and affix their thoughts in a tangible medium, writers, artists, computer programmers, and web designers would have to have their hands tied down to keep them from creating unregistered copyrights all day every day. Moreover, the Copyright Act says that copyrights "may" be registered, implying that they don't have to be, and since a fee is charged and time and effort is required, the statute sets up a regime in which most copyrights won't ever be registered.

Though Congress must have contemplated that most copyrights would be unregistered, it only provided for protection of security interests in registered copyrights. There is no reason to infer from Congress's silence as to unregistered copyrights an intent to make such copyrights useless as collateral by preempting state law but not providing any federal priority scheme for unregistered copyrights. That would amount to a presumption in favor of federal preemption, but we are required to presume just the opposite. The only reasonable inference to draw is that Congress chose not to create a federal scheme for security interests in unregistered copyrights, but left the matter to States, which have traditionally governed security interests.

For similar reasons, we reject Aerocon's argument that congressional intent to preempt can be inferred from conflict between the Copyright Act and the U.C.C. There is no conflict between the statutory provisions: the Copyright Act doesn't speak to security interests in unregistered copyrights, the U.C.C. does.

Nor does the application of state law frustrate the objectives of federal copyright law. The basic objective of federal copyright law is to "promote the Progress of Science and useful Arts" by "establishing a marketable right to the use of one's expression" and supplying "the economic incentive to create and disseminate ideas." Aerocon argues that allowing perfection under state law would frustrate this objective by injecting uncertainty in secured transactions involving copyrights. Aerocon conjures up the image of a double-crossing debtor who, having gotten financing based on unregistered copyrights, registers them, thus triggering federal law, and gets financing from a second creditor, who then records its interest with the Copyright Office and takes priority. We decline to prevent this fraud by drawing the unreasonable inference that Congress intended to render copyrights useless as collateral unless registered.

Prudent creditors will always demand that debtors disclose any copyright registrations and perfect under federal law and will protect themselves against subsequent creditors gaining priority by means of covenants and policing mechanisms. The several *amici* banks and banking association in this case argue that most lenders would lend against unregistered copyrights subject to the remote risk of being "primed" by subsequent creditors; but no lender would lend against unregistered copyrights if they couldn't perfect their security interest. As we read the law, unregistered copyrights have value as collateral, discounted by the remote potential for priming. As Aerocon reads the law, they would have no value at all.

Aerocon's argument also ignores the special problem of copyrights as after-acquired collateral. To use just one example of the multi-industry need to use after-acquired (really after-created) intangible intellectual property as collateral, now that the high-tech boom of the 1990's has passed, and software companies don't attract equity financing like tulips in seventeenth century Holland, these companies will have to borrow more capital. After-acquired software is likely to serve as much of their collateral. Like liens in any other after- acquired collateral, liens in after-acquired software must attach immediately upon the creation of the software to satisfy creditors. Creditors would not tolerate a gap between the software's creation and the registration of the copyright. If software developers had to register copyrights in their software before using it as collateral, the last half hour of the day for a software company would be spent preparing and mailing utterly pointless forms to the Copyright Office to register and record security interests. Our reading of the law "promotes the Progress of Science and useful Arts" by preserving the collateral value of unregistered copyrights, which is to say, the vast majority of copyrights. Aerocon's reading of the law — would force producers engaged in the ongoing creation of copyrightable material to constantly register and update the registrations of their works before obtaining credit — does not. . . .

---

### A Note on Perfecting Security Interests in Copyrights, Internationally

The *Peregrine Entertainment*, *AEG Acquisition* and *World Auxiliary Power* cases explain what creditors must do to their perfect security interests in copyrights under *United States* law.

None of those cases, however, indicates what creditors should do to perfect their security interests under the laws of *other countries*. The two "foreign" movies at issue in *AEG* were treated just like the American movie, because the payments made by the bankrupt company (AEG) to its creditor (Zenith) – for all three movies – were made in the United States using money the bankrupt had in a bank account in the United States. (The "security interest" issue in the case, and the outcome, would have been the same, if AEG had failed to make required payments to Zenith; and, as a result, Zenith claimed to have a right to be paid that was superior to AEG's other creditors.)

Though the *AEG Acquisitions* case did not involve the law of other countries, it could have. Suppose for example that AEG had made payments to Zenith from a bank account maintained by AEG in London; and suppose that the money used to make those payments had been earned by AEG from its distribution of the three movies in the United Kingdom. In that case, the payments made by AEG would have resulted from AEG's exploitation of the movies' British (not U.S.) copyrights.

Registering copyrights and recording security interests in the U.S. Copyright Office – as required by the *Peregrine Entertainment* and *AEG Acquisition* cases – perfects security interests in U.S. copyrights, but not in British copyrights. Recording security interests under the U.C.C. for unregistered copyrights also perfects security interests in U.S. copyrights, but what does it do with respect to British copyrights?

Since copyrighted works often will be exploited – and thus earn income – outside the United States, as well as in the U.S., what procedures should creditors use in order to be certain they become secured creditors and thus have superior claims to *all* of the income earned by those works, from *outside* as well as inside the United States?

Surprisingly, there is no certain answer to this question. Instead, there are two arguments about how to perfect security interests in non-U.S. copyrights and in the proceeds from their exploitation outside the U.S., *where the borrower is an American whose assets – in the event of bankruptcy – would be administered in the U.S.*

*Argument 1*

One argument is that security interests in foreign (i.e., non-U.S.) copyrights are perfected by filing financing statements in the state where the borrower is located. This view is based on Uniform Commercial Code section 9103(3) which provides: "The law (including the conflict of laws rules) of the jurisdiction in which the debtor is located governs the perfection and the effect of perfection or nonperfection of the security interest" in "accounts . . . and general intangibles."

This may seem to be the same argument that was rejected in the *Peregrine Entertainment* and *AEG Acquisition* cases; but it's not. Those cases were based, in part, on UCC section 9302(3)(a) which provides: "The filing of a financing statement otherwise required by this Article is not . . . effective to perfect a security interest in property subject to . . . a statute . . . *of the United States* which provides for a national . . . registration . . . " (emphasis added). Thus this section is not applicable to security interests in foreign copyrights and proceeds, because foreign copyrights are not subject to a statute "of the United States."

*Argument 2*

The second argument is that security interests in foreign copyrights are perfected by complying with the registration or recording provisions of the copyright law, or the commercial law provisions that govern the perfecting of security interests in intangibles, in the foreign country where the copyright is to be exploited and proceeds are to be earned.

The rationale for this argument is that Uniform Commercial Code section 9103(3)(b) makes the "conflict of laws rules" of the debtor's state applicable to the perfection of security interests in intangibles; and the conflict rules of most states would look to foreign law to determine the method for perfecting security interests in foreign copyrights and proceeds.

This is not a surprising result, because the general rule is that perfection is determined by the law of the jurisdiction where the collateral is located. That is, UCC section 9103(1)(b) provides that the "perfection and the effect of perfection or non-perfection of a security interest in collateral are governed by the law of the jurisdiction where the collateral is when . . . the security interest is perfected or unperfected." Since the collateral is a foreign copyright, this would mean that the law of the foreign country would determine how the security interest would be perfected.

*Rebuttal in favor of Argument 1*

There does not appear to be any authority establishing that *other* countries would conclude (as *Peregrine* and *AEG* did in the U.S.) that a security interest in the *proceeds* from the exploitation of a copyright-protected work is the same thing as a security interest in the *copyright* itself. Thus, compliance with foreign copyright registration or recording requirements to may not be necessary or effective to perfect security interests in proceeds from the exploitation of foreign copyrights.

*Surrebutal in favor of Argument 2*

If other countries do distinguish between copyrights and their proceeds, then foreign commercial law – rather than U.S. law – on the perfection of security interests in intangibles must be consulted. And foreign commercial law may not be the same as the Uniform Commercial Code.

*If Argument 2 turns out to be correct*

If Argument 2 turns out to be correct, the method to be used to perfect security interests in other countries will depend on the copyright laws of those countries. The copyright laws of the following countries provide for registering or recording transfers of copyrights or interests in copyrights in a manner that is significant with respect to priorities among conflicting transferees – that is, in a manner that could determine (under their own laws) which parties are secured and the priority of their security interests: Canada, France, Japan, Spain, and the United Kingdom. (Australia and Italy may as well.)

Other countries may have commercial law provisions governing the perfection of security interests in intangibles that may be applicable to copyrights and the proceeds from their exploitation.

*Conclusion*

The conclusion to be drawn from this is that cautious lenders *to American borrowers* will want to:

- register in the U.S. Copyright Office the copyrights that are desired as collateral, and record in the U.S. Copyright Office their security interests (or copyright mortgages) in those copyrights;
- file Uniform Commercial Code financing statements with the Secretary of State (or other state) offices in the states where the borrowers are located; and
- file or record – in the government offices of other countries – whatever documents seem to have a bearing on security interests in copyrights and their proceeds, in those countries where the copyrighted works will be distributed.

---

## 3.2 GOVERNMENT INCENTIVE FINANCING

In addition to quotas (discussed below in Chapter 6), tax incentives have proven to be a favorite method of encouraging local production throughout the world.

Canada has pursued this approach very aggressively, adopting federal and provincial tax initatives which have increased annual volume to some C$10 billion, including approximately C$2.8 billion in "runaway" productions from the U.S. At the federal level, Canada provides two tax schemes, the Film & Video Production Tax Credit, which is essentially available only to Canadians and Canadian productions, and the Film Production Service Tax Credit, which is available to Canadian productions as well as to foreign producers who maintain permanent Canadian production bases. In either instance, the tax credit is a refundable portion of Canadian labor expenditures. Provincial tax schemes are quite similar but, of course, require that expenditures be made in the particular province in order to be eligible.

Ireland, Australia and New Zealand have tax programs which are philosophically similar to those in effect in Canada, but operate on a far smaller scale.

The UK's "sale and leaseback" tax scheme allows producers, whether domestic or foreign, to obtain government contributions of up to 10% of the budget of a film. As is the case with Canada, the UK scheme is aimed at promoting the utilization of UK creative and technical personnel.

In each case, the country adopting a tax credit/refund scheme is betting that the government's investment will be met or exceeded by incoming investments from foreign producers, whether such investments are directed toward indigenous films or foreign productions shot locally and/or that the volume of work going to local creative and technical personnel will improve and expand the capabilities of the local film industry. This has certainly been the case in Canada, and positive effects have been felt in Ireland, Australia and New Zealand as well. "Lord of the Rings: Fellowship of the Rings" was conceived by New Zealand director Peter Jackson, and the film was shot and post-produced in New Zealand, including special effects. Years ago, Hollywood enjoyed a virtual monopoly in the special effects area. "Lord of the Rings" serves notice that times have changed.

Indeed, other countries' film production incentives have been so successful that the United States Department of Commerce studied whether those incentives have induced producers to take productions abroad that othewise would have been produced in the United States. The Department of Commerce concluded that the answer is "yes." Ironically, the Department's published report entitled *The Migration of U.S. Film and Television Production* includes is an excellent guide for American producers (and their lawyers) who may be interested in taking advantage of some of those foreign incentives – though it's also a guide for U.S. lawmakers who may want to respond to foreign competition by enacting incentives of their own for productions made in America.

---

**The Migration of U.S. Film and Television Production**
**Chapter 6 - Incentive Programs in Other Countries**
**U.S. Department of Commerce (2001)**

Foreign governments around the globe increasingly recognize the tangible and intangible benefits of attracting film production to their countries. Many have taken steps to actively attract film production, primarily from the United States, through financial incentives. Indeed, many of the top destinations for runaway production . . . , Australia, Canada, Ireland, and the United Kingdom, offer substantial government incentive packages. These incentives have contributed to the propensity of the U.S. film industry to produce U.S. films abroad in recent years.

*Canada*

The Canadian government (federal and provincial) offers a number of programs in support of the country's film industry. As highlighted in the Ernst & Young "Guide to International Film Production," the support of the film industry through Canadian government incentive programs is a "well-known national legacy." In October 2000, the Minister of Canadian Heritage announced a new Canadian Feature Film Policy. This policy establishes several new incentive programs and nearly doubles the federal government's investment in Canada's feature film industry from C$51 million to C$100 million.

As part of a comprehensive program to encourage growth in the domestic film industry, both Federal and provincial governments in Canada offer a wide range of incentives to both assist domestic producers and attract foreign production. These packages may include direct financial and tax incentives, labor credits, and aggressive marketing campaigns promoting Canada as a destination for production. According to the Monitor Report, U.S.-developed productions located in Canada have been able to realize total savings, including incentives and other cost reducing characteristics of producing in Canada, of up to 26 percent, with approximately 60 percent of the direct savings coming from "below-the-line" labor cost differences. The Canadian incentive programs have been so successful, that it appears that the Canadian incentive system may be used as a model for other countries in the future that are attempting to build a film industry.

At the federal level, the Canadian government offers tax credits to compensate for salary and wages, provides funding for equity investment, and provides working capital loans. At the provincial level, similar tax credits are offered, as well as incentives through the waiving of fees for parking, permits, location, and other local costs. While these programs at both the federal and local levels typically require Canadian establishment, Canadian-controlled corporations, and/or a threshold of costs incurred in Canada, these programs have become less stringent over time. Many have argued that Canada has utilized their cultural exclusion under the NAFTA to defend such programs, but there is much debate on the validity of such cultural claims. For example, Congressman Jerry Weller of Illinois, concerned with the application of this exemption, pointed out that a movie filmed in Canada starring Dennis Rodman and set in Chicago was labeled Canadian cultural content.

Canadian experience suggests that administering tax incentive programs is not without problems. Cinar Corporation of Montreal, a producer of children's programming, has been under investigation since early in 2000 concerning whether the company falsely claimed film tax credits. The primary allegation has been that Cinar put the names of Canadian authors on screenplays in fact written by U.S. authors. As of the end of the year, the investigation was not yet completed, but the scandal has shaken the Canadian administration of film tax credits.

Foreign film makers can also take advantage of Canadian tax shelters, which were phased out in 1997, but reintroduced in 1999. These shelters allow Canadian financiers to offer structured film-financing incentives of three percent to four percent of non-Canadian labor expenditures (NCLE), in addition to production services tax credits. Because taking advantage of the NCLE tax shelter requires complex film financing arrangements, typically only large U.S. studios use the shelter arrangement.

U.S. film makers appear to benefit the most from Canada's federal and provincial Production Services Credits. These credits "are designed to promote and encourage foreign production in Canada, and thereby develop and grow Canadian production service industries." The Federal Production Services Credit, announced in October 1997 and effective in 1998, provides an 11 percent refund on qualifying Canadian labor expenditures. Assuming that labor expenditures total about 50 percent of production costs, such a credit can mean a potential savings of 5.5 percent (11 percent of 50 percent) on total production costs. There are no Canadian content requirements; U.S. producers qualify primarily through contracting for production services directly with Canadian companies. Expenditure criteria determine eligibility: a minimum of CAN$200,000 (US$135,000) per episode for a television series or pilot production, or CAN$1 million (US$675,000) for any other type of film or television production, including a feature film. All ten Canadian provinces have implemented similar measures. These credits can be combined with federal credits up to a certain maximum level (see Canadian incentive table below).

The Canadian government, particularly at the provincial level, has actively advertised their incentive packages and other benefits to producers. Many provinces have elaborate websites to highlight the benefits for companies willing to shoot their productions in Canada. Ontario's website is a good example. The province's website not only highlights the tax breaks, the local support and incentives, but provides extensive information on local companies, wages and salaries, listing of locations that provide the appearances of U.S. and international settings, and even an exchange rate converter between two currencies – the U.S. and Canadian dollar.

According to information from provinces where foreign film production data is readily available, U.S. film production surged after the introduction of provincial tax credits. For example, in British Columbia, foreign production growth, in terms of percentage change from year to year in production dollars spent in the province, was in the teens in 1996 and 1997; that growth percentage slumped to 3.5 percent in 1998 and then grew 51.2 percent in 1999. The British Columbia Credit was enacted in June 1998. For the fiscal year ending March 31, 2000, the British Columbia Film Commission (BCFC), the provincial government's domestic film and television tax credit program, issued tax credit eligibility certificates totaling $9.7 million to production companies and supported 51 film and television projects, representing $112 million worth of production in British Columbia. In July 1999, the province announced a CAN$50 million (US$34 million) expansion program for sound stages in Vancouver, CAN$14 million (US$9 million) of which are in the form of a government loan from the province.

In a press release this past summer, the British Columbia Film (BCF), the province's film development agency, announced production commitments for 2000/2001. The agency has alread committed CAN$2.5 million (US$1.68 million) in equity financing to produce 35 film and television projects through its Television and Film Financing Program (TFFP). In addition, nine television series and 3 feature films are to receive production support, 22 broadcast singles/documentaries have financing commitments, and 2 projects, a feature film (Protection) and a documentary special (Lilith Fair), will receive support through completion funding. This announcement by the BCF relates to funding commitments made through British Columbia's TFFP and the Market Incentive Program (MIP) and does not include activity through the provincial government tax credit programs Film Incentive BC and the Production Services Tax Credit.

Similar to British Columbia, where foreign film production had dropped in 1997, Ontario saw a 65 percent surge in 1998. The Ontario production credits, specifically the services tax credit (OPSTC), were introduced in November 1997. Similarly, film production credits were introduced in Quebec in February 1997. Notably, provinces with less-developed film production infrastructures (Manitoba, Saskatchewan, and Nova Scotia) are attempting to boost their film production industry by offering incentives of over 20 percent.

*Canada Incentive Programs for Film Production*

| | |
|---|---|
| *Federal* | *Film Production Service Tax Credit (PSTC)*: This is a tax credit equal to 11% of salary and wages paid to Canadian residents, with no cap on the amount. Eligibility: Available to taxable corporations with a permanent establishment in Canada whose primary business is the production of film and videos. Production costs must be at least C$1.0 million for a film, or C$100,000 for a pilot or episode of less than 30 minutes.<br><br>*Canadian Film or Video Production Tax Credit (CPTC):* This credit is equal to 25% of eligible labor costs, to a maximum of 12% of total production costs. Total production costs are reduced by provincial tax credits and other grants. Eligibility: Available to Canadian-controlled taxable corporations whose primary business is Canadian films and videos. A minimum of 75% of production costs must be paid to Canadian individuals and 75% of production must take place in Canada.<br><br>*Canadian Television Film (CTF) Fund*: An equity investment program, with a budget of C$200 million per year, to enhance the Canadian broadcasting and production sector's capacity to make and distribute television programming in the two official languages. (Generally, foreign co-production companies cannot qualify for CTF funds.)<br><br>*Culture Industries Development Fund (CIDF)*: Provides loans from C$20,000 to C$250,000 for working capital, expansion projects, and special initiatives for Canadian-owned cultural businesses. (Foreign-owned companies cannot generally use this program.) |

| | |
|---|---|
| | *Feature Film Fund:* This fund, which is administered by Telefilm Canada, assists the development and production of English- and French-language feature films destined for theatrical release.<br><br>*Multimedia Fund:* This fund supports the development, production and marketing of educational and entertainment multimedia products intended for the general public and is administered by Telefilm Canada.<br><br>*Feature Film Distribution Fund:* This fund is aimed chiefly at recognized Canadian distributors, providing lines of credit for use in acquiring the distribution rights to Canadian feature films.<br><br>*Versioning Fund:* This fund serves to make Canadian works more widely accessible in both official languages, on television and in movie theaters.<br><br>*Canadian Production Marketing Fund:* This fund has two components: national (test marketing, launch, advertising and promotion) and international (promotional campaigns, advertising in specialized publications, marketing, etc.). |
| *Alberta* | *Film Project Grants*: The Alberta Film Commission offers grants of up to C$500,000 per project per year. |
| *British Columbia* | *Film Production Services Tax Credit*: A credit of 11% of the labor costs paid to taxable Canadian residents and corporations. Taxable Canadian corporations or foreign-owned corporations with permanent facilities in British Columbia are eligible for this program. Production costs must be at least C$1.0 million for a film, or C$200,000 for an episode of a series.<br><br>*"Certified Canadian" Film Incentive BC Tax Credit*: A tax credit of 20% of labor costs, which are capped at 48% of production costs. An additional 12.5% regional credit for doing principal photography outside of Vancouver. All claimants must be BC-based production companies and 75% of production and post-production must be done in British Columbia. The film must be "certified Canadian" by meeting four out of ten "Canadian content criteria." |
| *Manitoba* | *Film Production Tax Credit:* Rebates 35% of approved Manitoba labor expenditures, up to a maximum of 22.5% of eligible production costs.<br><br>*Winnipeg Film Incentive Package:* Free parking, waivers of permit fees and location fees.<br><br>*Deeming Provision:* If there are no qualified production personnel available in Manitoba, then production staff can be brought in from outside the province, as long as training is taking place. If this is the case, salaries will be considered for the Film Production Tax Credit. |

| | |
|---|---|
| *New Brunswick* | *Labor Incentive Tax Credit*: The credit is equal to 40% of wages paid to New Brunswick residents, up to a maximum of 50% of total production costs of a film. The eligible film production company must have permanent facilities in New Brunswick and have less than C$25 million in assets.<br><br>*Film Development & Production Assistance*: Up to C$500,000 available per project to New Brunswick-controlled corporations. |
| *Newfoundland & Labrador* | *Labor Tax Credit*: The amount of the credit is 40% of the eligible Newfoundland/Labrador labor expenditures, to a maximum of 25% of the total production costs. Eligible labor must be resident in Newfoundland/Labrador, though in some cases the residency requirement may be waived. There is an annual tax credit maximum of C$1.0 million per project, and C$2.0 million per associated group of corporations. |
| *Nova Scotia* | *Film Tax Credit*: For production in the Greater Halifax Region, the amount of the credit is 30% of eligible Nova Scotia labor expenditures, up to a maximum of 15% of total production costs. (Outside of the Halifax Region, this is 35% and 17.5%, respectively.) This credit is available only to Canadian taxable corporations with a permanent establishment in Nova Scotia. |
| *Ontario* | *The Ontario Film Development Corporation (OFDC)* administers a tax credit program worth an estimated C$50 million a year. The OFDC administers four tax credits based on eligible Ontario labor expenditures.<br><br>*Ontario Film & Television Tax Credit:* A rebate of 20% on labor costs, available to Canadian-controlled, Ontario-based production companies.<br><br>*Ontario Production Services Tax Credit*: An 11% refundable tax credit on Ontario labor costs, available to foreign-based and domestic productions. A bonus of 3% is provided for projects with at least five production days in Ontario, and at least 85% of production days outside of the Greater Toronto Area.<br><br>*Ontario Computer Animation & Special Effects Tax Credit*: A 20% rebate of qualifying labor expenditures. Available to Canadian or foreign-owned corporations.<br><br>*Ontario Interactive Digital Media Tax Credit*: This 20% refundable tax credit on labor costs is eligible for projects involving interactive digital media. |
| *Prince Edward Island* | *Development Loan Programs*: Loans are available to qualifying companies that are provincially or federally incorporated and which have headquarters on PEI. Though no tax credits for labor are available, loans are available to finance development and production of film or video projects on PEI. |

| | |
|---|---|
| *Quebec* | *Film Tax Credits*: An 11% refundable tax credit for film or television productions, applicable to labor costs. There is also a special 31% tax credit for certain labor expenditures related to computer animation and special effects. Minimum production costs are C$100,000 for a 30-minute TV episode, C$200,000 for a longer episode, and C$1.0 million for a film production.<br><br>*Refunds of Provincial Sales Tax*: A refund to non-residents of the 7.5% tax on the cost of goods and services.<br><br>*Quebec City Film Incentives*: Granted to foreign film producers when billing for municipal services. This eliminates the 20% administration fee, as well as approximately 30 % of the gross cost of municipal services provided. |
| *Saskatchewan* | *Film Employment Tax Credit*: A rebate of 35% of total wages of all Saskatchewan labor, up to 50% of eligible production costs. There is additional 5% bonus for Saskatchewan labor expenditures for productions based in smaller centers and rural areas.<br><br>*Deeming Provision:* If there are no qualified production personnel available in Saskatchewan, then production staff can be brought in from outside the province, as long as training is taking place. If this is the case, salaries will be considered for the Film Employment Tax Credit. |

Source: Research conducted by the US&FCS – December 2000 and Canadian Audio-Visual Certification Office Information Bulletin

### *United Kingdom*

The United Kingdom (U.K.) has been successful in attracting foreign investment in the film industry through an array of programs offering taxation assistance, investment and financing arrangements. One of the major incentives is a 100 percent tax write-off for both feature film and made-for-television production that is provided if specific criteria are met: majority use of U.K. or European Union nationals or residents for production purposes, use of U.K. studios for production, and supply of half of all technical production equipment by U.K. companies. The United Kingdom imposes no minimum cultural requirement qualifications. Additionally if a foreign production cannot qualify for a 100 percent tax write-off, it can apply for benefits under a U.K. sponsored "leaseback" scheme. In a "leaseback" transaction, a non-qualifying foreign production company sells its film rights to a leasing company, which, in turn, leases back the film rights to the production company. The transaction allows the U.K. lessor to take advantage of tax reliefs; the value of the benefits are divided between the U.K. partner and the foreign production company.

In addition to the tax incentives, the U.K. government established in April 2000, the British Film Council (BFC) under the umbrella of the Department of Culture, Media and Sport. The BFC serves as a lottery distributor for film production and is responsible for:

- The British Film Commission (promoting inward investment)
- The Arts Council of England's Lottery Film Department (investing in film

production)

- The British Film Institute's Production Department (investing in film production)
- British Screen Finance (a publicly supported film investment company, which will be incorporated into the Film Council)
- The British Film Institute (BFI) (an independent body funded by the Film Council to deliver cultural and educational opportunities for the public).

Various incentive programs are available under the auspices of the British Film Council and range from providing funds for development including writer's, writer's research fees, and other aspects of development of the production to providing production funds for commercially viable projects. According to the BFC, generally funding is repaid to the BFC either through premiums on its loans, or through a profit sharing role taken by the BFC commensurate with its participation in the project. Some of the programs administered by the BFC are available to individuals; however, most of the funded programs are available only to companies or corporations. In addition, though funding is targeted at the British film industry, foreign production companies may be eligible for certain programs. Specific programs funded by the BFC include the *New Cinema Fund* and the *Premiere Fund.*

Other programs are offered in Britain as follows:

- 100% capital allowances write-off in the first year on expenditures on production and acquisition of British films with budgets under a certain amount and, film franchises financed by national Lottery funds and grants for British film production
- 'Sale and leaseback' arrangements are offered by British banks, while other financial institutions offer portfolio investment in the form of risk capital spread across a parcel of films
- British Screen Finance (British Screen) offers commercial loans for film projects from British film makers which are unlikely to receive commercial backing. Investments are offered up to $810,000 per project or 30 percent of its budget, whichever is lower.
- The ECF is administered by British Screen and offers funding for production companies based in Britain whose film project qualifies as British under the terms of the 1985 Films Act.

Regional programs that are offered in the United Kingdom include:

- The *Moving Image Development Agency* (MIDA) which funds Liverpool-based and other film production companies which spend at least twice the level of any investment made by the fund in the Merseyside area in North West England.
- *Glasgow Film Fund* which supports productions filmed around Glasgow. Funding is available for film production companies in the region, or produced by or with a Glasgowbased company.
- Funds may be provided by *Yorkshire Media Production Agency* for production loan financing to feature and short films and to television and multi-media projects. Some funding is available to media production and companies which are based outside the region, provided they agree to spend in the area at least double the amount of money they receive as a loan.
- *The Manx Scheme* (Isle of Man Film Commission) is aimed at low and medium-budget films. It offers tax credits for film producers. To qualify for this program, at least 20 percent of the production costs have to be spent on the island using island-based companies and individuals.

Finally, the European Union announced in mid-December 2000, that it had earmarked EUR 50 million (approximately $45 million) in a *Venture Capital for Creative Industries* fund "to help European media companies compete with

Hollywood and Silicon Valley." The money will be provided by the European Investment Bank (EIB), in cooperation with the European Investment Fund, over three years in the form of loans, credit lines, and backing for venture capital funds in order to support small- and medium-sized film production companies with low-cost loans, and for larger recipients to build high-tech studios and digital installations. This money may aid state and regional programs as well.

### *Australia*

Although the Australian government is a major financial supporter of the domestic film industry, it offers few federal incentives to foreign producers. Australian film incentives at the federal level for feature or television films have requirements for Australian content as well as significant participation of Australian partners. Australian state-based incentives, however, do not always have such restrictions. In fact, state-based incentives ranging from payroll tax rebates and exemptions to producers are very attractive to foreign film makers.

#### *Queensland*

The Pacific Film and Television Commission in Queensland, with the assistance of the Queensland State Government, offers payroll tax rebates and cast and crew salary rebates for productions filming in Queensland. The Queensland payroll taxes are fully refunded for projects spending at least $A3.5 million (US$2.0 million) in Queensland with no Australian content requirements or restrictions on foreign film companies. Cast and crew salary rebates of 8 percent to 10 percent are available only for below-the-line workers. The exact rebate amount is based on the value of the production's expenditures in Queensland. Queensland also offers free police and fire services during production.

#### *New South Wales*

Payroll tax rebates are available for certain productions filmed at Fox Studios in Sydney. In addition, the New South Wales Film and Television Office (FTO), which is funded by the New South Wales government, provides financial assistance and other aid to productions filmed in New South Wales. While some of this aid is specific to Australian productions, such as the Regional Film Fund which begins January 1, 2001, other production aid may be available to foreign filming companies.

#### *South Australia*

Payroll tax exemptions are available for feature films shot mostly in South Australia. In addition, the South Australia Film Corporation, a government-financed organization, provides loans, grants, and other funding opportunities.

#### *Tasmania*

The state government in Tasmania offers payroll tax exemptions and funding for film productions through a state agency, Screen Tasmania. Funding guidelines for Screen Tasmania indicate that priority is given to funding Tasmanian projects or projects which will benefit Tasmania. Although projects originating outside Tasmania may apply for aid, the project must be primarily filmed in Tasmania and generate "substantial employment opportunities for the local industry." Funding from Screen Tasmania may be provided for production (equity investment or loan), script development (Screen Tasmania will share in copyright ownership), producer's assistance (limited recourse loans which are repayable on the first day of filming at an interest rate to be determined by the board), and industry and cultural development, including marketing assistance (grants).

#### *Victoria*

Victoria's newly established Production Investment Attraction Fund (PIAF) is available for productions that spend a minimum of 70 percent of their total production budget in Victoria and spend a minimum of $A3.5 million (US$2.0 million) in the state. In addition, a Regional Victoria Film Location Assistance Fund (RLAF) was established to provide $A100,000 (US$57,000) annually to promote filming in regional Victoria. Projects considering a regional Victoria location (i.e., outside of Melbourne) for filming for a duration of at least one week may apply for funding.

### *Ireland*

Ireland is becoming an increasingly attractive country for international film production. Due to the unique countryside, the weakened currency, the generous tax incentives, and avoidance of the EU quotas, more and more producers are considering Ireland for their film production. In an effort to cultivate a healthy foreign and domestic film industry, the Irish government offers the Section 481 tax incentive, a non-refundable subsidy of up to 12 percent for film production. With Ireland's government ratifying the EU Coproduction Convention, films produced in Ireland not only gain access to the 20 European countries, but to the support measures provided by each of these countries as well. However, government support for Section 481 has been erratic, which has made U.S. film makers uneasy about filming in Ireland. In fact, Section 481 has been gradually reduced since 1996, and until 2000 was being extended only for one year at a time.

Given that Hollywood production planning is done 12 to 18 months in advance of the start of filming, a one-year tax incentive that had suffered cutbacks stimulated little interest among U.S. studios. In fact, Kevin Moriarty, managing director of Ardmore Studios, a major Irish production facility, blames the uncertainty surrounding Section 481, along with increasing competition from Australia and Canada for U.S. films, for a drop of more than 50 percent in activity at his studios in 1999. A Film Industry Strategic Review Group came to the same conclusion in August 1999. Referring to the report, Irish Screen Commission Chief Executive Roger Greene commented:

> The single most important issue for the inward production industry (foreign or U.S. companies wishing to produce here) is the recommendation to renew Section 481 for a further seven years. . . . Long-term tax incentives are vital for the industry as a whole – indigenous and incoming. Because of the uncertainty about the future of S481 this year, foreign producers have shied away from Ireland as a potential location. The impact of this, coupled with a general downturn in production world wide, has meant a considerable reduction in production in Ireland for 1999.

Today, however, Section 481 has been renewed for another five years and helps to maintain the tax relief level at 80 percent. Since Section 481 was extended by the Minister of Finance, production is reported to have increased. In February 2000, 11 films were reported in production or postproduction, and in May 2000, 18 films were awaiting certification by the Department of Arts and Heritage. All 18 of the latter films had applied for the Section 481 tax incentive. Most recently, the Minister for the Arts, Heritage, & the Islands indicated that with several projects already certified and additional projects still awaiting approval, figures for the year 2000 (US$66.5 million) have already exceeded 1999's production spending of US$61.9 million. The tax incentives, coupled with the ability to avoid the EU's quotas, have made Ireland an extremely attractive location to shoot production.

Filmmaker and President of New Concorde, Roger Corman, has established a presence in Ireland. Today, with the help of grant money from the Irish Government, Concorde has constructed a state-of-the-art studio (Concord Anois) featuring two major sound stages, post production facilities, full wardrobe and a manor house for cast and crew. This studio has shot 11 films with an additional four in pre-production. The studio has been very successful and Corman has even rented out his studio and recruited others to film in Ireland. Mark Amin, Chairman and CEO of Trimark Pictures indicated that when Corman first suggested Ireland for a location to shoot *Warlock*, he was very skeptical. However, after careful consideration, financial incentives being the driving force, he was pleased with the results of filming in Ireland.

*The Netherlands*

In the Netherlands, funding for film production is made available through the government-funded Dutch Film Fund (Nederlands Fonds voor de Film) which is responsible for coordinating national support to the film industry in the Netherlands. Various methods of funding may be provided including loans for development, production and distribution of fiction films and documentaries, and animation films. Generally speaking, the loans are made available through a Dutch-based producer and support for development is only available for essentially Dutch projects. In addition to film development assistance, the Fund also sponsors a marketing and promotion program that directs as much as $30,000 per year in matching funds for distribution purposes.

In 1998, the latest year for which data were available, the Dutch Film Fund, as well as other publicly-financed organizations, significantly contributed to feature film production. In addition to the Fund, aid is provided by the COBO-fund, the Dutch Cultural Broadcasting Promotion Fund, national Dutch broadcasting companies, Eurimages, and others.

In addition to programs which are offered on a country-wide basis, there are some regionally specific programs in the Netherlands. In Rotterdam, for example, the Rotterdam Film Fund (RFF) provides grants for the production of feature films, documentaries and TV productions made partly or entirely in the Rotterdam region. Funds for these grants are provided by the Rotterdam Development Corporation. In addition to grants, the RFF also may provide interest free loans and ‘extra development contributions’. Funds disbursed by the RFF may be granted to Rotterdam-based producers, producers based elsewhere, and foreign producers with co-producers based in Rotterdam. One of the conditions to receive aid under the RFF is that 50 percent of the sum that is borrowed must be spent in the Rotterdam region. Further conditions include that of this fund, at least 25 percent must be used in the audiovisual sector (staff, facilities, materials) and 25 percent in other sectors.

*South Africa*

In South Africa, the majority of funding for film is provided through the government-developed National Film and Video Foundation (NFVF), established in October 1999. The NFVF oversees film policy, public funding, promotion of South African films, and awards yearly government funded grants for film development and production for features and shorts. The NFVF offers funding in the form of grants or low-interest loans to individuals, companies, and organizations for a variety of film- and video-related expenses, including: education and training, development funding, production funding and marketing and distribution and is currently discussing the possibility of funding in the areas of information, research, advice and endorsement. Also, in certain cases, the NFVF may enter into equity arrangements with companies whose production will yield commercial success. The NFVF also provides aid in the form of grants or repayable loans for local and international marketing and distribution purposes. In order to qualify, independent producers and local distributors must be in possession of locally-produced, completed film and television product. The following aspects of film marketing and distribution qualify for support:

- Test screenings
- Film launches
- Entry costs and freight costs for the submission of films to local and international festivals and markets
- Travel to local and international markets
- Theatrical exhibition costs (print and advertising)
- Video promotion costs (launches, video sleeves, catalogues, posters)
- International film and video marketing costs.

In the case of production funding, priority is given to South African-owned production companies that have reasonable experience and to new and emerging filmmakers that would not otherwise have the opportunity to participate in the local film industry. Other criteria taken into consideration include:

- Credible track record in production
- Distribution intent or financial commitment from other partners
- Guaranteed rural or township exposure on screen
- Language diversity
- South African perspectives and leading roles for South African actors.

For commercial film production, the NVFV will fund a maximum of 25 percent of the budget through an equity investment scheme. Qualified applicants include those with proof of South African identity. Foreigners may apply for NFVF funding, though they must be able to explain how their project, organization, or skills would benefit the development of the South African film and television industry. Other criteria and priorities taken into consideration when funding is being considered include:

- Positive impact on the local film industry
- Advancement of people from historically disadvantaged communities
- Projects or organizations that are of national importance
- Proposals that contain local content

*Other Countries*

This program summary is intended to highlight the programs being utilized by countries that are the primary benefactors for runaway film production. What is clear from this study is that many countries outside the United States have recognized the importance of the industry and have developed programs and incentives to attract U.S. film production to their shores. The programs and incentives are particularly aimed at courting U.S. film production to overseas locations. While the benefit and impact of the various programs can be debated, it is undeniable that these programs threaten the market position of the U.S. industry and jobs of the U.S. workers they employ.

---

**Note on Direct Production Subsidies**

Although the main purpose of tax incentive programs is to upgrade production and marketing budgets, in order to permit local productions to compete more strongly against Hollywood films, and to attract foreign productions as well, Canada, the European Union and other countries with film and television production interests have other priorities as well, such as the preservation and promotion of local culture and the discovery and nurture of new talent.

To this end, Canada, Australia, the EU and other countries and groups of countries make direct subsidies available for less-commercial films, for the development of screenplays, and for films by novice directors.

Some of these subsidies take the form of equity investments, while others are cast in the form of loans repayable from film and television revenues. Some (almost always involving small payments to beginning filmmakers) are outright grants.

These subsidies are rather meager (compared to U.S. feature film budgets). The Eurimages fund, for example, to which producers, distributors and exhibitors from some 28 European countries have access, provides approximately $70 million per year *in all*, an amount which would scarcely cover the production and marketing costs of a single major-studio Hollywood film.

---

## 3.3 CO-PRODUCTION FINANCING

Still another way foreign countries try to upgrade their production and marketing budgets in order to compete more strongly against Hollywood products is the co-production treaty. Movies produced pursuant to co-production treaties enjoy two types of benefits. First, they are eligible for tax and subsidy programs in *both* countries that have signed the treaty (or, in the case of the European Co-Production Convention, in three or more countries) – benefits that otherwise would be available only to producers who are nationals of the country offering the program. Second, movies produced pursuant to co-production treaties will satisfy the "domestic content requirements" of both countries (about which you will read in Chapter 6).

The UK is party to just seven such treaties, Canada to more than 50.

While non-signatory "third countries" may participate in such productions, co-production treaties commonly provide for (1) minimum financial contributions from each signatory country, (2) creative control in the hands of the producers from the signatories, (3) specific levels of creative and technical participation by citizens or residents of the signatories, and similar thresholds. Third-country personnel are not completely excluded, but lead actors are usually permitted only where the story calls for it. (For example, Cher is seen in "Tea With Mussolini," an Italian/English co-production, because the script calls for an American woman and Cher fit the profile perfectly.)

To avoid having co-production monies frittered away on commercially suicidal projects, administering authorities in signatory countries (and especially at the Eurimages fund) place considerable weight on the prior track records of applicant producers.

Lawyers who represent Canadian or Australian producers will find the following materials both interesting and immediately useful. Some American producers (and their lawyers) have found these materials interesting and useful too. The United States is not a party to co-production treaties with Canada or Australia or any other country of the world. As you read the following materials, though, consider whether there is some way an American producer could benefit from Canadian or Australian co-production treaties. (Some Americans have.)

---

## Canadian Official Coproductions Guidelines 2000-2001

*Mission*

Telefilm Canada is a federal cultural agency dedicated primarily to developing and promoting the Canadian film, television and new media industry, both in Canada and abroad.

On behalf of the Canadian government, Telefilm Canada administers all international agreements governing official coproductions. In this capacity, through its Coproductions Department, the Corporation:

- receives and evaluates *applications for certification* of projects as official coproductions and recommends to the government either approval or denial of national production status;
- receives *applications for financial assistance* submitted under the Canada-France mini-treaties or the English-Language Cinema Plan and evaluates them in relation to the specific objectives of these programs.

Projects certified as official coproductions by the Department of Canadian Heritage, through the Canadian Audio-Visual Certification Office (CAVCO), are recognized as Canadian productions. As such, they are eligible for all programs and benefits offered to national audiovisual productions by the governments of the coproducing countries. Applications for assistance are received and evaluated by the departments or agencies concerned, in accordance with the criteria for each program.

*Basic Policies and Requirements – Official Coproductions*

Official coproduction treaties signed between Canada and other countries enable Canadian and foreign producers to pool their resources in order to coproduce audiovisual works of all types and all lengths that enjoy national production status in their respective countries.

The treaties currently in force appear in the table at the end of this document. The full text of each treaty is available at http://www.telefilm.gc.ca. It should be noted that, unlike the certification of wholly Canadian productions, which is recommended to the Department of Canadian Heritage by CAVCO, the certification of official coproductions, which is recommended by Telefilm Canada's Coproductions Department, is not based on a point system.

The Coproductions Department recommends to the Canadian government the certification as international coproductions of projects that comply with the agreements, policies and requirements established by the competent authorities. The process involves two stages:

- Advance Ruling
- Final Approval

Canadian and foreign coproducers must respect the spirit of the coproduction agreements and Telefilm Canada policy, as well as meeting a number of administrative requirements.

To obtain certification, applicants must complete the relevant forms, available on Telefilm Canada's website (http://www.telefilm.gc.ca) and at all the Corporation's Canadian offices. These forms are:

- Application for Advance Ruling
- Application for Final Approval
- Application under the Canada-France Mini-Treaty

- Application under the English-Language Cinema Plan (ELCP)

Foreign coproducers must also submit an application for certification to the competent authority in their own country.

*Official Coproductions*

Applications for advance ruling, duly completed and signed by an authorized representative, must be submitted to the Coproductions Department, in Montréal, *at least 30 days* prior to the commencement of principal photography. . . . In the case of projects applying for financial assistance from the Canadian Television Fund (CTF), applications for advance ruling should be submitted as early as possible or at least 30 days before the deadline for each eligible genre. . . . Applications for final approval must be submitted as soon as production is completed or *no later than 19 months* following the end of the Canadian coproducer's taxation year in which principal photography began or, in the case of animation projects, in which key animation of the first episode was undertaken. . . .

*Certification Policies, Requirements and Conditions*

The policies and requirements outlined below are intended to inform Canadian coproducers about the procedure to be followed when applying for certification of an international coproduction. . . .

*1. A Few Definitions . . .*

- A "coproduction" is an audiovisual work produced in accordance with the stipulations of a certification awarded under a coproduction treaty by the competent authority of each contracting party, acting jointly.
- A "two-party coproduction" means an audiovisual work produced jointly by a Canadian coproducer and a foreign coproducer from a country where a coproduction treaty with Canada is in place.
- A "multipartite coproduction" means an audiovisual work produced jointly by a Canadian producer and a producer from a country with which Canada has a coproduction agreement (leading coproducer) and one or more other producers from countries having a coproduction agreement either with Canada or one of the other coproducing countries.
- A "twinned coproduction" means two audiovisual works that are certified together. (For more information, see Section 6 of these guidelines.)
- A "third-party country" means any country not party to the coproduction agreement between two signing countries. In the case of a coproduction with a country that is a member of the European Union (EU), "third-party country" means any country that is not a member of the EU. . . .
- "Competent authorities" means the authorities designated respectively by the Department of Canadian Heritage (Telefilm Canada) and by the foreign government that has signed a coproduction agreement with Canada.
- "Canadian" means: a Canadian citizen as defined in the *Citizenship Act*, a permanent resident as defined in the *Immigration Act* or a corporation under Canadian control, as determined for the purposes of sections 26 to 28 of the *Investment Canada Act*.
- "Foreign" means: a citizen or resident of a foreign country who fulfills all the conditions relative to his or her status as such under the relevant laws of his or her country.
- A "producer" is defined as an individual or corporation who: controls the production and is the principal decision-maker; is directly responsible for acquisition of the production rights or script and for the development, creative and financial control, and exploitation of the production.

2. *Eligible Projects and Applicants*

Any project aimed at the creation of an audiovisual coproduction of any length, technical medium or genre that meets the requirements and conditions described in the applicable agreements or established by the competent authorities will be certified.

Any Canadian-owned company under the effective control of Canadians, as defined principally in the *Investment Canada Act* and Section 1106 (1) (c) of the Regulations of the *Income Tax Act*, that is headquartered and operated in Canada; and that meets the following criteria:

a. It coproduces with foreign producers from countries that have signed a coproduction treaty with Canada or, in the case of multipartite coproductions, with one of the other coproducing countries.
b. It complies with the minimum financial and creative participation requirements for the Canadian and foreign coproducers as laid out in the international coproduction treaties with the applicable signing country.
c. If the Canadian company is affiliated or associated with a foreign corporate group, it must be incorporated and operated independently from that group.

. . .

d. The company owns the rights and options necessary for production. It owns the exploitation and distribution rights in Canada and has retained a fair share of the net revenues from all other territories, including the coproducing country or countries.
e. The producer, the crew and the personnel exercising control over the creative, financial and technical aspects of the Canadian share of the project are Canadian citizens or permanent residents, in accordance with the provisions of the *Citizenship Act* or the *Immigration Act*.

*Key creative personnel (excluding animation) refers to:*

- Producer and key production personnel
- Director
- Scriptwriter(s)
- 1st lead performer (based on onscreen time)
- 2nd lead performer (based on onscreen time)
- Director of Photography
- Production Designer
- Picture Editor
- Music Composer

*Key creative personnel in animation refers to:*

- *Conventional Animation (2D)*

  Producer and key production personnel
  Director
  Head scriptwriter and scriptwriters
  Storyboard Supervisor
  Design Supervisor (Art Director)
  1st lead voice (based on onscreen time)
  2nd lead voice (based on onscreen time)
  Picture Editor
  Music Composer

- *3D Animation*

  Producer and key production personnel
  Director
  Head scriptwriter and scriptwriters
  Storyboard Supervisor

Design Supervisor (Art Director)
Character model Supervisor
Motion capture Supervisor
Animation Director
1st lead voice (based on onscreen time)
2nd lead voice (based on onscreen time)
Picture Editor
Music Composer

f. The director(s) and scriptwriter(s) must be citizens or permanent residents of Canada or of a coproducing country or, in the case of coproductions with a European Union member country, of an EU country.
g. The key personnel (creative and financial) responsible for the project possess the experience and competence required to successfully complete the project.

3. *Relevant Documents – Advance Ruling and Final Approval*

*Advance Ruling*

- A duly executed coproduction contract (Telefilm Canada proposes an example at http://www.telefilm.gc.ca)
- The Canadian company's incorporation documents
- The company's organizational chart
- A list of the main shareholders
- The shareholders' agreement
- The company's financial statements
- Contracts establishing full title to the property
- If the scriptwriter is Canadian, the producer and scriptwriter must produce an affidavit certifying the originality and authenticity of the script.
- The contracts with the scriptwriter(s), director(s) and music composer
- The documents relating to the sharing of production and distribution rights between the coproducers, in Canada and the rest of the world, should such terms not be stipulated in the coproduction contract.
- Subcontracting agreements in the case of animation projects
- Letters of interest, deal letters, or agreement with distributors or broadcasters
- A preliminary list of creative and technical personnel
- A legible photocopy of passports or other documents approved by Telefilm Canada, providing proof of citizenship for Canadian key creative personnel.
- The resumes of director(s), scriptwriter(s), and producer(s)
- An itemized project budget (in CA$), including both the Canadian and foreign shares.
- A cost breakdown by country (in CA$), including third-party expenses, if applicable
- An itemized financial structure (in CA$) for the Canadian coproducer, together with letters, contracts and other relevant financial documents, including the producer's contribution, the list of and contracts relating to deferred costs, and the project's recoupment schedule. An itemized financial structure for the foreign coproducer is also required should there be common sources of financing.
- A detailed production schedule giving the dates and locations of each phase of the coproduction.
- A temporary credit list, approved by Telefilm Canada, with the nationality of all participants.

Advance ruling letters will be modified only in the case of changes to the country of coproduction, a change in coproducing partner or to the financial structure of the project.

*Final Approval*

- The contracts between the producer and key personnel
- The complete list of head and tail credits, giving the nationality of each participant. This list must be approved and signed by the producer. In the case of series, the Canadian coproducer must provide a signed and approved list of credits for the first and last episodes, as well as a list of any credits that differ in other episodes.
- Any alternate versions of the credit list must be provided to Telefilm Canada for approval.
- Videocassette(s) of the production

*For the Canadian coproducer:*

- An audited production cost report, prepared by a certified accountant independent of the production company for productions with a budget of $500,000 or more.
- A review engagement report for productions with a budget of between $100,000 and $499,000
- An approved affidavit attesting to the production cost for productions with a budget of less than $100,000

*For the foreign coproducer:*

- A final cost report (in CA$), approved by the foreign coproducer.

*For all the coproducers:*

- Each coproducer's final financial structure, accompanied by all of the Canadian coproducer's related contracts; and a final itemized breakdown of costs by country (in CA$).

4. *Financial, Technical and Creative Participation*

The requirements and conditions outlined below are set out in the coproduction treaties or have been established by the competent authorities to ensure the balanced financial, technical, and creative participation of each country.

*a. Animation*

The competent authorities require that a significant portion of the creative animation work be undertaken by Canadians. Also, much of the technical activities must be undertaken in one or other of the coproducing countries (or an EU member country, if the coproducing country is part of the EU). Occasional exceptions may be made with the joint approval of the competent authorities in the coproducing countries, predominantly in the case of subcontracted technical work in third-party countries.

*b. Financial and Creative Contribution*

Creative and/or technical participation is proportionate to the financial contribution of each coproducing country. Some treaties stipulate minimum contribution requirements (e.g. if the financial contribution of the Canadian coproducer represents 25% of the total budget, 25% of the creative and/or technical positions must be filled by Canadians). The Canadian financing serves to cover the costs of Canadian elements. In the case of coproductions with more than one partner country, a minimal creative and/or technical contribution is required of each participating country.

*c. Intellectual Property Rights*

Intellectual property rights must be shared between the coproducers in proportion to their financial participation.

*d. Development and Scriptwriting*

The acquisition of rights pertaining to works originally conceived for purposes other than audiovisual production is allowed, regardless of country of origin. (For instance, a literary work from any country is eligible, provided it has been published and the rights to it have been acquired. However, if the work was conceived for an audiovisual medium, it must come from one of the coproducing countries.)

*e. Financing*

The minimum financial participation of each country varies from 15% to 30%, depending on the treaty. In the case of Canada-France feature film coproductions made in French with a budget of more than $3.5 million, the minimum financial participation of either country can be 10%.

*f. Distribution*

If a production company has signed a distribution agreement with a distributor or broadcaster that is participating in the project's financing, a copy of the interest or deal letter will be required. The market and revenue shares are established equitably between the coproducers based on their respective financial participation. All exploitation rights for the Canadian market are under the effective control of a Canadian distributor or producer. Third-party country investors should not demand more than 10% of the Canadian share of net revenues generated outside of Canada by a certified coproduction. The net revenues generated in Canada must belong to the Canadian producer in all cases. The distribution agreements or contracts will be analyzed with respect to cross-collateralization, revenue and territory sharing, and commission and expense percentages.

*g. Participation of Third-Party Countries*

The exceptional participation of personnel from a third-party country is permitted in the following cases to satisfy production requirements, subject to the approval of Telefilm Canada and the coproducing country authorities:

- Performers

*Feature Films or Made-for-TV Movies*: 1 third-party country performer and 1 third-party country cameo per project (*Cameo* means the brief appearance of an internationally known personality from a third-party country, involving no more than three shooting days)

*Television Series*

*For series of up to six episodes:* 1 lead performer + 1 cameo or 1 guest star (*Guest star* means the participation of a third-party country performer in one or more episodes of a series. . . .)

*For series of 7 to 13 episodes:* 1 lead performer + 2 cameos or 1 lead performer + 1 cameo + 1 guest star or 1 lead performer + 2 guest stars

*For series of 14 to 26 episodes:* 1 lead performer + 4 cameos or 1 lead performer + 2 cameos + 2 guest stars or 1 lead performer + 4 guest stars

*For series of more than 26 episodes*, the same ratio shall apply.

*Important:* The use of an actor/actress in a cameo appearance or as a guest star will be allowed on a trial basis for a period of three years.

- Credits

Two courtesy credits, at most, are permitted for third-party country participants provided their functions in no way interfere with the coproducers' financial and creative authority and they are related either to distribution or financing, or to the provision of production services under the strict control and supervision of the producer. A sworn declaration to this effect must be submitted to Telefilm Canada. In the case of animation projects, subcontractors for technical work are allowed credits customary in such circumstances. Moreover, the Canadian and foreign coproducers must be clearly and predominently identified in the head and tail credits. The coproducers' copyright must appear in the credits without fail. No more than two credits will be authorized for any one company and/or its representatives. The credits must be used in all exploitation territories as well as in all marketing material, and must be those authorized by Telefilm Canada.

*Screen Credits*

| [For] | [From] Canada and Co-producing Countries | [From] Third-Party Countries |
|---|---|---|
| Individuals | At the co-producers' discretion. | Two exemptions may be allowed for individuals from third-party countries: executive producer; senior executive/executive in charge of production; supervising producer/executive; production supervisor; associate produce Apart from these two courtesy credits, Telefilm Canada may authorize one other courtesy credit: production associate; executive production consultant; creative consultant. |
| Third-party country production companies | At the co-producers' discretion. The company's country of origin must have signed a co-production treaty with Canada or with a country that has signed a treaty with Canada. | No credits for production companies or co-producers from countries that have not signed a co-production treaty with Canada will be allowed. |
| Distributors | At the co-producers' discretion. | One credit for a foreign distributor may be given when authorized by Telefilm Canada. Telefilm Canada may agree to "in association with" or a similar formulation for distributors, taking into account the terminology used in the distributor's country of origin. |
| Broadcasters | At the co-producers' discretion. | One credit may be given for a foreign broadcaster holding a broadcast license to the production when authorized by Telefilm Canada. Telefilm Canada may agree to "in association with" or a similar formulation for broadcasters, taking into account the terminology used in the broadcaster's country of origin. |

| | | |
|---|---|---|
| Other foreign corporations, including finance companies | At the co-producers' discretion. | Other foreign corporations, such as finance and syndication companies, may be given a credit when authorized by Telefilm Canada. |
| Logos | | The logos of foreign distributors, broadcasters, syndication companies and finance companies may appear in the tail credits provided those of the co-producing companies and other Canadian participants appear in an equally prominent position. |

*h. Shooting and Production Locations*

Subcontracting technical animation work to a third-party country for up to 25% of the project's total budget is allowed. This regulation applies only to subcontracted services performed in third-party countries.

However, projects must respect the financial participation minimums stipulated in the coproduction treaties. All subcontracting agreements must be included with the application and require the approval of Telefilm Canada. Studio shooting must take place in one or other of the coproducing countries (or an EU member country, if the coproducing country is part of the EU). Location shooting in a third-party country is allowed where required by the script. A list of allowable expenses is available from Telefilm Canada.

*i. Screen Credits*

Audiovisual works produced as coproductions must be presented with the mention "A Canada-[coproducing country] Coproduction" or "A [coproducing country] -Canada Coproduction." This mention must appear separately in the screen credits and must be included in all commercial advertising and promotional material of audiovisual works, and in all presentations. Also, the credits must clearly identify the Canadian producer and production company. A draft credit list approved by the coproducers and indicating the nationality of each participant must be submitted.

*5. Ineligible Projects and Applications*

a. All applications submitted by a company or concerning a project that does not meet the eligibility requirements set out in these guidelines or in the relevant coproduction agreements [are ineligible].

b. The following types of production are not eligible for certification:

- pornography
- any project containing elements of excessive violence, sexual violence or sexual exploitation, or of a defamatory, obscene or otherwise illegal nature as defined in the Criminal Code of Canada.

c. The acquisition of concepts, screenplays or bibles from a third-party country is not allowed.

d. All projects conceived, developed or scripted by professionals from a third-party country are ineligible.

e. No studio shooting in a third-party country is allowed.

*6. Twinning*

Some coproduction treaties permit twinning, which involves the pairing under a single certification of two distinct audiovisual works of a similar kind and budget, one Canadian and the other foreign. In addition to complying with the treaties and the requirements established by the competent authorities, all twinning agreements must meet the following criteria:

a. The same producers are involved in both of the twinned works.

b. The Canadian producer must invest the minimum stipulated in the applicable coproduction treaty in one or other of the twinned productions. However, the coproducers may agree to share their artistic and technical contribution between the two projects or to concentrate it in their own project, so long as overall reciprocity is maintained.

c. Each coproducer holds the exploitation rights for the two works in their own territory.

d. The two productions are of the same genre and of similar length.

e. The maximum interval allowed between the end of production of the first work and commencement of principal photography for the second is one year. . . .

*Co-production treaties with Canada currently in force*

| **Country** | **Minimum Participation** | **Categories** | **Twinning** |
|---|---|---|---|
| Algeria | 30% | Cinema, Television | N/A |
| Argentina | 30% | Cinema, Television | N/A |
| Australia | 30% | Cinema, Television | Cinema, Television |
| Austria | 20% | Cinema, Television | Cinema, Television |
| Belgium | 30% | Cinema, Television | N/A |
| Brazil | 20% | Cinema, Television, Multimedia | N/A |
| Chile | 20% | Cinema, Television, Multimedia | N/A |
| China | 15% | Cinema, Television | N/A |
| Cuba | 20% | Cinema, Television, Multimedia | N/A |
| Czech Republic | 20% | Cinema, Television | N/A |
| Denmark | 20% | Cinema, Television, Multimedia | Cinema, Television |
| Finland | 20% | Cinema, Television, Multimedia | Cinema, Television |

| France | 20% | Cinema, Television | Television |
|---|---|---|---|
| Germany | 20% | Cinema, Television, Multimedia | Television |
| Greece | 20% | Cinema, Television, Multimedia | Cinema, Television |
| Hong Kong | 20% | Cinema, Television, Multimedia | N/A |
| Hungary | 20% | Cinema, Television, Multimedia | N/A |
| Iceland | 20% | Cinema, Television, Multimedia | N/A |
| Ireland | 20% | Cinema, Television | N/A |
| Israel | 20% | Cinema, Television | N/A |
| Italy | 20% | Cinema, Television, Multimedia | N/A |
| Japan | 20% | Cinema, Television, Multimedia | N/A |
| Luxembourg | 20% | Cinema, Television, Multimedia | Cinema, Television |
| Malta | 20% | Cinema, Television, Multimedia | N/A |
| Mexico | 20% | Cinema, Television, Multimedia | N/A |
| Morocco | 20% | Cinema, Television | N/A |
| Netherlands | 20% | Cinema, Television | N/A |
| New Zealand | 20% | Cinema, Television | N/A |
| Norway | 20% | Cinema, Television, Multimedia | Cinema, Television |
| Philippines | 20% | Cinema, Television, Multimedia | Cinema, Television |
| Poland | 20% | Cinema, Television, Multimedia | N/A |

| | | | |
|---|---|---|---|
| Romania | 20% | Cinema, Television, Multimedia | N/A |
| Russia | 20% | Cinema, Television | N/A |
| Senegal | 20% | Cinema, Television | Cinema, Television |
| Singapore | 20% | Cinema, Television | N/A |
| Slovak Republic | 20% | Cinema, Television | N/A |
| South Africa | 20% | Cinema, Television, Multimedia | Cinema, Television |
| South Korea | 30% | Television | Cinema, Television |
| Spain | 20% | Cinema, Television, Multimedia | N/A |
| Sweden | 20% | Cinema, Television, Multimedia | Cinema, Television |
| Switzerland | 20% | Cinema, Television | N/A |
| United Kingdom | 20% | Cinema, Television | Cinema, Television |
| Venezuela | 20% | Cinema, Television, Multimedia | Cinema, Television |
| Community of Independent States (treaty signed with the ex-USSR in force in the following countries): Armenia, Azerbaijan, Belarus, Georgia, Kazakhstan, Kyrgyzstan, Tajikistan, Turkmenistan, Ukraine, Uzbekistan | 20% | Cinema, Television | N/A |
| Former Yugoslavia including: Bosnia-Herzegovina, Croatia, Macedonia, Slovenia | 20% | Cinema, Television | N/A |

*Chapter 4*

# PRODUCTION

---

Hollywood travels to other countries for a variety of reasons. It went for the cast in "Harry Potter: The Sorcerer's Stone"; for the location in "Lord of the Rings: The Fellowship of the Rings" and for Helsinki as a surrogate for Leningrad in "Gorky Park"; for economics, e.g., the use of the Irish Army (as well as the Irish seashore) for the opening sequence of "Saving Private Ryan." As the costs of shooting films in Hollywood have mounted, however, the studios (as well as independent producers) have sought new and less expensive venues. In the U.S., for example, production facilities have thrived in Texas, Florida and North Carolina.

More and more, however, U.S. productions are going to other countries, most noticeably Canada. In part, this is due to the strength of the U.S. dollar; Canadian, Australian and New Zealand currencies trade at tremendous discounts against the dollar. In addition, thanks in large part to tax incentives and subsidies, many foreign countries now possess state-of-the-art production and post-production facilities (long almost a Hollywood monopoly), and highly trained technical staffs. What's more, new technologies for the storage and transmission of information make it possible for a U.S.-based producer to control filming taking place in a foreign countries. "Dailies," for example, can be transmitted and edited digitally. Years ago, in order to maintain control, the processing lab had to be on or near the studio lot. Now the vast majority of television movies-of-the-week are shot in Canada (mostly in British Columbia). Many smaller-budget films, and even some bigger-budget theatrical features, are going north too.

This has caused consternation among the Hollywood creative and technical communities, who fear an immediate diminution in their income and, long-term, erosion of the skill base which has made Southern California the capital of the film world. Los Angeles film development experts have estimated that close to 400,000 LA-area jobs are directly or indirectly related to the film and television industries. Next to tourism, filmed entertainment is the most important component of the Southern California economy.

There are larger implications, of course: after aerospace, entertainment is America's most important export (and yields the most positive trade surplus). At the present time, some 75% of the members of the Screen Actors Guild earn less than $1,000 per year from acting in films and television. The experience of other film/TV industry unions is not dramatically different. For these reasons, there has been recent agitation for solutions such as retaliatory tariffs and/or U.S. tax/subsidy schemes, to offset the advantages provided by the foreign programs.

These issues, however, were discussed in Chapter 3 in connection with finance. Other issues – concerning the legal significance of *where* movies and television programs are produced, and by whom – will be covered in Chapter 5 in connection with trade law barriers to distribution and in Chapter 6 in domestic content requirements.

Why, you may be wondering, is this Chapter 4 so short? "Production," after all, is the pivotal point in the entertainment business – the point at which rights, talent and finance come together to create the entertainment that will be distributed, exhibited and sold. The reason this chapter is short is that if pre-production legal work has been properly done (all necessary legal rights have been obtained, talent has been hired, and financing has been obtained), fewer legal issues arise during production than before or after.

There are legal issues associated with actual production: location permits may be necessary; recording studios, sound stages or concert venues may have to be rented; and equipment, costumes and props may have to be acquired. But none of these requirements present any cross-border issues that are unique to *international* entertainment law. Renting a sound stage in London involves the very same legal considerations as renting one in New York City, even for an entertainment company whose home office is in Los Angeles.

So, unless and until countries begin imposing legal requirements on foreign companies that they don't impose on local companies, in order for production to be done there – an unlikely event in today's business climate – this chapter will remain short.

# *Chapter 5*

# DISTRIBUTION

Revenues from foreign exploitation of U.S. entertainment products make entertainment the source of the United States' second-largest trade surplus (after aerospace). In some areas (for example, music publishing) the vast majority of revenues are derived from foreign sources. Films such as "Titanic," "Schindler's List" and "Harry Potter: The Sorcerer's Stone" will often derive as much as two-thirds of their box office revenue from non-U.S. sources. Some years ago, the Clint Eastwood/Kevin Costner film "A Perfect World" delivered a disappointing $40 million in U.S. box office, but more than $100 million elsewhere around the world.

U.S. producers and distributors customarily seek the fullest possible control of the distribution and exploitation process. There are many reasons for this. Products may be marketed differently in different places (for example, as you will read in the *Quality King* case, products may be marketed through limited, upscale channels in the U.S. – and therefore sold at higher prices – but not elsewhere). Products may cost more to manufacture in some countries than in others. It costs substantially less, for example, to manufacture compact discs in the U.S. than in some other countries, due to volume, and so imports of U.S.-made products into such countries can seriously undermine local manufacturing operations. Additionally, if a U.S. company can set up a network of foreign distributors with exclusive rights in limited territories, those distributors have incentives to make more intense marketing and sales efforts and to avoid cutthroat competition. Moreover, local involvement helps to foster heightened copyright protection and anti-piracy activities. Piracy is a major problem in all areas. In the recording industry, for example (which does approximately $40 billion per year in legitimate sales), it is estimated that 25% of sales are pirated products.

On the other hand, consumerism often leads governments to undercut or prohibit efforts to limit distribution on a territorial basis. Australia, for example, with a small population barely sufficient to sustain an indigenous record industry, no longer prohibits the "parallel importation" of records made legitimately in other countries, which regularly undersell their Australian equivalents. Article 36 of the Common Market Treaty (the basic organizational document of the European Union) expressly requires the free movement of goods, so that any attempt by a record company to license its products country by country will be a nullity in the (currently) 15 member states.

On the other side of the coin, some countries make strenuous efforts to protect their own industries from outside competition, and this, too, is illustrated by the materials which follow.

---

## 5.1 COPYRIGHT BARRIERS TO INTERNATIONAL DISTRIBUTION

### Quality King Distributors, Inc. v. L'Anza Research International, Inc.
### 523 U.S. 135 (1998)

Justice Stevens delivered the opinion of the Court.

Section 106(3) of the Copyright Act of 1976 (Act), 17 U.S.C. § 106(3), gives the owner of a copyright the exclusive right to distribute copies of a copyrighted work. That exclusive right is expressly limited, however, by the provisions of §§ 107 through 120. Section 602(a) gives the copyright owner the right to prohibit the unauthorized importation of copies. The question presented by this case is whether the right granted by § 602(a) is also limited by §§ 107 through 120. More narrowly, the question is whether the "first sale" doctrine endorsed in § 109(a) is applicable to imported copies.

I

Respondent, L'Anza Research International, Inc. (L'Anza), is a California corporation engaged in the business of manufacturing and selling shampoos, conditioners, and other hair care products. L'Anza has copyrighted the labels that are affixed to those products. In the United States, L'Anza sells exclusively to domestic distributors who have agreed to resell within limited geographic areas and then only to authorized retailers such as barber shops, beauty salons, and professional hair care colleges. L'Anza has found that the American "public is generally unwilling to pay the price charged for high quality products, such as L'Anza's products, when they are sold along with the less expensive lower quality products that are generally carried by supermarkets and drug stores." App. 54 (declaration of Robert Hall). L'Anza promotes the domestic sales of its products with extensive advertising in various trade magazines and at point of sale, and by providing special training to authorized retailers.

L'Anza also sells its products in foreign markets. In those markets, however, it does not engage in comparable advertising or promotion; its prices to foreign distributors are 35% to 40% lower than the prices charged to domestic distributors. In 1992 and 1993, L'Anza's distributor in the United Kingdom arranged the sale of three shipments to a distributor in Malta; each shipment contained several tons of L'Anza products with copyrighted labels affixed. The record does not establish whether the initial purchaser was the distributor in the United Kingdom or the distributor in Malta, or whether title passed when the goods were delivered to the carrier or when they arrived at their destination, but it is undisputed that the goods were manufactured by L'Anza and first sold by L'Anza to a foreign purchaser.

It is also undisputed that the goods found their way back to the United States without the permission of L'Anza and were sold in California by unauthorized retailers who had purchased them at discounted prices from Quality King Distributors, Inc. (petitioner). There is some uncertainty about the identity of the actual importer, but for the purpose of our decision we assume that petitioner bought all three shipments from the Malta distributor, imported them, and then resold them to retailers who were not in L'Anza's authorized chain of distribution.

After determining the source of the unauthorized sales, L'Anza brought suit against petitioner and several other defendants. The complaint alleged that the importation and subsequent distribution of those products bearing copyrighted labels violated L'Anza's "exclusive rights under 17 U.S.C. §§ 106, 501 and 602 to reproduce and distribute the copyrighted material in the United States." The District Court rejected petitioner's defense based on the "first sale" doctrine recognized by § 109 and entered summary judgment in favor of L'Anza. Based largely on its conclusion that § 602 would be "meaningless" if § 109 provided a defense in a case of this kind, the Court of Appeals affirmed. 98 F.3d 1109, 1114 (CA9 1996). Because its decision created a conflict with the Third Circuit, see *Sebastian Int'l, Inc.* v. *Consumer Contacts (PTY) Ltd.*, 847 F.2d 1093 (1988), we granted the petition for certiorari. 117 S. Ct. 2406, 138 L. Ed. 2d 173 (1997).

II

This is an unusual copyright case because L'Anza does not claim that anyone has made unauthorized copies of its copyrighted labels. Instead, L'Anza is primarily interested in protecting the integrity of its method of marketing the products to which the labels are affixed. Although the labels themselves have only a limited creative component, our interpretation of the relevant statutory provisions would apply equally to a case involving more familiar copyrighted materials such as sound recordings or books. Indeed, we first endorsed the first sale doctrine in a case involving a claim by a publisher that the resale of its books at discounted prices infringed its copyright on the books. *Bobbs-Merrill Co.* v. *Straus,* 210 U.S. 339, 52 L. Ed. 1086, 28 S. Ct. 722 (1908). . . .

The statute in force when *Bobbs-Merrill* was decided provided that the copyright owner had the exclusive right to "vend" the copyrighted work. Congress subsequently codified our holding in *Bobbs-Merrill* that the exclusive right to "vend" was limited to first sales of the work. Under the 1976 Act, the comparable exclusive right granted in 17 U.S.C. § 106(3) is the right "to distribute copies . . . by sale or other transfer of ownership." The comparable limitation on that right is provided not by judicial interpretation, but by an express statutory provision. Section 109(a) provides:

> "Notwithstanding the provisions of section 106(3), the owner of a particular copy or phonorecord lawfully made under this title, or any person authorized by such owner, is entitled, without the authority of the copyright owner, to sell or otherwise dispose of the possession of that copy or phonorecord . . . ."

. . .

III

The most relevant portion of § 602(a) provides:

> "Importation into the United States, without the authority of the owner of copyright under this title, of copies or phonorecords of a work that have been acquired outside the United States is an infringement of the exclusive right to distribute copies or phonorecords under section 106, actionable under section 501 . . . ."

It is significant that this provision does not categorically prohibit the unauthorized importation of copyrighted materials. Instead, it provides that such importation is an infringement of the exclusive right to distribute copies "under section 106." Like the exclusive right to "vend" that was construed in *Bobbs-Merrill,* the exclusive right to distribute is a limited right. The introductory language in § 106 expressly states that all of the exclusive rights granted by that section – including, of course, the distribution right granted by subsection (3) – are limited by the provisions of §§ 107 through 120. One of those limitations, as we have noted, is provided by the terms of § 109(a), which expressly permit the owner of a lawfully made copy to sell that copy "notwithstanding the provisions of section 106(3)."

After the first sale of a copyrighted item "lawfully made under this title," any subsequent purchaser, whether from a domestic or from a foreign reseller, is obviously an "owner" of that item. Read literally, § 109(a) unambiguously states that such an owner "is entitled, without the authority of the copyright owner, to sell" that item. Moreover, since § 602(a) merely provides that unauthorized importation is an infringement of an exclusive right "under section 106," and since that limited right does not encompass resales by lawful owners, the literal text of § 602(a) is simply inapplicable to both domestic and foreign owners of L'Anza's products who decide to import them and resell them in the United States.[14] [n14 Despite L'Anza's contention to the contrary, the owner of goods lawfully made under the Act is entitled to the protection of the first sale doctrine in an action in a United States court even if the first sale occurred abroad. Such protection does not require the extraterritorial application of the Act any more than § 602(a)'s "acquired abroad" language does.]

Notwithstanding the clarity of the text of §§ 106(3), 109(a), and 602(a), L'Anza argues that the language of the Act supports a construction of the right granted by § 602(a) as "distinct from the right under Section 106(3) standing alone," and thus not subject to § 109(a). Otherwise, L'Anza argues, both the § 602(a) right itself and its exceptions would be superfluous. Moreover, supported by various *amici curiae*, including the Solicitor General of the United States, L'Anza contends that its construction is supported by important policy considerations. We consider these arguments separately.

IV

L'Anza advances two primary arguments based on the text of the Act. . . . [And a] . . . textual argument [is] advanced by the Solicitor General [as well]. . . .

[But] . . . we are not persuaded by either L'Anza's or the Solicitor General's textual arguments.

V

The parties and their *amici* have debated at length the wisdom or unwisdom of governmental restraints on what is sometimes described as either the "gray market" or the practice of "parallel importation." In *K mart Corp.* v. *Cartier, Inc.,* 486 U.S. 281, 100 L. Ed. 2d 313, 108 S. Ct. 1811 (1988), we used those terms to refer to the importation of foreign-manufactured goods bearing a valid United States trademark without the consent of the trademark holder. We are not at all sure that those terms appropriately describe the consequences of an American manufacturer's decision to limit its promotional efforts to the domestic market and to sell its products abroad at discounted prices that are so low that its foreign distributors can compete in the domestic market. But even if they do, whether or not we think it would be wise policy to provide statutory protection for such price discrimination is not a matter that is relevant to our duty to interpret the text of the Copyright Act.

Equally irrelevant is the fact that the Executive Branch of the Government has entered into at least five international trade agreements that are apparently intended to protect domestic copyright owners from the unauthorized importation of copies of their works sold in those five countries.[30] [n30 The Solicitor General advises us that such agreements have been made with Cambodia, Trinidad and Tobago, Jamaica, Ecuador, and Sri Lanka.] The earliest of those agreements was made in 1991; none has been ratified by the Senate. Even though they are of course consistent with the position taken by the Solicitor General in this litigation, they shed no light on the proper interpretation of a statute that was enacted in 1976.

The judgment of the Court of Appeals is reversed.

It is so ordered.

Justice Ginsburg, concurring.

This case involves a "round trip" journey, travel of the copies in question from the United States to places abroad, then back again. I join the Court's opinion recognizing that we do not today resolve cases in which the allegedly infringing imports were manufactured abroad. See W. Patry, Copyright Law and Practice 166-170 (1997 Supp.) (commenting that provisions of Title 17 do not apply extraterritorially unless expressly so stated, hence the words "lawfully made under this title" in the "first sale" provision, 17 U.S.C. § 109(a), must mean "lawfully made in the United States"); see generally P. Goldstein, Copyright § 16.0, pp. 16:1-16:2 (2d ed. 1998) ("Copyright protection is territorial. The rights granted by the United States Copyright Act extend no farther than the nation's borders.").

---

**Deutsche Grammophon Gesellschaft GmbH**
**v. Metro-SB-Grossmarkte GmbH & Co. Ltd**
**[1971] ECR 487, [1971] CMLR 631, 2 IIC 429**
**(Court of Justice of the European Communities 1971)**

The facts of the case . . . may be summarized as follows.

Deutsche Grammophon . . . produces grampohone records (for which it has certain artists under exclusive contracts) and markets its products under a number of marks. In the German Federal Republic the records are supplied direct to retailers and to two book-wholesalers which exclusively supply retail bookshops. The retail prices of the records are mostly controlled; in any event, all the numbers that are sold under the "Polydor" mark are subject to a retail price-maintenance system. Retailers have to sign an appropriate form to this effect. The form in addition provides that the price-maintenance undertaking also applies to Deutsche Grammophon records acquired from third parties and that such products can only be imported from abroad with the authorisation of Deutsche Grammophon (and the consent is only given if the retailer also undertakes to observe the price-maintenance system in this respect). Deutsche Grammophon, on its part, is bound to supply solely to retailers who sign the undertaking. In addition, it has to ensure that the price-maintenance system is kept watertight and proceed against infringements. The records are marketed abroad through subsidiaries of Deutsche Grammophon or Philips. This is the case in particular in France where Polydor SA, Paris (99.55 per cent of the capital of which is held by Deutsche Grammophon), supplies the market from its factories in Paris and Strasbourg. Deutsche Grammophon has concluded a licensing agreement with it, whereby the licensee has inter alia the exclusive right in . . . France to exploit Deutsche Grammophon recordings through . . . through retailers and to use the appropriate marks. For this purpose Deutsche Grammophon supplies matrixes for reproduction against payment of licence fees. In special cases records manufactured in the Federal Republic are also supplied to Polydor Paris.

Metro-SB-Grossmarkte . . . bought Polydor records from Deutsche Grammophon in the period from April to October 1969 but did not observe the retail price-maintenance system. Since Metro was not prepared to sign a retailer's undertaking, business relations were broken off at the end of October 1969. However, in January and February 1970 Metro succeeded in obtaining Polydor records manufactured by Deutsche Grammophon in Germany from a Hamburg wholesaler.

Apparently these records had been supplied by Deutsche Grammophon to its Paris subsidiary. They had then reached the Hamburg wholesaler through the Strasbourg branch and a Swiss enterprise. Metro also sold these recrods to retail customers at a price below that fixed by Deutsche Grammophon for the Federal Republic.

When Deutsche Grammophon learned of this it obtained a provisional injunction from [a German court] on 20 March 1970 prohibiting Metro from selling or distributing in any other way Deutsche Grammophon records with certain serial numbers under the Polydor mark. The application and the court's decision were based on the [German copyright statute] which, in accordance with the [Rome] Convention . . . , created an original protection right, similar to copyright, for manufacturers of sound recordings. . . . The [German court] invoked sections 85 and 97 of the German [copyright] statute, which provide as follows:

> Section 85: "The manufacturer of a sound recording has the exclusive right to reproduce and to distribute the recording."
>
> Section 97: "Any person who unlawfully infringes the copyright or any other right protected by this statute may, at the suit of the person whose rights are infringed, be ordered to abate the infringement, or, if there is a danger of repetition, be restrained by injunction, and if he is found to have acted with intent or negligence he may be ordered to pay damages."

In addition, the court evidently found that the exclusive right attibuted to Deutsche Grammophon to distribute its records in Germany had not been exhausted by the delivery to Polydor Paris. Thus it held that there was no exhaustion of the right as provided in the appropriately applicable section 17 of the [German] Copyright Statute in the following words:

> "If the original or reproductions of the work have been brought into circulation with the consent of the person entitled to distribute them in the territory to which this statute applies by means of alienation their further distribution is permitted."

In the view of the court, this provision would only have applied if a distribution had occurred in the German Federal Republic. Otherwise the marketing of re-imported records in Germany had to be regarded as impermissible.

The protest lodged by Metro against the provisional injunction was unsuccessful. In a judgment of 22 May 1970 all the arguments submitted against the order of the court were held to be of no avail. Metro then lodged an appeal against this judgment and the matter thus came before the Hanseatische Oberlandesgericht [a German appeals court]. In support of the appeal it was submitted inter alia that Deutsche Grammophon no longer had the distribution rights in the records in question as these rights had been extinguished by the delivery to the French subsidiary. In addition it was contended that the contractual relations between Deutsche Grammophon and its French licensee constituted a division of the market and made inter-state trade more difficult, which, in conjunction with the price-maintenance system practised in the Federal Republic, justified the assertion that Articles 85 and 86 of the EEC Treaty were infringed.

In view of these arguments the Oberlandesgericht [the German appelas court], by an order of 8 October 1970, suspended the proceedings and in accordance with Article 177 of the EEC Treaty submitted the following questions for a preliminary ruling [by this court, i.e., the Court of Justice of the European Communities]:

1. Does an interpretation of Sections 97 and 85 of the [German] Statute concerning Copyright, whereby a German manufacturer of sound recordings, by

virtue of its distribution rights, can prohibit the marketing in the German Federal Republic of recordings which it has itself supplied to its subsidiary France which is legally separate but economically completely dependent, conflict with Article 5(2) or Article 85(1) of the EEC Treaty? . . .

According to Article 177 [of the EEC Treaty] the Court [of Justice of the European Communities] can only give preliminary rulings regarding the interpretation of the [EEC] Treaty and the measures taken by the organs of the Community or concerning the validity of these measures, and not with regard to the interpretation of a provision of national law. Nevertheless, it may extract from the wording of the question submitted by the national court, in the light of the facts found by that court, the questions that relate to the interpretation of the Treaty.

From the findings of the Hanseatische Oberlandesgericht, Hamburg, [the German appeals court,] it must be supposed that the question posed really seeks to ascertain whether [European] Community law is infringed if the exclusive right conferred on a manufacturer of recordings by national legislation to distribute the protected products can be used to prohibit the domestic marketing of products that have been brought into the market in the territory of another member-State by this manufacturer or with his consent. Thus the Court is asked to ascertain the content and scope of the applicable Community rules, particularly with regard to Article 5(2) or 85(1) of the Treaty.

According to Article 5(2) of the Treaty the member-States must "abstain from any measures which could jeopardise the attainment of the objectives of [the] Treaty." This provision imposes a general obligation on the member-States the concrete content of which depends in a particular case on the provisions of the Treaty or the rules of law derived from the general system of the Treaty.

According to Article 85(1) of the Treaty "all agreements between undertakings, all decisions by associations of undertakings and all concerted practices, which may affect trade between member-States and the object or effect of which is to prevent, restrict or distort competition within the common market are incompatible with the common Market and prohibited." The exercise of the exclusive right mentioned in the question may always come within this prohibition if it is proved that it is the object, means or consequence of a cartel agreement which effects a division of the Common market by prohibiting imports from other member-States of products duly brought onto the market in those States.

Nevertheless, if such an exercise of rights does not fulfil the requirements of the definition of an agreement or concerted practice under Article 85 of the EEC Treaty, to answer the question it must further be decided whether the exercise of the protection right in issue conflicts with other provisions of the Treaty, in particular those relating to the free movement of goods.

For this purpose reference must be made to the principles for the realisation of a uniform market among the member-States which are laid down in the Title "The Free Movement of Goods" in the second part of the Treaty devoted to the "Foundations of the Community" and in Article 3(f) of the Treaty which provides for the establishment of a system to protect competition within the Common Market against distortions.

Although the Treaty otherwise permits prohibitions or restrictions on the movement of goods between member-States laid down in Article 36, it nevertheless sets clear limits to these prohibitions or restrictions by providing that these exceptions may not amount "either to a means of arbitrary discrimination or to a disguised restriction on trade between the member-States."

According to these provisions, in particular Articles 36, 85 and 86, it must therefore be considered to what extent the marketing of products imported from another member-State may be prohibited in exercise of a national protection right similar to copyright.

Article 36 mentions among the prohibitions or restrictions on the free movement of goods permitted by it those that are justified for the protection of industrial and commercial property. [It may] be assumed that a right analogous to copyright can be covered by these provisions[.] [Nevertheless] it follows . . . from this Article that although the Treaty does not affect the existence of the industrial property rights conferred by the national legislation of a member-State, the exercise of these rights may come within the prohibitions of the Treaty. Although Article 36 permits prohibitions or restrictions on the free movement of goods that are justified for the protection of industrial and commercial property, it only allows such restrictions on the freedom of trade to the extent that they are justified for the protection of the rights that form the specific object of this property.

If a protection right analogous to copyright is used in order to prohibit in one member-State the marketing of goods that have been brought onto the market by the holder of the right or with his consent in the territory of another member-State solely because this marketing has not occurred in the domestic market, such a prohibition maintaining the isolation of the national markets conflicts with the essential aim of the Treaty, the integration of the national markets into one uniform market. This aim could not be achieved if by virtue of the various legal systems of the member-States private persons were able to divide the market and cause arbitrary discriminations or disguised restrictions in trade between the member-States.

Accordingly, it would conflict with the provisions regarding the free movement of goods in the Common market if a manufacturer of recordings exercised the exclusive right granted to him by the legislation of a member-State to market the protected articles in order to prohibit the marketing in that member-State of products that had been sold by him himself or with his consent in another member-State solely because this marketing had not occurred in the territory of the first member-State. . . .

The Court, for these reasons, giving judgment on the questions submitted to it by the Hanseatische Oberlandesgericht Hamburg in its order of 8 October 1970,

Hereby decides:

1. It conflicts with the provisions regarding the free movement of goods in the Common Market if a manufacturer of recordings so exercises the exclusive right granted to him by the legislation of a member-State to market the protected articles as to prohibit the marketing in that member-State of products that have been sold by himself or with his consent in another member-State solely because this marketing has not occurred in the territory of the first member-State. . . .

---

**Warner Bros. Inc. v. Christiansen**
**[1988] ECR 2605, [1990] 3 CMLR 684, [1991] FSR 161**
**(Court of Justice of the European Communities 1988)**

The film "Never Say Never Again" was produced by one of the plaintiffs in the main proceedings, Warner Brothers Incorporated, which assigned the video-production rights [i.e., homevideo manufacturing and distribution rights] for Denmark to the second plaintiff in the main proceedings, Metronome Video ApS.

In July 1984, while video-cassettes of the film could be purchased in England but were not available either for purchase or for hire in Denmark, the defendant in the main proceedings, Mr. Christiansen, who manages a video shop in Copenhagen, bought a copy of the film in London for the purpose of hiring it out [i.e., renting it to customers] in Denmark.

It is common ground between the parties that, as is stated in the order of the [Danish] national court,

– the video-cassette in question was lawfully manufactured, marketed and purchased in the United Kingdom;

– it was lawfully imported into Denmark by Mr. Christiansen;

– British copyright law does not confer any right of dissemination within the United Kingdom of the author or producer, so that the purchaser of a film recorded on video-cassette may hire it out in the United Kingdom without the consent of the owner of the exclusive rights;

– by virtue of . . . Danish Law . . . , the exclusive right to authorize the hiring-out of a musical or cinematographic work is not exhausted when the copyright owner sells a copy of the work but only when he authorizes the hiring-out of the work. Those articles therefore make it possible to prohibit the hiring-out to the public of a video-cassette without the copyright owner's consent, irrespective of how the video-cassette was purchased.

On the basis of that Danish legislation the two plaintiffs in the main proceedings obtained an injunction from the Copenhagen City Court restraining the defendant from hiring out the video-cassette in Denmark.

The plaintiffs then requested confirmation of the injunction from the Ostre Landsret [the Eastern Division of the Danish High Court] which, before giving judgment, made an order dated 11 June 1986 staying the proceedings and referring the following question to the Court of Justice [of the European Community] for a preliminary ruling:

> Must the provisions of Chapter 2 in Title I of Part 2 of the EEC Treaty, on the elimination of quantitative restrictions between Member States, namely Articles 30 and 36, in conjunction with Article 222 of the Treaty, be interpreted as meaning that the owner of exclusive rights (copyright) in a video cassette which is lawfully put into circulation by the owner of the exclusive right or with his consent in a Member State under whose domestic copyright law he may not prohibit the (resale and) hiring-out of the video cassette is prevented from restraining the hiring-out of that video cassette in another Member State into which it has been lawfully imported, where the copyright law of that State allows such prohibition without distinguishing between domestic and imported video-cassettes and without preventing the actual importation thereof? . . .

It should be noted that, unlike the national copyright legislation which gave rise to the judgment of 20 January 1981 in Musik Vertrieb Membran v GEMA, the legislation which gives rise to the present preliminary question does not enable the author to collect an additional fee on the actual importation of recordings of protected works which are marketed with his consent in another Member State, or to set up any further obstacle whatsoever to importation or resale. The rights and powers conferred on the author by the national legislation in question comes into operation only after importation has been carried out.

None the less, it must be observed that the commercial distribution of video-cassettes takes the form not only of sales but also, and increasingly, that of hiring out to individuals who possess video-tape recorders. The right to prohibit such hiring-out in a Member State is therefore liable to influence trade in video-cassettes in that State and hence, indirectly, to affect intra-Community trade in those products. Legislation of the kind which gave rise to the main proceedings must therefore, in the light of established csae-law, be regarded as a measure having an effect equivalent to a quantitative restriction on imports, which is prohibited by Article 30 of the Treaty.

Consideration should therefore be given to whether such legislation may be considered justified on grounds of the protection of industrial and commercial property within the meaning of Article 36 – a term which was held by the Court, in Coditel v. Cine-Vog, to include literary and artistic property.

In that connexion it should first be noted that the Danish legislation applies without distinction to video-cassettes produced in [Denmark] and video-cassettes imported from another Member State. The determining factor for the purposes of its application is the type of transaction in video-cassettes which is in question, not the origin of those video-cassettes. Such legislation does not therefore, in itself, operate any arbitrary discrimination in trade between Member States.

It should further be pointed out that literary and artistic works may be the subject of commercial exploitation, whether by way of public performance or of the reproduction and marketing of the recordings made of them, and this is true in particular of cinematographic works. The two essential rights of the author, namely the exclusive right of performance and the exclusive right of reproduction, are not called in question by the rules of the Treaty.

Lastly, consideration must be given to the emergence, demonstrated by the Commission, of a specific market for the hiring-out of such recordings, as distinct from their sale. The existence of that market was made possible by various factors such as the improvement of manufacturing methods for video-cassettes which increased their strength and life in use, the growing awareness amongst viewers that they watch only occasionally the video-cassettes whch they have bought and, lastly, their relatively high purchase price. The market for the hiring-out of video-cassettes reaches a wider public than the market for their sale and, at present, offers great potential as a source of revenue for makers of films.

However, it is apparent that, by authorizing the collection of royalties only on sales to private individuals and to persons hiring out video-cassettes, it is impossible to guarantee to makers of films a remuneration which reflects the number of occasions on which the video-cassettes are actually hired out and which secures for them a satisfactory share of the rental market. That explains why, as the Commission points out in its observations, certain national laws have recently provided specific protection of the right to hire out video-cassettes.

Laws of that kind are therefore clearly justified on grounds of the protection of industrial and commercial property pursuant to Article 36 of the Treaty.

However, the defendant in the main proceedings, relying on Dansk Supermarked v Imerco and Musik Vertrieb Membran v GEMA, contends that the author is at liberty to choose the Member State in which he will market his work. The defendant in the main proceedings emphasizes that the author makes his choice according to his own interests and must, in particular, take into consideration the fact that the legislation of certain Member States, unlike that of certain others, confers on him an exclusive right enabling him to restrain the hiring-out of the recording of the work even when that work has been offered for sale with his consent. That being so, a maker of a film who has offered the video-cassette of that film for sale in a Member State whose legislation confers on him no exclusive right of hiring it out (as in the main proceedings) must accept the consequences of his choice and the exhaustion of his right to restrain the hiring-out of that video-cassette in any other Member State.

That objection cannot be upheld. It follows from the foregoing considerations that, where national legislation confers on authors a specific right to hire out video-cassettes, that right would be rendered worthless if its owner were not in a position to authorize the operations for doing so. It cannot therefore be accepted that the marketing by a film-maker of a video-cassette containing one of his works, in a Member State which does not provide specific protection for the right to hire it out, should have repercussions on the right conferred on that same film-maker by the legislation of another Member State to restrain, in that State, the hiring-out of that video-cassette.

In those circumstanes, the answer to be given to the question submitted by the national court is that Articles 30 and 36 of the Treaty do not prohibit the application of national legislation which gives an author the right to make the hiring-out of video-cassettes subject to his permission, when the video-cassettes in question have already been put into circulation with his consent in another Member State whose legislation enables the author to control the initial sale, without giving him the right to prohibit hiring-out. . . .

On those grounds, the Court, in answer to the question referred to it by the Ostre Landsret, Copenhagen, by order of 11 June 1986, hereby rules:

Articles 30 and 36 of the EEC Treaty do not prohibit the application of national legislation which gives an author the right to make the hiring-out of video-cassettes subject to his permission, when the video-cassettes in question have already been put into circulation with his consent in another Member State whose legislation enables the author to control the initial sale, without giving him the right to prohibit hiring-out.

---

**Australian Competition & Consumer Commission**
**v. Universal Music Australia Pty Limited**
**Federal Court of Australia**
**[2001] FCA 1800 (14 December 2001)**

Justice Hill:

*REASONS FOR JUDGMENT*

*Introduction*

1 The Australian Competition and Consumer Commission ("ACCC") seeks pecuniary penalties and other relief in two proceedings brought by it under the *Trade Practices Act* 1974 ("the Act"). The first is a proceeding against Universal Music Australia Pty Limited ("Universal"). . . . The second is a proceeding against Warner Music Australia Pty Limited ("Warner"). . . .

2 The two proceedings were heard together. . . .

3 Universal was formerly named PolyGram Pty Limited. It changed its name as a result of a merger in March or April 1999 between what may be referred to as PolyGram and Universal. . . .

4 Each proceeding is concerned with conduct which is alleged to contravene the [Trade Practices] Act and which related to the marketing in Australia by Universal and Warner of compact discs ("CDs"). The background to each is the amendment of the *Copyright Act 1968* ("the Copyright Act") in 1998 by the Copyright Amendment Act (No 2) 1998 (the relevant amendments are here referred to as "the Copyright Amendments") to make it possible, legally, for the importation into Australia of CDs from other countries, so long as they did not infringe the

copyright laws of the country in which they were manufactured. Prior to the Copyright Amendments the importation into Australia of CDs manufactured outside Australia (at least where copyright protection was available in Australia) without the licence of the owner of copyright in Australia was an infringement of copyright and an offence. Such imports were and are popularly referred to as "parallel importing." However, as and from 30 July 1998, as a result of the Copyright Amendments, but subject to the provisions of the Copyright Act, parallel importing was, generally speaking, no longer illegal, at least so long as the imported CD did not infringe the copyright laws of the country in which it was manufactured. . . . Those CDs which were able to be imported legally into Australia without the consent of the Australian copyright owner are here referred to as "non-infringing copies." Those which were not, because they were manufactured overseas without the licence of the copyright owner, are here referred to as "infringing copies." Where in these reasons reference is made to the legalisation of parallel importing that reference is intended to refer to the legalisation of the importation into Australia and without consent of the Australian copyright owner of non-infringing copies.

5 It is not surprising that the legalisation of parallel importing into Australia was not greeted with enthusiasm by those who manufactured and sold CDs in Australia with the consent of the copyright owner for Australia. Whereas prior to 30 July 1998 these manufacturers (and both Universal and Warner were such manufacturers) had a statutory monopoly on the manufacture in Australia and thus wholesale sale of CDs as a result of the copyright protection they enjoyed, that statutory monopoly substantially disappeared and the prospect opened of the importation into Australia for sale by others of non-infringing copies that were effectively the same as the Australian manufactured CDs. The importation could be effected by those who wished to sell the non-infringing copies by wholesale to record retailers or by the retailers themselves for sale to the public.

6 It is well known that the record companies in Australia lobbied long and hard to have the amendments to the Copyright Act defeated in Parliament. In that they were not successful. However, they did succeed in having the amendments passed in a form which, to some extent at least, rendered the position of the importer somewhat uncertain. The uncertainty arose because of the requirement of the amendments that it would continue to be an infringement of copyright in Australia to sell imported CDs (and other musical works, such as records and cassettes) unless the importer or vendor was able to establish that the musical work was manufactured with the licence of the copyright owner overseas. Given that the question of who the owner of copyright might be in other countries is not a matter of public record and given also that many of the record companies are members of international groups of companies, where the ownership of the relevant copyrights may be in the hands of more than one company in the group situated, perhaps, not in the country where the CD was manufactured, but in rather more obscure locations which international taxation laws might render advantageous, the burden of proof placed upon the importer or vendor to show the imported copy was a non-infringing copy might well be thought to be difficult if not impossible to satisfy. Indeed, as will be seen, the effect of the legislation and particularly the burden of proof provisions made it not unlikely that the manufacturers of CDs in Australia might, with little reason to believe it to be the case, allege that CDs imported or sold were infringing copies and thus stop the sale of what were alleged to be, although in fact were not necessarily, infringing copies.

*The Copyright Act Provisions*

7 Under the Copyright Act, copyright will subsist at the least in both the words and the music of a musical work which is embodied in a CD. Such copyright

is infringed if the work is reproduced on a sound recording. Likewise, copyright may subsist in the recording itself. It will be an infringement of a relevant copyright if a person not the owner of the copyright does anything in Australia without the licence of the copyright owner which the Copyright Act stipulates that the copyright owner has the exclusive right to do. It will thus be an infringement in Australia to reproduce a musical work as a sound recording, to reproduce a sound recording or to sell or distribute for trade the sound recording, without the licence of the relevant copyright owner. It also constitutes an infringement of copyright to import into Australia a CD for the purpose of selling it, where, if the importer had manufactured the CD in Australia, that manufacture would constitute an infringement, unless the CD imported is a "non-infringing copy of a sound recording." "A non-infringing copy" is defined in s 10AA of the Copyright Act to mean:

> ". . . [a copy] made by or with the consent of:
>
> (a) the owner of the copyright or related right in the sound recording in the country (the copy country) in which the copy was made; or
>
> (b) the owner of the copyright or related right in the sound recording in the country (the original recording country) in which the sound recording was made, if the law of the copy country did not provide for copyright or a related right in sound recording when the sound recording was made . . .
>
> (2) If the sound recording is of a work that is a literary, dramatic or musical work in which copyright subsists in Australia, the copy is a non-infringing copy only if:
>
> (a) copyright subsists in the work under the law of the copy country; and
>
> (b) the making of the copy does not infringe the copyright in the work under the law of the copy country; and
>
> (c) the copy country meets the requirements of subsection (3)."

[Subsection (3) is generally concerned with whether the country is a party to the international copyright convention or a member of the World Trade Organisation.]

8 Section 130A of the Copyright Act provides that in an action for infringement involving a copy of a sound recording: " . . . it *must* be presumed that the copy is not a non-infringing copy unless the defendant proves that the copy is a non-infringing copy." (emphasis added)

9 Each of the present cases is concerned with steps alleged to have been taken by Universal and Warner respectively to deter importers and others from parallel importing in the period shortly after the Copyright Amendments were passed. In general terms it is alleged that each engaged in conduct which constituted a breach of ss . . . 46 and 47 of the [Trade Practices] Act. Each denies that such conduct as it engaged in was a contravention of these sections. . . .

*Relevant Provisions of the [Trade Practices] Act . . .*

11 Section 46 [prohibits] . . . "Misuse of market power. . . ."

12 Section 47 [prohibits] . . . "Exclusive dealing. . . ."

*Outline of the Matters Dealt with in Evidence*

27 There was a veritable flood of evidence at the hearing which came to resemble a royal commission into the record industry in Australia. . . .

290 Australia is a significant world market for music sales. In the 1997 calendar year Australia ranked eighth in the total world retail sales of recorded music (the data would seem to include cassettes and vinyl recording as well as CDs), with an overall $US739.1 million of sales ($AUD972.1 million). The following year Australia had slipped to ninth place with overall sales of $606.7

million ($AUD964 million). There was thus a 1% reduction in sales when valued in Australian currency, said to be a result of the legalisation of parallel importing.

328 The legalisation of parallel importation removed the statutory monopoly (at least in theory) which the record companies had as a result of the copyright laws which prevented importation without the licence of the holder of the Australian copyrights. Since approximately 80% of the sales of retailers were derived from some 20% of titles, it was obvious that importers would target those titles. The record companies took seriously what they perceived to be a threat to their business by the opening up of the Australian market to imported product. There was an increase in the level of imports from South East Asia in the last four months of 1998. However the overall level of imported CDs increased dramatically only in January 1999. Most of the imports were from Indonesia, a country which offered at that time the dual benefit of cheap prices and weak currency. . . .

331 Non-infringing copies from the Australian catalogues of the major record companies, at least if released internationally, were available to be imported from various overseas suppliers once parallel importation became legal. It seems at that time that prices in the US, Canada and the UK were comparable to Australian prices and hence importation from these countries was not financially viable. However, CDs could be imported from a number of South East Asian countries at a landed price well below the prevailing wholesale price in Australia. As already noted, at that time Indonesia was the most attractive source of supply. . . .

332 It was not possible to source from overseas all of the chart music within the Australian catalogue of the majors. It was unusual for Australian titles, and especially Australian singles, to be released overseas (unless they made the charts, of which only a relatively small percentage did). This meant that the majors were, and would continue to be, the only source of supply for most Australian titles within their respective catalogues. Moreover, there was no certainty of titles being released overseas being available at the right time or in sufficient quantities to meet demand in Australia, yet timeliness of supply for new releases was of critical importance to a traditional music retailer. Not all back catalogue was available overseas from a particular supplier. . . .

*The Case Under s 46*

*General*

402 The object of s 46 [is] . . . to protect the interest of consumers and . . . to promote competition . . . . It does this by proscribing conduct which involves the use by a corporation of power in the market, which is unconstrained by competitive forces, for a purpose which Parliament has identified as anti-competitive. The section is not, as senior counsel for Warner emphasised on more than one occasion . . . to regulate behaviour merely because it may be seen to be reprehensible, or blameworthy. Nor . . . is the section concerned to protect the private interests of particular persons or corporations.

403 For a case such as the present to fall within s 46 of the Act it will be necessary for the following matters to be found:

(i) a corporation with power in a market;

(ii) that the corporation has that power to a substantial degree;

(iii) the taking advantage of that power by the corporation; and

(iv) the requisite purpose, here, the preventing the entry of a person into a market or, perhaps, the preventing a person from engaging in competitive conduct in a market.

It is necessary to consider each of these elements in turn.

*Power in a market . . .*

417 One constraint preventing both Universal and Warner from behaving independently of competitive forces in the recorded music market is the presence of the large retailers in the market. While they, no doubt, would be both unhappy and indeed, inconvenienced if they were unable to purchase from any of the five major record companies (and the need for warehousing and distribution facilities to cope with imports if access to any or all the companies' catalogues were unavailable would present initial difficulty and cost), the fact is that the record companies needed the large retailers at least as much as the large retailers needed the record companies. That is ultimately the explanation why it was possible for HMV [an Australian record store chain] to refuse to purchase the product of Sony as a means of extracting better trading concessions. It is the explanation why none of the large retailers were unduly perturbed by such threat as there was contained in the Universal policy [that it might cease to have a trading relationship with them should they choose to stock imports which were non-infringing copies of Universal's catalogue] as conveyed to them both in writing and in conversation. It may also explain why the Warner letter of 20 July 1998 [in which Warner advised its Australian retailers that if they ceased to source recorded music in the Warner catalogue exclusively from Warner or sourced supply through parallel imports of non-infringing copies, Warner would no longer provide trading benefits, including support of sales and promotional teams, extensive point of sale material, television, print and radio advertising and promotional visits] left little impression upon those from the large retailers who gave evidence before me.

418 The small retailers were in a quite different position. They lacked the countervailing power of the large retailers. They lacked the ability to import competitively. They required access to chart music [that is to say music that is highly popular, although usually for a relatively short period, such that it appears on a chart, for example, "the Top 40"] (assuming they did not specialise in a particular genre of music where chart music played no part) and some part, at least, of the back catalogue. I think it likely that many would not survive if they could not purchase directly from the record company and on reasonable terms. A consequence would be that there would most likely be a reduction in competition at the retail level if the record companies refused to deal with the small retailers unless they purchased all their needs directly. . . .

423 There is . . . no really significant barrier to entry to the record industry generally, as indeed the growth from time to time of independents demonstrates. (The fact that new entrants may ultimately be absorbed by the major record companies does not seem to me to necessitate an opposite conclusion.) New entrants must compete with existing participants for artists. At least so far as new artists are concerned, new entrants might be expected to have no greater or less chance of recognising what is likely to be a "hit" than existing companies. Further, new artists might more readily be prepared to contract with new entrants to the market than established artists. Indeed it may be surmised that in some cases, not only might new artists be ignored altogether by the five major record companies, but even if they were not ignored might also be given more prominence by new entrants than would be the case with the larger established record companies. Production costs are relatively low for CDs. Distribution can be contracted out, as has been the case with many independents in the past. Publicity and promotion, the greatest cost ingredients in recorded music, are high in comparison with other costs, but save for a carryover effect from international publicity of international artists, are (perhaps subject to volume advertising discounts) neither more expensive for nor less accessible to new participants than for existing participants. It is not

suggested that radio, television or print media are less accessible to new entrants than to existing participants. On the other hand, it must be acknowledged that new entrants would not immediately have a large repertoire of existing product. That takes time to develop. More importantly it would be very difficult indeed for a new entrant to the market to be able to put on the market the constant stream of hits which constitute chart music.

424 The real question that arises in the present case is whether, having regard to the structure of the recorded music market and the significance which hit music has in that market, barriers to entry should be considered by reference to the overall flow of recordings in the market for recorded music generally, where they are not high, or whether regard should be had to the monopoly which is afforded to each record company in respect of such CDs as feature on the chart at a particular point of time as a result of the Copyright laws. Clearly enough, new firms can not enter the market of producing titles covered by copyright protection held by a particular record company. Absent any exclusive dealing conduct on the part of particular record companies directed at importers coming into the market, there would be no barrier for entry for them either. It must be added, however, that the drafting of the law permitting parallel importation, casting as it does the onus upon the importer to show each record imported was produced with the licence of the copyright holder in its place of manufacture, may in many cases make it almost impossible for an importer to avoid legal action by a determined record company wishing to impede competition.

425 I find the issue of market power and its related issue of barriers to entry extremely difficult to decide. It is really at the heart of the controversy between the parties. The case of a firm operating in an oligopolistic market with only 15% market share and unable to fix prices in the overall market above the competitive level but which has, as a result of a temporary monopoly power over a limited number of products in that market, substantial power to exclude competitors is not one which has been the subject of any authority in Australia or, so far as my researches indicate, in any other country. . . .

426 It is not unreasonable to ask what kind of power was Universal (or Warner) seeking to exercise when it set out to deter retailers from parallel importation by the conduct which it engaged in. It was only because it had power in the market that it could achieve its aim, at least with so much of the retail market as comprised the smaller retailers. The threat to refuse supply was not one which the small retailers could ignore, especially once it became clear that it was more than a threat and would be implemented. The retail business was threatened, particularly if more than 50% of customers were likely to go elsewhere to purchase the title which the retailer no longer stocked. Even the large retailers would be likely to think twice before importing CDs from overseas, if only because of the inconvenience of having to import their entire stock and in many cases having to establish a separate warehousing and distribution network. They would still not be able to stock some locally released titles unavailable overseas. In my view, whatever may be the view of economists, particularly, American economists, business people in Australia would regard such behaviour as involving both market power and the exercise of that power.

427 In reaching this conclusion I am conscious that the definition of the market requires that a common sense approach be taken so as not to concentrate on what is but a snapshot of the market at a particular point of time. I accept that the definition of market focuses in a case such as the present upon the continuous flow of product over time in a process where new albums displace old so as to compete for the attention of the public. But I do not think that acceptance of this definition of market

requires me to ignore the way that the market operates in considering the issue of market power. The fact is that chart music in particular has a significance in the market which can not be ignored. It is this significance which would empower a participant in the market such as Universal or Warner to take steps to prevent the entry of a person seeking to import non-infringing copies into the market. . . .

429 . . . All that can be said is that it is necessary for retailers to stock CDs drawn from all the major record companies to meet consumer demand and (except in the case of specialist stores) to stock chart music and have available for sale such parts of the back catalogue as it might wish commercially to order.

430 In deciding whether the action of Universal and Warner in refusing to supply stock to retailers who sold imported CDs was in breach of the [Trade Practices Act] Act, a relevant matter to be considered is whether it would be practical or even possible for retailers, big or small, to import their entire stock of recordings of Warner or Universal titles. It is also relevant to consider whether it would be practicable or even possible for wholesalers to import the whole of the Warner or Universal catalogue. There is no evidence which suggests that any wholesaler has sought to do so. Indeed, such importation as there has been by wholesalers has, on the evidence, been importation of particular popular titles.

431 While the evidence makes it clear that most of the catalogue of the major record companies is available to be imported from overseas sources at least in small quantities, it is also clear that both Warner and Universal can take steps in countries like Indonesia to ensure that stock will not be available to be exported in largish quantities at least to Australia for resale. Transportation delays can result in important titles not being available for sale. The evidence in the case varied from suggesting that only a few days would pass from order to delivery to suggesting that some weeks could pass. Delay of weeks would be commercially disastrous for a retailer wishing to have the title in store as soon as it is released in Australia and so as to take advantage of the pre-release publicity and subsequent advertising and promotion. So far as overseas hits are concerned, the advanced success of albums or singles overseas may offer a lead-time if releases occur overseas before they occur in Australia. If releases are simultaneous, then importation will invoke a time delay. How significant that delay would be would depend upon circumstances.

432 Another factor which would make importation of the entire range of a record company or even the chart range of that record company impractical would be that the cost of importation would be affected by exchange rate fluctuations. The same difficulty would have to be faced by a wholesaler who sought to import for sale the entire or substantially the entire catalogue of Warner or Universal. As rates fluctuated it could be necessary to change suppliers from country to country. History has not shown many occasions in recent times when the Australian dollar has increased in value. But manufacturing promotion and other costs, including general costs of living are likewise reflected in downward exchange adjustments.

433 Then there is the problem that some (although not all) Australian releases are never released overseas and thus are unavailable to be imported at all. There is a trend over time for Australia to lose the cultural cringe which existed in the past and indeed to value its own artists and culture. The inability to purchase those titles would put retailers unable to purchase them at a disadvantage.

434 . . . [W]arehousing and distribution facilities would present some difficulties for large chains of retailers (although it might be assumed that such large chains would more easily be able to pay the capital costs of setting up the necessary facilities). While smaller retailers would not have that problem if they purchased from wholesalers who imported or imported recordings themselves, the latter course would come with inconvenience and expense. . . .

*[To a substantial degree]*

435 The requirement that there be a substantial degree of market power is a requirement that the power in the market be neither trivial nor minimal. It is used in a relative sense and signifies the requirement that market power be real and of substance.

436 No doubt it can be said (and this was the submission made on behalf of the corporate respondents) that each record company (and for that matter, even the minor Jive Zomba) has, as a result of a particular hit recording or recordings in respect of which it has copyright protection, some degree of power in the overall market in the sense I have sought to use the expression. So, it was suggested, by way of reductio ad absurdem that a consequence of the view that Universal and Warner both had market power would be that Jive Zomba with only a few, although quite significant, artists and little in the way of back catalogue would have market power.

437 No doubt the concept of "substantial" market power is one of degree and one of judgment. The question whether Jive Zomba did have market power would require investigation into more facts than are before me. If Jive Zomba threatened not to supply if retailers parallel imported its titles, it is unlikely that the threat would have much teeth given the limited number of recordings it produced, even if such recordings are of popular artists. As presently advised I do not think it likely that Jive Zomba would have market power.

438 In my view both Warner and Universal did have market power in the sense that expression is used in s 46 of the Act and in the context of the structure of that market that market power was substantial.

*Was there a "taking advantage" of market power? . . .*

441 Here, once it is decided that Universal and Warner had each a substantial degree of market power in the market by virtue of each having hits or back catalogue which it was essential for retailers to access, I think that no other conclusion is open but that they had exercised that market power by threatening to refuse and thereafter refusing supply to retailers who imported non-infringing copies of Universal or Warner titles as the case may be. I should add that the so-called Universal policy, which went no more than to threaten retailers that if they dealt in imported titles Universal might consider whether or not to supply or reconsider trading terms, of its own would not be a breach of s 46. It was the implementation of the policy by actually refusing supply which constitutes the breach.

*Purpose*

442 In the present case the purpose alleged is the prevention of entry of other persons into the market, these being, essentially, persons desiring to import non-infringing CDs into the market. (There is no requirement that these other persons be identified, it suffices that they can be inferred to exist or potentially exist.)

443 Purpose in the present context involves intention to achieve a result. . . . On the evidence I have no difficulty in inferring that the refusal by Universal and Warner to supply was motivated by their intention to bring about the result that persons would not import recordings into Australia, whether those persons were wholesalers who carried on the business of importing or were retailers who purchased their requirements from overseas.

444 . . . Any attempt on the part of Universal to suggest that the action taken by it was taken to prevent piracy I would reject. In my view piracy or more accurately breach of the copyright law was not the principal matter of concern, although I accept it was a matter of some concern. What was of principal concern was the bringing into Australia of non-infringing copies at a price cheaper than that

prevailing in Australia and with the result of adversely affecting the bottom line profit of the respondent companies. . . .

445 In my opinion, not only did each of Universal and Warner take advantage of the substantial market power it had, but also each did so to prevent the entry into the wholesale market of persons who would sell imported recordings under Universal or Warner labels by wholesale or wholesalers from overseas with access to non-infringing copies who wished to export to Australia.

*The Case Under s 47*

*General. . .*

447 [The] . . . issues which need to be resolved before an offence under s 47 is made out . . .are:

– Whether Universal or Warner supplied or offered to supply goods (ie CDs) or services (ie aspects of its trading terms) on the condition that the acquirer would not acquire non-infringing copies of titles marketed by Universal or Warner as the case may be in Australia for resale from a competitor.

– Whether the conduct pleaded had the purpose, effect or likely effect of substantially lessening competition in a relevant market.

448 In its case against Universal the ACCC claims that each communication of the PolyGram Policy to a retailer constituted an offer to that retailer to supply either recorded goods or services being continued trading benefits on condition that the retailer agreed not to acquire product within the Australian catalogue of PolyGram from a competitor of PolyGram. . . . In its case against Warner it is alleged that the letter of 20 July 1998 constituted an offer to retailers to supply services (continued trading benefits) on condition that the retailers agreed not to acquire products within the Australian catalogue of Warner from a competitor. . . .

450 The evidence . . . shows that Universal did communicate with a number of retailers to the effect that it would be prepared to review the terms of its trading relationship with those retailers who chose to parallel import and that it reserved its right to cease supplying such retailers with PolyGram recordings. . . .

451 . . . In each case there is to be found in the conversations following closure of accounts an offer to supply only if parallel imported product were not acquired for resale in the future. In each of these cases I would find the requirement of an offer on condition satisfied.

452 In the case of Warner the ACCC relies on the letter of 20 July 1998 . . . to all retailers. . . . To aid understanding here it is convenient to set out that part of it as is relied upon by the ACCC:

> "As a key retail partner *dealing exclusively with us*, you will continue to receive the support of our sales and promotions teams, co-operative advertising, return privileges, favourable credit terms and the provision of extensive POINT-OF-SALE material. . . *[I]t is important you be aware of not only our future intentions, but also the large downside should you wish to alter your source of supply. Such a move will result in us being unable to provide any of the aforementioned trading benefits and will also result in a substantially reduced marketing and advertising spends."* (emphasis added) . . .

454 I think that the evidence makes clear that there was also an offer by Warner to supply services (relating to retailers' accounts) on condition that parallel imported titles not be acquired for resale. . . .

*Was there a purpose or effect of substantially lessening competition? . . .*

462 The purpose in question of the action taken by both Warner and Universal is not difficult to find, as the ACCC submits. It is to discourage retailers from

acquiring, whether by import or purchase, non-infringing copies of titles which were within the respective catalogues of Universal or Warner. . . .

475 . . . I have no doubt that the intention of those controlling PolyGram in Australia was to take such action as could be taken to prevent parallel importation and the steps it took were not necessarily the only steps which would have been taken but for the intervention of the ACCC. The same can be said of the steps taken by Warner.

476 The more difficult question is not that which goes to the purpose or effect of the conduct of Universal or Warner, it is the question whether such conduct as was engaged in . . . was capable of being characterised as substantially lessening competition. . . .

478 What the conduct of each company was designed to achieve and which was likely to have been achieved had it continued was to deter at least the small retailers or a substantial majority of them at least, and having regard to the inconvenience and cost to the large retailers, them also, from acquiring non-infringing copies of CDs for sale. Those CDs could either be imported directly by the retailer or by an Australian wholesaler or be exported to Australia for sale by an overseas wholesaler. It is thus not difficult to infer that the consequence of the continued conduct would be to prevent wholesalers operating in the market. That in turn would have the consequence of ensuring, in respect of Warner titles, that Warner had a monopoly of them in the wholesale market. It would in respect of Universal titles ensure that Universal had a monopoly of them in the wholesale market.

479 Put in another way, given the conclusion I have reached that both Universal and Warner had market power in the wholesale market in which they operated and that they took advantage of that power to prevent a competitor coming into that market, it must follow that there would be an impact upon competition by force of their conduct. Whether that impact was likely to be substantial is again a matter of degree. It is also a matter of judgment.

480 It is true that the evidence established that there was already competition in the overall wholesale market for recorded music comprising the continuous flow of CDs for sale to the public. In the overall market, chart hits would vary from week to week, although on average it would be expected that each major record company would have at least one recording on the chart each week. It is true that no one of the five major record companies dominated that market. But to ignore the monopoly each record company had with respect to its own CDs is to ignore the way the market in fact operated. Each recording with a Universal or a Warner label imported from overseas was virtually identical to the recording manufactured in Australia. Depending upon the country of source there could be a difference in the quality of printing on the packaging. Depending upon the country of source there could, at least in a particular case, have been a difference in the quality of the recording. Generally, however, they were indistinguishable but for the label pronouncing the country of origin. In my view and in these circumstances a requirement that retailers buy all Universal labelled product from Universal and all Warner labelled product from Warner would be likely to have a substantial effect on competition in the wholesale market. Indeed, the result of free importation of CDs from overseas appears to have been some increase in the discounts available to retailers and in consequence an overall reduction in the wholesale net price to dealers. This supports the view that the freeing up of importation of non-infringing copies has improved competition in the market and enables an inference to be drawn that the deterring such importation by the threat of refusal to supply and subsequent select

refusal would, had it been continued, have had the consequence of reducing competition and to a substantial degree. . . .

485 For these reasons I am of the view that the ACCC has made out its case that each of Universal and Warner contravened s 47 of the Act. . . .

*Conclusion*

531 It follows that I find that both Universal and Warner contravened ss 46 and 47 of the Act. . . .

532 . . . [I]t will also be necessary to consider the quantum of pecuniary penalty and what other consequential orders should be made, including possible injunctions and cost orders. I would stand the matters over to a date to be fixed with counsel to permit argument on the form such orders should take.

---

## 5.2 TRADE LAW BARRIERS TO INTERNATIONAL DISTRIBUTION

**Canada – Certain Measures Concerning Periodicals**
**World Trade Oganization – Report of the Appellate Body**
**WT/DS31/AB/R; AB-1997-2 (WTO 1997)**

Presiding Member Mitsuo Matsushita; Member Claus-Dieter Ehlermann; Member Julio Lacart-Muro

*I. Introduction*

Canada and the United States appeal from certain issues of law and legal interpretations in the Panel Report, *Canada - Certain Measures Concerning Periodicals* (the "Panel Report"). The Panel was established to consider a complaint by the United States against Canada concerning three measures: Tariff Code 9958, which prohibits the importation into Canada of certain periodicals, including split-run editions; Part V.1 of the Excise Tax Act, which imposes an excise tax on split-run editions of periodicals; and the application by Canada Post Corporation ("Canada Post") of commercial "Canadian", commercial "international" and "funded" publications mail postal rates, the latter through the Publications Assistance Program (the "PAP") maintained by the Department of Canadian Heritage ("Canadian Heritage") and Canada Post.

The Panel Report was circulated to the Members of the World Trade Organization (the "WTO"). . . . It contains the following conclusions:

> (a) Tariff Code 9958 is inconsistent with Article XI:1 of GATT 1994 and cannot be justified under Article XX(d) of GATT 1994; (b) Part V.1 of the Excise Tax Act is inconsistent with Article III:2, first sentence, of GATT 1994; (c) the application by Canada Post of lower "commercial Canadian" postal rates to domestically-produced periodicals than to imported periodicals, including additional discount options available only to domestic periodicals, is inconsistent with Article III:4 of GATT 1994; but (d) the maintenance of the "funded" rate scheme is justified under Article III:8(b) of GATT 1994.

The Panel made the following recommendation:

> The Panel recommends that the Dispute Settlement Body request Canada to bring the measures that are found to be inconsistent with GATT 1994 into conformity with its obligations thereunder.

. . .

*II. Arguments of the Participants*

A. *Canada*

Canada submits that the Panel erred in law by characterizing Part V.1 of the Excise Tax Act as a measure regulating trade in goods subject to the GATT 1994. In the alternative, Canada argues that, even on the assumption that the GATT 1994 applies, the Panel erred in law when it found Part V.1 of the Excise Tax Act to be inconsistent with Article III:2, first sentence, of the GATT 1994. . . .

1. *Applicability of the GATT 1994 to Part V.1 of the Excise Tax Act*

Canada submits that the Panel erred in law when it applied Article III:2, first sentence, of the GATT 1994 to a measure affecting advertising services. Canada asserts that the GATT 1994 applies, as the GATT 1947 had always applied previously, to measures affecting trade in goods, but it has never been a regime for dealing with services in their own right. In Canada's view, if the GATT 1994 applied to all aspects of services measures on the basis of incidental, secondary or indirect effects on goods, the GATT 1994 would effectively be converted into a services agreement. . . .

. . . In Canada's view, the advertising services of a publisher are not, like labour in the production of a car, an input into the production of a good. . . . Canada maintains that advertising is not an input or a cost in the production, distribution or use of magazines as physical products. Therefore, the taxation of magazine advertising services is not indirect taxation of magazines as goods within the meaning of Article III:2.

Canada asserts that the Panel mischaracterized Part V.1 of the Excise Tax Act as a measure affecting trade in goods. It is a measure regulating access to the magazine advertising market. Most magazines represent two distinct economic outputs, that of a good and an advertising medium for providing a service, depending on the perspective of the purchaser. According to Canada, the tax is not applied to the consumer good because it is not based on, nor applied to, the price of a magazine. Instead, the tax is calculated using the value of advertising carried in a split-run edition of a magazine and is assessed against the publisher of each split-run magazine as the seller of the advertising service.

In Canada's view, since the provision of magazine advertising services falls within the scope of the General Agreement on Trade in Services (the "GATS"), and Canada has not undertaken any commitments in respect of the provision of advertising services in its Schedule of Specific Commitments, Canada is not bound to provide national treatment to Members of the WTO with respect to the provision of advertising services in the Canadian market.

2. *Consistency of Part V.1 of the Excise Tax Act with Article III:2 of the GATT 1994*

Should the Appellate Body conclude that Part V.1 of the Excise Tax Act is properly subject to the jurisdiction of the GATT 1994, Canada submits, as an alternative argument, that such measure is consistent with Article III:2, first sentence, of the GATT 1994. . . .

3. *Consistency of the "Funded" Postal Rate Scheme with Article III:8(b) of the GATT 1994*

Canada submits that, consistent with the Panel's findings, the payments made by Canadian Heritage to Canada Post to provide Canadian publishers with reduced postal rates are payments of subsidies exclusively to domestic producers within the meaning of Article III:8(b) of the GATT 1994. . . .

B. *United States*

The United States agrees with the Panel's findings and conclusions concerning Tariff Code 9958, Part V.1 of the Excise Tax Act and the lower "commercial Canadian" postal rates . . . , but the United States submits that the Panel erred in determining that Canada's "funded" postal rate scheme is justified by Article III:8(b) of the GATT 1994.

1. *Applicability of the GATT 1994 to Part V.1 of the Excise Tax Act*

The United States submits that Canada's excise tax is not exempt from Article III of the GATT 1994 on the ground that it is a "services measure" subject only to the GATS. Canada has failed to demonstrate any significant conflict between the GATT 1994 and the GATS arising from this case or that, in any event, the GATS should be accorded priority over the GATT 1994. The United States argues that Canada is incorrect in suggesting that the GATT 1994 cannot apply to measures whose application affects both goods and services. . . .

2. *Consistency of Part V.1 of the Excise Tax Act with Article III:2 of the GATT 1994*

. . . In the United States' view, none of the three separate claims of legal error raised by Canada with respect to the Panel's findings and conclusions on Article III:2, first sentence, are persuasive. . . .

The United States requests the Appellate Body to affirm the Panel's conclusions that Part V.1 of the Excise Tax Act is inconsistent with Article III:2, first sentence, of the GATT 1994. . . .

3. *Consistency of the "Funded" Postal Rate Scheme with Article III:8(b) of the GATT 1994*

The United States submits that the Panel erred in determining that Canada's "funded" postal rate regime falls within the scope of Article III:8(b) of the GATT 1994. According to the United States, neither the intra-governmental transfers of funds between the Canadian governmental entities nor the application by Canada Post of lower postage rates to domestic periodicals amounts to "the payment of subsidies exclusively to domestic producers" within the meaning of Article III:8(b).

The United States argues that any "payment" under Canada's "funded" postal rate scheme is made from one government entity to another, not from the Canadian government to domestic producers as required by Article III:8(b). . . .

*IV. Applicability of the GATT 1994*

Canada's primary argument with respect to Part V.1 of the Excise Tax Act is that it is a measure regulating trade in services "in their own right" and, therefore, is subject to the GATS. Canada argues that the Panel's conclusion that Part V.1 of the Excise Tax Act is a measure affecting trade in goods, and, therefore, is subject to Article III:2 of the GATT 1994, is an error of law.

We are unable to agree with Canada's proposition that the GATT 1994 is not applicable to Part V.1 of the Excise Tax Act. First of all, the measure is an excise tax imposed on split-run editions of periodicals. We note that the title to Part V.1 of the Excise Tax Act reads, "TAX ON SPLIT-RUN PERIODICALS", not "tax on advertising". Furthermore, the "Summary" of An Act to Amend the Excise Tax Act and the Income Tax Act, reads: "The Excise Tax Act is amended to impose an excise tax in respect of split-run editions of periodicals". Secondly, a periodical is a good comprised of two components: editorial content and advertising content. Both components can be viewed as having services attributes, but they combine to form a physical product – the periodical itself.

The measure in this appeal, Part V.1 of the Excise Tax Act, is a companion to Tariff Code 9958, which is a prohibition on imports of special edition periodicals, including split-run or regional editions that contain advertisements primarily directed to a market in Canada and that do not appear in identical form in all editions of an issue distributed in that periodical's country of origin. Canada agrees that Tariff Code

9958 is a measure affecting trade in goods, even though it applies to split-run editions of periodicals as does Part V.1 of the Excise Tax Act. . . .

The Panel found that Tariff Code 9958 is an import prohibition, although it applies to split-run editions of periodicals which are distinguished by their advertising content directed at the Canadian market. Canada did not appeal this finding of the Panel. It is clear that Part V.1 of the Excise Tax Act is intended to complement and render effective the import ban of Tariff Code 9958. As a companion to the import ban, Part V.1 of the Excise Tax Act has the same objective and purpose as Tariff Code 9958 and, therefore, should be analyzed in the same manner.

. . . The fundamental purpose of Article III of the GATT 1994 is to ensure equality of competitive conditions between imported and like domestic products. . . .

We conclude, therefore, that . . . the . . . measure at issue in this appeal, Part V.1 of the Excise Tax Act, is a measure which clearly applies to goods – it is an excise tax on split-run editions of periodicals. We will now proceed to analyze this measure in light of Canada's points of appeal under Article III:2 of the GATT 1994. . . .

*VI. Article III:2, Second Sentence, of the GATT 1994*

We will proceed to examine the consistency of Part V.1 of the Excise Tax Act with the second sentence of Article III:2 of the GATT 1994. . . .

B. *The Issues Under Article III:2, Second Sentence*

1. *Directly Competitive or Substitutable Products*

. . . Canada considers that split-run periodicals are not "directly competitive or substitutable" for periodicals with editorial content developed for the Canadian market. Although they may be substitutable advertising vehicles, they are not competitive or substitutable information vehicles. Substitution implies interchangeability. Once the content is accepted as relevant, it seems obvious that magazines created for different markets are not interchangeable. They serve different end-uses. . . .

According to the United States, the very existence of the tax is itself proof of competition between split-run periodicals and non-split-run periodicals in the Canadian market. As Canada itself has acknowledged, split-run periodicals compete with wholly domestically-produced periodicals for advertising revenue, which demonstrates that they compete for the same readers. The only reason firms place advertisements in magazines is to reach readers. A firm would consider split-run periodicals to be an acceptable advertising alternative to non-split-run periodicals only if that firm had reason to believe that the split-run periodicals themselves would be an acceptable alternative to non-split-run periodicals in the eyes of consumers. According to the United States, Canada acknowledges that "[r]eaders attract advertisers" and that, "... Canadian publishers are ready to compete with magazines published all over the world in order to keep their readers, but the competition is fierce". . . .

We find the United States' position convincing, while Canada's assertions do not seem to us to be compatible with its own description of the Canadian market for periodicals. . . .

We, therefore, conclude that imported split-run periodicals and domestic non-split-run periodicals are directly competitive or substitutable products in so far as they are part of the same segment of the Canadian market for periodicals.

2. *Not Similarly Taxed*

Having found that imported split-run and domestic non-split-run periodicals of the same type are directly competitive or substitutable, we must examine whether the imported products and the directly competitive or substitutable domestic products are not similarly taxed. Part V.1 of the Excise Tax Act taxes split-run editions of periodicals in an amount equivalent to 80 per cent of the value of all advertisements in a split-run edition. In contrast, domestic non-split-run periodicals are not subject to

Part V.1 of the Excise Tax Act. . . . [D]issimilar taxation of even some imported products as compared to directly competitive or substitutable domestic products is inconsistent with the provisions of the second sentence of Article III:2. . . .

With respect to Part V.1 of the Excise Tax Act, we find that the amount of the taxation is far above the *de minimis* threshold . . . . The magnitude of this tax is sufficient to prevent the production and sale of split-run periodicals in Canada.

3. *So as to Afford Protection . . .*

With respect to Part V.1 of the Excise Tax Act, we note that the magnitude of the dissimilar taxation between imported split-run periodicals and domestic non-split-run periodicals is beyond excessive, indeed, it is prohibitive. There is also ample evidence that the very design and structure of the measure is such as to afford protection to domestic periodicals. . . .

During the debate of Bill C-103, An Act to Amend the Excise Tax Act and the Income Tax Act, the Minister of Canadian Heritage, the Honourable Michel Dupuy, stated the following:

> . . . the reality of the situation is that we must protect ourselves against split-runs coming from foreign countries and, in particular, from the United States.

Canada also admitted that the objective and structure of the tax is to insulate Canadian magazines from competition in the advertising sector, thus leaving significant Canadian advertising revenues for the production of editorial material created for the Canadian market. With respect to the actual application of the tax to date, it has resulted in one split-run magazine, *Sports Illustrated*, to move its production for the Canadian market out of Canada and back to the United States. . . .

We therefore conclude on the basis of the above reasons, including the magnitude of the differential taxation, the several statements of the Government of Canada's explicit policy objectives in introducing the measure and the demonstrated actual protective effect of the measure, that the design and structure of Part V.1 of the Excise Tax Act is clearly to afford protection to the production of Canadian periodicals.

*VII. Article III:8(b) of the GATT 1994*

Article III:8(b) of the GATT 1994 reads as follows:

> (b) The provisions of this Article shall not prevent the payment of subsidies exclusively to domestic producers, including payments to domestic producers derived from the proceeds of internal taxes or charges applied consistently with the provisions of this Article and subsidies effected through governmental purchases of domestic products.

Both participants agree that Canada's "funded" postal rates involve "a payment of subsidies". The appellant, the United States, argues, however, that the "funded" postal rates programme involves a transfer of funds from one government entity to another, i.e. from Canadian Heritage to Canada Post, and not from the Canadian government to domestic producers as required by Article III:8(b). . . .

As a result of our analysis of the text, context, and object and purpose of Article III:8(b), we conclude that the Panel incorrectly interpreted this provision. For these reasons, we reverse the Panel's findings and conclusions that Canada's "funded" postal rates scheme for periodicals is justified under Article III:8(b) of the GATT 1994.

*VIII. Findings and Conclusions*

For the reasons set out in this Report, the Appellate Body:

(a) upholds the Panel's findings and conclusions on the applicability of the GATT 1994 to Part V.1 of the Excise Tax Act;

(b) reverses the Panel's findings and conclusions on Part V.1 of the Excise Tax Act relating to "like products" within the context of Article III:2, first sentence, thereby reversing the Panel's conclusions on Article III:2, first sentence, of the GATT 1994;

(c) modifies the Panel's findings and conclusions on Article III:2 of the GATT 1994, by concluding that Part V.1 of the Excise Tax Act is inconsistent with Canada's obligations under Article III:2, second sentence, of the GATT 1994; and

(d) reverses the Panel's findings and conclusions that the maintenance by Canada Post of the "funded" postal rates scheme is justified by Article III:8(b) of the GATT 1994, and concludes that the "funded" postal rates scheme is not justified by Article III:8(b) of the GATT 1994. . . .

The Appellate Body *recommends* that the Dispute Settlement Body request Canada to bring the measures found in this Report and in the Panel Report, as modified by this Report, to be inconsistent with the GATT 1994 into conformity with Canada's obligations thereunder.

---

**Note on aftermath of WTO Appellate Body Report**

Following its loss before the WTO Appellate Body, Canada notified the WTO that it would comply with its ruling "while pursuing its cultural policy objectives." The vehicle that Canada chose in an effort to do both of these things was legislation called the "Foreign Publishers Advertising Services Act," commonly referred to in Canada as "Bill C-55." As introduced, Bill C-55 did a good job of pursuing Canada's "cultural policy objectives." But it did nothing to comply with the WTO's ruling, in the opinion of the United States.

In fact, as far as the United States was concerned, Bill C-55 "accomplished the same result as the import ban and excise tax, and would have kept U.S. and other foreign-produced split run magazines from competing in the Canadian market." The United States' response was blunt: it threatened to impose punitive tariffs, under section 301 of the U.S. Trade Act, on Canadian exports of steel, plastics, textiles, pulp, paper and wood products. How, exactly, the U.S. could have imposed these penalties under its own Trade Act, without thereby violating U.S. obligations as a WTO member, was unclear. (The WTO-compatible process that should have been used, it seems, is the one being used by the EU in its WTO case against the U.S. over the Fairness in Music Licensing Act, about which you read in Chapter 1.)

Nonetheless, the U.S. threat got the attention of Canadian manufacturers of those products, thus setting the stage for negotiations between the two countries. In due course, a deal was struck between the U.S. and Canada calling for modifications to Bill C-55 before its enactment, as well as amendments to the Canadian Income Tax Act, and the liberalization of Canadian law concerning foreign ownership of Canadian magazine publishing companies.

The deal was apparently a good one, because both countries claimed victory. United States Trade Representative Charlene Barshefsky announced that the "agreement opens Canada's magazine market and . . . will create new opportunities for U.S. publishers to sell and distribute magazines in Canada." Canada, on the other hand, said that Bill C-55 simply needs to "be amended to allow two limited forms of access. . . ." And Canadian Heritage Minister Sheila exulted that "For the first time in its history, the American government has recognized the right a country, Canada, to require a majority of Canadian content in one of its cultural instruments."

The agreement did three things:

First, it permitted American magazines to be exported to Canada even if they contain advertising by Canadian companies. The amount of permissible Canadian advertising was limited to no more than 12% of total ad space per issue immediately after enactment of Bill C-55, no more than 15% after 18 months, and no more than 18% after 36 months. Canada itself describes these exemptions as "de minimis," but they are generous by comparison with Bill C-55 as it was first introduced. Originally, Bill C-55 would have made it a *crime* for non-Canadian publishers to export magazines to Canada if they contained any Canadian ads (and apparently it still will be a crime if magazines exported to Canada contain more than the permitted percentage).

Second, the agreement required Canada to amend its Income Tax Act to permit Canadian companies to take a standard business deduction for the cost of advertising in foreign-owned publications, though a deduction for 100% of those costs is permitted only if 80% or more of the magazine's editorial material is "original or Canadian content." If less than 80% of the editorial material is "original or Canadian content," only 50% of the advertising cost may be deducted. While this means that the 50% cap is certain to apply to all advertising in non-Canadian magazines, this aspect of the agreement is better than prior Canadian law for American publishers in two ways: prior Canadian law did not allow Canadian companies to deduct any part of their advertising costs in foreign magazines; now, Canadian companies can deduct 50% of their advertising costs in foreign magazines, even if those magazines are exported to Canada, so long as Canadian ads make up no more than the permitted percentage of the magazine's total ad space.

Third, the agreement required Canada to permit majority foreign ownership in Canadian magazine publishers, except those that are already Canadian owned. Prior law capped foreign ownership of Canadian magazines at 25%. The agreement now allows 100% foreign ownership of Canadian magazines. However, authorization for foreign ownership of Canadian magazines has not been made automatic. Foreign ownership of magazines will have to be approved, as before, under the Investment Canada Act; and authority to review and approve foreign investments in all "cultural industries," including magazines, was transferred from the Minister of Industry to the Minister of Canadian Heritage.

Moreover, foreign ownership of magazines will be approved only if it creates a "net benefit to Canada" and is compatible with "Canada's cultural policies." Canada quickly issued a Policy Statement indicating that these conditions will be satisfied only if the magazine will contain "a majority [50% or more] of original editorial content for the Canadian market in each issue. . . ." The Policy Statement defined "original editorial content" as non-advertising material that is "authored by Canadians" or is "created for the Canadian market and does not appear in any other edition . . . published outside Canada." The Policy Statement also indicated that a "net benefit" to Canada may result from the employment of Canadian residents as editorial and support staff, establishing a place of business in Canada, and having magazines edited, typeset and printed in Canada.

The advantage to non-Canadians of establishing a Canadian magazine publishing company will be that *all* (not just 15% to 18%) of the ads in its magazine can be sold to Canadian companies — though if less than 80% is Canadian content, advertisers will be able to deduct only 50% of the cost.

In return for Canada's agreeing to these provisions, the United States assured Canada that it will not take action against it (in response to the enactment of Bill C-55) before the WTO, or under NAFTA or section 301 of the U.S. Trade Act.

*Canada and United States Sign Agreement on Periodicals*, www.pch.gc.ca/in/News.dll/View?/Lang= E&Code=9NR031E (June 4, 1999); *Ottawa and Washington Agree on Access to the Canadian Advertising Services*

*Market*, Office of the Minister of Canadian Heritage, http://www.pch.gc.ca/bin/News.dll/ View?Lang=E&Code=9NR029E (May 26, 1999); *United States and Canada Resolve "Periodical" Differences*, Office of the United States Trade Representative 99-46, www.ustr.gov/releases/1999/05/99-46.html (May 26, 1999)

---

**Note on Canada's Feature Film Policy**

In 1998, the Government of Canada initiated a review of its feature film policies. The review was conducted by the Cultural Industries Branch of the Department of Canadian Heritage; and it began the process by releasing a 23-page Discussion Paper. (*A Review of Canadian Feature Film Policy, Discussion Paper*, Department of Canadian Heritage, Cultural Industries Branch (February 1998), available at www.pch.gc.ca/culture/library/filmpol/review-e.htm) The goal of the process, according to the Discussion Paper, was "a future where more Canadians have access to Canadian films playing in their local cinemas – films that reflect their own locales, their own stories and their own culture."

Canada is an active producer of motion pictures for a country of its size. In recent years, it has produced as many films per million residents as the United Kingdom, and more per million residents than Australia, Italy or Germany. Indeed, on a per capita basis, Canada produces almost as many films each year (2 films per million population) as the United States (2.6 films per million).

Moreover, Canadian films have won critical praise and international awards. The very year its Discussion Paper was released, "The Sweet Hereafter" received two Academy Award nominations, for Best Director and Best Adapted Screenplay. The film was produced with the participation of Telefilm Canada, a government agency that administers what was then a $40 million a year fund to support the development, production and distribution of Canadian feature films. "The Sweet Hereafter" also received assistance from the "Canadian Film or Video Production Tax Credit Program" which allows producers a tax credit of as much as 11% of the cost of Canadian labor for production services performed in Canada.

*Poor box office results*

Despite the number of films produced each year in Canada, and the critical success they enjoy, the Government of Canada was disturbed by this fact: Canadian films perform poorly at the box office, even in Canada. "In fact," the Department of Canadian Heritage said in the Discussion Paper, "the box office receipts of Canadian films in Canada have remained unchanged at around 2 percent of the total Canadian market since at least 1984."

In this area – percentage of domestic box office – Canada's 2% places it last among the major movie-producing countries of the world. German, Australian and Spanish films garner roughly 10% of the box office in their own countries. British films earn about 15% of the U.K. box office. Italian films generate more than 20% of the Italian box office. And French and Japanese films do some 35% of the box office in France and Japan. In the United States, more than 95% of the box office is earned by American movies.

What accounts for the disappointing performance of Canadian films, even at home? The Department of Canadian Heritage knew, though it buried the explanation in the middle of its Discussion Paper. "There appears to be a correlation between the value of a film's budget and its performance at the box office," the Government noted. And "Canada's average production budgets do not appear to be competitive relative to other countries." Indeed.

According to the Government's own figures, Canadian budgets average just $2.4 million for English-language films and $2.8 million for French-language films (in Canadian dollars) – amounts that are down 8% and 10% since the late 1980s. French and Australian average budgets, by comparison, are about three times as great, up 35% over the same period. British average budgets are almost five times as great, up 26%. And United States average budgets are more than 20 times as great as those of Canadian films.

Moreover, what the Canadians call "marketing budgets" are woefully inadequate as well. Two-thirds of the films financed by Telefilm Canada (between 1989 and 1995) had marketing budgets of less than $150,000 (in Canadian dollars). Only five films (out of 149) had marketing budgets greater than $450,000. The Discussion Paper does not indicate what the average marketing and production budgets were for these films. But if the average production budget is assumed to be $2.6 million, and the average marketing budget is (generously) assumed to be $150,000, Canadian marketing expenses average less than 6% of production costs. In the United States, marketing expenses often exceed 40% of production costs.

Why do Canadian distributors spend so little to bring their movies to market? Again, the Department of Canadian Heritage knew. It apparently asked distributors this very question. The answer: "Distributors maintain that they usually commit enthusiastically to a Canadian film project on the basis of the script and budget submitted to them. However, once they are committed, the budget is often reduced and the screenplay, the number of shooting locations and the casting are revised. The end result is that the film delivered is not as attractive to the public as they had anticipated. Distributors are therefore hesitant to dedicate marketing resources to films they have limited confidence in."

From these facts, reported in the Discussion Paper itself, some would conclude that Canadian films perform poorly even in Canada because of inadequate production and marketing budgets, and because revisions are made to scripts, locations and casting after distributors already have committed to projects. But the Department of Canadian Heritage did not reach this conclusion; or if it did, it seems to place responsibility for these facts on those outside of Canada.

*Foreign entertainment multinationals*

According to the Department of Canadian Heritage, "The film distribution industry in Canada . . . is dominated by subsidiaries of foreign entertainment multinationals which have, in the past, shown little interest in the distribution of Canadian films. Traditionally their interest has been in the distribution of their own productions." Though foreign distributors are only 15% of all film distributors operating in Canada, the movies they distribute there earn 85% of the revenue from film distribution in Canada.

As a result, "Many in the [Canadian film industry] believe that, with a few exceptions, Canadian distributors do not have sufficient market power to influence release dates and theatre locations to ensure that a Canadian film has a chance to reach a significant audience." Thus, they say, ". . . if Canadian films are to have a chance at reaching an audience, it is necessary to improve the performance of Canadian-owned distributors. An increase in their performances would enable Canadian distributors to provide more financing and marketing to Canadian films. As a result, with more money invested in the production and marketing of Canadian films, Canadian distributors would have a better chance with regard to obtaining key release dates and an adequate number of screens from exhibitors."

According to these members of the Canadian film industry, there is an "underlying structural challenge" to improving the performance of Canadian-owned distributors that "needs to be addressed." It is, they say, that "Canada is not treated as a distinct market for the purpose of film distribution. That is, the Canadian rights to foreign independent films are routinely bundled along with the U.S. rights into North American rights packages. Canadian distributors can seldom afford the cost of North American rights and for many foreign independent films, therefore they are priced out of the market."

Their suggested remedies: distribution legislation, stronger foreign investment guidelines, screen and shelf quotas for theatres and video stores, larger direct subsidy programs for Canadian distributors, and production subsidies such as grants or tax credits.

There is another point of view in Canada too. Some do "believe that market forces should govern"; and they "contend that Canadian films would reach a larger audience if bigger players in the industry, regardless of ownership, were permitted to distribute these films." The Discussion Paper noted that "This group usually favours an approach that includes replacing both the Canadian-ownership criteria supporting programs and the foreign investment guidelines with financial incentive programs that specifically support the marketing of Canadian films."

To help resolve the debate over what should be done, the Discussion Paper asked "interested Canadians" to respond to fifteen specific questions, including these:

"Is Canadian ownership and control of distribution companies fundamental to the distribution of Canadian feature films?"

"How important is the link between Canadian ownership and control of film companies and the production of Canadian feature films?"

"Should exhibitors and video stores in Canada be required to provide a certain minimum level of access to Canadian films? If not, how could these sectors be encouraged to increase above the historical average the performance of Canadian films?"

*International trade obligations*

The Department of Cultural Heritage noted that the film policy review "takes place in a broader context of . . . increasing trade liberalization. . . ." Ironically, however, the Department made no mention of Canada's membership in the World Trade Organization, nor did it request comments on whether any of the suggested remedies may violate Canada's obligations under GATT. This was surprising, for at least two reasons.

First, just a year before the Discussion Paper was released, Canada lost a WTO case brought against it by the United States involving Canadian government policies that were intended to protect that country's magazines from foreign competition in order to "strengthen Canadian identity and contribute to its cultural sector." (The case is reproduced earlier in this chapter.)

Second, just one month before the Discussion Paper was released, the European Communities initiated a WTO dispute resolution proceeding against Canada in which the E.C. complained that Canada's then-existing Film Distribution Policy violated the WTO-administered General Agreement on Trade in Services. Canada's Film Distribution Policy prohibits foreign takeovers of Canadian-owned and controlled film distribution businesses, permits new foreign distribution businesses to distribute only films for which the distributor owns world rights or is a major investor, and permits takeovers of foreign distribution businesses operating in Canada only if they will result in a net benefit to Canada. Since some Canadians believe that Canada's existing film policy provides inadequate support for the Canadian film industry, Canada has embarked on a course designed to strengthen that policy at the same time its legality was being challenged, in a forum that had ruled against it before. (The proceeding appears to have been settled, because the WTO's online records show only the E.C.'s Request for Consultation.)

*Responses to Discussion Paper*

More than 110 comments were submitted in response to the Discussion Paper.

One submission was from the Canadian Motion Picture Distributors Association – the Canadian representative for Disney, Columbia, MGM, Paramount, Twentieth Century Fox, Universal and Warner Bros. This submission provoked a rebuttal from the Canadian Association of Film Distributors and Exporters, an organization that represents Canadian companies, which complained "The Americans want it all." But other submissions revealed that there are lots of conflicts within the Canadian film industry, which have nothing whatever to do with "the Americans."

Screenwriters complained, for example, that less than 50% of development budgets are allocated to their fees, and they recommended that 85% be paid to them. The increase presumably would have come out of money the being paid to producers and others involved in development, so this is a suggestion producers and others had no reason to support.

Broadcasters wanted to be to be included in the creative development phase "to ensure that the final product has suitable production values for broadcast." Others suggested that "experienced script editors be mandatory in the screenwriting and development process" and that editors be brought in at the treatment or first draft stage of writing. Screenwriters of course would have been the recipients of the broadcasters' input, as well as the editing offered by script editors, so this is a suggestion that screenwriters had no reason to support.

Exhibitors sought tax credits for showing Canadian films. Currently, film-related tax credits go entirely to producers, so this is a suggestion that producers had little reason to support.

In short, each Canadian interest group made recommendations favorable to itself, usually at the expense of other Canadians rather than at the expense of Americans.

*Report and recommendations*

When the comment-and-submission phase of the process was completed, the Canadian Heritage Department drafted a 20-page summary of those comments (*A Review of Canadian Feature Film Policy*, Summary of Submissions, Department of Canadian Heritage (1998), available at www.pch.gc.ca/culture/cult_ind/filmpol/smiss/english.htm) and turned everything over to a Feature Film Advisory Committee. The Committee's 13 members represented Canadian producers, distributors and exhibitors. In addition to the written submissions, the Committee met with almost 100 individuals, associations and businesses, and also held round-table consultations with more than 80 feature film industry experts.

All of this input resulted in a 27-page report containing the Committee's recommendations. (*The Road to Success*, Report of the Feature Film Advisory Committee, Department of Canadian Heritage (1999), available at www.pch.gc.ca/culture/cult_ind/filmpol/ pubs/advcomm/toc.html)

Many of those recommendations were of little concern to entertainment companies on the U.S. side of the Canadian border. They involved purely internal matters like reorganizing existing Canadian film support funds and creating a new fund, creating partnerships with Canadian cultural institutions, and getting Canadian television broadcasters to increase their support for feature films. Three recommendations, however, could have affected American companies that do business in Canada.

First, the Committee recommended that the legislature amend the Canadian Competition Act, or enact new legislation, to prevent the tied sale of Canadian and U.S. distribution rights. "One of the key problems facing the Canadian distribution sector," the Committee reported, "is its lack of ability to compete for Canadian-only rights to non-proprietary films from outside Canada that are also distributed in the US." The reason that Canadian distributors can't compete, the Committee reported, is that "US film distributors, as a condition of distributing independently produced films to theatrical and home video markets, have uniformly insisted on obtaining Canadian distribution rights as well."

To prevent American distributors from continuing to do this, the Committee recommended new legislation that would "ensure that no person distributes a non-proprietary feature film in Canada if it or its affiliates is also distributing the same film in the US unless the availability of separate Canadian rights have been made known and other distributors have had an equitable opportunity to bid on those Canada-only rights."

Second, in order to raise $50 million in new government funding for Canadian feature films, the Committee recommended "a 3.5% levy on gross receipts of theatrical and video distributors operating in Canada." On its face, this levy would appear to apply equally to Canadian as well as American distributors. But in fact, its burden would have been much heavier – in absolute dollar terms – on American distributors than on Canadian distributors. This is so because American distributors account for 85% of the gross receipts from theatrical exhibition in Canada. Canadian distributors account for just 15%. Thus, unless and until movies distributed by Canadian companies become more successful at the Canadian box office, American distributors would have paid 85% of the proposed new levy.

Third, the Committee recommended that the Canadian federal government "revamp" its Production Services Tax Credit. As written, the Production Services Tax Credit is a refundable tax credit equal to 11% of the wages paid to Canadian residents for services provided in Canada in connection with movie and television production. There is no cap on the amount that can be claimed, and it is available to foreign-owned (as well as Canadian) corporations so long as they have permanent "establishments" in Canada. The Report pointedly noted that "This program benefits foreign producers – to the detriment of Canadian producers, who must compete for the services of Canada's professional film crews."

The Committee therefore recommended that the law be amended "to ensure that only Canadian feature film producers producing Canadian feature films for theatrical release" could claim the tax credit and its accompanying refund. The Committee calculated that if this were done, the credit could be increased from 11% to 20%, all of which would then flow to Canadian film producers.

*New Canadian Feature Film Policy*

The work done by the Canadian Heritage Department and its Feature Film Advisory Committee produced conclusive results when, in the year 2000, the Government of Canada adopted a new Feature Film Policy. The new policy, and the reasons for it, were described in a 10-page document titled *From Script to Screen*. (*From Script to Screen: New Policy Directions for Canadian Feature Film*, Minister of Public Works and Government Services (2000), available at www.pch.gc.ca/culture/cult_ind/pol/policy.htm)

*From Script to Screen* refers to "Hollywood," twice, both times in ways that implied that at least one of the three anti-Hollywood recommendations made by the Advisory Committee had been adopted.

First, *From Script to Screen* notes that "Filmmaking is an expensive and risky form of storytelling," and that "No matter how promising the script, how famous the cast or how large the budget, there is no assurance of success." These are propositions that even the biggest Hollywood studios would not dispute. But in *From Script to Screen*, the Canadian Government attributes a portion of the risk faced by Canadian filmmakers to their American counterparts, when it reported – as though this were an observed fact of nature – that "The problem is compounded by the ever-growing dominance of Hollywood – the world's largest exporter of filmed entertainment. . . ."

Second, after observing that the "average production budgets [of Canadian films] are too small to sustain the more expensive genres of story telling," *From Script to Screen* adds that "Average marketing budgets are also inadequate in the face of the well-financed and heavily-promoted competition from Hollywood."

Yet, in the end, the new Canadian Feature Film Policy did not incorporate any of the anti-Hollywood recommendations made by the Advisory Committee, or anyone else. "The Government's target goal," it reported in *From Script to Screen*, "is to capture 5% of the domestic box office in five years and to increase audiences for Canadian feature films abroad." In order to reach this goal – one that every studio head in Hollywood would both understand and applaud – the new Canadian Feature Film Policy aims to: "improve the quality of Canadian feature films by fostering an increase in average production budgets to at least $5 million; and encourage more comprehensive national and international marketing strategies by promoting an increase in average marketing budgets to at least $500,000."

In order to do so, the Canadian "federal government will double its total investment in feature film, adding an additional $50 million per year, starting in the 2001-02 fiscal year." These new funds will be used to do four things.

1. They will be used to "develop and retain talented creators by investing in screenwriting and professional development for filmmakers."
2. They will be used to "foster the quality and diversity of Canadian film by restructuring support programs to reward ongoing performance and by encouraging an increase in average production budgets." Some of this money will be used to reward producers' and distributors' performances in reaching Canadian audiences, because funding will be allocated to eligible Canadian producers and distributors based on a formula that relies on box office success, the degree of Canadian content in the film, and critical acclaim. The rest of this money will be used "to give priority to new players who do not necessarily have a track record in the industry, but are submitting promising projects," that are "innovative" and "culturally-relevant Canadian feature films."
3. They will be used to "build larger audiences at home and abroad through more effective support for marketing and promoting Canadian films" by providing financial assistance to distributors. And,
4. They will be used to preserve and disseminate Canadian films.

For now at least, Canada's Feature Film Policy does not prevent the tied sale of Canadian and U.S. distribution rights. It does not impose a levy on theatrical or video gross receipts. And it does not bar "foreign" producers from claiming the benefits of Canada's Production Services Tax Credit.

---

**United States Trade Representative Proposals to the World Trade Organization for GATS Negotiations [Regarding] Audiovisual and Related Services (December 2000)**

*Introduction*

The United States presents this proposal on audiovisual and related services for consideration by all Members. The proposal is intended to provide a framework for future work in the WTO that will contribute to the continued growth of this sector by ensuring an open and predictable environment that recognizes public concern for the preservation and promotion of cultural values and identity. At the same time, the proposal is intended to stimulate discussion of the significant role that the audiovisual sector plays in the digitally networked society.

*A. The "New" Audiovisual Sector*

The audiovisual sector in 2000 is significantly different from the audiovisual sector of the Uruguay Round period when negotiations focused primarily on film production, film distribution, and terrestrial broadcasting of audiovisual goods and services.

New technologies have given consumers worldwide access to a multitude of entertainment and information services and have stimulated the growth and development of audiovisual services and products from around the globe. Digital compression is providing less expensive means of creating audiovisual works while broadband capacity is opening opportunities for lower-cost distribution. The audiovisual sector today includes an international array of content producers and program packagers utilizing not just traditional single channel broadcasting, but new media, such as cable, Direct to Home satellite, and digital networks to distribute content locally and also internationally.

At the same time as new technologies have transformed the audiovisual sector, the audiovisual sector is playing a role in fostering new technologies. Electronically delivered audiovisual products and services, for example, which increase use of the network, are helping to create an environment that will encourage investment in the digital networks of tomorrow. The role of commercial entertainment in the creation and maintenance of advanced telecommunications infrastructure in turn benefits the development and distribution of local culture.

*B. Trade Rules and the Audiovisual Sector*

The debate over the audiovisual sector in the WTO, whose four cornerstones – the GATT, the GATS, TRIPs and dispute settlement – apply to the audiovisual sector, has sometimes been framed as an "all-or-nothing" game. Some argue as if the only available options were to exclude culture from the WTO or to liberalize completely all aspects of audiovisual and related services. Presenting such stark options obscures a number of relevant facts.

First is the fact that business and regulatory considerations affect the ability to make and distribute audiovisual products, both to domestic and foreign audiences. Creating audiovisual content is costly, and commercial success is uncertain. Access to international markets is necessary to help recoup production costs. Predictable and clearly defined trade rules will foster international exhibition and distribution opportunities and provide commercial benefits that audiovisual service providers must have to continue their artistic endeavors.

Second, the argument implies that because the audiovisual sector may have special cultural characteristics, the sector should not be subject to the trade disciplines imposed on other service sectors. Such an argument neglects that other sectors also have unique characteristics for the purpose of fulfilling important social policy objectives and that the GATS has shown the flexibility to accommodate such specific concerns. For example, in the Annex on Financial Services, regulators were given exceptional discretion to take prudential measures to ensure, inter alia, the integrity of their financial system. Similarly, in the basic telecommunications Reference Paper, regulators insisted that the vital goal of providing universal service could not be sacrificed in the name of trade liberalization.

- The "all-or-nothing" approach to the audiovisual sector in the WTO implies that trade rules are somehow too rigid to take into account the special cultural qualities of the sector. This is not the case: GATT Article IV provides a special, and unique, exception for cinematic films to GATT national treatment rules. In 1947, in recognition of the difficulty that domestic film producers faced in finding adequate screen time to exhibit their films in the immediate post-World War II period, GATT founders authorized continuation of existing screen-time quotas. It is worth noting that the scarcity of outlets available to local film producers to exhibit their films has in large part been alleviated by multiplex cinemas and multichannel TV, and will be further aided in the digital Video on Demand context.
- Today, in the WTO, when governments schedule commitments for audiovisual, or for any service sector, they have the flexibility to make full or partial commitments, should they so desire. Even when countries make commitments, they may continue to regulate services covered by commitments, so long as the regulation is not administered in a way that represents an unexpected trade barrier.
- Additionally, in both the GATS (Article XIV(a)) and GATT (Article XX(a)), the general exception for measures necessary to protect public morals provides further reassurance for Members concerned that commitments relating to content mean that they will not be able to apply regulations intended to preserve public morality.
- Finally, in its current form, the GATS does not prevent governments from funding audiovisual services, a sensitive issue for many Members where local theatrical film production, for example, is dependent on government support. While the GATS provides for future negotiations to develop disciplines on subsidies that distort trade in services, there is no presupposition as to what those provisions will contain. (For further discussion of this issue, see section C(3) below).

The choices are not, nor have they even been, a choice between promoting and preserving a nation's cultural identity and liberalizing trade in audiovisual services. Especially in light of the quantum increase in exhibition possibilities available in today's digital environment, it is quite possible to enhance one's cultural identity and to make trade in audiovisual service more transparent, predictable, and open. Indeed, as indicated in the above discussion on the role of the new audiovisual sector in helping to attract investment for advanced infrastructure, the two objectives may reinforce each other.

*C. A Negotiating Proposal for the Audiovisual Sector*

Our negotiating proposal for the audiovisual sector consists of three interrelated elements:

(1) Members need to review the different activities that constitute the audiovisual sector today to develop a clear, accurate and comprehensive understanding of where the different facets of the sector are classified in GNS/W/120 [the WTO document that classifies services by type and assigns a classification number to each]. Existing classifications used by many Members in scheduling their commitments may not cover some of these services, or may create

uncertainties as to which services are covered. In other cases, two or more existing sub-categories may extend to the same service. In carrying out this review, Members need to respect the principle of technological neutrality, which is a fundamental tenet of the WTO, and must refrain from pursuing reclassifications that could erode existing commitments.

(2) GATS disciplines are relevant to the audiovisual sector, as they are to virtually any services sector. We seek negotiated commitments for the audiovisual sector that establish clear, dependable, and predictable trade rules with due account taken of the sector's specific sensitivities.

(3) In conjunction with negotiated commitments for audiovisual services, Members may also want to consider developing an understanding on subsidies that will respect each nation's need to foster its cultural identity by creating an environment to nurture local culture. To this end, many Members subsidize theatrical film production. There is precedent in the WTO for devising rules which recognize the use of carefully circumscribed subsidies for specifically defined purposes, all the while ensuring that the potential for trade distortive effects is effectively contained or significantly neutralized.

# Chapter 6

# PERFORMANCE, EXHIBITION, AND SALE

## 6.1 DOMESTIC CONTENT REQUIREMENTS

One of the classic mechanisms used by foreign governments to reduce the impact of U.S. entertainment exports is the local-content quota. Canada, for example, has long maintained a requirement that at least 30% of radio programming be "Canadian content" by Canadian performers and/or creators. (By contrast, as you read in Chapter 5, the Canadian theatrical film business, which is not subject to screen-time quotas, is almost totally devoted to foreign films; Canadian films take only about 2% of the box office, in stark contrast to the 85% of revenues which go to American films.)

Under the European Union "Television Without Frontiers" Directive, a majority of primetime programming "where practicable" must be material produced in the EU. The Spanish government provoked a near-mutiny among that country's theatrical film exhibitors when it required that Spanish or EU films be shown for 25% of each theater's exhibition days.

Of course, such quotas have cultural as well as economic significance. Many countries – France being a prime example – have long been concerned with the impact of American films, television, books, music, consumer goods and fast-food methods upon their indigenous cultures.

Because of this mix of economic and cultural considerations, foreign countries successfully insisted that they be able to retain their quota systems as a condition of signing on to the 1994 Uruguay Round of the General Agreement on Tariffs and Trade (GATT), which established the global intellectual property rights regime of the World Trade Organization (WTO). In addition, Canada insisted on retaining its historic quota advantages as a condition of entering the North American Free Trade Association (NAFTA). (Since Mexico had no similar pre-existing quota, none was provided for Mexico under NAFTA.)

Quotas have definitely served to stimulate local production, especially in the EU, where aggressive companies such as Canal Plus have become major producers of television and films.

We start with a close look at the Australian local content requirement for television broadcasters, and the adverse effect that quota had on television producers in neighboring New Zealand. This legal battle in the South Pacific is of interest to producers (and their lawyers) in North America, because the Australian case raises at least two questions: (1) whether U.S. producers could successfully attack Australian broadcast quotas, the way the New Zealanders did; and (2) whether U.S. producers could successfully attack Canadian broadcast quotas, or those of other countries, using arguments similar to those successfully used by the New Zealanders in the following case.

---

**Project Blue Sky v Australian Broadcasting Authority**
**High Court of Australia**
**[1998] HCA 28**

Brennan CJ.

The Australian Broadcasting Authority ("the ABA") has a number of "primary functions" which are listed in s 158 of the *Broadcasting Services Act* 1992 ("the Act"), including, inter alia: . . . (j) to develop program standards relating to broadcasting in Australia . . . .

Section 159 allows for "additional functions" which may be conferred on it by the Act or another Act. Section 160 imposes general obligations on the ABA in these terms: "The ABA is to perform its functions in a manner consistent with: . . . (d) Australia's obligations under any convention to which Australia is a party or any agreement between Australia and a foreign country."

In these proceedings, the appellants (to whom I shall refer as "Blue Sky"), which have the objective of encouraging the profitable growth of the New Zealand film and television industry, challenge the validity of a standard determined by the ABA on the ground that the ABA has not performed its function consistently with Australia's obligations under an "agreement between Australia and a foreign country." The agreement relied on is the Protocol on Trade in Services to the Australia New Zealand Closer Economic Relations Trade Agreement. The Protocol came into force on 1 January 1989.

Article 4 of the Protocol reads as follows:

> "Each Member State shall grant to persons of the other Member State and services provided by them access rights in its market no less favourable than those allowed to its own persons and services provided by them."

Article 5(1) reads as follows:

> "Each Member State shall accord to persons of the other Member State and services provided by them treatment no less favourable than that accorded in like circumstances to its persons and services provided by them."

Blue Sky contends that, by reason of Arts 4 and 5(1), Australia is under an obligation not to create or maintain any legal impediment which would adversely affect the capacity of the New Zealand film and television industry to compete equally with the Australian industry in the Australian market for the broadcasting of film and television products.

The impugned standard, known as the Australian Content Standard, was determined by the ABA on 15 December 1995 in purported exercise of the power conferred on the ABA by s 122(1)(a) of the Act. Part 5 of the Australian Content Standard, headed "Transmission Quota" contains but one clause: cl 9, headed "Australian transmission quota." Clause 9 reads:

> "(1) . . . until the end of 1997, Australian programs must be at least 50% of all programming broadcast between 6.00am and midnight. . . .

(2) . . . from the beginning of 1998, Australian programs must be at least 55% of all programming broadcast between 6.00am and midnight. . . ."

The quotas specified in cl 9 guarantee minimum periods between 6.00am and midnight during which Australian programs are to be broadcast. New Zealand programs are left to compete with all other programs (including Australian programs) for the remainder of the periods between 6.00am and midnight. Even if New Zealand programs were successful in obtaining transmission for the entire 50% of the relevant periods which, until the end of 1997, were available after the Australian program quota was satisfied, the Australian Content Standard would preclude their achieving more than 45% from the beginning of 1998. The definition of an Australian program is contained in cl 7 which reads: . . .

"(4) . . . a program is an Australian program if: . . .

(a) the producer of the program is, or the producers of the program are, Australian (whether or not the program is produced in conjunction with a co-producer, or an executive producer, who is not an Australian); and

(b) either:

(i) the director of the program is, or the directors of the program are, Australian; or

(ii) the writer of the program is, or the writers of the program are, Australian; and

(c) not less than 50% of the leading actors or on-screen presenters appearing in the program are Australians; and

(d) in the case of a drama program – not less than 75% of the major supporting cast appearing in the program are Australians; and

(e) the program:

(i) is produced and post-produced in Australia but may be filmed anywhere; and

(ii) in the case of a news, current affairs or sports program that is filmed outside Australia, may be produced or post produced outside Australia if to do otherwise would be impractical. . . ."

The Australian Content Standard thus provides a minimum quota for the transmission of programs . . . classified by the circumstances in which they were made. It is the provenance of a program, not its subject matter, which determines whether it is an "Australian program" for the purposes of the Australian Content Standard. The Australian Content Standard gives a competitive advantage to programs having an Australian provenance over programs having a corresponding New Zealand provenance. Thus the Australian Content Standard appears not to be consistent with Australia's obligations under Arts 4 and 5(1) of the Protocol.

In the Federal Court, Davies J made a declaration that the Australian Content Standard "is invalid to the extent to which it fails to be consistent with the Protocol." . . .

On appeal to the Full Court of the Federal Court a majority (Wilcox and Finn JJ, Northrop J dissenting) upheld the validity of the ABA's Standard. The Full Court allowed the appeal and dismissed Blue Sky's application. Pursuant to a grant of special leave, Blue Sky appeals against the Full Court's orders and seeks in lieu thereof a declaration that the Australian Content Standard is invalid.

*The issues*

The power of the ABA to determine standards is conferred by s 122 which reads:

"(1) The ABA must, by notice in writing: (a) determine standards that are to be observed by commercial television broadcasting licensees. . . .

(2) Standards under subsection (1) for commercial television broadcasting licensees are to relate to: . . . (b) the Australian content of programs. . . ."

The standards which may be determined in exercise of the power conferred by s 122 are limited to standards relating to . . . "the Australian content of programs."

The majority of the Full Court pointed out that the term "Australian content" is not defined by s 122 or by any other provision in the Act. The connotation which their Honours attributed to "Australian" was "something particular to this country." Then, noting that "a New Zealand program is not an Australian program," their Honours reasoned that –

> "If the ABA specified the 'Australian content' of television programs in such a way as to allow any of that required content to be satisfied by New Zealand programs, however they might be defined, it would fail to carry out its statutory task. . . . The only standard the ABA could set, consistent with the Protocol, would be one that allowed for there to be no Australian content programs at all, provided that New Zealand programs were broadcast in lieu of programs having Australian content. While one may be able to describe this as determining a standard, it is not one that puts into effect the statutory obligation to determine a standard that relates to the Australian content of programs."

Herein lies a difficulty. The proposition that a New Zealand program does not, or cannot, satisfy the "Australian content" requirement of a standard to be determined under s 122 is not self-evident. No doubt the proposition depends on the meaning to be attributed to "Australian content." . . .

. . . The parties and the interveners [Australian television program producers] made their submissions principally on the basis that Australian content could be seen or heard only in a program having an Australian provenance. The adoption of that common basis is understandable.

First, it is in the interveners' interests to assert that Australian content is to be found only in programs having an Australian provenance. If that be correct, s 122(2) authorises the determination of a standard that, by safeguarding Australian content, safeguards programs having an Australian provenance.

Secondly, the commercial interests represented by Blue Sky presumably recognise that the content of programs made in New Zealand or by New Zealanders will not be recognisably Australian or will be less likely to be recognisably Australian than programs having an Australian provenance. Blue Sky did not seek to have the Australian Content Standard set aside on the ground that the power to determine standards could be used only to prescribe the content of programs, whatever the provenance of those programs might be. However, Mr Ellicott QC, senior counsel for Blue Sky . . . submitted: ". . . if a standard was confined to content in the sense of subject matter, then anybody in the world could make or produce with whatever actors or writers, et cetera, they wanted to such films. . . ." But Blue Sky was not willing to advance that as the true construction of "Australian content," perhaps because it was thought that success on that ground might yield little commercial benefit. . . .

Thirdly, the ABA relied on the legislative history relating to program standards in an attempt to show that "Australian content" in s 122(2)(b) requires the involvement of Australians in the making of the program and that cl 7 of the Australian Content Standard conforms with the historical understanding.

The issues for determination can now be stated: . . .

2. What is the meaning of "the Australian content of programs"?
3. Is the Australian Content Standard consistent with s 160(d)?
4. If not, is the Australian Content Standard valid?. . .

2. *"The Australian content of programs."* . .

The "content" of a "program" is what a program contains. The Act calls that content "matter": it is what the broadcast audience sees or hears. "Australian" is the adjective describing the matter contained in the program; but the matter contained in a program is not its provenance. The content of a program for broadcast may be difficult to define in a statute, for it has to do with the communication of sights and sounds that convey ideas and the classification of an idea as "Australian" is a rather elusive concept. But that is not to deny the reality of Australian ideas; they are identifiable by reference to the sights and sounds that depict or evoke a particular connection with Australia, its land, sea and sky, its people, its fauna and its flora. They include our national or regional symbols, our topography and environment, our history and culture, the achievements and failures of our people, our relations with other nations, peoples and cultures and the contemporary issues of particular relevance or interest to Australians. The conferring of power on the ABA to determine a standard relating to the Australian content of programs accords with one of the objects prescribed by the Act, namely, "to promote the role of broadcasting services in developing and reflecting a sense of Australian identity, character and cultural diversity."

The "Australian content of a program" is the matter in a program in which Australian ideas find expression. The ABA is empowered by s 122(1)(a) to determine a transmission quota for programs in which Australian ideas find expression and the manner in which and the extent to which such programs must contain Australian ideas. . . .

The provisions of the Act uniformly point to one meaning of "the Australian content of programs," namely, the Australian matter contained in a program. There is neither historical nor textual foundation for the proposition that the term can be used to classify programs by reference to their provenance. The determination of the Australian Content Standard adopts an impermissible basis for classifying programs as the subject of a standard under s 122. It follows that I would hold the Australian Content Standard to be invalid, but for a reason other than the reason advanced by Blue Sky and debated by the ABA and the interveners.

3. *Is the Australian Content Standard consistent with s 160(d)?*

If, contrary to my view, s 122(2)(b) empowered the ABA to determine and prescribe a transmission quota for programs having an Australian provenance, is it consistent with s 160(d)? . . .

Here, Arts 4 and 5(1) express unequivocally Australia's obligations under an agreement "between Australia and a foreign country." . . . Arts 4 and 5(1) of the Protocol impose an obligation on Australia to extend to New Zealand service providers market access and treatment no less favourable to New Zealand service providers than the market access and treatment available to Australian service providers. As there is nothing to show that Arts 4 and 5(1) do not truly impose obligations on Australia, s 160(d) has the effect of requiring the ABA to perform its functions in a manner consistent with Arts 4 and 5(1).

On the hypothesis that the prescription of a transmission quota for programs having an Australian provenance could be supported by an exercise of power conferred by s 122, s 160(d) directs the ABA not to exercise its power so as to breach Australia's international obligations. On that hypothesis, a majority of this Court, reading s 122 with s 160, holds that: "the legal meaning of s 122 is that the ABA must determine standards relating to the Australian content of programs but only to the extent that those standards are consistent with the directions in s 160."

Given the hypothesis, I would respectfully agree. And, as Australian program makers are given an advantage over the New Zealand program makers by cll 7 and

9 of the Australian Content Standard, I would hold those clauses to be inconsistent with s 160(d).

4. *Is the Australian Content Standard valid?*

Although I apprehend that, on the hypothesis stated, the majority and I would hold cll 7 and 9 to be inconsistent with s 160(d) of the Act, my analysis of the consequences is radically different. . . .

Here, s 160(d) is a provision which directs the manner of the exercise of the powers conferred on the ABA under the Act, including (so far as is relevant) the power conferred by s 122(1)(a). If the ABA purports to exercise its powers in breach of the injunction contained in s 122(4) and s 160(d), to that extent the purported exercise of the power is invalid and the purported standard (or the non-conforming provisions thereof) is invalid and of no effect. . . . The Act empowers the ABA to determine a program standard that relates to the Australian content of programs only to the extent that the standard is consistent with Australia's obligations under Arts 4 and 5(1) of the Protocol. On the hypothesis that the Australian Content Standard authorises the determination of a standard prescribing a transmission quota for programs having an Australian provenance, cl 9 does not conform with Arts 4 and 5(1). It is therefore invalid.

. . . I would allow the appeal. Allowing the appeal, I would set aside the order of the Full Court of the Federal Court and in lieu thereof order that the appeal to that Court be dismissed. . . .

McHugh, Gummow, Kirby and Hayne JJ.

The question in this appeal is whether a program standard, known as the Australian Content Standard, made by the respondent, the Australian Broadcasting Authority ("ABA"), is invalid. The appellants contend that it is invalid because it gives preference to Australian television programmes contrary to Australia's obligations under the Australia New Zealand Closer Economic Relations Trade Agreement ("the Trade Agreement") and the Trade in Services Protocol to the Trade Agreement ("the Protocol"). . . .

The appellants contend that par (d) of s 160 required the ABA in determining program standards to comply with the Trade Agreement and the Protocol. They contend that, because the Protocol requires equality of treatment and access to markets, the Australian Content Standard is invalid because it gives television programs made by Australians preferential treatment over programs made by New Zealand nationals. . . .

. . . Nothing in the objects of the Act requires the ABA to give preferential treatment to Australian over New Zealand nationals in determining "standards that are to be observed by commercial television broadcasting licensees." Nor were we referred to any notified policy or ministerial direction to that effect. . . .

*The Trade Agreement and the Protocol. . .*

It was common ground between the parties that the provisions of cl 9 of the Australian Content Standard are in conflict with the provisions of Arts 4 and 5 of the Protocol. That being so, two questions arise: (1) is cl 9 of the Australian Content Standard in breach of s 160(d) of the Act; (2) if it is, is cl 9 invalid? . . .

*The Australian Content Standard was authorised by the literal meaning of s 122*

The Australian Content Standard made on 15 December 1995 is plainly a standard that relates to "the Australian content of programs" within the literal and grammatical meaning of s 122(2)(b) of the Act. The term "Australian content" is not defined by s 122 or by the Act. But, given the history of the term, there can be no doubt that the standard made on 15 December 1995 relates to the "Australian content of programs" within the literal meaning of s 122(2)(b) of the Act. . . .

*The legal meaning of s 122...*

If s 122(1) and (2) were given their grammatical meaning, without regard to the provisions of s 160, they would authorise the making of standards which were inconsistent with Australia's obligations under international conventions or under its agreements with foreign countries. However, the express words of s 122(4) and the mandatory direction in s 160 show that the grammatical meaning of s 122(1) and (2) is not the legal meaning of those sub-sections. When s 122 is read with s 160, the legal meaning of s 122 is that the ABA must determine standards relating to the Australian content of programs but only to the extent that those standards are consistent with the directions in s 160. If, by reason of an obligation under a convention or agreement with a foreign country, it is impossible to make an Australian content standard that is consistent with that obligation, the ABA is precluded by s 160 from making the standard, notwithstanding the literal command of s 122(1) and (2). Accordingly, in making the Australian Content Standard in December 1995, the ABA was under an obligation to ensure that the Standard was not inconsistent with the Trade Agreement or the Protocol.

The majority judges in the Full Court in the present case were therefore in error .... The power conferred by s 122 must ... be exercised within the framework imposed by s 160.

*An Australian content standard must be consistent with the Trade Agreement and the Protocol...*

Clause 9 of the Australian Content Standard published in December 1995 is plainly in breach of Australia's obligations under Arts 4 and 5 of the Protocol. That is because cl 9 requires Australian programs to constitute 50 per cent (rising to 55 per cent) of programming broadcasts made between 6.00am and midnight. Consequently, Australian programs have an assured market of at least 50 per cent of broadcasting time while New Zealand programs have to compete with all other programs including Australian programs for the balance of broadcasting time. New Zealand programs therefore have less favourable access rights to the market for television programs than Australian programs have. As a result, cl 9 of the Australian Content Standard is in breach of Art 4 (access rights of persons and services to a market to be no less favourable) and Art 5 (treatment of persons and services to be no less favourable) of the Protocol and was therefore made in contravention of s 122(4)....

However, it does not follow that cl 9 of the Standard is void and of no force or effect....

... The Parliament has not said that the ABA must give preferential treatment to Australian programs. It has said that the ABA must determine standards that "relate to ... the Australian content of programs." The words "relate to" are "extremely wide." They require the existence of a connection or association between the content of the Standard and the Australian content of programs. What constitutes a sufficient connection or association to form the required relationship is a matter for judgment depending on the facts of the case. No doubt the association or connection must be a relevant one in the sense that it cannot be accidental or so remote that the Standard has no real effect or bearing on the Australian content of programs. But, without attempting to provide an exhaustive definition, once the Standard appears to prohibit, regulate, promote or protect the Australian content of television broadcasts the required relationship will exist....

... The phrase "the Australian content of programs" in s 122 is a flexible expression that includes, inter alia, matter that reflects Australian identity, character and culture. A program will contain Australian content if it shows aspects of life in Australia or the life, work, art, leisure or sporting activities of Australians or if its scenes are or appear to be set in Australia or if it focuses on social, economic or political issues concerning Australia or Australians. Given the history of the concept of Australian content . . . , a program must also be taken to contain Australian content if the participants, creators or producers of a program are Australian. Nothing in the notion of the Australian content of programs requires, however, that a standard made pursuant to s 122 must give preference to Australian programs. Nor does the phrase "the Australian content of programs" in s 122 require that such programs should be under Australian creative control.

. . . The ABA has complete authority to make a standard that relates to the Australian content of programs as long as the standard does not discriminate against persons of New Zealand nationality or origin or the services that they provide or against the members of any other nationality protected by agreements similar to those contained in the Protocol. . . .

It is of course true that one of the objects of the Act is "to promote the role of broadcasting services in developing and reflecting a sense of Australian identity, character and cultural diversity." But this object can be fulfilled without requiring preference to be given to Australian programs over New Zealand programs. Thus, the ABA could determine a standard that required that a fixed percentage of programs broadcast during specified hours should be either Australian or New Zealand programs or that Australian and New Zealand programs should each be given a fixed percentage of viewing time. Such a standard would relate to the Australian content of programs even though it also dealt with the New Zealand content of programs. . . .

*Does the failure to comply with s 160 mean that cl 9 of the Australian Content Standard is invalid?*

An act done in breach of a condition regulating the exercise of a statutory power is not necessarily invalid and of no effect. . . .

*An act done in breach of s 160 is not invalid. . .*

. . . When a legislative provision directs that a power or function be carried out in accordance with matters of policy, ordinarily the better conclusion is that the direction goes to the administration of a power or function rather than to its validity. . . .

In a case like the present, however, the difference between holding an act done in breach of s 160 is invalid and holding it is valid is likely to be of significance only in respect of actions already carried out by, or done in reliance on the conduct of, the ABA. Although an act done in contravention of s 160 is not invalid, it is a breach of the Act and therefore unlawful. Failure to comply with a directory provision "may in particular cases be punishable." That being so, a person with sufficient interest is entitled to sue for a declaration that the ABA has acted in breach of the Act and, in an appropriate case, obtain an injunction restraining that body from taking any further action based on its unlawful action.

*Order*

The appeal to this Court from the Full Court of the Federal Court should be allowed with costs. . . . In lieu of the orders made by the Full Court, however, there should be substituted the following orders: . . .

The Court Declares That cl 9 of the Australian Content Standard (the Standard) determined by the Appellant on 15 December 1995 was unlawfully made. . . .

**Review of Australian Content Standard –**
**Regulatory Impact Statement**
**Broadcasting Services (Australian Content) Standard 1999**

The Australian Broadcasting Authority is the author of the following document, and it is reproduced with the ABA's permission.

*Issues. . .*

On 28 April 1998, the High Court of Australia found the Australian Content Standard, was unlawfully made and was inconsistent with Australia's obligations under the Trade in Services Protocol (the Protocol) to the Australia New Zealand Closer Economic Relations Trade Agreement (CER).

Section 122 of the *Broadcasting Services Act 1992* (the Act) requires the ABA to determine a standard relating to the Australian content of programs. Section 160(d) of the Act requires the ABA to perform its functions in a manner consistent with Australia's international obligations. The High Court ruled that section 160 is the dominant provision which directs how the ABA's functions must be exercised, including the determination of the standard under section 122.

The High Court ruled that clause 9 of the standard (which sets the 'Australian transmission quota') was unlawfully made, and contrary to articles 4 and 5 of the Protocol. . . .

*Objectives*

The ABA has reviewed the standard to remedy the inconsistency and make it comply with the Act.

The aim of the review was to develop a standard relating to the Australian content of programs that meets Australia's international treaty obligations concerning New Zealand and, as far as possible, promotes the role of television in developing and reflecting a sense of Australian identity, character and cultural diversity. Options canvassed in the review seek to achieve the cultural objective of Australian content regulation and consistency with Australia's CER obligations. . . .

Throughout the review there was widespread concern from the production industry and members of the community about the impact of the High Court decision and whether this would lead to the displacement of Australian programs. It was argued that, to the extent that New Zealand programs may displace Australian programs under a new standard, the effectiveness of the standard in promoting Australian identity, character and cultural diversity would diminish. . . .

*Options*

*The process*

Section 126 of the Act requires the ABA to seek public comment before determining, varying or revoking a standard. In developing the new standard the ABA has consulted widely with industry and government representatives from Australia and New Zealand.

The ABA's discussion paper released on 15 July 1998 canvassed a number of options for amending the standard. In response to the discussion paper, the ABA received a total of 38 submissions.

After consulting with interested parties and considering views submitted on options the ABA released draft amendments to the standard . . . on 13 November 1998 for public comment. The draft amendments to the standard included proposals for incorporating New Zealand programs and some other changes of a minimal nature.

. . . Following a period of consultation on the proposed standard, which ended on 7 December 1998, the ABA considered final changes to the standard. . . .

This Regulatory Impact Statement (RIS) focuses on the final changes in the standard. In preparing this RIS the ABA has assessed the costs and benefits that various options might have on affected parties, in particular, television audiences and the community generally, the broadcasting and production industries, and government.

*The new standard*

Having considered all the options for amending the Australian Content Standard, put forward in the discussion paper and in submissions, the ABA adopted the following:

1. introduce separate and equivalent creative elements tests for Australian and New Zealand programs and recognise programs that have a mix of Australian and New Zealand creative elements;
2. not adopt any form of on-screen test in the revised standard. . . .

The structure of the standard has been preserved, with the new standard allowing that the obligations to broadcast Australian programs may be reduced by the extent to which equivalent New Zealand programs, Australia/New Zealand programs and Australian official co-productions are broadcast by the licensee.

*Section 160(d)*

A majority of parties to the review made it clear that their preferred approach would be for Parliament to repeal s 160(d) of the Act. The ABA noted that an alternative approach would be for Parliament to limit the application of s 160(d) to treaty obligations with New Zealand and Australia's international co-production obligations.

Except for the Department of Foreign Affairs and Trade, all Australian parties to the review submitted that the appropriate course of action is for Parliament to repeal section 160(d) of the Act. This is a matter for the Parliament, rather than the ABA, and was canvassed within the terms of reference of the Senate Environment, Recreation, Communications and the Arts Legislation Committee that inquired into section 160(d). The ABA's proper role is to determine a lawful standard, following the High Court's decision.

*Impact Analysis (Costs and Benefits) of Each Option*

For the purposes of the RIS the key parties potentially affected are:

- Australian television audiences;
- Australian commercial television broadcasters;
- the Australian production industry;
- the Commonwealth Government; and
- the Australian Broadcasting Authority.

The Australian Content Standard is primarily an instrument of cultural policy, and is therefore not easily reduced to measures of quantification. Indeed, as noted in ORR's *A Guide to Regulation* economists would refer to it as an 'intangible', since the standard is directed to having an impact on the role of television in developing and reflecting a sense of Australian identity, character and cultural diversity.

However, the ABA recognises that, to the extent to which the standard operates to support the local television and film production industry, it has a direct economic impact on the members of the industry. Similarly, compliance with local content requirements impacts significantly on the programming expenditure of Australian broadcasters.

The review of the standard was necessary to comply with Australia's obligations under CER. In doing so the ABA sought to ensure that the interests of Australian television audiences are served by a standard that provides viewers with continued access to Australian programs.

Views of New Zealand interests have been taken account of to the extent they focussed on CER compliance issues.

*Defining eligible programs - introduction . . .*

The definition of what programs are eligible to count towards fulfilment of a licensee's Australian content obligation is fundamental to the standard.

The current standard defines Australian content [by] . . . Australian collaborative authorship via control of key creative roles and decisions – called the creative elements test. . . .

After the High Court decision, the ABA was required to assess whether [this definition] should be retained in a standard that gives national treatment to New Zealand programs.

For the purposes of giving no less favourable treatment to New Zealand programs, a New Zealand program must be defined in a way which is consistent with the definition used for an Australian program.

Broadly, two options were canvassed for testing the Australianness of a program:

1. a creative elements test (the method currently used); and
2. a test of program content based on 'on-screen' criteria.

In either case, there are two alternative approaches for providing equivalent treatment to New Zealanders:

1. by providing New Zealanders and Australians with equal and equivalent access to the same test, eg. by treating a New Zealand and an Australian actor as equivalent; or
2. by developing separate but parallel tests for Australianness and New Zealandness, respectively. A parallel test recognises that New Zealand programs are not Australian programs, and are included in the standard solely because of Australia's obligations under the CER Protocol.

*1. Separate and equivalent Australian and New Zealand creative elements tests or a combined test.*

In general there was a strong preference for the maintenance of a creative elements test over an on-screen test for defining the Australian and New Zealand content of programs in the standard.

The Federation of Commercial Television Stations (FACTS) considered that a combined creative elements test the most 'prudent approach.' They argued separate tests could be open to challenge on the grounds that exclusion of hybrid programs, may discriminate, in practice, against New Zealand program producers. However, FACTS was prepared to consider separate creative elements tests.

The Production Industry Group (PIG) comprises the Australian Film Commission (AFC), the Australian Children's Television Foundation (ACTF), the Australian Film Institute (AFI), Australian Guild of Screen Composers (AGSC), Australian Screen Editors, Australian Screen Directors Association (ASDA), Australian Writers Guild (AWG), Communication Law Centre, Film Australia Limited, Media Entertainment and Arts Alliance (MEAA), Pacific Film and Television Commission, and Screen Production Association of Australia (SPAA). The PIG recommended a single quota, to be satisfied by separately defined creative elements tests for Australian and New Zealand programs.

A joint submission from production companies Artist Services Pty Ltd, Becker Group Limited, Beyond Films Limited, Crawford Productions Pty Ltd and the Southern Star Group Ltd (the 'Joint Production Companies submission') submitted that Australian and New Zealand programs be equally eligible for the quotas and subquotas, with separate creative elements tests for Australian and New Zealand programs.

SPAA submitted its preferred option is for separate and equivalent creative elements tests for Australian and New Zealand programs.

The Screen Producers and Directors Association of New Zealand (SPADA's) first choice was for a single test applied to establish qualifying programs (Australian, New Zealand and hybrid). This in effect would be a 'trans-Tasman' creative elements test such that a person who is a citizen of, or ordinarily resident in, Australia or New Zealand could fulfil any of the required creative roles and the resulting program would qualify as an 'eligible' program. SPADA also noted that separate but parallel tests would be acceptable, provided hybrid programs are covered and suggested these could be allocated to the originating country.

The New Zealand Government's first preference was for a single trans-Tasman creative elements test. However, it was prepared to accept parallel creative elements test providing that these met the market access and national treatment criteria of the CER Services Protocol.

Several submissions, in response to the proposed standard, requested further strengthening of the creative elements test to prevent foreign 'offshore' productions made in New Zealand or Australia from counting for quota.

The Joint Production Companies, PIG, Film Australia, FFC, AFC, Southern Star, ASDA, AWG and the MEAA made written and oral submissions that further measures were needed.

The joint production companies and Southern Star argued for ownership, management and control elements in the test. If these were not included, then they submitted that the test should mandate both writer and director. The PIG, AFC and MEAA argued that both writer and director should be required under the test and that, in addition, only projects originated by Australians or New Zealanders should count.

The other submitters considered that both writer and director were essential to ensure that offshore foreign programs do not displace Australian programs. The PIG also proposed that an Australian content on-screen test be included in the standard in addition to the creative elements test.

SPAA did not support compulsory writer and director. SPAA submitted that if the current test in practice allowed too many marginal programs, the issue should be revisited and an alternative test introduced.

*Separate or combined tests*

Separate and equivalent creative elements tests for Australian and New Zealand programs have the following advantages over a single 'trans-Tasman' test:

- recognition that Australian and New Zealand programs are different cultural products;
- consistency with the cultural policy rationale for Australian programs – object 3(e) of the Act; and
- enabling effective compliance monitoring and review of the impact of the new standard.

The majority of key stakeholders favoured separate and equivalent creative elements tests. FACTS and the New Zealand parties accept this approach provided hybrid productions are included.

While separate and equivalent creative elements tests are preferred, this approach would appear to be inconsistent with Australia's obligations under the Protocol if it did not permit a mix of Australian and New Zealand creative elements in an individual program.

The CER Protocol requires that the standard provide New Zealand persons (and services provided by them) no less favourable access rights in the Australian market for television programs and no less favourable treatment than that accorded to Australian persons (and services provided by them).

Articles 4 and 5 seek to prevent preferential treatment or access rights being given to persons and services of one country over another. A standard that determines Australian content by reference to persons being an Australian or New Zealander (for the purposes of a creative elements test) but not a combination of the two would directly conflict with article 4. For example, a standard that excluded a program with a New Zealand director which for all other intents and purposes would have satisfied the standard (namely writer, producer, actors and so on were Australian), would be contrary to article 4 in that a New Zealand person would not be given equal access rights to the market of television programs in Australia.

To comply with the CER Protocol the standard has to deliver an outcome that, in effect, allows Australians or New Zealanders to fulfil any of the specified creative elements. While a single trans-Tasman test would achieve this outcome, the preferred approach is to include two creative elements tests: one for Australian programs and the second for New Zealand programs, and to recognise programs with a mix of Australian and New Zealand creative elements. The second (New Zealand) test and Australian/New Zealand program clause are included in the new part of the standard, making clear that they are a result of compliance with Australia's international obligations. This approach maintains the distinction between Australia and New Zealand and is preferred for the reasons noted above.

*Increasing the involvement of Australians/New Zealanders required under creative elements test*

The Production Industry Group's initial submission was that the current creative elements test ought to be revised and extended to ensure only genuinely New Zealand programs qualify and to protect the integrity of the remaining Australian programming. They made extensive comments for revising the creative elements test and these include:

- a production company incorporated in Australia and managed by Australians;
- an origination test for productions developed by Australians;
- at least 2 out of these 3 criteria

(i) director(s) are Australian

(ii) the program is based on an original creative work written by an Australian/s or an interpretation developed and written by an Australian/s of an original creative work;

(iii) the production company is incorporated in Australia and is majority owned and controlled by Australians; and

- where the company is not majority owned and controlled by Australians both the writer and director must be Australian.

SPAA argued that the standard should admit only those New Zealand programs under the real creative and commercial control of New Zealanders. To do this the test needed to look beyond 'natural persons' to the controlling corporate entity to prevent essentially foreign controlled productions, that may be using significant Australian or New Zealand creative and technical resources, from qualifying as either Australian or New Zealand content. They suggested:

- examining the nationality of the corporate entities involved in key production decisions;
- the company be incorporated in New Zealand (or Australia);
- the company be majority owned and controlled by New Zealanders (or Australians); and
- to be eligible, a foreign company would have to demonstrate a firm commitment to Australian content through at least ten years continuous production of programs that have met the Australian content standard.

The joint production companies submission argued that the current creative elements test for Australian programs should include the following:

- made by companies incorporated in Australia [or New Zealand];
- made by Australian [or New Zealand] controlled and managed production companies with majority Australian [or New Zealand] ownership; and
- a more than nominal portion of the copyright of each Australian [or New Zealand] program to be Australian [or New Zealand] owned.

Some submitters noted in discussion that New Zealand involvement in *Xena: Warrior Princess* and *Hercules* has increased over the years to the extent that apart for the US location of post-production these programs would count under the proposed standard. The cast requirement of the standard allows up to half the leads to be foreign and it is now more common to use a high percentage of local cast as well as crew. Similarly long running offshore productions with a mix of foreign writers and directors could count under the standard.

Production industry submitters considered that there would be no adverse effects from requiring both writer and director as genuinely Australian or New Zealand programs would be meeting this requirement. The AFC and AWG both stated that they could not identify any Australian program that would be excluded under a writer and director test.

Many suggestions focused on the ownership of production companies operating in Australia. If adopted they would represent a major change in approach to the definition of an 'Australian program.' The creative elements test has been based on the concept of collaborative authorship – that if Australians have creative control, the programs they make will be Australian and have Australian content.

Proposals concerning ownership and control would introduce complexity to the standard and involve practical difficulties in their implementation. The ABA's experience with ownership and control investigations into the application of Schedule of the Act indicates the need for caution.

These proposals would entail resource intensive compliance analysis by the ABA as to the management and control structures of production companies and individual production arrangements.

The production industry suggestion that production companies should be incorporated in Australia or New Zealand on closer scrutiny would appear to have little practical impact on the operation of the standard, given this can be relatively easily achieved.

The proposal relating to the nationality of the originators of the production was also considered and rejected by the ABA. It is often a complex issue to identify the exact origin of a project. There can also be confusion with the origins of a project and the origins of an idea or story.

Strengthening the creative elements test to require both writer and director to be Australian (or New Zealand in the case of a New Zealand production) was initially put forward by the ABA as a means of guaranteeing the cultural specificity of the programs. While offshore productions made in Australia have in the past usually not met the current creative elements test, there may be increasing pressures on producers and broadcasters in the future.

It might be argued that the ABA, in tightening the creative elements tests to require both writer and director, would make the standard too restrictive for Australian producers. . . . Following consultation on the draft standard, the ABA formed the view that the proposal would result in the loss of a necessary level of flexibility.

The November draft proposed that the ABA have the discretion to exclude reversioned foreign programs that meet the creative elements test but which have significant foreign content.

This is similar to the discretion in s 6(3) of the Act relating to Australian drama programs for pay TV. It allows the ABA to declare that a program which was made wholly or substantially in Australia and which has significant Australian content, also has non-Australian content of such significance that it should not be treated as an eligible Australian drama program. . . . Most submissions identified the problem of uncertainty associated with this proposal, which may leave the new standard open to a challenge of invalidity. The proposal to introduce a discretion was not implemented by the ABA. Rather the specific issue of reversioning foreign documentaries is remedied in the new standard.

*2. On-Screen test for Australian Content*

Overall there was little support for using an on-screen test to define Australian or New Zealand content of programs. Submitters generally accepted that the approach had inherent difficulties as outlined in the ABA discussion paper and in the November paper accompanying the draft standard. An exception was the PIG which proposed in response to the standard a suggestion to integrate on-screen criteria with the current creative elements test. It proposed a 'two-pronged' test with personnel and on-screen elements, which would apply to adult and children's drama. The proposal would have incorporated a definition of an Australian program that referred to 'substantial Australian content and without substantial non-Australian content', where 'Australian content is material which presents or explores Australian identity, character and cultural diversity.' The proposed definition also noted that: 'in assessing the above, the primary question to be considered is: do Australians see and/hear themselves on the screen?

The PIG argued that this proposal does not contain the same policy difficulties that have been associated with previous broader proposals for an on-screen test. In particular, while programs made by New Zealanders could have qualified, programs made by persons other than Australians and New Zealanders would not have been eligible. . . .

The difficulties with on-screen tests were outlined in the initial discussion paper remain. They relate to possible CER inconsistency and practical administrative issues in operating a potentially uncertain test.

The relative merits of an 'on-screen' or a 'creative elements test' have been debated at length during the two previous reviews of the standard. During the course of the Project Blue Sky litigation, the ABA's use of a creative elements test was called into question, including by Chief Justice Brennan. It may be thought that Australian identity and character might be better promoted on commercial television by rules which mandate specific on-screen depictions, such as Australian locations, stories, characters, symbols, themes and language. However, the ABA and its predecessor the Australian Broadcasting Tribunal (ABT) rejected an on-screen test on both policy and administrative grounds.

Standards must establish general criteria which are fixed in advance, and certain in their meaning and application. Although it may be possible to specify objective criteria relating to an on-screen test for Australian programs it is difficult to frame criteria which are neither too specific nor too general. For example, if the standard were to attempt to capture all the topics which might legitimately be depicted in a wide range of program types, it is likely to be arbitrary and creatively restrictive.

Australian programs can usually be identified as such on screen, but the notion of tying creative representation to concepts of culture defined by time, place and ideas could be limiting. Difficulties in relation to certain genres, both fiction (for example, fantasy and science fiction) and non-fiction (such as news and current affairs) are obvious, but the involvement of foreign characters, stories or locations could make judgments about the 'Australianness' of productions problematic.

An on-screen test which established general criteria would rely heavily on the ABA's discretion as to whether a program met the criteria. To provide certainty for producers and broadcasters, some form of prior classification or at least guidance by the ABA would seem desirable. At present statutory provision for requiring prior classification is only made for children's programs (section 129 of the Act). A system of elective 'prior opinions' at pre-production stage could only provide certainty in cases where no further change to the production took place after the ABA had given its opinion. The ABA's opinion would not hold if the completed program failed to realise its preproduction description. Such a system is likely to be difficult to administer and open to problems of interpretation.

Elective prior opinions would impose financial and administrative burdens on producers and broadcasters. The possible need to submit scripts or program pilots to the ABA for opinions and the time spent in discussions about the potential eligibility of program concepts could add to costs and would need to be included in production schedules. There are also resource implications for the ABA in providing advice about the eligibility of programs prior to production and broadcast.

No new evidence or legal argument was submitted that would lead the ABA to consider changing its view concerning on-screen tests, as expressed in the discussion paper and the paper which accompanied the draft standard. . . .

*Conclusion and Recommended Options*

The ABA is of the view that the revised standard complies with s 160(d) as required by law. In ensuring that the standard continues to fulfil its cultural purpose the ABA has attempted to balance the interests of Australian television viewers, the broadcasting industry and the production industry as required by law.

- The new standard is intended to accord national treatment to New Zealanders and New Zealand programs as required by the High Court's decision, but still to retain its focus on Australian content obligations. . . .
- The structure of the current standard is preserved. The amendments allow that the obligations under the standard to broadcast Australian programs may be decreased by the extent to which equivalent New Zealand programs, Australia/New Zealand programs and Australian official co-productions are broadcast by the licensee.

*Implementation and Review*

The ABA proposes to implement the amended standard on 1 March 1999.

The ABA will closely monitor the impact of the new standard during the initial two years of operation, with detailed compliance information published annually.

The ABA will undertake a review two years after commencement, to assess how well the standard is achieving its cultural purpose.

In particular, the ABA will be reviewing the impact of the following proposals: . . . the extent of any displacement of Australian programs by New Zealand programs, and any secondary market price effects. . . .

The ABA intends to commence a review of the new standard by 1 July 2001.

---

**Review of the Australian Content Standard - Issues Paper (2001)**

The Australian Broadcasting Authority is the author of the following document, and it is reproduced with the ABA's permission.

. . .

*Impact of New Zealand programs . . .*

When determining the standard in 1999, the ABA undertook to monitor the impact of the changes and to undertake a review two years after commencement, to assess how well the standard was achieving its cultural purpose. To date, the inclusion of New Zealand in the standard has not had any appreciable impact on the broadcast of Australian programs on commercial television. The ABA's compliance monitoring shows that a very small amount of New Zealand programming has been broadcast by the networks – 8.9 hours of programming broadcast across the networks in 2000 and none in 1999. The ABA does not consider that the effect of allowing New Zealand programs to count for quota will be the major focus of the current review. However, it is appropriate to examine whether any of the changes introduced in 1999 (responding to the inclusion of New Zealand in the standard) should be reconsidered. . . .

---

**Canadian Content Rules**


[http://www.pch.gc.ca/culture/can-con/can_con.html]

*Introduction*

Canadian content definitions in the film/video, broadcasting and sound recording sectors are used for two main purposes:

1. to determine access to direct funding or to access the Canadian Film or Video Production Tax Credit Program and
2. to measure television and radio broadcasters' conformity with Canadian Radio-television and Telecommunications Commission (CRTC) Canadian content regulations.

All the Canadian content definitions in these sectors can trace their origins to CRTC radio and television initiatives in the late 1960s and early 1970s under the chairmanship of Pierre Juneau.

One of the main factors in determining whether a work is "Canadian" relates to the key creative personnel involved in its making: a minimum number of key creative positions (e.g. director, screenwriter, actor, performer, composer, etc.) must be filled by Canadians. Points are ascribed for each of them. The minimum number of points required varies depending on the program or regulation. Additional eligibility requirements must be met to qualify for Canadian content designation (such as 75% of production costs spent in Canada) and these also depend on the program and regulation. As a general rule, production and distribution companies must be Canadian-owned and controlled.

The various systems used to define Canadian content are described below:

*Sound Recordings and Radio Broadcasting of Musical Works*

*I – MAPL System*

The MAPL system refers to the four elements in the Radio Regulations used to qualify musical selections as Canadian. These elements were selected by the CRTC following an extensive public hearing process in 1969 and since then have been reviewed periodically to ensure that they are still appropriate. The MAPL system is designed to stimulate all sectors of the Canadian music industry and yet be as simple as possible for the industry to implement and regulate.

The primary objective is a cultural one: to encourage increased exposure of Canadian musical performers, lyricists and composers to Canadian audiences. The secondary objective is an industrial one: to strengthen the Canadian music industry, including both the creative and production components.

To qualify as "Canadian content" for the purpose of radio broadcasting Canadian content quotas, a musical selection must generally fulfill at least two of the following conditions:

M (music): the music is composed entirely by a Canadian

A (artist): the music is, or the lyrics are, performed principally by a Canadian

P (production): the musical selection is:
– recorded wholly in Canada, or
– performed wholly in Canada and broadcast live in Canada.

L (lyrics): the lyrics are written entirely by a Canadian.

The MAPL system is used by both the CRTC to check Canadian content compliancy by licensees and as a basis for eligibility to the federal Sound Recording Development Program (SRDP).

In general, 35% of the sound recordings played on a radio station between 6 a.m. and midnight must qualify as "Canadian content" as defined by the MAPL system.

*II – Sound Recording Development Program (SRDP)*

The SRDP is administered by three organizations and the Department of Canadian Heritage, each of which has determined Canadian content requirements appropriate to the Canadian music sector it supports:

FACTOR (Foundation to Assist Canadian Talent on Record) is a not-for-profit organization which administers the components of the SRDP related to the production, marketing, promotion, touring and business development of the English-language, mainstream sectors of the Canadian music industry. Applications requesting assistance for the production of sound recordings must meet the following Canadian content requirements: 1) the artist must be Canadian, 2) the record company must be Canadian-owned and controlled, 3) at least 50% of the material to be recorded on an album must be 100% Canadian (i.e. 4-part MAPL), and 4) the recording must be produced in Canada.

Musicaction is the sister-organization to FACTOR for the French-language mainstream music industry in Canada. Musicaction requires that applicants requesting assistance for the production of sound recordings meet the following Canadian content requirements: 1) the artist be Canadian, 2) the record company be Canadian-owned and controlled, 3) at least 50% of the lyrics or music be written or composed by Canadians, and 4) the album be produced in Canada.

Canada Council of the Arts administers the Specialized Music Production Assistance component of the SRDP (non-mainstream/non-market-driven music). The Council requires that 1) the artist be Canadian, 2) the record company be Canadian-owned and controlled, 3) the album be produced and manufactured in Canada, and 4) at least 50% of the music be written by Canadians (original compositions or original interpretations of traditional music).

The Department of Canadian Heritage administers the component of the SRDP directly related to Canadian content – Specialized Music Distribution Assistance (non-mainstream/non-market-driven music). This component requires that 1) the distribution company be Canadian-owned and controlled and 2) the distributor distributes at least 6 record labels owned by Canadian companies. In addition, only the titles of the record catalogue that are Canadian specialized music receive funding. To be Canadian, the recordings listed in the catalogue 1) must be by a Canadian artist; 2) 50% of the tracks on the recording must have two qualifying MAPL conditions; 3) must be produced by a Canadian record company; and 4) the ownership of the Canadian master recording must be held by a Canadian company.

*Film, Video and Television Broadcasting*

*I – Canadian Audio-Visual Certification Office (CAVCO)*

CAVCO recommends to the Minister of Canadian Heritage the certification as Canadian for productions that meet the criteria set out in the Income Tax Act and its Regulations. Certification allows the production to have access to the Canadian Film or Video Production Tax Credit. For a production to qualify for the credit, it must be of an eligible genre and obtain a minimum of six "Canadian content" points. In addition, the producer must be a Canadian and 75% of the production expenditures must be made in Canada. CAVCO limits eligibility to specific program categories. CAVCO uses one "Canadian content" points scale for live-action production and another for animation. A maximum of 10 points are available under each scale.

*Live-Action*

A live-action production of any length must earn six points, based on the following key creative people qualifying as Canadian:

| | |
|---|---|
| Director | 2 points |
| Screenwriter | 2 points |
| Highest paid actor | 1 point |
| Second highest paid actor | 1 point |
| Head of Art Department | 1 point |
| Director of photography | 1 point |
| Music composer | 1 point |
| Picture editor | 1 point |

Two mandatory criteria must be respected:

1. Director or Screenwriter must be Canadian, and
2. the highest or second highest paid actor must be Canadian.

In the case of a television series the points system is applied to each episode.

*Animation*

An animation production must earn six points, based on the following key creative people qualifying as Canadian, or the location where the function is performed is in Canada:

Persons:

| | |
|---|---|
| Director | 1 point |
| Scriptwriter and storyboard supervisor | 1 point |
| First or second voice (or 1st or 2nd leading performer) | 1 point |
| Design supervisor (art director) | 1 point |
| Music composer | 1 point |
| Picture editor | 1 point |

Locations where functions are performed:

| | |
|---|---|
| Layout and background | 1 point |
| Key animation | 1 point |
| Assistant animation/In-betweening | 1 point |

Persons and Location where function is performed (i.e. the camera operator must be Canadian and the work must be performed in Canada):

| | |
|---|---|
| Camera operator | 1 point |

Three mandatory criteria must be respected:

1. director or scriptwriter and storyboard supervisor must be Canadian,
2. key animation must be performed in Canada, and
3. or second voice (or first or second leading performer) must be Canadian.

In the case of a television series the points system is applied to each episode.

*Producer Requirement*

The producer (i.e. the individual who controls and is the central decision-maker of the production from beginning to end) must be a Canadian. Provision is made for the extension of a courtesy Executive Producer credit to non-Canadians under certain specific conditions, such as when the non-Canadian arranges for financing and/or assists with the foreign distribution of the production.

*Cost Requirements*

The cost requirements provide that

1. 75% of total amounts paid in the production services category is paid to Canadians, and
2. 75% of all expenses incurred in the laboratory and post-production work category is incurred for services in Canada.

*Production Requirement*

The production must be completed within two years after the end of the taxation year in which the principal photography began. There must be an agreement to have the production shown in Canada in the two years following its completion.

The following genres will not qualify as Canadian productions for the purpose of the Canadian Film or Video Production Tax Credit:

1. news, current events or public affairs, weather or market reports
2. talk shows
3. games, questionnaires or contests (except if directed primarily at minors)
4. sports
5. gala or awards
6. production that solicits funds
7. reality television
8. pornography
9. advertising
10. produced for industrial, corporate or institutional purposes
11. primarily stock footage (except if documentary), and
12. production for which public financial support would, in the opinion of the Minister of Canadian Heritage, be contrary to public policy.

*II – Canadian Television Fund*

The Canadian Television Fund (CTF) requires a production to have 10 points using the CAVCO scale. In addition, the underlying rights must be owned, and significantly and meaningfully developed, by Canadians, and the project must be shot and set primarily in Canada. The genres eligible for support through the CTF are Canadian drama, variety and performing arts, documentaries, children's and feature films with a Canadian broadcast licence.

To access the CTF (both the Equity Investment Program and the Licence Fee Program), a production must meet all of the following essential requirements:

1. The project must speak to Canadians about, and reflect, Canadian themes and subject matters.
2. The project must obtain 10 points on the CAVCO scale, as determined by the CTF. (Feature length films supported by the CTF require 8 points.)
3. Underlying rights must be owned and significantly and meaningfully developed by Canadians. Eligible projects must be developed by Canadians. Canadian creators must have significant and meaningful involvement in the project, from concept to final script. The project may not be based on foreign television productions, foreign feature

films (unless based on a published Canadian literary work) or foreign fully developed, final-version scripts.

4. The project must be shot and set primarily in Canada.

These guidelines were strengthened in 1999-2000. Previously, productions required a minimum of 8/10 CAVCO points. However, given excess demand, the CTF Board raised the minimum access requirement to 10/10, giving the CTF the highest Canadian content entry threshold of any assistance program.

*III – Telefilm Canada*

Both Telefilm Canada's Canada Feature Film Fund and the feature film component within the CTF use the same basic requirements as those used by CAVCO, but require that a production obtain at least 8 points.

*Official International Co-Productions*

Telefilm Canada administers co-production treaties on behalf of the Government of Canada and can provide financial assistance with regard to the Canadian portion of the budget.

Official co-production agreements are binding international legal accords between governments. They are intended to encourage production by pooling creative, technical and financial resources under carefully prescribed conditions. Canada currently has more than 50 official co-production agreements with various countries around the world.

Official international co-productions receive 100% Canadian content credit; however, no points system is applied to co-productions. The creative portion must be equal to the financial portion. In other words, if a Canadian producer is responsible for 20% of the financing of a co-production, it is expected that the Canadian producer will have control over at least 20% of the creative elements of the production and 20% of the production costs must be spent in Canada.

Under these agreements, productions with a minimum of 20% Canadian participation (i.e. creative and financial) are recognized as Canadian content for broadcasting purposes. Moreover, the Canadian portion of the budget can have full access to the Canadian Film or Video Production Tax Credit Program and access to the CTF under certain conditions.

*IV – Canadian Radio-Television and Telecommunications Commission (CRTC)*

The CRTC was established pursuant to the Broadcasting Act to provide for the regulation and supervision of the Canadian broadcasting system. The Commission specifies that Canadian broadcast licensees must broadcast a certain percentage of Canadian content productions (i.e. Canadian content quota).

In television, the CRTC pioneered the Canadian content points system in the late 1960s. Today, it uses the same basic criteria as those used by CAVCO in determining whether a production is Canadian, and also requires the producer to be Canadian. In addition to those production genres eligible under CAVCO, the Commission also recognizes sports, talk shows, news, video clips, etc., using an identical points scale.

For the largest conventional broadcasters, the CRTC has introduced a requirement of a minimum of 8 hours of priority programming per week between 7 and 11 p.m. The eligible categories of priority programs are: Canadian drama, music and dance, and variety programs, long-form documentaries, entertainment magazine programs, and regionally produced programs in all categories except news, current affairs and sports.

The CRTC also requires Canadian content from pay and specialty broadcasters, tailoring the requirement according to the service, setting individual levels of Canadian content as a condition of licence. This can take two forms – a minimum percentage of programming, and/or a specific level of expenditure for Canadian content. The Weather Network, for example, has a 100% Canadian content requirement. YTV has conditions of licence that require it to exhibit 70% Canadian programming in primetime (between 6 p.m. and midnight) and to expend 38% of annual gross revenues on Canadian programs.

*International Co-Ventures*

Unlike CAVCO, the Commission recognizes co-ventures as Canadian for broadcast purposes. Co-ventures are international co-productions that are not undertaken under an official co-production treaty signed by the Government of Canada and a foreign government.

Co-ventures are generally required to meet the same minimum 6 points and 75% cost requirements as under CAVCO to obtain credit as Canadian content. The increased flexibility with a co-venture stems from the fact that a non-Canadian producer is allowed an equal decision-making responsibility on creative elements of a production along with a Canadian producer. In such a case, however, the Canadian producer is responsible for the Canadian elements of the production budget.

Co-ventures with Commonwealth or member countries of La Francophonie provide additional flexibility. The production will be considered Canadian if the director or the writer, and at least one of the two leading performers, are Canadian, and if:

1. it meets a minimum of 5 points for key creative personnel;
2. a minimum of 50% of the total remuneration is paid to Canadians, and;
3. at least 50% of processing and final preparation costs are paid for services in Canada.

*Canadian Content Bonuses*

For the purpose of a broadcaster's Canadian content quota, the CRTC provides an incentive for programming certain production types and genres. For example:

- A non-Canadian program that
  1. is produced either in French, English or in a native Canadian language, and
  2. is dubbed in any other of those languages using Canadian resources, will be awarded a 25% Canadian content credit.

On September 1, 2000, the CRTC implemented new Canadian content provisions for the largest TV broadcasters for prime time.

- Broadcasters will be required to schedule a minimum of 8 hours a week in the "priority programming categories of Canadian drama, music, variety, long-form documentaries and regionally produced programs in genres other than news, current affairs and sports."
- A bonus for Canadian drama programs:
  1. 150% for a 10/10 drama;
  2. 125% for a 6/10 to 9/10 drama; . . .

---

## General Agreement on Tariffs and Trade (GATT)

*Article IV: Special Provisions relating to Cinematograph Films*

If any contracting party establishes or maintains internal quantitative regulations relating to exposed cinematograph films, such regulations shall take the form of screen quotas which shall conform to the following requirements:

(a) Screen quotas may require the exhibition of cinematograph films of national origin during a pecified minimum proportion of the total screen time actually utilized, over a specified period of not less than one year, in the commercial exhibition of all films of whatever origin, and shall be computed on the basis of screen time per theatre per year or the equivalent thereof;

(b) With the exception of screen time reserved for films of national origin under a screen quota, screen time including that released by administrative action from screen time reserved for films of national origin, shall not be allocated formally or in effect among sources of supply;

(c) Notwithstanding the provisions of sub-paragraph (b) of this Article, any contracting party may maintain screen quotas conforming to the requirements of sub-paragraph (a) of this Article which reserve a minimum proportion of screen time for films of a specified origin other than that of the contracting party imposing such screen quotas; *Provided* that no such minimum proportion of screen time shall be increased above the level in effect on April 10, 1947;

(d) Screen quotas shall be subject to negotiation for their limitation, liberalization or elimination.

---

## North American Free Trade Agreement (NAFTA)

*Article 1202: National Treatment*

1. Each Party shall accord to service providers of another Party treatment no less favorable than that it accords, in like circumstances, to its own service providers.

2. The treatment accorded by a Party under paragraph 1 means, with respect to a state or province, treatment no less favorable than the most favorable treatment accorded, in like circumstances, by that state or province to service providers of the Party of which it forms a part.

*Article 1203: Most-Favored-Nation Treatment*

Each Party shall accord to service providers of another Party treatment no less favorable than that it accords, in like circumstances, to service providers of any other Party or of a non-Party.

*Article 1204: Standard of Treatment*

Each Party shall accord to service providers of any other Party the better of the treatment required by Articles 1202 and 1203.

*Article 2106: Cultural Industries*

Annex 2106 applies to the Parties specified in that Annex with respect to cultural industries.

*Article 2107: Definitions*

For purposes of this Chapter: *cultural industries* means persons engaged in any of the following activities:

(a) the publication, distribution, or sale of books, magazines, periodicals or newspapers in print or machine readable form but not including the sole activity of printing or typesetting any of the foregoing;

(b) the production, distribution, sale or exhibition of film or video recordings;

(c) the production, distribution, sale or exhibition of audio or video music recordings;

(d) the publication, distribution or sale of music in print or machine readable form; or

(e) radiocommunications in which the transmissions are intended for direct reception by the general public, and all radio, television and cable broadcasting undertakings and all satellite programming and broadcast network services. . . .

*Annex 2106 Cultural Industries*

Notwithstanding any other provision of this Agreement, as between Canada and the United States, any measure adopted or maintained with respect to cultural industries . . . shall be governed under this Agreement exclusively in accordance with the provisions of the [pre-NAFTA] *Canada-United States Free Trade Agreement*. . . .

---

**Canada-United States Free Trade Agreement**

*Article 2005: Cultural Industries*

1. Cultural industries are exempt from the provisions of this Agreement. . . .
2. Notwithstanding any other provision of this Agreement, a party may take measures of equivalent commercial effects in response to actions that would have been inconsistent with this Agreement but for Paragraph 1.

---

**Radio Television S.A. de C.V. v. Federal Communications Commission**
**130 F.3d 1078 (D.C.Cir. 1997)**

Sentelle, Circuit Judge:

Radio Television, S.A. de C.V., the licensee of Mexico-based XETV, and its domestic affiliate Bay City Television, Inc. (collectively "XETV"), seek review of an FCC order granting Fox Television's application under § 325 of the Communications Act for permission to transmit live television programming to XETV for rebroadcast into San Diego, California. . . .

*I. Background*

The Communications Act of 1934 (the "Act"), 47 U.S.C. § 151 *et seq.*, subjects radio and television stations that broadcast within the United States to licensing by the FCC, which must inquire as to whether the "public interest, convenience, and necessity will be served by the granting" of a license application. 47 U.S.C. § 309(a). To this end, the FCC must ask whether a broadcaster provides "issue-responsive programming," that is, whether it serves the public interest by providing programming that concerns local issues facing the community to which it broadcasts.

Because of the possibility that domestic broadcasters in some areas could evade the Act's requirements by transmitting their signals to a foreign station for rebroadcast into the United States, § 325(c) expressly prohibits such transmissions without an FCC permit. Section 325(d) provides that the "requirements of section 309" shall govern FCC consideration of applications for such permits; thus, in a § 325 proceeding, the FCC must determine whether the "public interest, convenience, and necessity will be served by the granting" of the permit. Since at least 1972, the FCC has considered issue-responsive programming as part of its "public interest" analysis under § 325.

XETV has for many years broadcast programming from its Tijuana, Mexico facilities to viewers in San Diego, California. In 1956, the FCC granted the § 325 application of American Broadcasting Companies, Inc. ("ABC") to transmit programming to XETV for rebroadcast into the domestic market. *See Channel 51 of San Diego, Inc. v. FCC,* 79 F.3d 1187, 1189 (D.C. Cir. 1996) ("*Channel 51*"). When ABC filed a renewal application in 1968, a new domestic station, KCST, filed a petition to deny the permit. Based in part on a finding that XETV's programming was "deficient in that it renders no local service meeting the needs and interests of the community," the FCC denied ABC's renewal application. *American Broadcasting Cos., Inc.,* 35 F.C.C.2d 1 (1972) ("*ABC 1972*"), *aff'd per curiam,* 26 Rad. Reg. 2d (P & F) 203 (D.C. Cir.), *cert. denied,* 412 U.S. 939 (1973).

More recently, XETV has served as the San Diego affiliate of the Fox Television network. Until 1994, Fox and XETV relied on a practice called "bicycling": Fox transmitted its programming to a U.S. receiving station, which made tapes and physically transported these across the border for XETV to rebroadcast into San Diego. This practice legally avoided the § 325 licensing regime, but did not allow live broadcasts of any sort, which became a problem when Fox acquired the right to broadcast live games of the National Football League in 1994. Fox accordingly sought a § 325 permit for crossborder electronic transmission.

A domestic San Diego broadcaster, Channel 51, filed a petition to deny Fox's § 325 application, arguing that XETV's "issue-responsive programming" was deficient. The FCC eventually granted Fox's permit, in the process reviewing the *ABC 1972* standards in light of the North American Free Trade Agreement ("NAFTA"). The FCC concluded that NAFTA had invalidated its prior position, expressed in *ABC 1972,* that "all of the public interest criteria used in domestic proceedings [should apply] to Section 325 proceedings." *See Fox Television Stations, Inc.,* 10 F.C.C.R. 4055, 4064 (1995) ("*Fox 1*"). Although recognizing that NAFTA permitted it to continue considering programming matters, the Commission held in *Fox 1* that its standards must be more lenient under § 325 than those applied in domestic proceedings. NAFTA's Annex VI directs the Commission to consider electrical interference as the "primary criterion" for evaluating the public interest under § 325, and prohibits discrimination based on nationality and other unnecessary restrictions on trade. Under its reading of NAFTA, the FCC found the issue-responsive programming requirement discriminatory and unnecessarily restrictive of trade, and consequently held that it should no longer apply in § 325 proceedings.

In *Channel 51* we vacated that portion of the FCC's decision in *Fox 1* which ruled, based on NAFTA, that the § 309 issue-responsive programming analysis no longer applied to applications under § 325. . . . For reasons set forth more fully in *Channel 51,* we concluded that the FCC's reliance on Annex VI was misplaced and that NAFTA did not support the departure from the reasoning of *ABC 1972.* Indeed, we observed that it would be "well-nigh impossible to concoct" an explanation for "why subjecting a foreign station to the same issue-responsive programming requirement to which domestic stations are subject constitutes discrimination against a foreign station on the basis of its nationality," in violation of NAFTA. Thus, we vacated the order granting Fox's § 325 permit and remanded for further proceedings.

On remand, the FCC reconsidered its position . . . and decided to reaffirm its original position articulated in *ABC 1972,* namely, that its "Section 325 analysis must include an analysis of the public interest convenience and necessity consistent with Section 309." *Fox Television Stations, Inc.,* 11 F.C.C.R. 14870, 14877, P 21

(1996) ("*Fox 2*"). It then granted the Fox application for a § 325 permit, but conditioned this grant "on XETV's provision of programming that meets the Commission's issue-responsive requirement during the five year authorization term." If and when Fox seeks renewal of its permit, it "will be required to show ... whether the programming broadcast by XETV has met the issue-responsive requirement during the term of the initial authorization."

*II. Justiciability*

Fox has not challenged the Commission's conditional grant, but XETV seeks review of the condition imposed on Fox, and indirectly upon its own programming, by the FCC's order in Fox 2. XETV claims that it has standing as a "person . . . aggrieved" by the Commission's order, and that the appeal is ripe for review. . . .

XETV's allegations of injury, at the heart of both standing and ripeness inquiries, amount to this: as a result of the Commission's allegedly unlawful condition on a future renewal application by Fox, XETV must alter its behavior, expending time and money to produce, air, and document the broadcast of issue-responsive programming during the next five years. Even though in five years time Fox might not seek renewal of its § 325 permit, the terms of the FCC order place a burden on XETV to comply with the issue-responsive programming requirement if it wants to preserve any chance of retaining its status as an affiliate of Fox, or any other U.S. network. . . . Although the Commission's order was directed to Fox, not XETV, we hold that the condition placed on the grant of Fox's permit would, if unlawfully imposed, adversely affect the interests of XETV. . . .

*III. Merits*

Having prevailed in its skirmish over standing and ripeness, XETV is doomed to lose its battle on the merits. We have already held that the Commission's application of the § 309 issue-responsive programming requirement in proceedings under § 325 does not constitute discrimination between foreign and domestic stations under NAFTA. . . .

*A. NAFTA*

. . . XETV repeatedly protests that the Commission has no authority to condition the "grant of a Section 325 permit on the provision of issue-responsive programming by the *recipient foreign station.*" Under § 325, the licensee is a *domestic* broadcaster: in this case, Fox Television. The foreign station, XETV, is *never* the recipient of a § 325 permit; at best, it is a third-party beneficiary of a domestic broadcaster's license. Thus, the condition set forth in *Fox 2* is a condition not on the foreign station's permission to broadcast a domestic network's programming, but on the domestic network's permission to use a foreign station to serve a domestic market. There is nothing unreasonable or discriminatory in the Commission's order which we can summarize as requiring a domestic network to serve a local market only via an intermediary which adequately serves the public interest, regardless of whether the local affiliate is located within U.S. borders.

*IV. Conclusion*

The order of the Commission in *Fox 2* is affirmed in all respects.

---

## 6.2 GOVERNMENT REGULATION OF OFFENSIVE CONTENT

### Yahoo!, Inc. v. La Ligue Contre Le Racisme et L'Antisemitisme
### 169 F. Supp. 2d 1181 (N.D.Cal. 2001)

Jeremy Fogel, District Judge

*I. Procedural History*

Defendants La Ligue Contre Le Racisme Et l'Antisemitisme ("LICRA") and L'Union Des Etudiants Juifs De France, citizens of France, are non-profit organizations dedicated to eliminating anti-Semitism. Plaintiff Yahoo!, Inc. ("Yahoo!") is a corporation organized under the laws of Delaware with its principal place of business in Santa Clara, California. Yahoo! is an Internet service provider that operates various Internet websites and services that any computer user can access at the Uniform Resource Locator ("URL") http://www.yahoo.com. Yahoo! services ending in the suffix, ".com," without an associated country code as a prefix or extension (collectively, "Yahoo!'s U.S. Services") use the English language and target users who are residents of, utilize servers based in and operate under the laws of the United States. Yahoo! subsidiary corporations operate regional Yahoo! sites and services in twenty other nations, including, for example, Yahoo! France, Yahoo! India, and Yahoo! Spain. Each of these regional web sites contains the host nation's unique two-letter code as either a prefix or a suffix in its URL (e.g., Yahoo! France is found at http://www.yahoo.fr and Yahoo! Korea at http://www.yahoo.kr). Yahoo!'s regional sites use the local region's primary language, target the local citizenry, and operate under local laws.

Yahoo! provides a variety of means by which people from all over the world can communicate and interact with one another over the Internet. Examples include an Internet search engine, e-mail, an automated auction site, personal web page hostings, shopping services, chat rooms, and a listing of clubs that individuals can create or join. Any computer user with Internet access is able to post materials on many of these Yahoo! sites, which in turn are instantly accessible by anyone who logs on to Yahoo!'s Internet sites. As relevant here, Yahoo!'s auction site allows anyone to post an item for sale and solicit bids from any computer user from around the globe. Yahoo! records when a posting is made and after the requisite time period lapses sends an e-mail notification to the highest bidder and seller with their respective contact information. Yahoo! is never a party to a transaction, and the buyer and seller are responsible for arranging privately for payment and shipment of goods. Yahoo! monitors the transaction through limited regulation by prohibiting particular items from being sold (such as stolen goods, body parts, prescription and illegal drugs, weapons, and goods violating U.S. copyright laws or the Iranian and Cuban embargos) and by providing a rating system through which buyers and sellers have their transactional behavior evaluated for the benefit of future consumers. Yahoo! informs auction sellers that they must comply with Yahoo!'s policies and may not offer items to buyers in jurisdictions in which the sale of such item violates the jurisdiction's applicable laws. Yahoo! does not actively regulate the content of each posting, and individuals are able to post, and have in fact posted, highly offensive matter, including Nazi-related propaganda and Third Reich memorabilia, on Yahoo!'s auction sites.

On or about April 5, 2000, LICRA sent a "cease and desist" letter to Yahoo!'s Santa Clara headquarters informing Yahoo! that the sale of Nazi and Third Reich related goods through its auction services violates French law. LICRA threatened to take legal action unless Yahoo! took steps to prevent such sales within eight days. Defendants subsequently utilized the United States Marshal's Office to serve

Yahoo! with process in California and filed a civil complaint against Yahoo! in the Tribunal de Grande Instance de Paris (the "French Court").

The French Court found that approximately 1,000 Nazi and Third Reich related objects, including Adolf Hitler's *Mein Kampf, The Protocol of the Elders of Zion* (an infamous anti-Semitic report produced by the Czarist secret police in the early 1900's), and purported "evidence" that the gas chambers of the Holocaust did not exist were being offered for sale on Yahoo.com's auction site. Because any French citizen is able to access these materials on Yahoo.com directly or through a link on Yahoo.fr, the French Court concluded that the Yahoo.com auction site violates Section R645-1 of the French Criminal Code, which prohibits exhibition of Nazi propaganda and artifacts for sale. On May 20, 2000, the French Court entered an order requiring Yahoo! to (1) eliminate French citizens' access to any material on the Yahoo.com auction site that offers for sale any Nazi objects, relics, insignia, emblems, and flags; (2) eliminate French citizens' access to web pages on Yahoo.com displaying text, extracts, or quotations from *Mein Kampf* and *Protocol of the Elders of Zion*; (3) post a warning to French citizens on Yahoo.fr that any search through Yahoo.com may lead to sites containing material prohibited by Section R645-1 of the French Criminal Code, and that such viewing of the prohibited material may result in legal action against the Internet user; (4) remove from all browser directories accessible in the French Republic index headings entitled "negationists" and from all hypertext links the equation of "negationists" under the heading "Holocaust." The order subjects Yahoo! to a penalty of 100,000 Euros for each day that it fails to comply with the order. The order concludes:

> We order the Company YAHOO! Inc. to take all necessary measures to dissuade and render impossible any access via Yahoo.com to the Nazi artifact auction service and to any other site or service that may be construed as constituting an apology for Nazism or a contesting of Nazi crimes.

The French Court set a return date in July 2000 for Yahoo! to demonstrate its compliance with the order.

Yahoo! asked the French Court to reconsider the terms of the order, claiming that although it easily could post the required warning on Yahoo.fr, compliance with the order's requirements with respect to Yahoo.com was technologically impossible. The French Court sought expert opinion on the matter and on November 20, 2000 "reaffirmed" its order of May 22. The French Court ordered Yahoo! to comply with the May 22 order within three (3) months or face a penalty of 100,000 Francs (approximately U.S. $13,300) for each day of non-compliance. The French Court also provided that penalties assessed against Yahoo! Inc. may not be collected from Yahoo! France. Defendants again utilized the United States Marshal's Office to serve Yahoo! in California with the French Order.

Yahoo! subsequently posted the required warning and prohibited postings in violation of Section R645-1 of the French Criminal Code from appearing on Yahoo.fr. Yahoo! also amended the auction policy of Yahoo.com to prohibit individuals from auctioning:

> Any item that promotes, glorifies, or is directly associated with groups or individuals known principally for hateful or violent positions or acts, such as Nazis or the Ku Klux Klan. Official government-issue stamps and coins are not prohibited under this policy. Expressive media, such as books and films, may be subject to more permissive standards as determined by Yahoo! in its sole discretion.

Notwithstanding these actions, the Yahoo.com auction site still offers certain items for sale (such as stamps, coins, and a copy of *Mein Kampf* which appear to violate the French Order. While Yahoo! has removed the *Protocol of the Elders of Zion* from its auction site, it has not prevented access to numerous other sites which reasonably "may be construed as constituting an apology for Nazism or a contesting of Nazi crimes."

Yahoo! claims that because it lacks the technology to block French citizens from accessing the Yahoo.com auction site to view materials which violate the French Order or from accessing other Nazi-based content of websites on Yahoo.com, it cannot comply with the French order without banning Nazi-related material from Yahoo.com altogether. Yahoo! contends that such a ban would infringe impermissibly upon its rights under the First Amendment to the United States Constitution. Accordingly, Yahoo! filed a complaint in this Court seeking a declaratory judgment that the French Court's orders are neither cognizable nor enforceable under the laws of the United States.

Defendants immediately moved to dismiss on the basis that this Court lacks personal jurisdiction over them. That motion was denied. . . .

*II. Overview*

As this Court and others have observed, the instant case presents novel and important issues arising from the global reach of the Internet. Indeed, the specific facts of this case implicate issues of policy, politics, and culture that are beyond the purview of one nation's judiciary. Thus it is critical that the Court define at the outset what is and is not at stake in the present proceeding.

This case is *not* about the moral acceptability of promoting the symbols or propaganda of Nazism. Most would agree that such acts are profoundly offensive. By any reasonable standard of morality, the Nazis were responsible for one of the worst displays of inhumanity in recorded history. This Court is acutely mindful of the emotional pain reminders of the Nazi era cause to Holocaust survivors and deeply respectful of the motivations of the French Republic in enacting the underlying statutes and of the defendant organizations in seeking relief under those statutes. Vigilance is the key to preventing atrocities such as the Holocaust from occurring again.

Nor is this case about the right of France or any other nation to determine its own law and social policies. A basic function of a sovereign state is to determine by law what forms of speech and conduct are acceptable within its borders. In this instance, as a nation whose citizens suffered the effects of Nazism in ways that are incomprehensible to most Americans, France clearly has the right to enact and enforce laws such as those relied upon by the French Court here.[6] [n6 In particular, there is no doubt that France may and will continue to ban the purchase and possession within its borders of Nazi and Third Reich related matter and to seek criminal sanctions against those who violate the law.]

What *is* at issue here is whether it is consistent with the Constitution and laws of the United States for another nation to regulate speech by a United States resident within the United States on the basis that such speech can be accessed by Internet users in that nation. In a world in which ideas and information transcend borders and the Internet in particular renders the physical distance between speaker and audience virtually meaningless, the implications of this question go far beyond the facts of this case. The modern world is home to widely varied cultures with radically divergent value systems. There is little doubt that Internet users in the United States routinely engage in speech that violates, for example, China's laws against religious expression, the laws of various nations against advocacy of gender equality or homosexuality, or even the United Kingdom's restrictions on freedom of the press. If the government or another party in one of these sovereign nations were to seek enforcement of such laws against Yahoo! or another U.S.-based Internet service provider, what principles should guide the court's analysis?

The Court has stated that it must and will decide this case in accordance with the Constitution and laws of the United States. It recognizes that in so doing, it necessarily adopts certain value judgments embedded in those enactments, including the fundamental judgment expressed in the First Amendment that it is preferable to permit the non-violent expression of offensive viewpoints rather than to impose viewpoint-based governmental regulation upon speech. The government and people of France have made a different judgment based upon their own experience. In undertaking its inquiry as to the proper application of the laws of the United States, the Court intends no disrespect for that judgment or for the experience that has informed it. . . .

*IV. Legal Issues. . .*

The French order prohibits the sale or display of items based on their association with a particular political organization and bans the display of websites based on the authors' viewpoint with respect to the Holocaust and anti-Semitism. A United States court constitutionally could not make such an order. The First Amendment does not permit the government to engage in viewpoint-based regulation of speech absent a compelling governmental interest, such as averting a clear and present danger of imminent violence. In addition, the French Court's mandate that Yahoo! "take all necessary measures to dissuade and render impossible any access via Yahoo.com to the Nazi artifact auction service and to any other site or service that may be construed as constituting an apology for Nazism or a contesting of Nazi crimes" is far too general and imprecise to survive the strict scrutiny required by the First Amendment. The phrase, "and any other site or service that *may be construed* as an apology for Nazism or a contesting of Nazi crimes" fails to provide Yahoo! with a sufficiently definite warning as to what is proscribed. Phrases such as "all necessary measures" and "render impossible" instruct Yahoo! to undertake efforts that will impermissibly chill and perhaps even censor protected speech. "The loss of First Amendment freedoms, for even minimal periods of time, unquestionably constitutes irreparable injury.." . .

Defendants next argue that this Court should abstain from deciding the instant case because Yahoo! simply is unhappy with the outcome of the French litigation and is trying to obtain a more favorable result here. Indeed, abstention is an appropriate remedy for international forum-shopping. . . .

No legal judgment has any effect, of its own force, beyond the limits of the sovereignty from which its authority is derived. However, the United States Constitution and implementing legislation require that full faith and credit be given to judgments of sister states, territories, and possessions of the United States. The extent to which the United States, or any state, honors the judicial decrees of foreign nations is a matter of choice, governed by "the comity of nations." Comity "is neither a matter of absolute obligation, on the one hand, nor of mere courtesy and good will, upon the other." United States courts generally recognize foreign judgments and decrees unless enforcement would be prejudicial or contrary to the country's interests.

As discussed previously, the French order's content and viewpoint-based regulation of the web pages and auction site on Yahoo.com, while entitled to great deference as an articulation of French law, clearly would be inconsistent with the First Amendment if mandated by a court in the United States. What makes this case uniquely challenging is that the Internet in effect allows one to speak in more than one place at the same time. Although France has the sovereign right to regulate what speech is permissible in France, this Court may not enforce a foreign order that violates the protections of the United States Constitution by chilling protected speech that occurs simultaneously within our borders. The reason for limiting comity in this area is sound. "The protection to free speech and the press embodied in [the First] amendment would be seriously jeopardized by the entry of foreign [] judgments granted pursuant to standards deemed appropriate in [another country] but considered antithetical to the protections afforded the press by the U.S. Constitution." Absent a body of law that establishes international standards with respect to speech on the Internet and an appropriate treaty or legislation addressing enforcement of such standards to speech originating within the United States, the principle of comity is outweighed by the Court's obligation to uphold the First Amendment.[12] [n12 The Court expresses no opinion as to whether any such treaty or legislation would or could be constitutional.] . . .

*V. Conclusion*

Yahoo! seeks a declaration from this Court that the First Amendment precludes enforcement within the United States of a French order intended to regulate the content of its speech over the Internet. Yahoo! has shown that the French order is valid under the laws of France, that it may be enforced with retroactive penalties, and that the ongoing possibility of its enforcement in the United States chills Yahoo!'s First Amendment rights. Yahoo! also has shown that an actual controversy exists and that the threat to its constitutional rights is real and immediate. Defendants have failed to show the existence of a genuine issue of material fact or to identify any such issue the existence of which could be shown through further discovery. Accordingly, the motion for summary judgment will be granted. The Clerk shall enter judgment and close the file.

---

**Note on further developments in Yahoo case**

Judge Fogel's decision in the *Yahoo* case reflects its status at just one moment in time. La Ligue Contre Le Racisme Et l'Antisemitisme and L'Union Des Etudiants Juifs De France – the defendants in the U.S. case – have appealed Judge Fogel's ruling to the U.S. Court of Appeals for the Ninth Circuit. In France, Yahoo has appealed the decision of the French court to the Court of Appeals in Paris. As a result, the *civil* aspects of this case – those involving the French injunction and money judgment against Yahoo, and the question of whether that judgment may be enforced in the United States – are not yet concluded.

Moreover, a *criminal* dimension was injected into the case as well when the French court that rendered the civil judgment against Yahoo! announced that it would bring Yahoo! US and Timothy Koogle, its former CEO, to trial on criminal charges of inciting racial hatred by permitting Nazi memorabilia to be sold via websites carried by Yahoo! US. A criminal trial was in fact held in Paris. Yahoo! was charged with violating French criminal law by allowing the sale of Nazi memorabilia from websites it hosted on servers located in the United States. Yahoo! however was acquitted.

French law prohibits "justifying a crime against humanity" and "exhibiting a uniform, insignia or emblem of a person guilty of crimes against humanity." The penalty for doing so can amount to as much as five years in jail and a fine of some $45,000. A Paris criminal court judge ruled that "justifying war crimes" means "glorifying, praising, or at least presenting the crimes in question favorably." And the judge decided that Yahoo! did not do these things, simply by allowing Nazi memorabilia to be sold from websites it hosted.

---

**Note on Free Speech Law in Europe and Canada**

It should not be assumed from the French *Yahoo!* decision that France or other European countries embrace censorship wholeheartedly. To the contrary, Article 10 of the European Convention on Human Rights expressly recognizes the right of free expression:

> "Everyone has the right to freedom of expression. This right shall include the freedom to hold opinions and to receive and impart information without interference by public authority and regardless of frontiers. . . ."

However, there are exceptions to this broad declaration which should be of concern to American entertainment and media producers and distributors working in, or licensing to, the European market. Section 2 of the Article states, *inter alia*:

> "The exercise of these freedoms, since it carries with it duties and responsibilities, may be subject to such formalities, conditions, restrictions or penalties as are prescribed by law and necessary to a democratic society, in the interests of national security, territorial integrity, or public safety, for the prevention of disorder or crime, for the protection of health or morals, [and] for the protection of the reputation or rights of others. . . ."

The good news is that this rather sweeping language has been limited significantly by decisions of the European Court of Human Rights.

For example, in *Hertel v. Switzerland*, 28 E.H.R.R. 534, 1998 WL 1043159 (ECHR 1999), the Court upheld the right of a Swiss scientist to publish articles attacking microwave ovens as dangerous to health and dramatizing his comments by utilizing death's-head images in connection with his articles and speeches. This decision overturned (by an 8-1 vote) Hertel's conviction under the Swiss Unfair Competition Act for "denigrat[ing] others or the goods, work, services, prices or business of others by making inaccurate, misleading, or unnecessarily wounding statements." Article 10, the Court stated, applies "not only to 'information' or 'ideas' that are favourably received or regarded as inoffensive or as a matter of indifference, but also to those which offend, shock or disturb. Such are the demands of pluralism, broadmindedness and tolerance." Any exception to freedom of expression would have to be construed strictly, and its necessity established convincingly. So stating, the Court awarded damages and costs to Hertel.

And in *Oberschlick v. Austria*, 25 E.H.R.R. 357, 1997 WL 1104647 (ECHR 1998), the criminal conviction of a Viennese journalist for insulting right-wing political leader Jorg Haider by calling Haider a "Trottel" (idiot) was reversed, again with an award of damages and costs to the journalist. The Austrian courts had held that Oberschlick's comments (which were in reaction to a speech in which Haider appeared to many to approve of Hitler's actions) overstepped the bounds of "acceptable objective criticism," and that "insults [must not] replac[e] substance in political debate." Adopting a position reminiscent of the U.S. Supreme Court in *New York Times v. Sullivan*, 376 U.S. 254 (1964), the European Court stated that while some limitations under section 2 of Article 10 might apply to the media:

> "[the press's] task is nevertheless to impart information and ideas on political issues and on other matters of general interest. As to the limits of acceptable criticism, they are wider with respect to a politician acting in his public capacity than in relation to a private individual. A politician inevitably and knowingly lays himself open to close scrutiny of his every word and deed by both journalists and the public at large, and he must display a greater degree of tolerance, especially when he himself makes

public statements that are subject to criticism. He is certainly entitled to have his reputation protected, even when he is not acting in his private capacity, but the requirements of that protection have to be weighed against the interests of open discussion of public issues, since exceptions to freedom of expression must be interpreted narrowly."

However, it would be a mistake to equate Article 10 of the ECHR with the United States' First Amendment. There are differences, as is illustrated by *Wabl v. Austria*, 31 E.H.R.R. 51, 2000 WL 33348533 (ECHR 2001). Wabl, a member of the Austrian parliament from the small Green Party, became involved in a scuffle with a policeman during a political protest, resulting in Wabl's infliction of two scratches on the policeman's arm. Austria's largest newspaper (with 40% of total national newspaper circulation) published an article with a scare headline indicating that the policeman was demanding that Wabl take an AIDS test. Wabl demanded a retraction, which was published on the same day that Wabl answered a question at a press conference by accusing the newspaper of "Nazi journalism." One of the Nazis' favorite tactics was to accuse their opponents of having loathsome diseases. Nazi-type activity was specifically prohibited by the National Socialist Prohibition Act in the State Treaty of 1955. Upholding the Austrian courts' grant of an injunction pursuant to the Austrian defamation statute prohibiting Wabl from repeating his accusation, the ECHR stated that the Austrian Supreme Court "duly balanced the interests involved . . . [and] had particular regard to the special stigma which attaches to activities inspired by National Socialist ideas." While the newspaper's article was defamatory, the ECHR stated, Wabl's statement was an overreaction. Adequate alternative remedies were available; indeed, Wabl had secured the neewspaper's conviction for defamation under Austria's Media Act.

A somewhat similar situation exists in Canada, where Section 2 of the Canadian Charter of Rights and Freedoms guarantees "freedom of thought, belief, opinion and expression," but Section 1 of the Charter permits the government to establish "such limits . . . as may be demonstrably justified in a free and democratic society."

Using the latter clause, the Supreme Court of Canada upheld a statute which made criminal the distribution of entertainment materials which "unduly" exploited sex (in this case, by depicting women in "degrading or dehumanizing" sexual situations), thereby violating a nationwide "community standard of tolerance." *Regina v. Butler*, [1992] 1 S.C.R. 452, 1992 R.C.S. LEXIS 44. Although conceding that its decision constituted a limitation upon free expression, the Court stated that its result was justified by "the actual causal relationship between obscenity [under the expansive definition of the statute in question] and the risk of harm to society at large [which might result from emulative behavior by consumers of the targeted products.]"

And in a case of "hate speech," *Regina v. Keegstra*, [1990] 3 S.C.R. 697, 1990 R.C.S. LEXIS 674, the Supreme Court of Canada again cited Section 1 to justify suppression of speech. Keegstra, a high school teacher in Eckville, Alberta, was convicted of unlawfully promoting hatred against an identifiable group by telling his students: that Jews are "treacherous," "subversive," "sadistic," "money-loving," "power hungry" and "child killers"; that Jewish people seek to destroy Christianity; that they are responsible for "depressions, anarchy, chaos, wars and revolution"; that Jews "created the Holocaust to gain sympathy"; and that, unlike the open and honest Christians, were "deceptive, secretive and inherently evil." Students who failed to reflect his teachings on exams suffered lower grades.

By contrast, in *American Booksellers Association v. Hudnut*, 771 F.2d 323 (7th Cir. 1985), summarily aff'd, 475 U.S. 1001 (1986), an Indianapolis ordinance similar to the Canadian statute (and drafted by the same feminist activists who drafted the Canadian statute) was held to violate the First Amendment; and in *R.A.V. v. City of St. Paul*, 505 U.S. 377 (1992), the Supreme Court invalidated the city's hate speech ordinance.

---

## 6.3 PERFORMANCE, REPRODUCTION, TRANSMISSION, AND SALE

In addition to feeling the impact of the exclusionary effects of the regulations and decisions discussed in the preceding sections of this chapter, American producers and distributors face enormous challenges from "pirates" – those who unlawfully duplicate or transmit entertainment properties owned by others. As the Biden Report indicates, piracy is ubiquitous throughout the entertainment industries, and results in enormous losses in one of the most important segments of the American economy. Senator Biden outlines number of areas in which the U.S. and the international community have taken steps to eliminate (or at least minimize) the threat of piracy.

The damage from piracy has been exacerbated by new technology. For example, because of the availability of digital transmission, international piracy of Hollywood films is so rampant that there have been cases in which illegal DVD's of major films have been put on sale in foreign countries before the films' initial release in the United States. This, in turn, has prompted studios to abandon their previous practice of delaying foreign releases for several months following U.S. release, in order to build up the public relations "buzz," in favor of "day/date" (i.e., simultaneous) releases in the U.S. and major foreign territories. As you will read in the *Playboy v. Chuckleberry* and *NFL v. TVRadioNow* cases, foreign trademark and copyright infringers have not merely exploited U.S.-owned materials in their own countries, they also have reached back for customers in the U.S., and those activities have subjected them to the jurisdiction of U.S. federal courts.

However, as is shown by cases involving MP3.com (*UMG Recordings, Inc. v. MP3.com, Inc.*, 92 F.Supp.2d 349 (S.D.N.Y. 2000)) and Napster (*A&M Records, Inc. v. Napster, Inc.*, 239 F.3d 1004 (9th Cir. 2001)), as well as *Universal City Studios, Inc. v. Reimerdes*, 82 F.Supp.2d 211 (S.D.N.Y. 2000)(involving "DeCSS" code permitting circumvention of encryption technology designed to prevent duplication of DVDs), piracy is far from unknown in the U.S. And, as you will see in the *HitBit* decision, a U.S. company may be held liable in a foreign country where access to infringing material posted to its U.S. website is accessed by customers of one of its foreign affiliates, even though not available directly through the subsidiary itself.

Moreover, as you read in the *John Houston* "colorizing" decision in Chapter 1, the rules in other countries concerning what may be done with entertainment materials may well differ from our own. The European Union 2000 Directive requiring royalty payments to fine artists on the resale of their works is another example of this phenomenon. While the state of California has a resale royalties act, and the U.S. Artists Visual Rights Act of 1990 protects certain fine artists against the distortion, mutilation or other modification of their work under (17 U.S.C. sec. 106A), neither the Artists Visual Rights Act nor any other *federal* law provides artists with royalties on the resale of their works.

Piracy and inconsistency are not the whole story of international performance, reproduction, transmission and sale. Billions of dollars in entertainment industry royalties flow across national borders every year, to their rightful recipients, without litigation or even the threat of it. So this chapter, and the book, end with a Note on how this occurs.

---

**Theft of American Intellectual Property: Fighting Crime Abroad . . .**
**A Report from Senator Joseph R. Biden, Jr.**
**Chairman, Senate Committee on Foreign Relations**
**(2002)**

*Introduction*

The *New York Times* recently reported that illegal copies of "The Lord of the Rings," a film just recently released to movie theaters here in the United States, are already on sale on the streets of Jalalabad, Afghanistan. . . . Every episode of "Seinfeld" is now available for download free to anyone with access to the Internet. In September of 2001 alone, 1.5 billion songs were downloaded from Grokster.com, an Internet website that enables users to steal music. Video games that would cost $50 each in the United States are sold for the equivalent of 75 cents on the streets of some Chinese cities.

Everyday, thieves steal millions of dollars of American intellectual property from its rightful owners, and hundreds of thousands of American jobs are lost as a result.

American innovation – and the protection of that innovation by the government – has been a critical component of American economic growth throughout our history. The Founding Fathers had the foresight to provide for protection of intellectual property, giving Congress the power to "promote the progress of science and useful arts" by providing copyrights and patents. The federal government's vigilance in shielding intellectual property rights remains essential: innovation would slow, businesses would suffer, and jobs would dissolve if technological advances were left unprotected. The American arts and entertainment industry could not survive without the ability to protect and earn income from its ideas. Would U2 continue to make records and go on tour if all of their records, videos, and fan paraphernalia were given out for free? Would the tens of thousands of Americans who staff their concerts and produce their CDs keep their jobs?

Copyrights and trademarks mean nothing if government authorities fail to enforce the protections they provide intellectual property owners. . . . It has been estimated that . . . the government loses a billion dollars in revenue to piracy each year. To put that in perspective, with the $1 billion in lost revenue, the American government could pay for child care services for more than 100,000 children annually. Alternatively, $1 billion could be used to fund a Senate proposal to assist schools with emergency school renovation and repair projects.

This report aims to (1) highlight some of the problems that have emerged in America's continuing struggle to protect innovators from those who would steal their products, and (2) list some potential solutions for combating piracy . . . abroad.

If we intend to nurture growth and development, the government will have to take a long look at how best to approach the global technological marketplace, and address those who would take advantage of American innovation.

*The Problem*

When an American owns property, the government has a responsibility to protect that property from theft. When that property is an idea, it deserves our protection no less than if it were land, or a personal object. Who among us would want to expend the effort required to develop a new product if the government were not prepared to punish those who would steal it? If we want to protect American innovation, and by extension American jobs, we need to maintain a vigilant stand against what is commonly known as "intellectual property theft."

American intellectual property is an immensely valuable – perhaps our most valuable – resource. Not to protect it is equivalent to letting coal be stolen from our mines or water taken from our rivers. With that concern in mind, the American government has developed an infrastructure to protect Americans who rightfully own pieces of intellectual property.

Copyrights protect the authors of "original works of authorship," including literary, dramatic, musical, artistic, and certain other intellectual works. Trademarks provide businesses with exclusive use of "any word, name, symbol, or device" to indicate the source of the goods and to distinguish them from the goods of others.

Unfortunately, the integration of the global economy and emergence of the Internet have eroded some of the walls which protect intellectual property rights from thieves: some of our efforts to protect intellectual property at home have become outmoded, and certain nations around the world are not doing enough to combat the problem. Advances in digital media have made it tremendously easy to steal and reproduce a variety of media.

This report addresses two types of intellectual property theft: (1) "piracy" is the unlawful theft of a protected product; and (2) counterfeiting, a type of piracy, is the unauthorized reproduction of a good, in an attempt to pass it off as the original. . . . Both types of crime represent an enormous threat to the . . . entertainment industries. It is clearly the responsibility of governments around the world to protect intellectual property owners from those who would steal their goods.

Let me begin by illustrating the breadth and pervasiveness of intellectual property theft. The International Intellectual Property Alliance estimates that the world of intellectual property represents the largest single sector of the American economy, almost 5% of the nation's gross domestic product. By comparison, defense spending occupies approximately 3% of U.S. GDP. While I could provide an endless list of industries affected by piracy and counterfeiting around the world, this report will focus primarily on the following industries: computer software including business applications and entertainment software; motion pictures; television programs; DVDs and home videocassettes; music, records, CDs, and audiocassettes; and textbooks, tradebooks, reference and professional publications, and journals (in both electronic and print media). What makes these industries particularly vulnerable is the degree to which their products can be stolen, reproduced, and distributed with ease through emerging technologies like the Internet, CD-Rs, and DVDs.

. . . According to the International Intellectual Property Alliance, trade losses for five industries in 58 countries amount to almost $8 billion [see table, next page].

But what is most important is not the sheer enormity of the intellectual property sector, but rather the number of people it employs here in the United States. 4.3 million Americans are employed by the intellectual property sector, representing 3.24% of total U.S. employment. To provide some perspective, intellectual property businesses export more American value to the world than the automobile, automobile parts, agricultural, and aircraft industries combined. In other words, theft of intellectual property does not just affect media moguls or software titans; it robs the American economy of valuable jobs.

*Estimated Trade Losses Due to Copyright Piracy in 58 Selected Countries in 2000*

| Industry | Estimated Revenue Losses |
|---|---:|
| Motion Pictures | $1,242,500,000 |
| Sound Recordings and Musical Compositions | $1,835,600,000 |
| Business Software Applications | $2,490,900,000 |
| Entertainment Software | $1,658,400,000 |
| Books | $675,100,000 |
| Total | $7,903,300,000 |

*Piracy*

Piracy has had a particularly dramatic effect on American businesses and the entertainment software industry. . . .

- Disks and CD-ROMS are copied illegally, and then re-sold. . . .
- Software and entertainment can be sent illegally from one user to another through the Internet. By accessing so-called "warez" sites, pirates can transfer any sort of digital media electronically.

Together, these . . . forms of piracy have taken a real bite out of intellectual property industry revenues. And to what degree does software affect the American economy? . . . The Interactive Digital Software Association estimates that $3 billion in revenue was lost to the entertainment software industry in 2000, money which industry experts believe could have been used to develop 1,600 new games.

The music industry has also been victimized by piracy. Modern technology has enabled thieves to employ inexpensive, portable, CD factories which take up no more space than a small room to manufacture illegal reproductions; such facilities, each of which can produce upwards of 100,000 CDs per year, have been built all over the world. Additionally, user-friendly, piracy-enabling websites like Grokster in the West Indies, iMesh in Israel, Morphius in Tennessee, and KaZaA in the Netherlands, allow users all over the world to download music illegally at no expense. In addition, the advent of decentralized "peer-to-peer" technology, such as that used by the Gnutella network to permit maintenance of large databases of music without any central location, makes pursuit and prosecution of these criminal activities exceedingly difficult. To date, over 100 million copies have been made of commonly used peer-to-peer software for downloading music. The music industry estimates that piracy cost it $4.2 billion worldwide in 2000.

Finally, the movie industry is yet another victim of the growing spate of piracy. The Motion Picture Association of America estimates that as many as one million movies are downloaded illegally from the Internet each day. DVD copies of "Harry Potter and the Sorcerer's Stone" were available in parts of China even before the film had hit theaters anywhere in the world, let alone been released for home viewing. Imagine the number of people who choose not to go to the movie theater or rent a film because they are able to obtain a pirated copy; imagine the amount of money sapped from our economy; and imagine the number of jobs lost as a result.

*Counterfeiting*

In their attempts to develop a customer base, companies often "trademark" their product names or symbols. . . .

The same industries which have been victimized by piracy are getting hammered by counterfeiting. . . .

*Piracy Around The World – A Snap Shot*

Piracy rates around the world are dispiritingly high. The International Planning and Research Corporation estimates that software piracy rates are as high as 94% in China, 81% in Bolivia, 97% in Vietnam, and 89% in the Ukraine. Brazil, Mexico, Paraguay, the Philippines, Poland, the Netherlands, the Bahamas, South Africa, Egypt and Indonesia are also known to be afflicted with widespread piracy. By comparison, piracy rates in the United States hover around 24%, a figure which needs to be reduced further, but is comparatively impressive.

That discrepancy points to an important problem: while the American government is relatively vigilant in trying to stem intellectual property theft, other countries have not enacted the requisite laws to prosecute intellectual property thieves. Others willingly look the other way as property is pirated and stolen, and/or lack the resources needed to police the intellectual property market adequately.

At first glance, one might assume that developing economies would benefit from loose intellectual property rights enforcement. Piracy would appear to enable firms to employ software at a diminished cost, and foreign governments often expect that any cost savings will advance economic development by increasing efficiencies and output.

In the long run, however, weak intellectual property protections stifle local innovation. Music, software, and entertainment companies simply do not invest in nations that fail to honor or protect intellectual property rights. Ultimately, that lost investment costs nations much more than pirating and counterfeiting will ever provide. As important, local innovators are provided an enormous *disincentive* to create new products if they believe that thieves will steal whatever profit they might make. It is not uncommon for native-born innovators, such as software engineers, to leave their countries reluctantly, because their government will not protect their creations. Essentially, foreign countries that fail to enact and enforce anti-piracy laws end up doing themselves more harm than good.

Unfortunately, once a country enacts the requisite laws, summons the adequate will, and provides the necessary resources to combat piracy and counterfeiting, the criminals who profit from stealing intellectual property often simply change venue. Combating intellectual property theft is like squeezing a balloon: when you apply pressure in one area, the air inside simply adjusts and moves elsewhere. For example, when Bulgaria, once rampant with illegal piracy operations, cracked down, much of its pirating industry moved to the Ukraine, which continues today to be an important haven for intellectual property thieves.

When China began cracking down on some of the factories producing pirated compact discs, those production facilities (which, as noted earlier, are sometimes no more than a roomful of equipment) were largely moved to Hong Kong. When authorities in Hong Kong began to crack down, facilities sprouted in Macao and then Malaysia, where a civil case against a pirate can take six years to be heard in court. Hence, the balloon squeezing analogy: when one nation's government puts pressure on intellectual property thieves, they simply move to another part of the world.

Finally, international markets are debilitated by intellectual property theft on two dimensions. First, significant damage is done when a government fails to crack down on intellectual property theft and effectively corrupts its domestic market; this aspect of the problem is restricted to within a country's borders. Unfortunately, stolen material often floods across borders and into countries around the globe – even markets here in the United States – making pirated and counterfeit goods a problem even for countries doing an adequate job patrolling their own industries. As such, even when American authorities successfully prosecute copyright and trademark infringers here in the United States, our domestic market is affected by foreign production. Particularly as more theft moves onto the Internet, it will become difficult for a country to combat intellectual property theft initiated beyond its own borders. As such, it is tremendously important that every country participate in efforts to combat the problem.

*Advances in Technology*

What is it exactly that makes intellectual property so vulnerable to theft? First, the global economy has expanded tremendously during the last 20 years, buttressing demand worldwide for international products (entertainment and software goods in particular). Second, intellectual property is now most often transferred as digital data, which pirates can duplicate easily in *identical* form. Today, criminals can reproduce discs (CDs in the music business, CD-ROMS in the software industry, and DVDs in the world of entertainment) without degrading the quality of the recorded material. In the past, criminals who reproduced analog recordings (cassette tapes and VHS cassettes, for example) unavoidably faced a significant loss in sound quality: second generation copies were not as good as the original, and after a few generations they became virtually unusable. As a result, consumers were generally willing to pay more to ensure the highest quality sound. But the sound of a reproduced CD, even after 100 generations of reproduction, is identical to that of the original. Thus, improved technology has broken a barrier that previously limited the scope of pirated products. That breakthrough has translated into an explosion in supply: in the year 2001, DVD production increased by 9% and production capacity in Asia grew by 35%.

Second, technology advances enable counterfeiters to produce packaging that fools even discriminating consumers into believing that they are buying the legitimate product. Often, a counterfeit CD's packaging will be nearly identical to that of the original. Sophisticated software and printing equipment enable counterfeiters to improve their illegal reproductions of trademarks themselves, copying even the markings (such as holograms) that trademark holders place on products to deter counterfeiting. Customs officials have even seen cases where the counterfeit packaging is of a *higher* quality than that of its legitimate counterpart.

Third, digital products can not only be marketed on the Internet, they can actually be *delivered* on line. A copy of a popular song, for example, can itself be transferred immediately through the web. Certainly, the pervasiveness of Napster's successors, such as Grokster, Morphius, and Gnutella, indicates the extent to which the music industry has already been victimized by online piracy; indeed, illegal downloading of songs is now at its highest level ever, despite any chilling effect brought about by the industry's suit against Napster and, as noted earlier, is becoming more difficult to prosecute because of decentralization. Until recently, only small files, such as individual songs, could be downloaded efficiently over the Internet. But the emergence of "broadband technologies," which dramatically increase the speed with which web-users can download large files, empowers consumers to download entire albums, television programs, and even full-length feature movies much more easily and quickly.

Thanks to broadband, a full-length motion picture can be downloaded in less than 15 minutes, as compared to the four to five hours with conventional Internet access.

In turn, groups of pirates who upload products to the web have developed so-called "warez" sites at which one can download all sorts of stolen digital media at little or no cost to the consumer. As broadband becomes more pervasive in the U.S., the problem of online piracy will only grow. In other countries, such as South Korea and some northern European countries, where broadband is already more widely available, the problem has already grown. A simple Internet search for the word "warez" draws over 2 million hits.

*Current Legal Framework*

A variety of laws, both domestic and international, empower governments around the world to combat, investigate, and prosecute intellectual property thieves. But the web of protection they provide is incomplete. Officials at the U.S. Copyright Office have suggested that nations intending to uphold intellectual property rights must meet three criteria:

- First, they must develop an adequate legal framework for prosecuting intellectual property theft.
- Second, they must have the political will to enforce intellectual property laws. If prosecuting authorities, or those involved in the enforcement process, are in league with those who will profit from intellectual property theft, any number of well-written laws will be ineffective.
- Third, they must devote sufficient resources to enforcement of piracy laws. Even if adequate laws are on the books, and the government retains the requisite political will, prosecutors and judicial systems which do not receive the resources they need to handle the sheer volume of crimes before them will be unable to corral the problem. . . .

*B. International Treaties To Protect Intellectual Property*

There is no such thing as "international copyrights" or "international trademarks." Rather, copyrights and trademarks are governed by national laws. That said, nations are obligated to protect copyrights and trademarks through a number of interrelated international treaties which impose minimum standards on countries party to the respective treaties. In this regard, there have been two important advancements for the international protection of copyrights and trademarks in the last decade. The first was the approval, during the Uruguay Round trade negotiations (concluded in 1994), of the Agreement on Trade-Related Aspects of Intellectual Property Rights, or "TRIPS." The second was the approval of the World Intellectual Property Organization (WIPO) Copyright Treaty and the WIPO Performances and Phonograms Treaty (concluded in 1996).

*TRIPS Agreement*

Members of the World Trade Organization are required to comply with the TRIPS Agreement. Article 66 of the TRIPS Agreement, however, permits "least developed countries" a ten-year transition period for implementation of the Agreement; at present, 30 members of the WTO qualify for least developed country status.

The TRIPS Agreement requires all members to comply with substantive provisions of two baseline treaties – one on copyrights (the Berne Convention for the Protection of Literary and Artistic Works) and one on trademarks (the Paris Convention for the Protection of Industrial Property).

Equally important, the TRIPS Agreement imposes obligations on members to enforce adequately the intellectual property rights protected by it. The TRIPS Agreement also provides a means to secure enforcement, if diplomacy and persuasion prove inadequate: it incorporates by reference the dispute settlement procedures of the WTO. The Dispute Settlement Understanding provides a quasi-judicial means for a member to complain about WTO violations, a process which has often been successful for the United States in a range of trade areas. The United States has initiated several proceedings against foreign governments for TRIPS violations, including against Ireland for its deficient copyright laws, Greece for television piracy, and Denmark for its failure to make available *ex parte* search remedies in intellectual property enforcement actions. These cases have all been settled to the satisfaction of the United States.

*WIPO Treaties*

. . . The WIPO Copyright Treaty . . . enter[ed] into force . . . on March 6, 2002, and . . . the Performances and Phonograms Treaty [entered into force on May 20, 2002].

*Enforcement*

Jurisdiction over piracy spans across not only a host of federal agencies, but also the community of nations. The Justice Department is the lead federal law enforcement agency while the State Department currently chairs a working group of U.S. Agencies that is involved in coordinating intellectual property assistance and training that is provided by the U.S. government overseas. . . .

The Justice Department has worked with other federal and international law enforcement agencies in bringing criminal prosecutions against high tech pirates. For example, U.S. authorities spear-headed a 15-month investigation entitled "Operation Buccaneer." Working in collaboration with officials in the U.K., Australia, Norway and Finland, the U.S. executed 58 warrants in 27 cities against "warez" groups operators, seizing more than 140 computers. The operation struck at highly structured, security-conscious criminal groups specializing in "obtaining the latest computer software, games, and movies; stripping ('cracking') copyright protections; and releasing the final product to hundreds of Internet sites worldwide."

. . .

*Potential Solutions*

As discussed above, substantial laws, both international and domestic, already exist to help fight intellectual property theft. It is likely, therefore, that any successful proposals at this stage would not revolutionize the legal landscape so much as enhance our abilities to enforce the laws and treaties that exist. Based on my discussions to date with government and industry representatives, it does not appear that a major sea change is needed with respect to the substantive law. With that in mind, the following suggestions have been made by experts in the field. . . .

*International*

On the international front, a key question is how can we in the United States convince foreign governments to join our effort to combat intellectual property theft. What will compel our counterparts around the world to institute and enforce proper intellectual property laws when many foreigners remain convinced that active enforcement will hobble their local economies?

First, we could use the type of bilateral trade negotiations and threats available to us in trade disputes, namely the "Special 301" process, authorized in Section 182 of the Trade Act of 1974. That statute empowers the United States Trade Representative (USTR) to "identify and investigate" priority foreign countries that fail to provide adequate and effective protection of American intellectual property rights. When foreign countries fail to provide proper relief, the USTR is empowered to impose trade sanctions. The U.S. Copyright Office notes that the process of investigation, in which foreign countries are placed on a so-called "watch list," has been a tremendously successful tool. Foreign countries are often disinclined to invest in a "priority country," so governments are often anxious to avoid that designation. Hong Kong and Malaysia were recently both compelled to do more to enforce intellectual property rights because the United States promised that failure to do so would impact their designation in the Special 301 process.

Second, we could use the power we wield in negotiating free trade agreements to compel foreign governments to implement and enforce adequate intellectual property protections. Under the TRIPS agreement, World Trade Organization members are required only to institute laws which are "sufficient to provide a deterrent" to intellectual property theft. We in the United States know that authorities must do much more than that – most notably, they must prosecute those who violate the law. So, as we work to shape bilateral free trade agreements with nations like Peru, Brazil, Chile and Singapore, we should insist that the laws and policy instituted with our trading partners conform to the more stringent standards we apply domestically.

Third, we might provide an expanded arsenal of resources to foreign governments inclined to write and implement the type of intellectual property laws which will guarantee, with enforcement, that companies operating within their market have adequate protection. Many countries with pervasive problems simply do not have the resources or expertise necessary to prevent intellectual property theft, even when they understand that implementing the proper enforcement mechanisms will spur investment and economic growth. If American advisors, technology or financial resources are provided to well-meaning foreign governments, those countries will be better equipped to produce the sort of legal framework we enjoy here in the United States. The United States government provided at least $7.1 million worth of aid to developing countries in the pursuit of improving their intellectual property laws between 1999 and 2001. We should make sure that such programs are effective, and if they are, make them more available to countries throughout the globe.

Fourth, developing foreign countries often lack the resources required to fund and maintain the law enforcement agencies which prosecute intellectual property thieves. Enforcement agencies are often ill-equipped to fight high tech, fast-paced, well-financed criminal enterprises, and they rarely place intellectual property crime at the top of their enforcement agendas. In turn, piracy and trademark prosecutions are often given the short shift, despite the economic cost of failing to regulate the market.

The United States could support foreign law enforcement, or at least foreign agencies, with some of the tools and training necessary to do an adequate job of prosecuting offending parties.

Fifth, we can encourage other countries that have already developed comparatively strong systems for protecting intellectual property to use their influence to persuade and cajole other governments to rise to their level. For example, the U.S. Government could press the European Union to do its utmost to raise the level of intellectual property protection in countries that seek to join its ranks. . . .

All of these proposals, of course, are for potential action by our government. As a Senator, that is logically my focus in reviewing this issue. Of course, any effort to fight the crime of intellectual property theft must involve substantial efforts on the part of the industries involved. For example, industries are currently working on technologies to protect their materials from illicit copying. Even as hackers and crooks become ever more sophisticated at cracking the codes, companies must continue to seek ways to thwart criminal efforts.

*Conclusion*

Intellectual property theft has, through the years, stolen billions of dollars from American businesses and hundreds of thousands of jobs from American workers. The robust global economy and the Internet have enabled worldwide commerce to flourish. As businesses struggle to adapt to the new economic landscape, we need to ensure that government authorities throughout the world, and at home, are prepared to address the new challenges before them.

As this report demonstrates, efforts to protect intellectual property are lacking, and represent an important hurdle for the development of economies around the globe. If those who invest in developing new and innovative ideas are consistently exploited, they may well give up efforts to improve technology and generate the type of art, music, literature, and entertainment that animates all our lives. More than that, if we fail to address this growing problem, millions of jobs will be lost, and we will have given into thieves and pirates.

Our efforts will inevitably be buoyed by the development of intellectual property industries around the world. As software and entertainment companies begin to flourish in foreign countries, foreign governments will realize that intellectual property theft poses a significant economic threat. The Indian film industry, as it matured, became increasingly aware that its product was being pirated. It successfully pushed the Indian government to institute adequate protections. In the future, countries may come to the United States asking for assistance in developing the type of legal framework needed to combat intellectual property crime. We ought to be prepared to assist them in our mutual interest. . . .

Only by being vigilant in investigating and prosecuting those who steal intellectual property will we be successful in continuing to nurture the development of the music, software, and entertainment industries which employ so many people both here and around the world. I look forward to assisting our government here at home in its battle against high tech pirates, as well as urging nations around the world join the United States in the fight against intellectual property theft, and I hope that I can continue to be helpful in that endeavor. Inevitably, the landscape will change, and I intend to reevaluate and readdress new problems in the coming years to ensure that creators and innovators are fully protected under the law.

---

**Playboy Enterprises, Inc. v. Chuckleberry Publishing, Inc.**
**939 F. Supp. 1032 (S.D.N.Y. 1996)**

Shira A. Scheindlin, U.S.D.J.:

*I. Background*

Plaintiff, Playboy Enterprises, Inc. ("PEI"), publishes the well-known male entertainment magazine "Playboy." Defendant, Tattilo Editrice, S.p.A. ("Tattilo"), has published a male sophisticate magazine in Italy under the name "PLAYMEN" since 1967. In 1979, after Tattilo announced plans to publish an English language version of PLAYMEN in the United States, PEI brought suit to enjoin Tattilo's use of the PLAYMEN name in connection with a male sophisticate magazine and related products. As a result, PEI was awarded an injunction ("Injunction") permanently enjoining Tattilo from . . . using "PLAYBOY" [or] "PLAYMEN" [in a variety of ways].

Fifteen years later, in January 1996, PEI discovered that Tattilo had created an Internet site featuring the PLAYMEN name (the "PLAYMEN Internet site" or "Internet site") which makes available images of the cover of the Italian magazine, as well as its "Women of the Month" feature and several other sexually explicit photographic images. The Internet site was created by uploading images onto a World Wide Web server located in Italy.

Tattilo offers two services on its Internet site. "PLAYMEN Lite" is available without a subscription and allows users of the Internet to view moderately explicit images. "PLAYMEN Pro," which offers more explicit images, is available only upon the purchase of a paid subscription. It appears that the main (if not sole) purpose of the PLAYMEN Lite site is to allow prospective subscribers to PLAYMEN Pro to sample the product before purchasing a subscription.

PEI moved for a finding of contempt against Tattilo. By Opinion and Order dated June 19, 1996 ("Opinion"), I determined that the Internet site violated the Injunction, and thereby found Tattilo in contempt. Tattilo was ordered, within two weeks, to: (1) either shut down its Internet site completely or refrain from accepting any new subscriptions from customers residing in the United States; (2) invalidate the user names and passwords to the Internet site previously purchased by United States customers; (3) refund to its United States customers the remaining unused portions of their subscriptions; (4) remit to PEI all gross profits earned from subscriptions to its PLAYMEN Pro Internet service by customers in the United States; (5) remit to PEI all gross profits earned from the sale of goods and services advertised on its PLAYMEN Internet service to customers in the United States; (6) revise its Internet site to indicate that all subscription requests from potential United States customers will be denied; and (7) remit to PEI its costs and attorneys' fees incurred in making that application. I further ruled that if those conditions were not met within two weeks, Tattilo shall pay to PEI a fine of $1,000 per day until it complies fully.

Defendant now requests that the Court amend its Order. . . . Defendant submits that the Court misconstrued the process by which a user of the Internet site accesses PLAYMEN Lite, resulting in the incorrect determination that the PLAYMEN Lite service violated the Injunction. Defendant argues that the continued availability of PLAYMEN Lite within the United States would not violate the Injunction. . . .

Plaintiff also moves for an amendment of the judgment. PEI requests that Tattilo be ordered to refrain from "publishing, promoting and selling in the English language PLAYMEN publications and related products." . . .

*III. Discussion*

*A. Whether PLAYMEN Lite Violates the Injunction*

In the Opinion, Defendant was found to have violated Subsection 1(c) of the 1981 Injunction which permanently enjoined Tattilo from:

> using "PLAYBOY", "PLAYMEN" or any other word confusingly similar with either such word in or as part of any trademark, service mark, brand name, trade name or other business or commercial designation, in connection with the sale, offering for sale or distributing in the United States, importing into or exporting from the United States, English language publications and related products.

The basis for this holding was the Court's finding that 1) the word PLAYMEN was used as part of a trademark, service mark, brand name, trade name or other business or commercial designation; 2) that such use was made in connection with an English language publication or related product; and 3) that such use was made in connection with a sale or distribution within the United States. The sole issue raised in this request for reconsideration is whether Tattilo has sold or distributed PLAYMEN Lite in the United States.

*1. The Previous Order*

The uploading of pictorial images onto a computer which may be accessed by other users constitutes a "distribution" because Defendant does more than simply provide access to the Internet. It also provides its own services, PLAYMEN Lite and PLAYMEN Pro, and supplies the content for these services. Moreover, . . . these pictorial images can be downloaded to and stored upon the computers of subscribers to the service. In fact, Defendant actively invites such use: the Internet site allows the user to decide between viewing and downloading the images. Thus this use of Defendant's Internet site constitutes a distribution.

This distribution occurred in the United States because of the direct contact between Tattilo and users of the PLAYMEN Internet site. Specifically, in order to subscribe to the PLAYMEN Pro service, prospective users fax an "order form" to Tattilo, along with a credit card number, and receive back a password and user ID via e-mail.

Although users of the PLAYMEN Internet site do not "subscribe" to PLAYMEN Lite, Tattilo nonetheless distributes this product in the United States because of the means by which a user accesses PLAYMEN Lite, which is described on the Internet site itself:

> Before I pay I want to see what you offer:
> For this reason, you will receive a temporary user name and password by email. With this password you can browse on the xxx pages of the lite version of Playmen. Once you are satisfied, you will have to fill the form and send it [to] us by fax, specifing [sic] all the details of your credit card.

2. *The Instant Motion*

Tattilo now claims that the above passage does not accurately describe the process by which a user accesses PLAYMEN Lite. According to Tattilo, not only is a password not necessary to peruse the PLAYMEN Lite service, but in reality no contact with Tattilo is required for a potential user to access PLAYMEN Lite.

On July 3, 1996, a hearing was held at which the parties demonstrated the process of accessing the PLAYMEN Internet site. No password or user ID was necessary. Defendant has therefore presented factual matter which was not before the Court that might materially have influenced its earlier decision. The question, then, is whether Tattilo's PLAYMEN Lite service still violates the Injunction.

While the Opinion held that deliberate and intentional contact with the United States was established based on the requirement that prospective customers fax subscription forms to Italy, and that user names and IDs are sent to United States customers from Italy, this is not the only basis for finding that a distribution occurred within the United States. The PLAYMEN Lite service allows (indeed invites) a user to download Tattilo's pictorial images onto his or her home computer. PLAYMEN Lite can thus be viewed as an "advertisement" by which Tattilo distributes its pictorial images throughout the United States. That the local user "pulls" these images from Tattilo's computer in Italy, as opposed to Tattilo "sending" them to this country, is irrelevant. By inviting United States users to download these images, Tattilo is causing and contributing to their distribution within the United States.

Moreover, the availability of PLAYMEN Lite within the United States violates the Injunction even if the user could not download the images. PLAYMEN Lite is nearly identical to PLAYMEN Pro. Both reveal many of the same images; both allow the user to download these images; both services purport to sell products such as movies and CD-Roms to their users. Most notably, as demonstrated at the hearing, the two services utilize many of the same screens and links.

This implies that PLAYMEN Lite and PLAYMEN Pro are not two separate and distinct services as Defendant has argued, but are actually one Service – the "PLAYMEN Internet Service" – part of which requires a password and part of which does not. In other words, PLAYMEN Lite is nothing more than an "advertisement" or "coming attractions" for the money-making PLAYMEN Pro service. This relationship is further demonstrated by the passage quoted above, which caused confusion as to how a user accesses PLAYMEN Lite. When a

PLAYMEN Lite user is considering purchasing a subscription to PLAYMEN Pro, but would like to sample the product first, Tattilo will provide a temporary password that will allow the user to access the pages of PLAYMEN Pro through PLAYMEN Lite.

As such, PLAYMEN Lite represents a free distribution of Tattilo's product, a product which has been banned in this country since the 1981 Injunction. I decline to hold that Tattilo may maintain some portion of its service but shut down other portions of its Internet site. Because PLAYMEN Lite and PLAYMEN Pro are essentially one entity, they must be treated as such.

Therefore, the PLAYMEN Lite service violates the Injunction. As ordered in the Opinion, Tattilo must either shut down PLAYMEN Lite completely or prohibit United States users from accessing the site in the future. The simplest method of prohibiting access by United States users is to adopt a method of access similar to the one which I had believed was already in place: require users of the PLAYMEN Lite service to acquire free passwords and user IDs in order to access the site. In this way, users residing in the United States can be filtered out and refused access.[4] [n4 If technology cannot identify the country of origin of e-mail addresses, these passwords and user IDs should be sent by mail. Only in this way can the Court be assured that United States users are not accidentally permitted access to PLAYMEN Lite.]

Because this motion raised serious issues, Tattilo may have two weeks from the date of this Order to either shut down PLAYMEN Lite or adopt procedures prohibiting United States users from accessing the site. . . .

*D. PEI's Request For an Additional Sanction*

PEI has . . . failed to set forth any ground for reconsideration. As previously stated, this Court has no power to restrict Tattilo from providing its PLAYMEN Internet service outside the United States. There are many English speaking countries throughout the world. This Court has no jurisdiction to control Tattilo's activities in those countries. As a result, PEI's motion for an order prohibiting Tattilo from using English on its Internet site is denied.

*V. Conclusion*

For the foregoing reasons, the motion for reconsideration is denied. Tattilo must shut down the PLAYMEN Lite service in accord with this Opinion.

---

**National Football League v. TVRadioNow Corp.**
**53 U.S.P.Q.2d 1831, 2000 WL 255989 (W.D.Pa. 2000)**

Ziegler, C.J.

. . . [D]efendants [the operators of the Canadian website iCraveTV.com] have streamed copyrighted professional football and basketball games as well as copyrighted programs such as "60 Minutes," "Ally McBeal," and "Star Trek Voyager," framed with advertisements obtained by defendants. Plaintiffs [the owners of the copyrights to those programs] allege that defendants have captured United States programming from television stations in Buffalo, New York and elsewhere, converted these television signals into computerized data and streamed them over the Internet from a website called iCraveTV.com. According to plaintiffs, any Internet user may access iCraveTV.com by simply entering three digits of any Canadian area code, one of which is provided to the user on the site itself, and by clicking two other buttons. Further, Internet users from the United States and elsewhere easily may revisit the site because iCraveTV causes a small file, or cookie, to be deposited in a user's computer during his or her initial visit so that the user can automatically bypass defendants' screening process. . . .

Defendants argue that their website is for Canadian viewers only and it is not intended for citizens of the United States and elsewhere. Thus, the argument continues, the alleged improper acts are limited to Canada.

[However,] Pennsylvania residents have accessed defendants' website and viewed the programs which were streamed thereon. Further, defendants posted an article on the website by a United States citizen noting that access to defendants' website could be obtained by any United States citizen with little or no difficulty.

Accordingly, when an allegedly infringing act occurring without [i.e., outside] the United States is publicly performed within the United States, the Copyright Act is implicated and a district court possesses jurisdiction. Subject matter jurisdiction exists because, although the streaming of the plaintiffs' programming originated in Canada, acts of infringement were committed within the United States when United States citizens received and viewed defendants' streaming of the copyrighted materials. These constitute, at a minimum, public performances in the United States.

The Court also possesses personal jurisdiction over each of the defendants. With respect to George Simons and William R. Craig, this Court finds that personal jurisdiction exists because Simons and Craig are Pennsylvania residents.

With respect to [Canadian-based] defendants iCraveTV, TVRadioNow Corp. and William R. Craig, the Court may also determine whether personal jurisdiction can be asserted on another basis. . . . [P]ersonal jurisdiction [can be asserted] over a nonresident to the extent permissible under the laws of the forum state. The forum state in this case is Pennsylvania, and Pennsylvania's long-arm statute . . . provides that jurisdiction is permitted to the fullest extent allowed under the Constitution of the United States and may be based on the most minimum contacts with the state. . . .

. . .When a state has general personal jurisdiction over a party, that party can be haled into court in the forum state regardless of whether the subject matter of the cause of action has any connection to the forum. A non-resident's contacts with the forum must be continuous and substantial to establish general personal jurisdiction.

The Court finds that general personal jurisdiction exists over the nonresident defendants [because] defendants have engaged in continuous and systematic contacts with Pennsylvania. For example, . . . defendants, through their agent, . . . have attempted to sell advertising out of an office maintained in the Pittsburgh area as well as others. Further, defendants maintain an office and have a sales agent, at least a former sales agent, located within this district, namely, George Simons. Defendants have also registered the iCraveTV.com domain name in the United States and have provided that the technical contact as well as the billing contact are within Pennsylvania. By maintaining an office and an agent in this state on an ongoing basis, entering into contractual relationships in this jurisdiction, and designating and maintaining billing and technical contacts within this state, the Court finds that the non-resident defendants purposely availed themselves of the privilege of conducting activities within Pennsylvania, thus invoking the benefits and protections of its laws. The Court further finds that due process is not offended by the assertion of personal jurisdiction when a defendant, such as the non-resident defendants here, has maintained substantial and continuous forum affiliation.

Additionally, because the defendants' activities within this forum were integrally a part of the activities giving rise to the cause of action asserted, the Court also finds that specific personal jurisdiction exists over the non-resident defendants. Further, defendants also streamed plaintiffs' programming to numerous other computer users throughout the United States and made efforts to sell advertising in the United States through agents in New York and Pennsylvania who had extensive advertising activities within the United States and with whom the non-resident defendants had extensive contacts.

[The court found that the plaintiffs had adequately demonstrated ownership of the copyrights and trademarks at issue in the case, and had made an adequate showing of irreparable harm and other factors so that a preliminary injunction was granted.]

---

**Hit Bit Software GmbH v. AOL Bertelsmann Online GmbH & Co. KG**
**Oberlandesgericht [County Court of Appeal Munich], Civil Division (2001)**

Presiding Judge Wörle and Judges Haußmann and Jackson

*Statement of Facts:*

The matter which the parties are disputing is a claim for damages by the Claimant on account of the distribution of music recordings over the Internet.

1. The Claimant is one of the largest producers of MIDI files in Germany. The MIDI software is a program for storing works of music in digital form; MIDI files are digital recordings of instrumental synthesiser versions of, in the main popular, musical works. They can be produced at a simple level with the aid of a computer and a suitable program by inputting the notes with the mouse; if the musical quality is sufficient, they are recorded on several tracks in a complicated process through playing on a keyboard, with the resulting electrical signals being directly digitised and recorded. They can be reproduced over a computer with the aid of a sound card or over an appropriately equipped keyboard with amplifier and loudspeaker equipment. Users of this technique are semi-professional and professional musicians – primarily solo entertainers – who, with the aid of MIDI files, perform current light music "hits" at occasions such as dances which they are able to supplement by their own improvisation of, for instance, the vocals. The Claimant distributes the MIDI files produced by it on disk by direct sale (mail order) and over the Internet. According to the claimant's assertion, it obtains prices of between DM 18 and DM 35 per file.

2. The Claimant has asserted that it produced (probably around 1995/1997) MIDI files of current hits by well-known groups with the titles Get Down, Samba de Janeiro and Freedom, and the file names GETDOWN.MID, samba~1.mid (*sic*) and 1067.mid. The witness Kist, a musician qualified to degree level, is said to have produced the instrumental version by "hearing out" the original recording, playing it over himself and making an arrangement suitable for a MIDI file in an expensive procedure using modern studio techniques. As far as the musical input of the witness is concerned, this was said to have involved an artistic and creative input. The Claimant later distributed the MIDI files at the price of DM 29.90 and up to 28.7.1998 sold nearly 2000 of them. It acquired the requisite utilisation rights in respect of the pre-existing musical work through agreements with GEMA [the German performing and mechanical rights society] and the utilisation rights in the MIDI files through agreements with the witness Kist.

3. The Defendant is a subsidiary owned in equal shares by AOL Online Inc., Dulles, Virginia, USA (hereafter AOL) and Bertelsmann Online AG, Gütersloh. AOL and its subsidiaries are the largest providers of online services in the world. AOL operates as a Content Provider supplying its own content, as a provider of outside content on its servers (as a Service Provider with hosting function) and finally also as an Access Provider for material offered by third parties (Service Provider without hosting function).

Among the services offered by AOL are also so-called "forums." Forums are in essence storage areas which are structured according to subject matter, but which are otherwise not subject to editorial supervision, into which members (customers who pay fees) can upload content of their choice, generated or stored on their computer. From there other members of AOL can download this material into the memory of their computer, bring it up, store it on the hard disk of their computer and transfer it to floppy disk. At the time the action was commenced, AOL also offered a forum for MIDI files which was subdivided according to music category. The stored MIDI files with their titles indicated were held within the individual categories.

If a member wants to upload a MIDI file on to AOL's server, first of all a compulsory window opens up in which it is pointed out that "the entering of data . . . must be done under consideration of third party rights and statutory provisions." If the user takes up the opportunity offered to him to read the Terms and Conditions of Use, then he will notice in Para. 8 that he is obliged "prior to and while entering and using content . . . (to comply with) . . . all possible third party rights (in particular copyright and to obtain the right to utilise such rights). In terms of Para. 12 of the Conditions AOL can terminate membership for good cause at any time with immediate effect. MIDI files uploaded by AOL members on to AOL's server are checked for viruses by "scouts" working for the Defendant by means of a suitable program and they are also checked with the aid of the Windows program for a copyright notice posted in the place provided for it within the MIDI format. If this check produces nothing untoward, the MIDI files are passed by the scouts and are then available to be downloaded.

4. . . .[I]t was not disputed that the provider of the services and forums described above is the Defendant, who "offers its members the use of its central server, which is located at the premises of a parent company of the Defendant in Dulles, for the independent uploading of members' own data." It was further undisputed that the seven scouts working for the Defendant were at that time responsible for around 850 MIDI files in the forum and that on average 20 - 30 new files were put on per week.

Among the MIDI files stored on AOL's server were also MIDI files with the titles Get Down (file name: GET DOWN. MID., uploaded on 17.9.1997), Samba de Janeiro (file name: SAMBAD ~1. MID, uploaded on 15.7.1997) and Freedom (file name: MACFREED. MID, uploaded on 29.5.1997).

5. The Claimant alleged that among the MIDI files mentioned above stored on the AOL server, there were copies of the MIDI files . . . produced by Claimant, which were uploaded by unknown AOL members. The Claimant stated that it had downloaded copies of the MIDI files from the AOL server on to the hard disk of its computer . . . and made a copy of the downloaded MIDI files on floppy disk. This floppy disk was submitted by the Claimant with its Pleadings. . . .

The Claimant contended that both the uploading and downloading of the MIDI files resulted in copies of these being produced. The utilisation rights in the rights resulting from the input of the witness Kist to which it, the Claimant, is entitled were thereby infringed. In relation to these acts of infringement, the Defendant was stated to be a joint perpetrator or infringer, as it had created the technical conditions necessary for the reproduction process. By creating storage areas not subject to editorial control and with anonymous access the Defendant was involved in nothing short of abetting in the uploading of copyright protected MIDI files. It is claimed that it was known to the Defendant that the utilisation of the entire content of the MIDI File forum on the AOL computer infringed the rights of third parties in the pre-existing musical works and/or the rights of the MIDI file producers, as it could not be counted on that AOL members had entered into relevant agreements for utilising the rights.

The Claimant originally sought judgment against the Defendant ordering it to delete the stored copies of its MIDI files and to pay a reasonable licence fee for facilitating the downloading of the MIDI files by third parties in the period up to 23.1.1998, and the determination that the Defendant was liable in damages with regard to the downloading of the MIDI files by third parties in the period after 23.1.1998. Immediately after the commencement of the action, the Defendant removed the disputed files from the area of the forum accessible to its users, following which the parties unanimously pronounced the case to be settled in this respect. With regard to the other two motions, the Claimant proceeded to an action for payment. It claimed a reasonable licence fee of DM20.80 for each of the disputed 4784 occurrences of downloading, with its claim therefore amounting to (4784 x 20.80 =) DM 99,507. . . . The Claimant applied for judgment against the Defendant ordering it to pay the Claimant the sum of DM 99,000 with interest at the rate of 5% while litigation was pending.

The Defendant applied for the action to be dismissed.

The Defendant . . . states that until the action was commenced it had no knowledge of the content of the files offered on the server. . . . The Defendant contends that in its legal arguments the Claimant overlooks the fact that in terms of Para. 5 subpara. 2 of the TDG [Teleservices Law] it, the Defendant, is only liable if it had positive knowledge of the content or of the illegality of the downloaded files. Thus, at best, the Claimant would have claims against the users of the forum, but not against the Defendant. In addition, there is no fault whatsoever on the part of the Defendant for what happened, as by putting on the notices about the inadmissibility of uploads which infringed the rights of third parties and by checking the uploaded files prior to release it had done all that it could do. Further technical restrictions were said not to be possible. The Defendant states that it thus had no knowledge of, for instance, rights on the part of the Claimant, nor was it in a state of negligent ignorance concerning such rights.

The Claimant challenges this. It alleged in particular that Para. 5 of the TDG applies only to content stored on servers, in relation to which the illegality of dissemination arises from the content itself; in cases of copyright infringement this provision has no application. . . . It is claimed that the Defendant is liable in any event from the point of view of there being sufficient causal contributory negligence in relation to the acts of infringement by its members and from the point of view of the infringement of the duty upon it to safeguard traffic.

After the taking of evidence had been undertaken . . . the Landgericht [trial court] held as follows:

The statement of claim is justified on the merits in as far as the Claimant claims an infringement of rights protected in accordance with the Copyright Law through having the MIDI files which are the subject matter of the action stored on the server of the Defendant's parent company.

In as far as it likewise asserts this with regard to the facilitating of the uploading, the case is refused. . . .

The Defendant's appeal is directed against this judgment. In its appeal, the Defendant contends . . . it is . . . not the proper defendant of possible claims by the Claimant; the Provider of the forum which is involved in the dispute is AOL Online Inc. Although in the context of the German AOL service the Defendant does also appear itself as Content Provider, in relation to the forum which is involved in the dispute it is neither Provider of its own nor of other people's content, but rather it is purely an Access Provider. It merely makes a point of presence available for the service. Contractual relations with the user only arise between the user and AOL Online Inc. Also, the formation of the forum goes back exclusively to the parent company. . . .

The Defendant applies for the judgment of the Landgericht to be set aside and the case to be dismissed.

The Claimant applies for the appeal to be refused. . . .

The Claimant has lodged a cross-appeal. . . . It applies for the judgment of the Landgericht to be set aside in so far as the action on the grounds of facilitating the uploading of the MIDI files which are the subject matter of the dispute was dismissed.

The Defendant applies for the cross-appeal to be refused. . . .

*Reasons for the Decision:*

The Claimant's appeal is proved to be well-founded, and that of the Defendant to be without sufficient cause. . . .

The admissible appeal by the Defendant does not succeed. The claim for payment asserted by the Claimant results on the merits as a claim for compensation based on . . . the Copyright Law. The following points apply:

The Defendant is liable in accordance with . . . the Copyright Law, in view of there being adequate causality, for culpably causing the infringement of the Claimant's ancillary copyright or of an ancillary copyright acquired by the Claimant from the witness Kist without a restriction on this liability in accordance with Para. 5 subpara. 2 of the TDG.

The question as to whether Para. 5 of the TDG finds application in cases of infringement of copyright or ancillary copyright has not yet been judicially determined as far as can be seen. In textbooks the point is controversial. It is to be answered in the negative.

Interpreting the text of the law for help in finding an answer to the question regarding the applicability of Para. 5 of the TDG to cases of infringement of copyright or ancillary copyright produces no conclusive answer. . . .

Difficulties arise with the interpretation of Para. 5 subpara. 2 of the TDG. An interpretation of the term "content" disregarding the remaining content of this provision could suggest that the term be understood in conformity with Para. 2 subpara. 1 of the TDG as meaning all "combinable data such as characters, pictures or sounds." Para. 5 subpara. 2 of the TDG, however, restricts liability for outside content but in accordance with whether the service provider knew about the outside content. This suggests, it is to be assumed, that with "content" only such data is intended in relation to which the content itself is the basis of evaluation of the legality or illegality of its being stored and in relation to which knowledge of it therefore – even possibly with great difficulty – facilitates the evaluation of the legality or illegality of the storage for the Service Provider. Such an interpretation would have as a result that Para. 5 of the TDG would apply to all criminal and civil provisions which regulate the permissibility of disseminating content (in the area of protection of industrial property, thus, for instance, also content inadmissible under competition law), but not, on the other hand, to content infringing copyright or ancillary copyright, as in determining legality in such cases it is not the content and having knowledge of it that is the decisive consideration but rather it is the legal classification of the content and having knowledge of that that is the decisive consideration. It would scarcely be comprehensible that a Service Provider should be "responsible" for the dissemination of copyright infringing content when he knew the content but did not know of the existence of a copyright in it, but that he should not be "responsible" when he did not know the content but did know of the existence of a copyright in the file merely from its description. An indication that

Para. 5 of the TDG was only intended to regulate responsibility for such data as that where the legality of its dissemination results from the content itself also follows from the fact that Para. 5 subpara. 4 of the TDG speaks of "illegal content" and treats it as equivalent to "content." As a result the wording of Para. 5 of the TDG speaks more against than for its applicability in cases of copyright or ancillary copyright.

On the other hand it has been contended that the area of application of the TDG (and the Media Services Treaty) must coincide to a large degree with the provisions on liability, as it is difficult to see why a provider should be subject to the provisions of the Teleservices Law but not able to enjoy the benefit of the provisions relating to liability contained in Para. 5 of the TDG. This argument does not appear to be compelling: it is hard to see why the validity of Para. 5 of the TDG should not be limited to the "illegal content" in the previously discussed sense and liability for inadmissible storing of content, not on account of the content itself, but rather on account of its legal classification, should yield to the rule in the Copyright Law because of the other fundamental principle of the illegality of the dissemination of such content.

Legislative history also supports the assumption that Para. 5 of the TDG has no application to copyright. . . .

As a result it is to be stressed that the validity of Para. 5 – in particular subpara. 2 – of the TDG is restricted to "illegal content". . . . The precise scope of the imprecise concept of "illegal content" does not require any clarification here. In cases of infringement of copyright or ancillary copyright the provision does not apply in any event. In the meantime there is a discussion draft out of a fifth law to amend the Copyright Law that is aimed at achieving the conformity of German copyright law to the requirements of new technology, taking into consideration international and European standards. . . . According to the statement of reasons for the discussion draft it is stated to be "on the one hand about guaranteeing the legal protection of the holder of rights in the digital sphere, and on the other hand . . . also to give users and exploiters of rights an adequate legal framework which permits the most efficient operation of the new technology and promotes the development of the information society."

Both the (once-off) uploading and downloading procedures resulted in copies of the Claimant's MIDI files through which the Claimant's rights . . . were illegally infringed . . . [under] the Copyright Law. Those responsible for the infringement are in the first place the AOL members who undertook the copying. Responsible alongside them is also the Defendant, for those liable for copyright infringement and for infringement of related protective rights include anyone who committed the infringement of a legal right or took part in it; this applies as long as there is a sufficient causal link between the conduct and the infringement of a legal right, whereby one of several causes is enough, if it is not unlikely according to common sense that it was this cause in particular that lead to such an outcome.

The liability of the Defendant is accordingly well-founded. There is no need for clarification of the question as to whether the Defendant was itself the provider of the forum as Host Provider, the differences between "Content Provider," "Host Provider" and "Access Provider" having been presented in detailed discussions; nor whether, as it submitted at the rehearing (second hearing), it had as its priority the task of developing marketing strategies suited to the German market, in order to be able to market the American style AOL online service to a German target audience and in this connection dealt with the translation of the texts constituting the forum which is the subject of the dispute and made a point of presence available for the purposes of the forum. The Court assumes that the foregoing is accurate. Even within this restricted sphere of activity the Defendant had adequate cause for the infringements of the Claimant's rights which then occurred: the typical consequence of opening up a forum which is designated as being a forum for MIDI files is that AOL members put MIDI files into the forum and download them from there. The occurrences of copying which, it is not disputed, were carried out over the point of presence provided by the Defendant, were thus jointly caused by the Defendant.

The Defendant was also at fault for these occurrences of copying. The Claimant accurately pointed out and it is essentially not denied that the setting up of a forum for MIDI files was nothing short of an invitation to infringement of copyright and ancillary copyright on a grand scale. MIDI files are . . . produced at a good level of quality by enterprises operating on a commercial basis and are exploited commercially by being sold to professional and semi-professional musicians. The repertoire consists in the main of current "hits." In these circumstances it was to be expected from the outset that in all likelihood, under the protection of anonymity afforded by the Internet, AOL members would go on to putting MIDI file versions protected by ancillary copyright of copyright protected works in the forum and from there download them, without acquiring the requisite rights thereto from the holders of the rights or performing rights societies. The Claimant pointed out quite rightly that the computer screen photograph submitted by it with its exclusive current titles is impressive confirmation of this suspected assumption. The Defendant's conduct thus amounted in general and with regard to the titles which are the subject matter of the dispute to gross negligence, if not even eventual intent.

The numerous notices to AOL members built in to the program to the effect that only non-copyright protected material could be uploaded cannot exculpate the Defendant. In view of the anonymity of the Internet these notices were not suitable to limit substantially the well-founded risk of infringement of rights by AOL members through the setting up of the forum, particularly since, as the refusal of the Defendant to notify the Claimant of the names of the "uploaders" shows, the Members could rely on their anonymity being preserved by the Defendant. It must rather have been reckoned on from the outset that a large portion of the members would at any rate not hesitate to disregard these notices.

The Defendant can also not exonerate itself by reference to the activities of its "scouts." The fact that it employed the scouts and had the uploaded files checked for copyright notices confirms first and foremost that the Defendant too had recognised the risk of copyright infringement and that it had also seen that its notices discussed previously about the inadmissibility of uploading copyright protected content could not prevent the infringement of rights. The check carried out on the files for the presence of copyright notices was not an appropriate way of establishing whether copyright and ancillary copyright existed or not with adequate certainty as such notices can be manipulated.

The claim for damages asserted by the Claimant thus subsists on the merits. . . .

---

**Note on the European Union Directive on Copyright in the Information Society**

Just one month after the Munich Court of Appeal rendered its decision in *Hit Bit v. AOL*, the European Union issued its *Directive on Copyright in the Information Society.* That Directive is intended to do two things: harmonize the copyright laws of EU members, and respond to the requirements of two treaties adopted in 1996 by the World Intellectual Property Organization – the the WIPO Copyright Treaty, and the WIPO Performances and Phonograms Treaty. (These are the treaties that required the United States to enact its Digital Millennium Copyright Act, in 1998.)

Two "Recitals" in the EU Directive address the the potential liability of Internet and Online Service Providers.

One Recital provides that "The mere provision of physical facilities for enabling or making a communication does not in itself amount to communication within the meaning of this Directive." This appears to mean that if a website operator – or other Service Provider customer – communicates a performance, recording or film to the public, without being licensed to do so, the Service Provider will not be liable for violating the exclusive communication right, even though the website operator (or other customer) itself will be. It is thus possible that had this Directive been implemented in Germany at the time the activities litigated in *Hit Bit Software GmbH v. AOL Bertelsmann Online GmbH*, AOL would not have been found liable for the infringing activities of its users.

A second Recital of significance to ISPs and OSPs provides "In digital environment . . . , the services of intermediaries may increasingly be used by third parties for infringing activities. In many cases such intermediaries are best placed to bring such infringing activities to an end. Therefore . . . , rightholders should have the possibility of applying for an injunction against an intermediary who carries a third party's infringement . . . in a network." From this, it appears that even if AOL would not have been liable for infringement in the *Hit Bit Software* case, Hit Bit would have been able to get an injunction against AOL requiring it to block access to the infringing midi files that were posted in its forum.

---

As you read the following EU Directive, consider whether it will give artists who are United States citizens and California residents the right to receive resale royalties if their works are resold in Europe. As noted above, the United States does not have a *federal* resale royalties statute. The state of California, however, does have such a statute; and it is reproduced immediately following this directive.

---

**Directive 2000 of the European Parliament and of the Council on the resale right for the benefit of the author of an original work of art (2001)**

[http://europa.eu.int/comm/internal_market/en/intprop/news/resale_en.pdf]

Whereas:

(1) In the field of copyright, the resale right is an unassignable and inalienable right, enjoyed by the author of an original work of graphic or plastic art, to an economic interest in successive sales of the work concerned.

(2) The resale right is a right of a productive character which enables the author/artist to receive consideration for successive transfers of the work. The subject-matter of the resale right is the physical work, namely the medium in which the protected work is incorporated.

(3) The resale right is intended to ensure that authors of graphic and plastic works of art share in the economic success of their original works of art. It helps to redress the balance between the economic situation of authors of graphic and plastic works of art and that of other creators who benefit from successive exploitations of their works.

(4) The resale right forms an integral part of copyright and is an essential prerogative for authors. The imposition of such a right in all Member States meets the need for providing creators with an adequate and standard level of protection.

(5) Under Article 151(4) of the Treaty the Community is to take cultural

aspects into account in its action under other provisions of the Treaty.

(6) The Berne Convention for the Protection of Literary and Artistic Works provides that the resale right is available only if legislation in the country to which the author belongs so permits. The right is therefore optional and subject to the rule of reciprocity. It follows from the case-law of the Court of Justice of the European Communities on the application of the principle of non-discrimination laid down in Article 12 of the Treaty, as shown in the judgement of 20 October 1993 in Joined Cases C-92/92 and C-326/92 Phil Collins and Others, that domestic provisions containing reciprocity clauses cannot be relied upon in order to deny nationals of other Member States rights conferred on national authors. The application of such clauses in the Community context runs counter to the principle of equal treatment resulting from the prohibition of any discrimination on grounds of nationality.

(7) The process of internationalisation of the Community market in modern and contemporary art, which is now being speeded up by the effects of the new economy, in a regulatory context in which few States outside the EU recognise the resale right, makes it essential for the European Community, in the external sphere, to open negotiations with a view to making Article 14ter of the Berne Convention compulsory.

(8) The fact this international market exists, combined with the lack of a resale right in several Member States and the current disparity as regards national systems which recognise that right, make it essential to lay down transitional provisions both as regards entry into force and the substantive regulation of the right, which will preserve the competitiveness of the European market.

(9) The resale right is currently provided for by the domestic legislation of a majority of Member States. Such laws, where they exist, display certain differences, notably as regards the works covered, those entitled to receive royalties, the rate applied, the transactions subject to payment of a royalty, and the basis on which these are calculated. The application or non-application of such a right has a significant impact on the competitive environment within the internal market, since the existence or absence of an obligation to pay on the basis of the resale right is an element which must be taken into account by each individual wishing to sell a work of art. This right is therefore a factor which contributes to the creation of distortions of competition as well as displacement of sales within the Community.

(10) Such disparities with regard to the existence of the resale right and its application by the Member States have a direct negative impact on the proper functioning of the internal market in works of art as provided for by Article 14 of the Treaty. In such a situation Article 95 of the Treaty constitutes the appropriate legal basis.

(11) The objectives of the Community as set out in the Treaty include laying the foundations of an ever closer union among the peoples of Europe, promoting closer relations between the Member States belonging to the Community, and ensuring their economic and social progress by common action to eliminate the barriers which divide Europe. To that end the Treaty provides for the establishment of an internal market which presupposes the abolition of obstacles to the free movement of goods, freedom to provide services and freedom of establishment, and for the introduction of a system ensuring that competition in the common market is not distorted. Harmonisation of Member States' laws on the resale right contributes to the attainment of these objectives.

(12) The Sixth Council Directive (77/388/EEC) of 17 May 1977 on the harmonisation of the laws of the Member States relating to turnover taxes . . . progressively introduces a Community system of taxation applicable inter alia to works of art. Measures confined to the tax field are not sufficient to guarantee the

harmonious functioning of the art market. This objective cannot be attained without harmonisation in the field of the resale right.

(13) Existing differences between laws should be eliminated where they have a distorting effect on the functioning of the internal market, and the emergence of any new differences of that kind should be prevented. There is no need to eliminate, or prevent the emergence of, differences which cannot be expected to affect the functioning of the internal market.

(14) A precondition of the proper functioning of the internal market is the existence of conditions of competition which are not distorted. The existence of differences between national provisions on the resale right creates distortions of competition and displacement of sales within the Community and leads to unequal treatment between artists depending on where their works are sold. The issue under consideration has therefore transnational aspects which cannot be satisfactorily regulated by action by Member States. A lack of Community action would conflict with the requirement of the Treaty to correct distortions of competition and unequal treatment.

(15) In view of the scale of divergences between national provisions it is therefore necessary to adopt harmonising measures to deal with disparities between the laws of the Member States in areas where such disparities are liable to create or maintain distorted conditions of competition. It is not however necessary to harmonise every provision of the Member States' laws on the resale right and, in order to leave as much scope for national decision as possible, it is sufficient to limit the harmonisation exercise to those domestic provisions that have the most direct impact on the functioning of the internal market.

(16) This Directive complies therefore, in its entirety, with the principles of subsidiarity and proportionality as laid down in Article 5 of the Treaty.

(17) Pursuant to Council Directive 93/98/EEC of 29 October 1993 harmonising the term of protection of copyright and certain related rights 1, the term of copyright runs for 70 years after the author's death. The same period should be laid down for the resale right. Consequently, only the originals of works of modern and contemporary art may fall within the scope of the resale right. However, in order to allow the legal systems of Member States which do not, at the time of the adoption of this Directive, apply a resale right for the benefit of artists to incorporate this right into their respective legal systems and, moreover, to enable the economic operators in those Member States to adapt gradually to the aforementioned right whilst maintaining their economic viability, the Member States concerned should be allowed a limited transitional period during which they may choose not to apply the resale right for the benefit of those entitled under the artist after his death.

(18) The scope of the resale right should be extended to all acts of resale, with the exception of those effected directly between persons acting in their private capacity without the participation of an art market professional. This right should not extend to acts of resale by persons acting in their private capacity to museums which are not for profit and which are open to the public. With regard to the particular situation of art galleries which acquire works directly from the author, Member States should be allowed the option of exempting from the resale right acts of resale of those works which take place within three years of that acquisition. The interests of the artist should also be taken into account by limiting this exemption to such acts of resale where the resale price does not exceed EUR 10 000.

(19) It should be made clear that the harmonisation brought about by this Directive does not apply to original manuscripts of writers and composers.

(20) Effective rules should be laid down based on experience already gained at national level with the resale right. It is appropriate to calculate the royalty as a

percentage of the sale price and not of the increase in value of works whose original value has increased.

(21) The categories of works of art subject to the resale right should be harmonised.

(22) The non-application of royalties below the minimum threshold may help to avoid disproportionately high collection and administration costs compared with the profit for the artist. However, in accordance with the principle of subsidiarity, the Member States should be allowed to establish national thresholds lower than the Community threshold, so as to promote the interests of new artists. Given the small amounts involved, this derogation is not likely to have a significant effect on the proper functioning of the internal market.

(23) The rates set by the different Member States for the application of the resale right vary considerably at present. The effective functioning of the internal market in works of modern and contemporary art requires the fixing of uniform rates to the widest possible extent.

(24) It is desirable to establish, with the intention of reconciling the various interests involved in the market for original works of art, a system consisting of a tapering scale of rates for several price bands. It is important to reduce the risk of sales relocating and of the circumvention of the Community rules on the resale right.

(25) The person by whom the royalty is payable should, in principle, be the seller. Member States should be given the option to provide for derogations from this principle in respect of liability for payment. The seller is the person or undertaking on whose behalf the sale is concluded.

(26) Provision should be made for the possibility of periodic adjustment of the threshold and rates. To this end, it is appropriate to entrust to the Commission the task of drawing up periodic reports on the actual application of the resale right in the Member States and on the impact on the art market in the Community and, where appropriate, of making proposals relating to the amendment of this Directive.

(27) The persons entitled to receive royalties must be specified, due regard being had to the principle of subsidiarity. It is not appropriate to take action through this Directive in relation to Member States' laws of succession. However, those entitled under the author must be able to benefit fully from the resale right after his death, at least following the expiry of the transitional period referred to above.

(28) The Member States are responsible for regulating the exercise of the resale right, particularly with regard to the way this is managed. In this respect management by a collecting society is one possibility. Member States should ensure that collecting societies operate in a transparent and efficient manner. However, Member States must ensure that amounts intended for authors who are nationals of other Member States are in fact collected and distributed. This Directive is without prejudice to arrangements in Member States for collection and distribution.

(29) Enjoyment of the resale right should be restricted to Community nationals as well as to foreign authors whose countries afford such protection to authors who are nationals of Member States. A Member State should have the option of extending enjoyment of this right to foreign authors who have their habitual residence in that Member State.

(30) Appropriate procedures for monitoring transactions should be introduced so as to ensure by practical means that the resale right is effectively applied by Member States. This implies also a right on the part of the author or his authorised representative to obtain any necessary information from the natural or legal person liable for payment of royalties. Member States which provide for collective management of the resale right may also provide that the bodies responsible for that

collective management should alone be entitled to obtain information,
HAVE ADOPTED THIS DIRECTIVE:

*Chapter I - Scope*

*Article 1- Subject matter of the resale right*

1. Member States shall provide, for the benefit of the author of an original work of art, a resale right, to be defined as an inalienable right, which cannot be waived, even in advance, to receive a royalty based on the sale price obtained for any resale of the work, subsequent to the first transfer of the work by the author.

2. The right referred to in paragraph 1 shall apply to all acts of resale involving as sellers, buyers or intermediaries art market professionals, such as salesrooms, art galleries and, in general, any dealers in works of art.

3. Member States may provide that the right referred to in paragraph 1 shall not apply to acts of resale where the seller has acquired the work directly from the author less than three years before that resale and where the resale price does not exceed EUR 10 000.

4. The royalty shall be payable by the seller. Member States may provide that one of the natural or legal persons referred to in paragraph 2 other than the seller shall alone be liable or shall share liability with the seller for payment of the royalty.

*Article 2- Works of art to which the resale right relates*

1. For the purposes of this Directive, "original work of art" means works of graphic or plastic art such as pictures, collages, paintings, drawings, engravings, prints, lithographs, sculptures, tapestries, ceramics, glassware and photographs, provided they are made by the artist himself or are copies considered to be original works of art.

2. Copies of works of art covered by this Directive, which have been made in limited numbers by the artist himself or under his authority, shall be considered to be original works of art for the purposes of this Directive. Such copies will normally have been numbered, signed or otherwise duly authorised by the artist.

*CHAPTER II - Particular provisions*

*Article 3 - Threshold*

1. It shall be for the Member States to set a minimum sale price from which the sales referred to in Article 1 shall be subject to resale right.

2. This minimum sale price may not under any circumstances exceed EUR 3 000.

*Article 4 - Rates*

1. The royalty provided for in Article 1 shall be set at the following rates:

(a) 4% for the portion of the sale price up to EUR 50 000;

(b) 3% for the portion of the sale price from EUR 50 000,01 to 200 000;

(c) 1% for the portion of the sale price from EUR 200 000,01 to 350 000;

(d) 0,5% for the portion of the sale price from EUR 350 000,01 to 500 000;

(e) 0,25% for the portion of the sale price exceeding EUR 500 000.

However, the total amount of the royalty may not exceed EUR 12 500.

2. By way of derogation from paragraph 1, Member States may apply a rate of 5% for the portion of the sale price referred to in paragraph 1(a).

3. If the minimum sale price set should be lower than EUR 3 000, the Member State shall also determine the rate applicable to the portion of the sale price up to EUR 3 000; this rate may not be lower than 4%.

*Article 5 - Calculation basis*

The sale prices referred to in Articles 3 and 4 are net of tax.

*Article 6 - Persons entitled to receive royalties*

1. The royalty provided for under Article 1 shall be payable to the author of the work and, subject to Article 8(2), after his death to those entitled under him.

2. Member States may provide for compulsory or optional collective management of the royalty provided for under Article 1.

*Article 7 - Third-country nationals entitled to receive royalties*

1. Member States shall provide that authors who are nationals of third countries and, subject to Article 8(2), their successors in title shall enjoy the resale right in accordance with this Directive and the legislation of the Member State concerned only if legislation in the country of which the author or his successor in title is a national permits resale right protection in that country for authors from the Member States and their successors in title.

2. On the basis of information provided by the Member States, the Commission shall publish as soon as possible an indicative list of those third countries which fulfil the condition set out in paragraph 1. This list shall be kept up to date.

3. Any Member State may treat authors who are not nationals of a Member State but who have their habitual residence in that Member State in the same way as its own nationals for the purpose of resale right protection.

*Article 8 - Term of protection of the resale right*

1. The term of protection of the resale right shall correspond to that laid down in Article 1 of Directive 93/98/EEC.

2. By way of derogation from paragraph 1, those Member States which do not apply the resale right on [the entry into force date referred to in Article 13], shall not be required, for a period expiring not later than 1 January 2010, to apply the resale right for the benefit of those entitled under the artist after his death.

3. A Member State to which paragraph 2 applies may have up to two more years, if necessary to enable the economic operators in that Member State to adapt gradually to the resale right system whilst maintaining their economic viability, before it is required to apply the resale right for the benefit of those entitled under the artist after his death. At least 12 months before the end of the period referred to in paragraph 2, the Member State concerned shall inform the Commission giving its reasons, so that the Commission can give an opinion, after appropriate consultations, within three months following the receipt of such information. If the Member State does not follow the opinion of the Commission, it shall within one month inform the Commission and justify its decision. The notification and justification of the Member State and the opinion of the Commission shall be published in the Official Journal of the European Communities and forwarded to the European Parliament.

4. In the event of the successful conclusion, within the periods referred to in Article 8(2) and 8(3), of international negotiations aimed at extending the resale right at international level, the Commission shall submit appropriate proposals.

*Article 9 - Right to obtain information*

The Member States shall provide that for a period of three years after the resale, the persons entitled under Article 6 may require from any art market professional mentioned in Article 1(2) to furnish any information that may be necessary in order to secure payment of royalties in respect of the resale.

*Final provisions*

*Article 10 - Application in time*

This Directive shall apply in respect of all original works of art as defined in Article 2 which, on 1 January 2006, are still protected by the legislation of the Member States in the field of copyright or meet the criteria for protection under the provisions of this Directive at that date.

*Article 11 - Revision clause*

1. The Commission shall submit to the European Parliament, the Council and the Economic and Social Committee not later than 1 January 2009 and every four

years thereafter a report on the implementation and the effect of this Directive, paying particular attention to the competitiveness of the market in modern and contemporary art in the Community, especially as regards the position of the Community in relation to relevant markets that do not apply the resale right and the fostering of artistic creativity and the management procedures in the Member States. It shall examine in particular its impact on the internal market and the effect of the introduction of the resale right in those Member States that did not apply the right in national law prior to the entry into force of this Directive. Where appropriate, the Commission shall submit proposals for adapting the minimum threshold and the rates of royalty to take account of changes in the sector, proposals relating to the maximum amount laid down in Article 4(1) and any other proposal it may deem necessary in order to enhance the effectiveness of this Directive.

2. A Contact Committee is hereby established. It shall be composed of representatives of the competent authorities of the Member States. It shall be chaired by a representative of the Commission and shall meet either on the initiative of the Chairman or at the request of the delegation of a Member State.

3. The task of the Committee shall be as follows:

– to organise consultations on all questions deriving from application of this Directive;

– to facilitate the exchange of information between the Commission and the Member States on relevant developments in the art market in the Community.

*Article 12 - Implementation*

1. Member States shall bring into force the laws, regulations and administrative provisions necessary to comply with this Directive before 1 January 2006. . . .

---

**California Civil Code § 986**

(a) Whenever a work of fine art is sold and the seller resides in California or the sale takes place in California, the seller or the seller's agent shall pay to the artist of such work of fine art or to such artist's agent 5 percent of the amount of such sale. The right of the artist to receive an amount equal to 5 percent of the amount of such sale may be waived only by a contract in writing providing for an amount in excess of 5 percent of the amount of such sale. An artist may assign the right to collect the royalty payment provided by this section to another individual or entity. However, the assignment shall not have the effect of creating a waiver prohibited by this subdivision. . . .
  (7) Upon the death of an artist, the rights and duties created under this section shall inure to his or her heirs, legatees, or personal representative, until the 20th anniversary of the death of the artist. . . .

(b) Subdivision (a) shall not apply to any of the following:
  (1) To the initial sale of a work of fine art where legal title to such work at the time of such initial sale is vested in the artist thereof.
  (2) To the resale of a work of fine art for a gross sales price of less than one thousand dollars ($1,000).
  (3) Except as provided in paragraph (7) of subdivision (a), to a resale after the death of such artist.
  (4) To the resale of the work of fine art for a gross sales price less than the purchase price paid by the seller. . . .

(c) For purposes of this section, the following terms have the following meanings:

(1) "Artist" means the person who creates a work of fine art and who, at the time of resale, is a citizen of the United States, or a resident of the state who has resided in the state for a minimum of two years. . . .

---

**Note on International Payment of Performance and Reproduction Royalties**

As you read in Chapter 1, copyrighted works that originate in one country are entitled to protection in other countries, if certain requirements are satisfied. You also read about which country's law is applicable in cases involving cross-border uses of copyrighted works, and about which courts are proper for claiming the protection and remedies provided by copyright law.

International copyright litigation is not uncommon. But choice of law issues are rarely difficult where the cross-border uses involve the public performance or reproduction of songs, movies or television programs, because the copyright laws of virtually all countries protect against the unauthorized performance or reproduction of these types of works. As a practical matter, this means that if copyrighted works are publicly performed or reproduced, those who do so are legally required to pay royalties to copyright owners, even if they are in other countries.

In fact, billions of dollars in royalties flow across national borders every year, to their rightful recipients, without litigation or even the threat of it. Those royalties flow, in other words, without any need to think about which court would be the proper court for a copyright owner to enforce its rights or seek its remedies. Administrative formalities may have to be complied with to obtain those royalties; but in many cases, copyright owners receive royalties from abroad by doing virtually nothing.

To explain how so much money flows so smoothly from one country to another, it is first necessary to distinguish between two types of royalties: (1) those that are paid as a result of individually negotiated voluntary licenses; and (2) those that are paid as a result of collectively administered or compulsory licenses. For reasons you will soon see, most of this Note will be devoted to collectively administered or compulsory licenses.

*Individually negotiated voluntary licenses*

Individually negotiated licenses would be used to authorize:

- the foreign-language translation and publication abroad of a book written by an American author
- the performance of U.S.-authored play in London
- the theatrical exhibition abroad of a U.S.-produced movie
- television broadcasts in other countries of a U.S. program, and
- cable and satellite transmissions in other countries of original (as distinguished from retransmitted) programming, such as the programming carried on CNN, HBO and MTV.

These are just examples. Licenses to use other types of works in other ways are individually negotiated as well. What all of these types of works have in common is that the copyright laws of virtually all countries give copyright owners the right to license the use of these types of works – or not – as they see fit. Licenses to use these types of works, in other words, are voluntary. And when licenses for their use are granted, they are granted as a result of individually negotiated, two-party licenses between the owner of the work's copyright and the company that wants to use it.

The terms of individually negotiated licenses authorizing the use of American copyrighted works abroad are almost identical to domestic license agreements. In other words, a license authorizing the performance in London or Milan of an American stage play would be almost identical to a license authorizing its performance in San Diego. Likewise, a license authorizing the performance in Los Angeles of a British or Italian play would be almost identical to a license authorizing its performance in Oxford or Florence.

International licenses may have special provisions dealing with such issues as:

- the approval of translations and other adaptations of the work, in order to "localize" it for the licensee's expected audience
- ownership of the copyright to the translated version
- choice of law, personal jurisdiction and service of process, should litigation become necessary
- whether the licensee will be required to post a letter of credit to secure its payments to the copyright owner, and
- currency conversion.

Special provisions like these may make international license agreements somewhat longer than purely domestic licenses. On the other hand, they may not. Cultural norms in the licensee's country may have a greater influence on the length of a license agreement than the fact that it's international. Japanese contracts, for example, are typically much shorter than American contracts; and for that reason, a license from an American copyright owner authorizing the use of its work in Japan may be shorter than a license from that same copyright owner authorizing the use of its work in New York.

Relations between copyright owners in one country and their licensees in another usually are about as cordial (or not) as relations between copyright owners and licensees in the same country. Where, however, a copyright owner is in one country and a licensee in another – and the license is voluntary and individually negotiated – the process of negotiating and documenting the license will be a significant one. The way in which international law enables the smooth flow of copyright royalties across national borders is more dramatically illustrated by the international operation of collectively administered or compulsory licenses.

*Collectively administered or compulsory licenses*

Examples of collectively administered or compulsory licenses include licenses for:

- nondramatic public performances abroad of American musical compositions
- the manufacture and sale of recordings of American musical compositions in other countries, and
- cable and satellite retransmissions abroad of American movies and television programs that are broadcast on conventional (over-the-air) television.

Again, these are just examples. Licenses to use other types of works in other ways are collectively administered or are handled by compulsory license too. What these types of works have in common is that the licensing practices or copyright laws of many countries, including the United States, use collective administration or compulsory licensing to authorize these uses of these works.

"Collective administration" is the term used to describe the issuance of licenses for certain types of uses of many separate works, and the collection of royalties from licensees, done by a single organization on behalf many separate copyright owners. In the United States expecially, there are sub-categories of collective administration that differ from one another slightly (though in ways that may be significant to those involved). But for present purposes, these distinctions may be disregarded.

Classic examples of collective administration in the United States are the licenses issued by ASCAP, BMI and SESAC to broadcasters and concert venues authorizing them to perform musical compositions nondramatically. (Dramatic musical performances – that is, performances during a musical stage play – are not licensed collectively; they are licensed individually.) These collectively administered licenses are referred to as "blanket licenses," because they authorize licensees to use, for a single fee, any or all of the songs represented by the licensing organization. The licensee is not required to identify in advance which songs will be performed. Nor is the licensee charged more if it chooses to perform popular songs, or less if it chooses to perform songs that are not well known.

In the United States, the *law* does *not* require songwriters and music publishers to use ASCAP, BMI or SESAC to issue public performances licenses. Legally, songwriters and music publishers may, if they wish, issue their own public performance licenses directly to broadcasters, concert venues and others. As a practical matter, however, songwriters and music publishers could not possibly issue their own licenses. There simply are too many music users to keep track of; there would be too much paper work to do; and the costs of doing so would exceed the license fees that could could be charged or collected. For these practical reasons, songwriters and music publishers do appoint either ASCAP, BMI or SESAC to issue licenses and collect royalties on their behalves, even though American law does not require it.

"Compulsory licenses," also referred to as "statutory licenses," are those that are required by law – hence the names "compulsory" and "statutory." Copyright statutes around the world typically give copyright owners the "exclusive" right to do, or authorize others to do, certain things with their works. The word "exclusive" is misleading, however, because those same statutes typically contain other provisions that authorize certain types of uses of certain works, whether or not copyright owners like it. Of course, once certain uses are authorized – that is, licensed – by statute, the statute must provide a mechanism for establishing the license fee, as well as the procedure for collecting licensee fees from those that take advantage of this compulsory license, and for allocating and distributing to copyright owners the license fees that are collected.

In many (though not all) cases, collective rights organizations (like ASCAP, BMI and SESAC) participate in the process by which compulsory license fees are set; and in may (though not all) cases, compulsory license fees are paid or distributed to collective rights organizations for them to allocate among the copyright owners they represent.

The types of works and uses that are subject to compulsory licensing are determined by the copyright statutes of each country. The types of works and uses that are collectively administered are determined by the local practices of each country. Thus, to explain the international operation of collectively administered or compulsory licenses, it is necessary to consider them one type of use a time, one country at a time.

*Nondramatic pubic performances*

Royalties for nondramatic public performances (including broadcasts) of musical compositions are collected by performing rights organizations (often called "PROs" for short) in the countries where those performances take place. ASCAP, BMI and SESAC are the PROs that collect for performances in the U.S. Other PROs collect for performances in their own countries – SOCAN in Canada,

SACEM in France, GEMA in Germany, JASRAC in Japan, and PRS in the U.K. (These are only examples; there are at least 85 separate PROs in the world.)

ASCAP, BMI and SESAC have entered into agreements with their counterparts around the world, pursuant to which:

- other PROs collect royalties in their countries on behalf of American songwriters and music publishers whose songs have been performed abroad, which royalties are then paid to ASCAP, BMI and SESAC for distribution to those entitled to them in the U.S.; and
- ASCAP, BMI and SESAC collect royalties in the U.S. for foreign songwriters and music publishers whose songs have been performed in the U.S., which royalties ASCAP, BMI and SESAC then pay to PROs in other countries for distribution to those entitled to them.

From the point of view of an individual songwriter or music publisher, the system is virtually seamless. All that is required is membership (or affiliation) with a local PRO; and if performances occur abroad, royalties from abroad will be received eventually.

Songwriters and publishers may have to satisfy some administrative formalities. If, for example, a songwriter composes a song that is in the soundtrack of a movie or television program that is broadcast in another country, cue-sheets must be submitted to that country's PRO so the song is properly credited to the songwriter and music publisher entitled to royalties on account of that broadcast. Likewise, if singer-songwriters go on tour in another country, they may have to submit "tour itineraries" and "set-lists" to that country's PRO so their songs can receive credit, and they can be paid royalties, for their performances of the songs they've written. But the same or similar administrative formalities would have to be complied with in order for them to receive credit for performances in their own countries, so little or no additional burdens are required of songwriters and publishers to collect their performance royalties internationally. That burden has been assumed for them by the PROs of the world, by means of a remarkably efficient network of international agreements for the reciprocal collective administration of music copyrights.

*Manufacture and sale of music recordings*

The copyright laws of all countries require those who record, manufacture and sell music recordings to obtain licenses from the owners of the copyrights to the songs on those recordings (that is, from music publishers or songwriters). This is so, because the law gives copyright owners the right to reproduce and distribute their works. Recording songs and manufacturing records results in the "reproduction" of the songs on the record; and the sale of recordings results in the "distribution" of those songs.

Though in the language of copyright law, record companies need "reproduction" and "distribution" licenses, those in the music business refer to these licenses as "mechanical licenses." (The reason is historic. Player piano rolls were the first "recordings." At the time, piano rolls were considered to be "mechanical" parts of pianos. Hence: "mechanical licenses.")

In the United States, many music publishers (or songwriters) issue mechanical licenses directly to record companies who request them. More publishers, however, have appointed The Harry Fox Agency to handle mechanical licensing on their behalves. The Harry Fox Agency acts, literally, as the agent for its music publishing clients for this purpose. Publishers have a choice between doing it themselves, using their own staff employees, or having The Harry Fox Agency do it for them, in return for a fee.

United States copyright law contains a compulsory mechanical license that authorizes record companies to make new recordings of previously released songs, in return for the payment of a royalty of 8 cents per song for each recording sold. (That's the royalty at the time this book went to press; the rate is adjusted periodically.) The compulsory mechanical license is a license of last resort, however, for most record companies, because most record companies try to make better deals for themselves through voluntary negotiations directly with music publishers.

Other countries handle mechanical licensing somewhat differently than does the U.S. In other countries, all mechanical licenses are issued – by local practice or law – by "mechanical rights societies." In some countries the mechanical rights society is the same organization that serves as that country's performing rights organization. GEMA for instance is both the PRO and mechanical rights society for Germany; and JASRAC is both the PRO and mechanical rights society for Japan. Mechanical and performing rights are legally distinct, however, and many countries have two separate organizations – one for each of these rights.

Moreover, in other countries, the mechanical license royalty is calculated differently than it is in the U.S. (It's often a percentage of the wholesale price of the recording, divided equally among all the songs on the recording, regardless of how many or how few there are.) Also, in other countries, record companies do not seek better deals through direct negotiations with music publishers. They don't, because all mechanical licenses are issued by mechanical rights societies; publishers in those countries do not issue mechanical licenses themselves.

If a song by an American songwriter is recorded abroad, The Harry Fox Agency will collect the royalties that are due from the mechanical rights society in that country, on behalf of the U.S. publisher of that song. The Harry Fox Agency will then send the collected royalty to the publisher, and the publisher in turn will pay the songwriter, in accordance with the contract between the publisher and the songwriter.

To collect foreign mechanicals this way, the U.S. publisher must affiliate with The Harry Fox Agency – must, in other words, appoint the Fox Agency its agent for making those collections – and the publisher must notify the Fox Agency which of its songs have been recorded, manufactured and sold abroad.

The Harry Fox Agency has "affiliation" agreements with some two dozen mechanical rights societies in other countries. Those agreements also authorize The Harry Fox Agency to issue mechanical licenses to record companies in the U.S. for songs written by songwriters from those countries.

Things are a bit more complicated for U.S. music publishers that don't use The Harry Fox Agency to collect foreign mechanical royalties, and for the collection of foreign mechanical royalties from countries whose mechanical rights societies are not affiliated with The Harry Fox Agency. In those cases, U.S. publishers must enter into sub-publishing agreements with music publishers in other countries; and foreign music publishers must enter into sub-publishing agreements with U.S. publishers. Sub-publishing companies authorize music publishers to publish in their own countries songs that originated and were first published in other countries. In this fashion, sub-publishers collect mechanical royalties from the societies in their own countries, and then send those royalties (less their commissions) to the publishers in other countries with which they have entered into sub-publishing contracts.

Regardless of which technique is used – The Harry Fox Agency as intermediary, or sub-publishing agreements with foreign music publishers – American music publishers and songwriters are able to receive mechanical royalties from foreign record companies, without having to negotiate individual licenses, and without litigation. The same is true in reverse: songwriters and music publishers in other countries are able to receive mechanical royalties from U.S. record companies, without having to negotiate or litigate.

*Cable and satellite retransmissions of broadcasts*

The copyright laws of all countries now require cable systems and satellite television companies to pay royalties when they retransmit to their own subscribers the signals of over-the-air broadcasts. These royalties are owed to the owners of the copyrights to the retransmitted programming. When cable and satellite companies transmit original programming (like CNN, HBO and MTV), they must pay royalties too; but that type of programming is licensed by voluntary direct negotiations with copyright owners (as you read near the beginning of this Note). When cable and satellite companies retransmit over-the-air broadcasts, those retransmissions are licensed by statute or collective admininstration, somewhat differently in each country.

*Europe*

AGICOA (the Association for the International Collective Management of Audiovisual Works) is an organization whose members are *associations* of movie and TV program producers. U.S. producers are represented (within AGICOA) by MPAA (for the "majors"), AFMA (for the "independents") and the American Public Television Producers Association.

AGICOA negotiates license fees with cable and satellite companies in those European countries whose laws do not contain compulsory or statutory broadcast retransmission license provisions. AGICOA also collects retransmission royalties from cable and satellite companies; and it distributes those royalties to its association members, which then distribute them to the producers those associations represent.

To receive retransmission royalties, programs that are broadcast in Europe must be registered with AGICOA, a process that can be done on behalf of U.S. producers by the associations to which they belong.

*Canada*

Cable and satellite companies in Canada pay retransmission royalties to several "copyright collective societies" representing movie and TV producers, sports leagues (that own copyrights to sports broadcasts), and music publishers and songwriters. To receive royalties, those entitled to them must affiliate with (or form) a copyright collective society. The society proposes a "tariff," which may be challenged by cable and satellite companies in proceedings before the Copyright Board of Canada. That Board "certifies" the tariff to be paid to each society. And the societies collect the tariffs and distribute them to those it represents.

American copyright owners are represented in Canada by several such societies:

- Border Broadcasters, Inc. (TV stations, for local programming)
- Canadian Retransmission Right Association (ABC, CBS, NBC)
- Copyright Collective of Canada (MPAA, AFMA)
- FWS Joints Sports Claimants (NFL, NBA, NHL)
- Major League Baseball Collective of Canada (Major League Baseball), and
- SOCAN (ASCAP, BMI)

*United States*

Cable and satellite companies in the U.S. pay retransmission royalties as well, at rates established through proceedings administered by the U.S. Copyright Office. The royalties are paid to the Copyright Office, which then divides them among the owners of the copyrights to the retransmitted programs, in proportions determined by other proceedings administered by the Copyright Office.

When the signals of Canadian and Mexican television stations are retransmitted by cable and satellite companies in the U.S., the owners of the copyrights to those retransmitted programs are entitled to a share of the U.S. retransmission royalties. To get their shares, those Canadian and Mexican copyright owners participate in U.S. Copyright Office proceedings, side-by-side with American copyright owners.

*Other royalties*

Music performance royalties, mechanical royalties, and broadcast retransmission royalties are the most significant royalties paid as a result of collective administration or compulsory licensing, measured by the amount of money involved. There are, however, additional types of royalties, some of which are not required under U.S. law, but are under the laws of other countries. Though these royalties are not required by the international copyright treaties to which the U.S. adheres, some countries pay these royalties to American copyright owners anyway – even though the U.S. does not reciprocate (because U.S. law does not require these royalties to be paid to anyone).

*Private copying levies* (also known as blank tape and copier levies) are imposed by the laws of Austria, Belgium, Denmark, France, Germany, Netherlands, Spain and Switzerland. These levies are added to the price of blank tapes and copiers, and are then distributed to those whose works are likely to have been privately copied to blank media. American works are among those copied in the countries that impose these levies; and the Americans' share of these levies is collected on their behalf by the MPAA and AFMA (on behalf of movie and television producers) and ASCAP, BMI and SESAC (on behalf of music publishers and songwriters). (A narrow form of this levy exists in U.S. law, in the Audio Home Recording Act of 1992, about which more is said below.)

*Video rental and lending levies* are imposed by the laws of Germany, the Netherlands and Switzerland. The levy is collected by retail video stores from customers who rent or borrow videos, and it is eventually distributed to those whose videos were rented or lent. American videos are among those rented and lent in those countries. And the Americans' share is collected on their behalf by the MPAA and AFMA from those organizations within Germany, the Netherlands and Switzerland that collect them from retail video stores there.

*American dissatisfaction*

Though this system for collecting and distributing royalties across national borders works well, it is not entirely problem free, at least from the point of view of American copyright owers. Here is why some Americans are dissatisfied.

*Royalties not paid to Americans*

Some royalties are not paid to Americans even though they are paid to others. For example, royalties paid by European, Australian and Japanese radio stations on account of their broadcasts of music *recordings* by performers who are nationals of those countries are not paid for recordings by American performers released by American record companies. Similarly, royalties are paid to authors living in the European Economic Area on account of the loan of their books by libraries in the

U.K. and Germany; but those royalties are not paid to authors living in the U.S., even when their books are lent by U.K. and German libraries.

There is of course a legal reason that these royalties are not paid to Americans, even though they are paid to others. The copyright treaties to which the United States adheres – such as the Berne Convention, the TRIPs Agreement, and the WIPO Copyright Treaty – do not require adhering countries to grant recording performance or library lending rights, and the U.S. does not (except for very narrow digital performance rights). The Rome Convention *does* require adhering countries to pay royalties for broadcasts of recordings by nationals of adhering countries; but the United States has never adhered to Rome Convention, so American radio stations don't pay royalties to record companies or performers of any nationality – not even to Americans – for broadcasting their recordings.

*Royalties are paid, but not to "copyright owners"*

Compulsory license royalties are not always paid to "copyright owners." The country where the royalty originates determines who is entitled to receive it. And in some countries, royalties are divided *by law* among authors, performers and producers – as defined by the laws of those countries – rather than being paid to copyright owners. In the United States entertainment industry, most works are created as "works made for hire," so that under U.S. law, production companies usually are the "authors" as well as the "copyright owners" of their works. Not so, elsewhere.

In countries where private copying and video rental royalties are divided by law among producers, authors and performers, U.S. production companies collect the producers' share, and – by agreement with the DGA and the WGA – the directors' and writers' shares are split with production companies: two-thirds to producers, and one-third split between directors and writers. (No one yet collects the performers' share for actors, however.)

Of course, the concept of directing a portion of compulsory license royalties, by statute, to authors and performers, is no longer alien to American copyright owners. This very thing was done by the U.S. Congress in the Audio Home Recording Act of 1992 which statutorily allocates, by percentage, blank digital media and recorder royalties among featured recording artists, background vocalists, background musicians, record companies, songwriters and music publishers. The Act does not simply divide these royalties between record companies and music publishers, even though they are the copyright owners. (Copyright Act §1006) Congress did so again in the Digital Performance Right in Sound Recordings Act of 1995 which statutorily allocates, by percentage, digital public performance royalties among featured recording artists, backup vocalists, backup musicians, and recording companies. The Act does not permit record companies (which are the copyright owners) to get all these royalties. (Copyright Act §114(g)(2)) As a result, when American copyright owners complain that other countries direct royalties away from copyright owners, that complaint is simply the international part of a broader complaint about something the U.S. does too.

*Foreign collecting organizations sometimes retain royalties*

Royalties that might otherwise have been paid to Americans are sometimes retained by foreign collecting societies, for at least three reasons.

First, performing rights organizations sometimes have difficulty identifying songs that have been publicly performed in their countries. The public performance royalties earned by unidentified songs may be retained by PROs in a so-called "black box." These "black box" moneys are distributed eventually, but only to *local* music publishers, thus depriving American songwriters and publishers of their share.

Second, a portion of some collective and compulsory license royalties are diverted away from those who would otherwise receive them, and are used for local social and cultural purposes. In France, 25% of private copying royalties are used for French cultural purposes; and in Spain, 20% of private copying royalties are used for training and promoting young Spanish performers. French and Spanish recipients of these royalties get less than they otherwise would; the diversions are not just aimed at Americans. On the other hand, these diversions do benefit French and Spanish nationals, while they do not benefit Americans.

Third, a portion of some royalties are retained by local collecting organizations to fund health insurance, retirement programs, loans, grants and awards, and programs to promote live local performances. The royalties used for these purposes are retained from all that are collected – not merely from royalties collected for the use of American works. But again, these programs benefit only those who are members of the local collecting organizations; they do not benefit Americans.

### *Conclusion*

Despite the complaints of Americans, the cross-border collection and distribution of royalties described in this Note demonstrate that "international entertainment law" is a body of law that actually works. What's more, given the distances involved, and the differences in language, culture and business practices among nations, it works remarkably well.

# TABLE OF CASES AND OTHER MATERIALS

## CASES

## STATUTES, REGULATIONS, TREATIES, DIRECTIVES



## GOVERNMENT REPORTS AND RELATED MATERIALS

## COLLECTIVE BARGAINING AGREEMENTS AND GUILD RULES



## NOTES

# INDEX

## About the Authors

LIONEL S. SOBEL is the Editor of the *Entertainment Law Reporter* and a Distinguished Scholar at the Berkeley Center for Law & Technology. He was a Professor at Loyola Law School in Los Angeles. He also has taught Copyright and Entertainment Law at UCLA School of Law and at the University of California at Berkeley's Boalt Hall School of Law, and International Entertainment Law at Southwestern University School of Law in Los Angeles and for the University of San Diego Law School in London.

DONALD E. BIEDERMAN was a Professor of Law at Southwestern University School of Law in Los Angeles as well as the Director of Southwestern's National Entertainment & Media Law Institute. Formerly, he was Executive Vice President and General Counsel of Warner/Chappell Music, Inc. He also was Director of the USC Entertainment Law Institute from 1993 to 2000.